Limca

LIMCA BOOK of RECORDS

India at Her Best 2024

hachette INDIA

First published in 2024 by Hachette India
(Registered name: Hachette Book Publishing India Pvt. Ltd)
An Hachette UK company
www.hachetteindia.com

1

Information in the book has been updated to 31 August 2023, except in the Science and Technology, Education, Business and Economy, The Natural World, Literature, and Sports chapters, where select information relates to later dates.

All maps in this work are pictorial representations, not to scale, and are not meant to represent exact political boundaries. They are for general illustration only, and are not intended to be used for reference purposes or reproduction elsewhere. It is clarified that the representation of a particular theme, or data set across regions with colour demarcations do not reflect political boundaries. It is also reiterated that such pictorial maps do not either represent or contradict India's national sovereignty, jurisdiction or the recognition of political regions as mandated by the Surveyor General of India for maps showing political boundaries.

Old place names (such as Madras, Calcutta and Bombay) may have been used to retain the historicity of the information as well as avoid confusion with earlier presidencies and provinces of the same name.

All efforts have been made to verify the copyright ownership of photographs as well as the correctness of the information included in this edition. Any omissions are unintentional and regretted, and, following written communication, will be rectified in the next edition.

Subsequent edition/reprint specifications may be subject to change, including but not limited to cover or inside finishes, paper, text colour, and/or colour sections.

Paperback edition ISBN 978-93-5731-754-2
Ebook edition ISBN 978-93-5731-765-8

Hachette Book Publishing India Pvt. Ltd
4th & 5th Floors, Corporate Centre
Plot No. 94, Sector 44, Gurugram 122003, India

Designed and typeset
by Syed Salahuddin

Printed and bound in India
by Thomson Press India Ltd.

Dear Readers,

India is a powerhouse of talent, vigour, and ingenuity in every possible arena. Reflecting India's multifaceted progression towards an ever-evolving future, the *Limca Book of Records* has been a veritable chronicle of the country's achievements. This book is not merely a corpus of records, but an inspirational saga of overcoming challenges and epic journeys undertaken to attain marvellous feats.

As in all the previous years, this edition of the *Limca Book of Records* too showcases many new records, covering a variety of fields and featuring record holders from all parts of the country. Dr Anne Sai Pavan, a cardiothoracic surgeon at Aayush Hospital, Vijayawada, removed the longest blood clot, measuring 20 cm, in a femoral artery embolectomy. Constable Rajwinder Kaur of the Border Security Force performed the longest continuous ride of 32 km while sitting facing backwards on a Royal Enfield 350. The world's tallest reinforced earth structure has come up in Tindharia town in Darjeeling district, West Bengal. Akash Bhadsavle performed a total of 12 shows featuring three plays in a day in Thane, Maharashtra. Aditya L1, India's first-ever solar observatory, has taken India's status in space exploration to unprecedented heights. AIRAWAT-PSAI, India's fastest supercomputer, has secured the 75th position at the 61st edition of Top 500 Global Supercomputing List released at the International Supercomputing Conference (ISC 2023) in Germany

In sports, the year 2023 has been an extraordinary year for India, marked by the 100-plus medal haul at the Asian Games 2022 in Hangzhou, China. Neeraj Chopra and Kishore Kumar Jena finished at the top of the podium in the men's javelin throw, making for India's first-ever 1–2 finish in the event. Jyothi Yarraji won the first gold for India in the women's 100 m hurdles at the Asian Athletics Championships held in Bangkok in July 2023. Sumit Antil broke his own world record in the para men's javelin F64 category as an amputee track-and-field athlete – he scripted history by throwing 70.83 m at the World Para Athletics Championships 2023 in Paris. Veteran striker Sunil Chhetri became the first Indian football player to score 90 or more goals for the national team when he scored eight goals during the Intercontinental Cup and the South Asian Football Federation (SAFF) Championship 2023. The list is endless.

With a wide range of old and new records, reader-friendly infographics, at-a-glance tables and charts, stunning photographs, and carefully curated reference information, this edition of the *Limca Book of Records* stands true to its own legacy as India's first-ever record book.

LBR Marketing Team
Coca-Cola India

HACHETTE INDIA LBR TEAM

Consulting Editor: Vatsala Kaul Banerjee
Managing Editor: Anirban Sarkar
Research and Editorial Team: Shubhali Chopra, Arunima Dharanipragada, Yukta Vats

CONSULTANTS

ADVENTURE
Ajeet Bajaj

CINEMA
Diptakirti Chaudhuri

EDUCATION
Dr Alpana Neogy

MEMORY
Squadron Leader Jayasimha Ravirala

SPORTS
Jaydeep Basu: Football

Kamesh Srinivasan: Shooting

Meenakshi Pahuja: Swimming

K. Arumugam: Hockey

Rakesh Rao: Chess, Golf, Table Tennis

Aditya K. Halder: Archery, Athletics, Badminton, Basketball, Boxing, Cricket, Cue Sports, Gymnastics, Kabaddi, Powerlifting, Squash, Tennis, Weighlifting, Wrestling, General sports, Sports Statistics

LAST DATE FOR NEW ENTRIES (COMPLETE WITH DOCUMENTATION) FOR THE *LIMCA BOOK OF RECORDS* 2025 EDITION:

31 MAY 2024

Please see the revised and updated 'Rules and Guidelines' section for details.

Limca Book of Records does not have any branch offices or representatives.

General and Sales enquiries: **sales@hachetteindia.com**

Dear Readers,

Another exhilarating year of sifting through record applications finally leads us to the *Limca Book of Records 2024*. Each application, whether finally accepted as a record or not, speaks of fascinating talent and determination. India's most prestigious record book once again puts out the best Indian real-life stories of perseverance, patience, and sinewy performances.

The variety in the vast array of achievements we have been capturing in the *Limca Book of Records* never fails to impress us. This year it ranges from collecting newspaper clippings of India's famous personalities, including the president, to covering 95.42 km while standing on the side footrest of a Royal Enfield, and from a marathon quiz to most squares and cubes correctly solved in a minute. The year 2023 will be particularly known for two of India's headlining achievements in space technology: Chandrayaan-3's successful soft-landing on the moon, followed by the launch of Aditya-L1, India's first space-based solar observatory.

In sports, India's achievements in 2023 will be remembered for years to come. The unprecedented 107-medal haul at the Asian Games 2022 comprises records such as the women's kabaddi team becoming the first one in the history of the tournament to complete a hat-trick of gold medals in this discipline.

The year 2023 has been an extraordinary year for Indian athletes. Neeraj Chopra became the first Indian to win the gold medal at the World Athletics Championships, achieving the feat with 88.17 m in the javelin throw final in Budapest, Hungary. Teen archer Aditi Swami became the youngest-ever senior world champion in the World Cup era (2006 onwards) at the age of 17 as she won the gold medal at the World Archery Championships 2023 in Berlin, Germany, in August. The compound archer also claimed India's first-ever individual gold medal at the tournament.

Record-makers have not left any field untrodden. Sukraty Saxena, Rupam Devedi, Swaranjali Saxena, and Apala Rajvanshi completed the fastest Golden Quadrilateral expedition. Maharashtra Metro Rail Corporation Limited created the longest double-decker viaduct in the country. A team of urologists from ACE Hospital and Research Centre, Pune, Maharashtra, removed the largest adrenal cyst, measuring 23 cm, laparoscopically from a 58-year-old patient. The list goes on...

With a legacy of more than 30 years, the *Limca Book of Records* is not just a compendium of records but also a unique reference book for students, public service examination aspirants, and curious readers of any age. This special pre-general election edition has facts and figures that highlight intriguing aspects of India's complex democratic machinery. There is also a special section on the Parliament with quotable information about the new Sansad Bhavan building.

The awe-inspiring stories of passion and resolve, daredevil stunts, and philanthropic community development continue as ever, adding to the pride of India and to our very own *Limca Book of Records*. We express our heartfelt gratitude to all our applicants and to every Indian who is doing or planning to do something different, something meaningful, something that makes or breaks a record!

Anirban Sarkar
Managing Editor, *Limca Book of Records*
(Reference Division, Hachette India)

CONTENTS

THE HUMAN STORY

2 MEMORY
3 SKILLS
6 ENDEAVOUR
6 TALLEST
8 FASTEST
7 LONGEST
9 MOST
15 COLLECTIONS
24 YOGA
25 PHYSICAL FEATS
31 SMALLEST
37 BIGGEST
39 LARGEST
41 CURRENCY, COINS, AND STAMPS
47 COMMUNITY DEVELOPMENT
50 ONLINE FEATS

STRUCTURES

52 EARLY TIMES
54 MEDIEVAL AND MODERN ERAS
55 FORTS AND PALACES
59 RELIGIOUS STRUCTURES
66 STATUES AND IDOLS
67 BRIDGES
70 DAMS
73 LIGHTHOUSES
73 AMUSEMENT ZONES
74 MECHANICAL AND GENERAL STRUCTURES
77 MODERN STRUCTURES
77 SPECIALIZED STRUCTURES

AGRICULTURE

82 GENERAL
83 HISTORY
86 AWARDS AND HONOURS
86 FARMLANDS AND PRINCIPAL CROPS
90 HORTICULTURE
92 ANIMAL HUSBANDRY
97 POULTRY AND FISHERIES
98 FERTILIZERS, PESTICIDES, AND MACHINERY

5

92

52

12-13

91

98

EDUCATION
102 LITERACY
103 SCHOOLS
104 HIGHER EDUCATION
117 ARCHIVES AND LIBRARIES
120 MUSEUMS
125 QUIZZES

PERFORMING ARTS
128 DANCE
134 MUSIC
146 THEATRE

VISUAL ARTS
152 CINEMA
164 PHOTOGRAPHY
168 PAINTING AND CRAFT

104

123

136

130

172–173

CONTENTS

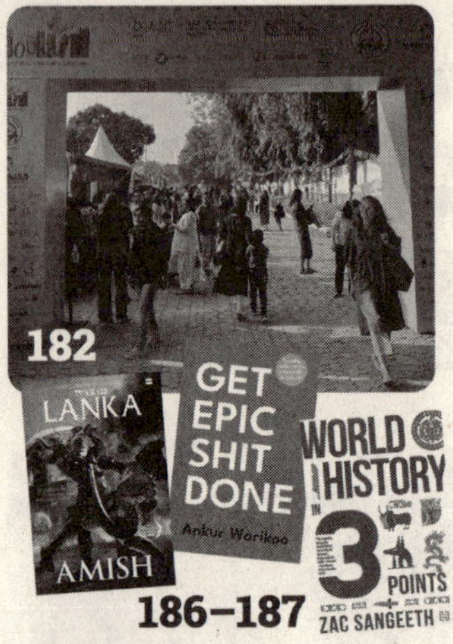

182

186–187

LITERATURE

178 BOOKS
182 PUBLISHING AND BOOK SELLING
185 AWARDS AND HONOURS

MEDIA AND COMMUNICATIONS

194 PRINT
202 RADIO
204 TELEVISION
207 POST AND PHILATELY
215 TELECOM
218 INTERNET, SOCIAL MEDIA, AND APPS

214

197

GOVERNMENT

222 HISTORICAL PERSPECTIVE
225 PARTIES AND ELECTIONS
231 PRESIDENTS AND VICE PRESIDENTS
233 PRIME MINISTERS
234 UNION GOVERNMENT
236 THE STATES
240 GOVERNANCE
241 AADHAAR
242 LAW AND ORDER
243 LEGAL MATTERS
247 THE CENSUS

227

238

249 PARLIAMENT

DEFENCE
262 ARMY
274 NAVY
281 AIR FORCE
292 COAST GUARD

SCIENCE AND TECHNOLOGY
296 FORMAL SCIENCES
298 PHYSICAL SCIENCES
309 OCEAN STUDIES
310 LIFE SCIENCES
312 INTERDISCIPLINARY AND APPLIED SCIENCES
315 METALLURGY
316 SPACE

253

277

263

268

319

312

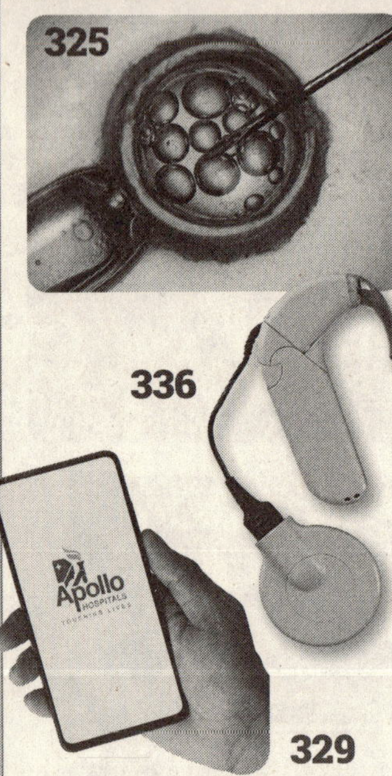

MEDICAL SCIENCES

324 GENERAL
324 FERTILITY, CHILDBIRTH, AND BABIES
325 MEDICAL INSTITUTIONS AND LABORATORIES
330 DOCTORS
331 PUBLICATIONS
331 HEALTH CHECK-UPS AND SCREENING CAMPS
332 MEDICINE AND SURGERY
336 TRANSPLANTS
337 MEDICAL MARVELS

THE NATURAL WORLD

344 PHYSICAL FEATURES
347 FOSSILS
347 MAMMALS
351 BIRDS
353 BUTTERFLIES
353 AMPHIBIANS
354 REPTILES
357 FISH AND MOLLUSCS
358 TORTOISES AND TURTLES
360 PLANTS
362 CONSERVING NATURE AND WILDLIFE
365 GARDENING
369 ENVIRONMENT AND SUSTAINABILITY

350

357

TRANSPORT

376 AIR
383 RAIL AND METRO
392 ROAD
396 WATER

378

386

BUSINESS AND ECONOMY

400 PLANNING
401 WORKFORCE AND HUMAN RESOURCES
403 COINS AND CURRENCY
405 BANKING
408 INSURANCE
409 FINANCIAL INSTRUMENTS
411 FINANCIAL INSTITUTIONS
412 POWER AND ENERGY
416 MINING
417 INDUSTRIES AND COMPANIES
422 RETAIL
424 ADVERTISING

400

412

ADVENTURE

428 AERO SPORTS
435 ROAD EXPEDITIONS
446 WATER SPORTS
455 MARATHONS
458 MOUNTAIN ADVENTURES
460 TREKKING
462 THE POLES

428

431

CONTENTS

SPORTS

464 GENERAL
468 ARCHERY
473 ATHLETICS
482 BADMINTON
490 BASKETBALL
490 BOXING
495 CHESS
503 CRICKET
515 CUE SPORTS
518 FOOTBALL
528 GOLF
536 GYMNASTICS
537 HOCKEY
544 KABADDI
546 LUGE
546 MARTIAL ARTS
547 POWERLIFTING
548 SHOOTING
554 SQUASH
557 SWIMMING
560 TABLE TENNIS
567 TENNIS
571 WEIGHTLIFTING
574 WRESTLING

499

531

559

570

573

581 ASIAN GAMES 2022

587 INDEX
630 IMAGE COPYRIGHT INFORMATION
639 RULES AND GUIDELINES

THE HUMAN STORY

MEMORY

Fastest to identify the flags of all the countries of the world

Taha Ammar Kheyroolla (b. 7 November 2013) from Chennai, Tamil Nadu, identified the flags of all the countries (195) of the world in 3 mins 1 millisec. on 16 May 2021 at Club Mahindra Resort, Puducherry.

Fastest to identify all the bones in the human body

Kudrat Kukreja (b. 23 February 2000) from Shimla, Himachal Pradesh, set a new record by identifying all the bones in the human body in 1 min. 53 secs on 21 August 2020 at Hotel Siddharth, Ram Bazar, Shimla.

Fastest solving of mirror cube while blindfolded

Mohammed Aiman Koli (b. 1 August 2004) from Mumbai, Maharashtra, solved a mirror cube (3 x 3), blindfolded, in 1 min. 0.8 sec. on 26 December 2017 at Veermata Jijabai Technological Institute, Mumbai, Maharashtra.

Fastest to recall 2,500 digits of π

Vimosh Venugopal (b. 23 May 1984) from Thrissur, Kerala, recalled 2,500 digits of the value of π correctly in 12 mins 18 secs 90 microseconds on 27 October 2019 at Hotel Joys Palace, Thrissur.

First winner of the Mental Calculation World Championship

Neelakanta Bhanu Prakash (b. 13 October 1999) from Hyderabad, Telangana, became the first Indian gold medallist at the Mental Calculation World Championship at Mind Sports Olympiad (MSO) held in London, UK, on 15 August 2020. He beat 29 contenders from 13 countries by a margin of 65 points.

Fastest identification of all elements of the periodic table

Jag Prasad Bhattarai (b. 27 July 1980) from Dehradun, Uttarakhand, identified all 118 elements of the periodic table by looking at the atomic numbers arranged in random order in 1 min. 30 secs on 19 February 2019 at the Choice Coaching Institute, Kaulagarh, Dehradun.

Fastest to arrange all elements of the periodic table in order

Meenakshi Agrawal (b. 5 March 1975) from Delhi arranged all the 118 elements of the periodic table in order in 2 mins 49 secs on 27 September 2019 at the Press Club of India, New Delhi.

Meenakshi Agrawal

Most number of national anthems sung by an individual

Yathaarth Murthy (b. 23 February 2006) from Bengaluru, Karnataka, sang the national anthems of 260 countries, as on 31 May 2019.

Most Rubik's cubes solved – 15 mins

S.P. Shankar (b. 1 March 2011) from Hyderabad, Telangana, correctly solved 49 Rubik's cubes (3 x 3) in 15 mins on 19 September 2020 at his residence.

Most 2-digit numbers multiplied correctly – 1 min.

Abhilakshya Arora (b. 9 February 2007), a student of Trendz Abacus, Kota, Rajasthan, solved 29 tasks of multiplication of a 2-digit number by a 2-digit number in 1 min. in an event held during 23–26 May 2019.

Most Rubik's cubes solved – 1 hr*

Satya Sudhai Kolipaka (b. 20 February 2011) from Hyderabad, Telangana, solved 93 scrambled Rubik's cubes (3 x 3) in 1 hr on 23 July 2019 in Hyderabad, Telangana.

Most Rubik's cubes solved – 5 mins

Peram Madhumitha (b. 23 May 2007) from Kamareddy, Telangana, successfully solved 20 Rubik's cubes (3 x 3) in 5 mins on 23 May 2020 at Hotel Hamsa, Kamareddy.

Peram Madhumitha

Most binary numbers memorized – 5 mins

Peram Madhumitha (b. 23 May 2007) from Kamareddy, Telangana, successfully recited 300 binary numbers in 5 mins on 10 June 2020 at Hotel Hamsa, Kamareddy.

SKILLS

Most juggling patterns on a balance board

Jaykishan Vimalbhai Hingu (b. 3 March 2000) from Jetpur, Gujarat, performed 28 juggling patterns using 3 balls while balancing on a balance board on 5 May 2021 at Radha Park, Jetpur. The patterns were: cascade, columns, fake columns, the machine, crossed columns, one going over the top, half shower, false shower, behind the back, box, clawed catches, Mangham's mangle, 'M', infinity, reverse infinity, Georgian shuffle, real tennis, tennis, yo-yo, oy-oy, outside throws, Statue of Liberty, shower, Ripley's rainbow, wiper, 'W', the weave, and Mill's mess.

WR Most tie knots tied – 1 min.

Dr Deepak M. Sharma (b. 2 June 1967) from Ahmedabad, Gujarat, knotted a tie around the neck seven times in 1 min. on 12 February 2020 at a stage performance in Surat.

Fastest to form the English alphabet on Rubik's cubes while blindfolded

Affan Kutty (b. 10 August 2005) from Thane, Mumbai, formed all 26 letters of the English alphabet from A to Z, while blindfolded, on 7 x 7 Rubik's cubes on 30 May 2020 at Noori Garden, Mumbai, in 5 mins 6 secs 55 microseconds. Each letter was formed on all six sides of the Rubik's cube.

Longest duration of non-stop hitting of a dangling cricket ball

Dr Arjun Anand Shirsath (b. 19 March 1977) from Ahmednagar, Maharashtra, knocked a dangling cricket ball with a 1.83 m (6 ft) cord length non-stop 10,332 times with a bat for 4 hrs 34 mins 35 secs on 24 April 2020.

* This category has been discontinued. Further and future claims for this category will not be accepted.

Most squares correctly calculated – 3-digit numbers – 1 min.

Virat Maken (b. 22 October 2013) from Ranchi, Jharkhand, correctly identified the squares of 24 three-digit numbers in 1 min. from 10:24 p.m. to 10:25 p.m. on 22 May 2023 at the Namkum Police Station, Ranchi.

Most cubes correctly calculated – 3-digit numbers – 1 min.

Viraj Maken (b. 22 October 2013) from Ranchi, Jharkhand, correctly identified the cubes of 22 three-digit numbers in 1 min. from 9:36 p.m. to 9:37 p.m. on 22 May 2023 at the Namkum Police Station, Ranchi.

Viraj Maken (*left*) and Virat Maken (*right*)

Longest basketball shot

Manisha Satyajit Dange (b. 8 December 1979) from Thane, Maharashtra, made a 21.4 m long basketball shot in 2 secs 72 millisecs at 10:03 a.m. on 22 May 2021 at the Central Railway Sport Complex, Parel, Mumbai, Maharashtra.

Longest time balancing a hockey stick on the middle finger

Arun Kumar Kannan Murthy (b. 15 September 1985) from Kanchipuram, Tamil Nadu, balanced an on-field hockey stick on his middle finger for 3 hrs 11 mins 50 secs on 18 August 2019 at Neat Trust, Vellore.

Reyaansh Pardeshi

Most dinosaur names identified – 1 min.

Reyaansh Pardeshi (b. 11 September 2015) from Doha, Qatar, correctly identified 85 dinosaurs by name in 1 min. on 28 May 2021 at the Indian Cultural Centre (ICC), Doha.

Most football rolls from eye to eye

Satish Kasi (b. 19 December 1990) from Bengaluru, Karnataka, performed 164 football rolls from eye to eye in 1 min. from 9:36 a.m. to 9:37 a.m. on 16 May 2019 at Sree Kanteerava Stadium, Bengaluru. He shifts the football from eye to eye while balancing the ball on the forehead.

Satish Kasi

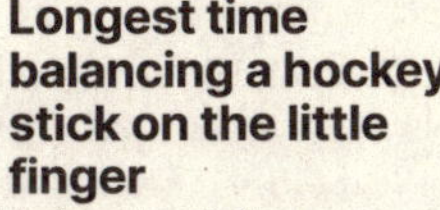

Longest time balancing a hockey stick on the little finger

Gagandeep Singh (b. 25 November 1998) from Fatehgarh Sahib, Punjab, balanced a hockey stick weighing 660 g on his little finger for 1 hr from 4:00 p.m. to 5:00 p.m. on 10 May 2019 in Sirhind–Fatehgarh.

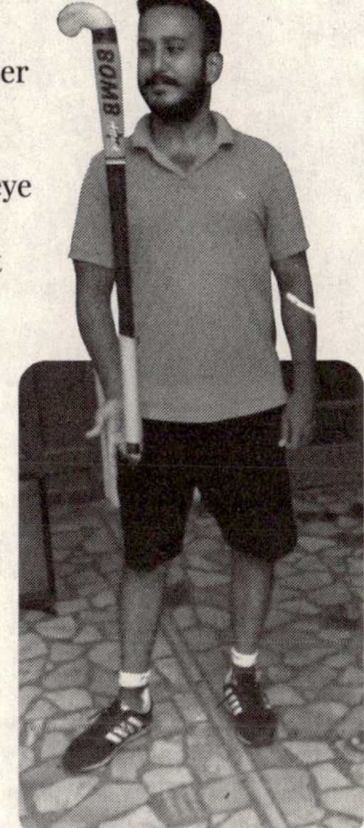

Gagandeep Singh

ENDEAVOUR

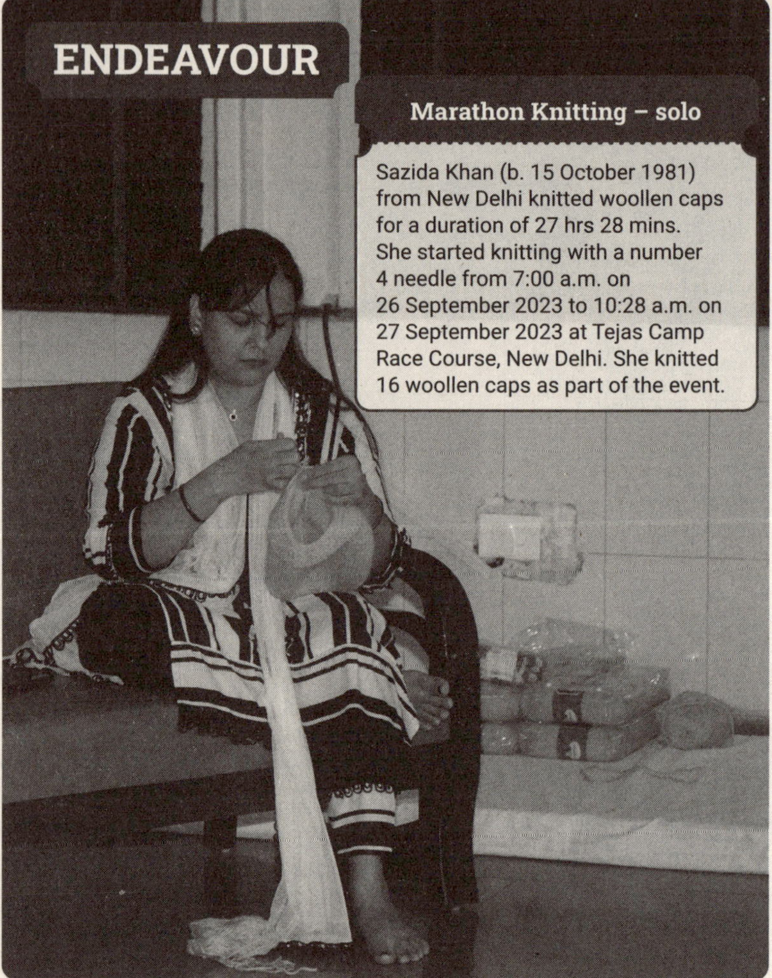

Marathon Knitting – solo

Sazida Khan (b. 15 October 1981) from New Delhi knitted woollen caps for a duration of 27 hrs 28 mins. She started knitting with a number 4 needle from 7:00 a.m. on 26 September 2023 to 10:28 a.m. on 27 September 2023 at Tejas Camp Race Course, New Delhi. She knitted 16 woollen caps as part of the event.

TALLEST

Tallest Man

Dharmendra Pratap Singh from Meerut, Uttar Pradesh, is the tallest man in India. Standing 8 ft 1 in tall, he is a feet taller than the Great Khali.

Tallest Santa Claus

Shoppers Stop Ltd made the tallest Santa Claus, 75.4 ft at Inorbit Mall in Malad, Mumbai, Maharashtra, for Christmas. Work on the Santa started on 10 December 2015 and was completed on 4 January 2016. Over 30 people worked round the clock to construct it.

Tallest Ravana effigy

Rana Tejinder Singh Chauhan is the founder of Shri Ram Leela Club, Barara, Ambala, Haryana. For Dussehra 2014 the Club made a 64 m (210 ft) tall Ravana effigy and burnt it with fire crackers on 3 October that year. The structure weighed 5 tonnes and used hardware like iron pipes, rods, and angles accounting for 3.5 tonnes while the bamboo, cloth, rope, and paper constituted the remaining 1.5 tonnes. The effigy was burnt as a symbolic representation of the destruction of social vices such as terrorism, communalism, casteism, corruption, foeticide, and adulteration etc.

Tallest man-made Christmas tree

Tallest man-made Christmas tree

Delhi International Airport Ltd, New Delhi, commissioned India's tallest man-made Christmas tree, 30.7 m (101 ft) tall (including the 2.4 m [8 ft] star on top). It had over 16,000 Christmas ornaments and 60,000 pine twigs as decoration. The 12 tonne installation was made in 23 days by a team of 80 members from Karmic Events India. It was inaugurated on 23 December 2019.

Tallest Snowman

Shoppers Stop Ltd made the tallest snowman, 28 ft tall and weighing 200 kg. It was displayed in three metros – Inorbit Mall, Malad, Mumbai; Rajouri Garden, Delhi; and Banerghatta, Bengaluru; from 12 December 2014 to 2 January 2015. Twenty people were involved in its making, and it took 15 days to complete.

FASTEST

Fastest assembling of cycles

Hindustan Petroleum Corporation Ltd organized the 'Velocipede Challenge', where 313 participants simultaneously assembled 60 bicycles from different segregated components in 45 mins at the Yuvantage 3.0 Grand Finale on 7 January 2019 at Ramoji Film City, Hyderabad.

Fastest lighting of diyas – group*

The NSHM Faculty of Hospitality and Tourism, Durgapur, West Bengal, with the help of 200 participants, lit 21,328 diyas in 13 mins 22 secs at the NSHM

*This category has been discontinued. Further and future claims for this category will not be accepted.

Knowledge Campus on 25 January 2019. The event was organized by the students, teachers, and management of the college. Teachers and students from neighbouring schools, eminent members of society, and underprivileged children also took part.

LONGEST

Longest sandwich

The St. Soldier Institute of Hotel Management and Catering Technology, Jalandhar, Punjab, made the longest sandwich on 22 December 2021. Led by Sandeep Lohani, the principal, 5 faculty chefs and 15 students prepared a sandwich, measuring 223 ft 2.4 in. in length and 8 in. in width, in 35 mins from 11:13 a.m. to 11:48 a.m. They used 123 slices of loaf spread with a combination of vegetables, noodles, cheese, pasta, and dressings for it.

WR Longest paper chain

Pavitra Patro (b. 29 September 1981) from Ahmedabad, Gujarat, made the longest paper chain, measuring 924.88 m (3,034 ft 4 in.), in 13 hrs 44 mins from 6:31 a.m. to 8:15 p.m. on 19 May 2019 at the Statue of Unity, Kevadia, Gujarat.

Longest charcuterie platter

Longest charcuterie platter

Spectra, a restaurant at The Leela Ambience Gurugram Hotel and Residences, Gurugram, Haryana, displayed a 9.448 m (31 ft) long and 30 cm (11.8 in.) wide Christmas charcuterie platter on 24 December 2018. It had a variety of cheeses, meats, compotes, crudités, sandwiches, canapés, truffles, and chocolates, among other dishes.

Longest kebab

NIMS University-Jaipur in Jaipur, Rajasthan, made a kebab measuring 49 ft 8.4 in. in length with a team of 45 participants under the supervision of Prof. Manoj Srivastava in 9 hrs 53 mins on 6 April 2022. The vegetarian *tawa* kebab was made on a customized tawa, 50 ft long and 2.5 ft wide, using seven industrial gas cylinders with 4 mm hot plate tawa with rail burners underneath. It was displayed at the Sundervan Garden of NIMS University. The kebab was made with 16 kg potatoes, 5 kg chickpea flour, 2 kg green peas, 2 kg of ghee, 1 kg mint leaves, 5 kg onion garlic paste, 2 kg capsicum, 1 kg green chillies, 5 kg soya nuggets, 7 kg spinach, and 900 gm ground garam masala.

Longest and largest human chain

The Government of Bihar, as part of its 'Jan Jeevan Hariyali' campaign, organized an 18,034 km long human chain with 5.16 crore (51.6 million) people on 19 January 2020. It took seven helicopters and over 100 drones to take aerial images of the human chain. The event championed the cause of conservation of environment along with other social causes.

Longest bill

Sanjay Dodrajka (b. 28 January 1972) from New Delhi ordered 420 burgers from the Burger King outlet in Dhaula Kuan for children of MCD School, Nangal Punya, New Delhi, on 7 December 2019. As a result, Sanjay got a 12 ft (144 in.) long bill.

Longest hair

Akanksha Yadav (b. 21 January 1988) from Thane, Maharashtra, has the longest hair, which is 3.01 m (9 ft 10.5 in.) long.

Akanksha Yadav

MOST

Most varieties of mini tarts

The School of Hospitality Management at IMS Unison University, Dehradun, Uttarakhand, organized a culinary challenge where a team – 'Fantastic 36' – headed by Chef Abhay Chamoli and Chef Devashish Pandey, prepared the most varieties of mini tarts on 21 April 2022. The event showcased 550 varieties of mini tarts with popular international types of fillings and toppings. The shells, prepared from shortcrust pastry, was filled with both sweet and savoury vegetarian and non-vegetarian fillings. Abhay and Devashish along with team 'Fantastic 36', made 1,100 mini tarts, each measuring 4 in., with two pieces of each kind. Assembling the mini tarts took 2 hrs 30 mins from 11:00 a.m. to 1:30 p.m. at IMS Unison University, Dehradun.

Most varieties of chaat

Team 35, coordinated by Chef Ashish Spencer, made 503 varieties of chaat in 2 hrs 20 mins from 10:25 a.m. to 12:45 p.m., on 12 March 2022 at Dewan VS Institute of Hotel Management, Meerut, Uttar Pradesh. The chaats were innovative and involved the fusion of ingredients into crunchy, sweet, and savoury chaat. The varieties of chaat included *sabudana papad sevpuri, khatta meetha bhel, dum aloo masala bhel, aloo paneer* chaat, coconut *puchka* chaat and pineapple chaat.

Most varieties of pastries

The Department of Hospitality and Tourism Management at Assam Down Town University, Guwahati, Assam, assembled 517 assorted pastries in 3 hrs 44 mins from 9:30 a.m. to 1:14 p.m. on 11 May 2022 on the university campus. A team of 25 in-house chefs comprising students and faculty, headed by Chef Jyotirmay

Choudhury and Chef Mridu Pawan Rabha, made the pastries. These included pistachio and blackcurrant pastry, chocolate red velvet pastry, pineapple and mango pastry, and litchi and mixed fruit pastry, among others.

Most varieties of vada

The Savoy, Mussoorie team led by Chef Rajeev Badola, Chef Varinder Singh Rana, Chef Smriti Sarin Hari and Junior Chef Khyati Hari prepared 551 varieties of vada on 7 September 2021. Regional varieties of vada including medu vada, keerai vadai, thavala, masala vada and kanji vada, were prepared in front of guests and the general public. To spread the message of sustainable cuisine, regional pahadi vadas were prepared using local ingredients. The vadas were served to the guests and staff.

Most varieties of wraps

A team of seven chefs and 32 students led by Chef Gaurav Khurana, dean of Institute of Hotel Management, Guru Kashi University, Talwandi Sabo, Bathinda, Punjab, prepared 1,348 varieties of wraps on their campus on 12 August 2021. The different fillings and sheets were chicken, mutton, fish, vegetables, dairy products, and sweets.

Most varieties of halwa prepared

Eight chefs – Varinder Singh Rana, Dhiraj Pathak, Ashish Raina, Paramjeet Singh, Vinod, Mohammad Kayamuddin, Tarunvir Singh and Amandeep Kumar – and 51 student chefs of GNA University, Phagwara, Punjab, made 213 kinds of halwa (sweet pudding) in 3 hrs on 22 January 2018. The varieties included suji halwa, turmeric halwa, fig and honey, pumpkin halwa, tomato halwa, and garlic halwa.

Most varieties of *phirni*

The students and faculty of the School of Hotel Management, Airlines and Tourism (SOHAD), CT University, Ludhiana, Punjab, in collaboration with Amul (under the Gujarat Cooperative Milk Marketing Federation Ltd) prepared 1,101 different types of *phirni* on 11 January 2021. A total of 167 ingredients were used to prepare the varieties of *phirni*.

Most varieties of *basundi*

Amity School of Hospitality, Jaipur, Rajasthan, made the most varieties of *basundi* on the university premises on 25 May 2022 under the guidance of Associate professor and chef Dr Saurabh Sharma, Prof. Sanjvee Pal, Chef Adity, Dr Yashwant, Dr Sushil, Dr Jai, Chef Himmat Singh, 4 staff members and 21 students. They made 515 varieties of *basundi* in 3 hrs 29 mins. The *basundi* was served to all guests, faculty, staff, and students of Amity University.

Most varieties of quiche

A team of students and faculty members from the Department of Hospitality Management of the Graphic Era Hill Deemed to be University, Haldwani, Uttarakhand, prepared 251 varieties of savoury quiche in 1 hr 45 mins between 11:00 a.m. and 12:45 p.m. on 24 May 2022 on the university campus. These included chicken and basil quiche, mushroom quiche, broccoli and salmon quiche, and leek and chillies quiche, among others.

Most varieties of tea prepared

Dr Rakesh Dani from the Department of Hospitality Management, Graphic Era Deemed to be University, Uttarakhand, with a team of 15 members (excluding him), prepared 500 varieties of tea. The varieties were prepared between 11:00 a.m. and 12:36 p.m. on 25 May 2023 at the Chanakya Block of the university. The varieties included – clove-flavoured Darjeeling tea, mint lemon tea, peach tea, and oolong tea.

Most varieties of dim sums

Amar Prakash Dabral, Mohsin Khan, Sunil Kumar Lal, Yogesh Upreti, and 'Team Incredible of 26' from the Department of hospitality Management, Graphic Era Hill Deemed to be University, Dehradun, Uttarakhand, assembled 624 varieties of dim sums as part of their event, 'The Dim Sums Quest'. A total of 2,496 dim sums were assembled in 1 hr 47 mins 6 secs between 11:10 a.m. and 12:57 p.m. on 6 May 2022 at the Chanakya block on the university premises.

Most kites on a single line

Dharampal Satyapal Foods Limited in association with MOMS Outdoor Media Solutions flew a train of 1,150 kites on a single line between 1:00 p.m. and 2:16 p.m. on 25 February 2023 at the Rann of Kachchh, Gujarat. The thread measured 1,155 m, and around 10 people participated in the event.

PULSE

Most varieties of biryani

The Institute of Hotel Management Catering Technology and Applied Nutrition, Hyderabad, Telangana, prepared 75 varieties of biryani in 8 hrs on 5 April 2022 in the university premises. The varieties included *goemchi* chicken biryani, Goan shrimp biryani, *bhatkal* biryani, *mawa ki* biryani, and *bharwan gosht ki* biryani, among others.

Most varieties of lassi

A team of 7 chefs and 38 students led by Chef Gaurav Khurana, Dean of the Institute of Hotel Management, Guru Kashi University, Talwandi Sabo, Bathinda, Punjab, prepared 1,813 varieties of lassi on their campus on 13 August 2021. The different flavours used included mango, apple, savoury flavours, vegetables, herbal plants, and sweets.

Most varieties of samosa

The faculty of hospitality, GNA University, Phagwara, Punjab, led by Chef Varinder Singh Rana, prepared 406 varieties of samosas using 217 ingredients in 2 hrs on 26 October 2018. The varieties included dry-fruit samosa, egg samosa, and beetroot samosa, among other flavours.

Most varieties of canapés

The School of Hospitality Management, IMS Unison University, Dehradun, Uttarakhand, assembled 351 varieties of canapés, in 2 hrs 30 mins from 10:30 a.m. to 1:00 p.m. at their campus on 24 April 2019. The canapés were prepared by the 'Fantastic 34' team and the event was anchored by Abhay Chamoli.

Most varieties of cakes made and displayed

Bakersville India Pvt. Ltd executed the largest display of cakes at the Bombay Exhibition Centre, Mumbai, Maharashtra. A team of 15 chefs made and displayed 598 cakes from 9:00 a.m. on 19 September to 8:15 a.m. on 20 September 2019. The cakes were kept on display during 20–22 September. All the cakes were unduplicated in design and flavour.

Most varieties of flavoured rasgulla

A team of 10 chefs and 20 students of Chandigarh University, Gharuan, Punjab, led by Chef Dev Raj, prepared 720 varieties of rasgullas at the campus on 14 August 2018. The flavours included mango, apple, green chilli, lemon, and mint, among others.

Most varieties of besan *chilla*s

Sandeep Lohani, principal, St. Soldier Institute of Hotel Management, Jalandhar, Punjab, along with five faculty members and 30 students, prepared 389 besan *chilla*s with various toppings in 1 hr 25 mins from 10:55 a.m. to 12:20 p.m. on 27 March 2019.

Most saree styles draped

Kalpana Bhagwandas Shah (b. 30 November 1948) from Mumbai, Maharashtra, draped a total of 226 unduplicated saree styles in 24 hrs on 9 April 2022. The sarees used varied from chiffon to georgette and crepe to Benarasi silk. A total of 3,914 ft of saree material was draped in total. The fastest saree drape was done within 1 min.

Most varieties of mocktails prepared

The Institute of Hospitality, Management & Sciences, Balbhadrapur, Uttarakhand, prepared 251 mocktails on 15 May 2023 in 1 hr 30 mins. The team consisted of 15 members and the different flavours included a pineapple sour, mango mash, sunny lemonade, cucumber sparkle, and a pomegranate mimosa.

COLLECTIONS

WR Credit cards

Manish Kumar Dhameja from Lucknow, Uttar Pradesh, has a collection of 1,638 valid credit cards from 25 banks. His first credit card was issued by the State Bank of India in 2014. The collection includes prepaid cards and add-on/supplementary cards. His collection was exhibited from 10:00 a.m. to 11:00 a.m. on 30 August 2022 at the Telecommunications Consultants India Limited (TCIL) Southern Regional Office, Hyderabad, Telangana.

Amitabh Bachchan memorabilia

Mohan Rajgopal Iyer (b. 12 February 1963) from Nagpur, Maharashtra, an ardent admirer of superstar Amitabh Bachchan, has a collection of his photographs, articles, press clippings, filmography, and correspondences and articles from the internet. The total number of items were 8,650 up to 31 May 2019.

Maps

Ravindranath Vishnu Newadkar (b. 22 August 1960) from Thane, Maharashtra, has a collection of 365 maps up to 31 May 2022. These include 100 maps of various countries and 265 maps of different cities.

Press clippings featuring Sridevi

Anuradha Gupta (b. 30 May 1968) from New Delhi has a collection of 1,270 press clippings about the late actor Sridevi from newspapers and magazines in many languages starting from 24 February 2018.

Foreign-language newspapers

Shashanka Sekhar Dash (b. 1 July 1978) from Jajpur, Odisha, has a collection of 981 newspapers in 63 languages from 102 countries. Started in 2005, his collection has newspapers from countries like Lesotho, Seychelles, Peru, Palestine, East Timor, and Papua New Guinea and in languages like Estonian, Yakut, Tok Pisin, Tetum, Hebrew, Dari, and Pashto.

Hindi-language newspapers

Dr Ashok Pandey 'Gulshan' (b. 25 June 1963) from Bahraich, Uttar Pradesh, has a collection of 12,634 different Hindi newspapers under 655 titles from Indian states, Nepal, China, and Thailand, all received by India Post in Uttar Pradesh since 1990. He has bound volumes alphabetically as Daily, Tri-weekly, Biweekly, Weekly, Fortnightly, Monthly, Bimonthly, Tri-monthly, and Annual Special Issues.

Matchboxes featuring horses

Matchboxes featuring horses

Sudhir Jain (b. 7 October 1954) from Satna, Madhya Pradesh, has a collection of 235 matchboxes featuring a horse in the design. None of the matchboxes in the collection is duplicated.

Ties

Dr Deepak M. Sharma (b. 2 June 1967) from Ahmedabad, Gujarat, has a collection of 4,589 ties including 2,611 theme-based ones.

Playing cards

Aditi Shailesh Agarwal (b. 27 July 1979) from Ahmedabad, Gujarat, has 6,000 sets of Indian and foreign playing cards, the largest such collection, which she started when she was 15 years old. The collection varies in theme, form, size, shape, and material. Aditi has a card deck that was used for a code during the First World War and a celebrity collection on Lady Diana, George Bush, Nelson Mandela, and Bollywood stars Amitabh Bachchan, Madhuri Dixit, Shah Rukh Khan, and others.

Airmail envelopes

Jinesh Joseph (b. 8 April 1984) from Bengaluru, Karnataka, has a collection of 1,858 airmail envelopes from 338 regions including recognized countries, disputed territories and autonomous republics.

Stickers

Nidhi Bansal (b. 6 June 1989) from Fatehgarh Sahib, Punjab, had collected 103,800 stickers, a hobby since 2007. She had categorized her collection into subjects like smiley faces, flowers, footballs, birds, trains, and cartoons, among others.

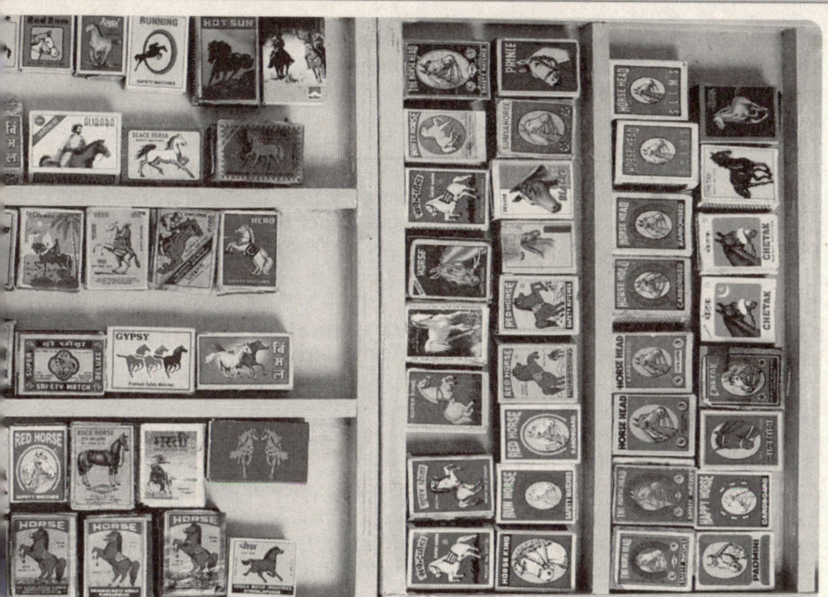

Autographs – national awardees
Praful Thakkar (b. 25 April 1940) has more than 4,300 autographs of Indian and world celebrities, collected in more than 40 years and arranged thematically into 50 categories. The collection includes autographs of 519 Padma Shri awardees and 101 Nobel laureates.

Chitra Kathayen comics
Ninad Jadhav (b. 11 July 1977) from Barkuhi, Chhindwara District, Madhya Pradesh, has the largest collection of Hindi-film *Chitra Kathayen*, numbering 123, a collection since 1997. Most of the comics feature Mithun Chakraborty, Dimple Kapadia, Madhuri Dixit, Vinod Khanna, Rajesh Khanna, Shahrukh Khan, and Navin Nischol. All *Chitra Kathayen* are from Diamond Comics. Amit Jain from Berasia, Bhopal, an ardent fan of Amitabh Bachchan, helped Ninad build this collection.

Hair clips
Sana Fathima (b. 24 October 2014) from Pudukkottai, Tamil Nadu, has 1,200 hair clips, a collection started on 24 October 2017 and completed on 24 March 2018.

Newspaper clippings featuring Mahatma Gandhi
Shiju Thomas (b. 25 February 1976) from Bengaluru, Karnataka, has a collection of 860 news clippings on Mahatma Gandhi in various Indian languages.

Owl-shaped jewellery
Dr Prashant Laxman Wagh (b. 16 June 1978) from Nashik, Maharashtra, has a collection of owl-shaped jewellery, which he started in 2016. He has

717 items in his collection – 478 pendants, 129 brooches, 62 earrings and 48 rings. The jewellery is made of materials like zinc alloy, stainless steel, rhinestone, synthetic turquoise stone, and semi-precious metals, among others.

Models of owls

Ramesh Kumar Bhatia (b. 27 March 1948) from Mumbai, Maharashtra, has a collection of 351 owl models (up to 31 May 2020) since 2013. The models of owls are from different countries including India, Bhutan, China, New Zealand, Australia, Iceland, Uzbekistan, and Morocco, among others.

Obituaries – from a single family

Ninad Jadhav (b. 11 July 1977) from Chhindwara, Madhya Pradesh, has the most obituary news clippings of the Kapoor family (of Hindi cinema) from 272 multi-language newspapers. The obituaries are of Shammi Kapoor (111), Shashi Kapoor (68), Rishi Kapoor (19) and Rajiv Kapoor (74).

Autographs of Ajit Laxman Wadekar

Satish Laxman Chaphekar (b. 5 February 1957) from Dombivli, Maharashtra, has 39 autographs of the late cricketer Ajit Laxman Wadekar, who played 39 international matches during his career including 37 Tests and 2 ODIs. Satish collected Wadekar's bats, balls, and gloves, among other things.

Seer (Indian weights)

Ranjeet Kumar Jha (b. 26 January 1989) from Bhopal, Madhya Pradesh, has a collection of 250 'seer' or 'ser', old Indian weights in various shapes from different Indian princely states like Bhopal, Gwalior, Mewar, Agra, Rajkot, and Indore. In total there are 25 kinds of seer. The scales carry different state seals with different values in different languages.

WR Aircraft models

Vikram Rajkumar Tirkannad (b. 13 April 1980) from Chennai, Tamil Nadu, has collected 719 models of aircraft over the last 38 years. The first model in his collection was an Air India Boeing 747. The largest are the Airways Concorde and a Jet Airways Boeing 737-800 Winglet, both measuring 0.6 m (2 ft). The smallest is the Air India ATR 42-320 measuring only 6 cm (2.36 in.).

Aircraft models

Largest collection of napkins

Parveen Gupta (b. 29 April 1969), his wife Anuradha Gupta (b. 30 May 1968), and daughter Dr Kanika Gupta (b. 7 December 1993) from New Delhi have collected 12,246 commercial and 9,325 non-commercial paper napkins from countries like Romania, Egypt, Slovakia, the UK, the US, the UAE, Germany, Australia, Switzerland, and India. They started their collection in 2014.

Nokia handsets

Nokia handsets

Jayesh Umesh Kale (b. 13 April 1985) from Thane, Maharashtra, has a collection of 1,600 Nokia handsets, a hobby he started in 2013. All the mobile handsets are in working condition.

Cinema press booklets – on a single personality

Ninad Jadhav (b. 11 July 1977) from Chhindwara, Madhya Pradesh, has a collection of 105 cinema press booklets on actor Mithun Chakraborty. The oldest booklet is of the film *Mera Rakshak*, which was released in 1978.

Soap covers – single brand

Mohanan Vareeth Vattapparuthayl (b. 25 May 1972) from Ernakulam, Kerala, who has been using only Medimix brand soap at home, started a collection of the soap covers in 1994. Since then he has collected as many as 1,300 soap covers of that single brand till 10 December 2021.

Toothpaste wrappers

Mankeerat Kaur (b. 11 October 2006) from Gurugram, Haryana, has toothpaste wrappers from different countries, a collection started in April 2020. She has 178 unduplicated toothpaste wrappers from India, the UAE, and the US. Her complete collection comprises 204 wrappers.

Newspaper clippings featuring Lata Mangeshkar

Gaurav Sharma (b. 24 November 1980) and Manju Lata Sharma (b. 5 June 1947) have collected 11,505 news clippings on the late singer Lata Mangeshkar. The oldest press clipping dates back to 1955. There are various original press articles on her from 1959 onwards in various languages - Hindi, Marathi, Odia, Bangla,

Gujarati, Konkani, Tamil, Telugu, Assamese, Malayalam, Punjabi, Urdu, and English. There are also original newspaper articles on her from Finland, the UK, and Bangladesh.

Pradhan Mantri Yojana matchboxes

Alok Mehrotra (b. 16 October 1970) from Kanpur, Uttar Pradesh, has a collection of 1,550 matchboxes of 21 Pradhan Mantri Yojanas including the Awas Yojana, the Amrit Kosh Yojana, the Garib Kalyan Yojana, the Sukanya Samriddhi Yojana, the Namami Gange programme, the Swachh Bharat Mission, the Pradhan Mantri Jan Aarogya Yojna, the National Sports Talent Yojana, the UMANG Yojana, the Jal Shakti Yojana and the Sovereign Gold Bond Yojana, among others. He started his collection in 2019.

Lapel pins

Arvind Sinha (b. 14 May 1955) from Mumbai, Maharashtra, has been collecting lapel pins since 1998 and had 53,228 lapel pins as on 31 March 2015. He exhibits his collection to create awareness on history through lapel pins. The world wars, development of guns, aviation history, space programmes – all depicted through his lapel pins.

Lighters

Hamed Husein Patel (b. 5 September 1959) from Mumbai, Maharashtra, has a collection of 1,042 gas and petrol lighters (till 30 June 2018). The most expensive lighter is the 2008 limited edition St. Dupont priced at ₹2,00,000. He also possesses a Dunhill lighter which was once owned by Elvis Presley.

Railway platform tickets

Naveen Kumar (b. 10 June 1974) from New Delhi has a collection of 100 unduplicated railway platform tickets. These tickets have been collected from Uttar Pradesh, Uttarakhand, Delhi, Haryana, Maharashtra, and Rajasthan between 30 April 2023 and 10 June 2023.

Railway platform tickets

MAGAZINE MANIA

1 Magazines

Daria Singh Yadav from Haryana has a collection of over 3,000 different magazines and periodicals. The magazines, which are not necessarily first issues, are in 17 languages covering 6 continents.

2 Magazines – Hindi

Dr Jawahar Karnavat (b. 12 August 1959) from Bhopal, Madhya Pradesh, has 93 Hindi magazines, a collection that started in 2002. The oldest magazine in his collection is the *India Opinion* published in 1903 in South Africa in Gujarati, Tamil, English, and Hindi. In all, there are 25 weekly, 3 fortnightly, 40 monthly, 18 quarterly, and 7 half-yearly magazines. The Deepawali special issue of *Shanti Doot* published from Fiji contains as many as 120 pages.

3 Magazines – Regional languages

A. Ramanan from Vellore, Tamil Nadu, has collected over 1,706 Tamil magazines, some of which have now stopped publication. The oldest *Varthaga Mitran* is dated 1917, and the second oldest is *Ramanujan* dated 1919.

4 Magazines – first issues

Mudappalam M. Sukumar from Mumbai, Maharashtra, has been collecting first issues of magazines since May 1979. He has a total of 662 issues of weekly, fortnightly, monthly, and bimonthly magazines in English, Tamil, and Hindi. There are 488 Tamil, 30 Hindi, 112 English and 32 magazines in other languages. His collection started with the very first issue of the Tamil magazine *Chaavi*.

5 Airline magazines

Mallikarjun M. Umadi (b. 1 June 1965) from Nashik, Maharashtra, has been collecting magazines printed by various airlines since 2006; and as of 30 June 2016, he had 175 different magazines of 33 different airlines, both national and international.

6 Magazines – personality covers – featuring a single personality

Anuradha Gupta (b. 30 May 1968) from New Delhi has collected 317 different magazines in various languages with Prime Minister Narendra Modi on the cover. The collection began in 2017.

Antique matchbox labels – uncut sheets

Samirkumar Hasmukhbhai Arya (b. 16 December 1977) from Valsad, Gujarat, has a collection of 225 uncut antique matchbox labels.

Badges – political theme

Ranjeet Kumar Jha (b. 26 January 1989) from Bhopal, Madhya Pradesh, has 250 badges from different years and of different shapes, sizes, material, and logos of political parties, such as the Congress, BJP, and BSP, in his collection. He started the collection on 9 April 2003 and completed it on 9 April 2021.

YOGA

WR Longest *setu bandhasana*

Prof. Dr S. Ramesh Babu (b. 12 February 1957) from Bengaluru, Karnataka, performed *setu bandhasana* (bridge pose) for 24 mins from 8:00 a.m. to 8:24 a.m. on 9 July 2019 at Vidyanjali Academy for Learning, Bengaluru.

Longest *ashtavakrasana*

Adesh Motiramji Karnase (b. 9 April 1997) from Gurugram, Haryana, performed *ashtavakrasana* (eight-angle pose) for 1 min. 4 secs on 10 June 2020 in Morshi, Maharashtra.

Longest *vishvamitrasana*

Nitin Mohanrao Prajapat (b. 2 April 1996) from Gurugram, Haryana, performed *vishvamitrasana* for 1 min. 13 secs on 10 June 2020 in Morshi, Maharashtra.

Longest *Hanumanasana*

Dr Narendra Kumar Sharma (b. 30 March 1978) from Jaipur, Rajasthan, performed *Hanumanasana* (monkey pose) for 23 mins 36 secs on 22 June 2020 in Malviya Nagar, Jaipur.

Longest *parshva poorna dhanurasana*

Amrutha Anand (b. 13 July 1991) from Chidambaram, Tamil Nadu, performed *parshva poorna dhanurasana* (full side bow pose) for 15 mins 10 secs, starting at 2:00 p.m., on 2 March 2019 at the Great Wall of China, Beijing.

Amrutha Anand: performing *parshva poorna dhanurasana*

Longest *padma mayurasana*

Mangal Raj (b. 11 August 1991) from Sitamarhi, Bihar, performed *padma mayurasana* (lotus in peacock pose) for 4 mins 14 secs from 5:49 p.m. to 5:54 p.m. on 19 November 2021 at Raj Classic Park, Versova, Mumbai.

Longest *mayurasana* – with one hand

Mangal Raj (b. 11 August 1991) from Sitamarhi, Bihar, performed *mayurasana* (peacock pose) with one hand for 56 secs on 4 February 2022 at Raj Classic Park, Versova, Mumbai.

Longest *purvattanasana*

Sandeep Krishna Murthy Karupakala (b. 27 January 1982) and Aruna K.S. (b. 2 January 1987) from Chintamani, Karnataka, held *purvattanasana* (upward plank pose) for 2 mins 10 secs on 10 April 2021 at Lalitha Nivas, Chintamani.

Longest *mandukasana*

Swapan Kumar Sur (b. 24 February 1974) from Faridabad, Haryana, performed *mandukasana* (frog pose) for 47 mins 11 secs from 8:33 p.m. to 9:21 p.m. on 14 April 2021 in Chhinamore, Hoogly, West Bengal.

Longest *niralamba ushtrasana*

Dr Narendra Kumar Sharma (b. 30 March 1978) from Jaipur, Rajasthan, performed *niralamba ushtrasana* (unsupported camel pose) for 10 mins 38 secs on 30 May 2021 in Bharatpur, Rajasthan.

PHYSICAL FEATS

Most push-ups – 1 hr

Umesh Sopan Vyavahare (b. 3 December 1988) of Adhegaon, Tal Madha, Solapur District, Maharashtra, performed 2,993 half push-ups in 1 hr from 5:30 to 6:30 p.m. on 13 July 2017.

Most two-thumb push-ups – 1 min.

Harpreet Singh (b. 4 October 1975) of Sultanpuri Lodhi, Kapurthala District, Punjab, performed 69 two-thumb push-ups in 1 min. at Lyallpur Khalsa College for Women on 17 April 2017.

Most fingertip push-ups – one arm – 1 min.

Shaikh Rejaul Haque (b. 3 May 1988) of Ulhasnagar, Maharashtra, performed 45 one-arm fingertip push-ups in 1 min. on 20 May 2015.

Most push-ups – 1 min. (woman)

Sunita Chhabra (b. 3 May 1972) of Jaipur, Rajasthan, performed 34 full push-ups at Manav Seva Trust's head office in 1 min. on 25 March 2018.

Most contortion push-ups – 1 min.

Rajendra Bishnoi (b. 5 November 1995) from Bikaner, Rajasthan, performed 132 unique contortion push-ups in 1 min. on 17 March 2019 at Swargiya Shri Balasaheb Thackeray Maidan, Mumbai.

Most half-knuckle push-ups – 1 min.

Ashif Khan (b. 30 September 1990) from Gurugram, Haryana, did 145 half-knuckle push-ups in 1 min. from 12:05 p.m. to 12:06 p.m. on 23 May 2019 at H2O Fitness gym, Gurugram.

Most diamond push-ups – 1 min.

V. Kaliraj (b. 3 October 1996) from Virudhunagar, Tamil Nadu, did 112 diamond push-ups in 1 min. on 26 May 2019 at D'Pearl Sport Academy, Ramapuran, Chennai.

Most clap push-ups – 1 min.

Jatin Goel (b. 10 April 1994) from Gurugram, Haryana, performed 85 clap push-ups in 1 min. from 12:05 p.m. to 12:06 p.m. on 10 May 2019 at H2O Fitness gym, Gurugram.

Most superman push-ups – 1 min.

Kuwar Amritbir Singh (b. 4 November 2001) from Gurdaspur, Punjab, performed 52 superman push-ups in 1 min. from 12:05 p.m. to 12:06 p.m. on 5 May 2021 in Umarwala, Punjab.

Most abdominal push-ups – 1 hr

Prof. Dr S. Ramesh Babu (b. 12 February 1957) of Bengaluru, Karnataka, did 1,700 non-stop abdominal push-ups in 1 hr, at Prof. Satish Dhawan Park, from 9:00 a.m. on 14 April 2018.

Most burpees – 1 min. (woman)

Ankita Nagpal (b. 2 January 1994) from Gurugram, Haryana, performed 48 burpees in 1 min. from 12:05 p.m. to 12:06 p.m. on 23 May 2019 at H2O Fitness gym, Gurugram.

Most two-finger push-ups – both arms – 1 min.

Arya Rishabh Rameshchandra (b. 26 September 1997) from Ahmedabad, Gujarat, performed 65 two-finger push-ups (index and middle finger) in 1 min. on 19 May 2019 at I-Can Gym, Ahmedabad.

Arya Rishabh Rameshchandra: most two-finger push-ups in 1 min.

Most parallel dips – 1 min.

Ashish Lohia (b. 10 July 1998) from Gurugram, Haryana, performed 75 parallel dips in 1 min. from 12:05 p.m. to 12:06 p.m. on 28 May 2019 at H2O Fitness gym in Gurugram.

Most side-jump push-ups – 1 min.

Anand S. (b. 18 May 1993) from Chennai, Tamil Nadu, performed 42 side-jump push-ups in 1 min. from 1:00 p.m. to 1:01 p.m. on 20 October 2021 in Potheri, Chennai.

Most reverse dips – 1 min.

Ankush Gurjar (b. 12 September 1992) from Gurugram, Haryana, performed 137 reverse dips in 1 min. from 12:06 p.m. to 12:07 p.m. on 4 May 2019 at H2O Fitness gym, Gurugram.

Most lunges – 1 hr

Kapil Arora (b. 28 September 1975) from Mumbai, Maharashtra, performed 948 lunges in 1 hr between 8:16 a.m. and 9:16 a.m. on 28 June 2020 at his residence.

Most jump squats – 1 min.

Himanshu Jadon (b. 28 November 1993) from Gurugram, Haryana, performed 82 jump squats in 1 min. from 12:05 p.m. to 12:06 p.m. on 28 May 2019 at H2O Fitness gym, Gurugram.

Most squats – 1 min.

Apoorv Ashok Mathur (b. 19 October 1988) performed 96 squats in 1 min. at H2O Fitness Gym, Gurugram, Haryana, on 28 April 2018.

Longest plank

Abhishek Sihag (b. 15 August 1997) from Sikar, Rajasthan, performed the longest plank for 8 hrs 5 mins from 6:51 a.m. to 2:56 p.m. at the Railway Community Centre, Sikar, on 1 January 2019.

Most squats – 1 min. (woman)

Priyanka Prasher (b. 14 February 1986) from Gurugram, Haryana, performed 97 squats in 1 min. from 12:09 p.m. to 12:10 p.m. on 10 May 2019 at H2O Fitness gym, Gurugram.

Most pistol squats – alternating legs – 1 min.

Shivam (b. 5 October 2000) from Lucknow, Uttar Pradesh, performed 45 pistol squats in 1 min. using legs alternately on 4 September 2019 at his residence.

Most sit-ups – 1 min.

Sandeep Arya (b. 20 March 1967) of Kolkata, West Bengal attempted 67 sit-ups in 1 min. at Tivoli Court, Kolkata, West Bengal, at 9.30 a.m. on 28 April 2018.

Most abdominal sit-ups – 1 min. (woman)

Shreya Bhardwaj (b. 21 October 1999) performed 85 abdominal sit-ups in 1 min. from 12:05 p.m. to 12:06 p.m. on 23 May 2019 at H2O Fitness gym, Gurugram.

LONGEST HOLD OF *ASANAS*

1 Longest *ekapada shirshasana*

Virendra Vikram Singh (b. 2 December 1954) from Balrampur, Uttar Pradesh, performed *ekapada shirshasana* (foot behind the head pose) for 10 mins from 10:00 a.m. to 10:10 a.m. on 20 February 2019 at M.L.K. PG College, Balrampur.

2 Longest *bakasana*

Virendra Vikram Singh (b. 2 December 1954) from Balrampur, Uttar Pradesh, performed the *bakasana* (crane pose) for 5 mins from 6:10 p.m. to 6:15 p.m. on 16 May 2022 at the M.P.P. Inter college, Balrampur.

3 Longest *janu shirshasana*

Virendra Vikram Singh (b. 2 December 1954) from Balrampur, Uttar Pradesh, performed *janu shirshasana* (head to knee pose) for 1 hr from 9:00 a.m. to 10:00 a.m. on 24 February 2021 at Late Ravindra Singh Memorial, Balrampur, Uttar Pradesh.

4 Longest *paschimottanasana*

Virendra Vikram Singh (b. 2 December 1954) from Balrampur, Uttar Pradesh, performed *paschimottanasana* (seated forward bend pose) for 40 mins from 9:00 a.m. to 9:40 a.m. on 19 May 2020 at Bagh Palace, Balrampur.

5 Longest *supta padangushthasana*

Virendra Vikram Singh (b. 2 December 1954) from Balrampur, Uttar Pradesh, performed *supta padangushthasana* (reclining hand to big toe pose) for 20 mins from 9:50 a.m. to 10:10 a.m. on 19 May 2020 at the Late Maharaj Dharmendra Prasad Singh Memorial, Balrampur.

Gaurav Singh Bhatti: most alternative squats in 1 min.

Most alternative squats – 1 min.

Gaurav Singh Bhatti (b. 11 April 1997) of Mandi Dabwali, Haryana, attempted 122 alternative squats in 1 min. at Big Gym on 7 July 2018.

Most bicycle crunches – 1 min. (woman)

Sunita Chhabra (b. 3 May 1972) from Jaipur, Rajasthan, performed 88 bicycle crunches in 1 min. from 7:32 p.m. to 7:33 p.m. on 18 February 2020 at the office of JVP Media Group, Jaipur.

Most jumping jacks – 1 min.

Venkata Sairam Reddy Pulusu (b. 11 April 1988) from Hyderabad, Telangana, performed 127 jumping jacks in 1 min. from 12:05 p.m. to 12:06 p.m. on 23 May 2019 at H2O Fitness gym, Gurugram.

Most tandem push-ups – 1 min.

Mandeep Singh Karir (b. 2 September 1992) and Baldeep Singh (b. 27 June 1998) of Singhbhum, Jharkhand, performed 28 tandem push-ups in 1 min. at Paul Fitness and Yoga Hub on 6 July 2022.

Mandeep Singh Karir and Baldeep Singh: most tandem push-ups in 1 min.

Most abdominal crunches – 1 min.

Mohit Bhardwaj (b. 29 March 1988) from Gurugram, Haryana, performed 108 abdominal crunches in 1 min. from 12:06 p.m. to 12:07 p.m. on 23 May 2019 at H2O Fitness gym, Gurugram.

Most full-contact kicks on a kickpad – alternate legs – 1 hr

Naman Bhardwaj (b. 6 February 2002) from Ghaziabad, Uttar Pradesh, performed 6,170 full-contact kicks in 1 hr from 10:20 a.m. to 11:20 a.m. on 26 May 2021 at Vasundhara Taekwondo Academy, Ghaziabad, Uttar Pradesh.

Most crunches*

Nitin Arora (b. 18 March 1977) of Ghaziabad, Uttar Pradesh, performed 1,000 abdomen crunches from 8:45 a.m. to 8:53 a.m. in 8 mins on 6 May 2018.

Most jumping jacks – 1 min. (woman)

Richa Maheshwari (b. 23 September 1988) from New Delhi performed 115 jumping jacks in 1 min. from 12:07 p.m. to 12:08 p.m. on 25 May 2019 at H2O Fitness gym, Gurugram.

Most jumping jacks – 1 hr

Jasjeet Singh (b. 21 March 1990) from New Delhi performed 4,479 jumping jacks in 1 hr from 9:12 a.m. to 10:12 a.m. on 17 February 2021 at his residence in Vikaspuri, Delhi.

SMALLEST

Smallest electric bike model

Santhosh (b. 7 May 1974) from Mysuru, Karnataka, made the smallest electric bike model, named Moosshiqk-3. It measures 145 mm (5.7 in.), with a 130 mm (5.12 in.) wheelbase, its total length being 230.4 mm (9.07 in.). It weighs 2.5 kg, with a payload of 64 kg.

WR Smallest rugby stadium model

Shaminder Singh (b. 13 January 1976) from Coventry, UK, constructed a model of the Ricoh Arena rugby stadium, 122 cm (48 in.) long, 76 cm (29.9 in.) wide, and 41 cm (16.1 in.) high, with 45,000 toothpicks. He worked on the model for a total of 900 hours over six months between 1 September 2017 and 2 March 2018.

Smallest functioning guitar

Prakash Chandra Upadhyay (b. 25 May 1973) from Haldwani, Uttarakhand, made the smallest functioning guitar, measuring 3 cm (1.2 in.) in length, using sandalwood, copper wire, and aluminium and iron pins on 29 April 2020. He took 4 hrs 30 mins to make it. The sound of the guitar is audible with audio speakers.

Smallest drill

Kiran Patil of Bengaluru, Karnataka, made the smallest working model of a drill machine on 19 April 2019. The dimensions of the drill are 6.1 mm (0.24 in.) in height, 6.7 mm (0.27 in.) in length, and 4.6 mm (0.18 in.) in width.

*This category has been discontinued. Further and future claims for this category will not be accepted.

Smallest model of Belur Math

Sudhakar Raghunath Shinde (b. 25 February 1955) from Pune, Maharashtra, carved the smallest model of the Belur Math out of wood measuring 218.5 cm (86 in.) in length, 102 cm (40 in.) in width, and 98 cm (38.6 in.) in height. The design included details such as carving of elephants, balconies, blooming lotuses, domes, pillars, Lord Ganesha, and Lord Hanuman. He has never visited the Belur Math and made this model using images downloaded from the Internet.

Smallest microwave oven

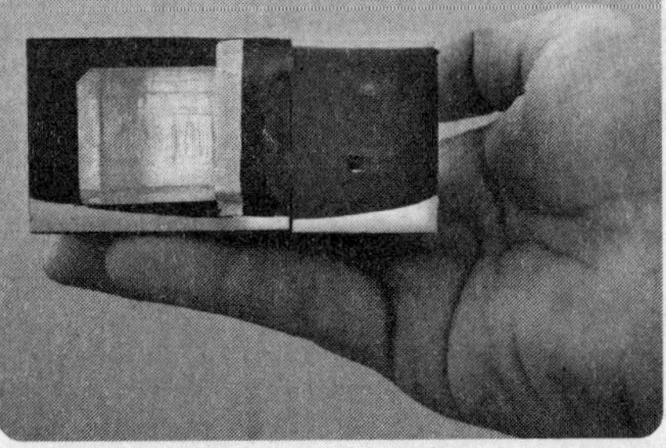

Smallest microwave oven

Salvendar Ghansheed Baba (b. 21 October 1999) from Vijayawada, Andhra Pradesh, made the smallest microwave oven, 80 mm (3.15 in.) long, 35 mm (1.38 in.) wide, and 40 mm (1.57 in.) high in 15 days, from 11 to 25 December 2018. He used plywood cardboard, green and orange LED lights of 3 volts, 1,000-ohm resistor, small wires, Nichrome wire, aluminium foil, Fevicol glue, a small switch, a design sticker, a 3.7-volt phone battery and a connecting pin to make the oven.

Smallest functioning water-level controller printed circuit board

Pranav Ramesh Rokde (b. 30 October 1995) from Nagpur, Maharashtra, made the smallest functioning water-level controller printed circuit board (PCB) with dimensions of 28 mm x 28 mm x 15 mm (1.1 in. x 1.1 in. x 0.6 in.) on 7 May 2021 at his residence. The water-level controller encompasses electronic components such as NPN (negative-positive-negative) and PNP transistors, capacitors, a few resistors, a diode, and a relay for switching water motor pump on and off.

Smallest iron

Pawan Sharma (b. 8 January 1977) of Surat, Gujarat, made the smallest electric iron of 17 mm (0.66 in.) height, 9 mm (0.35 in.) width, and 2.5 mm (0.09 in.) thickness, which he completed in seven days spending 1 hr every day until 17 October 2012. The iron is made using aluminium, a plastic handle, asbestos, tungsten wire, a steel stand, and a mobile charger with a 12V DC connection.

Smallest iron

Smallest juice blender

Vijaya Mohan Koppineedi (b. 18 November 1989) of Narasapuram, West Godavari District, Andhra Pradesh, made the smallest juice blender of 39 mm (1.53 in.) height and 16.3 mm (0.64 in.) width in 5 hrs on 7 January 2018. The blender was made using a button cell battery for power, a small switch, and a vibrator motor, an aluminium bottle cap, pen a cap, and two pieces of wires.

Smallest curd-churning machine

Vijaya Mohan Koppineedi (b. 18 November 1989) of Narasapuram, West Godavari District, Andhra Pradesh, made the smallest curd-churning machine at his residence, which is of 40.4 mm (1.59 in.) height and 20.4 mm (0.80 in.) width in

5 hrs on 8 January 2018. It operates on 1.5V DC supply and contains a vibrator motor, steel pipe, curd-churning blade, aluminium sheet, and two pieces of wire.

Smallest scissors

Mattewada Ajay Kumar (b. 7 December 1973) of Warangal, Telangana, created a miniature working pair of gold scissors in 3 hrs in 2015. It is 11 mm (0.43 in.) long and weighs 0.18 mg.

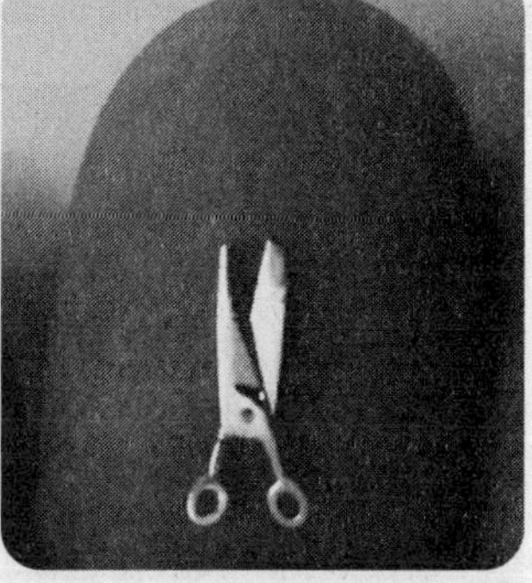

Smallest scissors

Smallest gold violin

Mattewada Ajay Kumar (b. 7 December 1973) of Warangal, Telangana, created a 20 mm (0.78 in) long miniature gold violin, weighing 0.74 mg, in 12 hrs in 2009.

Smallest gold violin

Smallest Wimbledon Centre Court model

Shaminder Singh (b. 13 January 1976) of Coventry, UK, made a replica of the Wimbledon Centre Court using 12,000 toothpicks over 40 hours each week in 10 months from 2 July to 25 September 2017. The structure is 36 in (91.44 cm) long, 28 in (71.12 cm) wide and 12 in (30.48 cm) in height.

Wimbledon Centre Court model

Smallest spinning wheel

Jayant Natthuji Tandulkar (b. 11 October 1976) from Nagpur, Maharashtra, designed the smallest spinning wheel (charkha) to spin yarn from cotton measuring 2.94 mm (0.12 in.) in length, 2.40 mm (0.09 in.) in width, 2.74 mm (0.11 in.) in height, and weighing 0.03 g on 22 April 2023. It took him 8 hrs to make it. He used materials such as steel wire, wooden sticks, and cotton thread to make it. The charkha was measured using a vernier caliper and a digital scale.

BIGGEST

Biggest Swachh Bharat logo made by arranging motorcycles*

Pavitra Patro (b. 29 September 1981) of Ahmedabad, Gujarat, made the biggest Swachh Bharat Abhiyan logo (Gandhiji's spectacles) using 667 motorcycles at TVS Oceanic Warehouse, Ahmedabad, on 8 April 2018. Pavitra alone arranged the bikes in 9 hrs from 9 a.m. to 6 p.m. The diameter of each lens was 19.5 m (63 ft 11.7 in.) and the frame's length was 3.6 m (11 ft 9.7 in.).

Biggest postcard

Suresh Kumar (b. 2 January 1980) from Marthandam, Kanniyakumari, Tamil Nadu, made the biggest replica of an India Post postcard using plywood. The postcard measured 3.65 m (11 ft 11.7 in.) long, 2.44 m (8 ft) wide and 18 mm (0.71 in.) thick. Balakrishna Matriculation Higher Secondary School, Vadakkankulam, got 1,686 students to sign the card. The card was made in 17 days from 15 April to 1 May 2019.

Biggest memento

A team of 11 members – consisting of Dr Abhilash Modi, Utkarsh Singh, Karan Sharma, Ajay Jhanwar, Sonali Dangi, Dinesh Teli, Ajay Singh Rawat, Jaswant Khati, Prateek Bapna, Surbhi Jain, and Diksha Dangi – created a memento, dedicated to Indian defence forces. It was 7.68 m (25 ft 2 in.) long, 4.60 m (15 ft 1 in.) wide, weighed 92 kg,and was made in 50 hrs.

Biggest jigsaw puzzle solved – group

Vodafone Idea Business Services created the largest jigsaw puzzle on 17 January 2019 at the Vodafone Idea office in Peninsula Towers, Mumbai, Maharashtra. The 6 m (19 ft 8.2 in.) long and 3.96 m (12 ft 11.9 in.) wide jigsaw had 912 pieces. The puzzle was completed by 264 employees from 18 cities in 3 hrs 20 mins from 9:45 a.m. to 1:05 p.m.

Biggest replica of ₹1 coin

Shailendra Kumar (b. 5 February 1983) of Sarai Dharampur, Fatehpur, Uttar Pradesh, made a replica of a ₹1 coin, with a diameter of 5 ft (1.52 m), and weighing 211 kg, using wheat and chaff, in 45 days.

Biggest replica of a ₹1 coin

Biggest Dharmachakra

The Buddhist Forum, Yamunanagar, Haryana, made the biggest Dharmachakra (Ashoka Chakra is a depiction of Dharmachakra) with mild steel in 240 days between 25 February and 22 October 2018. Created by Dr Satyadeep Neil Gauri and Sidhartha Gauri, the structure weighs 6 tonnes and has a diameter of 9.14 m (29 ft 11.8 in.).

*This category has been discontinued. Further and future claims for this category will not be accepted.

Biggest steel charkha

District Administration, Wardha, Maharashtra, Sevagram Ashram Pratishthan, and Sir J. J. School of Arts, Mumbai, unveiled the biggest functional mild-steel charkha on 2 October 2018. It is 9.75 m (31 ft 11.8 in.) long, 3.45 m (11 ft 3.83 in.) wide, 5.64 m (18 ft 6 in.) high, and weighs 5.5 tonnes. It was built in 21 days from 11 September to 1 October 2018 (both days included).

Biggest steel charkha

Biggest traditional lamp

Dr Braj Kishore Shukla (b. 3 June 1970) from Gandhinagar, Gujarat, created the biggest traditional lamp to spread the message of humanity. The 10.97 m (35 ft 11.8 in.) tall stainless steel lamp, with a bowl 4.8 m (15 ft 8.98 in.) in diameter, weighed 3,000 kg. Named the 'Lamp of Humanity', it has solar panels and was installed at the Sabarmati waterfront in Ahmedabad, Gujarat, on 25 September 2018. It has five flames, with four side flames representing Truth, Justice, Honesty and Compassion, and the central flame symbolizing Humanity.

Biggest jigsaw puzzle solved – solo

Heer Kalpakbhai Doshi (b. 10 March 2006) from Rajkot, Gujarat, completed the 32,256 Ravensburger jigsaw puzzle

Biggest jigsaw puzzle solved – solo

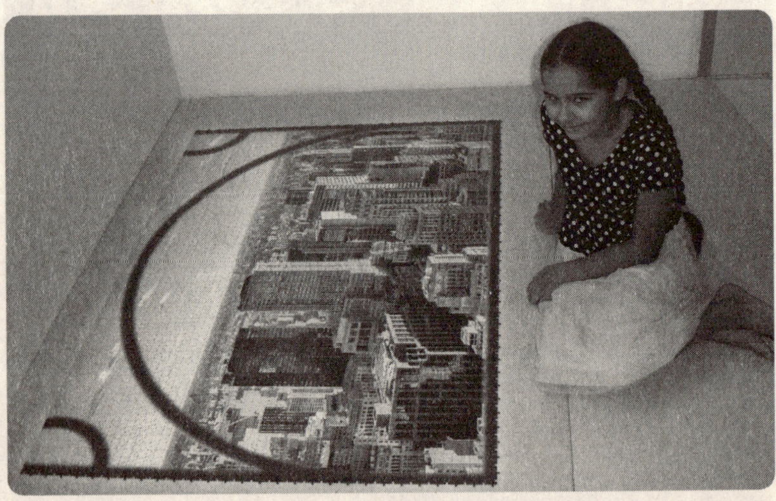

titled 'New York City Window' in 3 years 1 month between 18 October 2015 and 18 November 2018. The finished puzzle is 5.44 m x 1.92 m (17 ft 10 in. x 6 ft 3.59 in.) in area. LED lamps were used to illuminate it from behind. Celebrations started on 12 October and ended on 21 October 2018.

Biggest desk calendar

Revati Ravi Sonar (b. 19 December 2000) from Pandharpur, Maharashtra, received the biggest desk calendar as a gift from her brother, Omkar Ravi Sonar, on 19 December 2018. The area of the calendar is 6.503 sq. m (70 sq. ft) and it is 3.048 m (10 ft) wide and 2.134 m (7 ft) high. The flex calendar has seven pages.

Biggest thali – dishes

The Institute of Hospitality, Management and Sciences, Kotdwar, Uttarakhand, made the biggest thali with 301 dishes from various states. The event involved 57 participants, 49 students, and 8 faculty members making the dishes in 2 hrs 15 mins on 15 May 2022 on the college premises.

Biggest umbrella

The Rural Development and Research Centre, Haryana, made the biggest umbrella, measuring 52 ft (15.85 m) in height and having a diameter of 84 ft (25.60 m), at Aastha Science Park, Rewari, Haryana. The umbrella is made of tensile fabric. It has a steel frame and a cement-concrete base. It weighs 100 tonnes and covers an area of 5,760 sq. ft. (535.12 sq. m). Inaugurated on 19 March 2022, it has a digital lighting system and can be folded easily.

LARGEST

Largest wall clock

Nisha Jayesh Chheda (b. 16 June 1977) from Mumbai, Maharashtra, conceptualized and designed the largest wall clock, which was executed by Vipul Panchal, Saikrishna Vasam, Jayesh L. Chheda, Saachi J. Chheda, and Digvijay Singh. The 1.8 m (5 ft 10.8 in.) diameter clock was made using plywood, acrylic, stainless steel nuts, moulds, and colours. The clock was made in 49 days from 15 January 2019 to 4 March 2019.

Largest *kaju katli*

Kanti Sweets from Bengaluru, Karnataka, made the largest kaju katli (a sweet made with cashew nuts), measuring 3.3 m x 2.1 m x 0.2 m (10 ft 9.9 in. x 6 ft 10.6 in. x 7.87 in.) and weighing 1,051 kg, at Ganakallu Village on 15 January 2020. A total of 540 kg of ground cashew nuts, 486 kg of sugar, and ghee and silver foil were used. Twelve people were involved in the preparation that took 5 hrs.

Largest arrangement in the shape of a sanitary pad*

MyPadBank, an NGO in Bareilly, Uttar Pradesh, made the largest sanitary pad, 6.7 m (21 ft 11.7 in.) long and 3.35 m (10 ft 11.8 in.) wide, using 1,720 'NIINE Sanitary Pads' at Gandhi Udyan Ground, Bareilly, on 23 December 2018. Chitransh Saxena, Utkarsh Saxena, Shilpi Saxena, Saher Choudhry, Anil K. Razz, Rashi Udit, Yash Vajpai, Emmanuel Singh, Ajayank, Ana Khan, Jennifer Lal, Aishwarya Lal, Shilpi Jaiswal, Sunidhi Malick, and Amaan Siddiqui participated in the event.

Largest replica of ₹500 note

Largest replica of ₹500 note

Forty-three artists of the Kalabhumi Institutes of Fine Arts, Delhi, made a 6.70 m (22 ft) long and 3.35 m (11 ft) wide replica of the old Indian 500-rupee note in 2 hrs 20 mins on 16 December 2017 at Hotel Radisson Blu, Dwarka.

Largest broom

Ashok Kumar Bairwa (b. 1 August 1994) from Sawai Madhopur, Rajasthan, made a 20.11 m (65 ft 11.7 in.) long broom, along with Mangilal Rathor, Vinod Kumar, Sukhdev, and Pannalal. He sourced bamboo, palm leaves, waste materials and rope in 15 days and the finishing work was done in 6 hrs from 7:00 p.m. to 1:00 a.m. during 8–9 April 2019.

WR Largest moulded potato chip

Chandresh Himmatlal Bayad (b. 3 September 1985) of Helly & Chilly Foods, Ahmedabad, Gujarat, cooked the largest

Largest moulded potato chip

moulded potato chip, weighing 11 kg, at Rifle Club, Ahmedabad, on 7 October 2018. The potato fry was 291 cm (9 ft 6.567 in.) long, 6.4 cm (3.30 in.) wide and 6.2 cm (2.4 in.) thick. It was made in 3 hrs from 4:30 p.m. to 7:30 p.m. with five other persons.

Largest momo

Largest momo

Jackie's Chinese Restaurant, Vasant Kunj, New Delhi, made the largest steamed chicken momo, weighing 78.24 kg and measuring 1.52 m (4 ft 11.8 in.) in diameter on 25 March 2019 at the restaurant. It took 3 hrs from 12:30 p.m. to 3:30 p.m. to make it.

CURRENCY, COINS, AND STAMPS

Largest collection of ₹5 commemorative coins

Ravikumar K.S. (b. 27 March 1978) from Chennai, Tamil Nadu, has 175 unduplicated commemorative coins of 5-rupee denomination from the Republic of India by mint-wise, error and Mule coin, a collection started in 2010. The first coin in his collection is of former prime minister Indira Gandhi in 1985 and the latest was of south Indian actor and politician MGR (Maruthur Gopalan Ramachandran) in 2019. The collection includes the rare Tilak design error coin; and the extremely rare 1996 Crop Science Congress coin and 1991 Commonwealth and Tourism Year coin, among others.

Largest collection of stamps – mountain-theme

Dr Kamal Mohnani (b. 18 September 1954) of Vadodara, Gujarat, has a collection of 3,447 stamps, miniature sheets, and cancellation covers, all related to mountains, including their flora, fauna, pagodas, temples, and cuisine, from different countries.

Largest collection of stamps – Ramayana theme

Dr Upender Vennam (b. 14 December 1971) of Hyderabad, Telangana, held a philatelic exhibition on the story of the Ramayana on 80 A4 size sheets. Over 400 items including mint never-hinged stamps, miniature sheets, sheet-lets, souvenir sheets, rare proofs, scarce postcards, First Day Covers, and special covers were used for creating an exhibit of five frames.

Stamps from most countries – bird theme

Pushpa Khamesra (b. 19 March 1968) from Udaipur, Rajasthan, had 7,265 postage stamps featuring birds from 354 countries up to 28 December 2021.

FOR ALL THE CHOCOLATE LOVERS!

1 Largest chocolate wall

Windsor Chocolatier created the largest chocolate wall, which was 5.23 m (17 ft 2 in.) in length, 2.29 m (7 ft 6 in.) in height, 0.15 m (6 in.) wide, and weighed 1,050 kg. The chocolate wall was made between 3 March and 20 March 2020. They used dark chocolate, white chocolate, and chocolate colours for their attempt. The chocolate wall was initiated by Rhea Gupta and involved five persons.

2 Largest chocolate painting

Windsor Chocolatier created the largest painting with chocolate, measuring 2.44 m (8 ft) in length and 6.09 m (20 ft) in width, using light brown and dark chocolate. It featured 160 shades made from four Mona Lisa base colours like red, blue, yellow, and white, and was made in 200 hrs from 15 February to 10 March 2018 by six people, headed by Rhea Gupta at Windsor Chocolatier, Gurugram, Haryana.

3 Largest chocolate fall

Windsor Chocolatier created the largest chocolate fall with milk chocolate between 21 June and 28 June 2019. Headed by Rhea Gupta, the 2.84 m (9 ft 3.8 in.) high and 4.90 m (16 ft 1 in.) wide fall was made by 12 people.

Largest flower carpet

Largest flower carpet

TRENDS and Malayala Manorama Co. Pvt. Ltd made the largest flower carpet measuring 30,000 sq. ft (250 ft x 120 ft) at the Calicut Trade Centre, Kerala, on 30 August 2022. The carpet was completed in 8 mins 58 secs and saw the participation of 426 people. Different types of flowers were used such as oleander, marigold, rose, and chrysanthemum. A total of 40,000 kg of flowers were used to make the carpet.

Largest postal stamp

Deepak Sharma (b. 8 November 1985) of Moradabad, Uttar Pradesh, has the largest 11 cm x 6.5 cm postal stamp issued in China on 17 June 2014. The six-yuan stamp depicts Sahasrabhuja Sahasranetra (thousand-armed, thousand-eyed) Avalokiteshvara in Buddhism.

Largest postal stamp

Largest collection of smallest-value stamps*

Putsa Krishna Kameshwar (b. 1 August 1977) from Amalapuram, Andhra Pradesh, has collected 216 unduplicated stamps of smallest value. The collection includes stamp values ranging from 1 paisa to ₹2. It took him 22 years to collect all these stamps. The oldest stamp was released in 1957 and the latest stamp was released in 2016.

Smallest-value stamps

*This category has been discontinued. Further and future claims for this category will not be accepted.

Largest collection of one-quarter British anna coins

Rajendra Agrawal 'Shashi' (b. 12 May 1962) from Satna, Madhya Pradesh, has collected 10 varieties of one-quarter British anna coins issued between 1835 and 1942. His collection has 90 coins and includes the East India Company, Queen Victoria, King Edward II, King George V, and King George VI.

Largest collection of one-quarter British anna coins

Largest collection of ₹100 commemorative coins

Ashish Rajesh Ramrakhiani (b. 19 June 1988) from Thane, Maharashtra, has 68 commemorative coins of ₹100 issued by different mints between 1980 and 2020.

Largest collection of coins – Covid-19 theme

Putsa Krishna Kameswar (b. 1 August 1977) from Amalapuram, Andhra Pradesh, collected 18 coins from 15 countries – Australia, Egypt, France, Gibraltar, Hungary, Israel, Italy, Lithuania, Malta, Niue, Russia, Samoa, San Marino, Moldova (separatist enclave of Transnistria), Ukraine – one coin each from 12 countries and two coins each from three countries on the Covid-19 theme, released in 2020 and 2021.

Largest collection of coins – experimental

Ravikumar K.S. (b. 27 March 1978) from Chennai, Tamil Nadu, collects coins minted by the Indian government for experimental purposes. These coins are minted to check the quality of the die and to correct manufacturing mistakes. Since they minted only a few experimental coins, the collection is rare. These coins have EXP or EXPT stamped on the coin. He has seven experimental coins: three ₹5 coins from the Mumbai mint (featuring the Dandi March); two ₹1 coins from the Kolkata Mint; one ₹1 coin from the Mumbai mint; and one ₹2 coin from the Hyderabad mint.

Largest collection of commemorative currency notes – from most countries

Mitesh Dilipkumar Dave (b. 20 March 1989) from Morbi, Gujarat, has commemorative currency notes from 155 countries, a collection started in 1999.

Largest collection of 5-rupee notes with the same serial number

Raj Kishore Mahanta (b. 29 March 1994) from Keonjhar, Odisha, has the largest collection of 5-rupee currency notes with the same serial number. He has 108 notes in his collection with the serial number 999990. All notes have the signature of the former RBI governor D. Subbarao.

₹5 notes with the same serial number

Largest collection of coins – environmental theme

Parvathina Venkata Narayana (b. 1 July 1971) from Yeditha, Andhra Pradesh, a teacher by profession, has a collection of coins on environmental themes since 2001. He has 613 coins from 145 countries in his collection. The coins have captions like 'Protect Our World', 'Save the Environment', 'Forestry for Development', 'Forestry of Prosperity', 'Biodiversity', 'For a Better Environment', 'Preserve Planet Earth', 'Water for Life,' 'Endangered Animal Species,' and many more in English and foreign languages.

COMMUNITY DEVELOPMENT

Largest shoe donation

Inc.5 Shoes Pvt. Ltd in Mumbai, Maharashtra, distributed 5,000 pairs of shoes to women, girls, and the underprivileged in Mumbai and Navi Mumbai between 10:00 a.m. and 5:00 p.m. on 15 March 2019.

Most food donated in a single day – multiple venues

The ISKCON Temple in Dwarka, Delhi, under the chairmanship of Pradyumna Priya Das, in coordination with the district magistrate of south-west Delhi, Rahul Singh, cooked and distributed food to migrant labourers and other needy persons during the lockdown. Beginning in the third week of March 2020 with 5,000 meals a day, they increased the number of meals to 10,000 and subsequently 100,000 a day.

WOOLLEN CAPS FOR EVERYONE!

1 Most woollen caps donated – group – single day – single venue

The Air Force Wives Welfare Association (AFWWA) from New Delhi donated 9,071 woollen caps to Safe Approach, a shelter home in Delhi on 28 October 2022 between 9:55 a.m. and 12:51 p.m. There were 19 people involved in the donation. Each cap measured 22.86–26.67 cm (9–10.5 in.) in length and 43.18–50.8 cm (17–20 in.) in circumference.

2 Most woollen caps donated – group – single day – multiple venues*

The Air Force Wives Welfare Association (AFWWA) from New Delhi donated 17,071 woollen caps to three welfare organizations in Delhi on 28 October 2022 between 9:31 a.m. and 12:51 p.m. There were 58 people involved in the donation. Each cap measured 22.86–26.67 cm (9–10.5 in.) in length and 43.18–50.8 cm (17–20 in.) in circumference.

*This record was first featured in the hardback edition and is republished here with modified details.

Most benches donated – 1 year

The Ghanshyamdas Saraf Trust, a charitable trust in Mumbai, Maharashtra, donated 127 three-seater RCC pink benches to temples and police stations in and around Mumbai, between July 2021 and July 2022. A team of eight people were employed in making the benches and it took a week to make 20 benches.

Most food packets distributed among the poor

Swami Sunil Das Prabhakaran, chairman of the Muthalamada Charitable Trust in Palakkad, Kerala, has been distributing 1,000 food packets every day to the poor since 1992. He distributed nine million food packets and 70 million litres of drinking water to the poor up to September 2018.

Most ramps constructed – single day

J.K. Cement Ltd, Uttar Pradesh, set a record by constructing 249 cemented ramps for the specially abled on 5 August 2021 at different government schools around Jaipur, Rajasthan. The ramps were constructed for government schools of Jotwara City and Rural, and Sanganer City and Rural.

Most toys donated – single day

Children's University, Gandhinagar, Gujarat, has donated 5,100 toys on a single day, 12 May 2022, on its campus between 9:00 a.m. and 11:00 a.m. The toys were distributed to eight organizations and schools, as well as NGOs working with children. The donation drive was organized by the university's Departments of Toy Innovations and Social Work, and around 30 people participated in the drive.

ONLINE FEATS

Most participants in a training/workshop

The Department of Management Studies, B.K. Birla College of Arts, Science, and Commerce, Kalyan, Maharashtra, organized a training session on basic self-defence with 291 participants from 10:15 a.m. to 10:50 a.m. on 8 March 2021 on Microsoft Teams. The session was led by Revati Hunswadkar and the participants were taught three attack kicks, two defence blocks, and three punch types.

Longest lesson

Rajashri Sanjay Kabra (b. 21 July 1998) from Washim, Maharashtra, conducted the longest online lesson for 16 hrs 25 mins from 7:45 a.m. to 12:10 a.m. on 5 May 2022. The total break time was 1 hr 10 mins. The event was conducted on Google Meet from Deogiri College, Aurangabad, Maharashtra. The lesson was on Physics and targeted topics for preparation for competitive exams such as BARC, IIT, JAM, GIS, CSIRNET, and TIFR, among others.

Longest seminar

Dr Geetha Challa (b. 28 June 1971) from Hyderabad, Telangana, conducted an online seminar from 7:00 a.m. to 8:45 p.m. on 10 October 2020 with 140 participants. The seminar lasted for 12 hrs 19 mins with a total break time of 1 hr 26 mins. The seminar was on the effects of COVID-19 on mental health and coping mechanisms for the same.

STRUCTURES

EARLY TIMES

Oldest rust-free iron pillar

Earliest structures

The oldest structures excavated in Koldihwa in Allahabad (now Prayagraj) District, Uttar Pradesh, date to the first half of the seventh millennium BCE. Archaeological evidence has indicated that the site had circular huts made of timber posts and thatch and also had a cattle pen.

Earliest village settlement

A 4,000-year-old village settlement of the Chalcolithic period (Copper Age), along with remnants of subsequent Iron Age occupation, was unearthed at Balathal near Udaipur, Rajasthan. It included a massive mud rampart. It is the oldest village settlement in India outside of Harappan sites.

First architect

Maha Govinda, mentioned in the Buddhist work *Dhammapada*, is the first architect on record. He designed many north Indian cities in the fifth century BCE. Another treatise on housing architecture from the same period is the *Mayamata*.

Oldest rust-free iron pillar

The iron pillar in the Qutb (Minar) complex in Delhi has stood strong since the fifth century CE, when it was erected by King Chandravarman. A solid iron shaft, 7.32 m (24 ft) high, it has six lines in Sanskrit inscribed on it.

Earliest extensive drainage system

The Harappan towns of Lothal in Gujarat and Mohenjo-daro (now in Pakistan); with rectangular houses, chessboard streets, brick-lined bathrooms, drainage pipes, and cesspits; were unique in the ancient world. The toilets were equipped with water chutes, which carried dirty water away to covered street drains. The main sewer, about 1.5 m (4 ft 11 in.) deep and 91 cm (2 ft 11 .8 in.) across, is connected to north-south and east-west sewers.

An army deserter called Charles Mason chanced upon the mounds of Harappa in 1826. But then he thought it was the spot where Alexander the Great met King Porus in the famous fourth-century battle!

Earliest known fortified city

The remains of rubble masonry and mud bricks, excavated at the Harappan site of Kalibangan in Rajasthan, have been dated to 3000–2500 BCE. These excavations show that Kalibangan was a fortified city with a stone citadel, and surrounded by a massive rampart of mud bricks.

Earliest *stambha*

The oldest surviving examples of the *stambha*, or pillar, belong to the period of Emperor Ashoka (c. 268 to 232 BCE). The best known is the pillar and its edict at Sarnath near Varanasi, Uttar Pradesh. It was ordered by him 26 years after his coronation, to convey the teachings of the Buddhist scriptures.

Earliest open-air theatre

The third century BCE brick structure at Nagarjunakonda in Guntur District, Andhra Pradesh – similar to ancient Greek and Roman amphitheatres – has a pit with tiers on all four sides, which could seat at least 1,000 spectators. It encloses a rectangular room of 16.5 m x 13.7 m (54 ft 1.5 in. x 44 ft 11.4 in.). The structure has good acoustic properties.

The longest corridor in India, that of the Ramanathaswamy Temple in Rameswaram, Tamil Nadu, is 1,220 m (4,002 ft) long. It has 1,212 sculpted and painted pillars. It was built in the 17th century.

First known example of ancient hydraulic engineering

A first century BCE site in Singraur (Sringaverapura) near Allahabad, Uttar Pradesh, revealed the remains of a large rectangular brick tank, a unique example of ancient hydraulic engineering. Water from the Ganga River was brought through a feeding channel into a silting chamber, from which clean water flowed into a main tank.

Oldest man-made lake

Sudarshan Lake at the foot of Girnar Hills in Junagadh District, Gujarat, was built during the reign of Chandragupta Maurya (c. 321–297 BCE), according to the epigraph engraved on the Ashokan pillar a kilometre from the lake. It was restored by Emperor Ashoka around 273 BCE. Now the lake has shrunk due to silt and debris.

Oldest palace site excavated

Kumrahar in Patna, Bihar, dating to 250 BCE, is said to be one of Emperor Ashoka's palaces. The remains of the columns at the site indicate that the palace had an 84-pillar hall, originally made of wood.

Deepest stepwell

Chand Baori, located at Abhaneri in Dausa District, Rajasthan, is the deepest stepwell in India, extending to 30 m (98 ft 5 in.) down from the ground. It is also considered to be the largest ancient stepwell in the country and among the oldest wells in the world. Its oldest parts were constructed in the 8th century by King Chand and the upper storeys were built during the reign of the Mughals in the 18th century. The stepwell has 13 levels and 3,500 narrow steps. The temperature at the bottom of the well remains 6°C lower than the temperature at its surface.

Largest stupa

The great stupa at Sanchi in Madhya Pradesh, built with bricks by Emperor Ashoka between 273 and 232 BCE, was later enlarged and enclosed within another stone stupa. In its present form, the stupa now has a diameter of 37 m (121 ft 5 in.) and a height of 16 m (52 ft 6 in.).

MEDIEVAL AND MODERN ERAS

Largest silver article

A 1.8 m (5 ft 11 in.) tall silver jug at the City Palace in Jaipur, Rajasthan, was made for the maharaja of Jaipur to store drinking water during his visit to England in 1901 for the coronation of King Edward VII.

Largest corbelled cornice dome

The Gol Gumbaz, built in 1659 in the tomb complex of the Adil Shahi sultans at Bijapur in Karnataka, features a dome that measures 42 m (137 ft 9.5 in.) in diameter. Its corbelled cornice (the ornamental projection that crowns a building) projects more than 3 m (9 ft 10 in.). The dome is the largest of its kind in the world.

Largest bas-relief

The 'Descent of the Ganga' bas-relief, also known as 'Arjuna's Penance', in Mamallapuram in Chengalpattu District, Tamil Nadu, is 27 m (88 ft 7 in.) long and 9 m (29 ft 6 in.) high. Created during the Pallava period in the seventh century CE, it features over 30 large and small sculptures of animals, humans, sages, and gods.

Largest vaulted hall

The Bara Imambara in Lucknow, Uttar Pradesh, is not only India's but also Asia's largest hall without any external support of wood, iron, or stone beams. The hall measures 49.4 m x 16.2 m (162 ft x 53 ft 2 in.). The ceiling is more than 15 m (49 ft 2.5 in.) high.

Oldest known British inscription

The Fort St George cemetery in Chennai, Tamil Nadu, has a tombstone reportedly belonging to one Elizabeth Baker, dating back to 1632.

Largest maze

The Bhul-Bhulaiya, which is a set of passages on the top terrace of the Bara Imambara building in Lucknow, Uttar Pradesh, is a labyrinth of over 1,000 interconnected passages that can be approached through a narrow flight of steps but seem to lead nowhere. These passages reduced the load on the walls, which support the massive 4.88 m (16 ft) thick roof with an estimated weight of about 20,000 tonnes.

FORTS AND PALACES

Fort on three hills

Gingee Fort, located about 100 km from Chennai, Tamil Nadu, is built on three hills – Krishnagiri, Chandragiri, and Rajagiri – forming a triangle. Together they form a fort complex, each with its own citadel. The fort walls are 13 km long and the three hills are connected by walls enclosing an area of around 11 sq. km. Built by the Konar dynasty in 1190 CE, the fort was then improved upon by the Cholas and subsequently modified in Vijayanagara times.

Oldest extant marble structure

The white marble structure over Hoshang Shah Ghori's tomb, built by his son c.1440, at Mandu, Dhar District, Madhya Pradesh, is the oldest extant marble structure known.

Only palace with just a facade wall

Hawa Mahal ('the palace of winds') in Jaipur, Rajasthan, has a facade built on to a wall of the main palace compound. Royal ladies seated in its 953 niches and windows could look down at the street below.

WR Fort with largest metal ordnance

The Bijapur Fort in Bijapur District, Karnataka, houses the famous bell-metal cannon Malik-e-Maidan ('lord of the battlefield'), the largest piece of medieval bell-metal ordnance, which is 4.45 m (14 ft 7 in.) long, with a diameter of 1.5 m (4 ft 11 in.). It weighs 55 tonnes and has a bore of 0.71 m (2 ft 4 in.) from which an iron ball of over a tonne could be fired.

Only fort with a tiger reserve

The 'forest fort' of Ranthambore, a classical *vana durg*, is located in Ranthambore National Park, Sawai Madhopur District, Rajasthan. Built between 944 and 1110 CE by a Chauhan ruler whose name is disputed, it towers over the park from the top of a hill.

Vana durg: Only fort in India with a tiger reserve

STRUCTURES OF THE SULTANATE

1 Tallest brick minaret

The Qutb Minar in Delhi, made in fluted sandstone carved with verses from the Quran, is 72 m (236 ft) high with 379 steps inside leading to the top. It is a tapering tower of five storeys, with a base diameter of 14.3 m (47 ft), which reduces to 2.74 m (9 ft) at the top. Its construction began under Qutbuddin Aibak in 1193 CE, and his successor Iltutmish added three storeys. Firuz Shah Tughlaq completed the last storey in 1383 CE.

2 Earliest known monumental tomb

The Sultan Garhi tomb in Delhi was built over a *garhi* (cave) in 1231 for Prince Nasiruddin Mahmud by his father Iltutmish, the third sultan of the Slave dynasty, who ruled in Delhi from1212 to 1236. The octagonal tomb is like a fortress with a courtyard-like layout, uncommon for a tomb.

3 First garden tomb

The tomb of Sikandar Lodi (r. 1489–1517) of the Lodi dynasty is located in Lodi Garden near Lodi Road in New Delhi and was built during 1517–18 by his son Ibrahim Lodi.

Kumbhalgarh Fort and the longest wall of India

Longest fortification wall

A 36 km (22.37 miles) long fortification wall was built by Rana Kumbha (r. 1433–68) along the Aravallis in Rajasthan to protect his kingdom of Mewar. It enclosed 34 fortresses. At its widest sections, the wall is 15 m (49 ft) thick and has stone-brick masonry and decorative flourishes along the top.

Only palace with a bird sanctuary

The Bharatpur Palace in Rajasthan houses the Keoladeo National Park (earlier Bharatpur Bird Sanctuary) within its site. It is the only nature reserve in India. The maharaja of Bharatpur, who owned this palace, arranged the water supply in 1760 with an irrigation canal. Thus he created the habitat that became a stopover for the migratory Siberian crane. It was converted into a bird sanctuary in 1956 and a national park in 1981.

Highest gateway

Buland Darwaza, the highest gateway in India, is 53.5 m (175 ft 6 in.) high. It was built by Mughal emperor Akbar (r. 1550–1605) at Fatehpur Sikri, about 40 km from Agra in Uttar Pradesh, and commemorated his conquest of Ranthambore Fort and Khandesh.

One of the Oldest Forts of India

The Kalinjar Fort in Banda District of Uttar Pradesh has several temples dating to the rule of the Gupta dynasty from the 3rd to the 5th centuries. Built on a hill at one end of the Vindhya mountain range, at 367 m (1,204 ft), this enduring fort was used by several of the ruling dynasties of Bundelkhand, including the Chandela dynasty of Rajputs in the 10th century and the Solankis of Rewa.

Palace with the largest chandelier
The durbar hall of Jai Vilas Mahal of Gwalior, Madhya Pradesh, has two chandeliers, each 12.5 m (41 ft) high and weighing 3.5 tonnes. It is said that three (or eight!) elephants were hoisted to the roof (or suspended from it!) to make sure it would withstand the weight of the chandeliers.

Hazar Duari ('thousand doors'), the palace of Nizam Humayun Khan (r. 1824–38) in the Kila Nizamat premises in Murshidabad, West Bengal, has **1,000** doors, of which **100** are false. It was designed by the Scottish architect Duncan McLeod.

Oldest medieval amphitheatre
The Rang Ghar, about 3 km from Sivasagar in Assam, was built during the reign of Swargadeo Rudra Singha (r. 1696–1714) with bamboo and wood. It was rebuilt in brick by Swargadeo Pramatta Singha during 1744–50. It was the royal sports pavilion where Ahom kings watched cockfights and bullfights.

Longest time taken to build a mausoleum
The Taj Mahal, one of the New Seven Wonders of the World, was built by Mughal emperor Shah Jahan (r. 1627–58 CE) as a mausoleum for his wife Mumtaz Mahal, on the banks of the Yamuna River in Agra, Uttar Pradesh. It took 22,000 workmen 22 years (1631–53) to complete it. It is built on a 29 sq. m (312 sq. ft) marble platform on a sandstone base.

RELIGIOUS STRUCTURES

Earliest extant structural temple
A third century BCE circular brick-and-timber shrine excavated at Bairat (now Viratnagar) in Jaipur District, Rajasthan, is considered to be the earliest surviving structural temple. The shrine, with a diameter of 8.23 m (27 ft), was built with lime-plastered panels of brickwork alternating with 26 octagonal wooden pillars. The shrine, portico, and a 2 m (6 ft 6.7 in.) wide ambulatory were enclosed in a rectangular compound that measures 305 m x 21 m (1,000 ft 7.8 in. x 68 ft 10.7 in.).

Earliest extant Hindu temples
The Gupta period temples in Sanchi and Tigawa near Jabalpur in Madhya Pradesh belong to the fifth century CE. The Kankali Devi Temple in Tigawa is well preserved.

First single-aisle mosque
The Bara Gumbad Mosque, a single-aisle mosque in Delhi's Lodi Garden, was constructed by Sikandar Lodi in 1494 CE.

Earliest mosque
The Cheraman Jama Masjid in Kodungallur, Thrissur District, Kerala, is said to

In 2023 budget the ASI has been allocated ₹1,102.83 crore for protection, conservation, and preservation of centrally protected monuments and sites.

have been built in 629 CE. It is considered the first mosque in India and the second in the world where Juma prayers were started. Malik Ibn Dinar, who made this mosque under instructions from Maharaja Chereman Perumal, used Kerala style of architecture to build this mosque. He also became its first ghazi. The mosque is still in use. In the 1970s, it was reconstructed in a way that changed its look completely. In 2021, further renovation took place which brought back the original look.

First revolving minaret

The minaret of the 55-year-old Masjid-e-Chini ki Burj, also known as Chhoti Masjid in Jaipur, Rajasthan, was the first revolving minaret in India. The 10-tonne dome of the 30.5 m (100 ft) high minaret, with a 3 m (9 ft 10 in.) diameter, completed one round in a minute, running on a 1.5 HP motor.

First Baha'i house of worship

The Baha'i house of worship, or 'Lotus Temple', in Kalkaji, New Delhi, the first such structure in Asia, is built on 26 acres (10.52 hectares) of land. Built between 1980 and 1986, it is designed as a blossoming lotus. The main structure has three folds of nine concrete petals, each covered with Grecian marble. The temple rises to 35 m (114 ft 10 in.) and is surrounded by pools of water.

Oldest Buddhist monument

A stupa, which was estimated to be 2,500 years old, was excavated in 1898 in Piprahwa in Siddharthnagar District, Uttar Pradesh, by British colonial engineer and landowner W.C. Peppe. The solid brickwork stupa was 7 m (23 ft) high and its cupola measured 35 m (114 ft 10 in.) in diameter. Most of the other surviving stupas are from the reign of Emperor Ashoka (c. 273 to 232 BCE).

Oldest leaning temple

Built in the 17th century by Baliar Singh of the Chauhan dynasty, the 10.6 m (34 ft 9 in.) tall Shiva Temple at Huma, a village on the banks of the Mahanadi River in Sambalpur District, Odisha, leans at an angle of 13.8 degrees from the vertical. Its smaller shrines, bull pillar, and shivalinga, all lean at different angles and in different directions.

Only quadrangular yogini temple

The 10th century CE Chausath Yogini Temple in the famous Khajuraho complex in Madhya Pradesh is the only quadrangular yogini temple in the country. Built entirely of coarse granite, the temple stands on a terrace that is 7.6 m (25 ft) high and has peripheral shrines.

Oldest yogini temple

The Chausath Yogini Temple at Hirapur, around 20 km from Bhubaneswar, Odisha, is the earliest extant yogini temple, dated to the ninth century CE. Its inner diameter is 7.6 m (25 ft) and outer circumference is 27 m (88 ft 7 in.). In the middle of the enclosure is a rectangular open mandapa 2.8 m x 2.4 m (9 ft 2 in. x 7 ft 10 in.). The niches in the inner enclosure feature images of yoginis, and the outer surface has nine images of Katyayani, one of the nine forms of the Hindu goddess Parvati.

At present the Archeological Survey of India has 46 museums in the country.

Oldest extant temple with a shikhara

The earliest known extant temple with a rudimentary shikhara or pinnacle is the Vishnu Dashavatara Temple, belonging to the Gupta period (320–550 CE), at Deogarh in Jhansi District, Uttar Pradesh. It is one of the earliest to draw on the stories of Rama and Krishna to decorate the panels.

Oldest church

St Thomas Syro-Malabar Church, located in Palayoor in Thrissur District, Kerala, is dated to 52 CE. According to tradition, it was established by St Thomas. It was rebuilt in the 17th century by the Reverend Fenichi. The original altar survives.

Biggest temple lamp

A lamp with 1,000 wicks at the Chettikulangara Devi Temple in Alappuzha District, Kerala, is madc of 1,500 kg of gunmetal. It is 3.3 m (10 ft 10 in.) high with 13 tiers like banyan branches. The lowest rung is 2.1 m (6 ft 10.7 in.) in circumference and holds 101 wicks. The topmost is over 1 m wide with 53 wicks.

Biggest bathing tank

The Brahma Sarovar at Thanesar in Kurukshetra District, Haryana, is 1,370 mx 762 m (4,495 ft x 2,500 ft) and attracts thousands of pilgrims during solar eclipses. Its ancient water reservoir finds mention in the Mahabharata.

Oldest active synagogue

The Paradesi Synagogue in Mattancherry in Kochi, Kerala, was built by the descendants of the European Jews in 1568 CE. The synagogue is also the first one known to be built in a Commonwealth country.

Biggest queue complex

The Vaikuntam qucuc complcx at the Venkateswara Temple complex, Tirumala, Tirupati, Andhra Pradesh, permits the

Oldest active synagogue

free flow of around 35,000 pilgrims daily. It has a two-tier seating gallery, two corridors, and a floor at the ground level with amenities within a semicircular length of 238 m (781 ft). A new complex was added later for *sarvadarshan*, or free entry of devotees.

Biggest temple bell

The 110-year-old bronze bell at Tirumala Devaswom, Kochi, Kerala, is more than 1.8 m (5 ft 11 in.) high and weighs over 3 tonnes. The bell is suspended from a huge wooden frame that rests over four massive granite pillars.

Only Nataraja temple

The Thillai Nataraja Temple in Chidambaram in Cuddalore District, Tamil Nadu, built by a succession of kings and devotees between the 10th and the 17th centuries CE is unique because Shiva is worshipped here not as a lingam but as Nataraja, the Lord of Dance. The temple has four *gopurams* (monumental entrance towers) carved with 108 dance postures described in the *Natyashastra*, the ancient Hindu text on the performing arts.

Only rat temple

The 575-year-old temple of Karni Devi (one of the nine incarnations of Goddess Durga) has a large number of rats called *kaba*, believed to be the offspring of the presiding deity. Located at Deshnok, 35 km from Bikaner, Rajasthan, this temple is devoted exclusively to the 'holy' rats, which have the run of the place.

Only temple with an apsidal sanctum

The Durga Temple at Aihole in Bagalkot District, Karnataka, is a peripheral structure with a semicircular *garbhagriha* (sanctum sanctorum). The 18 m (59 ft) long and 11 m (36 ft) wide temple has a 7 m (23 ft) verandah. The flat roof, 9 m (29 ft 6 in.) above the ground, is surmounted by a gopuram. The temple is built on an earlier Buddhist chaitya hall.

Largest monastery

The largest Buddhist monastery in the country, and a functioning one, is located in Tawang District, Arunachal Pradesh. The three-storey structure spread over 140 sq. m (1,507 sq. ft) has 65 residential buildings that can house up to 450 lamas. This monastery's Tibetan name – Galden Namgey Lhatse – translates as 'celestial paradise on a clear night'.

Galden Namgey Lhatse: the largest Buddhist monastery in India

Only shaking minarets

Sidi Bashir Mosque: Shake one minaret and the other will vibrate too

At the Sidi Bashir Mosque in Ahmedabad, Gujarat, the minarets, which are three storeys high and have carved balconies, are known as the *jhulta*, or shaking, minarets. Dated to 1452 CE, the mosque was built either by Sidi Bashir, a slave of Sultan Ahmed Shah, or by Malik Sarang, a noble in the court of Sultan Mahmud Begada. The shaking of either minaret results in the other minaret vibrating after a few seconds, a fact that was first observed in the 19th century by an Englishman and Sanskrit scholar, Monier M. Williams. One minaret has been partly taken down to prevent it from falling over.

Most sculptures in a temple

The Meenakshi Sundareswar Temple in Madurai, Tamil Nadu, has more than 30 million sculptures in its shrines, halls, and colonnades. It covers an area of 243 m x 228 m (797 ft x 748 ft).

Largest cave temple complex

The cave temples in Ellora in Aurangabad District, Maharashtra, were built between the fifth and tenth centuries CE. There are 12 Buddhist, 17 Hindu, and 5 Jain cave temples and monasteries. The Kailasa or Kailasanatha Temple in cave 16 is the largest single monolithic rock excavation in the world.

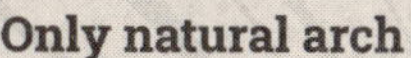

Only natural arch

The Silatoranam, a 7.62 m x 3.05 m (25 ft x 10 ft) natural arch at the Tirumala Hills, about 1 km north of the Venkateswara Temple in Tirumala town in Tirupati, Andhra Pradesh, is the only one of its kind in Asia. It is also a notified national geoheritage monument.

Largest sun temple
Built by Narasimha Deva I in 1200 CE, the Sun Temple in the historic town of Konark, Odisha, represents a huge chariot with 12 pairs of ornamental wheels, drawn by seven horses rearing up to the east. The original temple consisted of a sanctum sanctorum with a lofty curvilinear shikhara, a 34.14 m (112 ft) long and 38.4 m (126 ft) high jagmohana (assembly hall), and a dance hall. Along with many subsidiary structures, the Sun Temple, which is now the largest extant sun temple, was enclosed within a compound wall 264 m (866 ft) long and 165 m (541 ft) wide, with three gates.

Largest collection of temples
There are as many as 1,000 Jain temples and 12,000 idols in the Shatrunjai Hills of Palitana in Bhavnagar District of Gujarat.

Largest synagogue
Located on Moledina Street in Pune, Maharashtra, the Ohel David Synagogue is a 30 m (98 ft 5 in.) high tower, built in the Gothic style with a spire and four giant clocks.

TOP 10 CENTRALLY PROTECTED MONUMENTS UNDER ASI HAVING HIGHEST INDIAN VISITOR'S FOOTFALL DURING FINANCIAL YEAR 2022-23 (IN LAKHS, UP TO FEBRUARY 2023)

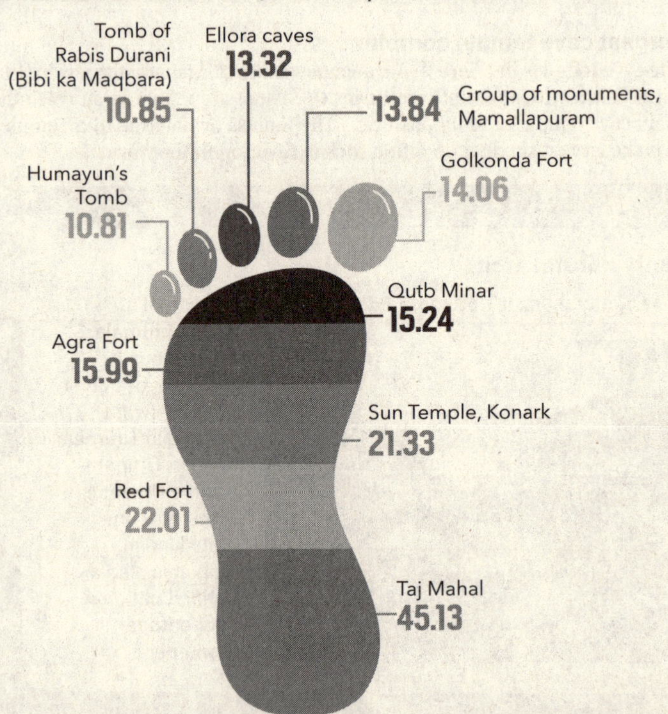

Largest mosque

The Taj-ul-Masjid, or Taj-ul-Masajid, in Bhopal, Madhya Pradesh, was built by Sultan Shah Jehan Begum between 1868 and 1901. Constructed over decades, the mosque was completed in 1985 by Maulana Sayed Hashmat Ali Sahab and Allama Mohammad Imran Khan Nadwi Azhari. Its name means 'the crown of mosques' and it has an interior area of 23,000 sq. m (247,570 sq. ft). The mosque is made of red stone and can accommodate 175,000 worshippers.

Largest chaitya hall

The Karla Caves near Lonavala, Maharashtra, house the largest known chaitya (Buddhist prayer hall) cave. Its dimensions are 37 m x 14 m x 14 m (121 ft 5 in. x 46 ft x 46 ft).

Largest church

The 76.2 m x 55 m (250 ft x 180 ft 5 in.) Se Cathedral at Old Goa, around 10 km from Panaji, is the largest in India. It was constructed between 1562 and 1619. It was consecrated in 1640. It had two towers, but one collapsed in 1776 and was not rebuilt.

Only mosque entirely of marble

Moti Masjid, built by Mughal emperor Aurangzeb during 1659–60 CE within the Red Fort in Delhi, is made entirely of marble.

WR Heaviest and highest single-stone shikhara

The 80-tonne single-piece granite shikhara atop the Brihadeeswarar Temple at Thanjavur, Tamil Nadu, is the largest and heaviest single-stone object on top of any temple in the world. This marvel of engineering was constructed from 1004 CE, during the reign of Rajaraja Chola, to 1009 CE. It is the world's first temple built with granite. Its *vimana* (a pyramidal tower built over the central shrine of a temple) is also the highest, at 66 m (216 ft 6 in.).

Highest gurdwara

The gurdwara at Hemkund-Lokpal in Chamoli District, Uttarakhand, stands at a height of 4,328.16 m (14,200 ft) above mean sea level. The place Hemkund finds mention in the Guru Granth Sahib and in Guru Gobind Singh's memoir, *Bachittar* (or *Bichittar*) *Natak*.

Highest monastery

The Tangyud Monastery at Komic Village near Hikkim in Spiti Valley, Himachal Pradesh, is India's highest monastery at an altitude of around 4,572 m (15,000 ft). Built like a fortified castle, it lies on the edge of the Kibber Wildlife Sanctuary.

Tallest temple tower

The 13-storey Sri RanganathaswamyTemple, built between 1982 and 1987 at Srirangam in Tiruchirappalli District, Tamil Nadu, has a 72 m (236 ft) high *rajagopuram* (main gateway).

Tallest church

The Gothic-style Basilica of Our Lady of Dolours, known locally as Puthanpally, is a minor basilica of the Syro-Malabar Catholic Church in Thrissur, Kerala. Its construction started in 1929. Its two front towers are 45 m (147 ft 8 in.) tall, and the central tower is 79 m (259 ft 2 in.) tall.

WR Tallest hollow stone structure

The Global Vipassana Pagoda at Gorai in Mumbai, Maharashtra, is one of the world's largest structures enshrining the relics of the Buddha. It was donated by the Sri Lankan government and the Mahabodhi Society, Bodhgaya, Bihar. Inaugurated on 8 February 2009, it contains the largest and tallest pillar-less hollow stone pagoda in the world. The height of the dome is 29 m (95 ft 1.7 in.), and the height of the building is 96.12 m (315 ft 4.2 in.). It took around 11 years and 2.5 million tonnes of stone to complete it.

STATUES AND IDOLS

WR Tallest statue

A 182 m (597 ft) 'Statue of Unity' of Sardar Vallabhbhai Patel, inaugurated on 31 October 2018, stands on the Sadhu Bet Island in the Narmada River near Rajpipla, Narmada District, Gujarat. Designed by sculptor Ram V. Sutar, it took nearly four years to build and cost an estimated ₹29.89 billion (2,989 crore).

WR Tallest monolithic statue

The Gommateshwara statue at Shravanabelagola, Karnataka, is the world's tallest monolithic statue. Dedicated to Bahubali and venerated by the Jains, it is 17.37 m (57 ft) high. It was carved from a single block of granite rock and weighs 80 tonnes. It was built between 978 and 993 CE by Chavundaraya, a minister of the Western Ganga dynasty.

WR Tallest shivalinga

The tallest shivalinga in the world was created by Maheswaram Sri Sivaparvathi Temple Trust, Thiruvananthapuram, Kerala. It measures 33.85 m (111 ft) and was constructed in six years and one day between 31 December 2012 and 31 December 2018.

Tallest Shani Dev statue

The Shani Dev Sewa Samiti, Shani Dham, Jammu, built and installed the world's tallest Shani Dev statue, which is 11.88 m (39 ft) high, including its 1.83 m (6 ft) base, in Jourian Village, Akhnoor District, Jammu and Kashmir. It weighs around 2,100 kg.

Tallest Ganesha Idol

A 6 m (19 ft 8 in.) high and 3.35 m (11 ft) wide Ganesha, weighing 190 tonnes and carved out of a single block of stone, was installed at the Mundhi Vinayagar Temple at Puliakulam, Coimbatore District, Tamil Nadu. Its *abhisheka* ritual needs 3 litres of oil and is performed using a ladder.

Tallest Durga structure

Nuruddin Ahmed from Bishnupur Village in Chirang District, Assam, built the tallest Durga structure, measuring 30 m x 14.5 m x 8 m (98 ft 5 in. x 47 ft 7 in. x

26 ft 3 in.), using only bamboo materials (including 5,000 bamboo sticks). No other material was used except cotton cloth as rope. It was made to promote the bamboo sector in Assam.

WR Largest bird sculpture

Jatayu, the largest bird sculpture in the world, is located at the Jatayu Earth's Centre (also known as Jatayu Rock or Jatayu Nature Park) in Chadayamangalam, Kollam District, Kerala. The sculpture, conceptualized and built by sculptor and film-maker Rajiv Anchal, is 60.96 m (200 ft) long, 45.72 m (150 ft) wide, and 21.33 m (70 ft) high. It houses a digital museum and a multidimensional theatre, making it a 'functional' sculpture.

Largest bust

Inaugurated on 24 February 2017, the 34.1 m (112 ft) tall 'Adiyogi' Lord Shiva statue made of steel and located in Coimbatore, Tamil Nadu, at the Isha Yoga Centre, has been funded by the Isha Foundation, and set up by Sadhguru Jaggi Vasudev. Built over 8 months, the structure reportedly weighs 500 tonnes. Its height signifies the 112 chakras in the human system to explore the 112 dimensions of life.

Largest Nandi statue

Nandi is the sacred bull and Lord Shiva's vehicle in Hindu mythology. The Nandi statue, about 200 m (656 ft) from the Veerabhadra Temple at Lepakshi Village in Anantapur District, Andhra Pradesh, is 4.57 m (15 ft) tall and 8.23 m (27 ft) long, and is carved from a single piece of granite.

Largest shivalinga

Located in Bhojpur, on the outskirts of the city of Bhopal in Madhya Pradesh, the Bhojeshwar Temple, built by Raja Bhoj (r. 1010–53 CE), houses the largest shivalinga, 5.5 m (18 ft) high and 2.5 m (8 ft 2 in.) in circumference.

BRIDGES

First iron bridge

The first iron bridge was built by Jessop and Company Limited in 1815 over the Gomti River in Lucknow in Uttar Pradesh. Designed by the Scottish engineer John Rennie the Elder, it was made at Butterfly Iron Works, England, for the nawab of Awadh.

First cable-stayed road bridge

The Akkar Bridge in Jorethang, over the Rangit River in Sikkim, is an all-concrete, cable-stayed road bridge built in 1988. It spans a 1.5 km (4,921 ft) wide and nearly 20 m (65 ft 7 in.) deep valley. The bridge consists of two 77 m (252 ft 7 in.) symmetrical spans supported from a single central pylon. With 17 pairs of cable stays, the 55 m (180 ft) high pylon supports the decking 21 m (69 ft) above the river bed.

Longest balanced cantilever bridge

The 3,015 m (9,892 ft) road bridge across the river Brahmaputra at Tezpur, Assam, called Kolia Bhomora Setu, is the longest bridge that has been provided with a central suspended span of 15 m (49 ft 2.5 in.) length because of its geographical location in a seismic zone. The bridge consists of 24 spans of 120 m (393 ft 8 in.) each and two shore spans of 67.5 m (221 ft 5 in.) each. With a carriageway of 7.5 m (24 ft 7 in.) width, it was constructed between October 1981 and April 1987.

Longest Bailey bridge

The 182.8 m (600 ft) long suspension bridge over the river Chubi in Wokha, Nagaland, connects the Mokokchung District and the Dimapur District of Nagaland.

Longest sea bridge

The Bandra–Worli Sea Link (also known as the Rajiv Gandhi Sea Link) in Mumbai, Maharashtra, the longest sea bridge in India, is 5.6 km (18,373 ft) long. It connects Bandra in the western suburbs of Mumbai to Worli in south Mumbai, across Mahim Bay. This cable-stayed bridge, which carries 8 lanes of traffic, was inaugurated on 30 June 2009.

Biggest cantilever bridge

Howrah Bridge (or Rabindra Setu) is India's biggest cantilever bridge. It spans the river Hooghly in Kolkata, West Bengal, and is 457 m (1,499 ft) long. It was completed in 1943.

Only bascule bridge

The only bascule bridge in the country is constructed on Tolly's Nullah (or Adiganga) at Khidirpur in Kolkata, West Bengal. Operated by the Kolkata Port Trust, it is built in two halves, each of which goes up to allow ships to pass through. The bridge has a span of about 35 m (114 ft 10 in.) and was built by Wagner Biro AG, Austria. It was commissioned on 5 November 1966 and replaced a swing bridge built in 1892.

Busiest bridge

With nearly 60,000 vehicles a day and countless pedestrians, Rabindra Setu, also called Howrah Bridge, in Kolkata, West Bengal, is India's busiest bridge.

Highest suspension bridge

At a height of 4,144 m (13,596 ft) above sea level, the Chicham Bridge is built over a deep gorge and connects Kibber and Chicham Rivers in Himachal Pradesh.

Highest Bailey bridge

The highest Bailey bridge in the country is at a height of 5,602 m (18,380 ft) at Khardung La in Ladakh. The 30 m (98 ft 5 in.) long bridge rests on ice. It consists of square diamond-braced panels that can be assembled on approach and then

First Cable-Stayed Rail Bridge Is Ready

India's first cable-stayed rail bridge, Anil Khad Bridge, in Jammu and Kashmir is ready, as announced by the government in April 2023. It spans across the Chenab River. It took 11 months to complete the bridge. The total length of cable strand used to build this bridge is 653 km.

pushed or pinned together at the corners to form a girder. It was designed and built by Lieutenant Colonel S.G. Vombatkere of the Border Roads Organization in August 1982.

WR Highest Railway Bridge

Chenab Bridge, placed 359 m (1,177 ft 10 in.) above the level of the river bed, is some 35 m (115 ft) higher than the Eiffel Tower in Paris, France. The rail bridge is part of the Udhampur-Srinagar-Baramulla rail link project (USBRL). Located in the Reasi District of Jammu and Kashmir, the bridge is 1,315 m (4,314 ft 3.6 in.) long and is aimed at boosting connectivity to the Kashmir Valley. The rail bridge is designed to withstand high wind speed of up to 266 kmph and bear strong earthquake forces of the highest intensity seismic zone-V in India. The height of its cable crane's pylon at the Srinagar end is 127 m, which is much taller than the Qutb Minar, which is 72 m (236 ft) high. Connecting Bakkal (Katra) and Kauri (Srinagar), the bridge was constructed using 24,000 tonnes of blast-proof steel by the Indian Railways in collaboration with the Defence Research and Development Organization (DRDO).

Longest bridge over water

The Bhupen Hazarika Setu, also referred to as the Dhola–Sadiya Bridge, connecting Dhola in Dibrugarh District and Sadiya in Lakhimpur District, Assam, is the longest bridge over water. The 9.15 km (5.7 miles) long bridge on the Brahmaputra River was inaugurated on 26 May 2017 by Prime Minister Narendra Modi. It is named after Bhupen Hazarika, a well-known Assamese musician and film-maker, who died in 2011.

Widest Double-Decker Steel Bridge

The North-South corridor of Nagpur Metro Rail Project comprises an 18.9 m (62 ft) wide double-decker viaduct: the lower level has a highway flyover and the upper level has a double-line metro rail. It is a two-level bridge over existing railway

The widest double-decker steel bridge is situated in Nagpur

lines, crossing the Indian Railways tracks at Gaddigodam at a skew angle of 19 degrees. The span is straight with an effective dimension of 80 m (262 ft) centre to centre of pier. The project was commissioned on 13 May 2022 and commercial operations began on 11 December 2022.

A Rashtrapati Bhavan rainwater harvesting initiative has yielded encouraging result. The water table has risen by an average of 1.90 m in the estate as on 4 August 2023.

Tallest bridge

The 64 m (210 ft) high Panval Nadi viaduct near Ratnagiri, Maharashtra, is the tallest bridge in the country.

Longest road-and-rail bridge

Bogibeel Bridge on the Brahmaputra River, between Dhemaji and Dibrugarh Districts, Assam, is the longest road-and-rail bridge, with a length of 4.94 km. Its construction was started in April 2002 and it was completed in December 2018. The bridge has a double-line 1.676 m (5 ft 6 in.) broad-gauge railway on the lower deck and a three-lane road on the upper one. It is India's first bridge with fully welded steel-concrete support beams to withstand earthquakes of magnitudes up to 7 on the Richter scale.

DAMS

Earliest canal system

Canal systems have existed since the pre-Harappan era (around 2500 BCE). Excavations at Dholavira in Gujarat have revealed ingenious systems for diverting water from seasonal nullahs.

Earliest dam and canal

The earliest dam discovered was built on Sudarshan Lake in Junagadh (then Girinagar) in Gujarat. It dates to 326 BC.

Longest canal

The Indira Gandhi Canal, or Rajasthan Canal, which starts in Punjab and ends in Rajasthan, is 959 km long, and is the world's second longest canal. Its schemes include 6,308 km of distributary canals.

Longest breakwater

The V.O. Chidambaranar Port (earlier Tuticorin Port) North Breakwater in Tamil Nadu is the longest at 4.14 km.

First hydroelectric project

Shivanasamudra Falls hydro-electric project in Chamarajanagar District, Karnataka, opened in 1902 and involved the harnessing of the Kavery River to supply electrical energy to run the machinery at the Kolar goldfields. The power station is still a functioning one.

STATE/UT-WISE LIST OF LARGE DAMS AND GROSS STORAGE CAPACITY

Legend: **No. of constructed large dams** | Gross storage capacity (in million cubic metre, or MCM) of constructed dams

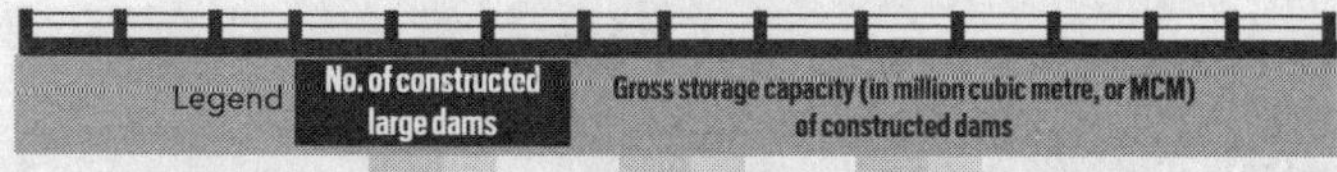

State/UT	No. of constructed large dams	Gross storage capacity (MCM)
Maharashtra	2,117	50,474.81
Karnataka	230	37,309.96
Madhya Pradesh	899	35,311.77
Odisha	200	32,529.84
Gujarat	620	32,134.26
Tripura	1	20,077.36
Himachal Pradesh	19	19,613.39
Uttar Pradesh	117	19,058.12
Kerala	61	16,522.93
Rajasthan	204	16,515.74
Andhra Pradesh	149	15,920.15
Chhattisgarh	249	8,982.92
Tamil Nadu	118	7,195.99
Jharkhand	55	5,881.91
Uttarakhand	17	4,760.77
Punjab	14	3,369.67
West Bengal	30	1,787.80
Mizoram	1	1,400.00
Bihar	24	984.90
Jammu and Kashmir and Ladakh	15	872.22
Nagaland	1	565.00
Meghalaya	8	403.17
Goa	5	299.61
Assam	3	245.30
Manipur	3	98.57
Andaman and Nicobar	2	15.28
Haryana	1	13.68
Sikkim	2	10.66
Arunachal Pradesh	1	6.17
Telangana	168	0.329

Total number of constructed large dams
5,334

Total Gross storage capacity (in MCM) of constructed dams
3,32,361 (approx.)

Source: Government press release posted on 07 August 2023

Grand Anicut Dam: the oldest dam in India that is still in use

Oldest extant dam

The Grand Anicut Dam, also known as the Kallanai Dam, built on the Kaveri River, 24 km from Tiruchirappalli in Tamil Nadu, is the oldest extant dam known in India. This masonry dam, which was built in the second century CE by the Chola king Aditha Karikalan (or Aditya II), is 330 m (1,083 ft) long, 5.49 m (18 ft) high, and 12–18 m (39–59 ft) wide. The ancient dam was remodelled, repaired, and fitted with sluice gates during 1899–1902. For centuries, it has irrigated more than a million acres (0.4 million hectares) of land.

Largest river dam

The Sardar Sarovar Dam is a gravity dam on the Narmada River near Navagam in Surat District, Gujarat. One of the 30 dams planned on the Narmada River, it is the largest such structure to be built and among the largest dams in the world. Four Indian states – Gujarat, Madhya Pradesh, Maharashtra and Rajasthan – receive water and electricity supplied from the dam.

Highest earth-fill dam

The Pong Dam, or Beas Dam, is an earth-fill embankment dam on the Beas River in Himachal Pradesh and the highest of its type at 133 m (436 ft 4 in.). Maharana Pratap Sagar Lake, created by the dam, is a bird sanctuary.

Oldest cement masonry dam

The Khadakwasla Dam on the Mutha River, 20 km from Pune in Maharashtra, was built on the suggestion of Colonel Fife of the Royal Engineers and a civil engineer N.G.K. Murti. It was started in 1869 and completed in 1879. The dam has since been rebuilt.

Largest water reservoir

Indirasagar Dam is a multipurpose project on the Narmada River in East Nimar District of Madhya Pradesh. The reservoir has a capacity of 12.2 billion cubic metre (9,890,701 acre feet) and, in terms of water storage, stands as the largest reservoir in India.

Largest barrage

The Farakka Barrage on the Ganga River was opened in 1972 to help maintain navigable depths in Shyama Prasad Mookerjee Port (earlier Kolkata Port). Its length of 2,245 m (7,365 ft 6 in.) contains 108 gated bays of 18 m (59 ft) each and two 8 m (26 ft) fish locks.

LIGHTHOUSES

Oldest lighthouses

- In 1766, two signal houses were built, one on Old Woman's Island (now part of Colaba) and the other at Malabar Point, in Bombay, Maharashtra.
- The former was replaced by the first proper lighthouse built in 1768–71. This threw a beam seven leagues seaward in clear weather at 45.72 m (150 ft). It was repaired in 1828 and 1853 but stopped operating when the Prongs Lighthouse was installed in 1874. Prongs Lighthouse is situated in a military area, so it has restricted access.

Oldest functional lighthouses

- The lighthouse built in 1821 on Sagar Island, at the mouth of the river Hooghly in West Bengal, was renovated in 1911. Its elevation from mean sea level is 26 m (85 ft 4 in.) and the tower is 25 m (82 ft) high. Its flashing light has a range of 31 km in clear weather. The second oldest was built more than fifty years later.
- The Prongs Lighthouse in the Colaba area in Bombay (now Mumbai), Maharashtra, is recorded to have been constructed in 1874 by Thomas Ormiston. The beam of the lighthouse can be seen at 30 km and it is still operational. Its height is 41 m (135 ft) and range is 43 km.

First unmanned lighthouse

Near Thalassery (earlier Tellicherry) in Kannur District, Kerala, stands the first unmanned lighthouse. It was built in 1835 and renovated in 1924. It is at an altitude of 27 m (89 ft) from mean sea level, and its range is 8 km.

Tallest lighthouse

The Jakhau Lighthouse in Gujarat is the tallest at 46 m (151 ft). It was established in 1957 and the present tower was built in 1965. Located on the main quay of Jakhau, a fishing port in western Kachchh, the lighthouse has a range of 33 km.

Tallest lighthouse (from mean sea level)

The tallest lighthouse from mean sea level is at Dolphin's Nose at Visakhapatnam, Andhra Pradesh. Its masonry tower rises 19 m (62 ft 4 in.) up from the ground level and it has an elevation of 173 m (567 ft 7 in.), which is 192 m (630 ft) from mean sea level.

AMUSEMENT ZONES

First indoor amusement play station

Funky Orbit at Ansal Plaza Mall on Khel Gaon Marg in New Delhi was launched on 15 June 2000 by Panoramic Entertainment Pvt. Ltd. The multi-tiered play station had an 8.53 m (28 ft) long curly slide and a ball pool. It closed down in 2011.

First amusement park

Appu Ghar at Pragati Maidan, New Delhi, the first family entertainment centre in India, opened during the 1982 Asian Games in Delhi. It was named after the Games' mascot – Appu the elephant. Shutting down in 2008, it reopened in Gurugram, Haryana.

MECHANICAL AND GENERAL STRUCTURES

First elevator

The first elevator was installed at Raj Bhavan, in Calcutta (now Kolkata), West Bengal in 1892. It used Otis's first design of an electric lift.

First hand-operated crane

The first hand-operated crane was built by Jessop & Company in 1850. The 5-tonne crane was installed at the then Calcutta Port (now Shyama Prasad Mookerjee Port) Customs.

First houseboat

The first houseboat, named *Victory*, was built in 1888 and stationed at the Dal Lake in Srinagar, Jammu and Kashmir.

First marine amusement park

In 1998, Dolphin City was set up by Amusements and Picnic Resorts Pvt. Ltd in Chennai, Tamil Nadu, with three performing dolphins and a performing sea lion show. Following the death of the performing dolphins, the marine amusement park featured sea lion performances, underwater viewing, and leisure boating.

First live entertainment, theatre, and leisure destination

Kingdom of Dreams in Gurugram, Haryana, is India's first live entertainment, theatre, and leisure destination. Spread over 6 acres (2.4 hectares), it is run by the Great Indian Nautanki Company (GINC), a joint venture of Apra Group and Wizcraft. It consists of two theatres, Nautanki Mahal and the Showshaa Theatre as well as a cultural and cuisine area known as Culture Gully.

Most names engraved on a monument

India Gate in Delhi carries the names of 13,516 British and Indian soldiers of the British

India Gate: It was built by Sir Edwin Lutyens, known for his planning of New Delhi

Indian Army, who died during 1914–21 at various fronts of the First World War and the Third Anglo-Afghan War. This constitutes the largest number of names inscribed on a monument. Designed by architect Edwin Lutyens, the arch was completed in 1921. It is 42.3 m (139 ft) high and 9.1 m (30 ft) wide.

Joseph Allen Stein, a US-born architect who came to India in 1952, was conferred an honorary doctorate, the first in architecture, by Anna University, Chennai, Tamil Nadu, in September 1999.

First floating restaurant

The first floating restaurant was built at Sirhind, Punjab, on the Bhakra Canal in 1979. The eight-room air-conditioned restaurant was part of a tourist complex.

First revolving restaurant

Neelkanth Patang at Ahmedabad, Gujarat, was the first revolving restaurant at 67.4 m (221 ft) above ground level. Opened in 1984, it has a 90-minute rotation, which unfolds a view of the old and new city of Ahmedabad.

First space-frame concrete structure

The first space-frame structure in reinforced concrete was the Hall of Nations at the Trade Fair Authority of India exhibition grounds in Pragati Maidan, New Delhi. Built during 1971–72, the hall offered an uninterrupted exhibition area of 6,700 sq. m (72,120 sq. ft) in a 82 m x 82 m x 27 m (269 ft x 269 ft x 88 ft 7 in.) pyramid supported at eight points.

Largest auditorium

The Sri Shanmukhananda Hall, inaugurated on 22 August 1963 in Bombay (now Mumbai), Maharashtra, has a total capacity of 3,012 seats. The ground floor seats 1,552, the first balcony 896 and the second balcony 564 people. The stage has a depth and width of 16 m (52 ft) and a height of 6.4 m (21 ft).

Largest glasshouse

A glass-covered hall in Davanagere, Karnataka, completed in 2018, covers 7,334 sq. m (78,942.5 sq. ft). It houses a horticultural information centre and a botanical garden.

First water park

Shanku's Water Park on the Ahmedabad–Mahesana Highway in Gujarat was launched by Shankarbhai Chaudhary in 1993, on a 75-acre (30.35 hectares) campus. It introduced a giant 15.24 m (50 ft) speed slide that ended in a shallow water pool, a spiral ride, a wave pool that simulated sea waves, and a kids' corner.

Largest table

The teakwood table in the Banquet Hall at the Rashtrapati Bhavan in Delhi can seat 104 people at a time.

Largest cooking vessel

The original badi deg (big vessel), christened Deg-i-Chittor-Kusba, or the 'Chittor-conquering vessel', said to be presented by the Mughal emperor Akbar to the dargah of Khwaja Moinuddin Chishti in Ajmer, Rajasthan, could hold 4,000 kg of food at a time that was enough for 12,000 people.

Largest official residence

The Rashtrapati Bhavan in New Delhi, the official residence of the president of India, has 340 rooms, 18 staircases, 74 lobbies, 37 salons, 1 km of corridors, 37 fountains, and 190 acres (76.9 hectares) of gardens. The residence covers 50 acres (20.2 hectares) of a 330-acre (133.5 hectare) estate.

Largest retractable roof

Kunta International Ltd, Noida, Uttar Pradesh, designed, built, installed, and commissioned an electrically driven retractable roof on a reusable structure on the presidential dais on Rajpath (now Kartavya Path), New Delhi, for Republic Day 2018. Made of steel and polycarbonate sheets with inbuilt sensors, it was 30.5 m (100 ft) wide and 6.4 m (21 ft) deep.

Longest conveyor

The longest single-belt international conveyor stretches from Nongtrai Village near Shella, East Khasi Hills District, Meghalaya, in India, to a cement factory at Chhatak in Sunamganj District, Bangladesh. It is about 17 km long (7 km in India and 10 km in Bangladesh) and conveys limestone and shale at 960 tonnes/hr. The conveyor was engineered by AUMUND France and Larsen & Toubro and installed by Beltpro. Its rollers are unusually designed to deal with both horizontal and vertical terrain curves.

Tallest chimney

The 275.2 m (903 ft) tall chimney of the Reliance Dahanu Thermal Power Station, Dahanu, in Palghar District, Maharashtra, is India's tallest RCC chimney. The base diameter of the chimney is 7 m (23 ft).

Largest multiplex

Mayajaal in Kanathur in Chennai, Tamil Nadu, has the largest movie multiplex with 16 screens and a seating capacity of 2,600. It is part of an entertainment centre that houses a shopping mall, a sports complex, and a resort.

Longest underground pipeline

The Hazira-Bijapur-Jagdishpur (HBJ) gas pipeline is India's first cross-country gas pipeline. This project by GAIL (India) Ltd began in 1986 to supply gas to fertilizer plants in Uttar Pradesh. The first phase, consisting of a non-branched 1,750 km grid, was later expanded to supply gas for industrial and domestic use in Rajasthan, Haryana, and the National Capital Territory (NCT). This extended the grid length to 3,474 km.

Oldest ice-skating rink

The ice-skating rink near Lakkar Bazaar in Simla (now Shimla), Himachal Pradesh, was founded in 1920 by one Mr Blessington. Initially out of bounds for

Indians during British rule, it is now managed by the Shimla Ice-skating Club and is open for skating between the winter months of December and February.

The first skyscraper

Usha Kiran, an apartment building of 26 storeys in Bombay (now Mumbai), Maharashtra, was the first of high-rise buildings. It was built between 1964 and 1967.

MODERN STRUCTURES

First architect to win the Pritzker Prize

Dr Balkrishna Vithaldas Doshi (b. 26 August 1927) won the famed Pritzker Architecture Prize on 12 March 2018, the first Indian to do so in the award's 40-year history. The Pritzker Prize is referred to as the Nobel Prize in architecture.

First reinforced-concrete building

The Golconde dormitory at Sri Aurobindo Ashram in Pondicherry (now Puducherry) was designed by Czech-American architect Antonin Raymond (1888–1976) and completed in 1948. All its features evolved from a study of the local climatic conditions and the occupants' needs.

First underground market

Palika Bazaar, the air-conditioned underground market at Connaught Place (now Rajiv Chowk) in New Delhi, was set up in 1978.

First permanent crafts market

Dilli Haat in Delhi opened in 1994, with 62 stalls selling handicrafts from all over the country and 25 food stalls.

First all-steel building

The ICICI headquarters in Mumbai, Maharashtra, designed by Raja Aederi and built in 1995, have a superstructure area of 39,948 sq. m (430,000 sq. ft), two-level basements with a total area of 21,368 sq. m (230,000 sq. ft), and a structural area of 14,000 sq. m (150,700 sq. ft).

Tallest escalator

The Janakpuri West metro station on the Magenta Line of the Delhi Metro features India's tallest escalator. The escalator is 15.6 m (51 ft 2 in.) high.

Tallest building

World One, a 280.2 m (919 ft 3 in.), 76-floor skyscraper in Mumbai, Maharashtra, is the tallest completed building in India. Developed by the Lodha Group, the building was completed in 2020.

SPECIALIZED STRUCTURES

Most elaborate stepwell

The Rani ki Vav ('queen's step well') at Patan, Gujarat, was built by Rani Udayamati, the queen of King Bhimadeva I (r. 1022–64 CE) of the Chalukya dynasty, in memory of her husband. It measures 65 m x 20 m (213 ft 3 in. x 65 ft 7 in.) and is over 28 m (91 ft 10 in.) deep. Originally, over 800 sculptures decorated it.

Oldest slide

The rock-cut slide at Mamallapuram in Chengalpattu District, Tamil Nadu, is said to be the world's oldest children's slide.

India's Biggest Demolition

Two illegally constructed towers at the Supertech Emerald Court Housing Society in Sector 93A, Noida, Uttar Pradesh, made headlines on 28 August 2022. The 103 m (338 ft) high towers were demolished by the 'waterfall implosion' technique in a mere 12 seconds! The demolition of these twin residential towers was ordered by the Supreme Court and carried out by a Mumbai-based company, Edifice Engineering, along with the South African firm Jet Demolitions as their expert partner. With the grounding of Apex (32 storeys) and Ceyane (29 storeys) towers, India joined the club of countries that have razed buildings taller than 100 m (328 ft).

First floating cottages

Kabeer Khader and M.R. Narayanan's Floatels India in 1999 launched 20 floating cottages at Poovar Island Resort in Thiruvananthapuram District, Kerala. Designed by architect N. Mahesh, they are built on laminated ferro-cement platforms.

First igloo stay

Keylinga's Manali Igloo Stay, near Sethan Village, about 16 km from Manali in Himachal Pradesh, was opened in 2017 by Vikas Kumar and Tashi Dorje of Keylinga Himalayan Adventures. Starting with two fully functional igloos, the duo provide guests sleeping bags with extra fleece, and hot-water bottles.

First igloo cafe

India's first cafe in the shape of an igloo opened in Gulmarg, Jammu and Kashmir, on 24 January 2021, at an altitude of 2,650 m (8,694 ft) in the Pir Panjal Range of the Himalayas. A part of the Kolahoi Green Group of Hotels and Resorts, the cafe is a 4.5 m (14 ft

9.17 in.) high structure completed by a team of 20 members in 15 days, and has a diameter of 7.3 m (23 ft 11.4 in.). The igloo cafe accommodates four tables that can seat around 16 people at a time and is currently the biggest igloo cafe in Asia.

WR Largest gazebo

Nirmala Nilayam Retirement Community at Theetipalayam near Siruvani in Coimbatore District, Tamil Nadu, completed the largest gazebo on 20 March 2021. It measures 242.25 sq. m (2,607.59 sq. ft). The gazebo serves as a yoga hall, a seminar hall, a space for art and music sessions, and a meditation space.

First eco-hotel

Asia's first certified eco-hotel, the Orchid, opened in Mumbai, Maharashtra, in 1997.

Largest tent structure

The largest permanent tent structure stood at the Osho International Commune in Pune, Maharashtra. Oval in shape – with a 62.75 m (205 ft 10 in.) major axis and a 32.8 m (107 ft 7 in.) minor axis – it had a floor area of 1,582 sq. m (17,029 sq. ft). The roof, which was 3.9 m (12 ft 9.5 in.) high, was a free-spanning, tensile

Tallest Reinforced Earth Structure

WR World's tallest reinforced earth structure came up in Tindharia town in Darjeeling District, West Bengal, in 2022. This was created by Terre Armée and was part of a landslide restoration process (under National Highway Circle No. III for Rehabilitation of Landslide Location with Slope Protection and Drainage Improvement at Tindharia on NH-55 at locations from 50.155 to 50.182 km, 52.650 to 52.929 km, and 53.452 to 53.475 km – covering a total length of 329 metres) in Darjeeling, West Bengal. The maximum height of the structure is 102.8 m in location 2 of the three locations where this earth structure was built. The project started in 2017 and took four years to complete.

Total area covered: 7724 sq m

Design life: 100 years

structure on a three-hinged steel arch covering 45.5 m (149 ft 3 in.). It used nylon reinforced PVC material, weighing 1,990 kg.

WR Largest pillar-less dome

The World Peace Monument is located at the Maharashtra Institute of Technology's World Peace University (MIT -WPU) campus at Loni Kalbhor near Pune, Maharashtra. At a height of 29 m (95 ft), the world's biggest pillar-less dome is built on top of the World Peace Prayer Hall and Library and has a diameter of 48.7 m (160 ft), larger than the dome of the Vatican 42.5 m (139 ft 5 in.). Completed in 2018, the dome has a bell hanging from the centre.

Largest underground aquarium

The Bagh-e-Bahu Aquarium at the Bagh-e-Bahu Garden that surrounds Bahu Fort in Jammu in Jammu and Kashmir is the largest underground aquarium in India. At more than 220 m (721 ft 9 in.) in length, this fish-shaped aquarium has freshwater and saltwater fish species in 24 caves with 13 smaller caves.

Highest and longest ropeway

The Gulmarg Gondola, a gondola lift that covers 2,540 m (8,333 ft), is a joint venture of the Jammu and Kashmir government and the French firm Pomagalski SA. Its first stage transfers people from Gulmarg at 2,600 m (8,530 ft) to Kongdori Station in Kongdori Valley. The second stage goes to 3,747 m (12,293 ft) on Kongdori Mountain, with the highest point at 4,200 m (13,780 ft).

Longest transportation railway tunnel

The 11.21 km long Pir Panjal or Banihal RailwayTunnel is the longest transportation tunnel in India. It connects Bichleri Valley, Banihal, to Qazigund in the Kashmir Valley. The first train here was flagged off on 26 June 2013.

Longest river ropeway

A 1.8 km (5,906 ft) long ropeway was opened in August 2020 across the Brahmaputra River in Guwahati, Assam. It connects the southern and northern parts of the city, cutting down travel time from an hour to eight minutes.

Guwahati Passenger Ropeway: The ropeway has two of its pillars directly on the river bed

AGRICULTURE

GENERAL

First fully organic state

Sikkim was declared India's first fully organic state on 18 January 2016. It has succeeded in converting around 75,000 hectares (185,329 acres) of its agricultural land to certified organic land by implementing organic practices as per the guidelines of the National Programme for Organic Production.

First nationwide farm loan waiver

The first nationwide farm loan waiver in independent India was implemented in 1990 by the V.P. Singh government. It cost the exchequer ₹10,000 crore (100 billion).

Biggest farm loan waiver

The then Maharashtra chief minister Devendra Fadnavis announced a farm loan waiver of ₹34,000 crore (340 billion) in June 2017. This unprecedented waiver was intended to provide relief to 89 lakh (8.9 million) farmers in the state.

First agricultural theme park

N.K. Kurian, a civil engineer, is the person behind Mango Meadows. It is India's first man-made agricultural theme park spread on 12 hectares (29.65 acres) of land, in Kottayam, Kerala. Work on the park began in 2004 and it was opened to the public in December 2016. With saplings and seeds collected from 15 countries, currently the park has 4,500 species of plants, including 1,900 medicinal plants, 700 trees, and 900 flowering plants.

First fruit train

A train exclusively carrying fruit – 980 tonnes of locally grown bananas – was flagged off from Tadipatri railway station in Anantapur District, Andhra Pradesh. It reached the Jawaharlal Nehru Port in Mumbai, Maharashtra, on 31 January 2020. The train was laden with 43 refrigerator containers of bananas that had been despatched for export to international markets.

Earliest ploughed field

Archaeologists B.B. Lal and B.K. Thapar of the Archaeological Survey of India (ASI) found a ploughed field dated to c. 2450–2300 BCE during excavations at Kalibangan in Pilibangan Tehsil in Hanumangarh District, Rajasthan.

Representative image

First state/UT to regulate crops

Telangana has become the first state in the country to

stipulate when and how much of which crops to grow for its farmers. From the beginning of the kharif season in 2020, the state decided to regulate the cropping pattern with the help of a detailed cropping map and a seed regulation authority. The emphasis is to drive supply according to the market demand.

First state/UT to enact a law on contract farming

Tamil Nadu became the first state in the country to pass a law on contract farming titled the Agricultural Produce and Livestock Contract Farming and Services (Promotion and Facilitation) Act in February 2019. Contract farming enables more transparency, and legally safeguards the interests of farmers, producer companies, and purchasers. The Act covers the produce of agriculture, sericulture, horticulture, apiculture, animal husbandry, and forest activities.

HISTORY

Earliest irrigation

Evidence of irrigation on agricultural land in the Indian subcontinent dates to the Chalcolithic period (3000–1000 BCE). The Inamgaon area of Maharashtra has a prehistoric mud embankment structure with a stone foundation. This was connected to the Ghod River by a number of channels. Floodwater was used effectively to irrigate the surrounding regions during the dry months by storing it and then distributing it.

Earliest cotton cultivation

The earliest evidence for cotton production comes from the Harappan civilization (2500–1700 BCE). The earliest sample of cotton material was discovered by archaeologist Daya Ram Sahni during 1921–22 in Mohenjo-daro (now in Pakistan). It was a small fragment of cotton clinging to the side of a vase and dyed red with madder pigment (*Rubia tinctorum*).

First famine commission

The Famine Commission set up in 1880 was the first famine commission in the country. Sir Edward Buck was its secretary, who had provincial agencies under his guidance. It was a forerunner of the later Ministry of Food and Agriculture of the government after India became independent.

First agricultural society

William Carey, a British Christian missionary, social reformer, translator, and anthropologist, founded the Agri-Horticultural Society of India in September 1820 in Calcutta (now Kolkata), West Bengal. It was set up to help disseminate scientific information among the people.

First society of soil sciences

The Indian Society of Soil Sciences was formed on 22 December 1934 in Calcutta with 28 members. It was

Cryobanks are facilities that store living tissue at very low temperatures. The temperature is maintained at -196° C using liquid nitrogen.

formally inaugurated on 3 January 1935 at the Presidency College (now Presidency University). Sir Bryce C. Burt, the then agricultural commissioner in the Imperial (now Indian) Council of Agricultural Research (ICAR), was its first president and Prof. J.N. Mukherjee, its first secretary.

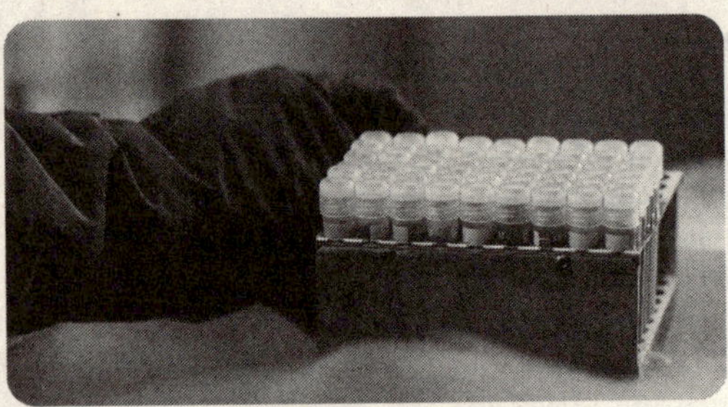
Biomaterial being stored in liquid nitrogen

First pollen cryobank

The first pollen cryobank (frost bank) was established in 1983 at the Indian Institute of Horticultural Research, Bengaluru, Karnataka, to conserve genetic biodiversity among plants and support the work of crop breeders.

First agricultural university

The G.B. (Govind Ballabh) Pant University of Agriculture and Technology (GBPUA&T), also known as Pantnagar University, was the first agricultural university in India. It was inaugurated on 17 November 1960 as the Uttar Pradesh Agricultural University (UPAU). Later, in 1972, its name was changed to Govind Ballabh Pant University of Agriculture and Technology after the first chief minister of Uttar Pradesh and Bharat Ratna recipient Pandit Govind Ballabh Pant.

First spices research institute

The regional station for spice research, set up at Kozhikode, Kerala, in 1975 is the apex research organization for spices in the country. It later evolved into the Indian Institute of Spices Research in 1986.

WR Oldest locust control programme

The Locust Warning Organization (LWO), set up in 1939 in Karachi (now in Pakistan) by the British, is the oldest locust control programme in the world. In 1946, the LWO moved to Delhi under the Directorate of Plant Protection, Quarantine and Storage, Ministry of Agriculture and Farmers' Welfare, Government of India. It surveys locust populations and issues bulletins.

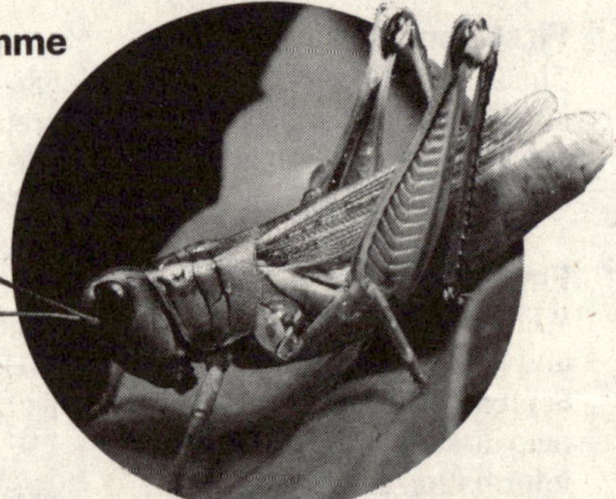
A locust on a leaf

First agricultural research institute

The Imperial Agricultural Research Institute, established in 1905 at Pusa, Samastipur District, Bihar, was India's first agricultural research institute. After the building was damaged in an earthquake in 1934, the institute was moved to New Delhi in 1936. It is now known as the Indian Agricultural Research Institute (IARI) and is the oldest agricultural institute in India.

Representative image

Micro-Irrigation Systems – What Is the Big Deal?

In recent years, micro-irrigation has received a lot of attention in light of the water crisis occurring across the globe. These systems employ methods to deliver smaller quantities of water in or below the surface of the soil to increase water use efficiency. Many efforts have been made by the Indian Government as well to implement this system. By 2022, the Indian government had covered an area of 137.8 lakh hectares (34051121.566 acres) under micro-irrigation. In March 2022, Kerala had the largest area under micro-irrigation with a total coverage of 24,29,315 hectares (6002968.1 acres).

Largest groundwater irrigation system

India has the largest groundwater irrigation system in the world with 39 million hectares (96.4 million acres) of land under this kind of irrigation. Besides groundwater, India's irrigation depends on canals from rivers, well-based systems, tanks, and other rainwater harvesting systems. About two-thirds of farmlands in the country still depend on the monsoon.

Oldest tea research station

Set up in 1911, the Tocklai Experimental Station in Jorhat, Assam, is the world's oldest and largest tea research station. Its many contributions include the invention of tea machinery and the development of 30 vegetative clones. The transfer of innovative technology to its member estates is carried out through its advisory network. This network covers 1,076 tea estates occupying 341,049 hectares (842,750.4 acres) of land spread over the Brahmaputra Valley, the Barak Valley, Tripura, the Dooars, Darjeeling and the Terai areas. Tocklai has its regional R&D centre at Nagrakata in Jalpaiguri District, West Bengal.

Only research centre for tropical tuber crops

The Central Tuber Crops Research Institute at Sreekariyam in Thiruvananthapuram District, Kerala, is the only institute in the world dedicated to research on tropical tuber crops. It was established in 1963.

Only weed research centre

The Directorate of Weed Science Research (DWSR), Jabalpur, Madhya Pradesh, set up the National Research Centre for Weed Science on 22 April 1989 – the only one in the world for weed management research.

Research institute located at the highest altitude

The Defence Institute of High Altitude Research (DIHAR), situated at 3,505 m (11,499 ft) in Leh, Ladakh, is a laboratory of the Defence Research Development

Organization (DRDO). It was established in 1962 to help Indian defence troops as well as farmers of the region with appropriate agro-animal technologies.

AWARDS AND HONOURS

First Indian scientist to receive the Ramon Magsaysay Award

Geneticist Dr M.S. Swaminathan received the Ramon Magsaysay award in 1971 for community leadership and became the first Indian scientist to do so. Known as the 'Father of the Green Revolution' for his leading role in food self-sufficiency in India, he was the director of the Indian Agricultural Research Institute in Delhi at the time. Dr Swaminathan advocates environmentally sustainable agriculture as well as preservation of biodiversity, culminating in what he has termed an 'evergreen' revolution.

First Indian fellow of the Royal Society

Dr Benjamin Peary Pal, the first director of the Indian Council of Agricultural Research, was also the first Indian agricultural scientist to become a Fellow of the Royal Society of London, UK, while in office, in 1972. He was also awarded the top national civilian awards: the Padma Shri (1959), the Padma Bhushan (1968) and the Padma Vibhushan (1987).

First Indian president of the International Society of Soil Sciences

Dr J.S. Kanwar was elected president of the International Society of Soil Sciences for the period 1978–82. The Society was founded in 1924, mainly by European agro-pedologists interested in establishing standardized methods of soil analysis.

First winner of the World Food Prize

In 1987, Dr M.S. Swaminathan became the first Indian to win the World Food Prize. He was an agronomist, agricultural scientist and plant geneticist. This global award is given to outstanding individuals who have advanced human development by improving the quality, quantity, or availability of food in the world. So far, eight Indians have won the World Food Prize and the most recent was Dr Rattan Lal, an India-born British scientist from the USA, in 2020.

FARMLANDS AND PRINCIPAL CROPS

Largest single farm

The Central State Farm at Suratgarh in Rajasthan, with an area of 6,296 hectares (15,557.8 acres), is said to be the largest farm in Asia.

Largest average farm holdings in a state/UT

As per the 2015–16 Agricultural Census, Nagaland has the largest farm holdings, with 4.87 hectares (12.03 acres) as the average size of an operational unit.

WR First hybrid Basmati rice

The IARI, New Delhi, developed and released RH-10 in 2001, the first hybrid superfine-grained, aromatic rice in the world. The optimum yield of this variety of rice, with typical Basmati traits, is 7 tonnes/hectare.

INDIA'S CONTRIBUTION TO CH4 EMISSIONS (IN KILOTONNES) FROM BURNING-CROP RESIDUES IN THE WORLD (IN %)

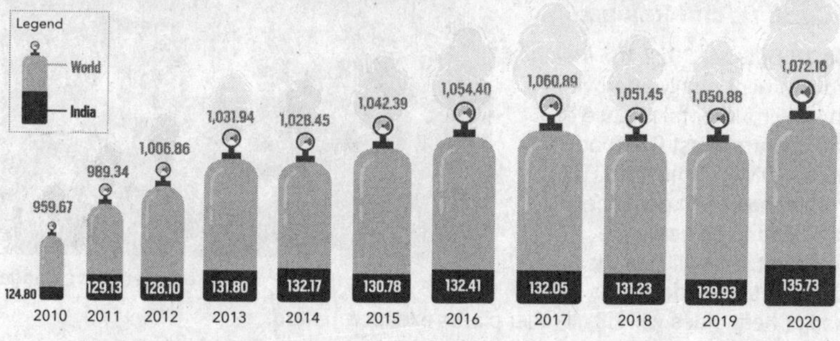

AREA UNDER ORGANIC CULTIVATION IN INDIA (2015-2020) IN THOUSAND HECTARES

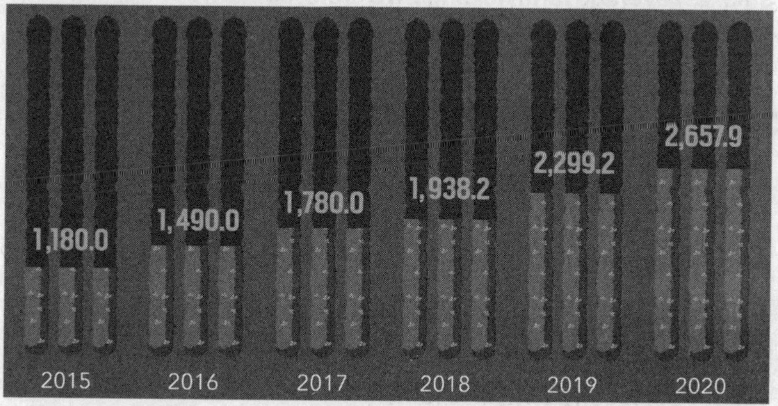

TOP 5 STATES WITH HIGHEST LAND COVERAGE UNDER MICRO-IRRIGATION IN HECTARES (2022)

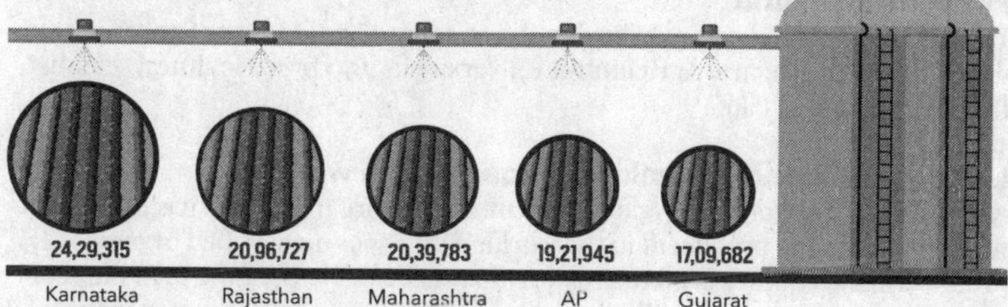

Source for all infographics on the page: Agricultural Statistics at a Glance 2022, Ministry of Agriculture and Farmers Welfare, Government of India

GM Mustard – India's First GM Food Crop Commercial Release

Representative image

On 18 October 2022, the Indian government finally approved the environmental release of the country's first GM food crop – DMH11 mustard. This variant has been genetically modified to be herbicide resistant. This will aid the farmers tremendously as the use of herbicides will kill all other plants except mustard. Field trials were conducted for three years to test its safety and effect on the environment and it was declared as safe for cultivation and consumption.

Smallest average farm holdings in a state/UT

The average size of an operational farm in Kerala is 0.18 hectares (0.44 acres) as per the 2015–16 Agricultural Census.

First genetically modified cash crop approved for commercial cultivation

Bt (*Bacillus thuringiensis*) cotton was the first genetically modified (GM) crop approved for commercial cultivation in 2002 by the Government of India. The Genetic Engineering Appraisal Committee (GEAC) has also approved confined field trials of 20 GM crops for the generation of bio-safety data from both private and public sector institutions. The crops are cotton, mustard, brinjal, okra, sorghum, groundnut, maize, potato, tomato, chickpea, pigeon pea, banana, castor, papaya, watermelon, sugar cane, wheat, rice, rubber tree and Indian wormwood.

WR First pigeon pea hybrid (arhar)

The International Crops Research Institute for Semi-Arid Tropics (ICRISAT) released the world's first hybrid pigeon pea, ICPH-8, in 1991. This variety recorded a yield potential of 2,057 kg/hectare.

First cotton hybrid

The first commercial cotton hybrid in the country, named H-4 or Sankar-4, was developed at the Gujarat Agricultural University in 1970 by agricultural scientist Dr Chandrakant T. Patel.

Largest number of organic producers in the world

According to the World of Organic Agriculture Report 2022, India has the largest number of organic producers in the world. With 1,599,010 certified organic producers, the country is home to more than 47.02 per cent of the total number of organic producers (3.4 million) worldwide. However, when it comes to the total area under certified organic cultivation, India only has 1.5 per cent of its entire agricultural area under organic cultivation.

Tea gardens in the Nilgiris

Highest tea garden

The Korakundah Tea Estate of the United Nilgiri Tea Estates Co. Ltd, near Coonoor in the Nilgiris in Tamil Nadu, has its highest tea garden at an altitude of 2,471 m (8,107 ft).

First tea estate

In 1837, the British East India Company set up the first tea estate at Chabua in Dibrugarh District, Assam. Now the estate is owned by Amalgamated Plantations Private Ltd. The first Tea Committee in India was set up in 1834 by the then Governor General of India, William Bentinck.

Tallest sugar cane

Vedant Rajendra Yadav (b. 28 January 1998) from Fursungi Village in Pune District, Maharashtra, grew a sugar cane plant that was 13.1 m (43 ft) tall in January 2021.

Tallest paddy plant

Tanaji Nikam, a farmer in Vannur Village in Kolhapur, Maharashtra, grew a paddy plant 2.8 m (9 ft 2 in.) tall in 2005 using organic manure.

Only producer of five commercial silk varieties

India is the only producer of all five commercial varieties of silk, viz. mulberry, oak tussore, tropical tussore, *eri* and *muga*. Golden muga is produced only in India. During 2018–19, India produced 31,906 tonnes of raw silk.

Tallest jowar

Dodda Ramachandra Reddy (b. 20 January 1951) from Peddapalli, Karimnagar District, Telangana, grew a jowar plant that was 5.3 m (17 ft 4 in.) tall as on 27 October 2018. It took 161 days to grow to this height.

State/UT with maximum cold storage capacity

Uttar Pradesh has 14,834,695 tonnes of cold storage capacity as on 31 January 2022.

In 2021-22, India's foodgrain production reached a record 315.7 million tonnes despite challenges posed by climate change.

A vineyard

Highest vineyard

At 1,585 m (5,200 ft) above mean sea level, Kookkal Vineyards (Domaine Kookkal) at Kookkal Village, near Udhagamandalam, Tamil Nadu, are the highest commercial-scale vineyards in the country.

HORTICULTURE

First seed company

The National Seeds Corporation, set up in 1963 by the Government of India, undertakes the production of certified seeds of nearly 600 varieties of 60 crops through its 8,000 registered seed growers.

First vanilla cultivation

The first cultivation centres of vanilla were set up more than a century ago at the Kallar Fruit Research Station, Thiruvananthapuram District, and the Ambalavayal Horticultural Research Station, Wayanad District, Kerala.

First non-narcotic poppy

Sujata, a poppy variety developed in 1998 at the Central Institute of Medicinal and Aromatic Plants, Lucknow, Uttar Pradesh, was the first poppy variety free of opium and opium alkaloids.

First mustard hybrid

In 2008, NRC Sankar Sarson (NRCHB 506), an Indian hybrid of mustard, was developed by a team of scientists led by Dr K.H. Singh at the National Research Centre on Rapeseed-Mustard (NRCRM; now called the Directorate of Rapeseed Mustard Research) in Bharatpur, Rajasthan.

First coconut hybrids

Researchers at the Coconut Research Station, now called the Central Plantation Crops Research Institute (CPCRI), Kasaragod, Kerala, produced the first coconut hybrids between the tall and dwarf palms in 1932, with two to three times more nuts than in each of the parent palms.

WR Tallest papaya plant

Jhantu Paul from Kolkata, West Bengal, owns the tallest papaya tree (*Carica papaya*) measuring 14.07 m (46 ft 2 in.) as verified on 22 January 2017.

Heaviest jackfruit

Kaithakkoli Kurichiya's family found a jackfruit weighing 57.9 kg on their compound in Thallappuzha, Wayanad District, Kerala, in May 2020. The jackfruit was 67 cm (26 in.) long, with a circumference of 1.35 m (4 ft 5 in.).

Jackfruit on a branch

Longest and biggest coconut

Dr Dilip Kumar Vitthaldas Patil, a scientist at the Central Institute for Cotton Research, Nagpur, Maharashtra, preserved for 12 years, the largest and biggest coconut (and the longest preserved) seen in India. Dr Patil found this giant coconut in a farm in Pilicode Village, Kasaragod District, Kerala. Even in the dried state, it was 27 cm (10.63 in.) from stalk to tip and its equitorial length was 67.5 cm (26.57 in.) as against normal green coconuts, which are 14 to 20 cm (5.51 to 7.87 in.) horizontally and 25 to 45 cm (9.84 to 17.72 in.) long. In its dried state the coconut weighed 1,450 g against an average of 300–500 g.

WR First onion hybrid

The world's first onion hybrid was developed at the Indian Agricultural Research Institute, New Delhi, in March 2002 with a potential of increasing yield by 20 per cent.

WR Largest producer of coconuts

India produces 34.73 per cent of the global production of coconuts. As per 2020–21 reports, the area and production of coconuts in the country is 2.18 million hectares (5.8 million acres) and 14.57 million tonnes, respectively. The four southern states of Kerala, Tamil Nadu, Karnataka and Andhra Pradesh account for 88.97 per cent of the area under coconut cultivation and 89.67 per cent of the coconut production in the country.

A coconut with a glass of coconut water

A variety of Indian spices

WR Largest producer of spices

India is the largest producer of spices and spice products. In 2020–21, India produced 16.6 million tonnes of spices.

Longest ash gourd

Dr Johnson Nayankara (b. 1 August 1961) from Mapranam in Thrissur District, Kerala, has grown the longest ash gourd as verified on 11 November 2020. It was 47.3 cm (18.62 in.) long, with a 6.2 cm (2.4 in.) stalk.

Hottest chilli

The *bhut jolokia*, or 'ghost chilli', is the hottest chilli in India. Rated at 1,041,427 Scoville heat units (SHUs), this variety is cultivated in the north-eastern states of Arunachal Pradesh, Assam, Nagaland and Manipur.

First castor hybrid

The Castor and Mustard Research Station in Sardarkrushinagar in Banaskantha District, Gujarat, developed the first castor hybrid named GCH 3 and released it in 1968–69 on a commercial scale. GCH 7, released in 2006, has the highest potential productivity (3,000 kg/hectare) in India.

WR Largest producer of mangoes

According to the first estimates for 2020–21, India's mango production stood at 20.82 million tonnes. Andhra Pradesh turned out to be the top mango-producing state with the production of 5,001,740 tonnes of mangoes.

ANIMAL HUSBANDRY

Early vet research

Research on animal healthcare began with the setting up of the Imperial Bacteriological Laboratory at Poona (now Pune), Maharashtra, on 9 December 1889, with Dr Alfred Lingard as the first bacteriologist in 1890. It was moved to Mukteshwar, Uttarakhand, in 1895. The Indian Veterinary Research Institute (IVRI) later began in 1913 at Izatnagar, Bareilly District, Uttar Pradesh.

First veterinary surgeon

William Moorcroft (1767–1825), a Britisher who was appointed veterinary surgeon in 1808 at the Pusa Stud Farm, Bihar, is the first one on record in India.

First frozen semen bank for bulls

The first frozen semen bank for bulls was established in 1963 in Mattupatti, Kerala, with Indo-Swiss collaboration. The objective was to evolve a new breed of cattle adapted to the local environment. The bank dealt with the collection, processing, storage, and transportation of the semen of bull breeds.

First artificial insemination in bulls

Artificial insemination was successfully attempted for the first time in 1939 by Sampath Kumaran, who crossed the Indian Hallikar breed with Holstein Friesian bulls.

First dairy research institute

Established in 1923 as the Imperial Dairy Institute of Animal Husbandry and Dairying in Bangalore (now Bengaluru), Karnataka, it was renamed National Dairy Research Institute (NDRI) after Independence. In 1955, its headquarters was shifted to Karnal, Haryana. It undertakes research, teaching and extension activities in dairy development.

First lamb from frozen embryo

Scientists at the Central Sheep and Wool Research Institute in Avikanagar in Tonk District, Rajasthan, implanted a cryo-preserved Bharat Merino embryo into a Kheri surrogate ewe, which birthed a lamb on 20 January 1999.

Only camel farm

The National Research Centre on Camel (NRCC), also a camel-breeding farm, was set up in Bikaner, Rajasthan, in 1957 for conducting scientific research on camels. The centre aims to study ways of optimizing the working capacity of camels. It is the only camel farm in the country.

Camels in National Research Centre on Camel, Bikaner, Rajasthan

CLONING RECORDS

1 First cloned pashmina goat

WR Noori, the first cloned pashmina goat, was born at the Faculty of Veterinary Sciences and Animal Husbandry, Sher-e-Kashmir University of Agricultural Sciences and Technology, Srinagar, Jammu and Kashmir, on 9 March 2012. With a birthweight of 1.3 kg, she was cloned by a team headed by Dr Riaz Ahmad Shah, using somatic cell nuclear transfer technique.

2 First calf cloned from frozen semen

In July 2014, a male calf named Rajat was cloned by the National Dairy Research Institute (NDRI), Karnal, Haryana, using a donor cell from the frozen semen of a highly ranked Murrah buffalo bull. This was the first time frozen semen was used for cloning a farm animal.

3 First cloned female buffalo by hand-guided technique

WR In June 2014, scientists of the National Dairy Research Institute, Karnal, Haryana, produced the world's first female cloned buffalo calf through 'hand-guided' cloning, using a donor cell from the ear of a high-yielding Murrah buffalo. The calf was named Lalima.

4 First cloned buffalo

WR On 6 February 2009, a team of six scientists – S.K. Singla, M.S. Chauhan, R.S. Manik, P. Palta, R.A. Shah and A. George – all from the Animal Biotechnology Centre at the National Dairy Research Institute, Karnal, Haryana, cloned the first female water buffalo calf in the world from a year-old buffalo of the Murrah breed. Although the calf died five days later, the team of scientists succeeded in testing the cloning and other technologies that helped them achieve one of their objectives of getting the desired gender of the cloned animal.

Ganga–the first cloned cow in India

On 16 March 2023, Ganga, the first cloned cow in India, was born. The scientists at NDRI, Karnal, Haryana, created her. The process of cloning a cow took much longer due to religious sentiments as the technology available back then was invasive. However, in 2018, the scientists got access to a non-invasive technology called ovum pick up that is used to separate oocytes from the cow without harming her. They chose Gir breed as it could withstand harsh weather and produce 2–3 times more milk, i.e., 15 to 20 litres per day.

5 Most calves cloned from a single bull

The Central Institute for Research on Buffaloes (CIRB), located in Hisar, Haryana, achieved the cloning of seven calves from a single superior breeding bull, named M-29, between October 2019 and January 2020.

Highest stud farm

The Zanskar Pony Breeding and Training Centre at Partapur in Nubra Block, Ladakh, is located at 3,146 m (10,321 ft) above mean sea level.

Most piglets in a single litter

An artificial insemination field project by scientists at the National Research Centre on Pig in Guwahati, Assam, achieved the largest litter size of 19 piglets in a single delivery in 2012.

Horse galloping in a farm in Gujarat

First cross-bred cow

The first cross-bred cow breed in India, called Taylor, was named after an Englishman, William Taylor, who was the one to initiate cattle cross-breeding in Patna, Bihar, in the mid-19th century.

WR First test-tube yak calf

The first test-tube yak calf in the world, a male weighing 19 kg, was born at the Nyukmadung farm of the National Research Centre on Yak (NRCY), Dirang Dzong, West Kameng District, Arunachal Pradesh, on 15 July 2013. The yak calf was named Norgayal.

WR First buffalo-milk powder

The Kaira District Cooperative Milk Producers Union (Amul Dairy), Anand, Gujarat, produced whole and skimmed milk powder from buffalo milk in 1955. They were also the first in the world to commercially produce cheese and baby food from buffalo milk in 1960.

WR Largest population of livestock

India had the largest population of livestock, with an estimated 536.76 million heads of cattle by 2019, making up as much as 31 per cent of the world's livestock population.

WR Top milk-producing country

India has led the world in milk production since 1997. Milk production in the country increased to 209.96 million tonnes during 2021. India contributes 21 per cent of the global milk production. The top milk-producing states are Uttar Pradesh, Rajasthan and Madhya Pradesh.

Heaviest goat

Asif Ali from Bhopal, Madhya Pradesh, reared the heaviest goat named King on his R.K. Goat Farm. King weighed 171 kg on 25 July 2019.

Heaviest and highest-priced bull

In March 2018, Haryana's first Murrah Ratan Award was won by a buffalo called Shahenshah, which weighed between 1,100 and 1,200 kg and was owned by Narender Singh from Didwari Village, Panipat, Haryana.

State with the most veterinary institutions

Rajasthan leads Indian states and UTs with 7,897 veterinary institutions (31 March 2018).

First and largest cattle farm

The District Livestock Farm in Hosur in Krishnagiri District, Tamil Nadu, is India's and Asia's largest cattle farm. It is spread over 664 hecatres (1,641 acres).

Largest dairy development programme

Project Operation Flood, launched in 1970 by the National Dairy Development Board (NDDB) and led by Dr Verghese Kurien, general manager and later chairman, AMUL and chairman, NDDB and the Institute of Rural Management Anand (IRMA), Gujarat. It involved forming a National Milk Grid that connected milk producers to consumers in over 700 towns and cities in India.

Oldest cow

Ruby, a cow owned by Dr Dipa Panjuani of Pune, Maharashtra, crossed 35 years in 2017. It was milking till six months before it turned 32 years old.

POULTRY AND FISHERIES

First broiler chicken variety

B-77, the first broiler variety of chicken, was released by the IVRI in Izatnagar in Bareilly District, Uttar Pradesh, in 1977.

First deep-sea fishing station

The Deep-Sea Fishing Station, Bombay (now Mumbai), Maharashtra, was set up in October 1946. It was renamed the Exploratory Fisheries Project (EFP) in 1974 when it systematically surveyed the coastal and offshore waters up to a depth of 70 m (230 ft). Engaged in oceanic surveys of Exclusive Economic Zones, it was renamed the Fishery Survey of India in 1979.

First and only licensed fisherwoman

In 2017, K.C. Rekha from Thrissur, Kerala, became India's only licensed deep-sea fisherwoman. Rekha accompanies her husband Karthikeyan to work every day.

First research institute for freshwater aquaculture

The Central Institute of Freshwater Aquaculture, Bhubaneswar, Odisha, began in the Pond Culture Division of the Central Inland Fisheries Research Institute, at Cuttack, Odisha, in 1949. The division was later upgraded as the Freshwater Aquaculture Research and Training Centre in 1976. It became an independent institute on 1 April 1987.

In the year 2021–22, Andhra Pradesh had the highest production of fish in the country. It produced 48.13 lakh tonnes of fish followed by West Bengal at 18.43 lakh tonnes.

First transgenic rohu fish

During 2004–05, a team of scientists led by Dr T.J. Pandian at the Madurai Kamaraj University, Madurai, Tamil Nadu, developed a genetically modified rohu fish that could grow 6–7 times faster than a normal one.

First transgenic rohu fish

Oldest fisheries research institutes

The oldest fisheries research institutes are the Central Marine Fisheries Research Institute (CMFRI), established in 1947, and the Central Inland Capture Fisheries Research Institute (CICFRI), also set up in 1947 under the name of Central Inland Fisheries Research Institute (CIFRI) in Calcutta (now Kolkata), West Bengal.

Largest poultry company

Suguna Foods Pvt. Ltd, which achieved a sales turnover of over ₹8,700 crore (87 billion) during 2019–20, is the largest broiler chicken company in India. Based in Coimbatore, Tamil Nadu, it ranks among the top 10 poultry enterprises worldwide and operates in 18 states in India, covering over 40,000 farmers in over 15,000 villages. Its products and services include hatcheries, feed mills, processing plants, valuc-added eggs, and broiler and frozen chicken.

First marine aquarium for ornamental fish

An aquarium for ornamental fish breeding and multiplication was established in 1998 in Vizhinjam near Kovalam in Kerala.

Biggest hen egg

A hen at the Dev Research and Breeding Farms of Sukhbir Singh of Ramrai Khera in Jind, Haryana, laid an egg weighing 167 g on 28 September 2014. It was 8.35 cm (3.3 in.) long and 5 cm (2 in.) wide.

Top shrimp-producing state/UT

Andhra Pradesh led with 634,672 million tonnes, followed by West Bengal with 35,392 million tonnes, in 2020–21.

FERTILIZERS, PESTICIDES, AND MACHINERY

Earliest soil treatment experiments

The earliest methods to find out the effects of inorganic fertilizers on the soil – its physical, chemical, and biological properties vis-à-vis crop yields – were started at the Agricultural College and Research Institute, Coimbatore, Tamil Nadu, in 1909.

First institute for farm machinery training and testing

The Central Farm Machinery Training and Testing Institute (FMTTI), established in 1959 in Budni, Sehore District, Madhya Pradesh, was the first of the four FMTTI centres in India. Since its inception and up to March 2020, the centre has trained a total of 69,056 trainees from across India.

First fertilizer factory

The first SSP (single superphosphate) factory that produced fertilizer mixtures, insecticides and fungicides was set up in 1906 in Ranipet District in Tamil Nadu by East India Distilleries Parry Ltd.

In 2022–23, Uttar Pradesh had the highest sales of tractors. The state sold 99,969 tractors that year.

First pesticide

Benzene hexachloride (BHC) was first commercialized by the Imperial Chemical Industries Ltd (ICI) in 1952 at Rishra in Hooghly District, West Bengal. A factory was set up in Calcutta (now Kolkata), West Bengal.

State/UT with the highest use of chemical pesticides and biopesticides

Maharashtra was the highest consumer of chemical pesticides (13,175 million tonnes) and biopesticides (934.44 million tonnes) in 2020–21.

First neem-based biocide

The first neem-based biocide was tested and commissioned by the National Tree Growers Cooperative Federation during 1997–98.

First use of lift irrigation

In 1926, an experimental lift irrigation system on 1,012 hectares (2,500 acres) of wasteland was started in the Rachna Doab region of Gangapur Village in Punjab (now in Pakistan) by Sir Ganga Ram, a member of the Regional Commission on Agriculture.

State/UT with the highest use of fertilizers per hectare

With a total consumption of 312.04 kg/hectare in 2021, Puducherry is the largest consumer of fertilizers (N, P & K).

Earliest use of tractors

Sardar Sir Jogendra Singh (1877–1946) experimented with steam tractors for wasteland reclamation in 1914 at Aira estate in Lakhimpur, Uttar Pradesh, and at Iqbal Nagar (now in Pakistan) in Punjab.

First pearl culture

The first cultured pearls, using the Akoya pearl oyster, were produced in 1973 at the Tuticorin Research Centre at the

Central Marine Fisheries Research Institute (CMFRI) building

Central Marine Fisheries Research Institute (CMFRI) in Thoothukudi, Tamil Nadu, in collaboration with the Tamil Nadu State Fisheries Department.

First semi-autonomous tractor

In April 2018, Mahindra and Mahindra Ltd rolled out a high-tech tractor, the Pack 1. This is an 'intelligent' tractor with a driver-assist system.

WR Largest seller of tractors

Mahindra and Mahindra Ltd is the largest-selling tractor brand in India, with total sales of 337,052 units in the financial year ended March 2022. It exported 17,646 units in the same period.

First synthetic pesticide

DDT (Dichlorodiphenyltrichloroethane) was introduced in 1946 for vector control and used in 1948. Its use was banned in May 1989.

Farmer spraying pesticide in the field

First agri-plane

Hindustan Aeronautics Ltd's HA-31 Basant monoplane was built in 1972 for agricultural needs. Its use was discontinued in 1980.

State/UT with most tractor exports

Maharashtra with exports worth US $186 million was the state with the most tractor exports in the year 2019–20. According to the Directorate General of Commercial Intelligence and Statistics data, Punjab exported tractors worth US $178 million in 2019–20 while Tamil Nadu exported tractors worth US $156 million.

First biocontrol agents

The ladybird beetle of Australia was introduced in 1898 to control mealy bugs on fruit crops.

Most sold farm equipment with largest market share

Tractors have the biggest share of the farm machinery market in India, at 80 per cent. In 2020–21, overall tractor sales in the country were 842,266 units.

Mahindra – the largest seller of tractors

EDUCATION

LITERACY

First state/UT to achieve 100 per cent literacy

On 18 April 1991, also the 81st birthday of Dr Malcolm S. Adiseshiah, the doyen of adult education in India, Kerala was declared 100 per cent literate.

First 100 per cent literate district

In 1990, Ernakulam, Kerala, with a population of three million then, became the first completely literate district in the country, with a literacy rate of 98.34 per cent in the age group of 5–60 years.

First national education council

The All India Council for Secondary Education (AICSE) was set up in 1955.

First minister of education

Independent India's first minister of education was Maulana Abul Kalam Azad (1888–1958) during 1947–58. Besides establishing the first Indian Institute of Technology (IIT), the Indian Institute of Science (IISc), the School of Planning and Architecture (SPA) and the University Grants Commission (UGC), he set up key cultural and literary organizations like the Sangeet Natak Akademi, the Lalit Kala Akademi, the Sahitya Akademi, and the Indian Council for Cultural Relations.

A stamp commemorating Maulana Abul Kalam Azad

State/UT with the highest literacy rate

Kerala, with 96.2 per cent, has the highest rate of literacy among all states, according to the 75th round of the National Sample Survey (NSS) conducted from July 2017 to June 2018.

State/UT with the lowest literacy rate

Andhra Pradesh, with 66.4 per cent, has the lowest rate of literacy among all states, according to the 75th round of the National Sample Survey.

State/UT with highest and lowest female literacy rate

The female literacy rate in Kerala was 95.2 per cent while Rajasthan recorded 57.6 per cent, according to the 75th round of the National Sample Survey.

State/UT with the highest percentage of graduates

Out of a total of around 68 million graduates in the country, Chandigarh, with 24.65 per cent, has the highest percentage of its population as graduates, according to the 2011 Census of India.

State/UT with the lowest percentage of graduates

Assam has the lowest percentage of graduate population, with only 4.83 per cent as per Census 2011.

SCHOOLS

Earliest schools for girls

St. Thomas School for Girls, which was founded in 1789 for the English-speaking community of Calcutta, Bengal (now Kolkata, West Bengal), was the first girls-only school in India.

Oldest extant school

St. George's Anglo-Indian Higher Secondary School, founded as the Military (later Madras) Male Orphan Asylum, was established in 1715 in Madras (now Chennai), Tamil Nadu.

First school for the hearing-impaired

Established in 1893, the Calcutta Deaf and Dumb School in Calcutta, West Bengal, was the first school for the hearing-impaired.

Oldest extant institute for the blind

The Institute for the Blind – Andh Vidyalaya – was established in Lahore (now in Pakistan) in 1939 and shifted to Delhi after Independence in 1947.

First Indian school abroad

The Indian High School, Dubai, set up in 1957, was the first Indian educational institution situated in a foreign country.

WR Largest open school

Set up as an autonomous institution under the Ministry of Human Resource Development in 1989, the National Institute of Open Schooling (NIOS) has a cumulative enrolment of 4.13 million students. It works through a network of 23 regional centres, two subregional centres, five departments, two NIOS cells, and over 7,400 study centres (accredited institutions and accredited vocational institutions). These centres are located in various parts of the world, viz., India, Nepal, and the Middle East.

Largest school science fair – single venue – single day

iScience World, a science club formed by science communicators in Prayagraj, Uttar Pradesh, in collaboration with Shri Mahaprabhu Public School, organized a science fair on 14 December 2019 at Delhi Public School, Prayagraj, in which 4,272 students from over 35 schools, participated.

The Gender Parity Index is 1 or over (in favour of girls) at all levels of education uptill 2021–22.

Largest school science fair – multiple venues – single day

More than 22,500 students from 637 upper primary schools of Bastar District, Chhattisgarh, conducted more than 35,000 scientific experiments at 116 centres on 18 January 2017. The Bastar Vigyan Mela, an annual event was organized by the Department of Education, Bastar District. The students demonstrated scientific activities and displayed innovative science models.

First solar-powered school

Sri Aurobindo International Centre for Education in White Town, Puducherry, became India's first fully solar-powered educational institute in 2014. It was set up in 1943 by Mirra Alfassa, the spiritual collaborator of Sri Aurobindo.

Largest chain of government schools

The Kendriya Vidyalaya Sangathan, an autonomous body under the Ministry of Human Resource Development, Government of India, since 15 December 1963, administers 1,252 schools, including three abroad, with 1,428,619 students, as of February 2023.

HIGHER EDUCATION

First steps

The first educational policy in colonial India was articulated in a document called the 'Dispatch of 1854 on "General Education in India"' sent by Sir Charles Wood to the then Governor General Lord Dalhousie. Sir Charles stressed the adoption of vernacular languages in local primary schools, Anglo-vernacular language in high schools and English-medium education in colleges.

First modern university

William Carey, a British Christian missionary, opened the first missionary college at Serampore, Bengal (now Srirampur, Hooghly District, West Bengal), in 1818. It was granted the status of a university in 1829.

Serampore College, West Bengal

First Sanskrit university

The Sampurnanand Sanskrit Vishwavidyalaya in Varanasi, Uttar Pradesh, was the first Sanskrit university in India and is said to have been established in 1791 as a Sanskrit college during the East India Company rule. It has 628 affiliated colleges across India.

First modern college

The first college to offer modern education in India was the Hindu College of Calcutta, Bengal, established in 1817. Scottish watchmaker and philanthropist David Hare was its first principal. It was renamed Presidency College in 1855. It became Presidency University on 7 July 2010.

First university act

The Indian Universities Act, 1904, was the first set of educational reforms, which stipulated that universities should offer more teaching and research opportunities and exert more control over affiliated colleges.

Longest functioning ancient university

Nalanda Mahavihara, located about 95 km south-east of present-day Patna in Bihar, functioned uninterrupted as a university from the Buddha's time in the sixth century BCE up to the 13th century CE, when it was destroyed by Muhammad bin Bakhtiyar Khilji. The university's curriculum then included many subjects such as logic, medicine, metaphysics, grammar, and the sciences. In an effort to emulate the ancient centre of learning, Nalanda University, an exclusively postgraduate and doctoral institution, was started in 2014 in Rajgir, Bihar.

First intermediate colleges

The University of Punjab (now in Chandigarh) and the University of Allahabad (now in Prayagraj, Uttar Pradesh) were the first to establish intermediate colleges in 1917, offering two-year courses between high school and degree college, as proposed by the Sadler Commission.

First five universities

The University of Calcutta, the University of Madras, and the University of Bombay (now renamed as the University of Mumbai), which were modelled on London University, were established in 1857 as non-teaching examining bodies. The University of Punjab in Lahore, Pakistan), was set up in 1881, and the University of Allahabad in 1887.

First Medical School

Established on 24 January 1857, the University of Calcutta was the first multidisciplinary and Western-style educational institution in Asia. It was also the first university in Asia to teach European classics, English literature, Indian philosophy and Occidental and Oriental history. At the time of establishment, it had a catchment area ranging from Lahore to Burma (now Myanmar) and Ceylon (now Sri Lanka).

The first medical school, the Calcutta Medical College, was affiliated to the

Bankim Chandra Chattopadhyay

Born in the Bengal Presidency (present-day West Bengal), Bankim Chandra Chattopadhyay (1838–94) was a government official and a prolific writer. He is best known for his novel *Anandamath* and for the composition of the national song, *Vande Mataram.* He had a significant role in the growth of Indian literature and specifically Bengali literature. He worked in many government administrative positions under the British rule and also served as editor to several newspapers, periodicals, and magazines. The influence of his work can be seen in the Indian independence struggle to a large extent. His notable works include, *Durgeshnandini*, *Kapalakundla,* and *Devi Chaudhurani* among others.

Enrolment Stats at a Glance

STATE-WISE TOTAL ENROLMENT

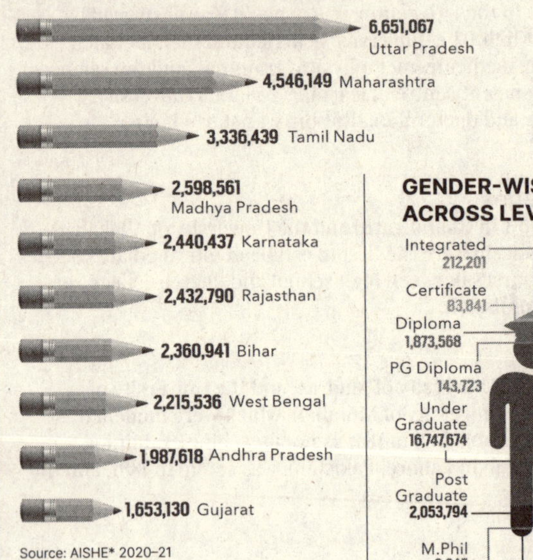

Source: AISHE* 2020–21

GENDER-WISE DISTRIBUTION ACROSS LEVELS

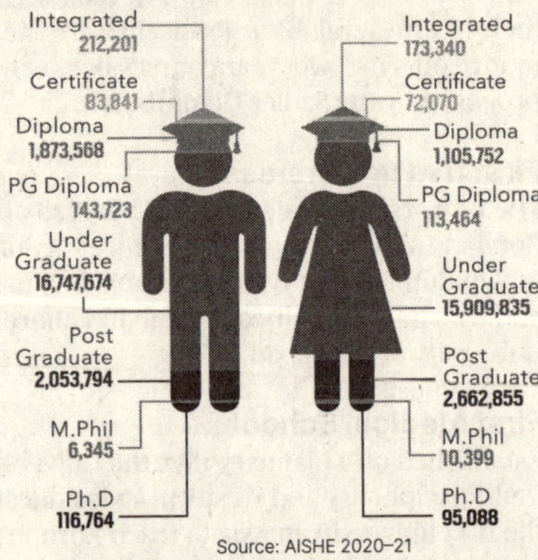

Source: AISHE 2020–21

ENROLMENT STATISTICS IN PRIVATE AND GOVERNMENT UNIVERSITY

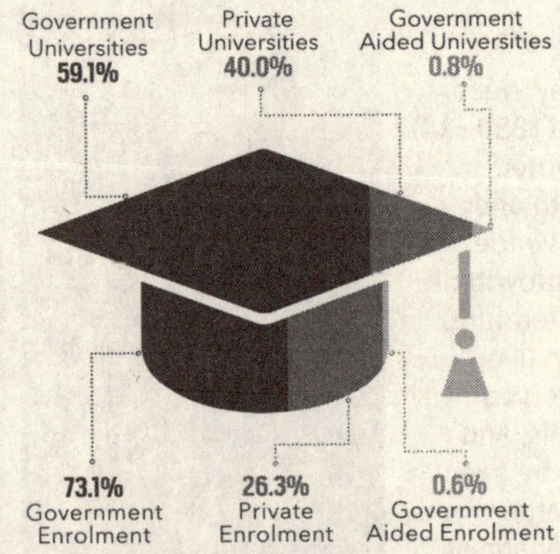

Source: AISHE 2020–21

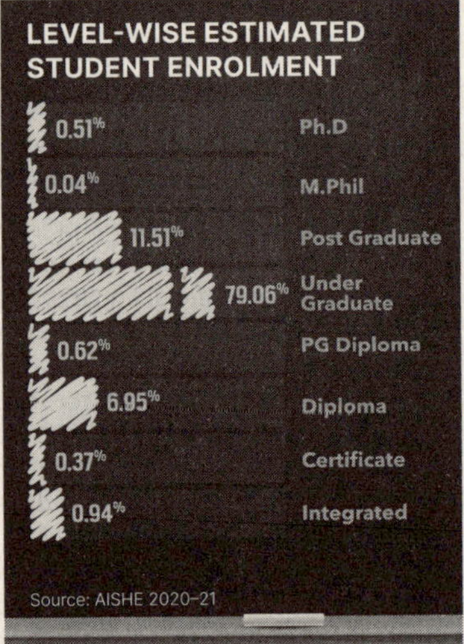

*AISHE - All India Survey on Higher Education

university in 1857. Five Nobel laureates (the highest number in South Asia) are associated with the university. They are Sir Ronald Ross, Rabindranath Tagore, Sir C.V. Raman, Amartya Sen, and Abhijit Vinayak Banerjee.

Bankim Chandra Chattopadhyay and Jadunath Bose were the first graduates of the university in 1858. Kadambini Ganguly and Chandramukhi Basu were the first female graduates in 1882.

First rural university

Mahatma Gandhi Chitrakoot Gramoday University, established in 1991 in Chitrakoot, Madhya Pradesh, to promote rural education, was the first rural university in the country.

First Pharmacy Education Course

A chemists and druggists course was initiated in Madras Medical College in 1874. It gained popularity and in 1898, a separate department of chemists and druggists was established at the college. The College of Pharmacy at Madras Medical College is the first institution in India to provide pharmacy education and training by offering a one-year certificate course called the 'Chemist and Druggist Course' training personnel for drug dispensing. However, formal pharmacy education in India was started in 1932 at the Banaras Hindu University (BHU) by Mahadeva Lal Schroff with the support of the vice chancellor of the university, Pandit Madan Mohan Malaviya. Initially, the course was known as B. Pharm (Bachelor of Pharmacy) and in April 1940 the first M. Pharm course was started at BHU.

First medical school to offer degrees in Oncology

The Cancer Institute (WIA–Women's' Indian Association), also known as the Adyar Cancer Institute, is a renowned non-profit treatment and research centre located in Chennai, Tamil Nadu. It was established in 1954 under the leadership of Muthulakshmi Reddy, with the motto 'Service to All.' The institute has played a vital role in cancer research and oncology in India. It is the first medical school to offer degrees in various sub-specialities of Oncology like radiotherapy, medical oncology, surgical oncology, etc. The Cancer Institute (WIA) is affiliated with both the University of Madras and Anna University, where it offers research programmes leading to MPhil and PhD degrees in areas of medical physics, psycho-oncology, and molecular oncology. It has also established the first department of nuclear medical oncology in the country and the first ever medical Physics Department.

Oldest dentist college in South-east Asia

In 1920, the legendary visionary Dr Rafiuddin Ahmed (1890–1965) set up the first Dental College in Calcutta, and since 1949 it is affiliated to Calcutta University, the same year that Dr Ahmed donated his college to the West Bengal government. Dr Ahmed served as principal of the college from 1920 to 1950. He established the Bengal Dental Association which became the forerunner for the Indian Dental Association. He also started the *Indian Dental Journal* in 1925 and was its editor till 1946. Dr Ahmed helped draft the Bengal Dentists Act in 1939, the first governmental dental regulation in India. It became the model for the Indian Dental Act passed in 1948.

First institute to teach modern architecture

The first course in architecture can be traced to the founding of a draftsman's class at the Sir J.J. School of Art (established in 1856), Bombay (now Mumbai), Maharashtra, in 1896. In 1913, the course was reorganized, and an independent Department of Architecture was formed.

A stamp commemorating the Sir J.J. School of Art

First virtual medical university

The first virtual medical university, Medvarsity, established in 2000, is an initiative of the Apollo Hospitals Group.

First energy studies university

The University of Petroleum and Energy Studies in Dehradun, Uttarakhand, established in 2003, is India's first university specializing in petroleum, energy, and power.

Main entrance to the Banaras Hindu University, Varanasi

First five residential universities

In 1915, the Banaras Hindu University (BHU) was established as a teaching and residential university, followed by the Universities of Mysore (1916), Patna (1917), and Osmania (1918), and the Aligarh Muslim University (1920).

First science college

The Government Science College, Jabalpur, Madhya Pradesh, was the first Indian science college and was affiliated to the Calcutta University from 1836 to 1890.

First college of nursing

The Christian Medical College (CMC) and Hospital, Vellore, is a private educational institute with a network of hospitals in and around Vellore, Tamil Nadu. It was started in 1902 by Dr Ida Scudder, a third-generation American missionary. In 1903, she began training women compounders and started the first school of nursing at CMC in 1909.

Only school of Tropical Medicine

The School of Tropical Medicine, Kolkata, also known as Calcutta School of Tropical Medicine (CSTM) was established in 1914 by Leonard Rogers. It is the only institution in the country dedicated exclusively in research, post graduate education and healthcare for tropical diseases. The institute is presently under the governance of West Bengal University of Health Sciences. The institute focuses on advanced research on HIV/HBV Co-infection and Hepatitis B anti-viral therapy.

First railway university

The National Rail and Transport University was established on 5 September 2018 at the Pratap Vilas Palace in Vadodara, Gujarat. It has now been subsumed by the Gati Shakti Vishwavidyalaya, announced as a central university in July 2022. It provides education and training in the latest technological applications related to the railways, such as radio frequency identification, artificial intelligence, and satellite-based tracking. It offers graduate degrees in subjects such as transportation management, transportation technology, rail infrastructural engineering, and electronics and communication engineering.

First women's university

The Shreemati Nathibai Damodar Thackersey (SNDT) Women's University was established in Pune, Maharashtra, by D.K. Karve (its first principal) on 5 July 1916. Dr R.P. Paranjpye was its first vice chancellor.

First college for women

The Bethune School of Calcutta, Bengal, set up in 1849, was reorganized after it merged with Banga Mahila Vidyalaya. In 1879, Bethune College classes started with one student, Kadambini Bose.

First technical university

The Thomason College of Engineering, established in 1847 at Roorkee (now in Uttarakhand), was India's first technical university. Its civil engineering department is the oldest one. It is now the Indian Institute of Technology (IIT), Roorkee.

First college alumni association

Dr William Miller, principal of Madras Christian College, Madras, Tamil Nadu, formed the first alumni association in 1891.

First technical university for women

The Indira Gandhi Delhi Technical University for Women (IGDTUW), New Delhi, was founded in 1998.

First IIT

The first Indian Institute of Technology (IIT) was established in 1951 at Kharagpur, West Bengal, at the site of the Hijli Detention Camp. There are 23 approved IITs in India currently.

First metro technology institute

The Institute of Metro and Rail Technology (IMRT) opened in October 2013 in Hyderabad, Telangana. It offers short- and long-term courses to design, build, and manage modern rail systems.

First institute for population sciences

The Institute for Population Sciences in Mumbai, Maharashtra, earlier known as the Demographic Training and Research Centre, was established in 1956 to prepare students for administrative, teaching, research, and consultancy careers in population sciences.

In 2020–21, out of total higher education enrolment, **22.89** per cent students were enrolled in STEM courses.

First school of mines

The Indian School of Mines – now renamed the Indian Institute of Technology – in Dhanbad, Jharkhand, opened in 1926.

First institute of oceanography

The National Institute of Oceanography, which was founded on 1 January 1966, is an autonomous research organization that undertakes scientific research and studies of special oceanographic features of the northern Indian Ocean. The institute has its main campus in Dona Paula, Goa, and regional centres have been set up in Mumbai, Kochi, and Visakhapatnam.

First university of fisheries and ocean studies

The College of Fisheries in Panangad, Cochin (now Kochi), Kerala, established in 1979, was a constituent college of the Kerala Agricultural University. The Kerala University of Fisheries and Ocean Studies (KUFOS) was established in 2010 with its headquarters at the College of Fisheries.

First statistical institute

The Indian Statistical Institute (ISI) was established in 1931 in Calcutta, Bengal, by scientist and statistician P.C. Mahalanobis.

First university for the study of outer space

The Indian Institute of Space Science and Technology (IIST) in Thiruvananthapuram, Kerala, is the first university in Asia to be solely dedicated to the study and research of outer space. It was set up by the Indian Space Research Organization (ISRO) under the Department of Space, Government of India, in 2007. The institute offers undergraduate, postgraduate, and doctorate programmes with a focus on space science, space technology, geoinformatics, earth system sciences, and their applications.

First gemmological institute

The Gemmological Institute of India (GII), a non-profit public institution founded by the Gem and Jewellery Exporters Association, was established in Bombay in 1971 to promote the scientific knowledge of gemmology.

First institute of mass communication

The first institute to provide a formal education in mass communication was the Indian Institute of Mass Communication (IIMC). Set up by the Government of India in 1965, it is now located in the Jawaharlal Nehru University (JNU) campus in New Delhi. It is an autonomous institution under the Ministry of Information and Broadcasting, and offers courses related to different media.

First institute of fashion technology

The Ministry of Textiles, Government of India, set up the National Institute of Fashion Technology (NIFT) in Delhi on 24 August 1987 to provide professional human resources for the textile industry. There are currently 18 NIFT campuses in the country.

First home science college

Lady Irwin College, established in 1932 in New Delhi, was the country's first home science college.

First institute for studying footwear design

The Footwear Design and Development Institute (FDDI), set up in 1986 at Noida, Uttar Pradesh, trains students in footwear technology, computer-aided designing, and pattern making.

First law university

The National Law School of India University (NLSIU) in Bangalore was established on 29 August 1987. Currently, there are 23 such national law universities in India.

First national institute of management

The Indian Institute of Management Calcutta was established for the pursuit of postgraduate studies in management on 17 November 1961 by the Government of India, in collaboration with the Sloan School of Management, Massachusetts Institute of Technology (MIT), US, the Government of West Bengal, the Ford Foundation, and several Indian industries.

First model-training school

Catwalk, set up in Bombay, Maharashtra, in 1990, by leading model Lubna Adams, was the first training school in India for fashion models.

First military school

The Prince of Wales Royal Indian Military College in Dehradun, Uttarakhand, now called the Rashtriya Indian Military College (RIMC), was inaugurated on 13 March 1922 by Prince Edward VIII, the Prince of Wales, to provide training to Indian boys to become officers in the armed forces. In a landmark move in 2021,

Rashtriya Indian Military College, Dehradun

women were allowed admission to the institute.

Number of colleges per lakh eligible population in the country is **31**.

First college of physical education

The YMCA College of Physical Education in Madras, Tamil Nadu, established in 1920 by Harry Crowe Buck of Pennsylvania, US, was Asia's first college for physical education. It is now affiliated to the Tamil Nadu Physical Education and Sports University, and is considered a pioneer in the promotion of sports for persons with disabilities.

First college for the hearing-challenged

The St. Louis Institute for the Deaf and Blind in Madras, Tamil Nadu, which opened on 8 September 1993, was the first college for the hearing-impaired in the country. It is affiliated to the University of Madras and offers graduate degrees.

First radio jockey training academy

The Academy of Broadcasting in Chandigarh, set up in July 2003, was the first academy for training radio jockeys.

First yoga institute

The Bihar School of Yoga, later the Bihar Yoga Bharati in Munger, Bihar, an institute for advanced studies in yoga, set up in 1964, was the first of its kind in Asia.

First defence academy

The National Defence Academy at Khadakwasla, Maharashtra, was opened on 16 January 1955, to give its students a military orientation to join any of the three services of the Indian armed forces.

First university for the disabled

The Jagadguru Rambhadracharya Handicapped University (now renamed as the Jagadguru Rambhadracharya Divyang State University) in Chitrakoot, Uttar Pradesh, was established as a private university on 27 September 2001 to provide higher and professional education only to persons with disabilities in four categories – the visually impaired, the hearing-impaired, the mobility-impaired, and the mentally impaired, as defined in the Persons with Disability Act, 1995.

First correspondence courses

The University of Delhi introduced non-formal education in 1962 with its first correspondence course.

First national institute for the visually impaired

The National Institute for the Visually Impaired was established in Dehradun, Uttarakhand, in 1979.

First college for sanitation workers

The Harpic World Toilet College, located in Aurangabad (now Chhatrapati

VETS FOR PETS

1 First college of veterinary science

The first college of veterinary science was established at Lahore in 1882. Before this, lectures on veterinary science were given to civilians at the Agricultural College at Saidapet, Madras, Tamil Nadu, and at the College of Sciences in Poona, Maharashtra.

2 First veterinary research institute

Established in 1889, the Indian Veterinary Research Institute (IVRI) at Izatnagar in Bareilly District, Uttar Pradesh, is India's premier advanced research facility in the field of veterinary medicine and allied branches. IVRI is currently under the Indian Council of Agricultural Research, New Delhi, and has six regional campuses for graduate, postgraduate, and diploma courses.

3 The first college to offer bachelor's degree in veterinary medicine

The Madras Veterinary College (MVC) in Madras was established on 1 October 1903 as a veterinary college. It later grew into and is affiliated with Tamil Nadu Veterinary and Animal Sciences University (TANUVAS). In 1936 it became the first college in the country to offer the Bachelor's degree in veterinary medicine. The MVC teaching hospital is the largest animal hospital in the country and is equipped with extensive facilities like radiology, ultrasound, CT scan, etc. There is a haemodialysis facility for small animals. Additionally, there is a special rabies ward.

4 First veterinary university

The Tamil Nadu Veterinary and Animal Sciences University (TANUVAS), which opened in 1989 in Madhavaram Milk Colony, Madras, was the first veterinary and animal sciences university in Asia.

Sambhajinagar), in Maharashtra, was established in August 2018. It is the first of its kind in the country and has trained more than 3,200 sanitation workers. It trains workers in the required skills and also makes them aware of the occupational hazards related to the job. It is run by British consumer goods company Reckitt Benckiser.

First university only for tribal students

The Kalinga Institute of Social Sciences, founded by Achyuta Samanta in Bhubaneswar, Odisha, became India's first exclusively 'tribal' university when it was granted university status by the Ministry of Human Resources in 2017. It admits students only from indigenous communities and is the only known university in the world to do so.

First National Institute of Watersports (NIWS)

The National Institute of Watersports (NIWS) was established in 1990 at Caranzalem, near Dona Paula Circle, Panaji, Goa, under the Ministry of Tourism. It is the first Institute of its kind in South-East Asia. NIWS serves as a centre for training, education, consultancy, and research for various water sports disciplines, including life-saving, power boat handling, sailing, windsurfing, scuba-diving, river rafting, and kayaking. The institute offers 20 courses designed for water sports professionals and tourists visiting Goa. Certification and licensing from NIWS are mandatory for operators handling different watercraft for tourists, swimming pools, water theme parks, etc.

First master's programme in Hindu studies

Two central universities, Banaras Hindu University (BHU) and Shri Lal Bahadur Shastri National Sanskrit University, have jointly launched a master's course in Hindu studies in 2022. The curriculum, developed by BHU, aims to provide a comprehensive understanding of the foundational principles underlying Hindu civilization, society, and culture, despite the endless variety. The course is interdisciplinary and covers various subjects, including Hindu philosophy, Mimamsa, the antiquity of Hinduism, and the meaning of the word Hindu. The programme is aligned with the recently introduced National Education Policy (NEP).

Oldest course in pharmacy

The Portuguese introduced the first pharmacy course with a medical course in 1842 at an old Portuguese school, the 'Escola Medica de Goa'. It was renamed the Goa College of Pharmacy in 1963 and moved to its current premises, a former Portuguese school in Panaji. The college is now affiliated to Goa University and is run by the Government of Goa.

Oldest school of art

Sir J.J. School of Art in Bombay, Maharashtra, was founded by Sir Jamsetjee Jeejeebhoy in 1833.

First postgraduate degree

Calcutta University in Kolkata, West Bengal, conferred the first postgraduate degree (MA) in India in 1862.

First Indian to receive a PhD from a foreign university

Agostino Lourenco of Margao, Goa, is considered to have received his PhD in chemistry in Paris, France, in 1860.

First to obtain a PhD in library science

In 1957, the University of Delhi awarded the first PhD in library science to D.B. Krishna Rao for his study on 'Facet analysis and depth of agriculture classification' under Dr S.R. Ranganathan and Dr S. Dasgupta.

First woman Bachelor of Medicine

Anandibai Joshi was the first Indian woman to obtain a Bachelor of Medicine degree in 1886 from the University of Philadelphia in the US, but she did not practise medicine.

First women graduates

Kadambini Ganguly née Bose and Chandramukhi Basu passed the BA examination from Calcutta University in 1883.

25,550
students received PhDs during 2020.

First woman doctor

Kadambini Ganguly née Bose obtained the Graduate degree from Calcutta Medical College to become the first woman doctor in 1888. She was the first woman to receive the degree from India and the first to practise medicine in the country.

First woman to receive a PhD in a scientific discipline

Kamala Sohonie (1912–98), a biochemist, received her PhD at the Indian Institute of Science (IISc) Bangalore, Karnataka, in 1939, for her work on vitamins and the nutritive values of pulses, paddy, and groups of food items consumed by the poorer sections of society.

First Indian vice chancellor

In 1890, Gurudas Banerjee became the vice chancellor of Calcutta University, Bengal.

First woman vice chancellor

Hansa Jivraj Mehta (1897–1995) made history when she became the first vice chancellor of the Maharaja Sayajirao University of Baroda, Vadodara, Gujarat, in 1949.

First woman law graduate

Cornelia Sorabji (b. 1866) graduated in law from the University of Bombay (now University of Mumbai) in 1894.

First gender-neutral certificate

The National Academy of Legal Studies and Research (NALSAR), Hyderabad, Telangana, issued the first gender-neutral graduation certificate in June 2015.

First to pass the Indian Medical Service examination

Surjo Kumar Chakraborty (1826–74), MRCS (Member of the Royal College of Surgeons), was the first Indian to pass the Indian Medical Service (IMS) examination in 1855. He subsequently became the first Indian professor of Materia Medica at Calcutta Medical College.

First to obtain a doctorate

In 1904, Annoda Prasad Sircar became the first to obtain a doctorate when the University of Allahabad (established in 1887) awarded him a DSc.

First to score 100 per cent in NEET

Kota-based ALLEN Career Institute's student Soyeb Aftab scored 720/720 with All-India rank no.1 at the National Eligibility-cum-Entrance Test (NEET) 2020 (UG).

Most PhDs awarded by a University in a year

Delhi University awarded 910 PhD degrees (512 females and 398 males) at its 99th Convocation on 25 February 2023.

Postgraduate qualifications from most number of universities

Dr Anil Kumar Yadav (b. 4 June 1968) from Chandigarh holds 32 postgraduate qualifications (PhD, MPhil and PG degrees and diplomas) from 20 universities across 17 states and Union Territories. His record begins with MA (sociology)

University of Delhi

With its humble beginnings of three colleges, the University of Delhi (estd 1 May 1922) has now grown into a network of 16 faculties, 86 departments, and 91 colleges. Running over 500 programmes, the university is one of the premier and distinguished educational institutions within the country. The departments of chemistry, geology, zoology, sociology and history have even been awarded the status of being Centres of Advanced Studies. In 1973, to meet the growing needs of the ever-expanding city scape, the university opened the South Campus to facilitate students from that area. With cut-throat competition for admissions, the university was ranked 13 on the National Institute Ranking Framework (NIRF) rankings in 2022. The university celebrated its centenary in 2022 and its notable alumni include Sheila Dixit, Aung San Suu Kyi, Shahrukh Khan, Amitabh Bachchan, Vikram Seth, Khushwant Singh, Geeta Chandran, and many more.

from Annamalai University in May 1995 and his latest degree is MA (sociology) from the University of Mumbai, Maharashtra, in May 2022.

48,035 foreign students from **163** countries are enrolled in Indian educational institutions.

Most master's degrees obtained – woman

Vandana Agrawal (b. 12 November 1954) from Alwar, Rajasthan, has 10 MA degrees, the highest number of postgraduate degrees attained by a woman in India.

WR First chartered scientist in aviation

Dr Bishnujee Singh (b. 27 October 1972), the chief executive officer of Cayley Aerospace Inc., from Lynnwood, Washington, US, became the world's first chartered scientist in aviation, with the Science Council, UK, in association with the Royal Aeronautical Society, on 26 September 2006.

First woman director of Indian Statistical Institute (ISI)

Dr Sanghamitra Bandyopadhyay, a computer scientist specializing in computational biology currently serves as director of the Indian Statistical Institute (ISI). She oversees all the five centres of ISI located at Kolkata, Delhi, Bengaluru, Chennai, and Tezpur.

Youngest chancellor

Dileep K. Nair became the youngest chancellor of a university in the country when he took office at the North East Frontier Technical University (NEFTU) in Along (now Aalo), West Siang District, Arunachal Pradesh, in April 2017. He was 38 years old at the time.

WR Largest open university

The Indira Gandhi National Open University (IGNOU) at Maidan Garhi, New Delhi, has the distinction of being the largest open university in the world, serving more than three million enrolled students through its 21 schools of studies, and a network of 67 regional centres, around 2,000 learner support centres and 25 overseas partner institutions in 15 countries.

ARCHIVES AND LIBRARIES

First library

Christian missionaries at Serampore, Bengal set up their first library (later the William Carey Library) in 1800, which became the hub of their educational activities. The Reverend John Fountain, sent to India in 1796 to assist William Carey, a missionary, was its first librarian.

First operational digital library network

DELNET was the first operational digital library network. It was started as a project of the India International Centre, New Delhi, in 1988 and registered as a society in 1992.

Oldest library

The Calcutta Public Library (established in 1836) was merged with the Imperial Library (established in 1891) in 1903. In 1953, it was inaugurated as the National Library with B.S. Kesavan as its first librarian.

First online Braille library

Launched in 2012 by the National Institute for the Visually Handicapped (NIVH), Dehradun, Uttarakhand, to commemorate the birth anniversary of Louis Braille on 4 January, the online Braille library provides access to 12,000 books in 10 languages in a user-friendly format. More information about the library can be found at https://nivh.gov.in/?page_id=6424.

First university library

The first university library began functioning at the University of Calcutta in 1870.

First mobile library

A bullock cart (in the shape of a small stall), laden with books at Melavasal, a village near Mannargudi in Tamil Nadu, on 21 October 1931, was possibly the first mobile library in the country. The brainchild of Rao Bahadur S.V. Kanagasabai Pillai, a Mannargudi-based engineer, the library was inaugurated by S.R. Ranganathan, called the father of library science in India. The mobile library carried books that dealt with bee-keeping and other cottage industries, aimed at providing vocational training to farmers. The cart would visit neighbouring villages in the months when there was less farming activity. A replica of the cart is now displayed in Tamil University in Thanjavur, Tamil Nadu.

First sports library

The Kanga Library at Wankhede Stadium, Mumbai, Maharashtra, has a collection of 13,000 books on sports. Around 10,000 of these are on cricket, including the entire collection of *Wisden Cricketers' Almanack* from 1864.

Biggest public library system

The Delhi Public Library, started as a UNESCO project in 1951 by the Government of India, is the biggest public library system in India and reportedly the busiest set of public libraries in South Asia. The library

Delhi Public Library, New Delhi

network consists of a central library, one zonal library, three branch libraries, 18 sub-branch libraries, one community library, seven resettlement colony libraries, one Braille library, 104 mobile library service points and 30 book-reading centres in the Union Territory of Delhi and the NCR. It has a collection of over 1.8 million books in English and other Indian languages.

First national medical library

This library was initially conceived as a departmental library with a small collection of books for the use of officers of the erstwhile Directorate General of Indian Medical Services (DGIMS). In 1947, DGIMS was merged with the Office of the Public Health Commission and the Directorate General of Health Services (DGHS) and the library became DGHS Library. As the need for a central library grew to support academic, research and clinical work by medical and health science professionals in the country, the DGHS Library was developed and was renamed Central Medical Library. In 1966, this library, located in New Delhi, was declared as the National Medical Library.

Only underground library

Almost 128 km from Jaisalmer, Rajasthan, in Bhadariya Village in Jaisalmer District, is an underground library 16 ft (4.88 m) below ground level. Above this library is a temple of Devi Bhadariya Mata. The library can seat 4,000 persons and is maintained by the trustees of the temple. Housing around 900,000 books, the library was started by Harbansh Singh Nirmal, an avid reader, popularly known as Bhadariya Maharaj.

Largest university library

The Maulana Azad Library, the central library of Aligarh Muslim University in Aligarh, is the largest university library in Asia. The current seven-floor library houses about 1,400,000 books, periodicals, and pamphlets, 43,000 e-journals and manuscripts, and also paintings and photographs. It was inaugurated by Jawaharlal Nehru, the first prime minister of India, in 1960.

Only bookshop-cum-library on a lake

Gulshan Books, a bookshop-cum-library set up in May 2016, has a reading room, a café and over 80,000 books. Located on Nehru Park Island on the Dal Lake in Srinagar, Jammu and Kashmir, it can be reached by a shikara.

Largest library

- *By built-up area:* The Anna Centenary Library in Chennai, Tamil Nadu, is the largest in terms of constructed area – close to 330,000 sq. ft (3.07 hectares). It houses around 1 million books.
- *By number of books:* The National Library, Kolkata, with more than 2.6 million books and over 500,000 manuscripts, is the largest library by number of books. The campus of the library is spread over 30 acres (12.14 hectares). However, the actual built-up area is around 1.5 lakh sq. ft (1.39 hectares).

First boat library

The Young Readers' Boat Library was set up on a boat by the West Bengal Transport Corporation in collaboration with a heritage bookshop. It was launched on 26 January 2021, and houses a collection of over 500 titles in English and Bengali. The boat library conducts three-hour ferries on the Hoogly River, starting from Millennium Park to Belur Math Jetty and back. It also offers free Wi-Fi facilities and various readership activities, and conducts three trips on all weekdays.

Largest film archives

The National Film Archives were set up in 1964 in Poona (now Pune), Maharashtra, as a media unit of the Ministry of Information and Broadcasting, Government of India. Besides over 100,000 films, it has 157,687 photographs, 23,748 film posters, 14,210 song booklets, over 100,000 press clippings and more.

MUSEUMS

Largest and oldest museum

The Indian Museum in Kolkata, West Bengal, one of the oldest museums in the world, founded by the Asiatic Society of Bengal in 1814 has rare collections of antiques, armour and ornaments, fossils, skeletons, mummies, and Mughal paintings.

First public museum in a university

Established in 1937, the Ashutosh Museum of Indian Art, located in the main campus of the University of Calcutta, West Bengal, is the first public museum in any university in India. It is named after Sir Ashutosh Mukherjee, the great educationist, who introduced the study of Indology – including Indian art and archaeology – at the university level, and was the vice chancellor of the university from 1906 to 1914 and 1921 to 1923. The museum houses more than 25,000 sculptures, paintings, folk-art objects, textiles, and terracotta items, among other artefacts from various phases of Indian art, with special emphasis on the art of Bengal.

First museum of textiles

The Calico Museum of Textiles in Ahmedabad, Gujarat, was set up by Gautam Sarabhai, chairman of Calico Mills, in 1949, at the suggestion of the pioneering art historian and philosopher Dr Ananda Coomaraswamy. The museum has a comprehensive collection of Indian textiles. The foundation of modern Indian textile studies was laid here and the catalogues of the Calico Museum textile collection are an indispensable reference.

First transport museum

Opened on 7 December 2013, the Heritage Transport Museum at Tauru, Nuh District, Haryana, has a rich collection of 2,500 objects, including howdahs, bullock carts, palanquins, a 1924 Ford, vintage scooters, a 1946 Piper aircraft, transport toys from the 1920s to now, and other related artefacts.

First national museum of Indian cinema

The country's first National Museum of Indian Cinema (NMIC) was inaugurated in Mumbai, Maharashtra, in January 2019. Conceived in 1997, it has been designed by the National Council of Science Museums and implemented by the Films Division, under the Ministry of Information and Broadcasting,

Government of India. It is placed in a period 19th century heritage bungalow called Gulshan Mahal, and extends to another new high-technology five-floor building with two mezzanine floors. On display are projectors, recording equipment, cameras, archival posters of old films, and biographies of actors and other film personalities.

First railway museum

Inaugurated by Kamlapati Tripathi, the then minister of railways, on 1 February 1977, the Rail Transport Museum at Chanakyapuri, New Delhi, was the first rail museum in India. it was renamed the National Rail Museum in 1995 and features historical exhibits and artefacts related to the history of rail transport in India.

WR First Partition museum

The Arts and Cultural Heritage Trust, set up on 24 October 2016 in Amritsar, Punjab, is the world's first museum on Partition of India. Housed in a restored portion of the Town Hall, it is dedicated to Partition of the subcontinent in 1947. The museum commemorates Partition's victims, its survivors and its legacy. On display are photographs, clothes, utensils, and other memorabilia of the time.

First kite museum

A museum dedicated to the rarest kites in the world is housed in Ahmedabad, Gujarat, a city popular for its annual International Kite Festival. Established in 1985, the museum was the brainchild of Bhanubhai Shah, who donated his rare collection of over 50 years to the Ahmedabad Municipal Corporation. The only kite museum in the country, it is located in the basement of Sanskar Kendra and boasts of kites of many shapes and sizes, with some that measure up to 6.7 m x 4.88 m (22 ft x 16 ft).

WR First museum of toilets

The Sulabh International Museum of Toilets at Mahavir Enclave in New Delhi, a museum dedicated to toilets, has 300 objects with a mix of originals, models, and photographs. The museum traces 4,500 years of the history of toilets.

First underground museum

India's first underground museum opened in the Rashtrapati Bhavan on 2 October 2016. The museum showcases a collection of artefacts associated with each of the past presidents of India, including their personal belongings and vehicles, with a range of materials highlighting the history of India's freedom struggle. The museum displays more than 2,000 artefacts in a sprawling 12,077.39 sq. m (130,000 sq. ft) space.

First Sports Museum – organization

The National Institute of Sports, also known as the Netaji Subhas National Institute of Sports (NSNIS) in Patiala, Punjab, houses within the campus a Sports Museum. Established in 1972, which showcases a remarkable collection of rare photographs, kits, and medals of renowned Indian sportsmen including the gold medal won by Dhyan Chand at the Amsterdam Olympics in 1928, the Adidas spikes worn by Milkha Singh during the Rome Olympics in 1960, P.T. Usha's shoes, and a donut-shaped exercise equipment used by Gama Pehalwan among others. There is a cricket bat on display signed by the Indian Cricket Team lead by Kapil Dev which won the World Cup in 1983. The museum also houses replicas of different national awards given for Sports like the Arjuna Award and the Dronacharya Award. A part of the museum displays numerous rare photographs and personal items contributed by the royal family of Patiala.

First sports museum – personal collection

Fanattic Sports Museum is located over 6,700 sq. ft (622.45 sq. m) at Ecospace in New Town, Rajarhat, around 25 km from central Kolkata. Opened in 2017, this multi-sports museum displays memorabilia from cricket, hockey, football, the Olympics, and Paralympics. It houses memorabilia collected by cricket historian Boria Majumdar for over 25 years. Highlights include Sachin Tendulkar's gloves, Lionel Messi's shoes, Didier Drogba's Chelsea jersey, and many artefacts donated by Olympic gold medallist Abhinav Bindra, Paralympics silver medallist Deepa Malik, and bronze medallist Devendra Jhajaria, among others.

First election museum

Inaugurated in 2016, the Election Museum, located in the office premises of the chief electoral officer at Kashmiri Gate, Delhi, depicts the election journey of the largest democracy in the world. The four sections – library, audio-visual, photo gallery, and electoral management – display more than 200 archived photographs, maps, artefacts, and references. Possibly the largest of its kind in the world, the museum showcases the electoral journey of India since the first general election in 1952.

First insect museum

An insect museum was unveiled by Tamil Nadu chief minister Edappadi K. Palaniswami, at the Tamil Nadu Agricultural University in Coimbatore, Tamil Nadu, in March 2018. Covering 621.61 sq. m (6,691 sq. ft), this museum displays insect specimens starting from the early 20th century. It has live butterflies in a natural setting, termite mounds, bee species, and insect-eating plants, along with images, videos and models of their behaviour and habitats.

First wax museum

Madame Tussauds Delhi, located in the vintage Regal Theatre in Rajiv Chowk, New Delhi, was part of the famed international chain of wax museums, the first of which opened in London in 1835. Set up in December 2017, the Delhi wax museum had on display over 40 life-size wax sculptures of political leaders and celebrities from sports and music, Bollywood, and Hollywood. The 23rd location for Tussauds museums, it was shifted to DLF Mall of India, Noida, Uttar Pradesh, in 2022.

First dinosaur museum

The Dinosaur Museum at the Balasinor Dinosaur Park in Raiyoli Village in Balanisor Taluka in Gujarat's Mahisagar District was inaugurated in June 2019. With an enhanced version of the Dinosaur Museum already existing there, the facility is equipped with modern technology like 3D projection, virtual-reality presentations, interactive kiosks and life-size dinosaur replicas. Its 10 galleries exhibit dinosaur remains and fossil records from the area as well as other regions of Gujarat and some other states of India, and show the history of these dinosaurs (such as the *Rajasaurus narmadensis*) from their origin to extinction.

Dinosaur Museum, Gujarat

First interactive museum of music

The Indian Music Experience (IME), established in 2018 in Bengaluru, Karnataka, is a rare museum that offers an interactive musical journey during which the visitor is encouraged to touch and feel the instruments on display to create one's own music. IME features a Sound Garden with 10 playable musical sculptures. It also has touchscreens, musical instruments, small theatres, and audio-video kiosks as well as a learning centre that offers music classes and workshops on a regular basis.

First science museum

The first science museum was set up by the industrialist Ghanshyam Das Birla at Birla Institute of Technology and Science (BITS), Pilani, Jhunjhunu District, Rajasthan, in 1954. Located in a hall 185 sq. m (1,991 sq. ft) of the Tower Building, it depicts the industries and business enterprises of the Birla family along with curricular scientific concepts and shows on current trends in science and technology. It is the only museum of industry and technology located inside a university campus.

First archaeological site museum

The first archaeological site museum was established adjacent to the excavated site of Sarnath, near Varanasi, in Uttar Pradesh. The Archaeological Museum Sarnath is the oldest site museum of the Archeological Survey of India and houses the findings and excavations from the Sarnath archaeological site. The idea of archaeological site museums was first proposed by Sir John Marshal, the then Director General of Archaeology in India, in 1905. Today there are 46 archaeological site museums spread over the length and breadth of the country displaying excavated antiquities in close proximity to their original site.

First culinary arts museum

Michelin-starred Indian chef Vikas Khanna opened India's first living culinary museum, the Museum of Culinary Arts, at his alma mater, the Welcomgroup Graduate School of Hotel Administration in Manipal, Karnataka, in April 2018. Over 2,000 utensils and artefacts from all over India and dating back centuries are housed in the museum, which is the shape of a giant pot (similar to Harappan ones). It is spread over 2,322 sq. m (25,000 sq. ft), as a part of the Department of Culinary Arts.

Largest chain of science museums

The National Council of Science Museums (NCSM), under the Ministry of Culture, Government of India, is the largest chain of science centres/museums under a single administrative umbrella in the world. There are 24 science centres or museums and an R&D laboratory and training centre of NCSM, located in different states in India.

First museum of utensils

Vechaar (Vishalla Environmental Centre for Heritage of Art, Architecture and Research), a museum that archives heritage utensils, including more than 5,400 pots, pans, serving vessels, nutcrackers, and other kitchen equipment, is housed in a village-like complex called Vishalla in Ahmedabad, Gujarat. The museum was set up in April 1981 by its collector and owner, Surendra C. Patel, and anthropologist Jyotindra Jain.

Largest terracotta museum – by collection

Formerly called the Allahabad Museum, it was established in 1931 by the Allahabad Municipal Board. The museum has the largest collection of terracoata artefacts in the country. Additionally, its rock art gallery showcases the largest collection of prehistoric paintings dating to 2000 BCE. The museum has achieved self-reliance in power generation by utilizing a solar power system, making it the first museum in the country to do so.

The Prime Ministers' Museum

The Pradhanmantri Sangrahalaya, located on the Teen Murti Estate in New Delhi, is a museum dedicated to celebrating all former prime ministers of India. It was inaugurated on 14 April 2022 by Prime Minister Narendra Modi marking 75 years of Independence. This museum consists of 43 galleries showcasing the lives and tenures of former prime ministers. It offers various interactive experiences like holograms, virtual reality, augmented reality, and more. The exhibits include personal items, gifts and memorabilia, and medals and commemorative stamps, provided by families of former prime ministers.

The Pradhanmantri Sangrahalaya, New Delhi

Only Leprosy Museum

The Acworth Leprosy Museum is located at Wadala Acworth Municipal General Hospital in Mumbai. The museum, inaugurated in 2003, showcases the early history of leprosy and honours the contributions by Mahatma Gandhi, Vinobha Bhave, and Ramachandra Vitthal Lad (also called Bhau Daji Lad) towards eradicating the disease and fighting against the discriminations and prejudices associated with leprosy. It is the only leprosy museum in the country and houses panels documenting the history of leprosy, therauptic experiments conducted by Mumbai doctors, social and legal histories related to leprosy, and the efforts of notable figures in the fight against leprosy.

Conflictorium Museum

The Conflictorium Museum in Ahmedabad, Gujarat, was inaugurated on 14 April 2013. It is housed in the Gool Lodge, a two-storey building, located between the Progressive West and the Historical East of the Sabarmati River. The museum was designed by Avni Sethi in collaboration with Janvikas, Centre for Social Justice and Nasarjan, aiming to document the violent and oppressive history of the state of Gujarat since its establishment in 1960. Originally owned by a Parsi lady, Bachuben Nagarwala, who was the first trained beautician and hairstylist of Ahmedabad, the building is now divided into several galleries each expressing people's voices and thoughts. The purpose of the Museum is to enable people to engage in various topics of conflict through artistic and creative ways in various forms of art and culture. It serves as a space for dialogue, reflection, and exploration of conflicts in society. Avni Sethi was declared the recipient of the Jane Lombard Prize for Art and Social Justice for 2020–22 by the Vera List Center for Arts and Politics.

QUIZZES

First live quiz on TV

Neil O'Brien, called the 'father of quizzing', brought the concept of quizzes to India in 1967, after watching them on TV in the UK in the 1960s. He moderated the Eddie Hyde Memorial Quiz Contest 1967 in the parish hall of the Church of Christ the King in Calcutta, West Bengal, before a 40-strong audience. The open live quiz had four teams with members from all walks of life.

First quiz show on radio

On 12 April 1972, the *Cadbury Bournvita Quiz Contest* for high-school students became the first English quiz show to be broadcast on radio (Vividh Bharati) in India. It became one of India's most famous quiz contests. It ran for over a decade and was later revived as a television quiz in June 1992. The original quizmaster on the radio show was Hamid Sayani, a prominent broadcast personality.

Longest-running open quiz

Instituted in 1992 in Chennai, Tamil Nadu, by the Landmark Bookstores, the annual Landmark Quiz is the longest-running open quiz in the country. A preliminary round of about 40 questions that come up on a screen is held due to the huge turnout. The quiz is hosted by Dr Navin Jayakumar and his team (which included his mother) since its inception, with the exception of 2006 when Derek O'Brien was the quizmaster.

Longest-running school quiz

The *Cadbury Bournvita Quiz Contest* was a weekly televised show that started in 1992 as the first televised school quiz in India. Anchored by reputed quizmaster Derek O'Brien, it ran continuously on Zee TV till 2001, after which it moved to the TV channel Sony, followed by Colors. Now it is conducted in a mobile application format.

First national TV quizmaster

Raman Kumar was the first quizmaster on national television. He hosted *Mashoor Mahal* during 1985–86 in the quiz genre, featuring famous personalities.

Longest-running televised quiz

Prashnottari, a twice-a-week (previously fortnightly) quiz, with participants from schools, colleges, and a general live TV audience, was first telecast on Prasar Bharati's Jaipur Doordarshan Kendra on 23 July 1993. Hosted by former IAS officer Dr Mahendra Surana since it began, it continued without break on the same channel, completing 900 episodes on 15 March 2020.

Longest-running state-level quiz

Initiated in 1986 by Vijaya Bank, Karnataka's oldest quiz competition, titled VGenUth Quiz Contest (now called the Baroda Champ Annual Quiz Contest), is open to all high-school students across Karnataka. Its 34th edition was held on 2 February 2020 in Bengaluru, in which more than 400 students from over 200 schools participated.

Most participants in an online quiz – single day

An e-quiz based on the theme 'AatmaNirbhar Bharat: Strengthen the Future', organized by the School of Entrepreneurship Skills, Bharatiya Skill Development University Jaipur, Rajasthan, and conducted in association with The Employers Association of Rajasthan and the Global Foundation for Skill Development and Entrepreneurship, had 5,058 participants on 1 June 2020. The purpose of this quiz was to disseminate knowledge about the AatmaNirbhar Bharat Abhiyan or self-reliance movement.

Most participants in an offline quiz – single venue – single day

Under the aegis of Dindayal Vichar Manch, Bhartya Janta Yuva Morcha conducted 'Jaane Humara Madhya Pradesh', the largest one-day general knowledge quiz with 15,000 participants from all walks of life at Nanakheda Stadium, Ujjain, Madhya Pradesh on 11 February 2013. Conducted between 9:30 a.m. to 11:00 a.m., there were 80 objective questions with over 900 invigilators present.

Most participants in an offline quiz – multiple venues – single day

The Haryana Police organized an hour-long state-level quiz competition on 8 November 2016 on the theme of road safety. As many as 2,447,744 students participated in it.

PERFORMING ARTS

DANCE

Dancing Girl of Mohenjo-daro

Earliest scriptural mention of dancers

The first known textual mention of dancers can be traced back to the Rig Veda (composed between c. 1500 and 1200 BCE), which has references to mythical apsaras (divine dancers) in the story of the celestial dancer Urvashi and the mortal king Pururava.

Earliest known treatise on the performing arts

The *Natyashastra,* said to be the work of Bharata Muni, is dated variously between the second and third centuries BCE and the fourth and fifth centuries CE. It is the earliest known treatise on the performing arts. The *Natyashastra* has 37 chapters with 5,569 slokas. It is the basis of classical Indian dance, music and drama, and is often referred to as the fifth Veda.

Earliest evidence of formalized dancing

The statuette of a dancing girl from Mohenjo-daro in the Indus Valley that dates to 2500 BCE is the earliest evidence of formal dance.

Earliest sculptures of Odissi

Sculptures depicting dancers in the Jain cave temples of Khandagiri and Udayagiri, such as the Machapuri and Hathigumpha caves (second century BCE) in present-day Odisha, show the existence of a dance form in the region, in which the dance of the female temple dancers called *maharis* (devadasis) formed a ritual during worship. Hundreds of figures depicting dance movements are carved on the walls of the Parashurameshwara, Kapileshwara, Brahmeshwara, Mukteshwara, Rajarani, and Lingaraj Temples in Bhubaneswar, Puri, and Konark in Odisha, displaying the complex vocabulary of Odissi.

Oldest surviving dance drama form

Mudiyettu from Kerala, now incorporated in Kathakali, is the oldest extant dance drama form. It is traced back to the ninth century CE.

First known dance drama form

In the early 17th century, Manaveda Raja, Zamorin of Calicut (now Kozhikode), Kerala, was inspired by Jayadeva's *Gita Govinda* to compose the *Krishna Geeti* in Sanskrit. He set it to a new dance drama form known as Krishnanattam – 'the dance of Krishna'. It combined ancient theatre traditions such as Kutiyattam, ritual performances like Theyyam and folk dances like Kaikottikali.

The most studied version of Natyashastra contains 6,000 poetic verses and is divided into 36 chapters.

Earliest text to mention Odissi

Odissi has been traced to a dance form that prevailed in present-day Odisha and Bihar. In ancient times it was in a region referred to as Odhra-Magadha in the *Natyashastra.* The dance was performed by maharis and male temple acolytes called gotipuas. It is also mentioned in Maheswar Mahapatra's *Abhinaya Chandrika* (15th–16th century CE). This dance form, which includes the *tandava* style and the *lasya* style, has its own repertoire, costumes, music, and grammar.

First modern translation of the *Natyashastra*

In 1950, Manmohan Ghosh translated the *Natyashastra* into English for the Asiatic Society. This was the first successful attempt at translating the definitive text on Indian performing arts.

First English periodical on Carnatic music and dance

Sruti, a periodical on music, was first published in October 1983 in Madras (now Chennai), Tamil Nadu, and gained 30,000 readers in its very first year. It was published by P.N. Sundaresan and edited by N. Pattabhiraman. It was the first known English periodical on Carnatic music and dance.

First revivalist dance school

The Kerala Kalamandalam in Trichur (now Thrissur) Kerala was founded in 1930 by the poet Vallathol Narayana Menon to re-establish Kathakali as a major regional theatre art and to revive Mohiniattam, a classical dance form from Kerala. These art forms flourished briefly under Maharaja Swathi Thirunal in the 19th century and then languished, until they were revived by Vallathol Narayana Menon.

First dance schools

- Santiniketan, which was founded in 1901 in Bolpur, Birbhum District, Bengal (now West Bengal) by Rabindranath Tagore, had a department of dance to which he invited gurus from regions as far-flung as Manipur and Kerala to live on

---

Nautch Girls of India

Nautch is an anglicized version of the term *nach* which means dance. Earlier devadasis performed ritual dance for the temple deities and during the Mughal period it became a form of popular court dance. British colonizers were often given nautch girls as presents and were much sought after. During the late 19th century reformers introduced the anti-nautch campaign prohibiting the performances by these women. Many of these nautch girls had fought back but eventually, the art of nautch began to be viewed as derogatory in modern society.

the campus and teach their dance forms to students. Santiniketan, which later evolved into the Visva-Bharati University, now has an institute of dance, drama and music, called the Sangit Bhavan.

- Kalakshetra, a premier school for classical dance, was established in 1936 at Adyar, Madras, Tamil Nadu, by Indian classical dancer Rukmini Devi Arundale. Initially called the International Academy of Arts, it was renamed Kalakshetra on the suggestion of Sanskrit and Tamil scholar Pandit P.S. Subrahmanya Sastri. Its first dance production was titled *Kutrala Kuravanji*.

Thickest make-up

The *chutti*, used in Kathakali, is a three dimensional mask-like attachment made of rice paste and paper, which may extend to 15 cm (6 in.) from the face. It is the thickest make-up used in any dance form in the world.

Thickest make-up

First classical dance to be revived

Odissi was rediscovered by dancer Indrani Rehman, who then popularized it abroad in the early 1940s, though it was recognized as a classical dance form only from the 1960s.

First modern work on dance

The book titled *Classical Indian Dance in Literature and the Arts* by scholar Dr Kapila Vatsyayan, published in 1968 by the country's premier institution of dance and music, the Sangeet Natak Akademi, was the first definitive modern work on dance, written in English. Dr Vatsyayan received the Sangeet Natak Akademi fellowship in 1970.

First national dance seminar

The Sangeet Natak Akademi held the first national seminar on dance from 30 March to 7 April 1958. Dr P.V. Rajammar was the Akademi's chairman then. The seminar's inaugural dance was performed by leading Kathak exponent Pandit Shambhu Maharaj.

First Kuchipudi dance couple to receive the Padma Shri

Raja and Radha Reddy were the first couple to receive the Padma Shri award for a single cause, individually and together, in 1984. Widely travelled, they popularized the Kuchipudi form of dance in India and abroad. They also won the Padma Bhushan in 2000.

First Sangeet Natak Akademi award for creative dance

Dance pioneer Uday Shankar was the first to be honoured by the Sangeet Natak Akademi with an award for creative dance in 1960. Two years later, he received the Sangeet Natak Akademi fellowship. In 1971, Uday Shankar became the first modern dancer to receive the Padma Vibhushan.

Earliest reference to musical performances

The grammarian Panini (c. fourth century BCE) in his comments on *nritya* (dancing) mentions composers of sutras on dancing. The *Pali Pitaka* (c. 300 BCE) mentions two disciples of Gautama Buddha attending one such recital.

First woman to perform chhau

Sonal Mansingh, the well-known exponent of Kuchipudi, was the first woman to learn the chhau dance form. It is a semi-classical dance with martial and folk origins, and is found in three styles drawing their names from the region where they are traditionally performed.

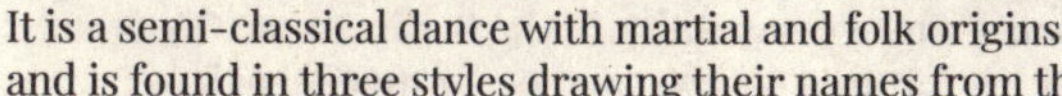

Sculpture of Panini

First campaign for revival of Bharatanatyam

E. Krishna Iyer, a lawyer based in Madras, was the first to fight the anti-nautch campaigns of the 1920s by learning the dance form Bharatanatyam in 1926 from the famous Natesa Iyer from Melattur, Kerala. For six years, he lectured and wrote for his cause, and presented devadasis in public performances outside of temples. Finally, it was with T. Balasaraswati's dance performance at the All-India Music Conference in Varanasi, Uttar Pradesh, in 1935, that the dance became accepted as a respectable art form.

First Kuchipudi solo

Vedantam Lakshminarayana Sastri (1886–1956) performed the first solo recital in the traditional dance drama form of Kuchipudi. He learnt the dance form from Sri Vempati Venkatanarayana. He also introduced the popular *tarangam* into the form, during which the dancers have to balance themselves on the edges of a thali.

First Sangeet Natak Akademi award winners for dance

T. Balasaraswati and Shambhu Maharaj won the first Sangeet Natak Akademi awards for dance in 1955 for their contribution to Bharatanatyam and Kathak, respectively. The awards were instituted in 1952 to honour performing artistes.

First known Kathak teacher

Pandit Birju Maharaj (1938–2022) is the first known Kathak teacher. Born in Lucknow, Uttar Pradesh, to Shri Achhan Maharaj, a Kathak exponent, he was the popular face of the dance form globally. He was invited to teach Kathak at the age of 13 at Sangeet Bharati, and later at the Bharatiya Kala Kendra, New Delhi. He received the Sangeet Natak Akademi award in 1966 and the Padma Vibhushan in 1986.

First ballet film
Classical–folk fusion guru Uday Shankar's film *Kalpana,* released in 1948, used the ballet form for a major part of its narration, making it the country's first ballet film.

First dance theatre form recognized by UNESCO: Kutiyattam
Kutiyattam, a traditional Sanskrit performing art form originating in Kerala, is recognized by UNESCO as a 'Masterpiece of the Oral and Intangible Heritage of Humanity'. It is considered to be at least 2,000 years old and the oldest living theatre tradition globally. UNESCO usually considers only monuments and heritage sites, and this was the first art form recognized for its exceptional value. Mizhavu, a large percussion instrument, is the primary musical instrument that accompanies Kutiyattam. Considered to be sacred, Kutiyattam was traditionally performed only in temple theatres, called *koothambalam*.

First to win an international dance competition
Madame Menaka (1899–1947), whose real name was Leila Sokhey, was the first Indian to win an international dance competition at the Berlin Dance Olympiad in July 1936. Her troupe, which featured on two days, performed Menaka's original ballet, *Deva Vijaya Nritya*, and won the first three individual prizes, along with the first prize in the competition.

First celebrity dance competition
Ten famous television couples participated in the first ever celebrity dance competition, *Nach Baliye*, on TV channel Star One. The show premiered on 11 October 2005. The judges were choreographer Saroj Khan, film-maker Farhan Akhtar and VJ-and-model Malaika Arora Khan. TV stars Sachin and Supriya Pilgaonkar were the first winners of the contest.

First Indian–European fusion
Versatile dancer Uday Shankar (1900–77), who was born in Udaipur, Rajasthan, is known as the father of modern dance in India. He combined European theatrical dance techniques with the classical and folk dance forms of India. Uday Shankar danced with Anna Pavlova, the Russian ballerina, during the 1920s and created *Hindu Wedding* as well as the duet *Radha and Krishna*, which was included in Pavlova's performance *Oriental Impressions*. In 1971, he was awarded the Padma Vibhushan, the second highest civilian award in India.

Only extant pre-Vedic dances
Bhutam and Theyyam are ritual dances of Karnataka and Kerala, respectively. The dancers represent local gods and ancestral spirits, based on a pre-Vedic belief system.

Only pan-Indian dance text
Jayadeva's Sanskrit book of verse, the *Gita Govinda* (12th century CE), has been choreographed in all major Indian dance

Purandara Dasa's works in the 16th century set the foundation for the Carnatic form of Indian classical music.

styles. It is sung in both Hindustani and Carnatic modes, and has been translated into many European languages.

Oldest recipient of President's Award

Asan Chandu Panikkar (1873–1969), a pioneer of 20th-century Kathakali, received the President's Award in 1958 at 84 years. He danced at the award ceremony, in front of the then prime minister Jawaharlal Nehru and the then president Dr Rajendra Prasad.

Only dance form varied in three states

Chhau, the classical folk dance with martial overtones, has three versions based on the regions it is performed in – Seraikela Chhau in Jharkhand (masked), Mayurbhanj Chhau in Odisha, and Purulia Chhau in West Bengal.

Only dance drama performed by women alone

Kuravanji, a form of musical play popular at the beginning of the 18th century, was meant only for devadasis and was performed at the annual festivals of some temples in Tamil Nadu.

Only Asthana Nartaki

In 1978, Bharatanatyam exponent Yamini Krishnamurthy was awarded the title of 'Asthana Nartaki', meaning 'resident dancer' of Lord Venkateswara Temple, Tirupati, Andhra Pradesh.

Only classical dancer with an artificial foot

Accomplished Bharatanatyam dancer Sudha Chandran, who lost a leg in a car crash in 1981, resumed her dancing career with a prosthetic Jaipur Foot in 1984. She was rehabilitated by Dr P.K. Sethi of the Sawai Man Singh Hospital in Jaipur, Rajasthan.

Only Persianized classical dance

Kathak is a classical dance form that derives its name from the female professional storytellers or *kathika*s who recited verses from the Ramayana and the Mahabharata, along with explanatory gestures, appropriate choreography, and music, as part of a system of ritualistic worship. This dance form, with its fast and intricate movements, attracted the attention of the Mughal rulers. Over time, the dance form split into two main schools: 'Temple Kathak', with its emphasis on *bhava* (or emotion), and a court dance or 'Darbari Kathak', with its focus on rhythmic display.

WR Largest Bharatanatyam ensemble

The Department of Tourism, Government of Tamil Nadu, organized the largest Bharatanatyam ensemble with 10,176 dancers on 8 February 2020. The event, 'Sathir 10000', which based the dance on the famous Tamil text *Thirukkural*, was held at S.I.V.E.T College in Chennai, Tamil Nadu.

Largest arts festival

Soorya Festival, organized annually by the Soorya Stage and Film Society, Thiruvananthapuram, Kerala, is the largest of its kind in India, both in terms of membership and the number of activities. The festival is held across 111 days between September and January each year. The 30,000-plus members of Soorya Society, founded in 1978, conduct around 200 programmes annually.

Marathon performance of Ottanthullal

Jaimon V.J. (b. 10 February 1974) from Kottayam, Kerala, performed a non-stop marathon session of Ottanthullal, a dance drama form, depicting 10 stories in 12 hrs from 5:00 a.m. to 6:45 p.m. on 12 May 2019 at the Karippadavathu Temple, Uzhavoor, Kerala. The break time was 1 hr 45 mins.

MUSIC

First raga

The first raga is believed to be the Carnatic Mayamalavagowla (equivalent to the Hindustani raga Bhairavi) that Purandara Dasa (c. 1484–1565), the Bhakti poet and musician, also known as Adi Guru, used as the teaching scale. Called Adi Raga, it is said to have emanated from Lord Shiva.

Earliest form of classical song

The Dhrupad, originally called Dhruvapada, was the prevailing mode of music until medieval times. While this form traces its roots to the *Natyashastra,* it was developed by Swami Haridas and the legendary singer Tansen in the 15th century.

Only multilingual classical songs

Manipravalam *kriti*s are songs in the Carnatic tradition in which two or even three languages are used and the lines are sung alternately in these languages, which include Tamil and Sanskrit.

Earliest form of music

The Rig Veda has references to *saman* hymns, the earliest form of music in India. Saman singing is also mentioned in the *Brahmana*s as well as the Upanishads, and features as a part of spiritual observances and exercises.

Earliest royal composer of ragas

Maharaja Swathi Thirunal (r. 1813–46), the ruler of the erstwhile princely state of Travancore (now in Kerala), created more than 400 classical compositions in both the Carnatic and Hindustani modes.

Earliest musical notes

The Sama Veda, which is believed to date to c. 1200–1000 BCE, mentions seven musical notes in saman singing, viz., Krushta, Prathama, Dvitiya, Tritiya, Chaturtha, Mandra/Panchama and Antya/Atisvara.

First medieval treatise on music

The Chalukyan king, Someshvara III, who ruled in the Karnataka region in the 12th century CE, wrote the *Manasollasa*, an encyclopaedic work in Sanskrit on a variety of topics, including music, with 2,500 verses dedicated to the topic. The music section, one of the largest sections in the book, is considered the earliest treatise on music.

The Trinity of Carnatic Music

The three prolific 18th-century composers – Thyagaraja, Muthuswamy Dikshitar and Syama Sastri – are known as the trinity of Carnatic music as the music system is based centrally on compositions attributed to them. The compositions of Syama Sastri are known for their intricate rhythmic patterns, those of Thyagaraja for the blend of emotion and melody, and those of Dikshitar for their depiction of melodic beauty and variety.

Stamp depicting Muthuswamy Dikshitar

Earliest ballad singing

Both Vedic and epic literature mentions minstrels singing *akhyanas* (texts narrated by professional storytellers), sung to the veena, in the *marga* style of singing. While the Vedas mentions both instrumental music and akhyana recitation in yagnas, the Ramayana also has several references to the singing of ballads.

Earliest mention of raga

The word *raga* in its modern connotation appears first in the classical Sanskrit text *Brihaddeshi* by Matanga (c. eighth century CE). It is described as 'a combination of tones which, with beautiful illuminating graces, pleases people'.

Earliest Prakrit (popular) songs

The *Natyashastra* mentions dhruvas, i.e., songs of five different kinds that were an integral part of drama. These songs indicate the context, place, and people in a scene. *Dhruva*s were originally in Prakrit and were mostly sung by a choir.

First to standardize music

Purandara Dasa (1484–1564) is revered as Sangeet Pitamaha (grandfather of music). He standardized Carnatic music for teaching, besides classifying 35 types of *tala*. He pioneered a musical notation system that is still being used.

Most prolific composer

Purandara Dasa (1484–1564), the philosopher-saint and Bhakti poet, is credited with as many as 475,000 compositions.

Early treatise on Carnatic music

Rama Amatya, a royal composer at the court of King Ramaraja of Vijayanagar, gave the first detailed exposition of the Carnatic system of music in his text titled *Swaramela Kalanidhi*, around 1550 BCE. He described the first collection of ragas.

First codifier of Carnatic concert format

Ariyakudi Ramanuja Iyengar (1890–1967) was the architect of modern Carnatic concert music. He pioneered the transition of the Carnatic concert from temples and courts to modern concert halls, codifying and adapting its format, order and duration. He introduced the largest number of compositions from the trinity of Thyagaraja, Muthuswamy Dikshitar and Syama Sastri to the concert repertoire, new *pallavi*s (opening phrase of a song), the order of *tukkada*s

MUSIC OF INDIA

Music in India is usually divided into two broad categories: Hindustani classical in the north and Carnatic music in the south. There are regions in India with their own schools of music that don't necessarily fit into the above categories. The musical instruments most popular in Hindustani music are the sitar, sarod, tambura, shenai, sarangi, and tabla. In Carnatic classical music the most popular instruments are veena, mridangam, kanjira, and violin. Bamboo flutes are commonly used in both traditions.

1 Mridangam

The mridangam is a percussion instrument used in Carnatic music. In ancient Hindu sculpture, painting, and mythology the mridangam is used as a choice instrument of numerous deities. Over the years the mridangam was made from different kinds of wood. Today the wood of the jackfruit tree is used for increased durability. The tala (rhythm) system in both Hindustani and Carnatic music was developed with the introduction of the mridangam.

2 *Shehnai*

The *shehnai* is a wind musical instrument made of wood or bamboo, with a double reed at one end to blow into, and a flared bell of metal or wood at the other. It is thought to produce the sound of auspiciousness and sanctity. It is almost similar to the nadaswaram used in south India, although the nadaswaram has a longer body. It is played at temples and is an integral instrument played during any Indian wedding.

3 Veena

The veena comprises many stringed instruments used in Indian musical traditions. The two main veenas are the Rudra veena used in Hindustani classical music and the Saraswati veena used in Carnatic classical music. The veena is mentioned in much of vedic literature including the Rig veda and Sama veda. The Rudra veena has a body of about 3 to 4 feet with two large resonating gourds at each end. However, the Saraswati veena is a long-necked pear-shaped lute with a pear-shaped wooden piece at one end. Both veenas have 24 frets.

4 Tabla

The tabla is a percussion instrument usually used in Hindustani classical music. It can be played solo or as a part of an ensemble. It is the main instrument used during bhajans or kirtans and other devotional music. There are two drums of different sizes and shapes in the tabla, and each is made of hollowed-out wood or clay. The smaller drum is called dayan (right side) while the bigger drum is called bayan (left side).

5 Bansuri

A bansuri is an ancient side-blown flute. It is usually made from a single hollow shaft of bamboo with seven finger holes. The bansuri is usually between 30 centimetres and 75 centimetres in length. The bansuri is generally associated with the Hindu mythological god Krishna, and is referred to as his divine instrument. It is also discussed as an important musical instrument in the *Natya Shastra*.

6 Sitar

The sitar is a stringed instrument normally used in Hindustani classical music. It was invented in medieval India and the word 'sitar' is taken from the Persian word *sehtar* meaning three-stringed. A sitar can have 18, 19, 20, or 21 strings. It is constructed using teak wood or tun wood for the neck and faceplate while calabash gourds are used for the resonating chambers.

7 Sarod

A sarod is a stringed instrument used in Hindustani classical music. Traditionally, a sarod is a lute like instrument with 17 to 25 strings. The strings are made of steel or phosphorus bronze and are plucked with a triangular plectrum. The word *sarod*, comes from Persian *sorud* which means song, melody, or hymn.

8 Ghatam

The ghatam is a percussion instrument used across India, especially in Tamil Nadu. It is a pot with a narrow mouth made of clay baked with brass or copper fillings. The pitch produced depends on the size of the ghatam and is a metallic sound. Ghatam is mainly manufactured in Manamadurai near Madurai, Tamil Nadu. It is a difficult instrument to play but is preferred for its sweet metallic sound.

(composition played towards the end of a Carnatic concert) and *padams* (other songs) that follow the main item of *ragam-thanam-pallavi*.

Flutes are an ancient musical instrument. Their origin can be dated to over **40,000** years ago.

First fusion melody

The 14th century saw the introduction of Persian models into Indian music. Amir Khusrau (1253–1325), the famous singer at the court of Alauddin Khilji (r. 1296–1316) introduced the qawwali mode of singing, a mixture of Persian and Indian music. He also introduced the sitar, a modification of the veena.

Oldest gharana

The Gwalior gharana was founded in the 16th century by Nathan Khan Pir Bakhsh.

Oldest sabha for dance and music

Sri Parthasarathy Swami Sabha at Triplicane, Madras (now Chennai), was established in 1900. The Bangalore Gayana Sabha, Bangalore (now Bengaluru), Karnataka, set up on 5 August 1905, is the second oldest private cultural organization with programmes in dance and music.

Oldest south Indian stringed instrument

The *yazh*, a seven-stringed lute is mentioned in Tamil Sangam literature (first to fourth century CE), making it the oldest south Indian stringed instrument known.

Oldest known percussion instrument

The ghatam or mud pot, still in vogue in Carnatic concerts, is mentioned in the Ramayana. It was used in folk music for centuries and later elevated to concert status by maestro Palani Krishna Iyer (1876–1908). This tradition continued with maestros such as Kodandarama Iyer and T.H. 'Vikku' Vinayakram, who popularized it.

Oldest musical instrument

A lithophone (stone chimes comparable to a xylophone), around 3,000–4,000 years old, was identified by German archaeologists in Sankarjang Village in Angul District, Odisha. All the 20 similar-shaped polished basalt stones found possibly formed fragments of a lithophone, with excellent acoustic quality, as the edges were ground thin to achieve a specific pitch.

First mention of the drum

The *Mahajanaka Jataka* (c. second century BCE) mentions the drum, along with horns, gongs and cymbals.

Earliest musical instruments

Drums came into being during the Vedic period. The earliest drums included the *dundubhi* and *adambara*, ordinary drums; *bhumi dundubhi*, an earth drum made by digging a hole in the ground and covering it with hide; and *vanaspati*, a wooden drum. Early stringed instruments included the *skanda veena* and *karkari*, ordinary lutes; *vana*, a lute with a hundred strings; and the veena (similar to the present-day one). Wind instruments included the *tunava*, a wooden flute; the *nadi*, a reed flute; and *bakura*, whose shape is unknown.

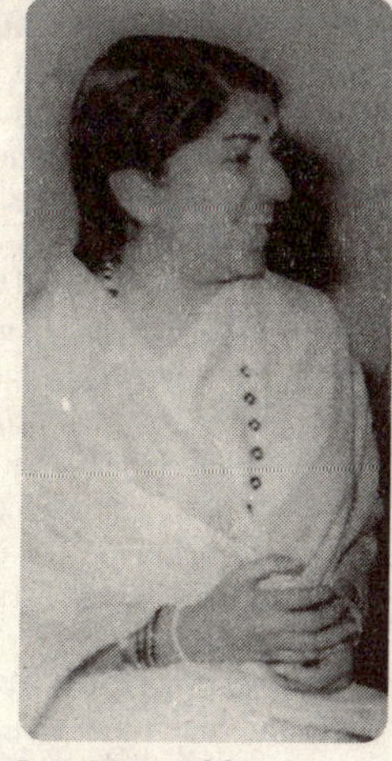
Lata Mangeshkar

First Indian performer at the Royal Albert Hall
The first Indian singer to perform at the iconic venue, the Royal Albert Hall, in London, UK, was Bollywood playback singer Lata Mangeshkar, who gave a performance at the venue in 1974. Other Indians who have also performed here include sitar players Pandit Ravi Shankar and Anoushka Shankar, flautist Hariprasad Chaurasia, and singer Shreya Ghoshal.

First three-in-one classical instrument
The *mridanga veenai*, a stand-up instrument that is framed in wood and played sitting on a chair, was invented by Audanoor P. Haridass, who demonstrated it on 23 September 1984 at the Purasawalkam Arts Academy, Madras, Tamil Nadu. Played with bamboo sticks, it not only reproduces the sounds of percussion and strings, but also simulates the sound of cymbals used in *natuvangam* (rhythmic sound play) and the tinkle of *gajjai* (ankle bells).

Earliest use of the Carnatic veena
Govinda Dikshitar modified the Saraswati veena into the Carnatic veena to enable the playing of all ragas. He was a minister of King Raghunatha Naik of Thanjavur (r. 1614–32 CE), Tamil Nadu.

First singer to be recorded on gramophone
Gauhar Jaan (1873–1930) was selected to sing when Fred Ginsberg introduced the gramophone in India with the first disc being cut in Calcutta (now Kolkata), West Bengal, in 1902. She was paid ₹3,000 for the recording session.

First recorded song
Sashi Mukhi of Classic Theatre in Calcutta recorded the first song *'Kanha Jeevan Dhan'* in 1902, from the play *Srikrishna* on a 22.86 cm (9 in.), one-sided disc made by the Gramophone and Typewriter Ltd.

First voices recorded on gramophone
The voices of Dr Harnamdas and Ahmed were recorded by the Gramophone Company in 1899 in London, UK. They sang songs based on the Ramayana and recited the *aayat*s of the Quran for the recordings.

First gramophone company
On 7 July 1901, J. Watson Harrod opened a branch of the Gramophone Company Ltd at Calcutta, West Bengal, which was further developed by T.W. Gainsberg. In 1908, the first factory to process and press records was set up in Beliaghata, Calcutta.

First female professional saxophone players

M.S. Subbulakshmi

Sisters M.S. Lavanya and M.S. Subbulakshmi from Chennai, Tamil Nadu, have given a new dimension to Carnatic music by playing ragas on the saxophone. Daughters of mridangam exponent M.R. Sainath, the duo, called the 'Saxophone Sisters', learnt the instrument from Padma Shri Dr Kadri Gopinath. They have performed at venues such as the Soorya Festival in Thiruvananthapuram, Kerala, the Sri Thyagaraja Festival at Thiruvaiyaru, Tamil Nadu, and the Malleswaram Sangeetha Sabha, Bengaluru, Karnataka. They have also performed at the 'One City One World Festival' in Nottingham and the Bath International Music Festival in the UK.

Only gramophone museum

Discs and Machines – Sunny's Gramophone Museum and Records' Archive in Kottayam, Kerala is a unique repository of around 110,000 records and more than 260 gramophones. Owner Sunny Matthew has been collecting them for the last 33 years and opened the museum to public on 25 January 2015. A copy of the first recorded song in India is also on display here. The museum may be visited by appointment.

First gramophone record

Indian music was first produced on a gramophone record in 1898 at the Beliaghata factory of the Gramophone and Typewriter Ltd. In July 1908, the production of disc records was started at the Sealdah factory located on Beliaghata Road, Calcutta, West Bengal. In 1928, the Sealdah factory was closed and building work commenced at the new factory on Jessore Road, Dum Dum, Calcutta.

First electronic instrument

The first electronic tala aid called talometer was invented by M.G. Raj Narayan of Bangalore, Karnataka, in June 1978. It helps musicians to get a precise, unerring, and continuous course of cycles in all the talas.

First duo to introduce jugalbandi

Pandit Ravi Shankar and Ustad Ali Akbar Khan formed the first musical duo to introduce instrumental duets popularly known as jugalbandi. Shankar and Khan performed the jugalbandi for the first time at the debut performance of the former in 1939, with Shankar playing the sitar and Khan playing the sarod. The duo was also among the first to popularize Indian classical music abroad.

The Indian Musical Industry's value is estimated to reach **33** billion rupees by the end of 2025.

First use of shehnai in Hindustani classical music

The shehnai, like the *sundari* and *surnayi*, was originally a folk instrument that was played on festive occasions. It was Ustad Bismillah Khan

(1916–2006) who brought it into the realm of classical music, at par with other classical instruments.

First harp player

Meagan Pandian from Mumbai, Maharashtra, is the first harp player from India and the first Indian harpist to participate in A.R. Rahman's concerts. She received the 'Young Musician of the Year' award from the Olga and Jules Craen Foundation in 2014.

First woman instrumentalist

Renowned sarod player Sharan Rani Backliwal (1929–2008) was a leading exponent of Hindustani instrumental music and the first female instrumentalist to give a public recital in the 1930s. She trained under sarod maestros Baba Allauddin Khan and Ustad Ali Akbar Khan. Popularly known as Sarod Rani, she was given the Sahitya Kala Parishad award and the Sangeet Natak Akademi award for classical Hindustani instrumental music in 1974. She received the Padma Shri in 1968.

First woman nadaswaram player

Madurai M.S. Ponnuthayi from Madurai, Tamil Nadu, was the first professional woman player of the nadaswaram, long considered a male bastion. Born into a family of musicians, she was introduced to the instrument by her father. After receiving training under Natesa Pillai, she gave her first performance at the age of nine in the 1940s.

First woman shehnai player

Bageswari Gamar was crowned 'Shehnai Queen' at Chandigarh in 1983, the year she made her debut. A disciple of Ustad Bismillah Khan, she recorded a jugalbandi with the maestro, besides releasing solo cassettes. She represented India at the Bharat Mahotsav in Russia in 1988.

India's Musical Genius

A.R. Rahman's career began with writing jingles for advertisements. He worked with Mani Ratnam on the film *Roja* for which he was acclaimed all over India. He made scores for numerous movies after that. He worked on the film *Lagaan* which was the first Bollywood film to be nominated for an Academy Award. Rahman also worked with Andrew Llyod Webber, Shekhar Kapur on *Elizabeth: The Golden Age*, and on the film *127 Hours*. For *Slumdog Millionaire*, Rahman not only won an Oscar and Grammy but also won a BAFTA for best score and a Golden Globe.

First woman ghatam player

Sukanya Ramgopal (b. 13 June 1957) from Bengaluru, Karnataka, became the first woman to play the ghatam in the Carnatic music tradition. Among many of her innovations are the 'Ghata Tarang', a melody created out of six ghatams, and the 'Sthree Taal Tarang', an all-woman percussion ensemble, experiments that have taken her to stages across India and abroad. She received the Sangeet Natak Akademi Award in 2014.

First to perform at the UN

M.S. Subbulakshmi (1916–2004) was the first Indian to perform at the United Nations (UN) in a concert at the UN General Assembly on UN Day, 23 October 1966. She received the Padma Bhushan in 1954 and the Padma Vibhushan in 1975 and became the first musician to be awarded the Bharat Ratna in 1998. Subbulakshmi was also the first Indian musician to receive the Ramon Magsaysay Award for Public Service in 1974.

First music school

Pandit Vishnu Digambar Paluskar (1872–1931) set up the Gandharva Mahavidyalaya – India's first known music school – in Lahore (now in Pakistan) on 5 May 1901. It was run on public donations and funds raised by his concerts. Another branch was opened by him in Bombay in September 1908, and Pandit Vinayakrao Patwardhan started a branch in Poona (now Pune), Maharashtra, on 8 May 1932. Later, the Lahore school was shifted to Bombay after Independence in 1947.

First foreign concert tour by a woman instrumentalist

According to a report in *Amrita Bazar Patrika*, dated 11 September 1912, Satyabala Devi, an 18-year-old Bengali girl, had gone to America in the summer of 1911 to play the veena. The article stated that she was the first Indian woman to have gone abroad to perform in an instrumental music concert and it was declared a great success.

WR Most recorded artiste

Asha Bhosle is the most recorded artiste in the history of music. Having begun her career in 1948 with the Hindi film *Chunariya*, she had recorded 11,000 solo, duet, and chorus songs by 2011. In a career spanning more than six decades, she has sung in over 20 Indian and foreign languages. She received the Dadasaheb Phalke Award in 2000 and the Padma Vibhushan in 2008. She was also the first Indian singer to be nominated for the Grammy Awards.

First compact disc

Pankaj Udhas's album titled *Shagufta* was the first to be formally released in a compact disc (CD) format by Music India in December 1987.

First recorded music

In the 1930s, an organization called Shining Star Society recorded sets of discs with mythological themes. A mix of music and dialogue, the sets ran into several records. A 10 disc *Ramayana* by Saraswati Stores was very popular, followed by other drama sets like *Tukaram* (four discs), *Purandara Dasa* (five discs), *Siruthondar* (three discs) and *Thirugnana Sambandhar* (four discs). Their recording was supervised by the Katcheri set pioneer, Thuraiyur Rajagopala Sharma.

First fusion album

Violinist Yehudi Menuhin and sitar maestro Pandit Ravi Shankar collaborated on a double album called *West Meets East,* which was released in Britain in January 1967, where both played Western and Indian classical pieces alternately.

First set of records

Renowned businessman H. Bose's Talking Machine Hall, a recording shop in Calcutta, released the first set of phonograph records on 19 March 1906. The set featured eight songs by Rabindranath Tagore and four by D.L. Roy.

WR First portable digital audio player

Carvaan, by Saregama India Ltd, is the world's first portable digital audio player with over 5,000 inbuilt songs. The songs are categorized based on singers, lyricists, music composers, and moods. Using a jog dial, music stations can be selected, from Kishore Kumar classics and R.D. Burman's hits to timeless love songs and soulful Sufi tracks. Carvaan can function as an FM radio, and also has Bluetooth and USB features.

First all-woman Hindustani–Carnatic music band

Tabla soloist Anuradha Pal from Mumbai, Maharashtra, founded Stree Shakti, the first all-woman Hindustani–Carnatic music band, in 1996. It performed in India as well as other countries, including in international festivals such as BBC Music Live and Rhythm Sticks.

Grammy Award for the Best World Music Album

Music composer and tabla player Sandeep Das won a Grammy Award for the Best World Music Album in 2017 for his collaboration with Yo-Yo Ma and The Silk Road Ensemble on the album *Sing Me Home*.

Only Indian to win both an Oscar and a Grammy Award

Composer and singer A.R. Rahman won two Grammys following his Oscar wins for the soundtrack from Danny Boyle's *Slumdog Millionaire*, becoming the first Indian to win an individual Grammy. He won the first Grammy in the Best Compilation Soundtrack for the Motion Picture category. The second was for the song '*Jai Ho*' in the Best Motion Picture Song category for the same in 2009.

First Indo-jazz (fusion) albums

Indo-jazz came into its own in India in the 1970s with Shakti, a group formed by jazz guitarist John McLaughlin, along with L. Shankar on the electric double violin (which he invented), Zakir Hussain on the tabla and T.H. 'Vikku' Vinayakram on the ghatam.

First Grammy Award–winning Indian percussionist

T.H. 'Vikku' Vinayakram was the first Indian percussionist to win the Grammy Award in 1991. He won it for his participation in *Planet Drum* by Mickey Hart.

Vinayakram, well-known for playing the *ghatam* and popularizing Carnatic music, was honoured with the Padma Shri in 2002 and the Padma Bhushan in 2014. He also won the Sangeet Natak Akademi fellowship in 2012.

First Asian to win the Golden Reel Award

Resul Pookutty was the first Asian to win the 63rd American Motion Picture Sound Editor's Golden Reel Award in 2016 for best sound for the documentary *India's Daughter*. A sound designer, editor and mixer who works in Hollywood and Indian cinema, he also won the Academy Award (Oscar) in 2009 for best sound mixing for the movie *Slumdog Millionaire,* along with Richard Pryke and Ian Tapp. He was awarded the Padma Shri in 2010 and the National Film Award for best audiography in the same year.

First whistling LP

An album of Carnatic and Hindustani ragas entirely whistled by Siva Prasad from Hyderabad (now in Telangana) was released on 15 June 1985.

First female rapper

Taran Kaur Dhillon (b. 29 July 1979), aka Hard Kaur, was the first female rapper of Indian origin. A British citizen, she topped the UK charts with her song, '*Ek Glassy*' in 2007. Her first solo album *Supawoman* released the same year had 11 tracks. She marked her Bollywood debut with the title track (which she co-wrote) of the film *Johnny Gaddaar* (2007).

First Indian band on MTV

Rana Banerjee and Sanjoy Sengupta's band, Extinct, was the first Indian group to be featured on MTV Asia, in September 1993.

First disabled DJ

Varun Khullar, aka DJ Aamish, from New Delhi, is the first disabled professional disc jockey (DJ) in India. He began his career in May 2017 and is currently a resident DJ with Kitty Su, New Delhi, a part of the Lalit Group and Hotels. He has performed at festivals like Time Out 72 and Greeshma Utsav.

India's only music director couple

Samir and Mana Raval from Ahmedabad, Gujarat, are India's first and only music director couple, having composed music for more than 100 songs in 35 feature films in Gujarati and Hindi. Having started with music direction for *Teenagers Gang*, a Gujarati film, in 2013, the couple continues to compose music for Hindi and other films, TV serials, and jingles.

WR Longest innings as a conductor

Western music maestro Zubin Mehta (b. 29 April 1936) from Bombay (now Mumbai), Maharashtra, spent over 13 years as the music director and principal conductor of the New York Philharmonic Orchestra from 1978 to 1991. Currently, he is the music director of the Israel Philharmonic Orchestra.

First virtual music festival

Sunburn Home Festival, a two-day virtual music festival, was organized from

11 to 12 July 2020. The festival featured a line-up of international stars such as Bassjackers, Vini Vici, and Ummet Ozcan. The highlight of the event was the application of extended reality (XR) technology offering a mixed reality and holistic environment, also used for the first time.

Longest *ravanhatha*

Praveen Singh Rathore along with Shiv Pal Ram, Sugana Ram, and Manwari from Jodhpur, Rajasthan, made the longest ravanhatha, a folk string instrument of Rajasthan. The ravanhatha, measuring 224 cm (7 ft 4.19 in.), was made in two weeks at Bhakrasani, Jodhpur, using bamboo, mango wood, goat leather, bull horn, iron, cotton threads, plastic threads, *baval* (babul) wood, *ghungroo* (bells) and fabric.

Marathon flute performance

Ananthakrishnan S.R., a flautist from Thiruvananthapuram, Kerala, played the flute for 33 hrs 36 mins, from 6:30 a.m. on 13 July to 6:30 p.m. on 14 July 2017 in Thrissur, Kerala, with a total break time of 2 hrs 24 mins.

WR Marathon qawwali performance

Haji Mohammad Idris and Mohammad Ilyas, known as the Qutbi brothers of Dargah Hazrat Qutbuddin, performed Sufi qawwali for 12 hrs. They began at 9:00 p.m. on 12 November 2016 and ended at 9:00 a.m. on 13 November 2016 at the Sangeet Natak Akademi in Delhi. Sixteen singers accompanied them.

Marathon duet singing

Venkatesh and Sangeetha Rajeshkumar from Chennai, Tamil Nadu, sang duets for 28 hours at the Akshaya Mahalakshmi Mahal, Chennai, Tamil Nadu, during 28–29 January 2017. They sang 342 Tamil film songs starting at around 4:00 a.m. on 28 January and ended by 12:30 p.m. the next day. The total break time was 4 hrs 30 mins.

Marathon Carnatic vocal performance

Sajna Sudheer (b. 1 August 1984) from Thiruvananthapuram, Kerala, performed a marathon Carnatic vocal recital for 37 hrs 50 mins at the Ganesham Natakakalari of Soorya Stage and Film Society. She began her performance at 3:15 a.m. on 21 January 2019 and ended at 9:15 p.m. on 22 January 2019, with a total break time of 4 hrs 10 mins.

Most people playing the harmonica together

Hindustan Petroleum Corporation Ltd, as part of its mega festival – Yuvantage BLITZ during 6–7 January 2019 – set a record for most people playing the harmonica simultaneously. The music was played by 457 of the company's employees on their harmonicas for 6 mins 17 secs on 6 January 2019 at Ramoji Film City, Hyderabad, Telangana.

Most events in a day

Pernod Ricard India Pvt. Ltd organized 104 musical events on a single day – 29 November 2019. These events were held at different venues across 27 cities in the country, including Delhi, Mumbai, Pune, Chennai, Visakhapatnam, and

Chandigarh. Titled 'Play for a Cause', this campaign raised awareness on issues such as pollution, nature, plastic use, and meals for the underprivileged. Bands and artistes including Perfect Strangers (Bengaluru), Parikrama (Gurugram), Ankur Tiwari and the Ghalat Family (Mumbai), Cherry Singh (Chandigarh) and Usha Uthup (Kolkata) performed at these events.

THEATRE

Oldest extant play

Palm-leaf fragments belonging to the Kushana period (around first century CE) feature a nine-act Buddhist play titles *Sariputra Prakarana*, by Ashvaghosha, the court poet of King Kanishka. It follows all the rules for drama laid down in the *Natyashastra*.

Early dramatic references

There are references to drama, dancing, music, and acting in the Ramayana, the Mahabharata and the Puranas. Buddhist and Jain texts mention that monks were forbidden from watch dramatic performances. Panini (c. fourth century BCE) mentions dramatic works in his *Ashtadhyayi*. Patanjali (variously dated from second century BCE to the fourth century CE), describes the conditions of dramatic performers. Kautilya also refers to music, dance, and drama in the *Arthashastra*.

Earliest plays

- Patanjali mentions plays such as *Kamavadha*, *Balibandhan*, and *Sariputra-Prakarana* in his text *Mahabhashya* (c. third century BCE).
- Bharatamuni also mentions plays such as *Devasura Sangrama*, *Amrita Manthana* and *Tripuradaha* in his *Natyashastra*.
- *Uparupakas* (secondary dramas) are found in the Rig Veda in the form of dialogue hymns. The most famous one tells the story of Pururava and Urvashi. Eighteen such uparupakas are mentioned in the *Sahitya Darpana*, a book on rhetoric and dramaturgy from the 14th century, authored by Pandit Vishwanath Kaviraj. These plays pre-date even the *Natyashastra*. Uparupakas were probably enacted before the public on royal occasions and temple festivals.

Early political plays

Mrichchhakatika by Shudraka (dated between the third and the fifth century CE) and Vishakhadatta's *Mudrarakshasa* (dated between late fourth and the eighth century CE), both depict clashes between different powers, political intrigue, espionage, and counter-espionage. They are considered to be the first plays with political themes.

Earliest playwright

Bhasa (third to fourth century CE) of the Chola era in south India is believed to be the earliest playwright. Well known plays by him include *Abhisheka*, *Swapnavasavadattam* and *Pratimanatakam*.

Oldest cave theatre

The cave theatres at Sita Bengra and Jogimara in the Surguja District of

Jogimara cave of Chhattisgarh

Chhattisgarh are estimated to be around 3,000 years old. Sita Bengra, which predates the Lomas Rishi caves of the Mauryan period (322–187 BCE), was chiefly used for dance and drama.

Earliest street plays

Therukoothu, a theatre form originating during 200 BCE–200 CE in ancient Tamilakam, literally means 'street play'. It was performed on streets on an improvised stage with very few props and hardly any special costumes. Themes were taken from the epics. Therukoothu as well as other forms of street plays like Pallu, Kuravanji, and Nandi Natakam are still performed in south India.

First 'protest play'

Nil Darpan, a play in Bengali about the plight of indigo farmers, was written by Dinabandhu Mitra in 1860. The play was banned by the British authorities.

First foreign translation of a Sanskrit play

Poet Kalidasa's *Abhijnana Shakuntalam* was translated into German in 1791 by revolutionary Georg Forster and into English by Anglo-Welsh philologist Sir William Jones in 1795.

First modern Indian plays (translations)

Gerasim Lebedev, a Russian adventurer, founded the first European-style proscenium drama theatre in Calcutta, West Bengal, in 1795. He was helped by the local intellectuals. Along with his Bengali tutor, Goloknath Das, he presented the plays *The Disguise* and *Love Is the Best Doctor* on 7 November 1795. These English comedies, translated into Bengali, were the first urban theatrical performances.

Marathon nukkad natak performance

The Mayaar Group of the Bhopal School of Social Sciences in Bhopal, Madhya Pradesh, organized a street-play marathon to celebrate Mahatma Gandhi's

150th birth anniversary. A record was set with a team of 17 members performing 151 street plays from 5:00 a.m. on 3 March 2019 to 3:56 a.m. on 4 March 2019 at different locations in the city. The performance time added up to 22 hours 56 mins, with a break time of 2 hrs 26 mins. The plays conveyed the importance of the Swachh Bharat Mission of the Government of India.

The National School of Drama (NSD), set up by the Sangeet Natak Akademi in **1959**, became autonomous in **1975**.

Oldest children's theatre

Children's Little Theatre, the oldest children's theatre in the country, was founded in Calcutta (now Kolkata), West Bengal, by Samar Chatterjee (1908–86) in May 1951. It included dance, drama, music, and puppetry.

First public theatre hall

The Star Theatre in Calcutta, West Bengal, was inaugurated on 21 July 1883 with the play *Daksha Yajna*. Among the first to produce plays here was the acclaimed playwright, novelist, theatre director, and actor Girish Chandra Ghosh. The theatre shifted to its present site on Bidhan Sarani in 1888 and now mainly functions as a cinema hall with plays also being staged.

First dramatic club

The first dramatic club was the Parsi Natak Mandali established in 1853 in Bombay, Maharashtra. They performed their first play *Roostum Zabooli and Sohrab* that year, followed by *King Afrasiab and Rustom Pehlvan* and *Padshah Faredun*. Other Parsi theatre clubs were the Elphinstone, established in 1860, and the Victoria, established in 1867. These drama clubs inspired Gujarati theatre.

First full-fledged opera

The Fakir of Benares, an Indo-French opera, was staged at the Siri Fort Auditorium, New Delhi, on 27 February 2002. The opera was directed by Muzaffar Ali while his wife Meera Ali designed the costumes.

First and only play on Broadway and West End

The Ramayana by Gopal Sharman, enacted in a one-woman tour de force by Jalabala Vaidya, was played at the Barbizon Plaza Theatre, Manhattan, New York, in February 1975. The play was also performed at other venues, such as the Smithsonian Institution, Washington DC, the United Nations headquarters, New York, USA, and Sedler's Wells Theatre, London, UK.

Play performed in most languages – single day

Yugpurush – Mahatma's Mahatma, a two-hour play based on the relationship between Mahatma Gandhi and his spiritual guide, Shrimad Rajchandra-ji, was performed in five languages, viz., English, Hindi, Bengali, Gujarati, and Tamil, on 11 August 2017. It was organized by the Shrimad Rajchandra Mission in Dharampur, Valsad District, Gujarat, as one of the 808 performances for the 150th birth anniversary celebrations of Shrimad Rajchandra-ji.

Origins of social theatre

The folk theatre form of Bhavai in Gujarat is said to have been introduced in the early 15th century by Asaita Thakar, a brahmin of the Andichya clan. Legend goes that Asaita, after being ostracized for saving a lower-caste girl from dacoits, composed playlets attacking social injustice and the caste system. Bhavai is partly entertainment and partly a ritual offering made to Goddess Amba. It is usually performed in open spaces in front of a temple.

First Marathi musical

Shakuntala was staged as a Sangeet play on 31 October 1880 by Balwant Pandurang 'Annasaheb' Kirloskar and his Kirloskar Natak Mandali. Written in Marathi, it featured simple songs. This format was followed by Marathi stage in the musical drama genre called Sangeet plays. It attracted giants like Bal Gandharva (Narayanrao Rajahansa) and Keshavrao Bhonsle.

First commercial theatre

The first commercial Parsi theatre, started by Pestonji Framji in 1870, was the first aimed at mass entertainment, while dealing with social problems. Though based in Bombay (now Mumbai), Maharashtra, the theatre company travelled widely all over north India.

First opera in English by an Indian

Well-known author Vikram Seth's *Arion and the Dolphin*, which premiered in the UK in June 1994, was the first opera written in English by an Indian. Commissioned by the English National Opera, it was performed at the 964-seat drill shed of HMS *Drake*, a high-security naval base. The opera was directed by Rebecca Meitlis.

Most theatrical performances

The Gujarati stage actor Pransukhlal Nayak (1910–89) had 22,455 theatrical performances to his credit by December 1986. He had played 241 roles in stage productions in a career he started at the age of nine.

Akash Bhadsavle

Most stage plays performed in a day - solo

Akash Bhadsavle (9 February 1996) has performed a total of 12 shows in 3 plays of 45 minutes each on Sunday, 9 October 2022. The plays were performed in Gadkari Rangayatan, Thane in two sessions from 8:00 a.m. to 11:00 p.m. and 11:00 a.m. to 2:30 p.m.; in Dada Kondake Amphi theatre, Thane, from 4:00 p.m. to 7:30 p.m.; and in Mahakavi Kalidas Natya Mandir Mulund from 8:30 p.m. to 11:45 p.m.

Asia's biggest theatre festival

Bharat Rang Mahotsav, the annual theatre festival of the National School of Drama (NSD), is the biggest theatre festival in Asia. Established in 1999, the Bharat Rang Mahotsav includes theatre groups from around the world. The 20th edition of the Bharat Rang Mahotsav concluded in February 2019 and featured 111 national and international acts including folk theatre, plays by groups invited for this, and plays by NSD students.

Most performances as a personality – stage and screen

Deepak Madhukant Antani (b. 20 August 1964) from Ahmedabad, Gujarat, is a professional actor who has performed the most times as Mahatma Gandhi on screen and stage. His maiden venture enacting the role of the Mahatma was on 20 June 2000 in *Sardar Patel*, a play written by him for Sardar Vallabhbhai Patel's 125th birth anniversary celebrations. As a Gandhi lookalike, he has performed in one advertisement, two feature films, 21 short films, one TV serial, 190 stage plays, three documentaries, four voice-overs and a 200-km *padyatra* completed in nine days.

Most performances as a character – (mythological) stage

V.S. Narayanan (b. 20 November 1943) from Mumbai, Maharashtra, has been performing the role of Hanuman for the annual Ramnavami festival held by the Mulund Bhajana Samaj, Mumbai, since 1967. He has performed each year for 53 years.

Longest-serving director of the NSD

Ebrahim Alkazi (1925–2020) was appointed as the second director of the National School of Drama (NSD) in 1962 and served till 1977.

First recipient of the Kalidas Samman (theatre)

Shambhu Mitra (1915–1997) from Kolkata, West Bengal, was the first recipient of the Kalidas Samman for his contribution to Bengali theatre.

VISUAL ARTS

CINEMA

PIONEERS

First film shot in India

Coconut Fair is said to be the first short film shot in India in 1897, and it was made by an unknown foreign photographer. Shortly after, another 'film' made in India, a short dancing scene from the Bengali opera, *The Flower of Persia*, was exhibited at the Star Theatre, Calcutta (now Kolkata), West Bengal, on 9 February 1898.

First films exhibited

The first screening of six short films, by France's famed Lumière Brothers, Louis and Auguste, was held on 7 July 1896. They were: *Entry of Cinematographe*, *Arrival of a Train at la Ciotat Station*, *Sea Bath*, *Workers Leaving the Factory*, *A Demolition*, and *Ladies and Soldiers on Wheels*.

First film shot by an Indian

H.S. Bhatavadekar was the first to import a Riley camera from the UK. He shot two short films – *The Wrestlers*, which featured a wrestling match, and *Man and Monkey*, which was about a juggler training his monkeys – both released in November 1899.

First indigenous feature film

Dadasaheb Phalke's silent feature film *Raja Harishchandra* was released at the Coronation Theatre in Bombay (now Mumbai), Maharashtra, on 3 May 1913. It was a fully Indian venture and was shown along with four imported short films, together making up a 90-minute show. It ran for 23 days and was screened again later at multiple venues.

First talkie

Alam Ara, made in Hindustani language by Ardeshir Irani and released on 14 March 1931 in Bombay, Maharashtra, became India's first talkie feature. The first talkie stars were Master Vithal as hero, Zubeida as heroine, Prithviraj Kapoor in a supporting role and W.M. Khan as a singing fakir. The first music directors were Pirojshah Mistry and B. Irani. It was a costume fantasy with seven songs. The film reel was 3,048 m (10,000 ft) long and it ran for seven weeks.

First female actor of the talkies

After silent performances in 36 movies, Zubeida Begum acted in the first Indian talkie *Alam Ara* (1931).

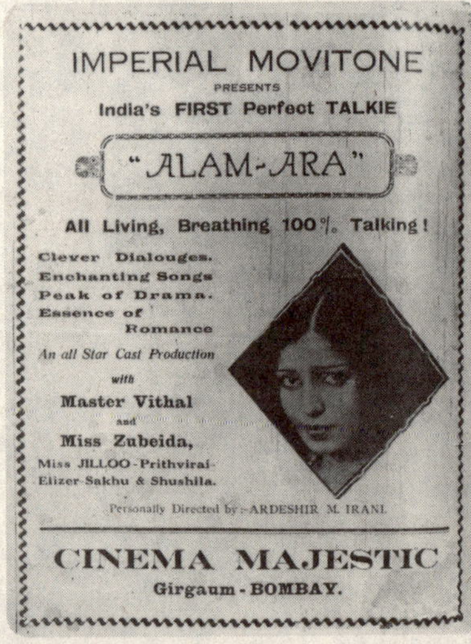

An advertisement for the talkie *Alam Ara*

First advertisement for a film

The first advertisement for a film appeared in *The Times of India*, Bombay, on 7 July 1896. It gave the night's programme for the screening of the six short films by the Lumière Brothers and called it, 'The marvel of the century' and 'The wonder of the world'.

First woman film-maker

Fatma Begum was the first woman to produce, direct, and script a film in the silent era. She formed Fatma Film Corporation and made *Bulbule Paristan* in 1926.

LANGUAGE

First Indian film in English

Ardeshir Irani's *Noor Jahan*, directed by Ezra Mir in 1931, starring Mazhar Khan, Nayampally, Mubarak, and Vimala, was given an English version a year later for foreign markets.

A. Sreekar Prasad: editor of films in most languages/ dialects

Films edited in most languages/dialects

A. Sreekar Prasad (b. 12 March 1963) from Chennai, Tamil Nadu, has edited films in 17 languages/ dialects: English, Hindi, Tamil, Telugu, Malayalam, Kannada, Odia, Assamese, Bengali, Punjabi, Nepali, Marathi, Sinhalese, Karbi, Mishing, Bodo, and Pangchenpa.

First film in multilingual versions

J.B.H. Wadia's *Court Dancer* (*Raj Nartaki*), directed by Madhu Bose and featuring Sadhana Bose and Prithviraj Kapoor, was shot in Hindi, Bengali, and English in 1941.

FIRSTS

First film concern

Royal Bioscope Company was started in 1898 by Hiralal Sen and his brother Motilal. Initially they bought films that were made in England and showcased them in India.

First cinemascope films

- Guru Dutt made *Kaagaz Ke Phool* in 1959 in black-and-white Cinemascope.
- Mahesh Kaul made *Pyar Ki Pyaas* in Cinemascope and colour in 1961.

First film in 70 mm

- The first Indian film in 70 mm (using the blowing-up method) was director Pachhi *Around the World*, starring Raj Kapoor and Rajshri, in 1967. It was in Technicolor and had stereophonic sound.
- G.P. Sippy's multi-starrer blockbuster *Sholay* in 1975 was shot on the 70 mm format in India, along with stereophonic soundtrack, the four channels of which could be connected to amplifiers in cinema theatres. Those not equipped for it

Adipurush and the Tradition of Ramayana Remakes

The Ramayana's moment of rediscovery happened in 1987 when Ramanand Sagar's 78-episode TV show brought alive the epic right into Indian drawing rooms. Cities reported curfew-like traffic situations as the entire country retreated indoors to watch the righteous prince of Ayodhya go into exile and then fight the demon king of Lanka. The TV series is one of India's most abiding cultural moments with abiding shared memories among the entire country's population, including south Indian states with low adoption of Hindi.

Om Raut's *Adipurush* released across India in multiple Indian languages and once again proved the pull of the Ramayana. The opening weekend saw unprecedented rush on the back of the epic story and superstar Prabhas (playing Ram). The screenplay, dialogues, and especially the visual effects (VFX) came in for a lot of criticism, and the film's collection crashed once the word of mouth kicked in. Despite that, the film made nearly ₹400 crore worldwide and was one of the highest-grossing films of 2023. (Thanks to the film's massive budget, it is also one of the biggest flops of Indian cinema.)

Some of the notable adaptations of the Ramayana for the Indian screen:

Film	Context
Lanka Dahan (1917) Dir. Dadasaheb Phalke	Phalke's second* feature film starred Anna Salunke as both Ram and Sita, thus making it Indian cinema's first double role. The film was a box-office hit and a cultural phenomenon, with people taking off their shoes and standing up to worship whenever Ram appeared on screen.
Bharat Milap (1942) and *Ram Rajya* (1943) Dir. Vijay Bhatt	Both films were commercially successful and managed to draw a lot of attention through political leaders watching them. *Ram Rajya* is said to be the only full-length film Mahatma Gandhi watched (in a special screening organized for him in Bombay).
Sampoorna Ramayana (1958, Tamil) Dir. K. Somu	Starring N.T. Rama Rao (future chief minister of Andhra Pradesh) as Ram and Sivaji Ganesan (future Tamil superstar) as Bharat, the film not only became a massive success, but also ushered in a long term trend of mythological films in Tamil cinema.
Lava Kusa (1963, Telugu and Tamil) Dir. C.S. Rao, C. Pullayya	The first full-length colour film of Telugu cinema, it was simultaneously shot in Tamil as well. N.T. Rama Rao again played Ram (a role he kept returning to); and the film is considered to be one of the classics of Telugu cinema, which was dubbed and remade several times.
Sita Kalyanama (1976, Telugu) Dir. Bapu	Jaya Prada, who went on to become a star in Telugu, Tamil, and Hindi cinema, played Sita around whose marriage to Ram the film was based. It was dubbed in Hindi and Malayalam as well.
Ramayana: The Legend of Prince Ram (1992, Japanese) Dir. Yugo Sako	After the massive popularity of *Ramayan* on television, this anime version was proposed as an Indo-Japanese co-production to take the story global. The film was dubbed in English and Hindi as well (with Arun Govil providing the voice-over for Ram), and the film ran for many years on Cartoon Network.
Raavan (2010, Tamil and Hindi) Dir. Mani Ratnam	Master director Mani Ratnam reimagined the epic tale into a modern setting with Ram being a righteous police officer in search of a Naxal leader who has kidnapped his wife. Leading stars played the main roles in the very unusual retelling of the epic, which also questioned Ram's moral choices for the greater good.

*Phalke's first film – *Raja Harishchandra* – was based on Ram's ancestor, a scion of Raghukul and ruler of Ayodhya. The same story was remade as *Ayodhyecha Raja* by V. Shantaram in 1932, as a bilingual film in Hindi and Marathi. Since the earliest talkie's (*Alam Ara*) print was lost in a fire, *Ayodhyecha Raja* is the earliest talkie of which a print is still available.
As a footnote to highlight the Ramayana's enduring popularity (if made in an acceptable style), it might be worthwhile to mention the re-release of the 1987 *Ramayan* in March and April 2020, at the peak of the Covid lockdown. It promptly became the most-watched television show in India and one of the most-watched in the world.

were provided flat (35 mm) single-track prints.

• Tarachand Barjatya's *Maine Pyar Kiya* (1989) was made in Cinemascope with a new system of four-track magnetic stereophonic sound. This could be fitted in theatres. Later, mobile equipment was provided for the stereophonic effect in small towns and touring cinemas.

First film serial

Ram Vanvas (The Exile of Rama) was made by Patankar Friends and Company, and released on 14 September 1918. It was shown in four parts, each running for a period of a few weeks.

WR First one-actor, one-set film

Sunil Dutt made *Yaadein* in 1964, the first experiment of its kind in the world with only one actor (himself) emoting on only one set. In 2005, Kannada film *Shanthi* became the second movie with a single actor to be released.

First adult film

Social Evil, a docudrama, was made by the Social Purity League of Bombay, Maharashtra, in 1929 to provide information about sex problems. It was also the first sex educational film. It was shown free of cost and was the first film given the label 'For Adults Only'.

First cinema hall

Elphinstone Picture Palace was started by J.F. Madan in Calcutta, West Bengal, in 1905. It was first renamed the Minerva Theatre and then later called Chaplin Cinema. This piece of history was demolished in 2013 by the Kolkata Municipal Corporation (which owned it).

First use of surround sound

Khuda Gawah (1992), when screened in big cities, used stereophonic four-track sound with special gadgets fitted into theatre walls and ceilings. This gave the impression of sound surrounding the audience, to give more impact to scenes of fights, horse riding, and the Afghan game of *buzkashi*, among others.

First animated film

Directed by R.C. Boral, *On a Moonlit Night* (1934) was the first Indian animated film with a soundtrack.

First 3D film

My Dear Kuttichathan (1984), produced by M.C. Punoos and directed by his son, Jijo, was the first Indian 3D. It was a Malayalam-language film.

WR Longest-running film

Yash Raj Films' *Dilwale Dulhania Le Jayenge* (*DDLJ*) is still running at Mumbai's Maratha Mandir theatre – twenty-eight years after the film premiered there. The single show at 11:30 a.m. is the result of an arrangement between Yash Raj and the theatre, which agreed to run the film there for (what seems like) eternity. But even before the arrangement, *DDLJ* ran to semi-packed houses for over two decades, making it the longest-running film in the world.

First studio

Khan Bahadur Ardeshir Irani (1886–1969) started his first studio – Star Films – in 1920.

First censor boards

- The first film censor boards were set up in Bombay, Calcutta, and Madras (now Chennai) in 1920.
- Film censorship was centralized under a central board, the Central Board of Film Certification (CBFC) in Bombay, Maharashtra, in 1951.

The Elephant Whisperers and its resounding success

When director Kartiki Gonsalves and producer Guneet Monga collected their Academy Award trophies for the Best Documentary (short subject), they became the first Indian film-makers to win a competitive Oscar. The heart-warming tale of Bomman and Belli, the caretaker couple of an orphaned elephant in Mudumalai National Park, was nearly five years in the making.

The 2023 Oscars were a particularly fruitful year for Indians, as Shaunak Sen's *All That Breathes* was also a nominee in the Best Documentary Feature category and a near-favourite after a stellar run at top film festivals like Sundance, Cannes, London, and Hong Kong.

In 2022, India was represented by *Writing With Fire* (directed by Sushmit Ghosh and Rintu Thomas), a film about Dalit women journalists running a newspaper called *Khabar Lahariya*.

The Elephant Whisperers' win is the happy ending of India's tryst with the Short Documentary Oscar, which started in 1978. Director Vidhu Vinod Chopra's *An Encounter With Faces* – about children in an orphanage – was the first Indian film to be nominated in a competitive category at the Academy Awards. The first-time director took frantic help from all quarters to be present at the ceremony, though unfortunately, he didn't win.

Four decades on, it is time to script a winning story.

First box-office hit

Dadasaheb Phalke's *Lanka Dahan* (1917), which ran for 23 weeks, was India's first box-office hit. It is on record that the money collected at the ticket counters had to be transported in bullock carts protected by armed guards!

In 2023–24, the Central Board for Film Certification (CBFC) issued 16,203 certifications.

INTERNATIONAL

First Academy Award for Best Documentary (short subject)

The Elephant Whisperers, directed by Kartiki Gonsalves was awarded the Best Documentary (short subject) award at the 95th Academy Awards held on 13 March 2023 in Los Angeles, US.

First Academy Award

Bhanu Athaiya (1929–2020) became the first Indian to win an Academy Award (Oscar) in 1983, for designing the costumes for the acclaimed film *Gandhi* (1982), directed by Sir Richard Attenborough.

First Indian winner of the Legion d'Honneur

Satyajit Ray is the only Indian film personality to be awarded the Commandeur level of France's highest civilian award, the Legion d'Honneur on 2 February 1989 – one of only two film-makers in the world to have received it. He is also the only Indian film-maker to receive the Magsaysay Award.

First to act in a Hollywood film

The first Indian actor to feature in a role that was credited in a Hollywood movie was Dastagir, who was also known as 'Sabu' in the film world. He hailed from the princely state of Mysore (now Mysuru), Karnataka. He acted in Robert Flaherty's film *Elephant Boy* (1937). His other films included *The Thief of Baghdad* (1940) and *Jungle Book* (1942).

Dastagir 'Sabu'

First foreign film award

The film *Seeta* (1934) by East India Films Co., Calcutta, West Bengal, which was directed by Debaki Bose, was the first film from India to win the gold medal at the Third International Exhibition of Cinematographic Art in Venice, Italy, in 1935.

PERFORMANCE

Maximum roles in a single film

- Harish Raj enacted 16 roles in the Kannada film *Shri Sathyanarayana*, which released on 11 March 2016. He essayed the role of the lead character named Sathyanarayana as well as 15 other cameo roles with screen time ranging from one to five minutes for each.

- Priyanka Chopra played 12 roles (one for each sign of the zodiac) in Ashutosh Gowariker's *What's Your Raashee?* (2009).
- Kamal Haasan played 10 different roles in K.S. Ravikumar's *Dasavathaaram* (2008), including one as former US president George W. Bush.

Akshay Kumar

Highest-earning actor

Forbes magazine placed Akshay Kumar sixth on its list of the 'World's Highest- Paid Actors of 2020', with estimated earnings of US $48.5 million (₹356.97 crore), making him the country's highest-earning actor. His earnings include remuneration for films (ranging from US $5 to 10 million – around ₹35.58 to 71.17 crore), endorsement deals, and appearance fees.

First woman stunt actor

Nadia, India's legendary woman stunt actor, has been described as 'Zorro, Tarzan and John Wayne rolled into one'. Born Mary Evans, she swung from chandeliers, jumped from moving trains and performed many other incredible stunts that earned her the title of 'Fearless Nadia'. Her best-known film is the 1935 hit, *Hunterwali*.

Most films as a lead

Prem Nazir, born as Abdul Kadar in Chirayinkeezhu, Kerala, played the lead role in as many as 600 films. He starred in Malayalam, Tamil, Kannada, and Telugu films, and co-starred in films with at least 85 female actors.

WR Roles in the most numbers of films

- *Women*: Manorama, a popular Tamil heroine of the 1950s and '60s, who later became a character actor, acted in over 1,000 films. Her first film was *Malayitta Mangai* (1958). Her real name was Gopishantha. She received the Padma Shri in 2002.
- *Men*: Brahmanandam Kanneganti, a well-known comedian of Telugu cinema, has received credits for acting in 1,178 films. He achieved this feat over an acting career of more than 30 years and he is still going strong. He received the Padma Shri in 2009.

WR Most pairings

Actors Prem Nazir and Sheila paired together in 107 films and hold a world record for the highest number of movies done together. They did 92 films more than the Hollywood husband–wife pair of Charles Bronson and Jill Ireland, who starred together in 15 films.

Oldest debut actor in a film

Ninety-three-year-old Chinnakrishnan Kaliyaperumal from Ariyalur, Tamil Nadu, acted as the lead in the Tamil short (20-minute) film, *93* Not Out* (2016),

India @ Cannes

Cannes Film Festival is held annually in Cannes, France to celebrate and showcase new films across genres and from around the globe.

Chetan Anand's *Neecha Nagar* (an adaptation of Maxim Gorky's *The Lower Depths*) was one of the joint winners of Grand Prix du Festival International du Film in 1946 – along with legends of cinema like David Lean, Billy Wilder, and Roberto Rossellini – which was also the first year of the festival.

After that, Bimal Roy's *Do Bigha Zamin*, child artiste Baby Naaz (for *Boot Polish*), and Rajbans Khanna for (short film) *Gotoma the Buddha* won prizes or special mentions at the festival.

Satyajit Ray won the special jury prize – Best Human Document – for *Pather Panchali* (in 1956) and went on to become India's best-known director globally.

The presence at Cannes was surprisingly muted in the subsequent decades, and it was only in the 1980s that an Indian film won at the festival. Veteran film-maker Mrinal Sen won a special jury prize for *Kharij* (1983). Mira Nair's *Salaam Bombay* (1988) won the Camera d'Or – a special prize for first feature films – and Shaji N. Karun's *Piravi* won a special mention in the same category that year.

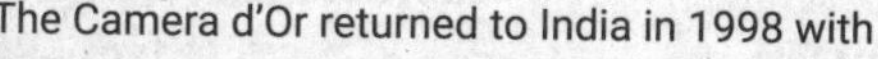

The Camera d'Or returned to India in 1998 with Murali Nair's *Marana Simhasana*.

Starting with the new millenium, the Indian entries expanded to a wider range of categories and wins. Un Certain Regard (for films outside of the main competition) has been a happy hunting ground for Indian films for the last two decades with many promising films making their appearance there and some of them winning.

Awards won @Cannes

2002	2006	2013	2015	2021	2022
Manish Jha's *A Very Very Silent Film*	Gitanjali Rao's *Printed Rainbow*	Ritesh Batra's *The Lunchbox*	Neeraj Ghaywan's *Masaan*	Payal Kapadia's *A Night of Knowing Nothing*	Shaunak Sen's *All That Breathes*
Jury Prize for Short Film	Grand Rail d'Or Audience Award Kodak Discovery Award Young Critics Award for Best Short Film	Grand Rail d'Or Audience Award	FIPRESCI Award for Un Certain Regard Prix Avenir prometteur (Most promising future) Award	Golden Eye*	Golden Eye

* Golden Eye (L'Oeil d'Or) is the prize given to the best documentary and has been won by two Indians since it was instituted in 2015.

directed by engineer-turned-film-maker Arudra Saravanakumar. It is the story of an old man who, after a pacemaker implant, has the desire to ride a cycle and to buy a book, and how he finally achieves it at the age of ninety-three. The film has won several awards, besides a jury mention at the Dadasaheb Phalke film festival 2017, and has been showcased at national and international film festivals.

LENGTH

Most episodic films in a single feature film

BSB Films, a film-making company from Jaipur, Rajasthan, made a Hindi-language film, titled *Prabhu Mahaveer Ki Divyavani,* under their banner. The film features 23 episodic films as part of it, the highest in a single feature film. The film has a total duration of 157 mins and 27 secs and was released on 30 September 2021.

Poster of *Mera Naam Joker*: one of the films with longest footage

Films with longest footage

- Vithalbhai Jhaveri's documentary on Mahatma Gandhi, *Mahatma: Life of Gandhi, 1869–1948* (1968), was 5 hrs 30 mins long, and was broken up into many segments for general screening.
- Gemini's *Chandralekha* in 1948, the first big Hindi film from south India, ran for over 3 hrs.
- R.K. Films' productions *Sangam* (1964) and *Mera Naam Joker* (1970) were the first to be run with two intervals.

WR Shortest film**

KVV Studioz produced the shortest film, *Uyiri–Bio War* (2023), with a run time of four seconds. There are additional two seconds that cover the CBFC certificate bringing the total duration to six seconds. The film is written, directed, and produced by M. Karthikbalan.

MUSIC

Most songs recorded in a day

In 1993, playback singer Kumar Sanu recorded 28 songs in a single day at the Musicians Studio in the Juhu area in Mumbai, Maharashtra. The session was made for Sterling Records and Cassettes and the chief recordist was Vishram More, who was on the machines for 24 hours.

WR Most number of songs in a Hindi film

Madan Theatre's film *Indra Sabha*, made in 1932, featured 71 songs. Based on an Urdu play and opera written by Agha Hasan Amanat and first staged in 1853, the 211-minute-long film was made by Jamshedji Framji Madan's company, Madan Theatre.

WR Most prolific lyricist

Shitala Pande, better known as Sameer 'Anjaan', holds the world record for

**This category has been discontinued. Further and future claims for this category will not be accepted.

writing lyrics for the most number of songs. Starting in 1983 with the Hindi film *Bekhabar*, he had written lyrics for 3,524 songs for Hindi and Bhojpuri films by 15 December 2015. He has also written lyrics for music albums. He has done the highest number of films (146) with the music director duo Anand–Milind, writing around 899 songs for them.

MAKERS

Most film-making aspects handled

Narasimha Raju (b. 4 March 1955) from Bengaluru, Karnataka, handled 18 segments of film-making for the Kannada film *The Fire* (2017). He was credited for direction, story, screenplay, dialogues, fight, stunt, direction of cinematography, editing, special effects, grading, Digital intermediate (DI), sound, dubbing, voice dubbing, Background music (BGM) placing, re-recording, poster design, and acting in the film. The 113-minute film participated in the 10th Bengaluru International Film Festival in March 2018.

WR Tallest film cut-out

The world's tallest cut-out – 65.5 m (215 ft) high – advertised a film in Thiruttani town, Tiruvallur District, Tamil Nadu. It featured actor Suriya (in a folded *veshti*, holding a flaming torch) to promote his film *Nandha Gopalan Kumaran (NGK)* in 2019.

Most expensive film produced

Directed by Om Raut, *Adipurush* (2023), starring Prabhas, Kriti Sanon and Saif Ali Khan in leading roles, was made on an estimated budget of ₹700 crore (7 billion). It was made in Hindi and Telugu, along with dubbed versions in Tamil, Kannada, and Malayalam.

WR Largest film poster

Global United Media Co. Ltd, in collaboration with Impresario Event Management (I) Ltd, unveiled a 75.28 m (247 ft) long and 63.39 m (208 ft) wide poster of *Baahubali,* to mark the launch of the film's Malayalam audio, at the Sacred Heart College football field in Thevara, Kochi, Kerala, on 27 June 2015. The poster, designed by the director of the movie, S.S. Rajamouli, and made by Sign Maker Digital Solution at Vyttila, Kochi, took 30 hrs to print.

The Dada Saheb Phalke Award has been awarded to 52 individuals so far.

Most tickets booked in advance

BookMyShow, a ticket-booking app, saw a record sale of advance tickets when it sold over a million tickets online in a day. The tickets for Marvel's *Avengers: Endgame* were booked in a manic frenzy as soon as they were available on 22 April 2019. The sale averaged about 18 tickets per second!

Most films produced

Well-known director and producer of Telugu films, Dr D. Ramanaidu holds the record of having produced 110 films (including 11 dubbed films) in six languages over a span of 36 years. He started his career with *Anuragam* in 1963.

WR Largest film city/studio

Ramoji Film City in Hyderabad, Telangana, spread over a little more than 1,666 acres (674 hectares), is the largest film city/studio in the world. It has sound stages and permanent sets ranging from railway stations and temples to gardens and residential streets, among others. It is also a tourist attraction because of its unique cinema-like experience.

Ramoji Film City

Telugu movie mogul, Ramoji Rao, conceived this 'city' in 1996 as a one-stop shop for all sorts of filming requirements. Designed and executed by award-winning art director, Nitish Roy, it has gone on to become a place of wonder.

Ramoji Film City's land is spread over jungles and mountains, has water-bodies running through it, and the facilities were built using them to provide natural locations in addition to studios and pretty much every artificial set that could ever be required in an Indian film. A railway station (with an engine and two coaches), an airport, a jail, a temple (where the God is changed as per the script), streets, gardens, restaurants, apartments, palaces, caves, towns, villages, and every recognizable location in Indian films are within the precincts of Ramoji Film City, the world's largest film studio and complex.

It was also turned into an amusement park, with hordes of tourists going around buses and vintage cars matching their memories with movie locations. Since the pan-India success of the *Baahubali* franchise, their sets have been left untouched and is a major attraction at the Film City.

India is the largest film-producing country in the world but not a major consumer market due to lower per capita incomes. This is also the reason why movie merchandise and tourism are still relatively nascent here. It is changing in recent times and places like Ramoji Film City are bringing about that change.

Most feature films directed

Dr Dasari Narayana Rao (1947–2017) has directed 148 films and among women, Vijaya Nirmala has directed 35 films in Telugu and Tamil.

Most horror films produced

The seven Ramsay brothers – Kumar, Keshu, Tulsi, Kiran, Shyam, Gangu, and Arjun - made more than 30 horror films on low budgets, of which the well-known ones are *Purana Mandir* (1984), *Veerana* (1988), and *Purani Haveli* (1989).

Poster of *RRR*: film released on highest number of screens

Highest number of screens

RRR – a period drama about two legendary revolutionaries and their journeys – directed by S.S. Rajamouli, was released worldwide on over 10,200 screens.

RRR and 'Naatu Naatu'

RRR was a sensation in the US, well before Oscar season. The turbo-charged, VFX-plastered film about two heroes of India's freedom struggle made director S.S. Rajamouli a cult figure, and there were calls to nominate *RRR* in the Best Film category (no, not the Best Foreign Film one). That didn't go past, but the music-action-emotion-driven extravaganza had found more than a niche audience in the US. Rajamouli's earlier films were rediscovered and a Hollywood film for him could materialize sooner than later.

However, *RRR*'s symbolic representation at the Oscars was for the set piece in the movie that India is now inalienably associated with – the song-and-dance number. It was the first song from an Indian-language film to be nominated in the Best Song category, and the audience erupted in whoops and cheers when it was performed on stage during the ceremony. And almost predictably, composer M.M. Keeravani and lyricist Chandrabose won, beating global superstars like Lady Gaga, Rihanna, and the like. Choreographer Prem Rakshith – while not part of the song's Oscar credits – deserves a lot of the credit for the impossibly energetic dancing that was also a large part of its charm.

RRR was the first Indian film to be nominated for Best Song, but Indians have made it before. A.R. Rahman and Gulzar were the first winners of Best Song for their *Jai Ho*, created for Danny Boyle's *Slumdog Millionaire*. And while at it, *RRR* also won the Best Score!

PHOTOGRAPHY

Earliest commercial studio

Bourne and Shepherd was well known for its studio portraits of the ruling classes, both Indian and British. Its photographers attended royal events, state visits and the imperial durbars of 1877, 1903, and 1911. After Independence, Bourne and Shepherd was bought over by Indian proprietors, who operated under the same name in Calcutta. The studio was closed down on 20 April 2016 after 176 years of operations.

First commercial photographer

Lala Deen Dayal of Hyderabad, the 'photographer of kings', is India's best-known photographer from the British times. His career began in the mid-1870s, and he went on to set up studios in three cities in three different states – Indore, Bombay, Maharashtra, and Hyderabad (now in Telangana). He was appointed as the photographer to the viceroy of India in 1885. His lens captured India's rich culture, architecture and landscapes.

Earliest recorded commercial album

A gilded and bound album of a hundred photographs of Indian buildings, scenery, races, costumes, and bazaar incidents was sold for ₹12 in Bombay in 1884. It used to be a popular souvenir among the British.

First photo exhibition

The first All-India Photographic Exhibition was organized by the Photographic Society of India in Bombay, in 1856. The exhibition was inaugurated by the then Governor General of India, Lord Canning.

First use of the daguerreotype

Within a year of its first use in England, the daguerreotype (early photography process using an iodine-sensitized silvered plate and mercury vapour) was used in Calcutta, in January 1840. They were brought to document India's architecture and landscape.

Earliest book on photography

Pagoda Hallibee written by R.B. Gakley in 1859 was the first book on photography published in India.

First woman photojournalist

Homai Vyarawalla (1913–2012), born into a priestly family in Navsari, Gujarat, in December 1913, was the first Indian woman photojournalist to document Indian life. Her very first photographs were published in *Bombay Chronicle* in 1936. She and her husband even covered wartime activities for *The Illustrated Weekly of India* and the *Far Eastern Bureau* of the British Information Service. *Life* and *Time* magazines also featured her photographs of the Indian independence movement.

Homai Vyarawalla

WR Largest camera museum

Museo Camera Museum

The Museo Camera Centre for the Photographic Arts, Gurugram, Haryana, houses more than 2,500 cameras, which is the world's largest collection of vintage and other cameras on display. Inaugurated on 27 September 2019, it is spread over 1,672.2 sq. m (18,000 sq. ft) of built-up space and can accommodate up to 200 visitors at a time. It is a collaboration between acclaimed photographer Aditya Arya and the Municipal Corporation of Gurugram.

First Kodak Express outlet

Established in 1978, Skylab was the first colour lab in suburban Bombay, Maharashtra. Initially the lab catered to advertising agencies, but gradually the focus shifted to providing a photo colour lab and studio for amateurs and ordinary people.

First personal studio

Maharaja Sawai Man Singh of Jaipur, Rajasthan, was a 19th century amateur photographer. Thousands of photographic plates of his work were discovered in the 1980s in the storerooms of the City Palace in Jaipur. He recorded the life of the people in his state.

First photo film-manufacturing company

Hindustan Photo Films Manufacturing Co. (HPF), a public sector unit, was set up in 1960 at Ooty (now Udhagamandalam), Tamil Nadu, to make photosensitive materials for the Indian film industry, still photography, and X-ray films for medical and industrial use. It introduced the Indu brand of raw film.

Oldest extant portrait studio

Sir Victor Sassoon, who was passionate about photography and constructed many public buildings in Bombay, set up Hamilton Studios in the E.D. Sassoon Building, which he owned, in 1928. Photography sessions at these studios were held by appointment, and the rich and famous personalities of Bombay were seen coming for quick and glamorous shoots. Currently, the studios are run by Ajita Madhavji and can be found in Ballard Estate.

First course in photography

The first photography course began in Elphinstone College, Bombay, in 1855. The J.J. School of Art, Bombay, and the Madras School of Art, Madras, Tamil Nadu, began similar courses around the same time.

First photographic society

The Bombay Photographic Society was founded in October 1854 with British captain Harry J. Barr as its first president. It had more than 200 people as members, many of them Indian. Divisions in Madras and Bengal followed in 1856.

Largest unit for photo production/distribution

The Photo Division, Press Information Bureau, under the Ministry of Information and Broadcasting, Government of India, provides photographs to media units, and Central and state government departments. In the year 2020–21, it acquired 51,929 digital images in-house and supplied 376 digital prints.

WR Largest collection of cameras

Dilish Parekh, a photojournalist from Mumbai, Maharashtra, has a collection of 4,425 cameras, some dating back to 1906. It includes brands such as Leica, Nikon, Kodak, Canon, Hasselblad, and Royal Mail Postage, and types such as watch, binocular, and button cameras. He began the collection in 1977 with 600 cameras given to him by his grandfather.

Most people in a selfie

During Ragam, the annual cultural festival at the National Institute of Technology Calicut (NITC) in Kozhikode, Kerala, actor Sreenath Bhasi clicked a selfie with a camera mounted on a selfie stick at the open air theatre on the campus, with 2,151 students on 26 March 2015.

Selfie with the most people

Marathon photography – models

Photographer Vivek Ashok Somani (b. 7 August 1995) from Surat, Gujarat, conducted a marathon photo shoot on 12 May 2019. He clicked 11,076 photographs in 15 hrs 55 mins. Using a Nikon D5300 camera, and a 18–55 mm lens, he photographed 70 models at Future Dance Studio, Surat.

Marathon photography – city/structures

Hariohm N. Gurjar from Vadodara, Gujarat, set out to document his city's various dimensions at 7:00 a.m. on 14 March 2014. He travelled 95 km in the city, shooting for 13 hrs. He captured 3,555 unduplicated images of people, architecture, markets, monuments, and more.

AWARDS AND HONOURS

First to receive the Hasselblad Award

Dayanita Singh from New Delhi became the first Indian and the first South Asian laureate to receive the Hasselblad Award. She was handed the award on 14 October 2022 in a ceremony held in Gothenburg, Sweden. She won two million Swedish krona, becoming the first to receive the prize since it was upgraded. Awarded annually since 1982, the Hasselblad Award is considered to be one of the most prestigious awards in photography worldwide. Dayanita received commendation for her 'mobile museums' (she uses objects that allow for the artwork to be constantly arranged and rearranged) in the official citation for the award.

Sir Prodyot Coomar Tagore

First Indian fellow of the British Photographic Society

Sir Prodyot Coomar Tagore (1873–1942), a prominent landowner of the time in Calcutta, West Bengal, was an art collector besides being a keen photographer. He was the first Indian to be elected a Fellow of the British Photographic Society in 1896. He had a studio in his Tagore Castle home and exhibited his works. He was the founder and first president of the Academy of Fine Arts, Calcutta.

First Asian to win the International Photography Awards

Sharad Haksar from Chennai, Tamil Nadu, won one gold, one silver, two bronzes and 21 nominations in the International Photography Awards 2004. India finished fourth behind the US, the UK, and Canada.

First winner of the Wildlife Photographer of the Year title

The Wildlife Photographer of the Year, organized by the Natural History Museum, London, UK, is one of the most famed contests in the world. Rajesh Bedi became the first Indian to win the grand title in 1986 for his photograph of the Asiatic black bear.

First winners of the Pulitzer Prize for feature photography

- Anushree Fadnavis and Adnan Abidi were part of the Reuters team that won in the 'Breaking News Photography' category of the Pulitzer Prize for photography in 2020, for their work on the Hong Kong protests.
- Dar Yasin, Mukhtar Khan, and Channi Anand from Associated Press won in the 'Feature Photography' category of the Pulitzer Prize for photography in 2020 for their coverage of Jammu and Kashmir.

WR First winner of the Académie des Beaux-Arts Photography Award – William Klein

Raghu Rai won the first-ever Académie des Beaux-Arts Photography Award – William Klein (Fine Arts Academy award for Photography). He was named the laureate and was awarded the prize at the Palais de l'Institut de France on 30 October 2019. The award carries a prize money of 120,000 euros (approximately ₹10.79 crore). It was instated in honour of William Klein, a celebrated US-born French photographer and film-maker.

National Photography Awards 2023

The Eighth National Photography Awards were conferred on 7 March 2023. Here is a list of the winners:

Category	Recipient
Lifetime Achievement Award	Sipra Das
Professional Photographer of the Year	Sasi Kumar Ramachandran
Special Mention in professional category	Dipjyoti Banik, Manish Kumar Chauhan, R.S. Gopakumar, Sudipto Das, Umesh Harishchandra Nikam
Amateur Photographer of the Year	Arun Saha
Special Mention in the amateur category	C.S. Sreeranj, Mohit Wadhawan, Subhadip Bose, Tharun Aduragatla, Ravishankar S.L.

WR First permanent photo exhibition in space

Dr Hersh Chadha (b. 27 November 1957) is the first person to organize a permanent photo exhibition in space on the International Space Station (ISS). Five images of different flowers were sent to the ISS on 16 October 2016 with the ISS 49/50 team. The purpose of this was to help the astronauts staying in space for months to remain connected with nature. On 1 March 2017, Dr Chadha was honoured by the Yuri Gagarin Cosmonaut Training Centre, Russia, for this.

PAINTING AND CRAFT

FIRSTS

Earliest paintings discovered

Painted pottery, mostly in fragments, excavated at Mohenjo-Daro, Chanhu-daro, Harappa, and other places in the Indus Valley, are dated to 3000–2250 BCE.

Earliest use of tempera method

The Ajanta Caves are rock-cut Buddhist cave monuments in Aurangabad, Maharashtra, dating back from the 2nd century BCE to about 650 CE. The paintings in these caves used the tempera method. In this technique the rough mud plaster containing some organic matter like cow dung and animal hair was first pressed on the surface of the rocks and then a coat of fine lime plaster was laid all over it. This layer was allowed to dry thoroughly before applying colour on it. The scenes represented in these caves are mostly from Buddhist texts and events from the Buddha's life.

Oldest extant murals

Two 1,000-year-old Chola paintings, which were found at the Brihadeeswarar Temple in Thanjavur, Tamil Nadu, are believed to be the oldest existing mural paintings. They depict two women who are watching a procession from a balcony.

First Mughal illuminated manuscript

Emperor Humayun engaged Mir Sayyid Ali and a group of painters to paint the '*Dastan-i-Amir*' (the story of Amir Hamza), which featured as many as 1,375 miniatures painted on cotton cloth in the Persian Safavid style. The work on the manuscript was underway in the 1560s.

First painting gallery

Maharaja Ram Singh, a 19th century king of Jaipur, built a unique hall in the garden of the Ram Niwas Bagh Palace. It was fully displayed with paintings and called the Ram Vilas. The walls of this hall were covered with imitations of several Greek, Roman, Persian, and Chinese paintings.

First auction of contemporary Indian paintings abroad

Sotheby's hosted the first-ever auction of contemporary Indian paintings in New York, US, on 12 June 1995. The 38 artists whose works were displayed included Jogen Chowdhury, M.F. Husain, Arpita Singh, Ganesh Pyne, S.H. Raza, and Jamini Roy.

First modern art school

The Mechanical Institute was founded by Frederik Corbyn and Tarapada Chakrabarty in Calcutta, West Bengal, on 2 February 1839. First named 'Society for the Promotion of Industrial Art', it was finally called the School of Industrial Art on 16 August 1854. It held its first exhibition from 22 January to 3 February 1855.

First fine arts exhibition

The first fine arts exhibition was held in the Public Library, Calcutta, on 1 February 1831, by the Brush Club, with paintings drawn by foreign artists in India.

First art summit

The first India Art Summit was held at Pragati Maidan, New Delhi, on 22–24 August 2008. The 34 exhibition galleries exhibited over 550 artworks and sold more than half of them. The summit was brought to India by Hanmer MS&L Communications Pvt. Ltd.

Earliest rock paintings

The largest and the oldest collection of rock paintings in India is at Bhimbetka, about 46 km from Bhopal, Madhya Pradesh. The paintings, found in more than 700 rock shelters dated to around 30,000 years ago, depict people's everyday lives such as hunting, dancing, and decoration of bodies.

Rock paintings at Bhimbetka

First realist painter

Raja Ravi Varma (1848–1906) from the princely state of Travancore (now in Kerala) painted themes mainly from Indian mythology and legends in the realistic style of the West, making him the first realist painter in the country and the pioneer of a new movement in Indian art. In 1904, the then viceroy Lord Curzon bestowed the Kaisar-i-Hind Gold Medal on him.

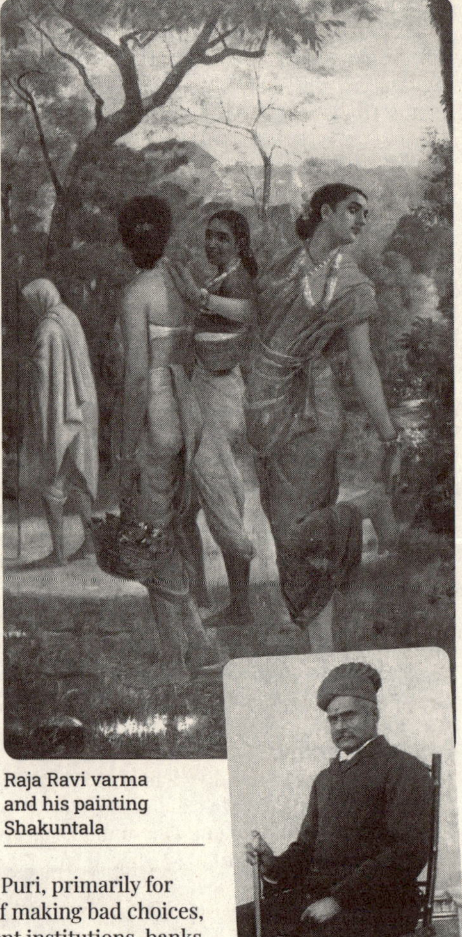

Raja Ravi varma and his painting Shakuntala

First academy for visual arts

The Lalit Kala Akademi, which was established in Delhi in 1954, started its work by organizing national exhibitions of contemporary Indian art. It also gives awards and honours and conducts Triennale-India (a global art show) and a Rashtriya Kala Mela (national art fair), where artists from across the country come together to present their work.

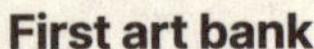

First art bank

The Art Bank, set up in 2007 and started by curator Adishwar Puri, primarily for novice collectors apprehensive of making bad choices, now has corporations, government institutions, banks, and hospitals as clients. The artists who register benefit by receiving 50 per cent of the rental value of the work.

First officially recognized female graffiti artist

Kajal Singh from New Delhi, who goes by the moniker 'Dizy', is the first recognized female graffiti artist from India. Her art form includes the use of bright colours and different font styles that instantly pop out. Besides India, she has left her signature in countries like Germany, China, the US, Russia, and Indonesia. She was part of the Indo-German Hip-Hop Urban Art Project (2012), Each One Teach One (2013), 25 Years of the Berlin Wall (2014), Hip-Hop Cultural Exchange (2015), and On The Run Exhibition (2016). She was honoured as the 'First Lady' of graffiti in India by the Ministry of Women and Child Development, Government of India on 20 January 2018.

First cartoon gallery

The Indian Institute of Cartoonists opened its 186 sq. m (2,000 sq. ft) gallery, the Indian Cartoon Gallery, at Midford House, Bangalore (now Bengaluru), Karnataka, on 16 August 2007. It has a seminar hall, a library and a cartoon bibliography from across the world.

GENERAL

Highest price at an auction for a work of Indian art

Vasudeo S. Gaitonde (1924–2001) was regarded as India's leading abstract painter. On 11 March 2021, a 1961 untitled painting by him was auctioned at the Saffronart Spring Live Auction for ₹39.98 crore (US $5.5 million) – a new record for the highest price achieved for a work of Indian art in an auction worldwide. It broke the painter's earlier record from 2020, when another of his untitled oil-on-canvas made in 1974 was sold for ₹36.8 crore at an auction by Pundole's.

Most National Awards won in a family

Nine members of the Jangid family have won the Master Craftsman Award, the national award for artisans and craft people between 1971 and 2017. Mal Chand Jangid, Richotmal Jangid, Vinod Kumar Jangid, Mahesh Chand Jangid, Sitaram Jangid, Kamlesh Jangid, Pawan Kumar Jangid, Navatmal Jangid, and Om Prakash Jangid won these awards.

LARGEST, SMALLEST, AND MARATHON ARTWORK

Largest collage – group

Forty-four students and three teachers from Christ University, Bengaluru, Karnataka, created the largest collage on 2 March 2018. The collage, which measured 85.34 m x 9.14 m (280 ft x 30 ft), was made in 2 hrs 12 mins.

Largest Zentangle Art

Twenty-five students from the NIFT-TEA (Tiruppur Exporters Association) College of Knitwear Fashion, Tiruppur, Tamil Nadu, created the largest Zentangle artwork measuring 185.8 sq. m (2,000 sq. ft), with 'Make in India' as its theme. The students completed the artwork in 34 hrs on 17–18 August 2018.

Largest drawing – pencils – solo

Megha Harsha (b. 12 July 1992) from Bikaner, Rajasthan, created the largest pencil drawing by an individual. The artwork measured 455.21 sq. m (4,900 sq. ft) and was completed in 86 hrs over the course of 17 days from 16 October to 1 November 2019 at Bikaner Boys School, Bikaner. The artwork created awareness regarding the United Nations' Sustainable Development Goals (SDGs) related to climate change, safety of women and pollution, among others.

WR Largest art competition – multiple venues***

Sakal Media Pvt. Ltd organized the largest drawing and painting competition at several locations across Maharashtra and Goa on 16 December 2018. The Sakal Chitrakala Spardha took place at 2,000 locations between 9:00 a.m. and 12:30 p.m., in which 763,264 students from classes 1 to 10 participated. The

***The rules regarding the age of participants have been modified. Please see *Rules and Guidelines*.

FIRST PUBLIC ART DISTRICT

The Lodhi Art District in New Delhi, inaugurated by the Central Public Works Department on 1 March 2019, is the first public art district in the country. Conceptualized and realized by the St+Art India Foundation, a not-for-profit that works on art projects in open spaces, the artistic transformation of the district began in 2015. With the support of the local community and civic and cultural bodies, more than 50 artists of 23 nationalities have reimagined the area's facades by creating murals that bring the viewer into a contemporary urban art museum. A total of 56 walls with an area of approximately 16,310 sq. m (175,565 sq. ft) have been painted by the artists. This was followed by the Mahim (East) art district in Mumbai, Maharashtra; the Maqta art district in Hyderabad, Telangana; and the Panjim (Panaji) art district in Goa.

FORTUNE
DELHI

painting centres were schools across the districts of Pune, Satara, Ahmednagar, Nanded, Mumbai, Nagpur, Akola, Jalgaon, Kolhapur, Solapur, and Nashik, besides the state of Goa.

Largest mandala artwork – solo

Radha Shankar Narayanan (b. 11 April 1977) from Bengaluru, Karnataka, created a 58.06 sq. m (625 sq. ft) mandala artwork in 89 hrs 20 mins over 12 days at BGS National Public School, Bengaluru. He started his painting on 15 June 2021 and finished on 28 June 2021.

Largest wall painting – single wall – solo

NIFT-TEA College of Knitwear Fashion, Tiruppur, Tamil Nadu, created a wall painting measuring 46.82 sq. m (504 sq. ft) in 250 hrs over 25 days in the college premises. The painting was made by R. Sanjay Kumar for the college. He started his painting on 17 June 2020 and finished on 11 July 2020.

Largest portrait – pencils – solo

Aman Gulati from Lakhimpur, Uttar Pradesh, created the largest pencil portrait, which measured 410.25 sq. m (4,416 sq. ft) in area. The portrait of Mahatma Gandhi was completed on 2 October 2019 to mark Gandhiji's 150th birth anniversary.

Largest mandala artwork – group

NIFT-TEA College of Knitwear Fashion in Tiruppur, Tamil Nadu, created a mandala artwork, which was 101.17 sq. m (1,089 sq. ft) in area, in 25 hrs over two days in the college premises. The participants began the artwork on 27 February 2021 and finished on 28 February 2021.

Largest quilling artwork – solo

Dr Jiji S. Deepak from Thrissur, Kerala, created a 6.71 m x 3.66 m (22 ft x 12 ft) artwork, using the paper-quilling technique. It took her 45 hrs 10 mins over a period of nine days. The artwork is based on the theme 'Mother Earth'.

Largest quilling artwork – solo

Largest portrait – acrylic paints – solo

Rajeev Ranjan (b. 1 March 1977) from Purnea, Bihar, who is popularly known as Rajeev Raj, created a painting of former prime minister Atal Bihari Vajpayee with acrylic paints on canvas. He began painting on 3 December 2018 at 4:43 p.m.

and completed the artwork at 11:18 p.m. on 4 December 2018 at the Vidya Vihar Residential School. He took 30 hrs 35 mins and used 225 pieces of canvas, each 0.762 m x 0.762 m (2.5 ft x 2.5 ft). The artwork covered a total area of 130.6 sq. m (1,406 sq. ft).

Largest doodle art – group

Students from the NIFT–TEA College of Knitwear Fashion, Coimbatore, Tamil Nadu, created a doodle artwork measuring 89 sq. m (960 sq. ft). The artwork depicts the historical development of the Tiruppur cluster. It took them 36 hrs on 14–15 July 2016.

Largest doodle art – group

Largest painting – oil paints – solo

Sandeep Sinha (b. 6 January 1982), an artist from Pune, Maharashtra, made an oil-on-canvas painting titled 'HiMakhan'. The artwork measures 48.78 sq. m (525.06 sq. ft) and is a single-scene painting of the Himalayas. He began in August 2018 and completed the work by October 2018. His painting was exhibited at the Raja Ravi Varma Art Gallery, Pune. Sinha dedicated this work to acid-attack survivors.

Largest painting – natural colours – solo

Sangeeta Gupta (b. 25 May 1958) from New Delhi created a painting using natural indigo and titled 'Aadiyogi Shiv – A Journey in Cosmic Indigo'. The artwork measures 169.16 sq. m (1,820.78 sq. ft) and is painted on *khadidar* fabric. She began the artwork on 25 February 2020 and completed it on 4 March 2020 at the Shilpi Sansthan, Rataliya Village, Jaipur, Rajasthan. The artwork was made to create awareness for sustainable living, using natural colours and dyes.

Smallest pencil-lead carving

Tribeni Kachari (b. 30 April 1997) from Kamrup, Assam, created the smallest pencil-lead carving of 'India Gate' on a graphite pencil lead. The artwork measures 5 mm (0.196 in.) in length and 3 mm (0.118 in.) in width. It was made on 31 August 2020.

Tallest sand castle

Sudarsan Pattnaik (b. 15 April 1977) from Puri, Odisha, created the tallest sandcastle

14.86 m (48 ft 9 in.) tall to symbolize the message of world peace in 2017.

Artwork from the marathon sand painting

Marathon sand painting

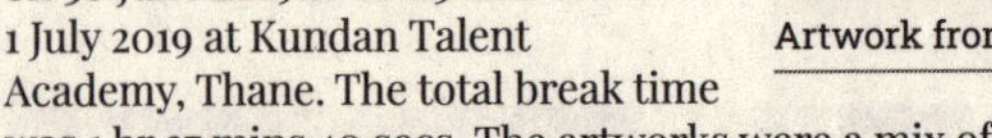

Neha Umak (b. 22 December 1990) from Thane, Maharashtra, completed 133 pieces of sand painting artwork in 24 hrs 49 mins 19 secs from 9:16 a.m. on 30 June 2019 to 10:05 a.m. on 1 July 2019 at Kundan Talent Academy, Thane. The total break time was 1 hr 37 mins 40 secs. The artworks were a mix of portraits and sceneries.

Marathon pencil-art session

Dinesh K. Gupta (b. 22 May 1978) from Mumbai, Maharashtra, completed 201 drawings in a marathon pencil-art session, starting at noon on 5 April 2019 and ending at noon on 6 April 2019. Using 6B pencils, he sketched famous people, natural sceneries, religious figures, and still life on A3 sheets. The event took place at Dr Babasaheb Ambedkar Art Gallery, Kalyan, Maharashtra. The total break time was 1 hr 50 mins.

Largest origami artwork – widest – solo

Radhika Chintalapati, an artist from Hyderabad, Telangana, created a butterfly with nine folds in 15 mins at Glendale International School on 21 February 2019.

Marathon portrait making – marker and ink – solo

Srushti Sandeep Ingale (b. 14 March 2000) from Kolhapur, Maharashtra, completed 157 portraits in a marathon marker-and-ink session, starting at 7:00 a.m. on 20 November 2021 and ending at 8:00 p.m. on the same day. Using four Montex Mega Tap black ball pens, she sketched portraits of political and sports personalities, amongst others, on A3 sheets. The event took place at Hotel Pearl, Kolhapur, Maharashtra. The total break time was 50 mins.

Marathon painting – acrylic colours – solo

Ramita Bhaduri (b. 27 September 1971) from Nazir Bagan, Kolkata, West Bengal, completed 213 artworks, using acrylic paints in 24 hrs from 4:05 p.m. on 5 June 2018 to 7:35 p.m. on 6 June 2018. The total break time was3 hrs 30 mins.

Marathon sculpture-making

Ramita Bhaduri (b. 27 September 1971) from Nazir Bagan, Kolkata, West Bengal, completed a marathon sculpture-making session during 29–30 April 2019, using clay and cement. She logged 15 hrs of sculpting and 3 hrs break time (30 mins after every 3 hrs), making 29 sculptures in all. The average dimensions of the sculptures were 30.48 cm x 30.48 cm x 33.02 cm (12 in. x 12 in. x 13 in.) for standing figures, 25.4 cm x 30.48 cm x 38.1 cm (10 in. x 12 in. x 15 in.) for lying-down ones and 25.4 cm x 25.4 cm x 30.48 cm (10 in. x 10 in. x 12 in.) for sitting figures.

The Lalit Kala Akademi has 7 regional centres.

LITERATURE

BOOKS

Oldest living language

Tamil, which belongs to the Dravidian group of languages, is the oldest living language of India. *Tholkappiyam,* the oldest known work in Tamil, is a work on Tamil grammar. Its composition has been variously dated to between the second century BCE and the fifth century CE.

Oldest surviving book

The oldest surviving Indian book is the Tamil work *Christiya Vanakkam,* a revised edition of the *Doctrina Christiana.* It was first published in 1560 in Goa and followed by its Tamil version published in 1564.

Earliest known grammar text

The Sanskrit grammar treatise *Ashtadhyayi,* which was composed around 500 BCE by Panini, a grammarian, is said to be the earliest formalized book on Sanskrit grammar. It contains 4,000 precise rules of grammar in as many sutras, expounding an array of topics such as syntax, root derivatives and moods.

First known printed book

The first known printed book in India, titled *Conclusoes e Outras Coisas,* was printed in Portuguese in Goa by Joao de Bustamante, a Christian missionary.

Earliest known anthology

Therigatha, the ninth book of the *Khuddaka Nikaya,* is the earliest known anthology. This Buddhist scripture, written in Pali, consists of short poems that were recited by the early members of the Buddhist sangha. It has 73 poems, which are organized into 16 chapters, and the text comprises 522 stanzas.

Earliest known Malayalam work

Samkshepa Vedartham, a catechism book by the Reverend Clement Pianius, was printed in movable type in Rome in 1772.

Earliest original Odia work

Lavanyavati, the first Odia epic, was an original work featuring the love story of a prince of Karnataka and a princess of Sri Lanka, by Upendra Bhanja (1680–1720), who belonged to a ruling feudatory family in Ghumsar in Bhanjanagar in present-day Odisha. Called *'Kavi Samrat',* he is said to have written many books.

Earliest known Gujarati work

The earliest work in Gujarati prose was *Balavabodha,* written by Tarunaprabha and dated to 1355 CE.

Earliest known Kannada works

- The earliest extant work in Kannada, the second oldest living language in India, is the *Kavirajamarga,* which was written (possibly in parts) by a Rashtrakuta king – Nrupatunga Amoghavarsha I (r. 814–78 CE). It is a work on the rhetoric, poetics and grammar of Kannada.
- The Kannada text in prose, titled *Vaddaradhane* (sixth to ninth century CE),

which is believed to have been written by Shivakotiacharya, consists of inspiring stories of 19 great Jain saints.

Earliest known Marathi works

- *Viveka Sindhu* was written by Mukundraj (1128–1200 CE) in Marathi verse, and preached Advaita bhakti. Mukundraj was a follower of Adi Shankaracharya's philosophy of Advaita or 'non-dualism', which inspired him to write this religious composition.
- *Leela Charitra* by Mahim Bhat is a biography of Chakradhara, a 13th century saint who founded the Mahanubhava sect and socio-religious movement. The work contains more than a hundred stories on the subject.

Earliest extant English work

Cavelly Venkata Boriah's *Account of the Jains,* published in 1809, is the first extant evidence of Indian writing in English.

Earliest known Tamil work

Tholkappiyam, a treatise on the grammar of the Tamil language, is the earliest known extant work in Tamil. It has been dated to between the second century BCE and the fifth century CE.The authorship is loosely attributed to the sage Tholkappiyar.

The original palm-leaf manuscript of *Tholkappiyam*

Earliest known Telugu work

The first printed prose work in Telugu, which was a part of the New Testament, was translated by Reverend Benjamin Schultze in the early 18th century.

First printed book to use Bengali type

A Grammar of the Bengal Language written in 1778 by Nathaniel Brassey Halhead constitued the first grammar book in Bengali. It was printed in Hoogly, West Bengal.

First printed book in Bengali

Krister Mangal Samacar (*The New Testament*) published in 1819, written by William Carey was the first translation of the Bible in Bengali. It was printed by the Serampore Mission Press, Serampore, Bengal (now Srirampur, West Bengal).

First known printed books in local languages

- **Assamese:** An early translation of the New Testament, titled *Dharmapustak,* printed by the Serampore Mission Press, Serampore, Bengal, in 1813.
- **Devanagari/Hindi:** *Grammar of Sanskrit and Grammar of the Hindustani Language,* published by the Chronicle Press, Calcutta (now Kolkata), in 1796.
- **Dogri:** *Valmiki Ramayana,* published by Sri Saraswati Press, Jammu in Jammu and Kashmir, in 1858.
- **Gujarati:** *Dabestan-e-Mazaheb,* the Gujarati translation of a Persian book, published by Fardoonjee Marazban in Bombay (now Mumbai), Maharashtra, in 1815.
- **Kannada:** *A Grammar of the Karnatic Language* by William Meckerell, published

by the Serampore Mission Press, Serampore, Bengal, in 1820.
- **Konkani:** *Doutrina Crista,* printed at the Society of Jesus Press, Goa, in 1556.
- **Maithili:** *Krishna Janma,* edited by Grierson, published by Vidyapati Press, Laheriasarai, Bihar, in 1936.
- **Malayalam:** *The Bible,* printed at the Courier Press, Bombay, Maharashtra, in 1811.
- **Odia:** A translation of the New Testament by Pandit Mrityunjaya Vidyalankar, printed at the Serampore Mission Press, Serampore, Bengal, in 1807.
- **Tamil:** *A Book of Prayers,* published by the Society of Jesus Press, Goa, around 1560.
- **Telugu:** *A Grammar of Telugu,* printed at the Serampore Mission Press, Serampore, Bengal, in 1813.
- **Urdu:** Hallhead's Urdu translation of Kannada laws, published by Honourable Company Press in Calcutta, in 1792.

First poet in English in India

Henry Louis Vivian Derozio (b. 18 April 1809), assistant headmaster of Hindu College, (now Presidency University, Kolkata), West Bengal, is considered to be the first Indian poet who wrote in English. The poems that he submitted to the newspaper *India Gazette* under the pseudonym 'Juvenis' were published as a collection in 1827. The second edition of the collection was released in the following year and included his most famous poem, 'The Fakeer of Jungheera', which featured aspects of life in colonial India.

First pseudonym

'Sujatha' was the pseudonym of the popular Tamil author S. Rangarajan (1935–2008), who wrote more than 100 novels, 250 short stories, 10 books on science, 10 stage plays and a volume of poems. He was a regular contributor to topical columns in Tamil periodicals such as *Ananda Vikatan, Kumudam* and *Kalki.* He served for a brief period as the editor of *Kumudam,* and also wrote screenplays and dialogues for Tamil movies.

Only Shakespeare folio

A rare copy of Shakespeare's First Folio (1623) was found at the Mahatma Gandhi Central Library, University of Roorkee, Uttar Pradesh (now IIT-Roorkee, Uttarakhand) as reported in 2019. The 900-page volume titled *Mr William Shakespeare's Comedies, Histories and Tragedies* was found in an old trunk in the librarian's office. It contains 36 of Shakespeare's 37 plays.

Longest novel

Avakasikal, written by M.K. Menon in Malayalam, runs into 3,958 pages, in four volumes, making it the longest novel in any Indian language. Menon received the Sahitya Akademi Award in 1981 and the Vayalar Award in 1983 for the novel.

First official sign language dictionary

Bridging the gap for the deaf and speech-disabled communities, *The Indian Sign Language Dictionary,* a first-of-its-kind book, was launched on 23 March 2018. Developed by the Delhi-based Indian Sign Language Research and Training Centre, it contains 3,000 words in Hindi and English, and their corresponding

Indian Sign Language Research and Training Centre

Established on 28 September 2015, the Indian Sign Language Research and Training Centre (ISLRTC) is an autonomous organization under the aegis of the Department of Empowerment of Persons with Disabilities under the Ministry of Social Justice and Empowerment. Located in New Delhi, the centre aims at promoting the Indian sign language (ISL), develop manpower in related areas and carry out research. It currently runs two courses – Diploma in Indian Sign Language Interpretation (DISLI) and Diploma in Teaching Indian Sign Language (DTISL). On 6 October 2020, they signed an MoU with the National Council of Educational Research and Training (NCERT) to make educational textbooks (classes I to XII) and resources available in the Indian sign language. In September 2022, the central government launched an android- and iOS-compatible mobile app called, 'Sign Learn' with 10,000 words from *The Indian Sign Language Dictionary.*

graphic representations. Available in both print and video formats, it brings uniformity to the various sign languages used. It divides the words into five categories: Everyday, Legal, Academic, Medical and Technical terms.

Scripture in the largest format

A special edition of the Bhagavadgita at the ISKCON temple in New Delhi is the world's largest-sized scripture. The book measures 2.8 m x 2 m (9 ft 2.2 in. x 6 ft 6.7 in.) and has 670 pages. Weighing 800 kg, it was printed in Milan, Italy, on YUPO synthetic paper, making it untearable and waterproof. It was unveiled on 26 February 2019.

Thickest book

Povitr Pustokantlem Bhanddar (*Roman Konkani Biblical Concordance*) is the thickest book. It is 149.09 cm (58.7 in.) thick, and measures 30.5 cm (12 in.) in length and 43.2 cm (17 in.) in width. The book was launched on 28 February 2021 at the Our Lady of Carmel Chapel, Navelim, Goa. The copyright owner of the book is Ives Joaquim Tavares.

Smallest book

B. Jameela from Madras (now Chennai), Tamil Nadu, had a copy of the Quran, which is 27 mm (1.06 in.) long, 19 mm (0.74 in.) wide and 10 mm (0.39 in.) thick, and weighed only 4.4 g.

Most translated Indian work

The most translated Indian work is the Bhagavadgita, which is an integral part of the Mahabharata. The Bhagavadgita was first translated into English in 1785 by British typographer and founder of the Asiatic Society, Charles Wilkins. Since then, it has been translated as many as 55 languages.

Longest audiobook

The longest audiobook, titled *Shree Haricharitramrut Sagar*, was voiced by Gyanjivandasji Swami – 'Kundaldham' and Ishwarcharandasji Swami – 'Kundaldham', and published on 27 October 2017. The audiobook is 146,444 mins 52 secs long.

PUBLISHING AND BOOK SELLING

Largest trade publishing house

Penguin Random House India is the subcontinent's largest English-language trade publisher. It publishes more than 300 new titles every year and has an active backlist of over 3,000 titles.

Largest literary publisher

DC Books in Kottayam, Kerala, started in 1974 by Dominic Chacko Kizhakemuri, is considered the publishing hub of south India. The translation programme of DC Books is considered to be the largest in India. It publishes around 1,500 books in a year (2024).

Entrance to the Bookaroo Festival 2022

First children's literary festival

Co-founded by Swati Roy, Jo Williams, and Venkatesh M. in 2008, Bookaroo was the first children's literary festival in India, with its first edition held in New Delhi.

First book fair

The First International Book Fair opened at New Delhi's Pragati Maidan on 18 March 1972 during the International Book Year. Around a hundred Indian publishers took part, displaying about 10,000 books in English and local Indian languages. Foreign participants included those from the USSR, the USA, France, New Zealand, Turkey and Sri Lanka.

First virtual literary festival

LitFest X, organized between 23 October and 1 November 2015 was the country's first virtual literary festival. The event used multiple platforms like YouTube, Google Hangouts, Facebook and Twitter to present the interactive sessions to readers including book launches and book readings.

First comic book convention

The Annual Indian Comic Book Convention (Comic Con) was organized for the first time on 19 February 2011 by Twenty Onwards Media at Dilli Haat, New Delhi. Fifty publishers participated in it, bringing together writers, gamers, cosplayers, games and films.

First literary agency

Neville Tuli of Osian, Rajasthan, set up the first professional agency for authors on 9 April 2007. The first author they signed on was Omair Ahmad on 1 June 2007. The literary agency was a division of Osian's Connoisseurs of Art Pvt. Ltd.

First independent publisher

The first Indian publisher to set up a press was Gangakishor Bhattacharya in 1821 in Calcutta, West Bengal, a former employee of the Serampore Press, Serampore, Bengal. He published 18th century ballads in Bengali and adaptations from classics.

First feminist publishing house

Kali for Women, a not-for-profit trust, publishing a wide variety of books by women and on women, was started in 1984 by Urvashi Butalia and Ritu Menon in New Delhi.

First book village

Bilhar, located in Satara District of Maharashtra, was identified as the first book village in India on 4 May 2017. Known as *Pustakanch Gaav*, the village has genre-specific libraries in 25 locations, housing more than 15,000 books, mostly in Marathi. The village is decorated with murals, paintings and artworks on the theme of books. The aim of the initiative is to share a passion for books and an appetite for knowledge. Perumkulam in Thiruvananthapuram District, Kerala was also announced to be converted into a village of books in June 2019.

Oldest bookshop

Higginbothams, the oldest bookshop in the country, was opened in 1844 by Abel Joshua Higginbotham in Madras, Tamil Nadu. It has a subscription division that helps educational institutions, corporate bodies and professionals to get journals and periodicals from more than 3,000 publishing houses abroad.

Biggest retail bookshop chain – high street

Crossword Bookstores Ltd, a wholly owned subsidiary of Shoppers Stop Ltd, is the largest high-street bookstore chain in India. Established in October 1992, the

THE SCALE OF SALES

1 Largest sales for a children's book – hardback

Harry Potter and the Cursed Child (Parts One and Two) is the official script book for the play of the same name written by J.K. Rowling, John Tiffany, and Jack Thorne. It is the eighth story in the Harry Potter book series. Released in India by Hachette India, Gurugram, Haryana, in July 2016, it sold 259,537 print copies (as of October 2017), making it the largest-selling children's book in India.

2 Largest sales on release for a fiction title – hardback

Dan Brown is a best-selling American author of thrillers. His book *Origin* was the fifth in his Robert Langdon series, following *Angels & Demons, The Da Vinci Code, The Lost Symbol,* and *Inferno*. It was released in India on 3 October 2017 by Penguin Random House India, with an initial subscription of 125,000 copies, breaking all records in the fiction hardback category.

3 Largest adult non-fiction seller – hardback

Cricket legend Sachin Tendulkar's autobiography, *Playing It My Way,* co-authored with Boria Majumdar, was published in India by Hachette India, Gurugram, Haryana, and released on 6 November 2014. It broke all previous records in the adult non-fiction (hardback) category with 150,289 copies confirmed on order subscriptions.

4 Largest-selling bilingual dictionary

The *English–English–Malayalam Dictionary* by T. Ramalingam Pillai was first published in May 1983. Published by DC Books, based in Kottayam, Kerala, it is in its 55th impression now. As on September 2019, around 2.4 million copies had been sold.

5 Largest lifetime sales – hardback

The Secret by Rhonda Byrne, published by Simon and Schuster, US, in 2006, is a best-selling self-help book, based on the pseudoscientific 'law of attraction', which claims that a person's thoughts can change the world directly. The book has sold over 700,000 copies in India and has also been translated into 50 languages.

company had 88 stores, including franchises, across India by August 2023. These stores are across the country in cities such as Mumbai, Bengaluru, Ahmedabad, Gurugram, Delhi, Chennai, and Pune, among others.

Largest book market

College Street in Kolkata, West Bengal, is the venue of the largest book market in the country and possibly the largest used-books market in the world. Known locally as *boi para* (the neighbourhood of books), this 1.5 km long street sees a large number of book lovers and buyers every day. The street suffered major damage due to cyclone Amphan in May 2020, but crowd funding efforts and the resilience of the shopkeepers brought it back in business.

Largest bookshop

Sapna Book House in Gandhinagar, Bengaluru, Karnataka, was started in 1967 by Suresh C. Shah. Spread over 3,716 sq. m (40,000 sq. ft), it has more than 220,000 titles covering many genres and topics. Sapna Book House has four more branches in Bengaluru and Mysuru – adding up to retail space of about 9,290.3 sq. m (100,000 sq. ft).

Most travel bookshops

Wheeler (A.H. Wheeler and Co. Pvt. Ltd) owns a bookshop chain co-founded by Emile Moreau and T.K. Banerjee in Allahabad (now Prayagraj), Uttar Pradesh, in 1877, with around 900 popular bookshops selling magazines and books at as many as 264 railway stations.

Largest literary festival

The Jaipur Literature Festival, founded in 2006, is an annual literary festival in Jaipur, Rajasthan, which brings together some of the most prominent thinkers and writers from across the world every January. The festival directors are authors Namita Gokhale and William Dalrymple, and it has been produced by Sanjoy Roy of Teamwork Arts since 2008. The festival has seen a footfall of 431,000 people, conducted 238 sessions in over 46 languages by around 370 speakers in 2023.

AWARDS AND HONOURS

First Sahitya Akademi Bhasha Samman Award

The Bhasha Samman Awards are given annually for contribution towards the development of a language. The first of these awards were given in 1996 to:

- Dharikshan Mishra for Bhojpuri,
- Bansi Ram Sharma and M.R. Thakur for Pahari (Himachali),
- K. Jathappa Rai and Mandara Keshava Bhat for Tulu (Karnataka), and
- Chandra Kanta Murasingh for Kokborok (Tripura).

First recipients of the Sahitya Akademi Award

- *Man*: Makhanlal Chaturvedi (1889–1968), a Hindi poet, was the first person to receive this award for *Him Tarangini* (Hindi) in 1955.
- *Woman*: The Punjabi poet and writer Amrita Pritam (1919–2005) received the award in 1956, the year after its inception, for *Sunehre* (Punjabi), a collection of poems.

TOP 10 FRONT-LIST TITLES* 2022

	TITLE	AUTHOR	VOLUME
ADULT FICTION	*War of Lanka* (Ram Chandra Series Book 4)	Amish Tripathi	74,597
	It Starts with Us	Colleen Hoover	64,110
	Tomb of Sand	Geetanjali Shree	24,650
	Verity	Colleen Hoover	20,705
	The Magicians of Mazda (Bharat Series 7)	Ashwin Sanghi	19,745
	The Hidden Hindu	Akshat Gupta	17,528
	When I Am with You	Durjoy Datta	17,189
	The Girl in the Glass Case: Keep Your Girls Safe. Boys safer.	Devashish Sardana	11,682
	Something I'm Waiting to Tell You	Shravya Bhinder	10,753
	The Seven Moons of Maali Almeida	Shehan Karunatilaka	10,019
ADULT NON-FICTION	*The Wisdom Bridge: Nine Principles to a Life That Echoes in the Hearts of Your Loved Ones*	Kamlesh D. Patel	31,535
	Youth and Truth: Unplug with Sadhguru	Sadhguru	16,165
	Get Epic Shit Done	Ankur Warikoo	15,914
	India, Bharat and Pakistan: The Constitutional Journey of a Sandwiched Civilisation	J. Sai Deepak	15,767
	Dear Stranger, You Deserve To Be Loved	Ashish Bagrecha	14,976
	*Mindf**ked: When It's 4 a.m. And You Can't Stop Overthinking* (Hinglish edition)	Anubhav Agrawal	11,233
	Build, Don't Talk: Things You Wish You Were Taught in School	Raj Shamani	10,667
	The India Way: Strategies for an Uncertain World	S. Jaishankar	10,176
	The Food Book	Subah Saraf	10,065
	Modi@20: Dreams Meet Delivery	BlueKraft Digital Foundation	9,694

	TITLE	AUTHOR	VOLUME
CHILDREN'S FICTION	*Diary of a Wimpy Kid: Diper Överlöde*	Jeff Kinney	17,901
	Moral Stories for Children	Om Books Editorial Team	15,211
	The Magic of the Lost Story	Sudha Murty	6,530
	Rowley Jefferson's Awesome Friendly Spooky Stories	Jeff Kinney	4,718
	Tales from Indian Mythology (Collection of 10 Books)	Wonder House Books	2,675
	Fantastic Beasts: The Secrets of Dumbledore – The Complete Screenplay	J.K. Rowling and Steve Kloves	1,843
	Unusual Tales from Indian Mythology (boxset)	Sudha Murty	1,755
	The Arabian Nights Illustrated Book for Children	Wonder House Books	1,676
	Into the Sideways World	Ross Welford	1,440
	Timeless Classics from Amar Chitra Katha	Chirstopher Baretto and Rituja Sawant	1,251
CHILDREN'S NON-FICTION	*Ikigai for Teens: Finding Your Reason for Being*	Héctor García and Francesc Miralles	8,660
	Unstoppable Us, Volume 1: *How Humans Took Over the World*	Yuval Noah Harari	4,375
	The People of the Indus	Nikhil Gulati and Jonathan Mark Kenoyer	1,799
	Listen to Your Heart: The London Adventure	Ruskin Bond	1,478
	The Gutsy Girls of Science	Ilina Singh	690
	The Puffin Book of 100 Extraordinary Indians	Venkatesh Vedam	685
	World History in 3 Points	Zac Sangeeth	645
	Mythonama: The Big Book of Indian Mythologies	Mudita Chauhan-Mubayi and Adittya Nath Mubayi	630
	Young Indian Innovators, Entrepreneurs and Change-makers	Rupangi Sharma	525
	Incredible Indians:75 People Who Shaped Modern India	Ashwitha Jayakumar	450

**NOTE: Titles published between 1 January and 31 December 2022. Data sourced from Nielsen BookScan retail panel market and © Nielsen BookData. Volume indicates the number of copies sold.*

Bibek Debroy (*left*)

Most prolific translator – published literary works

Prof. Bibek Debroy, an economist, policymaker and author, has translated into English, the Mahabharata (2.25 million words), *Harivamsha* (160,000 words, published in 2016), the *Valmiki Ramayana* (0.5 million words, published in 2017) the *Bhagavata Purana* (0.5 million words, published in December 2018). He is the third person (after Kisari Mohan Ganguli [published between 1883 and 1895] and Manmatha Nath Dutt [1855–1912]) to translate the unabridged version of the Mahabharata into English. His translation was published in 10 volumes (2010–14), and a box set released in 2015 by Penguin Random House India. He also translated the Bhagavadgita in 2019.

First recipients of the Jnanpith Award

The Jnanpith Award is presented annually by the Bharatiya Jnanpith to an Indian author for their contribution to literature. The first winners were:

- *Man*: Malayalam poet G. Sankara Kurup (1901–78) was the recipient of the first Jnanpith Award in 1965, the year of its inception, for his anthology of poems, *Odakkuzhal.*
- *Woman*: Ashapurna Devi (1909–95), Bengali novelist and poet, was the first woman author to receive the Jnanpith Award in 1976 for her novel *Pratham Pratishruti* (which was published in 1965), the first of a trilogy that included *Subarnalata* and *Bakul Katha.*

First Sahitya Akademi Fellowship

- *Man:* Former Indian president and eminent scholar Dr S. Radhakrishnan (1888–1975) was the first to receive this honour in 1968 for his contribution to Indian thought and universal humanism.
- *Woman:* The first woman to be elected Fellow of the Akademi was the poet Mahadevi Varma in 1979.

First novel in an Indian language to win the International Booker Prize

Tomb of Sand by Geetanjali Shree became the first Indian-language (Hindi) novel to win the prestigious International Booker Prize in 2022. Translated from *Ret Samadhi* into English by Daisy Rockwell, it is set in north India and follows the story of an 80-year-old woman.

First Indian winner of the Neustadt Prize

The Neustadt International Prize (given for an author's body of work) is one of the few international prizes for which poets, novelists, and playwrights are all eligible. Raja Rao was the first Indian to win it in 1988. Indian-Canadian writer Rohinton Mistry won the prize in 2012.

First winners of the Yuva Puraskar Award

The Yuva Puraskar Award is given by the Sahitya Akademi annually to writers below the age of 35 in 24 Indian languages. This award was introduced in 2011 and the Dogri and Sindhi languages were added later, in 2011 and 2015 respectively. The first year had only 22 languages. The first winners are:

- *Assamese*: Arindam Borkataki for *Anusilon.*
- *Bengali*: Binod Ghosal for *Danaowla Manus.*
- *Bodo*: Jaishree Baro for *Jeu Saharani Beduin.*
- *Dogri:* Yash Raina for *Do Kandhe* in 2012.
- *English*: Vikram Sampath for *My Name is Gauhar Jaan! – The Life and Times of a Musician.*
- *Gujarati*: Dhwanil Parekh for *Antim Yuddha.*
- *Hindi*: Uma Shankar Choudhary for *Kahte Hain Tab Shanshaah So Rahe The.*
- *Kannada*: Veeranna Madiwalara for *Nelada Karuneya Dani.*
- *Kashmiri*: Nisar Azam for *Patte Leji Zoon Daras.*
- *Konkani*: Jofa Gonsalves for *Nirnay.*
- *Maithili*: Anand Kumar Jha for *Hathat Parivartan.*
- *Malayalam*: Sushmesh Chandroth for *Marana Vidyalayam.*
- *Manipuri*: Devchand for *Nongthangna Mutkhrabada.*
- *Marathi*: Aishwarya Patekar for *Bhuishastra.*
- *Nepali*: Kamal Regmi for *Srijana Ra Abhista.*
- *Odia*: Gayatribala Panda for *Gaan.*
- *Punjabi*: Paramveer Singh for *Amrit Vela.*
- *Rajasthani*: Dula Ram Saharan for *Peer.*
- *Sanskrit*: Paramanand Jha for *Kavyakaveri.*
- *Santali*: Satilal Murmu for *Jagron.*
- *Sindhi*: Manoj Chawla 'Tanha' for *Pinjraa* in 2015.
- *Tamil*: M. Thavasi for *Sevalkattu.*
- *Telugu*: Vempalli Gangadhar for *Jumma.*
- *Urdu*: Vishal Khullar for *Dhund Mein Amaan.*

First Indian winner of the Ondaatje Prize

Sports journalist Rahul Bhattacharya's *The Sly Company of People Who Care* won the Royal Society of Literature Ondaatje Prize in 2012. It also won the Hindu Literary Prize (2011) and was the Kirkus Fiction Book of the Year in the USA.

First to win the DSC Prize for South Asian Literature

- *Man*: Poet and novelist Jeet Thayil won the DSC Prize for South Asian Literature 2013 for his novel *Narcopolis* (Faber & Faber).
- *Woman*: Jhumpa Lahiri was judged as the winner of the DSC Prize for South Asian Literature 2015 for her book *The Lowland*. The US $ 50,000 prize and the specially-designed trophy was awarded to her on 22 January 2015.

First Indian winner of the Commonwealth Writers' Prize

Author Nayantara Sahgal (b. 10 May 1927) won the Commonwealth Writers' Prize for Best Book in 1987, for her novel *Plans for Departure*.

First Winners of the Sahitya Akademi Translation Prize

Established in 1989, the award is presented for outstanding translation works in 24 languages. The awardees receive a plaque and a cash prize of ₹50,000. Here is a list of the first winners:

Language	Author	Original Title	Translator	Translation Title	Year
Assamese	Jawaharlal Nehru	*Autobiography* (English)	Narendranath Sarma	*Atmajivan Charit*	1990
Bengali	Vaikom Muhammad Basheer	*Pathummayude Adu and Balyakalasakhi* (Malayalam)	Nilina Abraham	*Patummar Chhagal O Balyaskhi*	1989
Bodo	Lakshinath Bezbarua	*Buri Aair Sadhu* (Assamese)	Pramila Narzary	*Aswini Solo*	2005
Dogri	Shudraka	*Mrichchakatikam* (Sanskrit)	Ram Nath Shastri	*Mitti Di Gaddi*	1989
English	Gopinath Mohanty	*Paraja* (Oriya)	Bikram K. Das	*Paraja*	1989
Gujarati	Maitreyee Devi	*Na Hanyate* (Bengali)	Nagindas Parekh	*Na Hanyate*	1989
Hindi	K.P.S. Menon	*Many Worlds* (English)	Noor Nabi Abbasi	*Malabar Se Masko Tak*	1989
Kannada	Kalidasa	*Collection of Kalidasa's Works* (Sanskrit)	S.V. Parameshwara Bhatta	*Kannada Kalidasa Mahasamputa*	1990
Kashmiri	Rajinder Singh Bedi	*Ek Chadar Maili Si* (Urdu)	Syed Rasool Pompur	*Pranwaar*	1991
Konkani	Jhaverchand Meghani	*Mansaeena Diva* (Gujarati)	Ravindra Kelekar	*Ani Tankan Manshant Hadle*	1990
Maithili	Saratchandra Chattopadhyay	*Vipradas* (Bengali)	Upendranath Jha 'Vyas'	*Vipradas*	1990
Malayalam	Tarashankar Bandyopadhyay	*Ganadevata* (Bengali)	K. Ravi Verma	*Ganadevata*	1989
Manipuri	Binay Mukhopadhyay	*Drishtipath* (Bengali)	T. Thoibi Devi	*Drishtipath*	1989
Marathi	S.L. Bhyrappa	*Vamshavriksha* (Kannada)	Uma Virupax Kulkarni	*Vamsavriksha*	1989
Nepali	Sukanta Bhattacharya	Collection (Bengali) poetry	Karna Thami	*Sakanta Ka Kavitaharu*	1994
Odia	Tarashankar Bandyopadhyay	*Ganadevata*, Parts I & II (Panchagram) (Bengali)	Basanta Kumari Devi	*Ganadebata*, Parts I and II (Panchagram)	1989
Punjabi	Tulsidas	*Ramcharitmanas* (Epic)	Rattan Singh Jaggi	*Tulasi Ramayan (Ramcharitmanas)*	1989
Rajasthani	Bhasa	*Swapna Vasavadatta* (Sanskrit)	Deo Dutta Nag	*Sapano*	1990
Sanskrit	Sarayu Prasad Gupta	*Vijnana Aur Samaja* (Hindi)	Ganesha Sharma	*Vijananam Samajasca*	1990
Santhali	Kalidas	*Meghdoot* (Sanskrit)	Sobha Nath Beshra	*Rahla Raybar*	2010
Sindhi	G.N. Dandekar	*Kuna Ekachi Bhramanagatha* (Marathi)	Jagat Assudomal Advani	*Rolak Ji Atam Kahani*	1989
Tamil	Krishnadeva Raja	*Aamukta Malyada* (Telugu)	M.G. Jagannatharaja	*Aamukta Malyada*	1990
Telugu	Rabindranath Tagore	*Bidayer Abhishap Chitrangada, etc.*, (Bengali)	B. Gopala Reddi	*Ravindruni Natikalu*	1989
Urdu	Basaveswara	*108 Vachanas* (Kannada sayings)	Hameed Almas	*Farmoodat*	1989

BOOKED THE PRIZE!

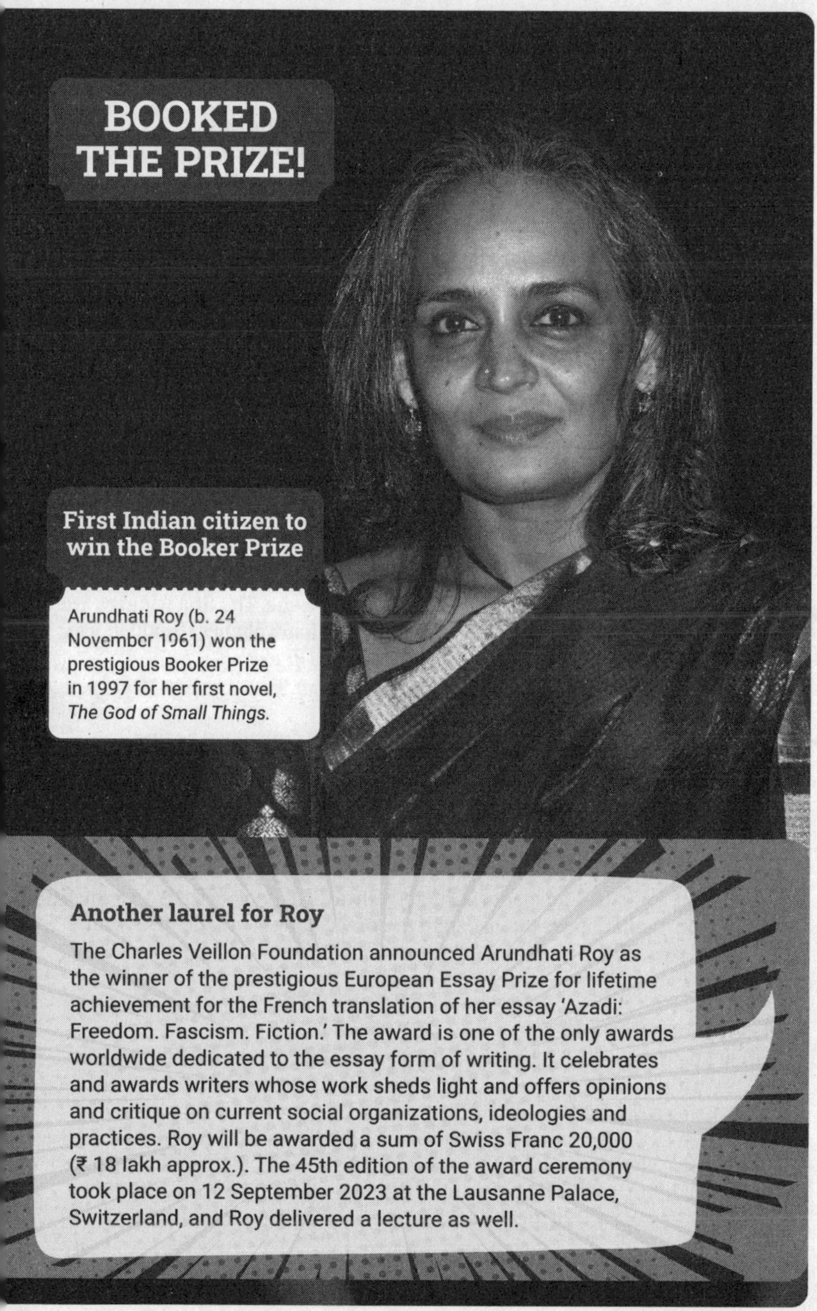

First Indian citizen to win the Booker Prize

Arundhati Roy (b. 24 November 1961) won the prestigious Booker Prize in 1997 for her first novel, *The God of Small Things*.

Another laurel for Roy

The Charles Veillon Foundation announced Arundhati Roy as the winner of the prestigious European Essay Prize for lifetime achievement for the French translation of her essay 'Azadi: Freedom. Fascism. Fiction.' The award is one of the only awards worldwide dedicated to the essay form of writing. It celebrates and awards writers whose work sheds light and offers opinions and critique on current social organizations, ideologies and practices. Roy will be awarded a sum of Swiss Franc 20,000 (₹ 18 lakh approx.). The 45th edition of the award ceremony took place on 12 September 2023 at the Lausanne Palace, Switzerland, and Roy delivered a lecture as well.

First winner of Grinzane Cavour award

Anita Desai won the lifetime achievement award of the Grinzane Cavour Prize in Piedmont, Italy, on 18 July 2005.

First Indian-origin winner of the Pulitzer Prize – fiction

Jhumpa Lahiri's *Interpreter of Maladies* (Mariner Books/Houghton Mifflin) won the Pulitzer Prize for Fiction in 2000.

First Indian winner of Newbery Medal

Dhan Gopal Mukerji (1890–1936), who was born in a village near Calcutta, West Bengal, and later went to the US, was the first Indian winner of the Newbery Medal for his novel, *Gay-Neck, the Story of a Pigeon,* in 1928. Indian-origin writer Veera Hiranandani received the Newbery honour for her work *The Night Diary* in 2019.

First winners of the Rabindranath Tagore Literary Prize

The Rabindranath Tagore Literary Prize, started in 2018, is awarded annually for valuable contributions to literature and poetry. Kabir (awarded posthumously) was the first awardee for *One Hundred Poems of Kabir* in 2018.

First winners of the Saraswati Samman

The Saraswati Samman was instituted by the K.K. Birla Foundation in 1991. Award winners receive ₹15 lakh along with a citation and a plaque. The first winners are:

- *Man*: Harivansh Rai Bachchan for Autobiography in four volumes (Hindi) in 1991.
- *Woman*: Balamani Amma for *Nivedyam* (Malayalam) in 1995.

First winners of the JCB prize

The JCB Prize was established in 2018 and is awarded annually. The first winners were:

- *Man*: Benyamin for *Jasmine Days* in 2018.
- *Woman*: Madhuri Vijay for *The Far Field* in 2019.

First winners of the Kamaladevi Chattopadhyay NIF Book Prize

Established in 2018, the Kamaladevi Chattopadhyay NIF Book Prize is an annual award for non-fiction books published in the preceeding year. The first winner of the award was Milan Vaishnav in 2018 for *When Crime Pays: Money and Muscle in Indian Politics*.

Highest monetary prize

- *Fiction:* The JCB Prize, established in 2018, is the most valuable prize in Indian literature, amounting to ₹25 lakh (2.5 million). Funded by JCB, a British manufacturing firm, the prize is awarded to the best work of fiction by an Indian citizen in English or translated from another language into English. Each of the five shortlisted books is awarded ₹1 lakh (0.1 million) and a separate prize of ₹5 lakh (0.5 million) is given if the winning entry is a translation. Mita Kapur, founder and CEO of Siyahi, a literary consultancy organization, now serves as its director.
- *Non-Fiction:* The richest prize for non-fiction writing is the New India Foundation Prize, valued at ₹15 lakh (1.5 million).

MEDIA AND COMMUNICATIONS

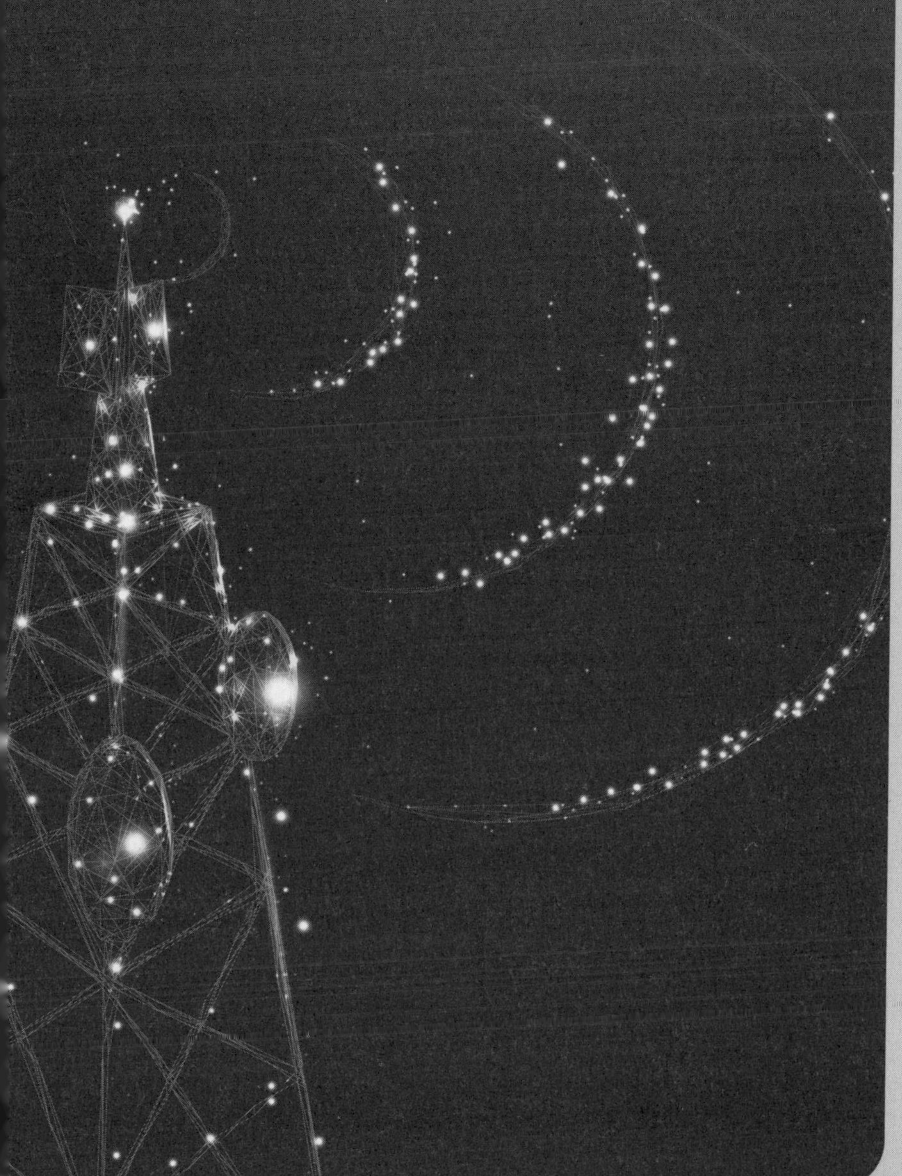

PRINT

First printing press

The first printing press came to India accidentally, in 1556, when the patriarch designate of Abyssinia (now Ethiopia, Africa) broke his journey at Goa and later died there. The printing press was left behind. The printers were a Spaniard named Joao de Bustamante and his Indian assistant, whose name is not known.

First paper-making machine

William Carey (1761–1834), a British Christian missionary, translator, social reformer, and cultural anthropologist, who founded Serampore College in Bengal, first set up a paper making machine in Calcutta (now Kolkata, West Bengal) in 1830.

First lithographic printing

Lithographic printing was introduced by the Calcutta Art Studio in 1878 in Calcutta (now Kolkata), West Bengal.

First multilingual press

A multilingual press for all the main local Indian languages was first set up in Serampore, Bengal (Srirampur, West Bengal), in 1800 by Christian missionaries.

Earliest type

The first types in any Indian language were cast in Goa in 1577 by João Gonçalves reportedly assisted by Father Pero Luis, who was a Tamil Jesuit priest.

First typewriters

The first typewriters were imported into India in 1896.

First indigenous typewriters

- Godrej & Boyce Manufacturing Company Ltd manufactured India's first manual typewriter in 1955. It was designed and created entirely by Indian engineers.
- Blackwood India Ltd in Calcutta, West Bengal, established in 1960 and then renamed J.K. Business Machines in 1961, were the first makers of portable typewriters in the country.
- The first indigenous electronic typewriters were manufactured by Hindustan Teleprinters Ltd in 1975.

First news agency

The Press Trust of India (PTI), which is a non-profit-sharing cooperative of Indian newspapers, was established on 27 August 1947. It took over the Associated Press of India and the Indian operations of

Press Trust of India

Bengal Gazette Banned

HICKY's
BENGAL GAZETTE;
OR THE ORIGINAL
Calcutta General Advertiser.

Hicky's Bengal Gazette was shut down in 1782 and its owner was thrown in jail. This was because Hicky used his paper to mock powerful men in British India. In 1781 Johann Zacharias Kiernander and Warren Hastings sued Hicky for libel. In many articles Hicky had called out to the army to mutiny against the British. Hicky was thrown in prison but continued to print his paper from jail. In 1782 the Supreme Court seized Hicky's printing press and banned the paper.

Reuters, and provided news, photographs, features, and infographics from February 1949 onwards.

First press regulation

The Censorship of Press Act of 1799 was the first censorship regulation to enforce wartime restrictions on the press. It was enacted by the then Governor General Lord Wellesley, who anticipated a French invasion of India. All news was scrutinized, including 'pre-censorship' before publication, by a special security administration unit with a view to preventing information leaks.

First newspaper

Hicky's Bengal Gazette or the *Original Calcutta General Advertiser*, India's and Asia's first newspaper, was launched on 29 June 1780 by James Augustus Hicky, an Irishman.

First newspaper for visually impaired people

Swagat Thorat's *Sparshdnyan*, launched in February 2008, is India's first newspaper for visually challenged. Its name means 'knowledge by touch', and it is published in Marathi on the 1st and 15th of every month.

WR First news agency to supply news in Urdu

On 5 June 1992, the United News of India (UNI) became the first agency in the world to supply Urdu news. It remains the only agency to do so.

First non-English newspaper

In 1794, the Reverend Harutyun Shmavonyan edited and published *Azdarar* in the Armenian script in Madras (now Chennai) Tamil Nadu. This was the first Armenian journal in the world and the first non-English one in India.

WR The only handwritten newspaper

The Musalman, the oldest Urdu language daily newspaper, published from Chennai, Tamil Nadu, is the only handwritten newspaper in the world. It is a four-page evening paper handwritten by four calligraphers or *katibs*, and printed. Established in 1927 by Syed Azmatulla, it has not missed a single day's publication. The paper has correspondents all over India and sells at 75 paise a copy to around 25,000 subscribers.

English daily with the largest readership

The Times of India, headquartered in Mumbai, Maharashtra, has a recorded readership of 17,344,000 (2019 Q4; Indian Readership Survey [IRS]).

The Times of India

First newsprint factory

The first paper mill in India to manufacture newsprint was a factory at Nepanagar, Burhanpur District, Madhya Pradesh, set up in January 1955.

First vernacular paper

Samachar Darpan was published in Bengali from Serampore, Bengal, by William Carey and John Clark Marshman from May 1818 onwards. Marshman was a British journalist, historian, and publisher of the *Friend of India* from which *The Statesman* newspaper descended.

First Hindi newspaper

Banaras Akhbar began in 1845, under the editorship of Govind Narayan Thatte, as the first Hindi newspaper.

First financial daily

The Economic Times, India's first financial daily, was launched by the Times of India Group in March 1961. Like the London-based *Financial Times*, it too was printed on salmon-pink paper.

First daily with an international edition

In February 1994, India's global newspaper *The Asian Age* was launched simultaneously from Delhi, Mumbai and London. It has a Kolkata edition too.

First magazine in Hindi

Saraswati, India's first Hindi monthly magazine, was published in January 1900. Its founder was the well-known printer and publisher Chintamani Ghosh and the magazine was published by the Indian Press, which was based in Allahabad (now Prayagraj), Uttar Pradesh.

First newspaper run entirely by women

Khabar Lahariya is the first newspaper in India that is entirely staffed, edited and published by women. The eight-page rural weekly newspaper in Hindi is sold in 600 villages in its print form

Indian magazines recorded a revenue of nearly ₹500 crore (5 billion) in the year 2020.

Pulitzer Prize in 2022

Danish Siddiqui along with Adnan Abidi, Sanna Irshad Mattoo, and Amit Dave from Reuters covered the Covid-19 pandemic in India and won a Pulitzer. Danish Siddiqui was killed while covering the war between Afghan troops and the Taliban. They won it in the feature photography category. In 2018 Danish Siddiqui along with Adnan Abidi was awarded the Pulitzer for covering the Rohingya refugee crisis.

and on multiple digital platforms. It was launched in 2002 in Chitrakoot District, Uttar Pradesh. In 2009, it was awarded the UNESCO King Sejong Literary Prize for its contribution to literacy.

First women's magazine in English

The Indian Ladies' Magazine was first published in English in 1901 by Kamala Satthianadhan in Madras, Tamil Nadu.

First women's magazine in an Indian language

Masik Patrika in Bengali, published from Calcutta, Bengal, in 1854, was the first women's magazine in an Indian language.

First magazine for visually challenged people

White Print was the first lifestyle magazine in English in India for visually challenged people. It was launched in May 2013 by Upasana Makati, a former communications student from the University of Ottawa, Canada. This 64-page monthly, printed at the National Association for the Blind, Mumbai, Maharashtra, and circulated across India, features articles about sports, politics, culture, fashion, and technology, besides short stories and reader contributions. *White Print* has also released Braille-tactile alphabet books in Braille, in both English and Hindi, which are called 'Tactabet'.

OWNERSHIP PATTERN OF PUBLICATIONS

DAILY

MONTHLY

0.10% Government
0.86% Society or Association
94.60% Individual
0.89% Trust
0.32% Firm or Partnership
3.23% Others

FORTNIGHTLY

WEEKLY

DAILY

Source: Press in India, 2021-22, RNI, Government of India

NUMBER OF PERIODICALS FOR 2021–22

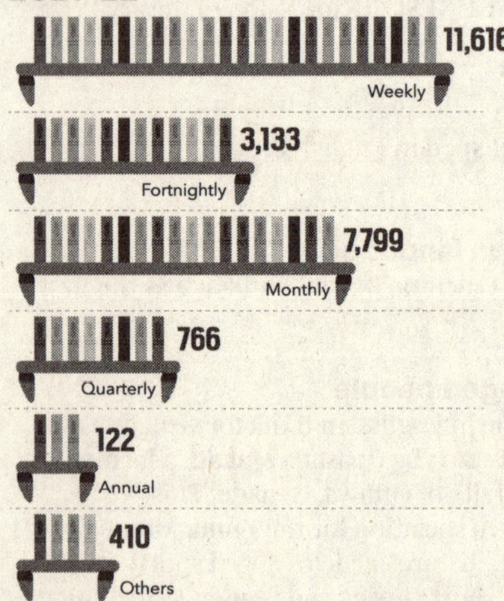

Source: Annual Report 2022-23, Department of Posts, Ministry of Communication, Government of India.

NUMBER OF DAILIES 2012–22

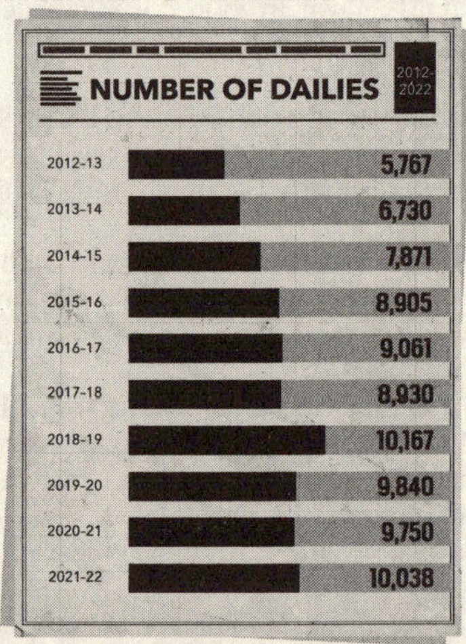

Source: Press in India, 2021-22, RNI, Government of India

First newspaper to be printed in colour
The Hindu, with its headquarters in Madras (now Chennai, Tamil Nadu), began as a weekly in 1878 and turned into a daily in 1889. A family-run newspaper, it was the first to be printed in colour in 1940. It was also the first Indian newspaper to own aeroplanes to distribute newspapers (1963), and the first newspaper to digitize and be available online (1995).

The total number of daily publications in 2021–22 was **20,278**.

First vernacular periodical
Digdarshan, a Bengali monthly, first appeared in April 1818.

First letters to the editor column
The letters to the editor column was introduced in the biweekly magazine *Calcutta Journal*, first published in 1878 in Bengal.

Multi-edition daily with the largest readership
Dainik Jagran, which has its headquarters in Kanpur, Uttar Pradesh, leads with 37 editions across 11 states and a readership of 68,667,000 (2019 Q4; IRS).

Daily with largest readership - Hindi
Dainik Jagran, which is headquartered in Kanpur, Uttar Pradesh, has a readership of 68,667,000 (2019 Q4; IRS).

State/UT with the most newspaper and periodical publications
Uttar Pradesh, with 21,166 publications, leads with the maximum number of publications in India. It is followed by Maharashtra, with 19,796 publications, and Delhi with 16,351 of them as of 2020–21.

State/UT with the most Indian-language publications
Delhi leads among all states and UTs in the most number of Indian language publications in as many as 15 languages. It is followed by Maharashtra, Uttarakhand, and Tamil Nadu with publications in 14 languages each. Gujarat comes after that with publications in 11 languages as of by 2020–21.

State/UT with most registered newspapers
Uttar Pradesh, with 21,336 registered publications, is the state with the most registered newspaper publications.

Largest read regional-language daily
Malayala Manorama, with its headquarters in Kottayam, Kerala, has a readership of 17,763,000 (2019 Q4; IRS).

Oldest children's magazine
Chandamama, founded by Telugu film-makers B. Nagi Reddy and Aluri Chakrapani was launched in July 1947 in Telugu. It was edited by Kodavatiganti Kutumba Rao. The magazine ceased publication in 1998. In 2007, it was acquired

by Geodesic Ltd. Its last edition came out in March 2013 and since then its status is unknown. In its heyday, *Chandamama* was published in 13 languages and had a readership of around 200,000 across the country.

Most read English magazine

India Today, a weekly published from Noida, Uttar Pradesh, by the India Today Group, has a readership of 9,493,000 (2019 Q4; IRS).

Most circulated government publication

Employment News, an English weekly that is published from New Delhi by the Publications Division, Ministry of Information and Broadcasting, Government of India, has the highest circulation of 239,498 among government publications (as of 2019).

Most read Hindi magazine

India Today (Hindi), a weekly published from Noida, Uttar Pradesh, by the India Today Group, has a total readership of 6,641,000 (2019 Q4; IRS).

Most read magazine in a regional language

Vanitha, a Malayalam fortnightly magazine, published from Kottayam, Kerala, by the Malayala Manorama Group, has a readership of 5,886,000 (2019 Q4; IRS).

State/UT with most publications in a single language

Uttar Pradesh, with 16,557 publications in Hindi, leads among all states and UTs with the most publications in a single language (Hindi). It is followed by Madhya Pradesh, with 11,973 Hindi-language publications, and Maharashtra, with 9,982 publications in Marathi.

First Indian-origin journalist to win the Pulitzer Prize

Gobind Behari Lal (1889–1982), a science journalist in the USA, won the Pulitzer Prize in 1937.

Longest-running women's magazine

Femina, which started in July 1959 with Frene Talyarkhan as its first editor, continues to be published. It is now published by Worldwide Media, which is owned by the Times Group. It was also the first lifestyle magazine of the country in English, and has the highest circulation in its category (108,560 in August 2019).

Longest spell as editor

Tushar Kanti Ghosh (1898–1994) was editor of the *Amrita Bazar Patrika*, based in Kolkata, West Bengal, for 64 years. He had founded the newspaper in 1928.

Oldest extant newspaper – regional language

The *Bombay Samachar*, now titled *Mumbai Samachar*, is the oldest continuously published newspaper in any language in India, and continues to be published. Launched on 1 July 1822 by Fardoonjee Marazban (1787–1847), the daily is published in both Gujarati and English. Marazban, who was from Bombay (now Mumbai), Maharashtra, was a printer and a newspaper editor. He established vernacular journalism in India and initiated the production of Gujarati types.

Oldest extant newspaper – English

The Times of India began on 3 November 1838 as a biweekly, initially called *Bombay Times and Journal of Commerce*. It was renamed *The Times of India* in 1850, with J.E. Brennan as its editor.

Most pages in a newspaper supplement

Kannada daily *Vijayavani*'s Mysuru edition brought out a special issue with 320 pages in 10 volumes on 25 March 2020. This supplement was dedicated to Shri Mayakara Madappa, a social reformer and spiritual leader of the 16th century. The newspaper was sold at a price of ₹4.

Most articles published in a year – single publication

Dr Prem Kumar Sharma (b. 9 November 1958) has been writing columns for *Hindustan Times* for a long time. He has written a total number of 415 articles in HT City in the year 2019, containing 362 daily horoscopes, 52 weekly astro queries, and 1 yearly horoscope.

Longest career as a journalist

B.P. Sharma, a journalist from Jammu and Kashmir, who died in 2005 at the age of 97, was an active journalist for over 70 years. He established the Jammu station of Radio Kashmir (All India Radio), and was its first director. He also worked with the news agency Reuters, *The Times of India, Hindustan Times* and *The Tribune*. Later, he served as the principal information officer of Jammu and Kashmir.

Longest letter to the editor

Vinod Chandrashekhar Dixit (b. 1 December 1964) from Ahmedabad, Gujarat, wrote the longest letter to the editor, which was published in *Free Press*, Gujarat, on 12 January 2023. He wrote a total of 3,321 words on the topic 'PM Narendra Modi – World's Most Powerful Leader'.

Most pages in a newspaper

Dainik Bhaskar's Indore edition brought out a special issue with 128 pages on 17 September 2020. This issue was on the theme 'AatmaNirbhar Indore'.

Most columns published in a year – multiple publications

Dr Prem Kumar Sharma (b. 9 November 1958) has the most number of columns published in a year. He has written nearly 1275 columns for multiple publications. His columns have been published in *Haribhoomi, Punjab Kesari, Voice Weekly, Hindustan Times* and other dailies.

Most articles published in a year - multiple publications

Vinod Chandrashekhar Dixit (b. 1 December 1964) from Ahmedabad, Gujarat, published the most number of articles in newspapers and magazines in a year. The total number of articles published by him between 1 March 2022 to 28 February 2023 was 1,846.

Delhi started an FM stereo station on 19 March 1988.

RADIO

First direct relay

A historic occasion, the first direct relay coincided with India's 'freedom at midnight' from British colonial rule. The ceremonies for the transfer of power from Britain to an independent India on the night of 14–15 August 1947 at the Central Hall of the Parliament House in Delhi were relayed by AIR.

First private radio station

On 10 September 1935, Akashvani Mysore, a private radio station, was set up in present-day Karnataka by Dr M.V. Gopalaswamy, professor of psychology and principal of the Maharaja's College, at his residence.

First private FM broadcaster

Times FM from Times Group commenced operations in 1993 from Ahmedabad, Gujarat. It ran till June 1998 and was relaunched as Radio Mirchi in 2000. Over the years, Radio Mirchi has expanded its presence across 63 cities in India and multiple stations in the UAE and the USA.

First private FM station

Radio City Bangalore, based in Bengaluru in Karnataka, started on 3 July 2001, becoming the country's first private FM radio station, after the Government of India opened up the FM broadcasting industry to private companies and competition.

First broadcasting service

The Madras Presidency Radio Club, under the stewardship of C.V. Krishnaswamy Chetty, started a broadcasting service in 1924, using a tiny 40-watt transmitter with an effective range of only 8 km.

First controller of broadcasting

Lionel Fielden took over as the first controller of broadcasting for the Indian State Broadcasting Service (ISBS) on 30 August 1935 in British India. A senior BBC producer, he spent five years in India, establishing a countrywide radio service. On 8 June 1936, the ISBS was renamed All India Radio.

Largest media organization

All India Radio (AIR), established in 1936, today reaches almost the entire population across the length and breadth of the country and nearly 92 per cent of the total area, making it the largest media organization by reach. It broadcasts in 23 languages and 179 dialects. Programmes of its External Services Division are broadcast in 11 Indian and 16 foreign languages.

AIR Logo

First frequency modulation (FM) service

AIR inaugurated the first ever FM service from Madras (now Chennai), Tamil Nadu, on 23 July 1977.

First broadcast

In June 1923, the Radio Club of Bombay made the first ever broadcast in the country from Bombay (now Mumbai), Maharashtra. This was followed by the setting up of the Calcutta Radio Club in West Bengal around five months later.

First national broadcast of music

AIR broadcast its first national music programme on 20 July 1952 with sitar maestro Pandit Ravi Shankar as the music conductor.

First broadcasting company

The Indian Broadcasting Company (IBC) was set up in Bombay, on 23 July 1927, with a medium-wave transmitter that had a range of 50 km.

First national broadcast of a play

On 15 August 1956, AIR first aired a play that was broadcast countrywide.

First news bulletin

The first news bulletin over radio was aired in English on July 23, 1927 from the Indian Broadcasting Company's station at Mumbai. As the station did not have a news bureau, the bulletin was based on news supplied by Reuters.

First sponsored programme

A musical programme, *Saridon Ke Saathi*, sponsored by Saridon, was aired on 3 May 1970 on the Mumbai–Pune–Nagpur radio network.

First cricket commentary

On 1 January 1936, Bertie Meyer provided commentary for a match between the All-India XI and the maharaja of Patiala's Australian XI, from Bombay station, Maharashtra, from 12:46 p.m. to 1:00 p.m.

Most commercial radio programmes anchored

The legendary radio announcer and programme anchor Ameen Sayani started his broadcasting career in 1951. During his career, he compèred more than 10,000 commercial radio programmes, and voiced 12,000 spots and jingles. He produced more than 38,920 publicity programmes for feature films.

WR Highest radio station

The Himbotingla station of AIR in Ladakh, located at an altitude of 4,053.84 m (13,300 ft) above mean sea level, is the highest radio station in the world. The 10 kW, high-power transmitters were inaugurated on 25 September 2021.

Longest running commentary

Melville de Mellow's running commentary on the last journey of Mahatma Gandhi on 31 January 1948, a day after his assassination, lasted for more than seven continuous hours.

First national programme of talks

On 29 July 1953, AIR aired the first national programme of talks in English.

First phone-in programme

Phone-in programmes were introduced on 10 January 1993 at AIR, Delhi.

First relay between radio stations

On 18 January 1939, an inter-station relay took place between Delhi and Bombay.

TELEVISION

First telecast

The first experimental telecast was carried out in Delhi on 15 September 1959 from a makeshift studio with the help of a single transmitter of 500W, which carried signals up to 25 km for an operational time of an hour a day. The studio was relocated to Rajpath for the first live telecast of the Republic Day parade in 1960.

First simultaneous tele-broadcast

Om Namah Shivay, directed by Dheeraj Kumar, was the first tele-serial to be telecast and broadcast at the same time on television and radio from March 1999.

First colour TVs

In 1982, the year India hosted the Asiad (Asian Games), colour TVs were introduced in India.

First colour transmission

An experimental telecast was conducted from the Madras TV station on 18 July 1980 for one hour. It was transmitted to Delhi viewers.

Longest running non-fiction TV series

Krishi Darshan, a TV programme aimed at disseminating useful information on farming to rural areas and agricultural communities, started on 26 January 1967 on DD National and still continues on the channel as well as on DD Kisan. It is considered to be the longest-running non-fiction TV series.

Mandi House, Delhi

First national telecast

Doordarshan started nationwide telecasts on 15 August 1982 from its TV studio in Mandi House in New Delhi.

First TV station to get a second channel

Delhi was the first TV station to get a second channel on 17 September 1984.

Doordarshan introduced five new channels on **15** August **1993** via Insat-1B.

First satellite linkage

The first satellite linkage experiment was launched on 1 August 1975 in six states in the country for one year. Later, satellite channels were available for the first time in 1991 to a select few who had access to the powerful dish antennas in embassies and five-star hotels.

First private channel

Zee TV, the first private television channel in the country, was launched in October 1992 in collaboration with Star TV and Zee Telefilms Ltd.

First business channel

Asia Business News International (ABNI), a 24/7 business channel, was launched on 14 February 1996 by the Hinduja Group in collaboration with Asia Business News (ABN) and TV18.

First central production centre

Set up in 1989 at the Siri Fort Complex, New Delhi, the Central Production Centre began with two large studios equipped with modern facilities to produce high-quality, well researched programmes.

First private satellite channel

Aaj Tak was the first private satellite channel permitted in 2000.

First 24-hour news channel

Star News, India's first 24-hour news channel, started on 3 February 1998, with news updates every hour from 6:00 a.m.

First infotainment channel

DD-3, which was Doordarshan's dedicated channel for infotainment, was launched on 14 November 1995.

First teleshopping programme

Shopping through TV was introduced on 1 January 1995, with an hour-long home-shopping show on Doordarshan's Metro channel in Delhi.

First telefilm

Satyajit Ray's *Sadgati* was telecast on the national network on 13 April 1981. This 52 min. telefilm was based on Munshi Premchand's short story. Produced by Doordarshan, it starred well-known actors, such as Om Puri and Smita Patil.

First serial

Teesra Rasta was the first fiction serial telecast from Doordarshan Kendra, New Delhi, starting from 2 May 1962.

First 24-Hour Channel

NDTV became India's first 24-hour news channel in alliance with Star in the year 1998, and at this time it produced 80 per cent of the content for BBC India. It also launched NDTV online in the same year and launched the first lifestyle channel in India. NDTV started out as a production house for news segments and gradually turned into the first independent news network in India.

First private producer of national news

In February 1995, New Delhi Television Ltd (NDTV) became the first private producer of national news with the show titled *The News Tonight*, which was hosted by Prannoy Roy at 8:00 p.m. They were the first private broadcasters for news on Doordarshan.

First video film

Teri Meri Kahani, the first video film, was produced by B.R. Chopra in 1981.

First Indian animation serial

Featuring Ghayab, the do-gooder ghost, *Ghayab Aya* was the first fully 'made-in-India' serialized animation film telecast on Doordarshan in 1986. The animator director was the well-known painter-illustrator Suddhasattwa Basu.

First director general of Doordarshan

P.V. Krishnamoorthy became the first director general of Doordarshan on 1 April 1976, the day Doordarshan and AIR were each given separate status.

First newsreader

Doordarshan began a five-minute news bulletin in 1965 with Pratima Puri as the first TV newsreader.

First high-definition channel

The first high-definition (HD) channel was introduced in India by Discovery Communications in March 2010.

First DTH service

Launched on 2 October 2013, Dish TV was the first Direct-to-Home (DTH) service in India.

Tallest TV tower

The tallest TV tower in India is located in Rameswaram, Tamil Nadu. The height of the tower is 323 m (1,060 ft). The tower was built in 1995 and is used by Doordarshan for television broadcasting. It is made of reinforced cement concrete and the mast is of lattice steel.

First sci-fi serial

Space City Sigma, produced by Studio Ifekt, was telecast from 21 May 1989.

Most watched daily soap

Anupamaa, starring Rupali Ganguly and Sudhanshu Panday, is the most watched daily soap in India between 21 and 27 October, according to the Broadcast Audience Research Council (BARC).

POST AND PHILATELY

Earliest postal communication

- In India, the earliest evidence of a systematic mail service is found during the reign of Chandragupta Maurya (r. 321–297 BCE), who ruled from Magadha (now in southern Bihar). In his empire, confidential reports were dispatched from the emperor to the outlying provinces, and from the provinces back to the ruler.
- The first recorded mention of a postal service was made by Ziauddin Barani, who wrote that Alauddin Khilji (r. 1296–1316) organized a regular foot-runner service, called *harkara,* as early as 1296. These harkaras carried a baton with bells and ran across allotted territory, carrying mail in a relay system with the runners changing every mile.
- Sikandar Lodi (r. 1488–1518), a ruler of the Lodi dynasty set up small posts across his kingdom and sent firmans daily to his armies.
- Babur (r. 1483–1530), the founder of the Mughal Empire, set up horse couriers from his capital at Agra up to Kabul, maintaining a regular 'postal' system.

First mail by steamboat

In 1828, mail was sent by a steamboat service between Calcutta (now Kolkata) West Bengal and Allahabad (now Prayagraj), Uttar Pradesh, along 1,266 km of the Ganga River. This is the earliest instance of mail delivery by steamer in Asia.

Post under British rule

- The first superintendent of post offices was appointed in Allahabad Uttar Pradesh, in 1870.
- British India became the first non-founding member of the General Postal Union in 1876.

First window delivery of letters

The Madras General Post Office or GPO (now in Chennai, Tamil Nadu) began the window delivery of letters from 1 June 1786 in the then Fort St George Square.

First postal training centre

Established on 2 April 1951, the postal training centre at Saharanpur, Uttar Pradesh, was the first training centre in Asia, set up exclusively for postal and telegraph personnel.

Madras General Post Office

ARTICLES DELIVERED THROUGH POSTMAN MOBILE APPLICATION (PMA) IN 2022

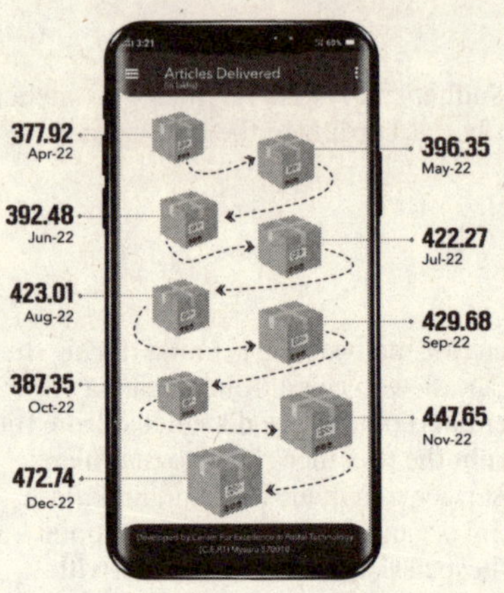

Source: Annual Report 2022–23, Department of Posts, Ministry of Communication, Government of India.

LETTER TRAFFIC DURING 2021–22 (IN CRORE)

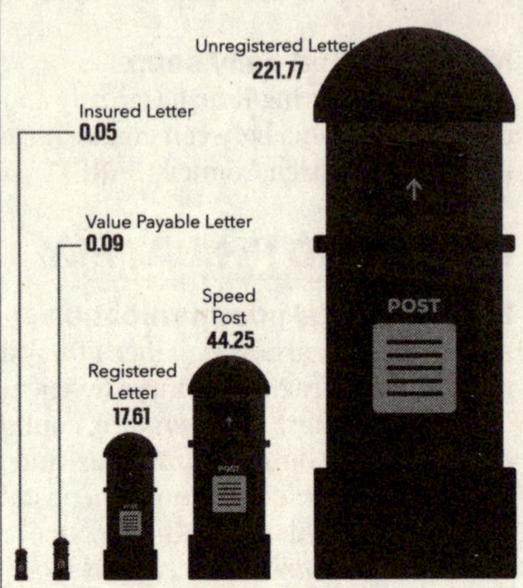

Source: Annual Report 2022–23, Department of Posts, Ministry of Communication, Government of India.

PARCELS HANDLED IN THE YEARS 2020–22

SPEED POST PARCEL

19,544,250

13,257,009

2020-21 2021-22

BUSINESS PARCEL

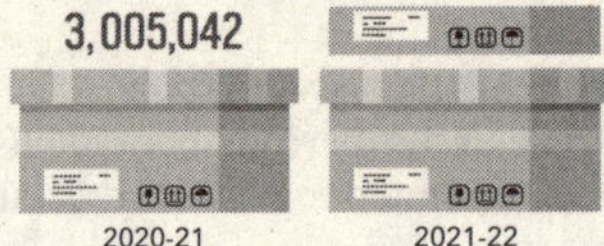

REGISTERED PARCEL

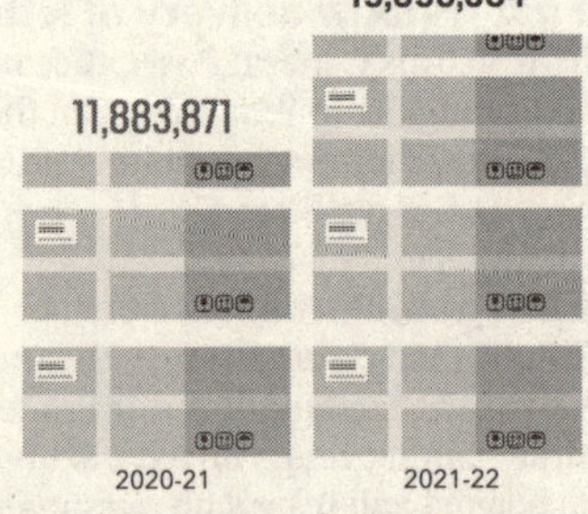

Source: Annual Report 2022–23, Department of Posts, Ministry of Communication, Government of India.

First electronic Indian Postal Order

On 22 March 2013, the first electronic Indian Postal Order (E-IPO) was introduced for Indian nationals living abroad. On 14 February 2014, the service was also extended to all Indian citizens.

The Government of India had allocated ₹1.23 lakh crore for postal and telecom projects in 2023.

WR Largest postal network

With a network of 156,434 post offices, the Indian Department of Posts has the world's largest postal network as recorded till 31 March 2021.

First postcard

The Postal and Telecommunications Department issued the first postcard on 1 July 1879.

First hot-air balloon carrying mail

A special postal cover was carried in a hot-air balloon carrier of India Post from Sakthi Mills Ground, Pollachi, Coimbatore District, Tamil Nadu, to the postmaster of Kovipalayam, Pollachi, on 3 January 2016.

First delivery peons

- Men: Postmen or delivery peons were first engaged on a security bond with a specific responsibility, as part of postal reforms carried out in Bengal in 1840. They were dressed in uniform and wore badges supplied by post offices. They were allowed to earn baksheesh of 2 pies (1 pie = 1/192 of a rupee) on each letter delivered, in addition to the collection of postage due to the post office.
- Women: K. Padmakshy Amma, who worked in the Thiruvananthapuram postal division in Kerala, joined service on 19 February 1959 as the country's first postwoman.

First Indian postmaster general

- *Man:* Rai Bahadur Saligram became the first Indian postmaster general for the North-Western Provinces in 1881.
- *Woman:* Sushila Chaurasia, who was born in Bijapur, Karnataka, in 1923, became the first woman to become postmaster general in the country. She assumed charge of the Madhya Pradesh circle on 24 May 1979.

First woman postal inspector

R. Santhakumari, who was from the Thiruvananthapuram postal division, Kerala, passed the inspector's examination in 1968 to become the first woman postal inspector.

The first Indian to be admitted to the Philatelic society was C.K. Dutt in 1907.

First letter by airmail

The first airmail letter was introduced in the country in November 1944. Priced at six annas, the airmail letter was called an 'aerogramme' and could be sent to the UK and other countries under the British Empire.

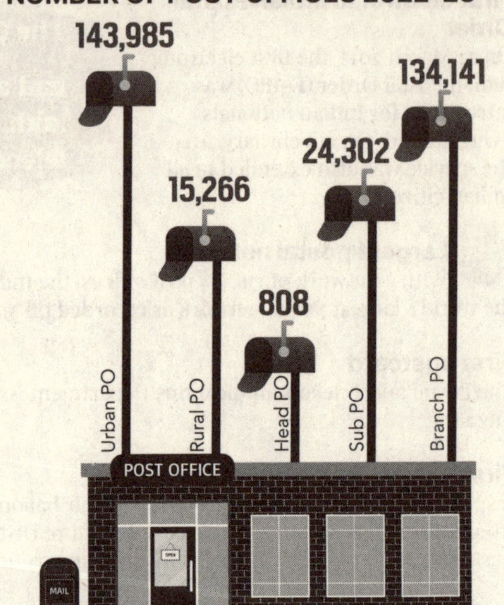

Source: Annual Report 2022–23, Department of Posts, Ministry of Communication, Government of India.

First insured mail service

The system of insurance post for letters and parcels, which was then called the 'insured mail service', was introduced on 1 January 1878.

First dead letter office

A post office for undelivered, unclaimed letters and letters with incomplete addresses was set up during 1834–37 in Benson Town in Bangalore. It was also called a Returned Letter Office.

First post office savings bank account

The post office savings bank, which started on 1 April 1882, introduced the then revolutionary concept of banking with a post office instead of a bank, which had been the usual method of keeping one's savings.

First all-woman post office

- Avinashilingam Home Science College post office at Coimbatore, Tamil Nadu, which opened in January 1966, was the first all-woman post office in India.
- A post office, which started functioning at Manoramaganj in Indore, Madhya Pradesh, on 31 March 1976, is also fully run only by women employees.

First computerized registration centre

The first computerized registration centre (CRC) was opened in June 1996 at the Market Road wing of the New Delhi General Post Office (GPO).

First mobile post office

On 1 November 2011, the Department of Post, Government of India, launched the Post Office on Wheels initiative with its first mobile van running in Pune, Maharashtra. The van worked from 8:00 a.m. to 8:00 p.m. daily covering 30 locations in a week, stopping at each location for two hours. The van offered all types of postal services, including e-enabled services, selling postcards, opening a new savings account, and selling postal life insurance, among others. The services were resumed during the COVID-19, related lockdown in 2020 to deliver pensions and provide mobile services in states such as Kerala and Uttar Pradesh.

First drive-in post office
A drive-in post office was inaugurated on 11 November 1975 in Pune, Maharashtra.

As of 2023 there are around **1,59,251** post offices in India.

First parcel service
Originally known as Bhangy post, parcel service was introduced on 2 December 1884. Its name came from the *bhangy* or bamboo stick with parcels on either end that the parcel carriers balanced on their shoulders.

Stamps from most countries in honour of a person
Stamps in honour of Mahatma Gandhi have been issued from over 150 countries up to 2019.

First registered mail service
The first mention of a system of registration being adopted by a post office to secure the safety of coins or documents in transit was found in an advertisement published on 20 February 1795. Actual registered post was introduced in Bombay Presidency on 1 November 1849 with a postal notice on 16 October 1849. In Bengal, it was established at Calcutta GPO on 1 January 1851 and later at Madras GPO. The fee was eight annas for registering a letter.

First online post office
The Head Post Office located at Sansad Marg, New Delhi, became fully computerized on 24 June 1998.

First letter boxes away from post offices
A great reform in the history of Indian post took place in October 1854 with the introduction of letter boxes located away from post offices.

First automatic mail processing centre (AMPC)
The first AMPC was launched at the Mumbai GPO, Maharashtra, on 29 April 1993, and a second one was established at Chennai, Tamil Nadu, in October 1995.

Longest-serving postmaster
Brother K.V.S.J. Peter, who received a Padma Shri in 1983, was the longest serving postmaster, for 68 years. He took charge of the Shenbaganur post office in Dindigul District, Tamil Nadu, on 12 September 1913, and was in service till 8 February 1982.

First express mail service
Speed Post was introduced by the Government of India on 1 August 1986, connecting seven cities in the country, and five other countries to India.

First stamp to be jointly issued with another country
India and the erstwhile USSR issued a set of two stamps on the Festival of India in the USSR, which was held in August 1990. Both countries issued the stamp with the same design.

First stamp

The Scinde Dawk (Provincial), India's first half-anna stamp, was issued with the help of Edward Lees Coffey, the postmaster of Karachi, on 1 July 1852 in Scinde District, Karachi (now in Pakistan). It was embossed on circular red wafers used as seals on letters, with the East India Company emblem and the legend Scinde District Dawk around the circumference. It was Asia's first ever adhesive stamp. It was withdrawn in 1854.

First airmail

India became the first country in the world to send mail by plane when 6,500 letters and postcards were flown from Allahabad to Naini (a distance of only 18 km!) in Uttar Pradesh in a Humber-Sommer biplane by Henri Pequet on 18 February 1911. A pictorial postmark showing the aeroplane was used.

A stamp commemorating the first aerial post

First Indian stamp featuring a woman

The Indian saints and poets series, issued on 1 October 1952, featured Mirabai, the 16th-century Bhakti poet-saint.

First customization of stamps

Initially introduced in India during the World Philatelic Exhibition 'INDIPEX-2011', 'My Stamp' is the scheme for personalized sheets of postage stamps of India Post. Such a sheet has a thumbnail image for example, the customer's photograph, logos of institutions, artwork, famous tourist places, historical cities, heritage buildings, and wildlife, on a selected template sheet featuring postage stamps. The facility is available for both non-corporate and corporate entities.

First state to issue a stamp (pre-1947)

Kathiawar state in Saurashtra (later Gujarat) issued a one-anna stamp in November 1864 with the inscription 'Saurashtra Post 1864–65'.

First differently shaped stamps

- **Polygonal:** The four-anna indigo-and-red stamp of India, issued on 15 October 1854, was polygonal, with the top and side panels raised from the main frame, which was slightly curved.
- **Circular:** The earliest circular stamp was the Scinde Dawk, though only the first printing was circular in the true sense since the later versions were issued on sheets that were usually cut square. It was the first circular stamp issued not only in India but in all of Asia. Later, the states of Indore (1889) and Jammu and Kashmir (1866–78) issued similar circular stamps.
- **Oval:** The half-anna red stamp, issued by the Indian state of Bhor (now in Maharashtra) in 1879, was oval in a horizontal format. It was imperforate and had to be cut out.
- **Triangular:** Stamps of this shape were issued on 10 October 1985 by the Border

Roads Organization.

- **Diamond-shaped:** Depicting Raja Ram Mohan Roy, these stamps were issued on 27 September 1964.
- **Trimmed:** These revenue stamps, reissued for postal use in 1866, had their inscriptions cut off at the top and bottom.
- **Octagonal:** A set of six octagon-shaped commemorative stamps to mark the 150th birth anniversary of Mahatma Gandhi was released on 2 October 2019 for the first time.

First stamp designer (pre-Independence)

Captain H.E.L. Thuillier, the deputy surveyor general of India, who was then stationed in Calcutta, Bengal, designed the first lithographic stamps, which were issued in 1854 and said to be engraved by an artist called Munirooddin.

First stamp of independent India

A 3.5-anna stamp with the inscription 'Jai Hind' was issued on 21 November 1947.

First one-rupee charity stamp

The first charity stamps were issued on 26 January 1950. Three 'Healthy India' charity stamps were brought out in denominations of one anna, four annas and one rupee.

First commemorative stamps

A set of six stamps was issued on 9 February 1931 on the laying of the foundation of New Delhi as the new capital of India. These were the first pictorial stamps depicting the important landmarks of the city.

First miniature sheet

To commemorate the India International Philatelic Exhibition 1973 in Delhi, a miniature sheet with a face value of ₹4.65 was issued on 14 November 1973.

First philatelic society

The Philatelic Society of India, the country's first philatelic society, was formed in Mumbai, Maharashtra, on 6 March 1897.

First autograph-inscribed stamp

A stamp issued on 7 May 1961 to commemorate the birth centenary of Nobel laureate Rabindranath Tagore had his signature inscribed on it.

Autograph-inscribed stamp

Largest philatelic bureau

Mumbai General Post Office Philatelic Bureau in Maharashtra, also an international philatelic bureau, is the largest in the country.

First Indian president of Federation Internationale de Philatelie (FIP)

Late D.N. Jatia, a reputed philatelist, was elected president at the 59th Congress of the FIP in London, UK, on 14 May 1990.

Birds and animals as carriers of mail

- Bullock mail: Between 1846 and 1904, bullock carts were used along the Grand Trunk Road between Allahabad, and Delhi to deliver mail. By 1875, as many as 41 government bullock 'trains' operated in the north-west provinces and Punjab. With the coming of the railways, bullock routes were used less, and the last line from Ambala in Haryana to Simla (now Shimla) in Himachal Pradesh was shut down in October 1904.
- Camel post office: A post office on camelback was started at Mithariya, Bikaner District, Rajasthan, on 27 October 1977. The postmaster here was given a special allowance for maintaining the camel. The office was later converted into a stationary post office.
- Pigeon post: The Odisha Police used pigeons as messengers till 2004. The force had a strength of around 900 homing pigeons.

First stamp featuring wildlife

The first Indian stamp depicting an animal was released in 1962, and it was a 15-paisa stamp showing the Indian rhinoceros. Next year, five more such stamps came out, featuring the Indian gaur (10 paise), the red panda (15 paise), the Indian elephant (30 paise), the Bengal tiger (50 paise) and the Asiatic lion (one rupee).

First philatelic exhibition

The Philatelic Society of Bengal held an exhibition of postage stamps at the art gallery of the Government School of Art (now renamed the Government College of Art and Craft) in Calcutta, Bengal, in December 1894.

First national philatelic museum

The National Philatelic Museum of India was established in New Delhi on 6 July 1968. It has large collections of postage stamps printed and issued by India and former princely states of India, early essays, proofs and colour trials, Indian stamps used abroad, early Indian postcards, postal stationery, and other thematic collections. It also has a philatelic bureau and postal objects such as letter boxes from Victorian times.

First Indian to design a stamp for the United Nations

Dipok Dey (b. 1938) from Calcutta, was the first Indian to design a stamp for the UN in 1985. The stamp was based on the theme of child survival.

First international stamp exhibition

'India 80' was the first international stamp exhibition held in Asia under the patronage of the Federation Internationale de Philatelie (FIP), held from 25 January 1980 to 3 February 1980.

TELECOM

First Indian radio telegraphy company

The Indian Radio Telegraphy Co. was established in 1923, which ushered in the era of wireless telegraphy.

First Indo-European telegraph line

The first independent double line of telegraph from London, UK, to Karachi (now in Pakistan) via Tehran, Iran, which was constructed by M/s Siemens and Co., was opened for operations on 31 January 1870.

First fibre-optic link

India's first fibre-optic link was made in 1979 when Hindustan Cables Ltd's office at Shivaji Nagar, Pune, Maharashtra, was linked to the Cotton Telephone Exchange, a distance of 4 km.

First submarine cable link

Madras (now Chennai), Tamil Nadu, was linked to Penang, Malaysia, in 1886 with a submarine telegraph cable.

First director general of the telegraph service

Sir William O'Shaughnessy was appointed as chief superintendent of telegraphs in 1857 in colonial India.

First manufacturer of telephones

- A telecommunication maintenance and repair shop was set up at Alipore, Calcutta, in 1860. The manufacture of minor components that were needed for the Baudot Telegraph and Line stores was initiated at the P&T workshop in 1913.
- The Indian Telephone Industries Ltd was established at Doorvaninagar near Bangalore, in July 1948 for manufacturing automatic and carrier equipment. The local assembly of phones from imported parts began in 1948 and the first phone off-the-line was produced on 26 January 1949.
- The first telephone with indigenous components was made in 1951.

First STD service

The facility for subscriber trunk dialling (STD) was first started between Lucknow and Kanpur in Uttar Pradesh on 26 November 1960.

Last telegram

India's 163-year-old telegram service ended at 11:45 p.m. on 14 July 2013. Its last message was booked at the Central

The telecom subscriber base in India grew to 117.075 crore (1170.75 million) January 2023.

Telegraph Office, Janpath, New Delhi, by Ashwani Mishra, who sent telegrams to Congress leader Rahul Gandhi and the DD news director general S.M. Khan.

First ISD service

The Arvi earth station for satellite communication, set up in 1971 in Arvi near Poona (now Pune), Maharashtra, marked the introduction of the first operator-dialled service to international subscribers. The first intercontinental telephone exchange was commissioned in 1973 and the first international subscriber dialling (ISD) telephone service was introduced between Bombay, and London, UK, in 1976.

First known use of SOS signal

On 1 November 1977, the duty operator in the astral wireless station at Ennore, near Madras, Tamil Nadu, received a weak SOS call from a cargo ship in the Bay of Bengal, stating that its engine room was on fire. The call was acknowledged and rescue ships reached in an hour.

First radio phone link

On 1 May 1933, Sir Samuel Hoare, the then Secretary of State for India under British rule, spoke from London, UK, to Sir Frederick Sykes, governor of Bombay, on radio phone, thus establishing a communication network between Britain and India.

First SMS provider

Hutchison Max offered a global text messaging service (SMS) in India in 2001.

First carrier to demonstrate 5G service capability

Bharti Airtel became the first carrier to successfully demonstrate live 5G service over a commercial network on 28 January 2021 in Hyderabad, Telangana. The carrier was capable of delivering 10x speed, 10x latency (the time it takes for data to pass from one point on a network to another) and 100x concurrency (the execution of multiple instruction sequences at the same time) in comparison with existing technologies.

First automatic telephone exchange

The first automatic telephone system in the country was commissioned at Simla (now Shimla, Himachal Pradesh), in 1914. The exchange had 400 working lines and another 300 lines in reserve.

First push-button telephone

The first Indian firm to manufacture electronic push-button phone answering machines was Bharti Telecom Ltd. It was also the first Indian company to launch cordless phones that were called 'Beetel'.

First cellular operators' association

The Cellular Operators Association of India (COAI), Delhi, was set up in 1995.

India had about **120** crore (1.2 billion) mobile subscribers in 2021.

Telecom revenue in FY2023

India's telecom revenues have crossed a record of Rs 3 lakh crore for the financial year 2023. This has happened for the first time ever as there is a higher consumption of data and content. The telecom industry saw some financial relief due to the government's reform packages. The top players who led the growth are Reliance Jio and Bharti Airtel. The government and mobile operators believe that revenues will continue to grow with the introduction of 5G across the country.

First call using a mobile phone

On 31 July 1995, the then Union telecom minister Sukh Ram and the then West Bengal chief minister Jyoti Basu spoke to each other using hand-held mobile phones, over Modi Telstra's MobileNet service.

First internet telephony service

On 25 July 2018, government-owned Bharat Sanchar Nigam Limited (BSNL) launched India's first internet telephony service that allows users to dial any phone number in India through its mobile app.

First circle launch

In 1996, Bharti Mobile Ltd, which was a joint venture of Bharti Enterprises with Telia Company of Sweden, launched Airtel, the first to provide services in a circle (outside metros) in Himachal Pradesh.

First national/international roaming service

On 12 September 1997, the Department of Telecommunications (DoT), Ministry of Communications, Government of India, cleared a national automatic roaming facility for cellular operators in Delhi, Mumbai, Calcutta and Chennai. International roaming facility was approved on 12 January 1998.

Service area with largest access subscriber base

Uttar Pradesh (East), with 98.14 million (9.814 crore) wireless and wireline subscribers, has the largest subscriber base (September 2020).

Largest wireline service provider

BSNL was the leading operator in wireline service, with 6,649,439 subscribers and 32.85 per cent of the market share as on 31 March 2021.

First telephone exchange

In 1881, the Government of India licensed the Oriental Telephone Company to set up telephone exchanges in Calcutta, Bombay, Madras, and Karachi (now in Pakistan). A 50-line exchange was set up in Calcutta in 1881 as one of the oldest exchanges in the world. It was set up only five years after the invention of the telephone.

First net fax service

Satyamfax, launched by Satyam Infoway on 25 April 2000 at Chennai, Tamil Nadu, in technical association with Singapore Telecom, was the first to provide fax to fax, web to fax, email to fax, and PC desktop to fax services.

For the fiscal year 2023, Reliance Jio reported a revenue close to ₹1 lakh crore (1.2 trillion rupees)

First cellular service

Modi Telstra, a joint-venture company of the B.K. Modi Group and the Telstra Corporation of Australia, inaugurated the first commercial cellular service in India on 23 August 1995. The network was constructed by Telecommunication Engineering Centre and the Modi Telstra team.

State/UT with highest tele-density

Delhi had 273.14 per cent tele-density (number of fixed [landline] telephone connections per 100 people in a specified area) up to 30 September 2020.

Largest wireless service provider

Reliance Jio was the leading wireless service provider with 422.92 million subscribers, followed by Bharti Airtel with 352.39 million subscribers, up to March 2021.

Mobile tower at the highest altitude

Installed by BSNL with the help of the Indian Army's Trishul Signallers, the highest mobile tower is located at 4,877 m (16,000 ft) in Chongtash in Ladakh. With this tower, even the remotest regions of Ladakh are connected by a communication link.

Service provider with number of rural subscribers – wireless

Reliance Jio has 179.31 million rural subscribers, which amounts to 33.47 per cent of total rural wireless subscribers. It is followed by Bharti Airtel with 168.63 million rural subscribers and Vodafone Idea with 149.93 rural subscribers up till March 2021.

INTERNET, SOCIAL MEDIA, AND APPS

First provider of internet services

Videsh Sanchar Nigam Limited (VSNL), under Department of Telecommunications (DoT), Ministry of Telecommunications, Government of India, was the first provider of Internet services in the country. It was launched on 15 August 1995.

First 3G operators

- The public sector telecom service provider Mahanagar Telephone Nigam Limited (MTNL) first provided 3G mobile service to parts of Delhi. This service started on 11 December 2008.
- Tata Docomo launched its 3G mobile service in many states – Rajasthan, Uttar

Pradesh (West), Gujarat, Maharashtra (except Mumbai), Haryana, Punjab, Kerala, Karnataka, and Madhya Pradesh – on 5 November 2010. It was he first private 3G operator in India.

First private internet service provider (ISP)

Satyam Infoway (Sify) became the country's first private internet service provider company on 22 November 1998.

First mobile app store

Airtel App Central was the first Indian mobile application store in the country. It was launched by Bharti Airtel Ltd on 9 February 2010.

First Aadhaar-based payment app

The Government of India launched Bharat Interface for Money (BHIM) app, an Aadhaar-based mobile app for digital payments, on 30 December 2016.

WR First free email service

Conceived by Sabeer Bhatia (and colleague Jack Smith), Hotmail was the first free email service that took the whole world by storm in 1996. Bhatia was a Bengaluru-born Indian-American businessman and led Hotmail as its president and CEO, until its eventual acquisition by Microsoft in 1998.

WR Largest WhatsApp user base in the world

India remained WhatsApp's biggest market with 40 crore (400 million) monthly active users, who exchange around 6,000 crore (60 billion) messages daily (as of July 2019). The country has been the biggest market for WhatsApp since November 2015.

Top internet subscription – service areas – both wired and wireless

The highest-subscription service areas in the country are the states of Uttar Pradesh (East+ West) (87.88 million/8.78 crore), Maharashtra (61.42 million/ 6.14 crore), Andhra Pradesh (56.73 million/5.67 crore), Tamil Nadu (50.42 million/ 5.04 crore) and Madhya Pradesh (47.23 million/4.72 crore).

Largest Facebook user base

With 310 million (31 crore) active users, India emerged as Facebook's largest country audience in July 2020.

Highest data consumption

India has the highest data consumption of 11 Gb/month per user on an average.

WR Most number of mobile app downloads

India had the most number of mobile app downloads, 7 billion (700 crore), on the Apple iOS Appstore as well as on Google Playstore in the second quarter of 2020. It is followed by the USA with 375 crore (3.75 billion) and Brazil with 300 crore (3 billion).

Most popular search engine

Google, with a user base of 93.4 per cent, is the favourite search engine in India.

Most popular mobile operating system

The favourite mobile operating system in India is Android with 62 per cent usage; next is Windows with 19.4 per cent usage.

Most popular browser

The most popular browser in India is Google Chrome, with a share of 51.91 per cent among all browsers.

Most viewed Indian video on YouTube

'Phonics Song with TWO Words', an alphabet learning video by ChuChu TV has garnered 4,348,214,171 views on YouTube as on 14 December 2021. The video was posted on 7 March 2014.

WR First and only 4G, all-Internet protocol network

Reliance Jio, which revolutionized the mobile Internet market in India when it rolled out 4G services in 2016, is the only network in the world to rely solely on 4G Long-Term Evolution (LTE) network, based on Internet telephony, without the backing of the legacy 3G/2G services.

Fastest 4G service provider

Vodafone Idea Ltd is the provider of the fastest 4G network in the country with a download speed of 13.74 Mbps and an upload speed of 6.19 Mbps. It is followed by Bharti Airtel and Reliance Jio.

WR Most subscribed YouTube channel

T-Series (Super Cassettes Industries Pvt. Ltd), a music record label and film production company, became the first YouTube channel in the world to reach 100 million subscribers in May 2019. As of October 2022, it had 226 million (22.6 crore) subscribers.

WR Highest concurrent video viewership

A new world record of 2.57 crore (25.7 million). concurrent viewers was set by Jio Cinema, the official digital streaming partner of the India Premier League (IPL). The record was set for the IPL 2023 match. Viewers came to watch Chennai Super Kings play with the Royal Challengers Bangalore. The previous record was held by Disney+Hotstar which had a record of 2.53 crore (2.53 million).

Most downloaded mobile application

Aarogya Setu, a COVID-19 contact-tracing app launched by the Government of India became the most downloaded application in India and the seventh most downloaded application in the world. It recorded 127.6 million (12.76 crore) installations up till July 2020.

Largest social network penetration

India is the world's second largest market with 34.997 crore (349.97 million) users in 2020. While there are many apps available to the Indian public, YouTube leads with an 82 per cent market penetration. It is closely followed by Facebook (76 per cent), WhatsApp (70 per cent), Instagram (64 per cent), and Facebook Messenger (53 per cent), according to the 2019 Q3 figures.

GOVERNMENT

HISTORICAL PERSPECTIVE

Earliest republic on the subcontinent

Vrijji, a *mahajanapada* (republic) of ancient India, dating to the sixth century BCE, is believed to be the earliest republic on the Indian subcontinent. It did not have a monarch, but instead a popular assembly of elders carried on the business of state. Vrijji was formed by the union of several clans, including the Lichchhavis, Jnatrikas, and Videhas. Its capital was at Vaishali, in the present-day region of Mithila, Bihar.

Early administration

During the time of the Mauryan rulers (322–180 BCE), the state maintained a vast bureaucracy with important functionaries called *tirtha*s. The top administrators were the minister (*mantri*), the high priest (*purohita*), the commander (*senapati*), and the prince (*yuvaraja*). An elaborate machinery was in place for taxation too.

First Indo-European alliance

Chandragupta Maurya met Alexander III of Macedon in 327 BCE – after the battle with Porus (or Puru) and the capture of Punjab – and teamed up with him for the capture of Magadha in what may be termed the first Indo-European treaty.

First War of Independence

The country's First War of Independence, which British historians called the Sepoy Mutiny or the Rebellion of 1857, was the first organized fight against the colonial rulers, and an important milestone in the long struggle for independence.

First colonial rule

Dom Francisco de Almeida was appointed the first Portuguese viceroy in India by King Manuel I of Portugal in 1505 – marking the first colonial rule in India.

First woman rulers

- Nayanika from the Satavahana dynasty (first century BCE) is considered the first woman ruler of India. She was a queen regent, who was holding the fort for her son, Satakarni II, when he was a child. She was the first woman ruler to have coins struck in her name. She was the wife of King Satakarni I.
- In 1236 CE, when Razia Sultan of the Mamluk dynasty ascended the Delhi throne, she became the first queen regnant in India. Unlike a queen regent, Razia ruled her territory in her own right. She was also the only woman ruler of the Delhi Sultanate.

Tomb of Razia Sultan in Old Delhi

First design of the national flag

The 'Flag of Indian Independence' was raised by freedom fighter Bhikhaiji (or Bhikaji) Rustam Cama (1861–1936) from Bombay (now Mumbai), Maharashtra, on 22 August 1907 at the International Socialist Conference in Stuttgart, Germany. It was based on the 'Calcutta flag', which was one of the first unofficial flags of India, designed by Sachindra Prasad Bose and Hemchandra Kanungo, and hoisted on 7 August 1906 at Parsi Bagan Square, Calcutta (now Kolkata), West Bengal. Cama's flag featured three colours: the top band was green, the middle one was saffron, and the bottom one was red. The upper band had eight lotuses, symbolizing the eight provinces of British India. The middle band had the words *Vande Mataram* in Devanagari script, and the lower band had a crescent and a sun, representing Islam and Hinduism respectively. The flag went through many versions before reaching its present form.

First rendition of the national song

'Vande Mataram', India's national song, composed by Bankim Chandra Chatterjee and published for the first time in his work *Anandamath*, was first sung at the Indian National Congress session in 1896 in Calcutta.

First rendition of the national anthem

'Jana Gana Mana', India's national anthem composed by Rabindranath Tagore, was sung for the first time on 27 December 1911 at the Calcutta session of the Indian National Congress. The song was formally adopted in its Hindi version by the Constituent Assembly as India's national anthem on 24 January 1950.

First satyagraha

In 1917, Mahatma Gandhi organized the first satyagraha, a non-violent protest, in Champaran, Bihar, for indigo cultivators, against British laws governing the cultivation of the plant.

First Republic Day parade

India became an independent nation on 15 August 1947, and declared itself a sovereign and democratic republic with the promulgation of the Constitution of India on 26 January 1950. The first Republic Day parade was held in 1950 at Irwin Stadium (now known as Major Dhyan Chand National Stadium) in New Delhi. Five years later in 1955 the R-Day parade found a new and permanent venue at Rajpath (now Kartavya Path), New Delhi.

Shortest reign

Following the death of Alauddin Khilji (Khilji dynasty) in 1316, Malik Kafur captured the throne of Delhi. His reign lasted between 25 and 30 days. He was ousted by Alauddin's son, Shihabuddin Omar.

Longest colonial rule

Goa, Daman, and Diu were under colonial rule for the longest period

Fundamental duties were added to the Constitution by the 42nd Amendment in 1976 on the recommendation of the Swaran Singh Committee.

A TIME LINE OF ACTS THAT SHAPED MODERN INDIA

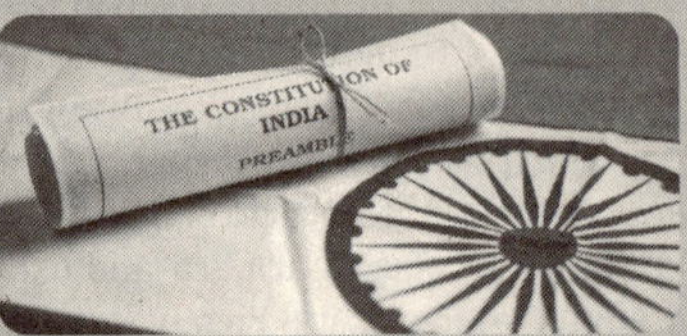

COMPANY RULE

1773
Regulating Act was passed by the British parliament to regulate affairs of the East India Company

1781
Amending Act was passed to amend the faults of the Regulating Act

1784
Pitts India Act introduced the system of decentralized administration

1786
Act of 1786 brought in judicial reforms; codification of civil and criminal laws; appointment of collector and registrar courts

1793
Charter Act extended the company's trade monopoly in India for 20 years

1813
Charter Act ended company's trade monopoly in the East; tea trading was allowed

1833
Charter Act drafted Indian Penal Code (IPC), Governor General of India appointed

1853
Charter Act formed Indian Central Legislative Council; legislative and executive functions separated

CROWN RULE

1858
Government of India Act transferred power of governance to British Crown

1861
Indian Councils Act included Indians in the law-making process; representative institutions came in

1892
Indian Councils Act included more Indians in legislative councils

1909
Indian Councils Act legalized 'communalism' (also called Morley–Minto Reforms)

1919
Government of India Act, also called 'mini constitution', forms the basis of Indian Constitution

1935
Government of India Act established the Federal Court (eventually leading to the formation of the Supreme Court of India in 1950); Burma was separated from India; steps taken towards establishment of 'Federation of India' (British India provinces and princely states)

1947
- **15 June:** The Mountbatten Plan of partition of India accepted by the All India Congress Committee

The process of drafting and adopting the Constitution after Independence and Partition of the country as India and Pakistan began.
- **29 August:** Drafting Committee appointed, Dr B.R. Ambedkar as chairman

1948
July 16: Vice presidents of Constituent Assembly appointed. They were H.C. Mookerjee and V.T. Krishnamachari

1949
November 26: The Constitution of India passed and adopted by the Constituent Assembly

1950
- **January 24:** The Constitution of India signed and accepted
- **January 26:** The Constitution of India came into force

in Indian history – over 450 years. For over a decade after the British had left India, the Portuguese ruled these pockets as 'Estado da India Portuguesa' (the Portuguese State of India). They were liberated by the Indian Army on 19 December 1961.

PARTIES AND ELECTIONS

First political organization

The first recorded political organization in the country was the Zamindari Association of Calcutta (now Kolkata), West Bengal. Formally launched in 1838, it was a body of landlords, which changed its name to Landholders' Association shortly after its inception. Its principal organizers were Radhakanta Deb and Prasanna Kumar Tagore. Set up to defend the landlords against government policies that the Zamindars thought were against their interest, it became defunct in 1851.

Oldest political party

Allan Octavian Hume (1829–1912), a member of the Imperial Civil Service, initiated the events that led to the formation of the first political party in India. Speaking out against British policies in India, in 1883, he exhorted Calcutta University graduates to form their own national political movement. This led to the first session of the Indian National Congress in Bombay (now Mumbai), Maharashtra, in 1885.

First party constitution

The first constitution of the Indian National Congress was drawn up in 1908, after the split in the party between the moderates and the extremists in the 1907 session held in Surat, Gujarat.

First woman president of the Indian National Congress

British socialist and women's rights activist Annie Besant (1847–1933), who was elected president of the Indian National Congress in 1917, was the first woman to head the party.

Longest-serving President of the Indian National Congress

Sonia Gandhi (b. 9 December 1946), the Italian-born Indian politician and widow of former Indian prime minister Rajiv Gandhi, she headed the Indian National Congress from 1998 to 2017, longest term served in this post in the party's history. With her at the helm, the Congress-led United Progressive Alliance (UPA) was victorious in the 2004 and 2009 general elections.

First chief election commissioner

Sukumar Sen (1898–1963) was India's first chief election commissioner, in office from 21 March 1950 to 19 December 1958. Under his leadership, the Election Commission of India conducted India's first two general elections, in 1951–52 and 1957. He also administered the first parliamentary elections in Sudan in 1953.

First general election

India went to the polls as an independent country for the first time during 1951–52, with 314 constituencies with one seat, 86 constituencies with two seats, and one with three seats. There were also two nominated Anglo-Indian members. At the time, the Election Commission of India recognized 14 political parties as multi-state parties and 39 parties as state parties. Voting in the election was based on the 'balloting system', i.e., casting votes in ballot boxes allotted to the respective candidates.

First use of single ballot paper and single ballot box

The general election of 1962 introduced the single ballot paper system, in which the voter had to mark one choice from the candidates and drop the paper in a ballot box. Earlier, during the 1951–52 and 1957 general elections, there were separate ballot boxes for each candidate with their name and party symbol on them.

Longest tenure as chief election commissioner

K.V.K. Sundaram (1904–92), India's second chief election commissioner, served for eight years, nine months and eleven days, from 20 December 1958 to 30 September 1967.

Shortest tenure as chief election commissioner

V.S. Ramadevi (1934–2013), the first woman chief election commissioner (acting) of the country, held the post of chief election commissioner for only 17 days from 26 November 1990 to 12 December 1990.

First electronic voting machines

Electronic voting machines (EVMs) were used for the first time in the assembly by-elections in Kerala in April 1982. The machines were introduced by the Electronics Corporation of India Ltd (ECIL).

First use of indelible ink

Indelible ink was used for the first time in the third Lok Sabha elections in 1962. Mysore Paints and Varnish Ltd, based in Mysore (now Mysuru), Karnataka, was authorized to manufacture the ink. The company continues to supply this ink to this date.

Voters showing the indelible ink on their fingers.

First app launched for voter vigilance

For the first time in elections, an application called 'cVIGIL' was launched for citizens to report any malpractice or violation of the model code of conduct before or during elections. This app includes a combination of live photo/ video and time-stamping with auto-location. A government official is bound to respond within 100 minutes. Launched in July 2018, the app was rolled out across India before the 2019 Lok Sabha election.

First 'Others' category of voters

A third gender category of voters, called 'Others', was introduced in the electoral rolls in 2014. As many as 28,314 voters enrolled in this category in 2014 and 38,970 voters in 2019.

First teenage vote

The 61st amendment of the Constitution of India in 1989 lowered the voting age for election to the Lok Sabha and the state legislatures from 21 years to 18 years. As a result, 35.7 million voters in the age group of 18–21 years voted.

First NOTA option

The 2014 general elections were the first to offer Indian voters the option of choosing 'None of the Above' (NOTA), also known as the 'against all' or a 'scratch' vote internationally. The NOTA option provides a neutral vote to those electors who do not wish to vote for any candidate on the electoral ballot. Around 1.04 per cent of voters polled NOTA in the 2019 elections.

First EVMs /postal ballot papers with photographs of candidates

For the first time in the history of elections in India, the EVMs/postal ballot papers carried the photographs of all the candidates in the constituency. This was done to enable the voters to identify the political leaders and to avoid confusion between candidates with similar names.

First transgender election ambassador

Gauri Sawant, a transgender activist from Mumbai, Maharashtra, was appointed as the first transgender election ambassador in the country in 2019.

Lowest voter turnout in the Lok Sabha general election

In the 1951–52 general election, which was the first election to be held in independent India, only 44.87 per cent of the electorate was recorded as having cast their votes.

Highest voter turnout in the Lok Sabha general election

The 2019 general election had the largest voter turnout to date with 613,136,854 voters, constituting 67.1 per cent of the total electorate of the country.

Most female candidates in a Lok Sabha general election

The 2019 general election registered a total of 723 female candidates.

Fewest women elected in a general election

Only 19 women were elected in the 1977 general election, which was the fewest ever in the history of general elections.

Most women elected in a Lok Sabha general election

Seventy-eight women were elected in the 2019 Lok Sabha general election, making it the election with the highest number of successful female candidates.

Most independent candidates elected in a general election

In the history of Indian elections, independent candidates had the most successful run in the 1957 general election, winning 42 seats.

Most independent candidates in a general election

The 1996 general election had a total of 10,636 independent candidates, the highest ever to date.

Fewest independent candidates elected in a general election

Only 3 of the 3,235 independent candidates in the 2014 general election were successful, the lowest win by independents in the history of general elections in India.

A-WEB Update

At the 11th meeting of the Executive Board of Association of World Election Bodies (A-WEB), chief election commissioner of India (CEC), Rajiv Kumar, raised two proposals:

1. Setting up an A-WEB portal which would serve as repository of electoral best practices and initiatives taken by member of the election management bodies (EMBs) worldwide in various aspects of electoral management.
2. Establishing A-WEB Global Awards for EMBs who make significant contribution and take important initiatives in the democratic processes.

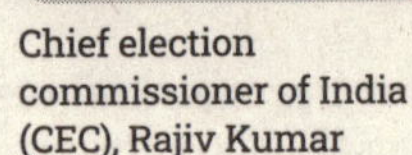

Chief election commissioner of India (CEC), Rajiv Kumar

Both the proposals were approved by the executive board.

The A-WEB is the largest EMBs worldwide; it has 119 EMBs as members and 20 regional organizations as associate members.

The most expensive election

The 2019 Lok Sabha election was estimated to be the most expensive election in the world. An estimated ₹55,000 crore (550 billion) was spent during these elections, according to a report brought out by the Centre for Media Studies.

Largest electorate

The number of voters in the 2019 general election was 908,722,153, making India the largest (most populous) democracy in the world.

Voter-verifiable paper audit trail in all constituencies for the first time

The Election Commission of India set up the voter-verifiable paper audit trail or VVPAT system in all constituencies in 2019. The VVPAT prints a slip with the serial number, name, and symbol of the candidate for whom the vote was cast.

State/UT with the largest electorate

Uttar Pradesh had the largest electorate in the 2019 general election, with 145,858,999 eligible voters.

Youngest winning candidate

Biju Janata Dal (BJD) member Chandrani Murmu was only 25 years old when she contested and won the Keonjhar seat in Odisha in the 2019 general election.

State/UT with the smallest electorate

The Union Territory of Lakshadweep had the smallest electorate in the 2019 general election, comprising a total of 55,057 eligible voters. The UT also holds the record for being the constituency with the smallest electorate in the country.

State/UT with the smallest voter turnout

In terms of percentage turnout, Jammu and Kashmir (before Ladakh was separated from it) had the smallest voter turnout in the 2019 general election, with 29.39 per cent of the voters turning out to vote. In terms of the number of voters, Lakshadweep, with 47,009 voters registered the smallest voter turnout.

State/UT with the largest voter turnout

Madhya Pradesh had the largest voter turnout in terms of the percentage of the total number of voters in the 2019 general election, with a turnout of 71.2 per cent. In terms of number of voters, Uttar Pradesh, with 86,481,398 voters, led all states.

Most voter IDs distributed – 1 hr

The district administration of Allahabad (now Prayagraj),

Currently the Constitution of India is divided into **25** parts and **10** schedules. There are **448** articles. So far it has been amended **105** times.

Local Self-government in India

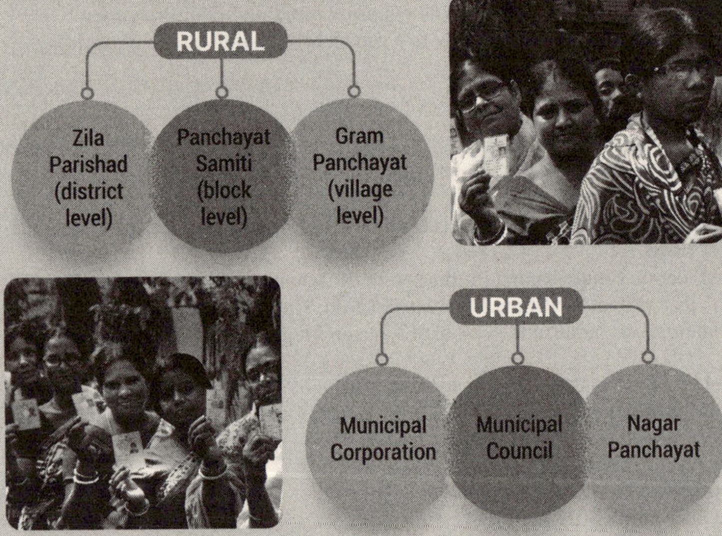

- **MUNICIPAL CORPORATION**: where population is over 10 lakh (one million) (large areas are further divided into wards)
- **MUNICIPAL COUNCIL**: where population is less than 10 lakh (one million)
- **NAGAR (TOWN) PANCHAYAT**: areas in the middle of transition from rural to urban

History of Local Self Government in India:

- Local self-government in villages have been practised in India since ancient times
- *Panch* means 'five', or, rule by an assembly of five village elderly,
- First elected local self-government was introduced by Lord Ripon in 1882
- Mahatma Gandhi supported and encouraged local self-government
- The Constitution of India made it compulsory to hold elections in the local level after every five years

Quick Facts:

- There are 250,000 local self-government bodies in India.
- Over 31 lakh (3.1 million) elected members.
- Thirteen lakh (1.3 million) members are women.
- All India Institute of Local Self Government, established in 1926, to guide the local bodies.
- Lord Ripon is known as the father of local self-government.

Uttar Pradesh, led by District Magistrate Sanjay Kumar and Chief Development Officer Andra Vamsi, conducted the largest ever voter ID distribution camp on 16 February 2017, distributing 12,594 voter ID cards in one hour. The distribution event took place from 11:00 a.m. to 12:00 noon at the Parade Ground in the city.

The size of the Indian electorate is as big as 36 democracies in the world combined. There were around 912 million eligible voters in India in 2019.

WR Highest polling station

The polling station at Tashigang in Spiti Valley, Himachal Pradesh, situated at an altitude of 4,650 m (15,256 ft), is the highest polling station in the world.

PRESIDENTS AND VICE PRESIDENTS

First presidential election

The first presidential election in the country was held in 1952 when Dr Rajendra Prasad (1884–1963) became the president of India.

First vice president

Dr S. Radhakrishnan (1888–1975) was vice president of India during 1952–62. He also had the longest tenure as vice president, that of 10 years, a record he shares with Hamid Ansari, who was in office from 11 August 2007 to 11 August 2017.

Oldest vice president to assume office

Bhairon Singh Shekhawat (1923–2010) became vice president on 19 August 2002, when he was 79 years of age.

Oldest to become president

K.R. Narayanan (1920–2005) became India's oldest president when he assumed the office on 25th July 1997. He was 76 years and 271 days old.

First woman president

Pratibha Patil (b. 19 December 1934) became the first woman to be appointed president of India. Earlier, Pratibha Patil had held the office of governor of Rajasthan during 2004–07. She was affiliated with the Indian National Congress. Pratibha Patil started the Shram Sadhana Trust. The trust runs hostels for working women in New Delhi, Mumbai, and Pune.

Shortest tenure as vice president

V.V. Giri (1894–1980) was vice president for two years during 1967–69, making his tenure the shortest for a vice president. He was elevated to the post of (acting) president on 24 August 1969, following the death of Dr Zakir Husain.

V.V. Giri: He left his legal career to join the non-cooperative movement in 1920

Youngest to Become President

Droupadi Murmu (b. 20 June 1958) became the youngest president of India when she assumed the office of president of India on 25 July 2022 at the age of 64 years and 36 days. The earlier record was held by former president Dr Zakir Husain who became president at 64 years and 67 days.

Shortest tenure as president

Dr Zakir Hussain (1897–1969), the third president of India, held the office of president from 13 May 1967 until his death, for a little less than two years. Dr Husain was also the first president to die in harness.

Longest tenure as president

Dr Rajendra Prasad (1884–1963), a lawyer and freedom fighter, was appointed as

Presidents of India

Name	Tenure
Dr Rajendra Prasad	26 January 1950–13 May 1962
Dr S. Radhakrishnan	13 May 1962–13 May 1967
Dr Zakir Hussain	13 May 1967–3 May 1969
Varahagiri Venkata Giri (acting)	3 May 1969–20 July 1969
Mohammad Hidyatullah (acting)	20 July 1969–24 August 1969
Varahagiri Venkata Giri	24 August 1969–24 August 1974
Fakhruddin Ali Ahmed	24 August 1974–11 February 1977
Basappa Danappa Jatti (acting)	11 February 1977–25 July 1977
Neelam Sanjiva Reddy	25 July 1977–25 July 1982
Giani Zail Singh	25 July 1982–25 July 1987
Ramaswamy Venkataraman	25 July 1987–25 July 1992
Shankar Dayal Sharma	25 July 1992–25 July 1997
Kocheril Raman Narayanan	25 July 1997–25 July 2002
Dr. A.P.J. Abdul Kalam	25 July 2002–25 July 2007
Pratibha Devisingh Patil	25 July 2007–25 July 2012
Pranab Mukherjee	25 July 2012–25 July 2017
Ram Nath Kovind	25 July 2017–25 July 2022
Droupadi Murmu	25 July 2022–present

Indian Executive System

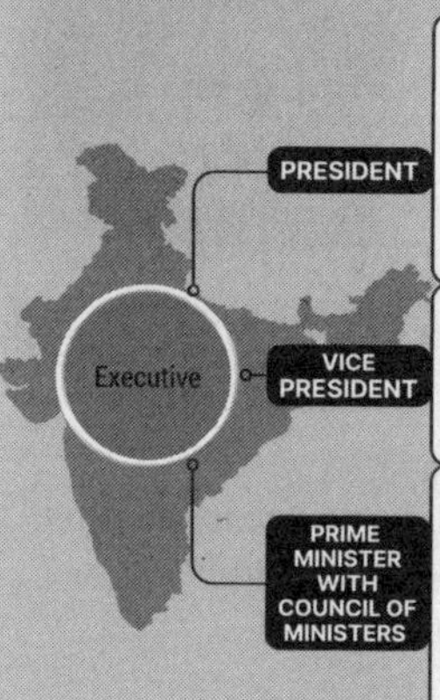

PRESIDENT

- fixed tenure of five years
- elected by electoral college (elected members of Parliament + state assembly members)
- ceremonial or nominal powers
- works on advice of the PM, except during an external or internal emergency
- is the supreme commander of defence forces
- can proclaim national emergency or impose president's rule, dissolve the Lok Sabha
- can grant mercy in case of capital punishment

VICE PRESIDENT

- fixed tenure of five years
- is chairperson of the Rajya Sabha
- acts as president when there is a sudden vacancy in the president's office
- may be removed from office by a resolution passed by both houses of Parliament

PRIME MINISTER WITH COUNCIL OF MINISTERS

- leader of majority party is appointed as prime minister by president
- PM forms government with his Council of Ministers
- PM cannot exceed five years' tenure; may be removed anytime before that by own party members
- rest of the ministers are appointed by president on the advice of the PM
- a person may be appointed as minister if the PM wants even if he/she is not an elected member. Must be elected to either House within six months
- most powerful post in India

the first president of India on 26 January 1950, a post he occupied for 12 years, three months, and 18 days until 13 May 1962.

Most presidents from a state

With three presidents to date, Tamil Nadu is the state that has given the country the most number of presidents. They are S. Radhakrishnan, R. Venkataraman, and A.P.J. Abdul Kalam.

- Dr S. Radhakrishnan,the first vice president and second president of India, held the position of president from 1962 to 1967.
- R. Venkataraman, the eighth president of India, held office from 1987 to 1992.
- A.P.J. Abdul Kalam, the 11th president of India, held the presidential office from 2002 to 2007.

PRIME MINISTERS

First prime minister

Jawaharlal Nehru (1889–1964) became the first prime minister of India on 15 August 1947. Previously, he headed the interim government as prime minister, starting 2 September 1946. He served as prime minister until he died on 27 May 1964.

First prime ministers to die in harness

- Jawaharlal Nehru, the first prime minister of India, passed away on 27 May 1964, after serving the office for 17 years. He was the first prime minister of India to die in harness.
- Jawaharlal Nehru's successor, Lal Bahadur Shastri, died at Tashkent, Uzbekistan, on 11 January 1966. He was the first prime minister of India to die in harness abroad.
- Indira Gandhi was the first prime minister to be assassinated while in office, on 31 October 1984.

Only woman prime minister

Indira Gandhi (1917–84), the first and only woman to become prime minister of India, was in office from 1966 until 1977. She was re-elected in 1980 and her second tenure lasted four years, until her assassination in 1984.

Indira Gandhi: the only woman prime minister of India to date

Oldest to become prime minister

Morarji Ranchhodji Desai (1896–1995), a freedom fighter during India's struggle for independence, became prime minister at the age of 81 years and 24 days on 24 March 1977. Earlier he had held many offices, such as those of minister of home affairs, deputy prime minister, and finance minister. He was also the chief minister of undivided Bombay state from April 1952 to October 1956.

First prime minister to resign

Morarji Ranchhodji Desai was the first prime minister of India to resign from the office. He assumed office on 24 March 1977 and resigned from his post on 28 July 1979, following a split in the Janata Party, which he was heading at the time.

First deputy prime minister

Sardar Vallabhbhai Patel was sworn in as the first deputy prime minister of India on 15 August 1947 in the first cabinet of independent India, which was headed by the then prime minister Jawaharlal Nehru.

Youngest to become prime minister

Rajiv Gandhi assumed office on 31 October 1984, when he was 40 years and 72 days, following the assassination of his mother, Prime Minister Indira Gandhi.

Shortest tenure as prime minister

- Chaudhary Charan Singh (1902–87) was prime minister for 171 days from 28 July 1979 to 14 January 1980, making him the shortest-tenured prime minister on record. He was the only prime minister of India who never faced the Parliament.
- Gulzari Lal Nanda had two shorter tenures as acting prime minister, once from 27 May to 9 June 1964, after Jawaharlal Nehru's death, and again from 11 to 24 January 1966, following Lal Bahadur Shastri's demise.

Rajiv Gandhi tops the list of prime ministers in terms of their physical height: only prime minister to date who is or was 6 ft tall.

UNION GOVERNMENT

First non-Congress government

The Janata Party, led by Jayaprakash Narayan, overthrew the Indira Gandhi government in the 1977 general election to form the first non-Congress

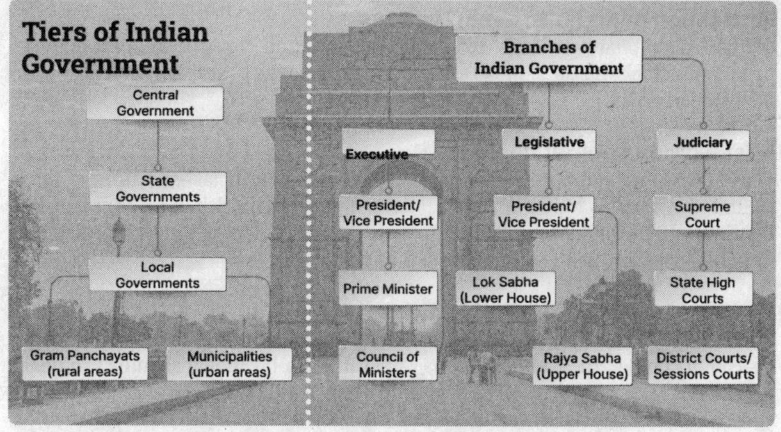

government in the history of independent India. Morarji Desai was appointed prime minister of the government formed by the Janata Party.

First electoral win by an Indian political party

In the elections held under the provisions of the Government of India Act, 1935, the Indian National Congress formed governments in seven states, in addition to a coalition ministry in Assam. They lasted till October–November 1939, after which they unanimously resigned in protest against the inclusion of Indians in the Second World War.

First woman full-time finance minister

Nirmala Sitharaman (b. 18 August 1959) became the first woman to be a time finance minister of India on 31 May 2019. She is the second woman finance minister after former prime minister Indira Gandhi, who held the finance ministerial office for some time while she was prime minister during 1970–71. Sitharaman was also the first woman minister with defence as her sole portfolio from 2014 to 2019.

First Union minister to resign

Dr Shyama Prasad Mookerjee (1901–53) resigned from the Union cabinet on 19 April 1950. After leaving the Nehru government and the Congress party, he founded the Bharatiya Jana Sangh in 1951.

Longest serving cabinet minister

Babu Jagjivan Ram (1908–86) was a Union minister for over 28 years from 15 August 1947 to 25 July 1979 with a break from 31 August 1963 to 24 January 1966. Some of the portfolios held by him included the Ministry of Labour, the Ministry of Defence, and the Ministry of Transport and Communications.

Shortest tenure of a cabinet minister

Justice H.R. Khanna (1912–2008) was in office as the minister for law and justice in the Charan Singh ministry for five days from 30 July to 3 August 1979.

First Union minister to die in harness

Sardar Vallabhbhai Patel (1875–1950), India's first home minister and first deputy prime minister, who died on 15 December 1950, was the first Union minister to die while in office.

First woman cabinet minister

Vijaya Lakshmi Pandit (1900–90) was elected to the provincial legislature of the United Provinces as minister for local government and health in 1937, making her the first woman cabinet minister. Later, she was president of the United Nations General Assembly from September 1953 to September 1954.

First use of Hindi at United Nations (UN)

Atal Bihari Vajpayee (1924–2018), former prime minister of India, gave a historic speech in Hindi at the United Nations General Assembly in 1977 as India's minister for external affairs. This was the first time when any Indian leader had given a speech in Hindi at any international platform. It was translated into English by an Indian diplomat. Vajpayee spoke again in Hindi in 1978.

THE STATES

First linguistic state (pre-1947)

The Orissa (now Odisha) province that was formed as a result of the division of the Bihar and Orissa province in 1936, was the first to be formed on a linguistic basis.

First linguistic state (post-1947)

The Telugu-speaking Andhra state was carved out of Madras state on 1 October

1953, with its capital at Kurnool. It was later merged with the Telugu-speaking areas of Hyderabad state to form Andhra Pradesh on 1 November 1956.

First modern Indian states/UTs

The Indian states of Bihar and Orissa were the first to be formed in British India. The Bihar and Orissa province of Bengal Presidency was carved out as a separate province on 1 April 1912, which included the present-day states of Bihar, Jharkhand, and parts of Odisha. On 1 April 1936, the then Bihar and Orissa province was divided into the separate provinces of Bihar and Orissa.

State sharing borders with most states

Uttar Pradesh shares its borders with nine Indian states – Rajasthan, Haryana, Himachal Pradesh, Delhi, Uttarakhand, Bihar, Madhya Pradesh, Jharkhand, and Chhattisgarh.

State with the longest coastline

Gujarat has the longest coastline of 1,214.7 km, followed by Andhra Pradesh with a coastal length of 973.7 km.

State with the longest international border

West Bengal shares a 2,216.7 km long border with Bangladesh, making it the state with the longest international border.

State with the largest area

With an area of 342,239 sq. km, Rajasthan is the largest state. It covers around 10.4 per cent of India's total area.

A panoramic view over Jodhpur, Rajasthan, with Mehrangarh Fort

State with the smallest area

Goa is India's smallest state with a total area of 3,702 sq. km.

Youngest state

Telangana was formed on 2 June 2014, after its separation from the state of Andhra Pradesh.

Youngest UTs

After abrogation of Article 370 on 5 August 2019, the former state Jammu and Kashmir was bifurcated into two union territories: a) Jammu and Kashmir and b) Ladakh.

First chief minister elected abroad

M.G. Ramachandran (popularly known as 'MGR') was elected chief minister of

Anganwadi centres

An anganwadi is a government-supported centre that works under the Integrated Child Development Services (ICDS). The anganwadis are mostly situated in rural areas. Each anganwadi caters to a population of 400 to 800 poeple.

Anganwadi provides six services: (i) Supplementary Nutrition; (ii) Pre-school Non-formal Education; (iii) Nutrition and Health Education; (iv) Immunization; (v) Health Check-up; and (vi) Referral.

The services are provided to children in the age group of 0–6 years, adolescent girls, pregnant women, and lactating mothers through anganwadi centres across the country. The three health services – immunization, health check-up, and referral services – are provided through National Health Mission (NHM) and public health infrastructure.

Tamil Nadu while he was admitted in a New York hospital. His nomination papers for the Andipatti assembly constituency were flown in from the United States and he was elected in absentia. He was sworn in on 10 February 1985, forty-three days after the election.

Shortest term as chief minister

- Jagdambika Pal was chief minister of Uttar Pradesh for one day – on 21 February 1998.
- Harish Rawat's second term as chief minister of Uttarakhand also lasted a day – 21 April 2016.

First woman chief minister

India's first woman chief minister was freedom fighter Sucheta Kripalani (1908–74). She was chief minister of Uttar Pradesh (1963 to 1967).

First state under president's rule

President's rule was imposed on Punjab from 20 July 1951 to 17 July 1952. The proclamation came after the resignation of the Congress ministry headed by Dr Gopichand Bhargava.

WR First elected communist government in power

On 5 April 1957, the Communist Party of India in Kerala formed the first communist government in the world to come to power by voting. It was led by E.M.S. Namboodiripad. It was dismissed by the Centre in 1959.

First 'film star' chief minister

M.G. Ramachandran or 'MGR' was the first film star to become chief minister when he assumed office in Tamil Nadu on 4 July 1977.

Oldest serving chief minister

Mizoram's chief minister Zoramthanga (b. 13 July 1944) at the age of 79, is the oldest serving chief minister of a state.

Youngest chief minister

- M.O. Hasan Farook Maricar, three-time chief minister of Pondicherry (now Puducherry), was the youngest chief minister when he came to power at 29 years in 1967. He died in office in 2012 as governor of Kerala.
- Pema Khandu, elected as chief minister of Arunachal Pradesh in 2016 at the age of 38 years, is the youngest serving chief minister of a state.

Most chief ministers in a year

Haryana had four chief ministers in nine months from November 1989 to July 1990: Devi Lal (November 1989), Om Prakash Chautala (December 1989), Banarsi Das Gupta (May 1990), and Hukam Singh (July 1990).

Chief minister with the longest tenure and most consecutive terms

Pawan Kumar Chamling (former chief minister of Sikkim) has been India's longest-serving chief minister, having served in that post for five terms from 12 December 1994 to 26 May 2019 (24 years 165 days). He has surpassed the record of Jyoti Basu, who held the office of chief minister of West Bengal from 1 June 1977 to 6 November 2000 (23 years 137 days).

Most Legislative Council elections won

Basavaraj Shivalingappa Horatti (b. 14 April 1946), currently chairman of Karnataka Legislative Council, scripted history in June 2022, when he got re-elected to the Legislative Council from the Karnataka West Teachers' Constituency for a record eighth time. He is the longest-serving member of a legislative council in India, a member since 1980.

GOVERNANCE

First woman sarpanch

Chhavi Rajawat, the first woman sarpanch (head of the village panchayat) in India, looks after Soda, a village in Tonk District, Rajasthan. She assumed office in February 2010 at the age of 30 years. She is an alumna of Rishi Valley School, Madanapalle, Andhra Pradesh; Mayo College Girls' School, Ajmer, Rajasthan; and Lady Shri Ram College, New Delhi. She also holds an MBA degree from Balaji Institute of Modern Management, Pune, Maharashtra. She left her corporate job to work in rural India.

First Indian in the Imperial Civil Service

Satyendranath Tagore, elder brother of Rabindranath Tagore, was the first Indian to join the service in 1863. He was recruited into the Covenanted Civil Service (later named the Imperial Civil Service). His first posting was in the Bombay Presidency (which included parts of present-day Maharashtra, Gujarat and Sindh).

First Indians in the Privy Council

In 1907, K.G. Puta and Syed Hussain Bilgrami were admitted to the Privy Council of India, the supreme appellate authority in British India, which advised the British monarchy.

First woman IAS officer

Anna Rajam George (b. 17 July 1927) from Calicut (now Kozhikode), Kerala, was the first woman to qualify for the Indian Administrative Service (IAS), in 1950. She was posted as a subdivisional officer in a small town in Tamil Nadu in 1951.

First municipalities

Municipal corporations for civic amenities were set up first between 1880 and 1884, when Lord Ripon was the viceroy of India.

First Public Service Commission

The Public Service Commission was first constituted under the chairmanship of Sir Charles Umpherston Aitchison, governor of Punjab, in 1926.

Chhattisgarh recruited **13** transgender people into the police force in **2021**.

First woman ambassador

Vijaya Lakshmi Pandit, the sister of India's

first prime minister, Jawaharlal Nehru, was India's first woman ambassador, to the erstwhile USSR from 1947 to 1949. She also served as ambassador to the US and Mexico (1949–51) and Ireland (1955–61). She held a post in the cabinet in pre-Independence India, the first Indian woman to do so. Her longest tenure was in London, as high commissioner to the UK, serving from 1954 to 1961. Her last posting as ambassador was in Spain. She served as governor of Maharashtra from 1962 to 1964 and as member of the Lok Sabha from 1964 to 1968.

First panchayats

Panchayats were first established in villages under the Panchayat Act in 1912, but with little success. It was in 1952 that a new Panchayat Act revived the system.

First woman career diplomat

Chonira Belliappa Muthamma from Coorg (now Kodagu), Karnataka, qualified for the Indian Civil Service and joined the foreign service in 1949. She served in France, the UK, and Burma (now Myanmar), and later as ambassador to Hungary and Ghana.

First woman mayor

Tara Cherian (1913–2000) was appointed mayor of Madras (now Chennai), Tamil Nadu, in 1957. She received the Padma Bhushan in 1967.

Youngest governor

Swaraj Kaushal was appointed governor of Mizoram in February 1990 when he was 37 years and seven months old.

Youngest mayor

Arya Rajendran (b. 12 January 1999), the Left Democratic Front (LDF) councillor from the Mudavanmugal ward, became the mayor of Thiruvananthapuram Corporation, Kerala, in December 2020 when she was 21 years old.

Youngest sarpanch

Anant Parag Khadilkar, the youngest sarpanch in India, secured the post in Nagargao Sattari Village in Goa in 2017 when he was only 21 years old. He was then a graduate in commerce.

Youngest woman sarpanch

Twenty-one-year-old Asruni Khan was elected as the sarpanch of Chulhera Village in Bharatpur District, Rajasthan, in January 2020.

AADHAAR

State/UT with least Aadhaar coverage

Nagaland, with a low saturation percentage of 61.08 as on 31 May 2023, has the lowest Aadhaar saturation among all states and Union Territories in India, on the basis of total projected population for the year 2023.

State/UT with highest Aadhaar coverage

Delhi, with a saturation percentage of 106.43 as on 31 May 2023, has the highest

Aadhaar coverage. The saturation percentage is calculated as the percentage of the number of Aadhaar cards assigned upon the total projected population for the year.

LAW AND ORDER

First Indian sheriff
Manackjee Rustomjee, a Parsi businessman and judge from Bombay (now Mumbai), Maharashtra, was appointed as the sheriff of Calcutta (now Kolkata, West Bengal) in 1873, the first Indian to be appointed to the position.

First forensic science laboratory
In 1853, the Government Examiners' Laboratory was established in Calcutta followed by labs in Madras (now Chennai), Tamil Nadu, Bombay, Lahore (now in Pakistan), and Agra, Uttar Pradesh. At present, there are seven central forensic science labs in India, viz., Hyderabad, Kolkata, Chandigarh, New Delhi, Guwahati, Bhopal, and Pune.

First all-woman police station
The first all-woman police station in the country was started in October 1973 at Calicut (now Kozhikode) in Kerala. Sub-inspector Padmini was in charge of it.

First Indian director of the Intelligence Bureau
T.G. Sanjeevi Pillai took over as the first Indian director of the Intelligence Bureau, Ministry of Home Affairs, from Sir N.P.A. Smith in April 1947 and held office till July 1950.

WR First fingerprint bureau
The first fingerprint bureau in the world was set up in Calcutta in June 1897. A murder case in 1898 in Jalpaiguri was the first to be solved on the basis of dactyloscopy, which is the science of fingerprint identification.

First Police Act
The Police Act of 1861 led to the creation of a police service. This Act introduced a uniform system applicable to entire British India.

First police dog squad
The Madras City Police Dog Squad, now called the Chennai City Police Dog Squad, was started in 1952 by a sub-inspector of police, Kanniah Naidu, in Chennai, Tamil Nadu. It was the first police dog squad in India.

First open prison
The first open prison in India, Durgapura Open Camp, was started in Rajasthan in 1956 by the then governor, Dr Sampurnanand, in the Government Agriculture and Research Centre campus at Jaipur. Prisoners who had spent six years behind bars could live with their families and go out in the day to earn.

First transgender sub-inspector
India's first transgender sub-inspector, K. Prithika Yashini, joined the Tamil Nadu

Police force on 2 April 2017. She was posted to Dharmapuri District in Tamil Nadu after a legal battle with the Madras High Court ruling in her favour.

First woman IPS officer

Kiran Bedi (b. 9 June 1949) was the first woman to join the Indian Police Service (IPS) on 16 July 1972. She retired in 2007 and was later the lieutenant governor of Puducherry (May 2016–February 2021).

Biggest cryptocurrency crime

India's biggest cryptocurrency crime involved US $300 million (₹ 2,498.26 crore approx). It happened through a multilevel bitcoin marketing scam allegedly perpetrated by Amit Bhardwaj, director of Gain Bitcoin. A case was registered against him in Pune, Maharashtra, in 2018. The victims allegedly claimed that the bitcoin investment company duped them into investing in bitcoins for higher returns. Bhardwaj died of a cardiac arrest on 15 January 2022.

Largest prison complex

Tihar Prisons, which started with the Central Jail in 1958, now includes nine central jails, apart from a district jail at Rohini, New Delhi, making it the largest prison complex in Asia. Starting with a capacity of 1,273 prisoners, it now houses 13,183 prisoners against the sanctioned capacity of 5,200 prisoners.

LEGAL MATTERS

First Penal Code

The Indian Penal Code (IPC) and the Criminal Procedure Code (CrPC), which were introduced in Bengal in 1862, were drafted on the recommendations of the first Law Commission of India set up in 1834, chaired by British historian and politician Thomas Babington Macaulay.

High court with the most judges

Allahabad High Court has the largest sanctioned strength of 160 judges, but has never held its full complement. As on 21 March 2023, it had 82 permanent judges and 21 additional judges (total 103).

Allahabad High Court, Allahabad (now Praygraj), UP

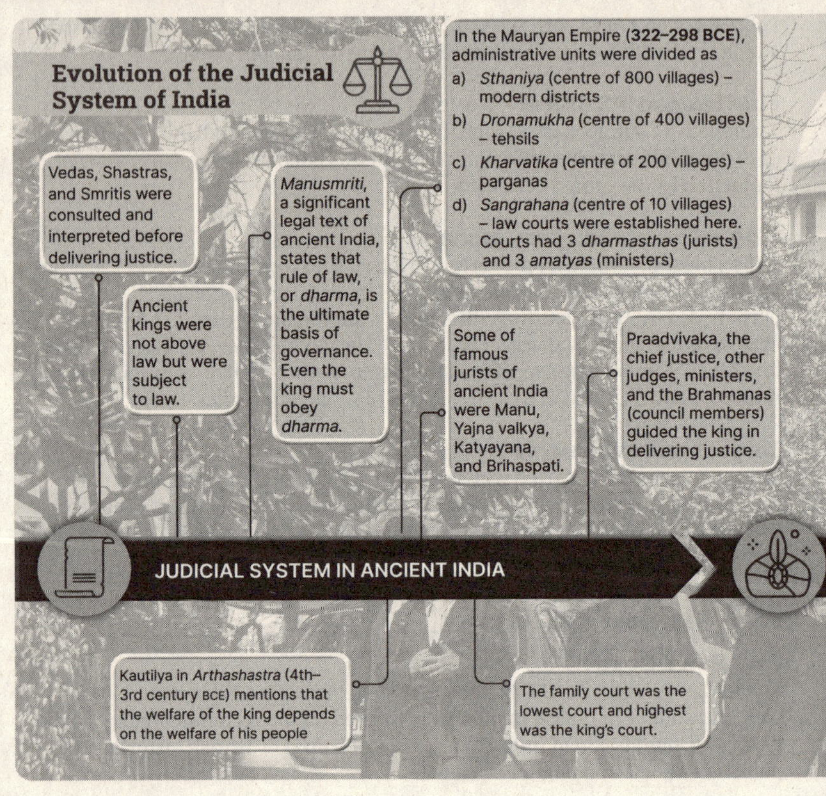

First British Indian Code

The East India Company's proposal for separate civil and criminal courts in districts of Calcutta (now Kolkata), West Bengal, on 15 August 1772 was the first British Indian Code.

First woman advocate

Cornelia Sorabji (1866–1954) was the first woman to graduate in law in 1894. However, law being a male bastion then, she was enrolled in the Allahabad High Court Bar only in 1923.

First public prosecutor

S. Subramania Iyer (1842–1924), jurist and freedom fighter, was appointed public prosecutor in Madras (now Chennai), Tamil Nadu, in 1887.

First barrister-at-law

Gyanendramohan Tagore (1826–90) passed the barrister-at-law examination from Lincoln's Inn in England on 21 June 1862, becoming the first Indian to do so. In November 1865, he was enrolled into the Calcutta High Court in the then Bengal Presidency (now in Kolkata, West Bengal) as the first Indian barrister.

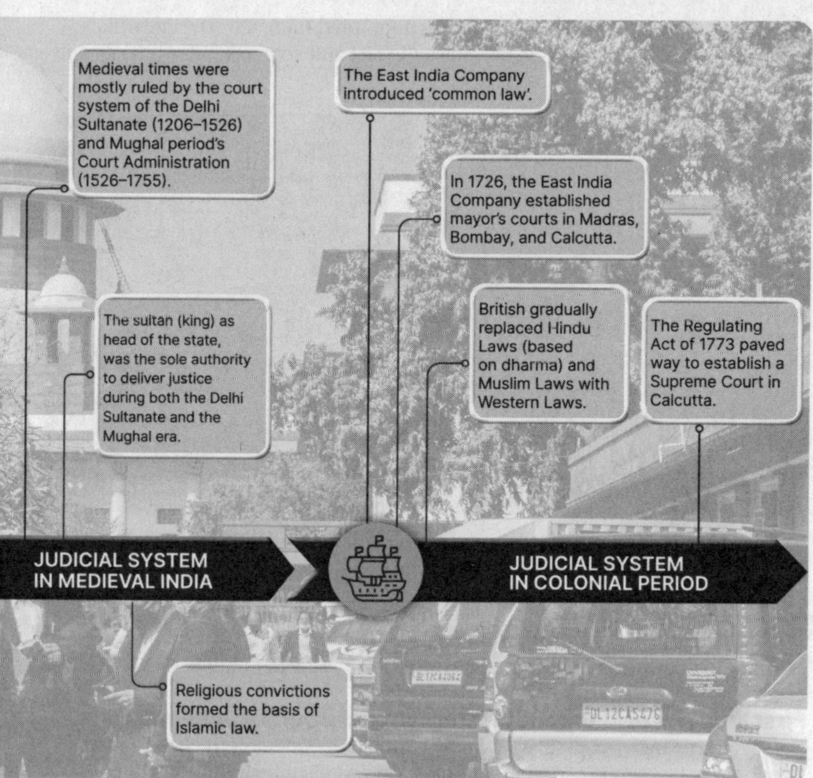

First woman judge of the Supreme Court

Meera Sahib Fathima Beevi (b. April 1927) was appointed as a judge of the Supreme Court in October 1989, the first Indian woman to hold this post. She was also the second woman in the world to hold such a position.

First high court judge

Shambhunath Pandit, a Kashmiri domiciled in Calcutta was appointed judge at the Calcutta High Court on 2 February 1863. His tenure ended in 1867.

First woman chief justice

Justice Leila Seth (1930–2017) was appointed the chief justice of Himachal Pradesh on 5 August 1991, becoming India's first woman chief justice of a high court.

First chief justice of India

India's first chief justice was Justice Sir Harilal J. Kania (1890–1951), who held the position from 26 January 1950 to 6 November 1951.

First woman judicial officer

Anna Chandy (1905–96), a member of the Travancore Legislative Council during

1923–24, graduated in law in 1930 and was appointed munsif by the erstwhile state of Travancore in 1937. She became a district and sessions judge in 1948, and a judge of the Kerala High Court in 1959.

Greater Chennai Corporation, Tamil Nadu.

Oldest civic body

The Greater Chennai Corporation, Tamil Nadu, was inaugurated under a royal charter issued by King James II of England, on 29 September 1688, as the Corporation of Madras. It is the oldest civic body in the country and the second oldest in the world. The first is in London, UK.

First Indian president of the International Court of Justice

Dr Nagendra Singh (1914–88) was the first Indian president of the International Court of Justice, serving from 1985 to 1988. He was also the first Indian to be a judge of the court. He received the Padma Vibhushan in 1973.

First Indian woman on the United Nations law board

Neeru Chadha, an international law expert, became the first Indian to be appointed to the International Tribunal for the Law of the Sea (ITLOS), being elected to the UN body in June 2017.

First citizen to have a 'no caste, no religion' certificate

M.A. Sneha Parthibaraja, a lawyer from Tirupattur, Tamil Nadu, became the first Indian citizen to win the right to not have a caste or religion, on 5 February 2021. She was granted the certificate after a nine-year-long court battle.

The Supreme Court of India has **33** judges as on 21 March 2023, apart from the chief justice. They are all appointed by the president of India.

Oldest high court

The Calcutta High Court, established on 1 July 1862, under the Indian High Courts Act, 1861, is the oldest high court in India. It has jurisdiction over West Bengal, and the Union Territory of

Andaman and Nicobar Islands. Its building was designed by British architect Walter Granville, who based it on the Cloth Hall at Ypres in Belgium. The seat of the high court is Kolkata. It also has a permanent circuit bench in Port Blair, the capital of the Andaman and Nicobar Islands. It has a sanctioned strength of 72 judges. T.S. Sivagnanam (b. 16 September 1963) is its current serving

First transgender judge

Joyita Mondal Mahi, India's first transgender judge, was appointed as a judge in the Lok Adalat in West Bengal in 2017. She was 29 years old at the time.

First transgender lawyer

Sathyasri Sharmila, a lawyer in the Bar Council of Tamil Nadu and Puducherry, is the first transgender lawyer in India. Although she completed her education in 2007, she enrolled as an advocate after the National Legal services Authority of India (NALSA) judgment of 2014, which recognized the third gender.
chief justice.

THE CENSUS*

First census

The first all-India census was conducted in 1872 in British India. However, the first regular census in the country was conducted in 1881, and then every 10 years. The last census was conducted in 2011. The census is conducted by the registrar general and census commissioner under the Ministry of Home Affairs, Government of India.

Most populated state

Uttar Pradesh is India's most populated state, with a population of 199,812,341.

Most populated Union Territory (UT)

Delhi is India's most populated Union Territory with a population of 16,787,941.

Least populated state

Sikkim is India's least populated state, with 610,577 people.

Least populated UT

Lakshadweep, with a population of 64,473, is the least populated union territory.

Most densely populated state

Bihar has a population density of 1,106 persons per sq. km, making it the most densely populated state in India.

Most densely populated Union Territory

Delhi, with a population density of 11,320 persons per sq. km, is the most densely populated UT.

Least densely populated UT

Andaman and Nicobar Islands have a population density of 46 persons per sq. km, making it the least densely populated UT.

*As per Census 2011

A French style street in Puducherry – a former French colony and now a union territory in south India

State v. Union Territory

A state is a larger division within the country. It has its own elected state government. A union territory (UT) is usually smaller than a state and is directly run by the Union government through a governor as the representative of the president.

The eight UTs of India are Andaman and Nicobar Islands, Chandigarh, Dadra and Nagar Haveli and Daman and Diu (one UT since the two separate UTs Dadra and Nagar Haveli and Daman and Diu were merged in 2019), Delhi, Puducherry, Jammu and Kashmir (J&K), Ladakh (Jammu and Kashmir Reorganization Act, 2019, reconstituted J&K as two UTs – namely, a) Jammu and Kashmir and b) Ladakh), and Lakshadweep.

Delhi, Puducherry, and Jammu and Kashmir are UTs that have received partial statehood. So they have their own elected legislative assembly and council of ministers with a chief minister.

Delhi was redefined as National Capital Territory and larger areas like Ghaziabad, Noida (in UP), and Faridabad and Gurugram (in Haryana) were added as National Capital Region (NCR).

Least densely populated state

Arunachal Pradesh, with a population density of 17 persons per sq. km, is the least densely populated state in India.

State/UT with the highest sex ratio

Ladakh has the highest sex ratio at birth among states and UTs, with 1,125 females per 1,000 males.

State/UT with the lowest sex ratio

Dadra and Nagar Haveli and Daman and Diu has a sex ratio at birth of 817 females per 1,000 males.

With inputs from Dr Sangita Sharma

PARLIAMENT

THE STORY OF THE INDIAN PARLIAMENT

INTRODUCTION

The Parliament of India is the supreme legislative body of the Republic of India. It is a bicameral legislature consisting of two houses – the Lok Sabha (House of the People) and the Rajya Sabha (Council of States), and the president of India acts as their head.

The significance of the Indian Parliament is best captured in the words of Nitish Kumar, chief minister of Bihar and former Union minister of railways: 'Since I joined politics my dream was to enter into this great parliament as a member. I was not alone, but it was a collective dream of our friends at that time in political circle. Never aspired to become a minister or party leader or an influential king maker ever. But to become an MP was the highest goal to achieve. Today I am proud not because I am a minister, but because I am an MP from Bihar.'

Prime Minister Narendra Modi, in speeches to bid farewell to the old Parliament building and welcome the new building (with a gap of 24 hrs), referred to the fact that Indian Parliament has so far had more than 7,500 members including 600 women lawmakers.

THE OLD BUILDING

This central area of New Delhi is also called Lutyens's Delhi, named after one of the two architects involved, Edwin Lutyens. He and Herbert Baker were selected for a project in British era to build the legislative council which became Indian Parliament after Independence. While Baker was a British architect of reputation who had designed

Eligibility to be a member of Parliament (MP)

To be eligible for membership in the Lok Sabha, a person must be 25 years of age or older and for membership in the Rajya Sabha, a person must be 30 years of age. A member of parliament (MP) must be mentally sound, should not be bankrupt, and should not be criminally convicted.

Parliamentary committees

Parliamentary committees are formed to deliberate specific matters at length. Parliamentary committees are of two types: standing committees and ad hoc committees. Standing committees are permanent committees constituted from time to time in pursuance of the provisions of an Act of Parliament or rules of procedure and conduct of business in Parliament. The work of these committees is of a continuing nature. Ad hoc committees are appointed for a specific purpose, and they cease to exist when they finish the task assigned to them and submit a report. The Parliament can also have consultative committees. Every Lok Sabha can create their own consultative committees. The 17th Lok Sabha has 40 such committees.

Question Hour

It is the time allocated in a sitting Parliament session when the MPs may ask questions to ministers about implementation of laws and policies by the government. The MPs use this time to seek information on matters that affect the day-to-day life of the citizens. For such matters, ministers are both collectively and individually answerable to the legislature.

prominent buildings in another British colony's city, in South Africa's Pretoria, Lutyens was not as well known.

At the coronation of George V as Emperor of India on 12 December 1911, the monarch announced, 'We have decided upon the transfer of the seat of the Government of India from Calcutta to the ancient Capital of Delhi.' The two architects would then build the Parliament House, Rashtrapati Bhawan, North and South Blocks, Rajpath, India Gate, the National Archives building and the princes' houses around India Gate.

It was in the year of 1913, Baker and Lutyens signed on to be the architects for the Imperial City at New Delhi, their brief only included the design of the President's House and North and South Block. In 1919, the British Parliament passed the Government of India Act which provided for a bicameral legislature for India. A new building was needed to accommodate the new Houses of the legislative council. The Parliament building's construction took six years (1921–1927). It was originally called the Council House and housed the Imperial Legislative Council, the legislature of British India.

In 1919, Lutyens and Baker settled on a blueprint for the Council House. They decided on a circular shape as the duo felt it would be reminiscent of the Colosseum, the Roman historical monument. It is popularly believed that the circular shape of the Chausath Yogini temple at Mitawli Village in Madhya Pradesh's Morena District provided inspiration for the Council House design, but there is no historical evidence to back this up.

The word *parliament* comes from the French word *parler*, which means 'to talk'.

Lutyens, in particular, was not

Old Parliament building

The old Parliament building – a quick look

The Old building is 21 metres (70 ft) tall, 170 metres (560 ft) in diameter and covers an area of 2.29 hectares (5.66 acres). It has 144 cream sandstone pillars, each measuring 27 feet. According to the official Central Vista website, around 2,500 stonecutters and masons were employed just to shape the stones and marbles required for the construction of the building. The Central Hall consists of the chambers of the Lok Sabha, the Rajya Sabha, and the library hall. Surrounding these three chambers is the four-storeyed circular structure providing accommodations for members and houses parliamentary committees, offices, and the Ministry of Parliamentary Affairs. The Central Hall is circular in shape and the dome is 30 metres (98 ft) in diameter. The Indian Constitution was framed in the Central Hall. The construction cost for the old building was ₹8.3 million.

in favour of adding hallmarks of Indian architectural traditions in his works, believing them to be inferior in quality. Soon after he arrived in India in March 1912, he wrote to his wife, 'I do not believe there is any real Indian architecture or any great tradition. There are just spurts by various mushroom dynasties with as much intellect as there is in any other art nouveau.'

On the other hand, Baker thought that the goal of ultimately projecting the strength of British imperialism and rule over India could also be achieved by mixing Eastern and Western styles. However, he did agree with Lutyens on the superiority of European classicism, upon which he said that Indian traditions had to be based.

As a result, a few Indian elements, such as jaalis (a latticed carving depicting objects like flowers and other patterns) and chhatris (a domed roof atop a pavilion-like structure) were finally added.

On 18 January 1927, Sir Bhupendra Nath Mitra, a member of the Governor General's Executive Council and in charge of the Department of Industries and Labour, invited Viceroy Lord Irwin to inaugurate the building. The next day, the third session of the Central Legislative Assembly was held there.

With the British rule in India coming to an end, the Constituent Assembly took over the building, and in 1950 it became the location of Indian Parliament as the Constitution of India came into force.

Paintings in old Parliament building

- 38 mural paintings depicting scenes from the Ramayana, Mahabharata, life of the Buddha, Shankaracharya, and so on
- 24 portraits of political leaders placed in the Central hall: Vallabh Bhai Patel, Rabindranath Tagore, Syama Prasad Mookerjee, Mahatma Gandhi, Gopal Krishna Gokhale, Sarojini Naidu, Veer Savarkar, Jawaharlal Nehru, Indira Gandhi, Rajiv Gandhi, among others
- 17 photographs of the old Parliament building
- 8 portraits of famous parliamentarians from the past
- 11 portraits of former chairmen

THE NEW BUILDING

At present, the Lok Sabha has 543 seats filled by elected representatives. The Rajya Sabha has 245 members, including 12 nominees from the expertise of different fields of literature, art, science, and social service.

In 2012, during the UPA (2nd) regime, the then Lok Sabha Speaker Meira Kumar gave approval for a high-powered committee to suggest an alternative complex to the old parliament house, according to an IANS report from the time. The report also mentions that the then Lok Sabha Secretary General T. K. Viswanathan stressed the need for an alternative complex as the existing building was heavily used and could not take the strain. Later, on 10 December 2020, Prime Minister Narendra Modi laid the foundation stone for the new Parliament House. He described the foundation laying as a 'milestone in India's democratic history', asserting that if the old Parliament House gave direction to the country after Independence, the new one would be a witness to the making of an Aatmanirbhar Bharat. The Central Vista Project, which includes the new Parliament House, was approved by the Modi government in 2019.

The new building, with a built-up area of approximately 65,000 sq m and a distinctive triangular shape, optimally utilizes space. It houses an expanded Lok Sabha Hall, accommodating up to 888 seats and a larger Rajya Sabha hall, accommodating up to 384 seats. As there is no Constitution Hall in the new Parliament building, the Lok Sabha can also accommodate 1,272 members for joint sessions.

The new Parliament building

Timeline of how the new Parliament House took shape:

2019

- The Central Vista Project was announced by the Government of India.
- HCP Design Planning and Management Pvt. Ltd was awarded the contract to draw up architectural plan for the project.

2020

- Tata Projects Ltd was awarded the contract to build the new Parliament House. Initially, the cost was estimated to be ₹862 crore. Last year, however, media reported that the cost had increased to over ₹1,250 crore.
- On 10 December, Prime Minister Narendra Modi laid the foundation stone for the construction of the new Parliament House.
- Writ petition filed against the project.

2021

- In January, the Supreme Court cleared the construction of the Parliament House. Later that month, the construction of the new Parliament House began.

Parliamentary debates

Debates are of two types:

(i) Those in which an MP may participate voluntarily, such as matters under Rule 377, matters of public importance and private member business

(ii) Those in which the MP is nominated by the party to speak, such matters related to government Bills and budget.

The Lok Sabha Hall draws inspiration from India's national bird, incorporating a peacock theme, while the Rajya Sabha hall is designed with a lotus theme, reflecting India's national flower. Additionally, a state-of-the-art Constitution Hall symbolically and physically places Indian citizens at the heart of democracy.

The building features secure and efficient office spaces equipped with the latest communications technology. Spacious committee rooms with advanced audio-visual equipment are one of the attractive features of the building.

As a 'Platinum-rated Green Building', the new Sansad Bhavan embodies India's commitment to environmental sustainability. It showcases Indian heritage, incorporating the vibrancy and diversity of modern India, along with its cultural and regional arts and crafts. According to the government, materials and designs had been brought in from all over India to reflect the country's cultural diversity and different architectural styles. The materials include marble from Rajasthan and teak from Maharashtra.

Ensuring accessibility, the new Parliament is divyang-friendly

Sansad TV

Sansad TV is directly run by the Indian Parliament. On 24 July 2006, the then-Speaker Somnath Chatterjee launched Lok Sabha TV. In 2011, the then-chairman of the Rajya Sabha, Hamid Ansari, launched Rajya Sabha TV. In 2021, the channels were merged and renamed Sansad TV. Sansad TV was launched by Prime Minister Narendra Modi on 15 September 2021. Through this TV channel, the Parliament has reached people's drawing rooms.

The need for a new building

In 2021, Union minister Hardeep Singh Puri said the older Parliament complex had become unsafe over the years and had other limitations too. His observation was: 'From a purely structural point of view, it is an unsafe building. When the building was constructed, it was in Seismic Zone II, and today that area is in Seismic Zone IV. It is not an exaggeration. We don't want to create panic, but you know you are above pushing the limit.'

The Central Vista Project's website also says the previous Parliament House is a 'distressed building'. It says, 'Over the period addition in services like water supply lines, sewer lines, air conditioning, firefighting, CCTV, audio-visual system, which were not originally planned, have led to seepages and destroyed the overall aesthetics of the building. Fire safety is a major concern as the building is not designed according to the present fire norms. Numerous new electric cables have been laid which are potential fire hazard.'

(handicapped-friendly), enabling people with disabilities to move freely within its premises. Besides the Parliament House, the Central Vista Project also consists of a common central secretariat, revamping of the 3 km Rajpath (now Kartavya Path) from Rashtrapati Bhavan to the India Gate, a new prime minister's residence and office, and a new vice president's enclave. Tata Projects Limited has constructed the new Parliament House.

THE INAUGURATION AND THE SENGOL

While inaugurating the new building, Narendra Modi installed the monarchical symbol of power, the Sengol (derived from the Tamil word *semmai*), near the Speaker's high chair in the morning. Then he threw the gates of the new building open to the members with a 40-minute speech in the afternoon.

A sacred Sengol, a gold sceptre from the southern state of Tamil Nadu that is said to have been received by India's first prime minister, Jawaharlal Nehru, on Independence in 1947, was also placed by Modi in the new Parliament chamber.

'This is not merely a building. The new Parliament is a reflection of the aspirations and dreams of 140 crore people. It is a temple of our democracy. It showcases India's determination and willpower to the world,' Modi said in his speech of new building inauguration.

The prime minister chose the occasion to draw a parallel between the new Parliament building and India's 'new direction, new goals, and a new vision' under his leadership, and claimed that the people's aspirations that are reflected in the new Sansad Bhawan will help the nation become 'developed' in another 25 years. India will become *atmanirbhar* (self-dependent), and set new records in the future.

The latest monsoon session of the parliament (July–August 2023) saw a productivity of approx 45 per cent in Lok Sabha and 63 per cent in Rajya Sabha.

Inauguration of the New parliament building

PM installs Sengol

By Agni Roy with inputs from Meenakshi Samanta Bhattacharya

ANIMALS ON PARLIAMENT DOORS

GAJA DVAR (north entrance): It is in the north direction of the building. *Gaj* means 'elephant'. Two statues of elephants are installed here. Elephant represents power, wisdom, and wealth. It is inspired by similar statues placed at the entrance of the ninth century Chalukyan Madhukeshvara Temple at Banabasi, Karnataka.
ASHVA DVAR (south entrance): At the southern entrance we can see an always-alert *ashva*. *Ashva* means 'horse'. The horse is a symbol of endurance, power, and dynamism. The statue of the horse is inspired by those in the Sun Temple of Konark, Odisha.
GARUDA DVAR (east entrance): The statue of garuda, a mythological bird is believed to have associations with Jain, Buddhist, and Hindu faiths. Garuda symbolizes aspiration, prosperity, and progress. The statue is inspired by the 18th-century Nayaka period sculpture from Kumbakonam, Thanjavur District, Tamil Nadu. The statue is currently located at Linden Museum, Stuttgart, Germany.
MAKARA DVAR (west entrance): Makara is a mythical aquatic creature. It combines the body parts of various animals, thus signifying unity in diversity among the people of the country. Makar is said to be inspired by the makara statues at Hoysaleshwara Temple, Halebeedu, Hassan District, Karnataka.

PARLIAMENT RECORDS

First session of Parliament

The first session of Parliament in free India was held on 13 May 1952 with Jawaharlal Nehru as prime minister and Dr Rajendra Prasad as president.

First Speaker of the Lok Sabha

Freedom fighter 'Dadasaheb' G.V. Mavalankar was the first Speaker of the Lok Sabha, holding the post from 15 May 1952 to 27 February 1956.

First deputy Speaker of the Lok Sabha

On 30 May 1952, Madabhushi Ananthasayanam Ayyangar was elected as deputy Speaker of the Lok Sabha.

First visually impaired member of Parliament

Sadhan Chandra Gupta (1917–2015), an Indian lawyer and politician, became the first visually impaired member member of Parliament (MP) in 1953. He later served as the advocate general of West Bengal. Gupta was elected to the Lok Sabha from the Calcutta (now Kolkata), West Bengal, South-east constituency in a 1953 by-election on a Communist Party of India (CPI) ticket.

First state legislative assembly

The maharaja of Travancore, Sree Moolam Thirunal Rama Varma, constituted an eight-member assembly in March 1888. A bicameral system was introduced on 28 October 1932 by King Chithira Thirunal Balarama Varma, who abolished the existing council and set up the Sree Moolam Assembly (Lower House) and the Sree Chitra State Council (Upper House).

SHARDULA DVAR (south-east entrance): Shardula refers to a mythical animal which is partly lion and partly tiger. It is a symbol of strength, grace, and victory. The statue of Shardula is said to be inspired by a statue from an 11th-century Shiva temple in Madhya Pradesh. Currently the statue is preserved at Gujri Mahal Museum in Gwalior, Madhya Pradesh.

HAMSA DVAR (north-east entrance): Hansa, or 'swan', at the public entrance is a symbol of the power of discernment, self-realization, and wisdom. It is inspired by the hamsa statue carved in Vijaya Vittala Temple built in the 15th century in Hampi, Vijaynagara District, Karnataka.

Difference between the old and new Parliament buildings

Points of difference	Old (now called Samvidhan Bhavan)	New (now called Sansad Bhavan)
Time taken	6 years	3 years
Cost (in ₹)	83 lakh (8.3 million) *not adjusted to inflation	861 crore (8.61 billion)
Seating capacity: Lok Sabha Chamber	550 members	888 members
Seating capacity: Rajya Sabha Chamber	250 members	384 members
Vehicle parking capacity	212	900
Central Hall	Yes	No
Shape	circular	triangular
Built-up area	24,281.16 sq. m	64,500 sq. m

By Meenakshi Samanta Bhattacharya

First representative in the British House of Commons

The 'Grand Old Man of India', Dadabhai Naoroji, was the first Indian-origin and non-white member of the British House of Commons, when he was elected as a Liberal Party member of Parliament in London from Central Finsbury in July 1892, by a bare majority of three votes. He held the position till 1895.

First Lok Sabha dissolution

The fifth Lok Sabha was dissolved by Indira Gandhi in 1971, for the first time in the history of the Indian Parliament. The second Lok Sabha dissolution came in 1979 under Charan Singh, and the third was the ninth Lok Sabha on 6 March 1991 under Chandra Shekhar.

First woman secretary general of Rajya Sabha

V.S. Ramadevi was the first woman to be appointed as the Secretary General of the Rajya Sabha on 1 July 1993, for three years. She was also acting chief election commissioner for some time in 1990.

First woman legislator

Dr S. Muthulakshmi Reddy was a social worker, educationist and physician, with many firsts to her credit. In 1926, she became the first woman legislator (Madras Legislative Council member) and in 1930, by way of the All India Women's Conference, pushed through the Child Marriage Restraint Act. She was also the first woman alderman of the Madras Corporation in 1937.

First hung Parliament

A hung parliament is a situation where no single political party has an absolute majority of seats in the Parliament. For the first time in nine general elections,

India's electorate did not give a decisive verdict in 1989. The Congress (I) was ousted in the north and the ruling regional parties were similarly ousted in the south.

First couple in Parliament

Joachim and Violet Alva from Karnataka were the first couple in Parliament. While Violet was elected to the Rajya Sabha in 1952, Joachim became a Lok Sabha member in the same year.

Longest tenure as Rajya Sabha chairman

Dr S. Radhakrishnan, the second president and first vice president of India, had the longest tenure as chairman of the Rajya Sabha, from 1952 to 1962.

Longest term as Speaker

Balram Jakhar served as Speaker from 1980 to 1989, for eight years and 329 days in two terms, becoming the Speaker with the longest tenure.

Shortest Lok Sabha term

The 12th Lok Sabha lasted from 10 March 1998 to 26 April 1999, a duration of around 13 months, due to the withdrawal of support by the All-India Anna Dravida Munnetra Kazhagam (AIADMK) from the National Democratic Alliance (NDA) government led by Atal Bihari Vajpayee.

Shortest term as Speaker

Neelam Sanjiva Reddy was Lok Sabha Speaker from 26 March to 13 July 1977, thus serving the shortest term as Speaker. He was the sixth president of India, from 1977 to 1982.

Shortest session of state legislative assembly

There was a one-minute session of the Rajasthan Legislative Assembly from 11:00 a.m. to 11:01 a.m. on 14 August 1972, the shortest session of a legislative assembly on record.

Lok Sabha with highest average age

The average age of the elected MPs in the current 17th Lok Sabha is 54 years, making it the Lok Sabha with the highest average age in the history of the Indian Parliament.

Lok Sabha with lowest average age

The first Lok Sabha (1952–57) had the lowest average age of 46.5 years.

Most bills passed in a year

The Parliament passed 118 bills in 1976, which is the highest number of bills ever passed by it in a single year.

National party with most votes

The Congress (I) secured a record 115,221,078 votes (78.5 per cent of the total votes) and won 412 out of the 513 parliamentary seats in the elections held in December 1984. This is the largest victory margin of any political party on record.

DEFENCE

ARMY

PERSONNEL

First Indian commander-in-chief

General (later field marshal in 1986) K.M. Cariappa (1899–1993) took over from the British commander-in-chief (C-in-C), General Sir Roy Bucher, on 15 January 1949 and held office till 14 January 1953. The only other C-in-C was General M. Rajendra Sinhji Jadeja, who took over as the first chief of army staff (CoAS) in April 1955, after which the post of C-in-C was abolished.

First chief of integrated defence staff

On 1 October 2001, Lieutenant General Pankaj Joshi was appointed the first chief of integrated defence staff (CIDS) in the country, reporting to General Sundararajan Padmanabhan, chairman of the Chief of Staff Committee at the time.

First chief of defence staff

On 31 December 2019, after demitting office as chief of army staff, General Bipin Rawat (1958–2021) took over as India's first chief of defence staff (CDS), serving as a tri-services chief and principal military adviser to the defence minister on all matters related to the army, navy, and air force. He also headed the Department of Military Affairs created within the Ministry of Defence.

First commissioned officer

Major General K. Bhagwati Singh (ID I-O-No. 1) was the first officer to be commissioned into the Indian Military Academy (IMA). He passed out of the Indian Military Academy in 1934, with his batchmate (and later field marshal) Sam Manekshaw.

First women in the army

The first batch of 25 women outside the Army Medical Corps (AMC) was commissioned in the Indian Army on 6 March 1993 at the Officers Training Academy in Madras (now Chennai), Tamil Nadu. They were inducted into non-combat departments, such as supply, legal, education, and logistics.

First field marshal

S.H.F.J. (Sam) Manekshaw, the then general, became field marshal in 1973. He was honoured with the Padma Bhushan in 1968 and the Padma Vibhushan in 1972.

S.H.F.J. (Sam) Manekshaw

First woman lieutenant general

Dr Punita Arora from Saharanpur, Uttar Pradesh, was promoted to the rank of lieutenant general on 1 September 2004. She was the first woman in any of the four services (army, navy, air force, and coast guard) to reach a three-star rank.

The highest altitude mountain warfare in history was fought when India and Pakistan fought in the Kargil war in **1999**.

First women in military police

On 25 April 2019, the Indian Army issued a formal notification inviting women applicants for the post of soldier – general duty. This was the first time that the army opened its ranks to women for personnel below officer rank (PBOR). The soldiers were to be inducted into the Corps of Military Police (CMP) to investigate offences such as theft, molestation, and rape. Their portfolio also included assisting civil police and the prevention of breach of regulations by army personnel.

MEDALS AND HONOURS

First Victoria Cross

The first Indian to be awarded the Victoria Cross was Sepoy (later Subedar) Khuda Dad Khan of the 129 Baluchis, on 31 October 1914, for gallantry at Hollebeke, Belgium, in the First World War.

Youngest to receive the Victoria Cross

At nineteen, Sepoy Kamal Ram of the Royal Indian Army was the youngest Indian to receive the Victoria Cross in 1944. Born in Bholupura Village of Karauli District, Rajasthan, he was with the 3rd Battalion of the 8th Punjab Regiment during the Second World War.

First prisoner of war and first Kirti Chakra recipient

Flying Officer Ulrich Anthony D'Cruz, whose aircraft was shot down by ground fire on 1 December 1947 in the 1947–48 Kashmir war, was taken prisoner by Pathan tribesmen and later by the Pakistan Army, and released after a year. He was awarded the Kirti Chakra in 1952 for bravery during captivity.

Victoria Cross

The Victoria Cross is an award of valour given to members of armed forces of some Commonwealth countries and British Empire territories. From 1857 to 1947, 152 members of the British Indian Army and civilians under its command received the Victoria Cross. Originally, Indian troops were not considered for the Victoria Cross because they had been eligible for the Indian order of Merit, a British gallantry award. At the end of the 19th century the call to award Indian troops the Victoria Cross intensified, and the first of the Indian troops to receive the award, Khuda Dad Khan and Darwan Singh Negi had their names in the *London Gazette*.

A stamp depicting the Param Vir Chakra

First George Cross

Havildar Nandlal Thapa of the Gurkha Rifles received the George Cross in 1935 for exceptional courage and devotion to duty. He was about 32 years old at the time, and was serving in the 2nd Battalion of the 8th Gurkha Rifles.

First Param Vir Chakra

Major Somnath Sharma, heading a detachment of the Kumaon Regiment at Badgam, Jammu and Kashmir, laid down his life in the effort to save Srinagar city and airport from a Pakistani attack during the Kashmir operations in 1947. He was given the award posthumously in 1950.

First Ashok Chakra

Naik Nar Bahadur Thapa of 5 Gurkha Rifles was awarded the Ashok Chakra Class I (now known as the Ashok Chakra). On 15 September 1948, during the Hyderabad police action, as the No. 2 Platoon of the A Company came under fire on the banks of the Tungabhadra River, he dashed across the 100-yard open ground and single-handedly silenced the gun crew.

First Republic Day commander and first army officer to receive Padma Bhushan

The first Republic Day parade of independent India, which featured inter-service contingents from the army, navy, air force, and police forces, was held on 26 January 1950, and was commanded by Brigadier (later Lieutenant General) Joginder Singh Dhillon, a Bengal Sapper. On 24 November 1965, as lieutenant general, he became the first Indian Army officer to receive the Padma Bhushan.

First Indian peacekeeper to win the United Nations Military Gender Advocate Award

Major Suman Gawani, an Indian Army officer, was awarded the UN (United Nations) Military Gender Advocate of the Year award on 29 May 2020 in a virtual ceremony, becoming the first Indian peacekeeper to receive the honour. She served as a peacekeeper in a UN mission in South Sudan (UNMISS) in 2019.

Most decorated regiment

The Sikh Regiment has to its credit the highest number of gallantry awards, i.e., 1,652. These include two Param Vir Chakras, eight Maha Vir Chakras, sixty-four Vir Chakras, and four Ashok Chakras among other decorations.

UNITS

First artillery unit

On 15 January 1935, A Field Brigade (now 1 Field Regiment SP), with four batteries of horse-drawn guns, was raised at Bangalore (now Bengaluru), Karnataka. This date was adopted by the Regiment of Artillery as its raising day.

First artillery company

- The first artillery company was raised temporarily in 1748 in India under

British rule with Indian troops, and was called the Gun Lascars.

- A company of Bombay Artillery, which still exists as 5 Bombay Mountain Battery, was raised on 28 September 1827, the date being celebrated as Gunners' Day.

India approved purchases of missiles, helicopters, artillery guns, and electronic warfare systems worth 8.5 billion dollars in 2023.

First administrative unit

The Army Service Corps (ASC) was established in 1748 when Stringer Lawrence, commander-in-chief in India, appointed Robert Clive as commissary. It was formally set up in 1760 in the Bengal, Madras, and Bombay Presidencies, and became a formal Supply and Transport Corps in 1901. The ASC was the oldest administrative component of the East India Company and was then known as the Commissariat.

Oldest infantry brigade

In September 1933, 5 Mountain Brigade was raised. Deployed in the Along (now Aalo) sector of Arunachal Pradesh, its area of responsibility comprises a frontage of more than 460 km.

Oldest infantry unit

Raised on 4 August 1768, the 1 Maratha Light Infantry or Jangi Paltan is the only unit that does not hang captured enemy flags upside down in its mess. It is also the only unit that was in constant battle for 20 years after it was raised, and in this duration, it earned 18 battle honours and five theatre honours.

First cavalry unit

The first Indian cavalry unit was raised in 1787 as 5 Regiment of Madras Native Cavalry. It became 1 Regiment in 1788 under Major Tonyn. Renamed 26 Light Cavalry in 1903, it was amalgamated with 30 Lancers in 1922 and became the 8th Light Cavalry.

First cavalry regiment

The first cavalry regiment before India's independence, the Scinde Horse, was raised in 1838 as the Scinde Irregular Horse by Captain Ward in Hyderabad (in Sind, now in Pakistan) under the command of Captain John Jacob. It last paraded its horses in April 1938 at Rawalpindi (now in Pakistan).

First rifle regiment

The rifle regiment as a tactical unit was introduced in 1841 and the first such unit was the 4 Bombay Native Infantry, which till 1947 was 1 Battalion Rajputana Rifles, and is now 3 Guard. They were issued Enfield muzzle-loaders and 577 bullets.

First tri-services affiliation

Bengal Sappers has been affiliated with the Indian Navy and Indian Air Force since 2002. Originally known as the Bengal Sappers and Miners, and headquartered in Roorkee (now in Uttarakhand), it has won 80 battle honours and 11 theatre honours.

First Special Operations Division

India's first Special Operations Division was announced on 15 May 2019. At its peak, this tri-services division will have around 3,000 commandos from the Indian Army's special forces, the Indian Air Force's Garud force, and the Indian Navy's marcos commando units. The raising is the first step for counterterrorism operations. Major General A.K. Dhingra, from the 1 Para Special Forces Regiment, was the first chief of the division.

First and oldest extant armament checker

The Proof and Experimental Establishment in Chandipur in present-day Odisha, called the Proof Department, was set up on 7 November 1895. It has been associated with major armament developments. Included under the Defence Research and Development Organization (DRDO) in 1958, it had Lieutenant Colonel B.N. Mitra as its first Indian director.

EQUIPMENT

First gun foundry

The Board of Ordnance was constituted in April 1775, but it took 27 years to establish a factory at Cossipore in Calcutta (now Kolkata), West Bengal, on 18 March 1802 as the Gun Carriage Agency. In 1830, it was renamed the Gun Foundry and, in 1905, this name was changed to Gun and Shell Factory.

First rifle factory

A rifle factory, set up at Ichhapore, Bengal (now Ishapore, West Bengal), began production on 20 September 1904. It produced the .303-inch Bolt-action rifles in large quantities for the First and Second World Wars.

Earliest tanks

The first three tanks of the Indian Army were two varieties of Medium-D tanks brought in 1920 before Indian independence. Fifty Vickers MkII-B light tanks were acquired for use in India in 1933.

First flying spy

Unmanned aerial vehicles (UAVs) were used first in the Kargil conflict in 1999 to detect the movement of enemy troops and locate bunkers. UAVs were brought in to counter Pakistan's Gultari guns and the US -made AN/TPQ-36-37 gun locating radars.

First indigenous tank

The first military tank that was made in India, named Vijayanta, rolled out of the assembly line on 12 December 1965 at the Heavy Vehicles Factory in Avadi in Madras (now Chennai), Tamil Nadu. It entered service on 29 December 1965.

Vijayanta: first indigenous tank

First indigenous armoured personnel carrier

In 1987, the first BMP-2 infantry fighting vehicle, Sarath, was assembled at the ordnance factory at Shankarapally, Andhra Pradesh (now in Telangana), from Soviet supplied components. Sarath was made indigenously subsequently in 1991.

First indigenous training simulator

On 20 February 2002, the Simulator Development Division, Secunderabad (now in Telangana), introduced the aiming- training simulator (ATS) for infantry combat vehicles.

Longest-range nuclear missile

On 26 December 2016, India successfully test-fired Agni-V, a surface-to-surface nuclear-capable missile with the longest range, from Abdul Kalam Island off the Odisha coast. Designed and developed by DRDO, this 17 m (55 ft 9 in.) long missile can carry a nuclear warhead of about 1.5 tonnes reportedly over 5,000–8,000 km. India is the sixth country after France, China, Russia, the USA and the UK to have a missile with a range of over 5,000 km.

Agni-V: longest-range nuclear missile

First bulletproof helmets

In July 2017, the army obtained bulletproof helmets for the first time. The 1.2 kg to 1.4 kg lightweight helmets are being made in Kanpur, Uttar Pradesh, by MKU Systems, which is manufacturing them for the Indian Army for the first time. The company had earlier manufactured such helmets for the UN and the North Atlantic Treaty Organization (NATO) forces.

First indigenous revolver

In 2002, the research and development wing of the Ishapore Rifle Factory near in Barrackpore, West Bengal, after around two years of research, developed a low-cost and high-tech revolver, which weighs barely 380 g. The .22-in. automatic revolver has a range of 20 m (65 ft 7 in.).

First indigenously manufactured bulletproof vests

Shantanu Bhowmik, professor at the Department of Aerospace Engineering at the School of Engineering, Amrita University, Coimbatore, Tamil Nadu, designed the first indigenous bulletproof vest for the armed forces in 2017. The 20-layer vest, made with indigenous-ultra-modern lightweight thermoplastic technology, is being developed in collaboration with DRDO. The vest is effective up to a temperature of 57°C and weighs 1.5 kg while the earlier jacket weighed 15 kg.

Lightest towed artillery

On 18 May 2017, the Indian Army received the first batch of two M-777 A-2 ultralight howitzers (ULH) from the USA. These ULHs, with a maximum range of 30 km, manufactured by BAE Systems, were test-fired at Pokhran, Rajasthan. The 155 mm, 39-calibre guns are equipped to fire Indian ammunition.

MADE-IN-INDIA LAUNCHES

In 2022 there were many path-breaking reforms made for the Ministry of Defence. New schemes such as the Aatmanirbhar were introduced and the armed forces were equipped with the latest weapons and technologies manufactured by industries in India. This happened in line with the 'Make in India, Make for the World' vision. There were also border areas development, expansion of National Cadet Corps, and setting up of new Sainik Schools. Here are some of the new equipment introduced to the Indian Defence forces in 2022:

1 LCH 'Prachand'

The Light Combat Helicopter was formally introduced in October 2022. It was designed and developed by Hindustan Aeronautics Limited (HAL) and is the first indigenous multi-role combat helicopter which has potent ground attack and aerial combat capability. It has elements of stealth, armour protection, and formidable night attack capability. It is capable of operating from a high-altitude terrain.

2 Advanced Light Helicopter (ALH) Mk-III

The ALH Mk-III was commissioned into the Indian Navy in a ceremony held at INS Utkrosh, Port Blair, Andaman and Nicobar Command in May 2022. This unit is the second ALH MK III Squadron commissioned into the Indian Navy. This was developed by HAL. It has advanced features such as electro-optical sensors, Shakti engines, full-glass cockpit, high-intensity search light, advanced communication systems, automatic identification system as well as a search-and-rescue homer.

3 Missile Destroyers/ Frigates

Two front line warships of the IN were launched in May 2022. These are *Surat* and *Udaygiri. Surat* is the fourth stealth-guided missile destroyer and *Udaygiri* is the second stealth frigate. *Surat* belongs to a class of ships that are the next-generation stealth guided missile destroyers and *Udaygir*i belongs to the P17 class which have improved stealth features, advanced weapons and sensors, and platform management systems. Another frigate, the *Taragiri*, belonging to the P17 class was introduced in September 2022, and the INS *Mormugao* was introduced in December 2022.

4 Driving Support/ Survey Vessels

DSV *Nistar* and DSV *Nipun* were launched in September 2022. These were built by Hindustan Shipyard Ltd. These are equipped with driving support systems and are capable of conducting search and rescue operations. In November, *Ikshak*, the third of the four survey vessels was launched. These contain a new-generation hydrographic equipment to collect oceanographic data.

5 ALH Squadrons and Offshore Patrol Vessels

A patrol vessel built for the ICG called *Saksham* was inducted in February 2022. It was designed and built by Goa Shipyard Ltd and has advanced-technology navigation and communication equipment, sensors, and machinery.

First robot sentry

In 2017, the Indian Army built Robot Sentry, a mobile robot specifically meant for patrolling and surveillance applications in urban campuses of the army. Another robot, the Snake, has 14 active joints for lateral undulation, sidewinding, and rolling. These help the robot to navigate difficult passages.

First set of next-gen Armoured Engineer Reconnaissance Vehicle

Indian Army chief General Manoj Mukund Naravane flagged off and inducted the first set of indigenously developed next-generation Armoured Engineer Reconnaissance Vehicles (AERVs) at Bombay Engineering Group (BEG) on 21 December 2021. The AERV, which can match the speed of tanks, will upscale the existing engineer reconnaissance capabilities of the Indian Army significantly, keeping in view the possibility of future conflicts.

First indigenous sniper rifles

SSS Defence, based in Bengaluru, Karnataka, has developed the country's first indigenous sniper rifle prototypes with 7.62 mm x 51 mm calibre and .338 Lapua magnum platforms. The barrel length ranges from 20 to 24 in. (50.8 to 60.96 cm) based on use environments and specific missions.

OPERATIONS

First heli-borne operations

In 1971, the Indian Army used helicopters to capture the 7,000-strong Sylhet garrison in East Pakistan (now Bangladesh). The 5 Gurkha Rifles (Frontier Force), which was led by Major M.M. Malik, landed with the first sortie of seven helicopters at Mirpara on the banks of the Surma River.

First heli-lifted battalion

The First Guards (2 Punjab), raised in 1762 as 10 Battalion of the Coastal Sepoys and redesignated 18 times since, was heli-lifted during the counter-insurgency operations in Nagaland during 1969–70.

First para-regiment in action

The 17 Para Field Regiment supported operations at Tangail in Bangladesh in 1971 by sending 49 Para Field Battery, a sub-unit of the regiment along with 2 Para.

First use of air cavalry

In May 2018, during Exercise Vijay Prahar carried out in the Mahajan Firing Range near Suratgarh, Rajasthan, Indian troops worked on the first use of the concept of air cavalry unleashed by the US Army in Vietnam during 1955–73. In these operations, weaponized attack helicopters carried out combined action against the 'enemy' in coordination with tanks and mechanized ground forces, while conventionally helicopters are called in only when ground forces cannot neutralize ground targets. This requires very precise coordination but speeds up the operation.

Highest battleground

Siachen is a 76.8 km river of ice abutted by knife-edged, fluted, serrated ridge lines, sometimes exceeding 6,400 m (21,000 ft), where temperatures dip to as low as –55°C. Army posts at altitudes from 4,572 m to 6,096 m (15,000 ft to 20,000 ft) face bitterly cold 200 km/hr blizzards.

Highest tank battle in the world

On 1 November 1948, an Indian brigade group, supported by the 7th Cavalry (using Stuart Tanks), broke through the Himalayan range at Zoji La in Jammu and Kashmir at 3,528 m (11,575 ft) to drive out a group of invaders from Pakistan intermixed with Pakistan-occupied Kashmir (PoK) battalions and tribal groups.

DEFENCE ALLOCATION IN 2023–24 (IN CRORES)

Ministry of Defence has the highest allocation in 2023-24

Source: Expenditure Budget, Union Budget 2023–24, GOI

GENERAL

First army veterinary school

A veterinary school was started at Kirkee in Poona (now Pune) District, Maharashtra, in 1862, for officers and men of artillery, cavalry, and mounted police. Similar schools also came up in Hapur (Uttar Pradesh)in 1877, Lahore (now in Pakistan) in 1882, Ambala (now in Haryana) in 1889, and Simla (now Shimla, in Himachal Pradesh) in 1891.

First military intelligence school

Opened in Karachi (now in Pakistan) on 20 January 1945, the first military intelligence school moved to Mhow (Dr Ambedkar Nagar) in Madhya Pradesh, and was renamed the Intelligence Corps Training School and Depot. On 29 February 1984, its name was changed to Military Intelligence Training School and Depot.

First board of ordnance

The Board of Ordnance was set up in 1775 at Fort William, Calcutta, West Bengal. Currently, the Indian Ordnance Factories Organization – a set of 41 ordnance factories under the aegis of its corporate headquarters, the Ordnance Factory Board (OFB), Kolkata – has more than 200 years of experience in the development and marketing of a range of land, sea, and air defence systems. At present, the OFB has nine training institutes, three regional marketing centres, and four regional controllers of safety under it.

First counter-insurgency school

The Counter-Insurgency and Jungle Warfare School was established at Mynkre, Meghalaya, in 1967. It was relocated to Vairengte in Mizoram on 1 May 1970.

Remount and Veterinary Corps

One of the oldest formations of the Indian Army is the Remount and Veterinary Corps and it is responsible for breeding, rearing, and training all of the animals used in the army. It was raised in Bengal in 1779 under the name The Stud Department. It actively participated in both the First and Second World Wars. Its motto is *Pashu seva asmakam dharma* which translates to, Service to animals is our duty. The corps also conducts training of dogs in the specialized fields as tracking, explosive detection, mine detection, avalanche rescue operation, search and rescue, infantry patrolling, and guarding.

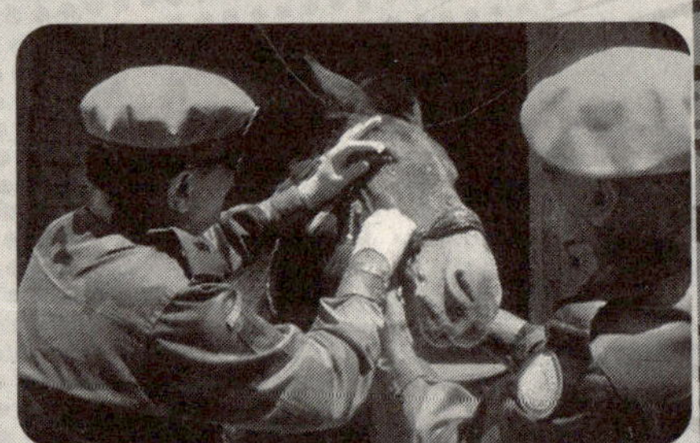

First military dog school

The War Dog Training School was opened in 1959 at the Indian Army Remount and Veterinary Corps Centre and School (now RVC Centre and School) in Meerut, Uttar Pradesh. Training for avalanche rescue operations began here in September 1976.

First high-altitude warfare school

Instituted as a formation ski school at Gulmarg, Jammu and Kashmir, the High Altitude Warfare School came into being on 8 April 1962. The courses at this institute include those on skiing and mountaineering.

First national war memorial

The armed forces first proposed a National War Memorial way back in 1960. On 25 February 2019, the memorial, designed by the Chennai-based WeBe Design Lab, led by Yogesh Chandrahasan, was inaugurated near India Gate, New Delhi. Covering over 40 acres (16.2 hectares), it has the names of Indian soldiers martyred in 1947–48 (Kashmir), 1961 (Goa), 1962 (China), 1965 and 1971 (Pakistan), 1987 (Siachen), 1987–88 (Sri Lanka), 1999 (Kargil) and other operations. It has concentric circles, with the Amar Chakra (Circle of Immortality) and an Eternal Flame in the centre. Around it are the Veerta Chakra (Circle of Bravery), a gallery depicting iconic battles and the Rakshak Chakra (Circle of Protection). The circles represent the *chakravyuh* or traditional Indian war formation. The Param Yodha Sthal has busts of 21 recipients of the Param Vir Chakra.

First drone show

For the first time ever a drone show was held during the republic day celebrations. This was for the 75th year of Indian independence celebration. The 10-minute show involved around 1,000 drones and they were conceptualized, designed, produced, and choreographed under the 'Make in India' initiative. It was organized by the start-up 'Botlab Dynamics' and supported by IIT Delhi and Department of Science and Technology.

Longest bridge built during war

The Indo-Pakistan war in 1971, termed the Sappers War, saw the construction of a 421.8 m (1,384 ft) composite bridge across the River Madhumati in East Pakistan (now Bangladesh) in a matter of 34 hours. It was the longest 'war' bridge to be constructed by India after the Second World War and the longest operational bridge constructed during a war involving India.

First nuclear shelter

DRDO, the Pune-based research and development laboratory, introduced an integrated battlefield shelter for all three services in 2002 to withstand nuclear or chemical strikes for up to 96 hours. The portable shelter, 28 m (91 ft 10 in.) long and with a diameter of 2.5 m (8 ft 2 in.), had chemical toilets, water tanks, pumps for sewage disposal, and two power generators. It could accommodate 30 people and could be used as a command post, an observation post, and a communication centre.

First Bactrian camels join the army

Since February 2017, the Bactrian camel was put through the paces at the Defence Institute of High Altitude Research (DIHAR), a DRDO laboratory in Leh, Ladakh. Bactrian camels are used to patrol the Line of Actual Control (LAC) in Ladakh and carry loads for the army.

First win at International Scout Masters Competition

Held in India for the first time, the host Indian Army team, trained by the Southern Command, won the Fifth Army International Scout Masters Competition (ISMC). Part of the International Army Games, it was held at Jaisalmer Military Station, Rajasthan, during 6–14 August 2019 and included five stages of competitions. Participants included teams from the armies of Armenia, Belarus, China, India, Kazakhstan, Russia, Sudan, and Uzbekistan.

First Indian dog breed in active duty

The Indian Army began to use dogs for active duty in 1959, the preferred breeds being the Labrador retriever, the Great Swiss Mountain dogs, and the German shepherd. In 2017, the Remount and Veterinary Corps introduced the first Indian breed, the Mudhol hound (or caravan hound), a sight hound used as a hunting hound first in Central Asia and later in the Deccan region, especially Karnataka. It is known for its courage, speed, and loyalty.

NAVY

PERSONNEL

INS *Mormugao* the second ship of Project 15B was commissioned in Mumbai on 18 December 2022

First naval pilot

Lieutenant Y.N. Singh of the Royal Indian Navy was deputed to England in 1941 for basic training and later to Canada where he obtained his wings in 1944 before serving in the escort carriers of the Royal Navy in the Second World War.

First commander-in-chief

- The first commander-in-chief of the Royal Indian Navy was Admiral Sir Edward Parry in August 1948.
- Rear Admiral I.T.S. Hall was the first post-Independence commander-in-chief of the Royal Indian Navy. The word 'Royal' was dropped on 26 January 1950.

First four-star admiral

Admiral A.K. Chatterji (1914–2001) became a four-star admiral on 1 March 1968. He joined the Royal Indian Marines as a cadet in 1933 and became chief of naval staff in 1966.

First chief of naval staff

- Admiral Sir Mark Pizey was the first chief of naval staff in 1955.
- The first Indian chief of naval staff was Vice Admiral Ram Dass Katari in 1958.

First woman maritime reconnaissance pilot

Shubhangi Swaroop became the first woman pilot in the navy who was trained to fly maritime reconnaissance aircraft in 2017. Three other women cadets – Astha Segal, Roopa A., and Sakthi Maya S. – passed out with her in the first batch of women officers from the Indian Naval Academy, Ezhimala, Kerala, on 22 November 2017, and were inducted into the naval armament inspection (NAI) branch. The Indian Navy had inducted its first woman officer in 1991. Its aviation branch had women working as air traffic control officers and as observers in aircraft.

INS Chakra

First nuclear submarine

INS *Chakra*, the navy's first nuclear-powered submarine belonging to the Victor 1 SSN class had a speed of 32 knots and a dive displacement of 5,000 tonnes. It carried 90 sailors. On lease from the USSR, it was commissioned on 3 February 1988 and sent back in 1991.

First woman pilot of naval aircraft

On 2 December 2019, 24-year-old sub

lieutenant Shivangi Singh graduated with two other trainee officers from the seventh Dornier Conversion Course (DOCC) at Kochi, Kerala. Originally from Muzaffarpur, Bihar, this Short Service Commission pilot entry scheme officer was commissioned into the Indian Navy in June 2018 and underwent a year of flying training at the Air Force Academy (AFA), Dundigal, Telangana, and Indian Naval Air Squadron (INAS) 550 and INS *Garuda* in Kochi. During training, she flew aircraft such as Pilatus PC 7 Mk-II, a basic trainer, at AFA before the Dornier Conversion Course.

First woman officers as 'Observers'

Sub lieutenant Kumudini Tyagi and Sub lieutenant Riti Singh graduated as 'Observers' (airborne technicians) in the Indian Navy's stream of helicopters to be deployed on warships for short- or long-term missions. They were awarded their wings in a graduation ceremony held at INS *Garuda* on 21 September 2020.

UNITS

First navy air squadron

On 17 June 1959, the Fleet Requirement Unit was commissioned as the Indian Naval Air Squadron 550. INS *Vikrant*, formerly HMS *Hercules*, joined the Indian Navy on 16 February 1961 as the first aircraft carrier and saw action during the Goa liberation struggle in December 1961. It has flown 14 types of aircraft, starting with Sealands to the Dornier maritime reconnaissance aircraft flown currently.

First unmanned aerial vehicle squadron

The navy's first unmanned aerial vehicle (UAV) squadron, intended to patrol the seas, was commissioned on 6 January 2006, with 12 UAVs from Israel. The Intensive Flying and Training Units were based in Kochi, Kerala.

Only training command

The Southern Naval Command is the only training command of the Indian Navy. It was augmented by INS *Magar*, which arrived at Kochi, Kerala, on 10 April 2018 to join the first Training Squadron for sea training of officers.

First exclusive naval base

INS *Kadamba*, inaugurated on 31 May 2005 near Karwar in Karnataka, is India's third operational naval base after Mumbai and Visakhapatnam, and the first under the sole control of the navy. Signifying another first, the inauguration speech was read out in Sanskrit. Sanctioned in 1985 as Project Seabird, its foundation stone was laid in 1986.

EQUIPMENT

First cruiser and flagship

HMS *Achilles*, a 7,030-tonne battleship, formerly of the Royal Navy, was commissioned as HMIS *Delhi* on 5 July 1948 in England, and became the first

Since April 2021, 9 Anti-narcotics operations have been undertaken by the Indian Navy.

Indigenous Nuclear-Powered Ballistic Missile Submarines

The Arihant-class submarines are India's first indigenously developed nuclear-powered ballistic missile submarines. The lead submarine of the class, INS *Arihant*, was commissioned in 2016. These submarines are designed to carry and launch nuclear ballistic missiles. It completed its first deterrence patrol on 5 November 2018.

cruiser and flagship of the Indian Navy. It arrived at Bombay (now Mumbai), Maharashtra, on 15 September 1948. HMIS *Delhi* (renamed INS *Delhi*) was 169.1 m (554 ft 9 in.) long and 16.77 m (55 ft) across its beam, with a speed of 32 knots. Its armaments included six 152 mm guns, eight 102 mm guns, fifteen 40 mm guns, four anti-aircraft three-pounders, and eight torpedo tubes.

First missile boat

INS *Vinash*, a Soviet OSA 1 commissioned on 21 January 1971, was fitted with four SS-N-2A surface-to-surface missiles and four 30 mm guns. With a complement of 30 crew, it could reach speeds exceeding 35 knots.

First submarine depot ship

INS *Amba*, an ex-Soviet Ugra-class ship with a displacement of 6,750 tonnes, is a submarine tender and was commissioned on 28 December 1968. INS *Amba* has two cranes (6 tonnes and 10 tonnes) and it can accommodate 750 personnel.

First indigenous patrol boat

Godavari-class frigate INS *Ajay*, commissioned on 21 September 1960, is a front-line warship equipped with missiles, guns, and anti-submarine equipment, as well as early warning navigation and electronic warfare systems. Built by Garden Reach Shipbuilders and Engineers (GRSE) Ltd, it could carry two Sea King helicopters.

First submarine base

On 19 May 1971, INS *Virbahu*, the Indian Navy's first submarine base, was commissioned near Visakhapatnam, Andhra Pradesh.

First submarine rescue ship

INS *Nistar* was converted from a fleet minesweeper to a submarine rescue ship and commissioned on 29 March 1971. An ex-Soviet Valday-class ship, it features a diving bell, a recompression chamber, two rescue chambers, and a lift of 10 tonnes.

INS *Viraat*

Largest aircraft carrier

INS *Viraat*, commissioned on 12 May 1987 at Devonport, UK, is the second and largest aircraft carrier of the Indian Navy. The 28,700 tonne INS *Viraat* (R-22), earlier called HMS *Hermes*, was launched in 1953 as the flagship of the South Atlantic Task Force in the Falklands War in 1982. The Indian Navy is among eight navies in the world to have aircraft carriers.

First missile corvette

INS *Kora*, the first indigenously built missile corvette, was commissioned on 10 August 1998. Capable of operating in nuclear, biological, and chemical confrontation zones, it had a displacement of 1,300 tonnes and an overall length of 91.16 m (299 ft). INS *Kora* had two indigenous fuel-efficient diesel engines and could touch 26 knots. Along with a helipad for advanced light helicopters and Chetaks, it had a complement of 11 officers and 110 sailors.

First indigenous modern warship

INS *Nilgiri*, which was commissioned on 3 June 1972, was the first modern warship built at Mazagon Dock Ltd, Bombay, Maharashtra. Based on the British Leander-class frigates, it had a hangar with a telescopic extension to take Alouette III helicopters. It was decommissioned on 31 May 1996.

First indigenous submarine

INS *Shalki*, the first of SSK Type-1500 submarines, built at Mazagon Dock Ltd, Bombay, Maharashtra, was commissioned in February 1992. It has a displacement of 1,450 tonnes and carries 14 AEG SUT torpedoes.

First ocean minesweepers

INS *Pondicherry* and INS *Porbandar*, built at the Isora Yard, Leningrad, USSR (now Russia), were given to the Indian Navy in 1978. These Natya-1-class sweepers have steel hulls with active mine detection sonars.

First dedicated cadet training ship

INS *Tir* (A86), named after HMIS *Tir*, a River-class frigate of the Royal Indian Navy that had served in the Second World War as HMS *Bann* (K256), was the first dedicated cadet-training ship built at Mazagon Dock Ltd. It was the senior ship of the First Training Squadron under the Southern Naval Command. Commissioned on 21 February 1986, it carried 120 cadets and 20 instructors.

First anti-ship missile

On 2 March 2017, the first anti-ship missile was fired from an indigenously built

Kalvari-class submarine, the first in a series of Scorpene-class submarines being built in India. The submarine was stationed in the Arabian Sea and the missile successfully hit a surface target.

First fast attacker

INFAC-T-80 (Indian Navy's extra-fast attack craft), commissioned at the Naval Dockyard in Mumbai, Maharashtra, on 24 June 1998, was the first fast-attack high-speed vessel and the first of an Indo-Israeli defence project. This aluminium-hull vessel could sustain 45 knots and it was the smallest ship in the Indian Navy.

First multi-warships

INS *Talwar* was launched in May 2000, INS *Trishul* in November 2000 and INS *Tabar* in May 2001. These Talwar-class guided missile frigates were designed and built by Russia.

First indigenous fleet replenishment tanker

INS *Aditya*, built by GRSE, Calcutta (now Kolkata), West Bengal, was commissioned at Visakhapatnam, Andhra Pradesh, on 3 April 2000. Manned by 16 officers and 140 sailors, the 172 m (564 ft) long fleet tanker has a deadweight tonnage of 1,700. It can touch a speed of 24 knots with an endurance of 10,000 nautical miles, and load six ships simultaneously on the high seas. It also carries a Sea King helicopter.

First Integrated Automatic Aviation Meteorological System

On 28 March 2017, the then chief of naval staff, Admiral Sunil Lanba, inaugurated the first Integrated Automatic Aviation Meteorological System (IAAMS) at INS *Rajali* (informally also known as the Arakkonam naval air station) in Tamil Nadu. The IAAMS has been established with the objective of modernizing the meteorological infrastructure and aviation safety of the nine naval air stations of the Indian Navy through automated monitoring of weather.

First 'green' ship

In February 2017, the survey vessel INS *Sarvekshak*, based at the Southern Naval Command in Kochi, Kerala, became India's first naval ship to go green by installing a zero-maintenance solar power system that can generate 5.4 kW of electricity. It replaces the ship's emergency diesel alternator. The customized power generating system has flexible, razor thin solar panels on the canopy of the retractable helicopter deck, which use no-fume solid electrolyte batteries and are maintenance-free for 24 years. The solar-power-generating system can be used to run communication equipment and on-board lights, and charge batteries. With an annual carbon emission of 60,225 kg, it will replace about 22,995 litres of diesel.

First indigenous ammunition

The Indian Navy received its first made-in-India, 30 mm ammunition for AK-630 rotary cannons fitted on warships, as reported on 29 August 2022.

Indian Navy has deployed 36 warships since June 2019.

The production of AK-630 guns was carried out by M/s Economic Explosives Ltd (EEL), Nagpur, Maharashtra, a subsidiary of Solar Industries India Ltd.

First indigenously developed naval anti-ship missile

The first indigenously developed naval anti-ship missile for the Indian Navy was test-fired on 18 May 2022. The missile was launched aboard a Sea King 42B Naval Helicopter from the Integrated Test Range (ITR) at Balasore in Odisha.

Longest-serving warship/aircraft carrier

INS *Viraat* – the second Centaur-class aircraft carrier in service – served India for 30 years after 27 years of service in the Royal Navy of the UK as HMS *Hermes*. The UK Royal Navy commissioned it in 1959 and it was later sold to the Indian Navy in 1986. It was decommissioned on 6 March 2017.

First pilotless drone

India's first passenger drone *Varuna* will be introduced into the navy. It is a pilotless drone with an ability to carry one person inside. Designed by the start-up Sagar Defence Engineering Company, this drone can cover a distance of 25 kilometres and can carry a payload of 130 kg.

GENERAL

First modern shipbuilder

In 1736, the East India Company invited Lowji Nusserwanji Wadia to build the first shipyard in Bombay (now Mumbai), Maharashtra. Since then, seven generations of the Wadias have built ships, including HMS *Minden* (the first constructed outside of Great Britain), HMS *Trincomalee* and HMS *Cornwallis*.

First modern shipbuilding yard

Garden Reach Shipbuilders and Engineers (GRSE) Ltd, located on the eastern bank of the River Hooghly in present-day Kolkata, West Bengal, dates to 1884. The company's name was changed to Garden Reach Workshop in 1916 and on 1 April 1960, it was taken over by the Government of India. The name was changed back to Garden Reach Shipbuilders and Engineers on 1 January 1977. It builds a range of ships, including warships, sophisticated commercial vessels, harbour craft and fast, powerful patrol vessels for the Indian Navy and the Indian Coast Guard. It built INS *Ajay*, India's first indigenous patrol boat, in 1960.

First naval dockyard

The Naval Dockyard at Bombay, Maharashtra, started with the Bunder Pier in 1693. A tiny dry dock was constructed in 1750. The old Bombay Dock and the Duncan Dock were built in 1765 and 1810, respectively. A wet basin was constructed in 1892. The largest naval dockyard today, it is the premier maintenance facility for ships and submarines of the Indian Navy.

First naval academy

The first naval academy was established in Kochi, Kerala, in January 1969. The first batch of cadets graduated in December 1970. Commander K. Ramdas was the first officer-in charge. Earlier, cadets used to be trained in England.

First naval school

The Signal School on INS *Venduruthy* was established at Bombay's Carnac Bunder in 1919 in Maharashtra. The next year, it was shifted to the Naval Dockyard, Bombay, Maharashtra, and in 1941, to HMIS *Talwar*, also in Bombay. In 1946, it finally moved to Kochi, Kerala.

First floating dry dock

The floating dry dock at Port Blair, Andaman and Nicobar Islands, commissioned in 1987, has a lifting capacity of 11,500 tonnes and can accommodate vessels that have a deadweight of up to 30,000 tonnes.

First indigenous floating dock

On 20 June 2017, FDN-2, the first indigenously designed and constructed floating dock of the Indian Navy was launched at the Larsen & Toubro Ltd shipyard at Kattupalli in Chennai, Tamil Nadu. The 185 m (607 ft) long and 40 m (131 ft 3 in.) wide platform has best-in-class machinery and control systems. It accommodates up to 8,000-tonne ships with draught up to 7 m (23 ft), including submarines.

First aircraft carrier dry dock

On 28 September 2019, the first aircraft carrier dry dock was inaugurated at the Naval Dockyard in Mumbai, Maharashtra. The largest dry dock of the Indian Navy, it can accommodate INS *Vikramaditya* (IAC-I), the indigenous aircraft carrier under construction at Cochin Shipyard Ltd, and ships with a tonnage of up to 90,000 tonnes. Started in 2010, the completed dock is 281 m (921 ft 11 in.) long, 45 m (147 ft 8 in.) wide and 17 m (55 ft 9 in.) deep. Unlike most dry docks that are made by excavating land, this one is built into the sea, for which 38 caissons or watertight steel sections drained out seawater before construction could begin.

First unified theatre command

Vice Admiral Arun Prakash took over as the first commander-in-chief of the Andaman and Nicobar Command in 2001, with operational control of all three services and the Indian Coast Guard in the Andaman and Nicobar theatre.

First helicopter training school

INS *Rajali* at Arakkonam, Tamil Nadu, houses the Indian Naval Air Station (INAS), which is a base for training helicopter pilots.

First deep-sea submarine rescue system

On 12 Dec 2018, the Indian Navy's first flyaway Deep-Sea Submarine Rescue System was inducted by Admiral Sunil Lanba at the Naval Dockyard, Mumbai, Maharashtra. The system has a non-tethered Deep Submergence Rescue Vehicle (DSRV) and associated equipment, which give the navy the capability to search, locate, and rescue crew. The rescue system can be mobilized from the naval base at Mumbai, to the nearest mobilization port by air, land, or sea to expedite rescue. On 5 June 2019, an entirely Indian crew conducted its first full submarine rescue drill on the Kilo-class submarine, INS *Sindhudhvaj*, off the eastern coast of India.

First all-woman crew to circumnavigate the world

On 21 May 2018, a six-member all-woman crew completed circumnavigating the globe in 254 days on-board INSV *Tarini*, becoming the first Indian all-woman crew to do so. The journey ended at INS *Mandovi* jetty in Panaji, Goa, from where they had set sail on 10 September 2017. The crew included Lieutenant Commanders Vartika Joshi, Pratibha Jamwal, P. Swathi, and Lieutenants S. Vijaya Devi, B. Aishwarya, and Payal Gupta. The 17 m (56 ft) sailing vessel was captained by Lieutenant Commander Joshi. The crew was mentored by Commander Dilip Donde, who became India's first solo circumnavigator in 2010.

First combat management system

A combat management system (CMS) for indigenous aircraft carriers has been developed by the Indian Navy along with the Tata Power Strategic Engineering Division (TPSED), in collaboration with the Weapon and Electronics System Engineering Establishment and MARS, Russia. On 28 March 2019, it was handed over to the navy. All tests and trials conducted on its hardware and software were successful. This is the first CMS developed by a private company for the Indian Navy.

Longest expedition with a mixed crew

INSV *Mhadei* and INSV *Tarini* set sail for the Bay of Bengal Offshore Sailing Expedition on 22 February 2020 from the Indian Naval Ocean Sailing Node in Goa. The crew comprised five naval officers, including two women officers in each boat, covering 6,100 nautical miles over 55 days. Captain Vipul Meherishi, the skipper of INSV *Tarini*, led the expedition. Captain Atool Sinha was the skipper of INSV *Mhadei*. The sailing vessels had scheduled halts at Colombo (Sri Lanka), Yangon (Myanmar), Chittagong (Bangladesh) and Phuket (Thailand).

First virtual reality centre

On 12 April 2019, Admiral Sunil Lanba inaugurated the first virtual reality centre (VRC) at the Directorate of Naval Design (Surface Ship Group). This centre boosts the design of indigenous warships and collaborative design reviews between designers and end-users of warships. It has developed 19 warship designs.

AIR FORCE

PERSONNEL

There were 220 sorties for casualty evacuation in the year 2022, including rescue of foreign nationals.

First Indian pilots

- Lieutenant Indra Lal Roy from Calcutta (now Kolkata), West Bengal, was the first Indian pilot with the Royal Flying Corps and later in the Royal Air Force during the First World War. He claimed 10 victories in air combat, all within two weeks, in July 1918. He was killed in action when only 19 years old and was posthumously awarded the Distinguished Flying Cross.
- The only other Indian pilots known to have flown in the First World War were Sardar Hardit Singh Malik, Lieutenant S.G. Welingkar, Lieutenant Errol Sharat Chandra Sen, and Lieutenant Naoroji.

INDIAN AIR FORCE

The Indian Air Force (IAF) is the aerial warfare branch of the Indian armed forces. It was officially established on 8 October 1932 and has since become one of the most prominent and powerful air forces in the world. The IAF's primary mission is to secure the Indian airspace and defend the country against any external threats, while also providing air support to the army and navy and conducting various other roles.

1 Aerial Defense

The IAF is responsible for safeguarding India's airspace from unauthorized incursions, intrusions, and attacks. It conducts continuous surveillance and maintains a state of readiness to respond to any threats. The IAF contains and operates a diverse fleet of fighter aircraft which includes the Sukhoi Su-30MKI, Mirage 2000, MiG-29, and Tejas Light Combat Aircraft. It also has radar systems, airborne early warning and control, training and exercises, strategic locations, and research and development.

1 Aerial Warfare

Aerial warfare is a crucial component of the Indian Air Force's (IAF) military strategy. It involves the use of aircraft and related technologies to gain control of the airspace, deter potential adversaries, and achieve various military objectives. The IAF performs a variety of functions such as offensive capabilities, air-to-air combat with BVR missiles, precision strikes, suppression of enemy air defences (SEAD), electronic warfare (EW), close air support (CAS), combat training and exercises, joint operations, and strategic deterrence.

3 Aerial Reconnaissance and Surveillance

The IAF utilizes aircraft and unmanned aerial vehicles (UAVs) for reconnaissance and surveillance missions to gather intelligence and maintain situational awareness. The IAF operates many reconnaissance aircraft such as MiG-25R, MiG-21 Variant, and Heritage Aircraft. It also employs Unmanned Aerial vehicles (UAVs) for reconnaissance and surveillance roles such as the Heron, Searcher, and Rustom. While not directly under IAF's control, satellite reconnaissance plays a significant role in gathering strategic intelligence for India.

4 Humanitarian Assistance and Disaster Relief (HADR)

The Indian Air Force (IAF) plays a crucial role in providing Humanitarian Assistance and Disaster Relief (HADR) during emergencies and natural disasters. HADR operations involve the IAF deploying its resources, including aircraft and personnel, to deliver aid, evacuate affected individuals, and support relief efforts. The IAF's ability to rapidly respond to emergencies is one of its key strengths in HADR operations. It utilizes transport aircrafts such as the C-17 Globemaster III and Ilyushin Il-76 to carry large amounts of relief supplies, including food, water, medical supplies, and equipment. The IAF's helicopters are also equipped for medical evacuation (MEDEVAC), and performs aerial surveys and rescues individuals stranded in floodwaters, on rooftops, or in other hazardous situations.

5 Search and Rescue Operations

The Indian Air Force (IAF) plays a critical role in search and rescue (SAR) operations, responding to emergencies and providing assistance in various situations, including natural disasters, accidents, and humanitarian crises. SAR missions involve locating and rescuing individuals in distress, often in challenging and remote environments. The IAF operates a range of helicopters such as Mi-17, Chetak, and ALH Dhruv which are equipped with searchlights, winches and hoists, and night vision equipment.

First air chiefs

Air Marshal Subroto Mukerjee became the first Indian chief of air staff when he succeeded Air Marshal Sir G.E. Gibbs on 1 April 1954. However, the IAF chief's rank was only equivalent to that of a lieutenant general of the Indian Army at the time. The IAF got its first air chief marshal only in 1966 when Air Marshal Arjan Singh was promoted to the post in recognition of the IAF's role in the 1965 war with Pakistan.

Subroto Mukerjee receiving a medal

First Indian station commander

Wing Commander Subroto Mukerjee was given command of the airbase RAF Kohat (now in Pakistan), the first all-Indian station with only Indian Air Force (IAF) squadrons, in 1944.

Longest tenure as air chief

Air Marshal Subroto Mukerjee served the longest tenure as air chief, from 1 April 1954 to 8 November 1960.

First marshal

On 26 January 2002, former chief of the Indian Air Force, Air Chief Marshal Arjan Singh, was given the rank of marshal, equivalent to a field marshal.

First woman air marshal

Air Marshal Padmavathy Bandopadhyay, AVSM, VSM, (b. 4 November 1944) took over as the director general of medical services (Air) on 1 October 2004. Having joined the IAF in 1968, she was also the first woman to reach the rank of air vice marshal in 2002.

First woman flight commander

Wing Commander Shaliza Dhami was the first woman to become a flight commander in the IAF. She was commissioned to the position on 26 August 2019 and took command of a Chetak Helicopter Unit at Hindon Airbase, Ghaziabad, Uttar Pradesh. She is also the first woman to be granted a permanent commission and the first to be an authorized instructor for IAF helicopters.

In 2022, Chetak helicopters of the armed forces completed 60 years of service to the nation

First chief of foreign air force

Air Commodore K. Jaswant Singh, who was on deputation to Ghana to plan and establish the Ghana Air Force, took charge on 25 March 1959 as its air chief.

First squadron commander

Flight Lieutenant Subroto Mukerjee took over command of 1 Squadron on

Women in Indian Air Force

Women are inducted into all roles in the Indian Air Force, including combat and support roles. They played key roles during India's most significant wars. Flight Lieutenant Kanta Handa was the first female IAF officer to receive a commendation for her service during the 1965 Indo-Pakistan war. Among the first women to fly in a combat zone during the Kargil war were Gunjan Saxena and Sreevidya Rajan. Indian Air Force opened new combat air force roles for women as fighter pilots in 2015.

3 September 1939 – later becoming the first officer to command a flight, a squadron, a station and finally the IAF.

First commissioned woman pilot by order of merit

Squadron Leader Priya Nalgundwar (b. 28 November 1970) was commissioned in the Indian Air Force in the Flying Branch on 17 December 1994 as part of the first batch of seven women pilots and stood first in the order of merit in her batch. She received her wings from the then chief of air staff Air Chief Marshal S.K. Kaul.

First technical officer

Harjinder Singh, one of 19 Hawai Sepoys recruited to the IAF in 1931 (who later became air vice marshal), was promoted to the rank of warrant officer in 1941 and became a flying officer in 1942. He was 41 years old when he learned to fly, earned his wings and became the air officer commander-in-chief of the then newly formed Maintenance Command in Kanpur, Uttar Pradesh, in 1955.

First woman medical officer

Dr Vijayalakshmi Ramanan (later, wing commander), an army doctor, was inducted into the IAF in 1955.

First women combat pilots

In July 2016, for the first time, women combat pilots were inducted into the Indian Air Force with the then defence minister Manohar Parrikar commissioning Mohana Singh, Avani Chaturvedi, and Bhawana Kanth.

First woman in the Defence Services Staff Course

Padmavathy Bandopadhyay (later air marshal) joined the Indian Air Force as a medical officer. Bandopadhyay was also the first woman to attend the prestigious Defence Services Staff Course (DSSC) in 1978, the first woman in Asia to specialize in aerospace medicine, and the first Indian woman to visit the North Pole (1989–90).

First woman pilot to lead the Republic Day fly-past

Flight Lieutenant Swati Rathore became the first woman pilot to lead the Republic Day fly past on 26 January 2021. She flew an Mi-17 V5 with the IAF flag in a formation of four choppers. Flight Lieutenant Bhawana Kanth also participated in the Republic Day fly-past. A total of 38 IAF and four army aircraft were part of the parade.

First helicopter pilot

On 28 March 1954, Flight Lieutenant A. Neil Todd and his co-pilot Squadron Leader S.K. Majumdar flew the then prime minister, Jawaharlal Nehru, from Palam, Delhi, to Tilpat Range in Faridabad, Haryana, and back.

MEDALS AND HONOURS

First couple to be awarded the Vishisht Seva Medals

Flight Lieutenant (Dr) Sati Nath Bandopadhyay and his wife Flight Lieutenant Padmavathy Bandopadhyay were honoured with the Vishisht Seva Medal (VSM) at the same investiture ceremony by Air Chief Marshal O.P. Mehra for their service to the nation in the 1971 Bangladesh operations. They are the only Indian Air Force couple to be awarded such a commendation.

First woman to be awarded the Yudh Seva Medal

Squadron Leader Minty Aggarwal, a woman fighter controller who essayed a stellar role in intercepting retaliatory air attacks by the Pakistan Air Force after the Indian Air Force's Balakot air strikes in February 2019, was awarded the Yudh Seva Medal on 15 August 2019. Aggarwal thereby became the first woman in India's military history to be awarded the medal for distinguished service of a high order during war, conflict or hostilities. Aggarwal was among seven fighter controllers on duty in an underground bunker at the Ambala airbase. She joined the air force in 2011.

First and only Sarvottam Yudh Seva Medal

On 15 August 1999, Air Marshal Vinod Patney was awarded the Sarvottam Yudh

Seva Medal (SYSM) for his exemplary leadership during the Kargil conflict in 1999. The award is the highest wartime distinguished service decoration. The medal has been conferred thrice to date and he is the only IAF officer to receive it.

First Param Vir Chakra

Flying Officer N.J.S. Sekhon of 18 Squadron is the only Indian Air Force officer to have been decorated with the Param Vir Chakra, the highest gallantry award. It was given posthumously after he was killed in an air battle over Srinagar in Jammu and Kashmir on 14 December 1971.

UNITS

First squadron

1 Squadron was formed at Karachi's Drigh Road Airfield with Royal Air Force (RAF) officer Flight Lieutenant C.A. Bouchier as the first commanding officer. The first six Indian officers commissioned into the IAF were: Subroto Mukerjee, H.C. Sirkar, A.B. Awan, Bhupendra Singh, Amarjeet Singh, and J.N. Tandon, along with 19 technicians who formed the complement. The six officers were pilots except Tandon, who was commissioned as first ground duty officer.

First transport squadron

The first transport squadron of the IAF was raised with Spitfire fighter aircraft under the command of Squadron Leader S. Sajad Haider at Kohat (now in Pakistan). It moved to Bhopal, Madhya Pradesh, in 1946 and converted to Dakotas, which it flew till 1954, when it then converted to Packets, a twin-engine cargo aircraft.

First heavy-lift transport squadron

In 1961, 44 Squadron, known as 'Himalayan Geese', was raised and equipped with the An-12 four-engine turboprop transport aircraft. In the 1980s, it was renamed the 'Mighty Jets'.

First squadron to have a jet bomber

106 SPR Squadron, though technically tasked with photo reconnaissance work, was the first unit to fly the famous English Electric Canberra in April 1957. The first squadron to have a jet bomber role again was No. 5 Squadron that took charge of the bomber variant of the Canberra in September 1957.

First bomber squadron

The No. 5 Squadron (Tuskers) was raised on 2 November 1948 on the Consolidated B-24 Liberator bomber. It is now equipped with Jaguar IS and based in Ambala, Haryana.

First attack helicopter squadron

On 1 November 1983, 125 Helicopter Squadron (also known as Gladiators), a fighter squadron, was formed with the Mil Mi-25 attack gunships. It was re-equipped with Mi 35 helicopters in April 1990. The squadron saw action in Sri Lanka during the operations of the Indian Peacekeeping Force (IPKF) between 1987 and 1990. It is currently based at the Pathankot air force station, Punjab.

EQUIPMENT

First aircraft

The biplane aircraft Westland Wapiti with a maximum speed of 362 km/hr was inducted into the IAF on 1 April 1933. Fitted with two machine guns, this aircraft could carry a load of 263 kg. Four Wapitis, which are believed to have been procured for 10 pounds sterling each, formed the A Flight of 1 Squadron, commanded by Flight Lieutenant C.A. Bouchier of the Royal Air Force (RAF).

First jet bomber

The twin-engine English Electric Canberra, which is a long-range and reconnaissance aircraft, was inducted into the Indian Air Force in 1957. Six IAF Canberras of 5 Squadron served with the UN forces on the Congo peacekeeping assignment in October 1961.

First supersonic aircraft

In February 1957, 1 Squadron (The Tigers) was equipped with the Dassault MD-452 Mystere Iva. The Mystere could break the sound barrier in a dive. However, the first squadron to fly a level-flight-capable supersonic aircraft was the 28 Squadron, raised in October 1963 on the MiG-21F. Aptly christened First Supersonics, 28 Squadron also has the honour of being the first squadron to fly a Mach 2-capable fighter.

First jet

The British single-seat Vampire was inducted in 1948, making India the first Asian country with jet fighters. In 1950, India entered into a licence agreement with de Havilland Aircraft Company Ltd, UK, and the first Vampire built by Hindustan Aeronautics Ltd (HAL) flew on 21 February 1952. Vampires were phased out in 1975.

First indigenous aircraft (trainer)

The HT-2-piston-engined elementary trainer was designed at HAL. It made its maiden flight on 5 August 1951 and was in operation from 1953 to 1990. It replaced the Tiger Moth and was used to train over 5,000 Indian and foreign pilots.

First indigenous light combat aircraft

Tejas is the first advanced fly-by-wire light combat aircraft (LCA) designed, developed, and manufactured indigenously by HAL, DRDO,

Tejas

NAL (National Aerospace Laboratories), and ADA (Aeronautical Development Agency). It is a lightweight single-seat multi-role jet fighter, and pegged as the world's smallest and lightest supersonic fighter. It is equipped with a satellite-aided inertial navigation system, a digital computer-based attack system, and autopilot mode. Tejas can fire air-to-air missiles, and carry bombs and precision-guided ammunition with a reach of over 400 km. It is mainly for use in close air-to-ground operations.

First indigenous fighter aircraft

The single seat Mach-2 combat jet fighter HF (Hindustan Fighter)-24 MkI (Marut Ground Attack Fighter), with two single-shaft turbojet engines, was designed at HAL, Bengaluru. It took its maiden flight on 17 June 1961.

First Gnat

The first Gnat or Ajeet, a single-seat, light, fighter bomber, about a third in size and half the weight of a conventional fighter, was inducted into the IAF in 1958. The first Gnat, made by HAL, flew on 18 November 1959. It won the IAF its only Param Vir Chakra, and was in front-line service for more than three decades.

First indigenous advanced light helicopter

The naval version of the advanced light helicopter (ALH), developed by HAL, took its first flight from INS *Viraat* on 8 March 1998. It had an integrated dynamic system, hinge-less main rotor and composite blades, bearing-less tail rotor, advanced cockpit, and high-power engines with electronic control. It could exceed a speed of 250 km/hr.

First indigenous tandem-seat jet trainer

The intermediate jet trainer (IJT) was designed in India, with the fastest design-to- first-flight time, and flown officially by Squadron Leader Baldev Singh for 20 mins on 21 March 2003. With a 10 m (32 ft 10 in.) wingspan and an overall length of 11 m (36 ft), the 3,500 kg aircraft can touch 750 km/hr. However, the credit of being the first tandem-seat jet trainer used for intermediate flying training in the IAF goes to the Polish PZL TS-11 Iskra.

First indigenous AEW&C class of aircraft

On 14 February 2017, the IAF was given its first indigenous Airborne Early Warning and Control (AEW&C) System class of aircraft in initial operational configuration (IOC) by DRDO, during Aero India 2017, a biennial air show and aviation exhibition, at the Yelahanka airbase in Bengaluru, Karnataka. It is built on an Emb-145 platform, and has an air-to-air refuelling capability to enhance surveillance time.

First AESA radar for IAF

The IAF gave the nod in July 2017 for the first Active Electronically Scanned Array (AESA) radar to be integrated into its aircraft. The radar is fitted on to Jaguar fighter aircraft. In conventional radars, the antenna is moved manually to scan enemy targets. The AESA radar moves electronically and rapidly, tracking multiple and long-distance targets, while also jamming enemy communications and radars.

HAL HJT-16 Kiran

The Hindustan Aeronautics Limited (HAL) HJT-16 Kiran is an Indian-built jet trainer aircraft designed for basic and intermediate flight training for pilots in the Indian Air Force and the Indian Navy. The Kiran has served as a staple in the training curriculum of the Indian armed forces for several decades. The name Kiran translates to ray of light in Sanskrit. The Kiran serves as a jet trainer aircraft for basic flight training, intermediate flight training, and weapons training. The Kiran had been gradually phased out from active service in the Indian Air Force. It was replaced by more modern and advanced trainer aircraft like the HAL HJT-36 Sitara, which is currently under development.

First Apache helicopters

On 3 September 2019, eight Boeing-made Apache Guardian attack helicopters were inducted into service at the Pathankot air force station. The AH-64E (I) Apache helicopter has been built keeping in mind the high mountainous terrain that the IAF operates in. It can also carry out precision attacks. This helicopter can receive and transmit images from the ground to its weapon systems and likewise transmit images from its weapon systems to the ground. The air crew and ground crew were trained to operate the helicopter at the US Army base, Fort Rucker.

First indigenous anti-radiation missile

Rudram-1, a new-generation air-to-surface anti-radiation missile (NGARM), developed by DRDO for the Indian Air Force was test-fired on 9 October 2020 on a radiation target on Wheeler Island off the coast of Odisha. The missile Rudram-1 was fired from a Sukhoi-30 Mk-I fighter aircraft, the potential launch-source aircraft for the same. With its ability to detect radio sources from 100 km away, the missile can disarm enemy radars and target the range of emitters. Its strike range is between 100 and 250 km.

First S-400 air-defence system

The Indian Air Force deployed the first S-400 Triumf air-defence missile system in the Punjab sector near Pakistan border, as reported on 21 December 2021. The deployment was to take care of any aerial threat from either Pakistan or China, using its capability to shoot down enemy fighter aircraft and cruise missiles at a long range (400 km).

OPERATIONS

First active operation

In September 1937, 1 Squadron operated from Miranshah in North Waziristan (now in Pakistan) against hostile tribesmen. The IAF men lived inside a fort for safety and had to wheel in their aircraft into the fort every evening. Flying Officer (later Air Marshal) Aspy Merwan Engineer was the first officer to be Mentioned in- Dispatches for the operations.

First flight to the true North Pole

The IL-76 aircraft of the 44 Squadron, representing the IAF, flew over the true North Pole in Exercise Cope Thunder-03 in Alaska, USA, with 14 crew members. The mission was launched on 19 June 2003 at 8:15 p.m. IST from USA's Eielson air force base, south-east of Fairbanks, Alaska, and the crew flew over the true North Pole on 20 June 2003 at 00:16 a.m. IST. The aircraft returned to base on 20 June 2003 at 5:51 a.m. IST after a flight lasting 9 hrs 36 mins.

Biggest rapid airlift

On 18 December 2018, the Western Air Command of the IAF airlifted a record 463 tonnes from the Chandigarh airbase and dropped the load in Ladakh. The massive airlift was done in a single wave and proved the IAF's rapid airlift capability. The feat was completed by 16 fixed-wing transport aircraft including the C-17 Globemaster, the Ilyushin-76 Gajraj and the medium-lift tactical aircraft, Antonov-32. The airdrop was done in less than six hours.

First airlift of Indian troops

During the Kurdish uprising in April 1923, the Royal Air Force flew 280 Sikh troops from Kingarban to Kirkuk, Iraq. Covering the distance that would normally require a five-day march, the flight covered 120.7 km in 10 hours.

GENERAL

Only vintage flight

A vintage aircraft flight was raised in Palam, Delhi, in 1988 for heritage aircraft, such as the Howard, Tiger Moth and Dakota planes.

First forward surgical centre

During an IAF military exercise, Gaganshakti-2018, which was conducted from 8 to 22 April 2018, the IAF set up a Forward Surgical Centre (FSC) at Naliya air force station in Gujarat. An FSC can be used for life- and limb-saving surgeries as also to help stabilize a patient.

First mobile health app launched by a defence service

MedWatch, a mobile health application, was launched by the IAF on 8 October 2018 for the IAF's 85th anniversary. With content from the Directorate General of Medical Services (Air), it was developed in-house by the Directorate of Information Technology (DIT) and is available on the Android platform for users. It provides a range of health information, reminders, and utility tools. The app shares important web links and helpline numbers along with a body mass index (BMI) calculator and health record cards.

COAST GUARD

PERSONNEL

First director general of the Indian Coast Guard

Vice Admiral V.A. Kamath, PVSM, was the first director general of the Indian Coast Guard (ICG) from 19 August 1978 to 31 March 1980.

First women combatants

In 2017, the Indian Coast Guard became the first Indian armed forces service to deploy women in combat roles on-board ships. Assistant Commandants Anuradha Shukla, Sneha Khatayak, Shirin Chandran, and Vasundhara Chouksey were trained at the Indian Coast Guard station at Mandapam, Tamil Nadu.

First and only Integral ICG contingent operating abroad

An ICG Dhruv helicopter – CG 853 – has been operating in Maldives along with an ICG contingent. Since its induction, the helicopter has aided in 168 medivac (medical evacuation) missions, saving 178 lives.

First woman hovercraft pilot

In 2017, Assistant Commandant Sneha Khatayak became the first woman hovercraft pilot in India.

First woman pilot

Assistant Commandant Monica Seth joined the Indian Coast Guard on 5 June 1998. She flew a total of 1,500 hours during her tenure. She flew on missions during the Kargil conflict in Jammu and Kashmir in 1999 and also for earthquake relief in Gujarat in January 2001.

ICGS *Sachet*

MEDALS AND HONOURS

In July, ICG rescued **22** lives in the Arabian Sea.

First Yudh Seva Medal

Deputy Commandant S.P.S. Basra and Deputy Commandant B.A.S. Bhar were awarded the Yudh Seva Medal (YSM) on 26 January 1989. Commanding the Indian Coast Guard ships ICGS *Ahalya Bai* and ICGS *Tara Bai*, respectively, they prevented the infiltration of the Liberation Tigers of Tamil Eelam (LTTE) in the Palk Bay.

First to receive President's Tatrakshak Medal

Commandant A.K. Dey received the award for his efforts in firefighting during the construction of an Indian Coast Guard ship, and preventing an oil spill off the coast of Goa in June 1994.

EQUIPMENT

First vessels

ICGS *Kuthar* and ICGS *Kirpan* (formerly of the Indian Navy) were commissioned on 19 August 1978 under Commander N.S. Achreja and Commander V.K. Tuli, respectively.

First indigenous offshore patrol vessel

On 21 February 2019, ICGS *Sachet*, the first indigenous offshore patrol vessel (OPV) of the Indian Coast Guard was launched at Goa Shipyard Ltd (GSL). This OPV is part of an indigenous project that was launched on 13 November 2016. Designed in-house, these OPVs will be used for protecting the Exclusive Economic Zone. The vessel weighs 2,400 tonnes and is equipped with features like quick-response boats for rescue and anti-piracy, gunnery simulators, and many more advanced features.

Latest training vessel

On 24 October 2018, ICGS *Varuna*, an indigenously designed training vessel built by Reliance Naval and Engineering Ltd (RNAVAL), was launched at the Pipavav Shipyard, Gujarat. ICGS *Varuna* is a 105 m (344 ft 6 in.) long vessel with a crew of 242 officers and sailors. It is powered by twin diesel engines and can reach a speed of 20 knots. It has ultra-modern navigation and communication systems. This is the largest ship built yet for the Indian Coast Guard.

OPERATIONS

First and longest deep-sea passage by hovercraft

On 13 January 2015, Indian Coast Guard Air Cushion Vehicle (ACV) H-198 undertook area deployment from New Mangaluru, Karnataka, to Androth Island in the Lakshadweep Islands, across the Arabian Sea. The ACV hovercraft, piloted by Commandant Amitabh Banerjee and Deputy Commandant

Konark Sharma, covered 142.5 nautical miles (264 km) in five hours. The ACV H-198 is the only hovercraft in India to venture into the lagoon islands of Lakshadweep. The return run of 146 nautical miles (270.39 km) was made on 22 January 2015.

First underwater clean-up

On 5 June 2019, celebrated as World Environment Day, the Indian Coast Guard (Eastern Region) conducted an underwater debris clean-up exercise in the Bay of Bengal near the Chennai (Tamil Nadu) coast, in association with Dive India. The operation lasted two hours during which nearly 500 kg of trash was collected. This was the first underwater clean-up in India to remove debris, nets, and plastic from the ocean.

GENERAL

Youngest defence service

The Indian Coast Guard or Sea Police, was constituted as India's fourth defence force under the Coast Guard Act on 18 August 1978, for the preservation and protection of the 2.01 million sq. km Exclusive Economic Zone. The force is under the direction and control of the director general, Indian Coast Guard.

First hovercraft berthing platform

In 2001, the first hovercraft berthing platform was built at Haldia, West Bengal, in eight months by the Military Engineering Services.

Largest integrated shipbuilding facility

Reliance Naval and Engineering Ltd (RNAVAL), known earlier as Reliance Defence and Engineering Ltd and Pipavav Shipyard Ltd, headquartered in Mumbai, Maharashtra, is one of the largest shipbuilding yards of its kind in the world. RNAVAL is the first private sector company in India to earn a licence and contract to construct warships. It has India's largest integrated shipbuilding facility with the shipyard located in Pipavav, Gujarat. Its dry dock measures 662 m x 65 m (2,172 ft x 213 ft). It has the only modular shipbuilding facility in India.

EXISTING FORCE LEVEL OF INDIAN COAST GUARD

Vessels	156
Dornier fixed wing aircraft	39
Ships	71
Chetak	19
Interceptor boats	67
Hovercrafts	18
Aircrafts	62
Advanced Light helicopters	4

Source: Annual report 2020-2021, Ministry of Defence, Government of India

SCIENCE AND TECHNOLOGY

FORMAL SCIENCES

MATHEMATICS

WR Earliest mention of mathematical series
Arithmetic and geometric series were mentioned in Vedic literature as early as 2000 BCE in the *Taittiriya Samhita* and in the *Panchavimsa Brahmana.*

WR Earliest treatise on geometry
The *Shulba Sutras* are the earliest known treatises that are related to geometry. Dating to the Vedic period, these texts are focused on the measurement and the building of altars. Baudhayana, who lived around 800 BCE, wrote the first *Shulba Sutra*.

WR First mention of geometry
In the first millennium BCE, Apastamba, the founder of a Vedic school, propounded practical geometry for the construction of sacrificial altars, which describes acute, obtuse, and right angles.

WR Earliest use of irrational numbers
The use of irrational numbers dates back to the *Shulba Sutras* (c. first millennium BCE).

Invention of algebra
Aryabhata (476–550 CE) from Kusumapura near Pataliputra (today's Patna) in Bihar is credited with the invention of algebra. He was also the first to approximate the value of π (pi) to 3.14159..., which is accepted today.

WR Earliest magic squares
The oldest magic square that can be dated in India occurs in polymath Varahamihira's encyclopaedic work the *Brihat-Samhita* (c. 550 CE). Varahamihira used a modified 4 x 4 magic square to indicate combinations and quantities of ingredients for making perfumes.

Earliest use of the decimal system
A Gupta inscription from 448 CE found in Allahabad (now Prayagraj) District, Uttar Pradesh, indicates that the decimal system was known in India at the beginning of the fifth century CE.

WR Use of sines and cosines in place of chords
In a significant contribution to trigonometry, Indian mathematicians changed the use of chords to sines and cosines, making the system much more convenient and the various theorems on triangles much neater. Starting with the *Arya-siddhanta* (c. fifth and sixth centuries CE), Aryabhata used a simple table for sines. Varahamihira gave the first clear statements of sin2A and sin2A + cos2A.

WR Firsts to understand the idea of 'zero'
- Brahmagupta (c. 598–668 CE) was the first mathematician to treat zero as a number and present its mathematical operations.

• Bhaskara I (c. 600–680 CE) was the first mathematician to understand the properties of both zero and infinity and to state that any number divided by zero equals infinity.

As per the National Science Foundation-2022, United States, report India's scholarly output increased from 60,555 papers in 2010 to 1,49,213 papers in 2020.

First study of infinite series

Founded in the 14th century by Madhava (c. 1340–1425 CE) of Sangamagrama, who is said to have been born in present-day Irinjalakuda in Thrissur District, Kerala; the Kerala school of astronomy and mathematics (or the Kerala school) was responsible for notable contributions to the study of infinite series, trigonometry, geometry, algebra, and calculus. The foundations for calculus laid by Madhava were further developed by his successors at the Kerala school, with many results that would later be repeated in Europe, including the infinite series for circular and trigonometric functions.

First textbook on arithmetic

Ganita Sara Sangraha, written by the great mathematician Mahavira in 850 CE, is the first known textbook on arithmetic. The subject matter and its arrangement is said to be practically the same as that in present-day textbooks. It only lacks a chapter on decimals.

WR Discovery of differential calculus

Bhaskara II (c. 1114–85 CE), said to have been born in Bijapur (now Vijayapura) in Karnataka, conducted mathematical operations that showed that he had invented calculus long before Isaac Newton and Gottfried Leibniz, who are considered its pioneers. Bhaskara II used calculus to determine the area and volume of a sphere and the daily motion of planets.

First to give the Gregory series

In 1502, Keḷallur Nilakantha Somayaji (1444–1545 CE) from Tirur in present-day Malappuram District, Kerala, devised the *Tantrasangraha* equation, which is employed to give the approximate value of π or pi (3.14159...). This is known today as the 'Gregory series' after it appeared in the works of later mathematicians James Gregory (1638–75) and Gottfried Leibniz (1646–1716).

Discovery of the Kaprekar Constant

D.R. Kaprekar (1905-81) discovered in 1946 what is known as the Kaprekar Constant in mathematics. Explained thus: Take a number, arrange its digits in descending order and in ascending order and calculate the difference. Arrange the digits of the result of the subtraction in the same way. Keep repeating. For any four-digit number, this leads in a few steps to 6,174 and then it becomes a constant. This does not work for repetitive numbers like 1,111 and 2,222, which lead to a difference of zero in the first step itself. So the numbers should have at least two different digits.

First mathematical society

The Indian Mathematical Society (IMS) was the oldest organization in India devoted to the promotion of the study of and research in mathematics. With its headquarters in Pune, Maharashtra, it was founded by V. Ramaswamy Aiyer in April 1907. The society's first president was Dr B. Hanumantha Rao.

Invention of the Mahalanobis distance

Pioneering statistician P.C. Mahalanobis (1893–1972) invented statistical tools such as the Mahalanobis distance and fractile graphical analysis in 1936. He was the first statistician to be elected a Fellow of the Royal Society, UK, in 1945.

First to propose a theory on infinite dimensional representations

Indian-born American mathematician-physicist Harish Chandra (1923–83) created a theory for infinite dimensional representations in 1947, which was used in quantum mechanics when it was necessary to analyse the effect of symmetries on the motions of particles and waves.

First Indian to win MSO

Twenty-year old Neelakantha Bhanu Prakash (b. 13 October 1999) became the fastest human calculator in the world after winning the gold for India in the Mental Calculation World Championship at Mind Sports Olympiad (MSO) in September 2020.

PHYSICAL SCIENCES

ASTRONOMY

Two firsts in astronomy

- Lagadha, who lived around 900 BCE near Srinagar, Jammu and Kashmir, was the first to systematize astronomy, the first to complete a text – *Vedanga Jyotisha* or *Jyotishavedanga* – on astronomy, and the first to work out simple formulae to derive unknown quantities from known ones.
- Aryabhata was the first astronomer to deduce that the earth is round and that it rotates on its own axis, causing day and night.

First manual on the astrolabe

The astrolabe is an instrument for measuring the altitude of stars. Mahendra Suri (c. 1340–1400 CE), an astronomer, wrote a manual on the astrolabe in Sanskrit while under the patronage of ruler Firuz Shah Tughlaq of the Tughlaq dynasty.

Earliest extant astrolabe

The Yantraraja, which was 276 mm (10.87 in.) in diameter, was designed and built in Ahmedabad, Gujarat, in 1607 for astronomer Damodara during the reign of the Mughal ruler Jahangir.

WR First chain of observatories

Sawai Jai Singh II (1686–1743), the maharaja of the kingdom of Amber in Rajasthan, was the first in the world to build a chain of astronomical observatories, in Mathura, Varanasi, Delhi, and Jaipur; from 1719 to 1737. It was about a century after European astronomers had verified Polish scientist Nicolaus Copernicus's theory that the sun (and not Earth) was at the centre of the universe.

First modern catalogue of stars

The Madras or Taylor catalogue was made by T.G. Taylor, astronomer to the British East India Company, in 1844. The catalogue contained the positions of 11,015 stars, based on his observations of the night sky in Madras (now Chennai), Tamil Nadu.

First astronomical observatory

On 5 December 1786, William Petrie, an officer of the East India Company, made the first astronomical observations to calculate the latitude and longitude of the Masulipatnam Fort from his private observatory. This observatory on the terrace of his residence was fitted with an astronomical clock, a transit instrument, and two or three telescopes. The first modern astronomical observatory, the Nizamia Observatory, was set up more than a century later in Hyderabad (now in Telangana) in 1908 by the Nizam's government.

Oldest planetarium

The M.P. Birla Planetarium at Calcutta (now Kolkata), West Bengal, was established on 29 September 1962 by the Birla Education Trust. The planetarium coordinates the various activities of the Amateur Astronomers Association, which include telescope fabrication, astrophotography, and organizing skywatching sessions.

Earliest observation of the Pole Star

Ancient astronomers Ashwalayana and Patanjali recorded observing the Pole Star (or *Dhruvatara*) in c. 1300 BCE.

The Pole Star

First to observe a nova

Radha Gobinda Chandra (1878–1975) from Jessore (now in Bangladesh) was the first Indian astronomer to observe a nova. A nova is a transient astronomical event that causes the sudden appearance of a bright and seemingly 'new' star that slowly fades over weeks or months. He sighted the nova in the Aquila constellation on 7 June 1918. A pioneer of observational astronomy in Bengal – now split into two parts, Bangladesh (a country) and West Bengal (an Indian state), Chandra was one of the first international members of the American Association of Variable Star Observers.

Discovery of the Bappu–Wilson effect

Indian astronomer M.K.V. Bappu (1927–82), in collaboration with Colin C. Wilson at Mount Wilson and Palomar Observatories, USA, discovered a relationship between the luminosity of particular types of stars and their spectral characteristics. Known as the 'Bappu–Wilson effect', this helps determine the luminosity and distance of these types of stars. It was discovered in 1957.

Rings of Uranus discovered

- Prof. J.C. Bhattacharya and Sri Kuppuswamy from the Indian Institute of Astrophysics, Bangalore (now Bengaluru), Karnataka, discovered the rings of planet Uranus in 1976 at the Vainu Bappu Observatory in Kavalur, Tamil Nadu.
- Around the same time, US astronomer James Elliot and his team, aboard the airborne Kuiper Observatory, discovered the same rings during an occultation of a star by the planet.

Discovery of solar radio burst

In 1958, Prof. Govind Swarup (b. 1929) and A. Maxwell discovered a burst, called 'type U solar radio burst'. A pioneer of radio astronomy, Swarup was behind the concept, design, and installation of the Ooty Radio Telescope near present-day Udhagamandalam, Tamil Nadu, and the Giant Metrewave Radio Telescope (GMRT) near Poona (now Pune) in Maharashtra.

First university to teach astronomy

Osmania University, based in Hyderabad (now in Telangana), was the first educational institution in the country to start teaching astronomy and astrophysics at postgraduate and research levels in 1959. The Astronomical Society of India was also registered in Hyderabad, in 1972.

Largest optical telescope

The Vainu Bappu telescope of 2.34 m (7 ft 8 in.) diameter at Kavalur, Tamil Nadu, is the largest in Asia. It was built indigenously (including the mirror) in 1986 by the Indian Institute of Astrophysics, Bangalore, Karnataka.

Highest astronomical observatory

Established in 2001, the Indian Astronomical Observatory, under the aegis of the Indian Institute of Astrophysics, Bangalore, is located in

Every year India manufactures **100** million km of optical fibre.

Hanle (at Digpa-Ratsa Ri, atop Mt Saraswati) in Ladakh. It has the world's second highest optical telescope at 4,500 m (14,764 ft) above mean sea level.

First discovery of an asteroid

R. Rajamohan (b. 1944), associate professor at the Indian Institute of Astrophysics, Bangalore, and his team discovered an asteroid (No. 4130) in 1988, through the optical telescope at Kavalur, Tamil Nadu.

WR Biggest sundial

The Samrat Yantra built by Sawai Jai Singh II, ruler of the kingdom of Amber in Rajasthan, in 1728 CE at Jaipur, Rajasthan, is the biggest sundial in the world. Its gnomon rises to 22.6 m (74 ft).

Discovery of the variability of stars

In 1958, astrophysicist K.D. Abhyankar (1928–2007), professor of astronomy at the Osmania University in Hyderabad, discovered the variability of two types of stars, called dwarf cepheid and the short period eclipsing binary.

First woman president of the Astronomical Society of India

In 2019, the Astronomical Society of India elected its first woman president, Dr G.C. Anupama, a senior professor and dean at the Indian Institute of Astrophysics in Bengaluru. She has projects such as the Himalayan Telescope at the Hanle Observatory in Ladakh to her credit and is a member of an international team setting up a 30 m (98 ft 5 in.) telescope (TMT) in Hawaii, USA.

First robotic telescope

India's first robotic telescope became functional on the night of 12 June 2018 at Hanle, Ladakh. It is the first one designed to observe dynamic or transient events in the universe. GROWTH-India, the facility at Hanle, is part of a multi-country collaborative initiative, known as the 'Global Relay of Observatories Watching Transients Happen' (GROWTH), to observe transient events in the universe.

PHYSICS

Earliest atomistic theory

Kanada, an ancient Indian natural scientist and philosopher, who lived between the sixth and second centuries BCE, composed the *Vaisheshika Sutra,* a text in which he explored and presented the relationship between cause and effect for the first time in relation to physics and philosophy.

WR First double radio source

Mrinal Kumar Dasgupta from the Institute of Radio Physics and Electronics, Calcutta, West Bengal, discovered the first double radio source Cygnus A in 1953 in collaboration with R.C. Jennison at the Jodrell Bank Experimental Station in Cheshire, UK.

First solar heater

Prof. Shri Krishna Joshi from Almora, who lived in Allahabad (now Prayagraj), Uttar Pradesh, invented an apparatus for utilizing solar heat as a substitute for fire, named 'Bhanu Taap'. Also called the 'heliotherm', it was patented in 1900 and awarded a gold medal at the Industrial Exhibition of Calcutta in 1901.

Crescograph: Invented by Jagadish Chandra Bose, it helps to measure growth in plants

First wireless demonstration

In 1894, scientist Jagadish Chandra Bose (1858–1937) at Presidency College, Calcutta, Bengal (now Presidency University, demonstrated the transmission of radio waves before Italian inventor Guglielmo Marconi did it in Europe, using very short radio waves or 'microwaves'. Jagadish Chandra Bose also scientifically proved that plants have feelings. He also wrote the first science fiction in Bengali.

First optical fibre

Narinder Kalpany from the Imperial College, University of London, UK, invented optical fibre in 1955. This is a thin and long fibre of glass through which light can travel without hindrance, whether it is bent or not. Optical fibres have a wide variety of applications in a range of fields, including medicine, computers, communications, and the automotive industry.

First multicore fibre

STL Multiverse launched India's first multicore fibre and cable in October 2022. This development allows the fibre to carry multiple beams of light (separated within the body of the optic fibre cable) through it making it more efficient than single-core fibre.

First molecular distillation unit

Major General Sir Singh Sokhey of Haffkine Institute, in Bombay (now Mumbai), Maharashtra, installed the first molecular distillation unit in India to separate vitamin A from shark liver oil in the early 1940s. He was also the first Indian scientist to receive the Lenin Peace Prize in 1947.

First nuclear implosion

On 18 May 1974, India imploded its first nuclear device at Pokhran in Rajasthan. The test, code-named 'Smiling Buddha', was conducted at a depth of 107 m (351 ft). It yielded energy equivalent to 8–10 kilotonnes of TNT, and produced a 47 m (154 ft) wide and 10 m (33 ft) deep crater.

First semiconductor laser

The Bhabha Atomic Research Centre, Bombay, Maharashtra, developed a semiconductor laser in 1965.

First synchrotron radiation facility

The first synchrotron radiation facility in India was INDUS-1, set up in 2002. An advanced, indigenously built nuclear particle accelerator, it is part of the Centre for Advanced Technology at Indore, Madhya Pradesh.

First to measure ozone in the atmosphere

In 1985, M. Vivekananda and R.S. Arora from the Raman Research Institute, Bangalore, first measured the density and height distribution of ozone in the atmosphere over Bangalore by a simple ground-based technique using radio waves.

First prediction of hot superconductors

S.N. Ekbote and A.V. Narlikar from the National Physical Laboratory (NPL), New Delhi, were the first scientists to predict the presence of 'hot' superconductors based on their new theory of superconductivity formulated in 1981, which challenged the then accepted Nobel Prize–winning theory.

WR First Liquid Mirror Telescope Only for Astronomical Observations

Aryabhatta Research Institute of Observational Sciences (ARIES), an autonomous institute under the Department of Science and Technology, now has the first liquid mirror telescope that is meant only for astronomical observations. It is called International Liquid Mirror Telescope (ILMT). This is also India's, as well as Asia's, largest. This telescope was inaugurated on 22 March 2023. It was designed and built by Advanced Mechanical and Optical Systems

First liquid mirror telescope designed only for astronomical observations: It is the largest in Asia, Inset: NGC 4274 Galaxy seen with the ILMT

(AMOS) Corporation and the Centre Spatial de Lie'ge in Belgium. The telescope will generate 10–15 gigabytes of data, which in turn will allow application of big data and machine-learning algorithms that will be used for classifying the objects observed through the ILMT.

First nuclear reactor

Apsara was the first Asian research reactor to achieve criticality, when it became operational, at the Bhabha Atomic Research Centre (BARC) in Bombay in 1956. It was shut down in 2009.

First advanced heavy water reactor

In 2016, the Bhabha Atomic Research Centre (BARC) in Mumbai, designed an advanced heavy water reactor, which employed thorium instead of uranium as fuel. It was the centrepiece of India's nuclear power programme.

First Nobel Prize in physics

Sir Chandrasekhara Venkata Raman (1888–1970) from Tiruchirappalli, Madras Presidency (now Tamil Nadu), won the 1930 Nobel Prize in physics for his groundbreaking work in the field of the scattering of light, or the 'Raman effect'.

Only nuclear safety institute

With the inauguration of the Safety Research Institute at Kalpakkam, Tamil Nadu, on 20 February 1999, India became the second country after France to have such a facility.

Discovery of the 'Krishnan effect'

In the 1930s, physicist Rappal Sangameswaran Krishnan (1911–99) from the Indian Institute of Science (IISc), Bangalore, discovered the 'Krishnan effect' – a new optical effect in the scattering of light. This led to the discovery of the presence of large clusters of molecules in liquid mixtures, glasses, and colloidal solutions. It also helps in assessing the size of the scattering particles.

New method for thermal conductivity

Suresh Chand Jain (1926–2009), former director of the Solid State Physics Laboratory and Defence Research and Development Organization (DRDO), and his mentor R. S. Krishnan developed a new method known as the Jain–Krishnan method in 1952, which is now a standard method for measuring the thermal conductivity of solids at high temperatures.

Discovery of bosons

In the late 1920s, famous physicist and German Nobel Prize-winner Albert Einstein and Indian scientist Satyendra Nath Bose worked together on the Bose-Einstein equations, which pointed to a state of matter comprising particles, now known as 'bosons'. As researchers at the Joint Institute of Laboratory Astrophysics, Colorado, USA, they cooled thousands of atoms of rubidium to create the 'Bose–Einstein condensate'.

Discovery of mesons

Indian nuclear physicist Dr Homi Jehangir Bhabha and German physicist

Dr Walter Heinrich Heitler presented the 'Cascade Theory of Electron Showers', called the 'Bhabha–Heitler Cascade Theory' in 1937 in Cambridge, UK, which explains the process of electron showers in cosmic rays. Bhabha recognized heavy electron particles in cosmic rays, which he named 'mesons'.

Discovery of helium isotope in cosmic rays

Dr K.M.V. Apparao (b. 1933), a scientist at the Tata Institute of Fundamental Research in Bombay discovered in 1961 an isotope of helium in cosmic rays, the energetic particles that fall down on earth like a continuous rain from outer space, in 1961.

Discovery of quantum Zeno paradox

Indian theoretical physicists Baidyanath Misra and E.C.G. Sudarshan, then conducting research at the University of Texas at Austin, US, discovered the quantum Zeno effect (or paradox) in 1977. It is the quantum mechanical analogue of the proverbial adage 'a watched kettle never boils'. In 1989, the paradox was experimentally proven – under continuous measurement, an unstable atomic nucleus that normally decays was found not to decay.

CHEMISTRY

First chemistry department

Chemistry was first taught as a subject in 1872–73 at Presidency College, (now Presidency University, Kolkata, West Bengal). Postgraduate courses were introduced in 1886. In 1889, chemist Prafulla Chandra Ray (1861–1944) set up the first organized laboratory here for research.

First heavy chemicals company

Behramji Sorabji Lalkaka (1880–1957) started the Pioneer Magnesia Works Ltd in 1915 at Kharagodha in the Little Rann of Kachchh, Gujarat, for the manufacture of magnesium chloride, the import of which was stopped from Germany due to the First World War. Magnesium chloride is used in a variety of ways in the chemical industry.

First tokamak

The first Indian tokamak – essentially a magnetic bottle that can maintain conditions present inside the sun wherein enormous energy from nuclear fusion reactions is produced – named Aditya was set up at the Institute for Plasma Research, Gandhinagar, Gujarat, in 1986.

First chemicals company

In 1892, Prafulla Chandra Ray set up Bengal Chemicals and Pharmaceutical Ltd at Calcutta, West Bengal, using locally available materials, which led to the production of many chemicals and medicines indigenously. He was also the first person to synthesize ammonium nitrite (NH_4NO_2) in its pure form.

First observation of spontaneous fission

Prof. Shyamadas Chatterjee (1909–95) from the Indian Physical Society in Calcutta, West Bengal, first observed spontaneous fission – the splitting of a

Bengal Chemicals Rejuvenated

Bengal Chemicals and Pharmaceuticals Ltd broke its 120 years' record in pheneol production in August 2020 – producing pheneol worth `8.3 crore (₹83 million). Lamp Brand pheneol is currently the flagship product of this public sector unit under the Ministry of Chemicals and Fertilizers.

heavy nucleus on its own in uranium – in 1940, almost at the same time when scientists in Western countries reported its discovery.

First Indian to receive the Chemical Landmark Plaque award

The Royal Society of Chemistry in 2011 honoured the life and work of Prafulla Chandra Ray with the first ever Chemical Landmark Plaque awarded to anyone from a country outside Europe.

Discoveries in terpene chemistry

Dr Sukh Dev (b. 1923) from the Indian Institute of Technology, Delhi, discovered many new fundamental types of terpenoids, a class of naturally occurring organic compounds found in plants.

Discovery of the isomerism of thiosulphuric acid

Prof. Priyada Ranjan Ray (1888–1982), director, Indian Association for the Cultivation of Science, Calcutta, established for the first time the isomerism (compounds that have the same molecular formulae but different molecular structures) of thiosulphuric acid.

Discovery of tetracycline

Tetracycline, a life-saving drug, was discovered as a natural product and developed in 1948 by a research group headed by Dr Yellapragada Subbarow at the Lederle Laboratories in New York, US. An anti-plague drug, it helped save many lives in the 1994 plague epidemic in Surat, Gujarat.

Largest scientific and industrial research organization

The Council of Scientific and Industrial Research (CSIR), which was set up in 1942, is India's largest research and development organization for scientific and industrial research for economic and environmental development.

Discovery of phosphocreatine

In 1927, Dr Yellapragada Subbarow (1895–1948) from Bhimavaram, Madras Presidency (now in Andhra Pradesh), and Cyrus H. Fiske discovered the function of adenosine triphosphate, an organic phosphorous compound, as an energy source in the human cell, connected with the chemical mechanism of muscle contraction. He also discovered methotrexate (still used in chemotherapy) and diethylcarbamazine (DEC), which is used for effectively treating filariasis).

First woman director general of CSIR

Dr Kalaiselvi N. (b. 5 February 1967) became India's first woman director general of the Council of Scientific and Industrial Research (CSIR), India's largest research organization. She primarily works on on electrochemical power systems.

First carbon dioxide laser

Chandra Kumar Naranbhai Patel (b. 1938), an Indian-origin scientist in the United States, invented the powerful carbon dioxide laser in 1963, which resulted in making lasers a valuable tool in scientific research.

GEOLOGY

First mention of seismological zones

Varahamihira, the ancient astronomer and scientist, was the first to mention seismological zones and the most earthquake-prone areas in his treatise *Brihat-Samhita* (c. 550 CE).

First geologist

Dr Henry Wesley Voysey, a doctor by profession, became the first professional geologist in India under British rule in 1818.

First geomagnetic observatory

The Colaba Geomagnetic Observatory in Bombay was the first geomagnetic observatory to be set up in pre-Independence India. It was established in 1846 by the scientists of the East India Company to study the earth's magnetic field by using geomagnetic instruments.

First megafossil from the Himalayas

In 1984, R.N. Lakhanpal, a scientist at the Birbal Sahni Institute of Palaeosciences, Lucknow, Uttar Pradesh, and his team discovered a leaf of the temperate palm *Trachycarpus*, the first definite megafossil record of the Miocene period (23 million to 5.3 million years ago) in Ladakh in the Himalayas.

First dinosaur fossils

- The Geological Survey of India (GSI) discovered dinosaur bone fossils from the Lameta formation of the late Cretaceous age (145 to 66 million years ago) at

Soil layers with dinosaur fossil illustration

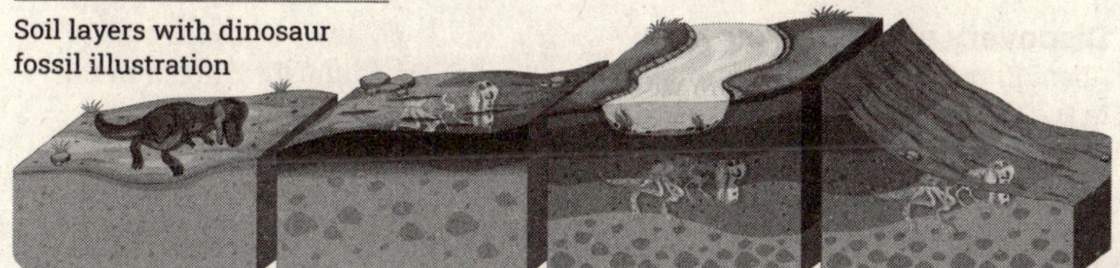

Raiyoli near Balasinor in the Kheda District, Gujarat, in 1981.

- Dinosaur egg clutches were also found at the site in 1982. Both the eggs and bones are preserved at the Indian Museum in Calcutta, West Bengal.

Largest number of dinosaur eggs, 256, were found in a single nest in India, in the Narmada Valley in January 2023.

First underwater mining system

The National Institute of Ocean Technology, Chennai, Tamil Nadu, in collaboration with the University of Siegen, Germany, devised an underwater mining vehicle called the crawler, which extracts mineral-rich polymetallic nodules from the ocean floor. The mining system consists of a crawler, cutter, and slurry pump. Mounted on board the ship ORV *Sagar Kanya*, its first test was conducted successfully on 14 March 2000 near Tuticorin (now Thoothukudi), Tamil Nadu.

First president of the International Geological Congress

Dr D.N. Wadia (1883–1969), president of the 22nd International Geological Congress, which was held in New Delhi in 1964, was the first and only Indian to become president of the International Geological Congress.

First course in geology

Geology as a degree course leading to postgraduation was started at Presidency College, Calcutta, for the first time in the country in 1892.

WR Periodicity of geomagnetic reversals

J.G. Negi and R.R. Tewari from the National Geophysical Research Institute, Hyderabad (now in Telangana), put forward, in 1983, the theory that the flipping of the earth's magnetic field, i.e., the North Pole becoming the South Pole and vice versa, is related to variations in the gravitational force of the earth. They found that the frequency with which the earth's magnetic field flips is directly correlated to the periodicity of the orbit of the sun.

Largest mineral explorer

The Mineral Exploration Corporation Ltd, established in October 1972, is a public sector company under the Ministry of Mines, Government of India with its corporate office at Nagpur, Maharashtra, and regional offices at Kolkata, Hyderabad, Ranchi, Jaipur, and Nagpur. Its functions include mineral targeting, deposit assessment, and mine development.

Discovery of vanadium

Abani Kumar Dey and J.A. Dunn discovered a new vanadium-bearing mineral in the Singhbhum–Mayurbhanj area, which is in present-day Jharkhand and Odisha, in the 1930s and called this mineral coulsonite (composition FeV_2O_4), the main source of vanadium in India. It is of strategic importance for making special steels. Abani Dey was the recipient of the First National Mineral Award in 1968.

The Geological Survey of India

First geoscientific data centre

The Geological Survey of India (GSI) set up a geoscientific data centre at Calcutta on 3 November 1998. It is the largest repository of knowledge on earth sciences in Asia, Australia, and Africa.

First official Indian geologist

Pramatha Nath Bose is considered to be the first official Indian geologist. He joined the Geological Survey of India (GSI) as an officer in 1880. He is known to have mapped the Vindhya Range as well as the igneous rocks of Raipur and Balaghat areas of what was then the Central Province.

Discovery of iron ore deposits

Pramatha Nath Bose discovered the first iron ore deposit in Mayurbhanj region in present-day Odisha, in 1904, paving the way for the modern iron industry.

OCEAN STUDIES

First course in oceanography

The first postgraduate course in oceanography was introduced in 1948 at Andhra University in Visakhapatnam in Andhra Pradesh.

First marine research institute

On 3 February 1947 the Central Marine Fisheries Research Institute was established in Chennai. Since 1971, it is headquartered in Kochi, Kerala.

First oceanographic research vessel

RV *Gaveshani,* commissioned on 1 December 1975, was the first oceanographic research vessel. It carried teams of scientific personnel on various marine expeditions that could last from a few days to months.

First Antarctic expedition

Dr S.Z. Qasim, director, National Institute of Oceanography, Goa, reached Antarctica on 9 January 1982. The 21-member team left Mormugao Harbour, Goa, on 6 December 1981 on a Norwegian ship, MV *Polar Circle*, and returned on 21 February 1982. During the expedition, the team built Dakshin Gangotri, the first Indian scientific research base station in the Queen Maud Land area in Antarctica.

First women on Antarctica

Structural geologist Sudipta Sengupta and marine biologist and oceanographer Aditi Pant were the first Indian women to visit Antarctica, during the third Indian expedition to Antarctica from 3 December 1983 to 25 March 1984. The expeditions aimed to study atmospheric, biological, earth, chemical, and medical sciences in the region.

Highest wave

Scientists on board the ship RV *Gaveshani* of the National Institute of Oceanography recorded a wave 13 m (42 ft 7.8 in.) high in the Arabian Sea off the coast of Goa in June 1979.

LIFE SCIENCES

BIOLOGY

Oldest biological fossils

Fossils of 3-billion-year-old photosynthetic blue-green algae of the Archaean era (4 billion to 2.5 billion years ago) were discovered at Kashia in Orissa (now Odisha) in 1998 by scientists of the Birbal Sahni Institute of Palaeosciences in Lucknow, Uttar Pradesh. The latest find includes 1.6-billion-year-old red algae fossils in the Chitrakoot region of central India.

Discovery of earliest multicellular organisms

In October 1998, Pradip K. Bose, a professor at Jadavpur University, Calcutta, found a site close to Churhat town in Sidhi District, Madhya Pradesh, where multicellular organisms with body fluid existed around 1.1 billion years ago. He discovered tracks on sandstone rock left by wormlike creatures about half a centimetre thick, while burrowing through the sea floor ages ago. This was the first evidence of macroscopic animals in India.

WR First zoologist

Rama Brahma Sanyal (1850–1908) joined the Calcutta Zoological Gardens in Calcutta in 1876. He wrote scientific papers on birds and sea snakes and books on zoology.

First methane plant

Biomethane was first put to use in India in 1857, when a methane plant was installed in a colony near Bombay.

WR First anther culture

S.C. Maheswari and Sipra Mukherjee from Delhi discovered the anther culture technique in 1967, in which anthers (part of a stamen that contains pollen, in a plant) were placed on a synthetic culture medium.

First national gene bank

R.S. Paroda, director general of the Indian Council of Agricultural Research, Delhi, established the first National Gene Bank in Delhi in 1985.

First synthesis of a workable gene

Indian-born US resident Dr Har Gobind Khorana (1922–2011), using off-the-shelf chemicals, synthesized a total gene of the simple microbe *Escherichia coli* (which lives in the intestines of humans and animals) in 1976. He was awarded the Nobel Prize for physiology or medicine in 1968 for discovering the genetic code, which opened up the possibility of producing DNA in a laboratory. He shared the prize with US scientists Robert W. Holley and Marshall W. Nirenberg.

First to extract insulin from a plant

In the early 1980s, Pushpa Khanna, professor at the University of Rajasthan, Jaipur, was the first to extract an insulin-like substance from bitter gourd. That substance is an active ingredient called polypeptide-P, which lowers blood sugar in the body. Insulin is currently extracted from animal pancreas for the treatment of diabetes.

First biocentre

The M.S. Swaminathan Foundation, Chennai, Tamil Nadu, opened a biocentre in Pillayarkuppam Village in Pondicherry (now Puducherry) on 10 April 1999. This centre functions as a demonstration, training, information dissemination, and service unit for sustainable food security.

WR First clone of hepatitis E virus

Dr S.K. Panda, professor of pathology, and his support team of scientists at the All India Institute of Medical Sciences (AIIMS), New Delhi, genetically engineered a clone of the hepatitis E virus in 1996.

First to isolate insulin-blocking enzyme

In 2013, Indian-born Kanwal Gambhir from Harvard University, US, and his co-workers isolated an insulin-blocking enzyme. As insulin controls sugar levels in blood, this discovery had far-reaching implications in the control of diabetes, cardiovascular diseases, and cancer.

WR Discovery of seminal plasmin

Pushpa M. Bhargava and E.S.R. Reddy from the Regional Research Laboratory, Hyderabad (now in Telangana), discovered the protein seminal plasmin in the seminal fluid of a bull in 1979. This is a potent antimicrobial agent active on a wide range of micro-organisms, such as yeast.

Discovery of gymnosperms

In 1948, Birbal Sahni (1891–1949), a pioneering palaeontologist, discovered Pentoxyleae (gymnosperms), a plant group belonging to the Jurassic period (208 to 145 million years ago).

Discovery of the cholera exotoxin

S.C. Seal from the All India Institute of Hygiene and Public Health, Calcutta, discovered cholera exotoxin in the early 1940s. The vaccine based on this helped in the eradication of cholera epidemics in India.

WR First bamboo tissue culture

A.F. Mascarenhas, R.S. Nadgauda, and V.A. Parasharami from the National Chemical Laboratory in Pune, Maharashtra, worked to produce a tissue culture of bamboo in 1990.

First human organ regeneration

In 2001, Dr Balakrishna Ganpatrao Matapurkar from Maulana Azad Medical College, New Delhi, was granted US Patent No. 6227202 (from 1995) for enabling regeneration of mammalian organs in the body at the site of old and diseased organs. He used unique stem cells in the body to regenerate organs like the uterus, urethra, and ureters in animals and large tendons in the human abdomen.

INTER-DISCIPLINARY AND APPLIED SCIENCES

COMPUTERS

First indigenous chip

The Graphics and Intelligence-based Script Technology (GIST), developed by the Centre for Development of Advanced Computing (C-DAC), hit the market in the 1990s. While it was designed especially for land records departments based in different climatic zones, where protection from dust and other vagaries is not always available, it was also used by industries and public information systems.

First analogue computer

Biswaranjan Nag (1932–2004), former professor of radio physics and electronics at the Institute for Radio Physics and Electronics (IRPE), Calcutta, built the first indigenous analogue computer (also called a differential analyser) in 1957.

First digital computer

The British-built HEC-2M was installed at the Indian Statistical Institute in Calcutta in 1955. In 1964, the first indigenous computer, ISIJU-1, was developed by the Jadavpur University and the Indian Statistical Institute.

First biologist to win the Linnean Medal

In 2018, Dr Kamaljit Bawa, president of the Ashoka Trust for Research in Ecology and the Environment (ATREE) and distinguished professor of biology at the University of Massachusetts, Boston, US, was awarded the Linnean Medal for his pioneering research in the field of conservation biology. He researched biodiversity, the evolution of tropical plants, deforestation, and non-timber forest products in Central America, the Western Ghats, and the Himalayas.

First human brain-like computing developed

A team of scientists led by Dheemahi Rao from the Jawaharlal Nehru Centre for Advanced Scientific Research (JNCASR), Bengaluru, have developed brain-like computing using industry-compatible nitride semi-conductors on 25 January 2023. For this, the scientists have used scandium nitrite, a semiconductor with great stability. The human brain is an extra-ordinary biological computer that is smaller than a traditional man-made computer and is more efficient because of a synapse (the connection between two neurons) that plays the role of both the processor and the memory storage units. Traditional computers take enormous energy and time to transfer data between these units because they are physically partitioned. The invention of brain-like computation will take artificial intelligence to new heights.

Fastest supercomputer

AIRAWAT-PSAI is currently India's fastest supercomputer, with a peak power of 13,170 teraflops (13.17 petaflops). The system is installed under National Programme on AI by Government of India. It was manufactured by Natweb Technologies and is currently installed in C-DAC, Pune, Maharashtra. It is currently ranked 75th among the top 500 supercomputers in the world (details on page 199). Earlier, in January 2018, India unveiled Pratyush and Mihir, an array of computers that are able to output a peak power of 6.8 petaflops. This was followed by PARAM Siddhi-AI, which was conceived by C-DAC, Pune, Maharashtra. Able to output a peak power of 6.5 petaflops, the supercomputer is used for research efforts in a wide range of areas, such as healthcare, agriculture, cybersecurity, and robotics. It was ranked 63rd among the top 500 most powerful supercomputers in the world in November 2020 (its current ranking is 131st).

First indigenous palmtop computer

In 1995, a team of engineers working for Signals and Systems India Private Ltd, headquartered in Gurugram, Haryana, built the country's first indigenous palmtop computer suitable for a variety of industrial and field applications.

First powerful commercial computer

In 2001, Tata Consultancy Services (TCS) commissioned the 64-bit z-Series e-Server from IBM to become the first organization in South Asia to adopt the then latest technology being used in mainframe computing.

First supercomputer

On 25 March 1989, the Supercomputer Cray XMP-14 was installed as a key facility at the National Centre for Medium Range Weather Forecasting, New Delhi, to facilitate medium-range weather forecasting and agrometeorology programmes.

First Indian to obtain a PhD in computer science

Dr Raj Reddy (b. 13 June 1937), the dean of the School of Computer Science, Carnegie Mellon University, Pittsburgh, US, was the first Indian with a PhD in computer science, which he obtained in 1966 from Stanford University, US. He was also the first person of Asian origin to receive the Association for Computing Machinery (ACM) Turing Award, in 1994, then the highest award in computer science, for his work in the field of artificial intelligence.

AIRAWAT Among Top 500

AIRAWAT–PSAI, Indian AI supercomputer, ranks 75th in top 500 supercomputing list. This was announced on 23 May 2023 at the 61st edition of Top 500 Global Supercomputing List at the International Supercomputing Conference (ISC 2023) in Germany. In total, India has four supercomputers in the list: PARAM Siddhi–AI, AIRAWAT–PSAI, Pratyush–Cray XC40, and Mihir–Cray XC40.

First indigenous supercomputer

Developed by C-DAC in Pune, in 1991, PARAM 8000 was capable of one billion calculations per second. The then director of C-DAC, Dr Vijay P. Bhatkar, under whom this project was conducted, is considered to be the architect of India's national initiative in supercomputing.

First powerful indigenous supercomputer

PARAM 10000, also developed by C-DAC under Dr Vijay P. Bhatkar's directorship, in 1998, was the first powerful indigenous supercomputer, capable of 100 billion calculations per second. It is housed at the National PARAM Supercomputing Facility (NPSF) at C-DAC, Pune.

First to invent a new and speedy algorithm

In 1984, Indian-born mathematician Dr Narendra Karmarkar from Bell Laboratories in New Jersey, USA, introduced a new algorithm, called 'Karmarkar's algorithm', which solved linear programming efficiently, and helped computers find solutions to simultaneous inequalities very quickly. It solved problems 50 to 100 times faster than the methods known at the time.

WR First smallest multimedia notebook

In 1997, Bangalore–Ncore Technology's multimedia sub-notebook computer called the Yantra, which weighed just 2.1 kg, was the lightest laptop in the world. The Yantra occupied less than half of a briefcase, had a CD-ROM, a built-in sound blaster, two PCMCIA (Personal Computer Memory Card International Association) card slots, and a small yet powerful battery built to last for more than three years.

First Super Fab Lab

The first super fab lab (fabrication laboratory) of the country was inaugurated via remote control from the Government Polytechnic College, Palakkad, Kerala, on 25 January 2020. Located at the Integrated Startup Complex of the Kerala Start-up Mission (KSUM), Kalamassery, Kochi, the lab offers digital fabrication and computation and was launched in collaboration with MIT (Massachusetts Institute of Technology, US). The brainchild of Dr Neil Gershenfeld, director of the MIT Centre for Bits and Atoms, it aims to enable researchers, innovators, and developers to do things beyond the purview of the existing fab labs of the country.

METALLURGY

Earliest zinc use

An artefact (No. 4189) containing 6.04 per cent zinc was found at the Harappan site of Lothal (dated to 2200–1500 BCE) in Gujarat. It indicated that the Harappan people could generate temperatures of above 1,000°C required for zinc metallurgy.

Earliest copper kiln

A copper smelting kiln, 35 cm (13.8 in.) high with an 18 cm (7 in.) rim diameter and 10 cm (3.9 in.) base diameter, was discovered at the Harappan site of Lothal (2200–1500 BCE) in Gujarat. Lothal copper was found to be very pure.

Earliest use of iron

Around 1000 BCE, iron was used in eastern Punjab, western Uttar Pradesh, and Rajasthan. Excavations show that iron weapons such as arrowheads and spearheads were commonly used in western Uttar Pradesh from about 800 BCE. Iron is called *shyama* or *krishna ayas* (black/dark metal) in later Vedic texts.

First metallurgist to work with plutonium

Dr P.R. Roy, a scientist and director at the Bhabha Atomic Research Centre (BARC), Bombay, was the first Indian metallurgist to handle plutonium. He played a crucial role in India's first nuclear implosion at Pokhran, Rajasthan, in 1974.

First manufacture of steel

Indian smiths manufactured crucible steel, known as 'wootz', which was exported to many countries in medieval times. Indian craftsmen were known around the world at the time for their steel swords. After the British banned the production of weapons following the Indian Rebellion of 1857 wootz technology was lost.

New class of quasicrystals

In 1985, P. Ramachandra Rao and G.V.S. Sastry from the National Metallurgical Laboratory, Jamshedpur, now in Jharkhand, discovered a new class of quasicrystals composed of aluminium, manganese, and zinc metals.

Earliest iron furnace

An iron furnace was found at Pandu Rajar Dhibi in Burdwan (now Bardhaman District), West Bengal, and was dated to 1100–800 BCE.

In 2022–23 budget, the government has allocated ₹32,225 crore (322,250 million) for scientific departments.

SPACE

First space venture

Launched from the base in Thumba near Trivandrum (now Thiruvananthapuram), Kerala, on 21 November 1963, a Nike-Apache rocket supplied by NASA kick-started the Indian space programme. Parts of this first sounding rocket launched by India were transported to the Thumba base on the carrier of a bicycle! St Mary Magdalene Church in Thumba is a preferred site for rocket launches because of its proximity to the magnetic equator. Quite fittingly, the church houses the Vikram Sarabhai Space Centre (VSSC) space museum.

First Indian space organization

Indian National Committee for Space Research (INCOSPAR) was India's first space research organization. It was formed in 1962 and helmed by Dr Vikram Sarabhai. When Indian Space Research Organization was formed in 1969, it superceded INCOSPAR.

First private sector space launches

On 24 June 2022, the Indian Space Promotion and Authorization Centre (IN-SPACe) authorized Dhruva Space Pvt. Ltd, Hyderabad, Telangana, and Digantara Research and Technologies Pvt. Ltd, Bengaluru, Karnataka, to launch their payloads. This marked the beginning of private sector space launches in India. Dhruva Space's Dhruva Space Satellite Orbital Deployer (DSOD 1U), a technology payload, along with Digantara's

First fully indigenous satellite

India's first fully indigenous satellite, Aryabhata, was launched into space from a Russian facility on 19 April 1975.

Mission	Scientific/Experimental
Weight	360 kg
On board power	46 Watts
Communication	VHF band
Stabilization	Spinstabilize
Payload	X-ray Astronomy, Aeronomy, and Solar Physics
Launch date	19 April 1975
Launch site	Volgograd Launch Station (presently in Russia)
Launch vehicle	C-1 Intercosmos
Orbit	563 x 619 km
Inclination	50.7 degrees
Mission life	6 months (nominal), Spacecraft mainframe active till March 1981
Orbital Life	Nearly seventeen years (Re-entered on 10 February 1992)

Source: https://www.isro.gov.in/aryabhata_1.html?timeline=timeline

ROBust Integrating Proton Fluence Meter (ROBI), a proton dosimeter payload, were carried onboard the PSLV Orbital Experimental Module (POEM).

First weather-cum-communications satellite

Indian National Satellite INSAT-1A, launched on 10 April 1982 on an American Delta-3920 launch vehicle, was India's first satellite employed for meteorological observations over India and the Indian Ocean, as well as for domestic telecommunications, including nationwide direct TV broadcasting, TV programme distribution, and meteorological data distribution.

First satellite centre

ISRO's Satellite Centre (ISAC), established in 1972, conducts research in satellite technology. Aryabhata, the first Indian satellite, Bhaskara I and II, and Rohini and APPLE satellites were all designed and built at ISAC. The spacecraft of the Indian Remote Sensing satellite series and the Stretched Rohini satellite series were also designed at ISAC.

First remote-sensing mission

IRS-1A, the first of a series of indigenous state-of-the-art remote-sensing satellites, was launched into a polar sun-synchronous orbit on 17 March 1988 from the then Soviet Cosmodrome at Baikonur. It carried two cameras, LISS-I and LISS-II, with a swathe width of 140 km during each pass over India.

First indigenous satellite series

Designed and built by ISRO, INSAT-2A was launched by the Ariane launch vehicle from Kourou, French Guiana, on 10 July 1992. INSAT-2B was also launched by Ariane on 23 July 1993. INSAT-2C, the third in this series of satellites, was launched on 7 December 1995 and put into operation in February 1996.

First man in space

Squadron Leader Rakesh Sharma (b. 13 January 1949), then an Indian Air Force pilot, flew aboard spacecraft Soyuz T-11, launched on 2 April 1984, as part of the Intercosmos programme and spent over seven days orbiting Earth. He was the first Indian person to travel to space.

Highest-resolution imaging satellite

CARTOSAT-3, considered to be India's highest-resolution civilian satellite to date, was successfully launched into space along with 13 US nanosatellites by ISRO on 27 November 2019. Weighing 1,625 kg, the observation satellite lifted off from the Satish Dhawan Space Centre, Sriharikota High Altitude Range (SHAR), Sriharikota, Andhra Pradesh. It is an advanced imaging and mapping satellite with a mission life of five years and a panchromatic resolution of 0.25 m (9.8 in.).

First oceanographic satellite

IRS-P4 (OceanSat), the first satellite built for ocean applications, was launched into a polar sun-synchronous orbit, 720 km high, by the PSLV from SHAR, Sriharikota, Andhra Pradesh, on 26 May 1999. A 1,050 kg satellite measuring 2.8 m x 1.98 m x 2.57 m (9 ft 2 in. x 6 ft 6 in. x 8 ft 5 in.), the IRS-P4 orbited Earth in 99.31 mins. It completed its mission on 8 August 2010.

FIRST LUNAR PROBE

Chandrayaan-1 was India's first lunar probe. It was launched by ISRO, using a PSLV-XL rocket on 22 October 2008 from Satish Dhawan Space Centre (SDSC), SHAR, Sriharikota, Andhra Pradesh. It operated until August 2009. The mission included a lunar orbiter and an impactor.

CHANDRAYAAN-2

Chandrayaan-2 mission was successfully launched on 22 July 2019 at 14:43 hrs by GSLV MkIII-M1 from SDSC, SHAR, Sriharikota. It was supposed to soft-land on the moon; however, ISRO lost contact with it just before the touchdown. Chanrdayaan-2 rotated 410 degrees instead of the planned 55 degrees and ended up crash-landing. Despite this, getting that close to the target has been hailed across the world.

CHANDRAYAAN-3

On 14 July 2023, ISRO, for the first time, successfully launched a spacecraft with a lander and rover to land on the moon — Chanrdayaan-3.
It successfully soft-landed on the moon on 23 August 2023.

Per media reports, Chandrayaan 3 landed near the moon's south pole, an achievement believed to be first in the world.

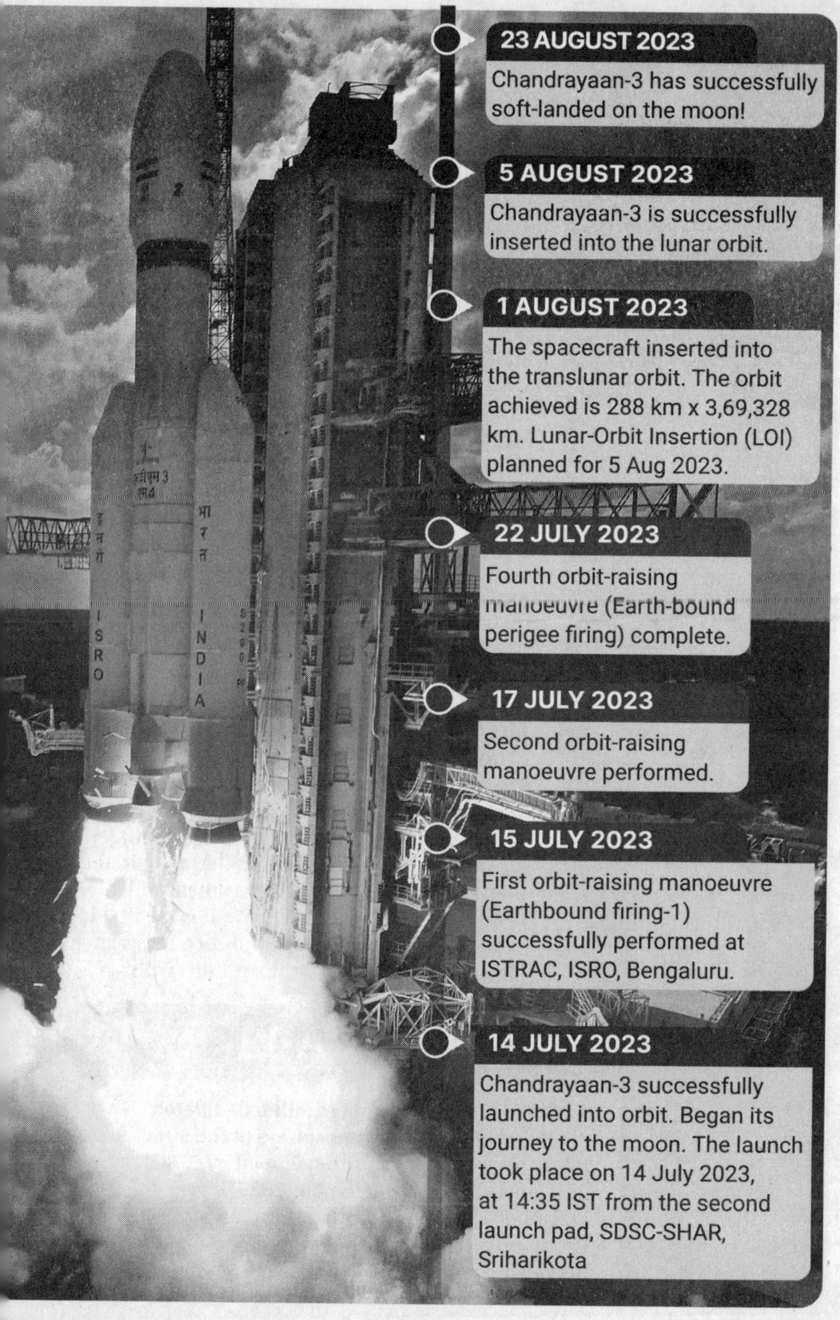

23 AUGUST 2023

Chandrayaan-3 has successfully soft-landed on the moon!

5 AUGUST 2023

Chandrayaan-3 is successfully inserted into the lunar orbit.

1 AUGUST 2023

The spacecraft inserted into the translunar orbit. The orbit achieved is 288 km x 3,69,328 km. Lunar-Orbit Insertion (LOI) planned for 5 Aug 2023.

22 JULY 2023

Fourth orbit-raising manoeuvre (Earth-bound perigee firing) complete.

17 JULY 2023

Second orbit-raising manoeuvre performed.

15 JULY 2023

First orbit-raising manoeuvre (Earthbound firing-1) successfully performed at ISTRAC, ISRO, Bengaluru.

14 JULY 2023

Chandrayaan-3 successfully launched into orbit. Began its journey to the moon. The launch took place on 14 July 2023, at 14:35 IST from the second launch pad, SDSC-SHAR, Sriharikota

First indigenous satellite launcher

The PSLV-D3, developed by ISRO, hoisted a 930 kg Indian remote-sensing satellite (IRS-P3) into an orbit of 807 km from Earth, 17 minutes after it shot into space on 21 March 1996.

First flight of PSLV

With a lift-off weight of 294 tonnes, the 44.4 m (145 ft 8 in.) tall Polar Satellite Launch Vehicle (PSLV) is a four-stage vehicle that employs two solid and two liquid propellant stages each. The first operational flight of PSLV took place on 29 September 1997, putting the satellite IRS-1D into a polar sun-synchronous orbit, from ISRO's SHAR centre in Sriharikota, Andhra Pradesh.

First flight of GSLV

India's first Geosynchronous Satellite Launch Vehicle (GSLV-D1) blasted off from the Satish Dhawan Space Centre, SHAR, Sriharikota, Andhra Pradesh, at 3:43 p.m. IST on 18 April 2001. The giant three-stage vehicle carried a 1,540 kg experimental communication satellite, GSAT-1, to be placed in the geosynchronous transfer orbit. There has been 15 GSLV launches from 2001 to 2023.

First university for the study of and research on outer space

The Indian Institute of Space Science and Technology (IIST), located at Valiamala in Thiruvananthapuram, Kerala, was inaugurated on 14 September 2007 by G. Madhavan Nair, the then chairman of ISRO. A government-aided institute and deemed university, it is the first in Asia to be dedicated to the study of and research on outer space. It was set up by ISRO with

ADITYA-L1

ADITYA-L1 is India's first satellite dedicated to studying the outer atmosphere of the sun. It has been indigenously developed by ISRO and launched on 2 September 2023. It will stay approximately 1.5 million km away from Earth, which is about 1 per cent of the distance between the sun and Earth.

former Indian president A.P.J. Abdul Kalam as its first chancellor. The university offers undergraduate, postgraduate, and doctorate programmes in engineering, focusing on space science, technology, and their applications.

First interplanetary mission

On 5 November 2013, PSLV-C25, the 25th flight of PSLV launched Mangalyaan, the Mars Orbiter Mission (MOM) spacecraft, from SHAR, Sriharikota, Andhra Pradesh. Under the aegis of ISRO, the mission was conducted to observe the physical features of Mars and the Martian atmosphere. With this mission, ISRO became the fourth space agency in the world to reach Mars. India is the first Asian nation to reach the Mars orbit and the first nation in the world to do so in its first attempt.

India's first private rocket builder

Skyroot Aerospace, India's first private rocket builder started operations in 2018. It is founded by a group of people that includes former ISRO scientists.

First dedicated commercial satellite mission

India's Polar Satellite Launch Vehicle PSLV-C51 successfully launched the satellite Amazonia-1, developed by Brazil, along with 18 co-passenger private satellites, from SHAR, Sriharikota, Andhra Pradesh, on 28 February 2021. The first dedicated commercial mission of NewSpace India Ltd (NSIL), under the Department of Space, Government of India, it was part of space reforms aimed at increasing the participation of private companies in the space sector. The co-passenger satellites included four from Indian National Space Promotion and Authorization Centre (IN-SPACe) and 14 from NSIL.

First private satellite launched

Exseed SAT-1, built by Exseed Space Innovations Private Ltd, founded by scientists Kris Nair and Asshar Farhan, became the first private Indian satellite to be launched in space. The amateur (ham) radio satellite hitched a ride on the Elon Musk-led company SpaceX's Falcon 9 rocket on 4 December 2018.

First woman in space

Dr Kalpana Chawla (1962–2003), an American cosmonaut who was born in Karnal, Haryana, was the first woman of Indian origin in space. She zoomed into orbit aboard space shuttle Columbia on 19 November 1997 on a 16-day scientific mission, along with five fellow astronauts, and returned to Cape Canaveral on 5 December 1997. In 2003, Chawla was

Kalpana Chawla, mission specialist, with astronauts Kevin R. Kregel, Leonid K. Kadenyuk and others

one of the seven crew members who died in the space shuttle Columbia disaster when it disintegrated during its re-entry into Earth's atmosphere.

Smallest spacecraft launched

On 23 June 2017, the world's smallest spacecraft, Sprites, was launched by ISRO's PSLV rocket and placed in the low earth orbit. The 3.5 cm x 3.5 cm (1.38 in. x 1.38 in.) space probe weighs just 4 g and runs on sunlight.

Heaviest satellite launched

GSAT-11, weighing 5,854 kg and laying claim to being the heaviest Indian satellite ever launched, was sent into space by ISRO on 5 December 2018 from the Ariane Launch Complex at Kourou in French Guiana. The satellite is expected to help boost communication services across India.

Lightest satellite in orbit

Kalamsat-V2 was launched by ISRO on 24 January 2019 from the Satish Dhawan Space Centre, SHAR, Sriharikota. Weighing only 1.26 kg, it is said to be the world's lightest satellite to be put into orbit. It was made by students belonging to Space Kidz India, a Chennai-based aerospace start-up pioneering in design, fabrication, and launch of small satellites, spacecraft, and ground systems. The satellite will also serve as a communications device for ham radio transmission, which is a form of wireless communication used by amateurs for non-commercial activities. It took six days to make and cost around ₹12 lakh (1.2 million).

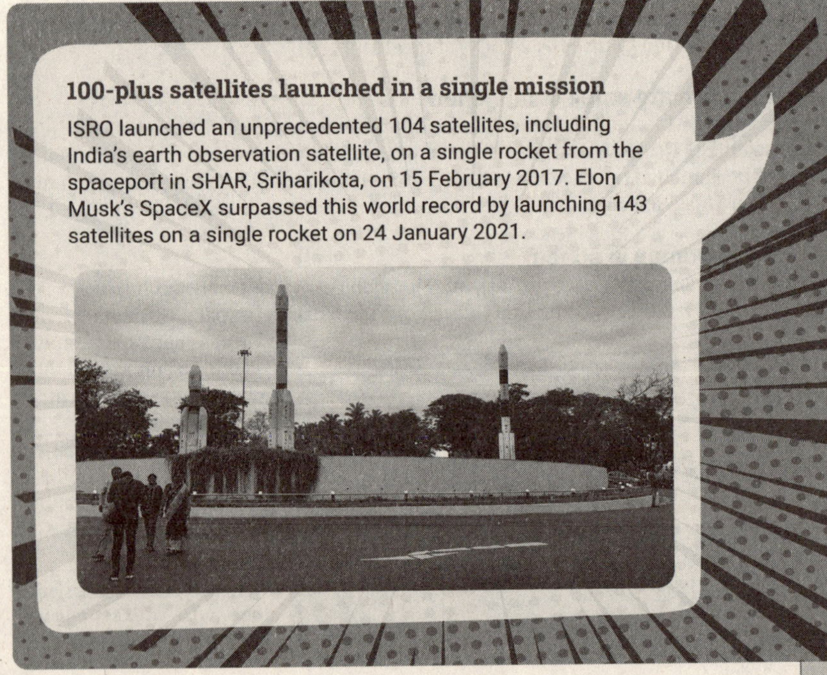

100-plus satellites launched in a single mission

ISRO launched an unprecedented 104 satellites, including India's earth observation satellite, on a single rocket from the spaceport in SHAR, Sriharikota, on 15 February 2017. Elon Musk's SpaceX surpassed this world record by launching 143 satellites on a single rocket on 24 January 2021.

MEDICAL SCIENCES

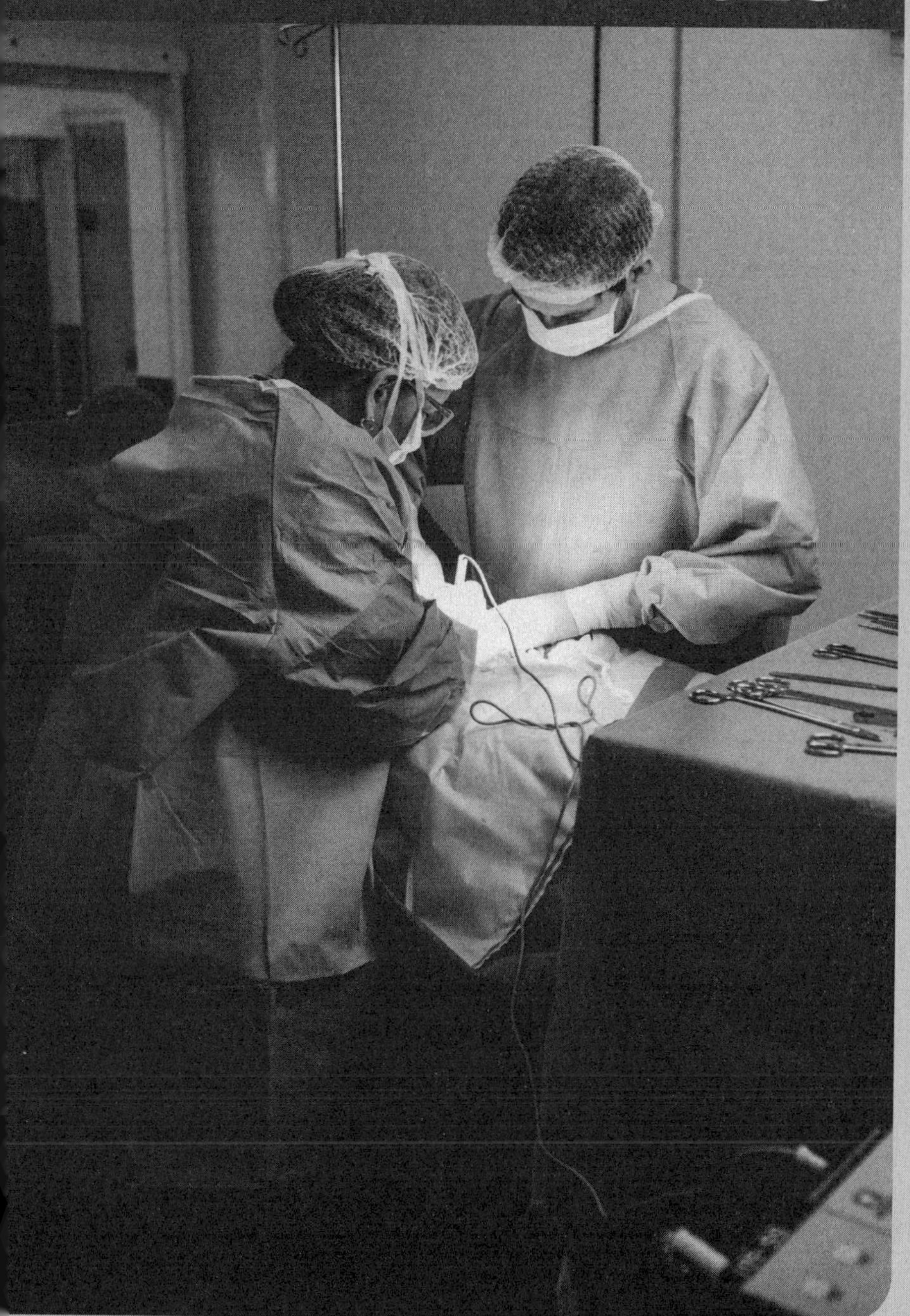

GENERAL

Earliest treatise on medicine

The Atharva Veda (1500–1200 BCE) is the earliest known treatise on human diseases and medicine.

First Persian text on medicine

Ma'dan-i-Shifa-i-Sikandar Shahi was the first Persian text on the Unani and Ayurvedic systems of medicine, authored by Hakim Bahwa bin Khwas Khan during 1512–13 CE. It was printed in 1987 by Naval Kishore Press in Lucknow, Uttar Pradesh.

WR Largest healthcare scheme

Ayushman Bharat Yojana, announced as a universal healthcare plan by the Government of India in February 2018, is the largest healthcare scheme in the world. Aimed at providing free healthcare access to around 50 crore (0.5 billion) people in the country, the Ayushman Bharat Pradhan Mantri Jan Arogya Yojana (AB-PMJAY) was launched in September 2018. A paperless and cashless scheme, it involves e-cards being issued to beneficiaries and health insurance coverage of up to ₹5,00,000 per family per year.

WR Largest survey sample

India's Annual Health Survey (AHS) is the first nationwide survey initiative to provide district-level fertility and mortality statistics. Begun with a baseline study in 2010–11 and a sample of 18.2 million people (3.6 million households), it is conducted in all 284 districts in eight Empowered Action Group (EAG) states, viz., Madhya Pradesh, Jharkhand, Bihar, Uttar Pradesh, Chhattisgarh, Uttarakhand, Odisha, and Rajasthan. It reports vital indicators such as crude birth and death rates, sex ratios (at birth, 0–4 years, and all ages) and mortality rates (maternal, infant, neonatal, and under-5), separated by urban/ rural and male/female data.

FERTILITY, CHILDBIRTH, AND BABIES

WR Oldest IVF mother

On 12 October 2019, 75-year-old Prabha Devi became the oldest woman to give birth, after conceiving through IVF. She delivered a baby girl, weighing 680 g, prematurely by Caesarean section performed at Kinker Hospital, Kota, Rajasthan.

First woman to give birth after a uterine transplant

Meenakshi Valand from Bharuch District, Gujarat, became the first Indian woman to deliver a baby after undergoing a uterine transplant on 19 October 2018 at Galaxy Care Hospital, Pune, Maharashtra.

First GIFT twins

The first twins, both male, were born through the gamete intra-fallopian transfer (GIFT) technology to Renuka and Vijay Thakkar on 5 September 1990 in Bombay (now Mumbai), Maharashtra.

First IVF baby

Baby Harsha was born to Mani and Shyami Chawda on 6 August 1986 by the in vitro fertilization and embryo transfer (IVF-ET) method. This technique was used after three years of research by Dr Indira Hinduja of King Edward Memorial Hospital and Seth Gordhandas Sunderdas Medical College, Bombay, Maharashtra.

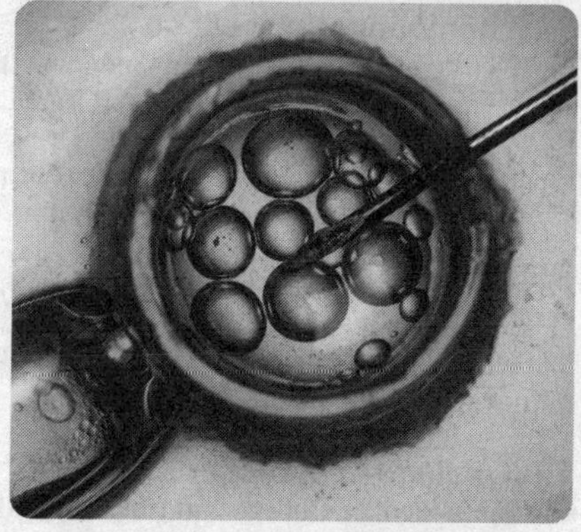

IVF – under the microscope

Heaviest baby at birth

On 26 May 2016, Nandini, a 20-year-old mother, gave birth to a baby girl by Caesarean section at a hospital in Hassan, Karnataka. The baby, whose birthweight was 6.8 kg, was reported to have been the heaviest one ever born in the country. The heaviest baby boy till then, who weighed 6.7 kg at birth, was recorded to have been born in November 2015.

Lightest baby

A premature baby girl, weighing 400 g and measuring 8.6 in. in length, was born by Caesarean section on 15 June 2017 at Jivanta Children's Hospital in Udaipur, Rajasthan. She was kept in the neonatal intensive care unit (NICU) at the hospital for 210 days under the care of Dr Sunil Janged, Dr Nikhilesh Nain, and trained nursing staff, and was discharged when she weighed close to 2.4 kg.

MEDICAL INSTITUTIONS AND LABORATORIES

First hospital

The first modern hospital was established at Fort St George, Madras (now Chennai), Tamil Nadu, in 1664.

Oldest eye hospital

The Madras Eye Infirmary in Madras was set up in 1819. It is said to be the oldest eye hospital in India and Asia. It was renamed the Government Ophthalmic Hospital in 1886 and is now called the Regional Institute of Ophthalmology and Government Ophthalmic Hospital. Locals refer to it as 'Ezhumbur Kanaaspatiri'.

WR First governmental family planning programme

India was the first country in the world to have government-sponsored family planning programmes in 1952. The first private family planning clinic was opened even earlier in Mysore (now Mysuru), Karnataka, in 1930.

First medical school to offer oncology degrees

The Adyar Cancer Institute in Chennai, Tamil Nadu, is a non-profit cancer treatment and research centre set up in 1954 under the leadership of Dr Muthulakshmi Reddy. It was the first medical school in India to offer degrees in various sub-specialities of oncology, recognized by the Medical Council of India.

First homoeopathic college

Dr L. Salzar from Austria began homoeopathic education in India in 1867. He influenced Dr P.C. Majumdar and Dr B.L. Bhaduri in Bengal, and in 1878, Dr Majumdar along with Dr D.N. Roy, Dr B.N. Banerjee, and Dr Younan set up the Calcutta Homoeopathic Medical College, Calcutta (now Kolkata), West Bengal, which was India's first homoeopathic college.

First homoeopathic company

M. Bhattacharya and Company Pvt. Ltd in Calcutta, was established in 1889 by Mahesh Chandra Bhattacharya from Comilla (now in Bangladesh), for making homoeopathic medicines.

First college of nursing

Christian Medical College and Hospital (CMCH), Vellore, Tamil Nadu, set up the first college of nursing in India in 1946.

First organized medical service

The Indian Medical Service was the formal collective name for the top echelon of the East India Company's and British Indian Army's medical service from the early 19th century up to 1896. Its three divisions – Bengal Medical Service, Madras Medical Service and Bombay Medical Service – were combined into a single service under government control in January 1897.

First dental college

Dr Rafiuddin Ahmed, the 'father of modern dentistry' in India, founded the Calcutta Dental College in Calcutta, in 1920. By 1928, it was a well-known institution for scientific dental education in India.

First biotechnology department

Dr Indira Nath set up the first department of medical biotechnology at the Al lIndia Institute of Medical Sciences (AIIMS), New Delhi, for teaching and research in 1986.

First medical college

Calcutta Medical College (now renamed Medical College and Hospital, Kolkata) set up on 28 January 1835 in Calcutta, was the first medical college to be established in India and Asia.

Calcutta Medical College – the first medical college in India

First centre for cancer rehabilitation

Dr Darab Jehangir Jussawala (1915–99) was a medical and surgical oncologist, medical writer, and director of the Lady Ratan Tata Memorial Centre in Bombay (now Mumbai), Maharashtra.

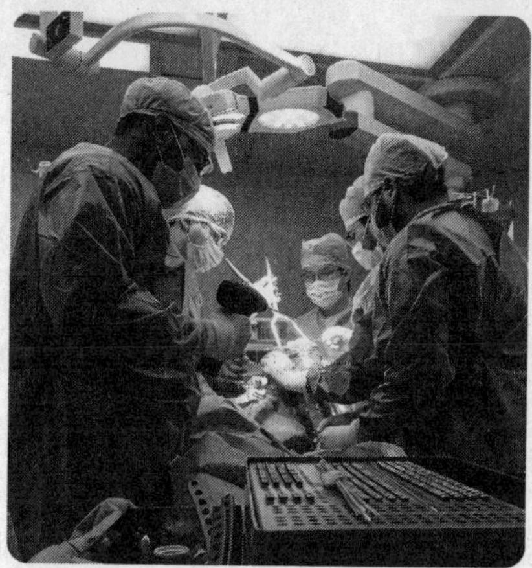

Revolutionizing Indian Medical Education!

In the last decade, the Indian government has taken many steps to provide proper medical education to aspiring doctors. From 2014 to 2023, the number of medical colleges has gone up 1.7 times from 387 to 660. The number of seats for MBBS and PG has also increased twofold and now stands at 101,043 and 65,335, respectively. AIIMS, which is the top medical institute in the country, now has 22 branches pan India.

Dr Jussawala was the co-founder of the Indian Cancer Society with Naval Tata in 1951 and established the Indian Cancer Rehabilitation Centre in Parel, Bombay, Maharashtra, in 1956, which was the first such centre in India. He received the Padma Bhushan in 1975 from the Government of India.

First online clinic

Homoeopath Dr Mukesh Batra set up Dr Batra's Positive Health Clinic in Bombay in 1982, which now has 230 clinics across 122 cities in India, Bangladesh, Dubai, and the UK. He went online in 1997, which made him the first online medical consultant in the country.

First medical laser facility

India's first medical laser to destroy tumours with minimal blood loss was set up at the K.B. Bhabha Hospital in Bombay in October 1993.

First hospital with a stealth neuro-navigation system

The Sri Sathya Sai Institute of Higher Medical Sciences, Whitefield, Bangalore (now Bengaluru), Karnataka, set up in 2001, is the first in India and second in the world to acquire a stealth neuro-navigation system (for image-guided surgeries). It is one of the cutting-edge technologies in precision neurosurgery.

First hormone replacement therapy clinic

A hormone replacement therapy (HRT) clinic was started by Urvashi P. Jha in March 1993 at the P.D. Hinduja National Hospital in Mumbai, Maharashtra, to deal with aspects of menopause.

First low-vision rehabilitation centre

L.V. Prasad Eye Institute, Hyderabad (now in Telangana), opened the Meera and L.B. Deshpande Centre for Sight Enhancement on 18 February 1997, to provide complete low-vision rehabilitation for patients by restoring optimal physical, psychological and social functioning.

First institute of advanced virology

The first Institute of Advanced Virology was inaugurated in February 2019 at Thiruvananthapuram, Kerala. It is affiliated to the Global Virus Network, which has 45 centres of excellence in more than 29 countries.

First indigenously developed vaccine

Rotavac, a rotavirus vaccine, was India's first indigenously developed vaccine, launched in 2015. It was developed by Bharat Biotech India Limited and the Gates Foundation, and supported by the Government of India and National Institute of Health of the US Government. Rotavirus is the most common cause of serious (often fatal) diarrhoea in children.

First department of minimal access surgery

Dr Pradeep Kumar Chowbey from Sir Ganga Ram Hospital, New Delhi, set up the first dedicated department of minimal access surgery (MAS) in Asia in 1995 and has trained nearly 1,000 doctors in laparoscopy in India and abroad.

First liver clinic

The first liver clinic was opened at Sir Ganga Ram Hospital, New Delhi, in 2002 for treating patients with liver diseases.

First hospital with a rooftop helipad

The eleven-storey Lakeshore Hospital and Research Centre, Kochi, Kerala, is the first super-speciality hospital in the country to have air, water, and road ambulance services at its doorstep. Inaugurated in January 2003, this hospital with its state-of-the-art medical services, has a helipad on its roof to facilitate heli-lifting of critically ill patients from airports in Kerala.

First rural medical college

Kasturba Health Society's Mahatma Gandhi Institute of Medical Sciences (MGIMS) in Sevagram, Wardha district, Maharashtra, was the country's first rural medical college. It was founded by Dr Sushila Nayar, a physician and politician, in 1969, and was affiliated to the Maharashtra University of Health Sciences.

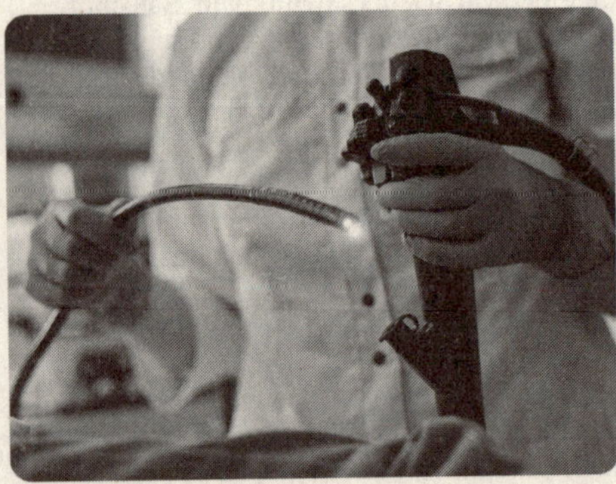

Endoscopy equipment

First endoscopy lab

The first fully equipped endoscopy centre was established at the Bhatia General Hospital in Mumbai, in October 1994. An endoscopy is performed to examine the interior of a hollow organ.

AIIMS: A hub of medical firsts

The All India Institute of Medical Sciences (AIIMS) is a public hospital and medical research university based in

New Delhi. Established in 1956, it operates autonomously under the Ministry of Health and Family Welfare. It was:

- The first to start a medical toxicology lab in a medical college in 1986.
- The first to develop a DNA profiling lab in a medical college in 1990.
- The first Indian centre to perform a successful cardiac transplant in 1994.
- India's first minimally invasive surgery training centre.
- The first in the public sector to have an in vitro fertilization (IVF) facility, in February 2008.

Apollo Hospital App

First corporate hospital

Apollo Hospitals, founded by Dr Prathap C. Reddy in Madras, Tamil Nadu, in 1983, was the first corporate hospital in the country.

WR Largest vaccine company

Thc Serum Institute of India in Pune, Maharashtra, founded by Cyrus Poonawalla in 1966, is the world's largest vaccine-making company by the number of doses produced and sold globally, with 1.2 billion vaccine doses supplied yearly to 147 countries.

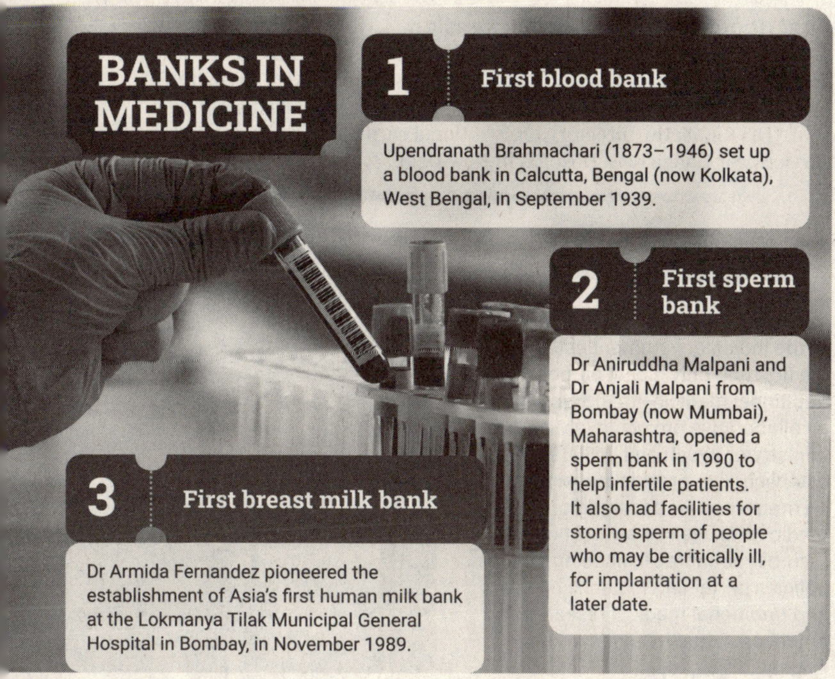

BANKS IN MEDICINE

1 First blood bank

Upendranath Brahmachari (1873–1946) set up a blood bank in Calcutta, Bengal (now Kolkata), West Bengal, in September 1939.

2 First sperm bank

Dr Aniruddha Malpani and Dr Anjali Malpani from Bombay (now Mumbai), Maharashtra, opened a sperm bank in 1990 to help infertile patients. It also had facilities for storing sperm of people who may be critically ill, for implantation at a later date.

3 First breast milk bank

Dr Armida Fernandez pioneered the establishment of Asia's first human milk bank at the Lokmanya Tilak Municipal General Hospital in Bombay, in November 1989.

DOCTORS

First doctor of western medicine

Pandit Madhusudan Gupta was the first Indian doctor to study western medicine in India. Initially an Ayurvedic practitioner based in Calcutta in the nineteenth century, he was trained in western medicine in 1835–36.

First neurosurgeon

Dr Jacob Chandy (1910–2007) started the department of neurology and neurosurgery in 1949 at Christian Medical College and Hospital, Vellore, Tamil Nadu. He initiated the first training programmes in neurosurgery in 1958 and in neurology in 1962.

First psychosurgeon

M.S. Govindaswamy (1904–62) was the first psychiatrist to start psychosurgery in India. He combined psychological, medical, psychiatric and nursing aspects for holistic treatment.

Discovery of a 'feeding' centre in the hypothalamus

Prof. Bal Krishan Anand (1917–2007) was a famous physiologist and pharmacologist, born in Lahore (now in Pakistan). He was credited with the discovery of the 'feeding' centre in the hypothalamus in 1951 and regarded as the founder of modern neurophysiology in India.

First doctor-to-doctor online session

A doctor-centric portal with the URL www.ranbaxyfordoctors.com hosted a discussion on 'Current trends in the management of cardiac arrhythmia' on 28 August 2000, where 69 doctors chatted online. It was moderated by Prof. (Dr) K.K. Sethi, director, interventional cardiology and cardiac arrhythmia services, Sir Ganga Ram Hospital in New Delhi.

WHO Global Centre for Traditional Medicine (GCTM)

In 2022, WHO along with the support of the Indian government established the first and only global outpost for traditional medicine in the world. It is a collaborative project involving the Ministry of Ayush and WHO. It was established to provide leadership on matters related to traditional medicine as well as support to member countries in shaping various policies pertaining to public health and traditional medical research and practices. It had its first summit in August 2023.

Entrance to PGIMER

First government-run department for disorders of sex development

The Postgraduate Institute of Medical Education and Research (PGIMER), Chandigarh, in July 2019, established the country's first government-run facility for children with disorders of sex development (DSD). The facility provides diagnosis of genetic and hormonal issues, surgical correction and psychological support for such children. Around 200 children per year can be treated here.

First cardiologist

Dr S Srinivas from Bihar was the first cardiologist of India, who started his medical practice in 1950. He was trained by Dr Paul Dudley White and was also the first to bring ECG machine in India.

First dissection

Pandit Madhusudan Gupta, the first Indian doctor of western medicine, was also the first to perform human dissection in Asia in 1836.

Most innovations by a medical professional

Dr Pankaj Garg (b. 27 December 1972), a colorectal surgeon from Panchkula, Haryana, has 16 innovations in the medical field to his name. Consisting of seven surgery procedures and nine treatment concepts, these have been published in national and international surgical journals from April 2015 to May 2019.

PUBLICATIONS

First to win a Pulitzer Prize for a health/medicine-related publication

Indian-origin American oncologist Siddhartha Mukherjee won the Pulitzer for General Non-Fiction in 2011 for *The Emperor of All Maladies: A Biography of Cancer*, published in 2010 by Scribner, New York, US. The book was acclaimed as one of the 100 most influential books of the last 100 years by *Time* magazine and one of the 100 best works of non-fiction by the *New York Times Magazine*.

HEALTH CHECK-UPS AND SCREENING CAMPS

Most people screened – multiple venues*

Lions Club International District 323 H-2, under the leadership of district governor Mohinder K. Aggarwal and district activity chairperson Dr Sanjay Vora, organized a vision screening camp in 2015 in which 140,388 students were screened from 7:00 a.m. to 7:00 p.m. in 13 districts of Maharashtra on 8 October (World Sight Day).

* This category has been discontinued. Further and future claims for this category will not be accepted.

Most people screened – single venue*

An eye check-up camp organized by Netra Kumbh on 26 February 2019, at Prayagraj, Uttar Pradesh, from 8:00 a.m. to 5:00 p.m., saw a record visit of 6,660 people. The check-ups were done by ophthalmologists and optometrists from accredited hospitals from across India. Free spectacles were also distributed to many visitors.

MEDICINE AND SURGERY

Christian Medical College and Hospital's many firsts

Christian Medical College and Hospital (CMCH), Vellore, Tamil Nadu, is a private educational and research institute, which includes a network of primary, secondary, and tertiary care hospitals. Founded in 1900 by an American missionary, Dr Ida S. Scudder, CMCH has many firsts to its credit:

- First reconstructive surgery for leprosy in the world (1948)
- First department of neurological sciences (1948)
- First successful open-heart surgery in India (1961)
- First kidney transplant in India (1971)
- First virology department (1978)
- First bone marrow transplant (1986)
- First successful ABO incompatible (organ donated by a donor of a different blood type) kidney transplant (2009)

Earliest cataract surgery

Ancient Indian physician Sushruta (c. sixth century BCE) had diagnosed that cataract was a disease of the eye lens, characterized by its opacity resulting in impaired vision, and had prescribed surgery as the only remedy. It was performed with a curved needle used to loosen the lens and push the cataract out of the field of vision. The eye would later be soaked with warm butter and then bandaged.

First medical symposium

The Vedic sage Bharadwaja, who is believed to have founded the Indian Ayurvedic system of medicine, presided over the first-ever symposium on medicinal plants in the seventh century BCE, possibly in the Himalayan region.

First international homoeopathic congress

The first International Homoeopathic Congress in India was held in 1967. It was organized and presided over by the renowned homoeopathic doctor Diwan Harish Chand. All the earlier ones, commencing from 1876, had been held in Europe and North America.

First separation of conjoined twins

Dr J. Dalal, paediatrics and neonatology specialist, surgically separated a set of conjoined twins (also known as Siamese twins) born to one Mrs Kambli on 11 August 1962 at Bhatia Hospital, Bombay (now Mumbai), Maharashtra.

First open-heart surgery

Dr Reeve H. Betts, an American missionary, founded the first department of

* This category has been discontinued. Further and future claims for this category will not be accepted.

thoracic and cardiovascular surgery in 1948 at the Christian Medical College and Hospital, Vellore, Tamil Nadu, with cardiac surgical work beginning in 1950. Along with Dr N. Gopinath, he performed the first successful open-heart surgery here on a 12-year-old patient, Beulah, in 1961.

First bloodless breast surgery

A team of doctors at the Dr B.R. Ambedkar Institute Rotary Cancer Hospital, AIIMS, New Delhi, carried out a major bloodless breast cancer surgery in September 1998, using ultrasonic waves.

First laser surgery on trachea

Dr Deepak Talwar, a leading pulmonologist, and his team at the Metro Hospital and Heart Institute, Noida, Uttar Pradesh, successfully opened up the lower part of a patient's windpipe, which had narrowed to 0.5 cm (0.2 in.) from the usual circumference of 2 cm (0.79 in.), in 1998. This was the first such surgery performed using laser technology.

First conference

The first medical conference, inaugurated by the then viceroy of colonial India, Lord Elgin, was held in Calcutta, Bengal (now Kolkata, West Bengal), between 24 and 29 December 1894.

First global telecast of surgery

On 11 June 1998, a team of doctors, led by leading cardiovascular and cardiothoracic surgeon Dr Naresh Trehan, operated upon six patients with heart ailments at the Escorts Heart Institute and Research Centre, New Delhi. The procedure was beamed live to 200 cardiac specialists and 1,000 delegates in San Francisco, US. The back-end support was provided by the Medical Products Group at Hewlett-Packard.

Father of plastic surgery

Sushruta is considered the 'father of plastic surgery'. He is believed to have lived around the sixth century BCE and pioneered the advancement of medicine in ancient India. His teachings of anatomy, pathophysiology and therapeutic strategies, featured in his *Sushruta Samhita*, were far ahead of his time.

Statue of Sushruta – father of plastic surgery

First craniopagus surgery

A team of 125 doctors and paramedical staff, led by Dr Deepak Kumar Gupta and Dr Ashok Kumar Mahapatra from the Department of

Neurosurgery at the All India Institute of Medical Sciences (AIIMS), New Delhi, successfully separated 28-month-old twins Jagga and Kalia, who were joined at the cranium. The twins belong to Milipada Village of Kandhamal district in Odisha. The complex surgery was conducted in two stages, on 28 August 2017 (25 hrs long) and 25 October 2017 (20 hrs long).

The doctor population ratio in India stands at 1 : 834 currently, which is much better than the WHO standard of 1 : 1000.

First video-assisted heart surgery

Video-assisted thoracic surgery (VATS) was used for the first time in heart surgery at the B.M. Birla Heart Research Centre, Calcutta on several children suffering from a congenital heart disease called patent ductus arteriosus (PDA), in August 1994.

First Maze III (atrial fibrillation) surgery

A heart surgery to cure arterial fibrillation (fast and irregular heartbeat) was performed for the first time in India by Dr Amit Banerjee, cardiothoracic surgeon, on 25-year-old Kiran Bir at the Govind Ballabh Pant Hospital, New Delhi, on 25 August 1994.

First heart-shrink surgery

Dr Naresh Trehan (b. 12 August 1946), a cardiovascular and cardiothoracic surgeon, performed the first successful heart-shrink surgery in India, which was also the first in Asia, with his team of cardiac surgeons, on a 50-year-old patient, Mani Ram Gurera, at the Escorts Heart Institute and Research Centre, New Delhi, on 21 May 1996.

Dr Naresh Trehan – renowned cardiothoracic and cardiovascular surgeon

First coronary artery bypass surgery

Dr K.M. Cherian performed India's first successful coronary artery bypass surgery in 1975. He has pioneered several transplants at the Madras Medical Mission and Institute of Cardiovascular Diseases in Chennai, Tamil Nadu.

First bi-ventricular pacemaker

Prof. Kewal Kishan Talwar, cardiologist and former chairman of the Medical Council of India, New Delhi, and Dr T.S. Kler of Escorts Heart Institute and Research Centre, New Delhi, implanted bi-ventricular pacemakers on end-stage heart-disease patients on 8 May 2000 in two separate surgeries. This pacemaker ensures that all chambers of the heart contract and expand simultaneously.

Pioneering cataract removal

Cataract surgery was normally done through a 10–12 mm incision until 15 August

WOMEN IN MEDICINE

1 First woman anaesthetist

WR Dr. Rupa Bai Furdoonji was one of five female students to join the Hyderabad Medical School in 1885. She received her diploma in 1891. As a medical student, she achieved great proficiency in delivering chloroform anaesthesia. She went to Edinburgh in 1909 to gain greater knowledge in the field of anaesthesia. She is probably the first lady anaesthetist in the world who took on anaesthesiology as a full-time career.

2 First woman nurse

Bai Kashibai Ganpat of Thane, Maharashtra, was the first Indian woman to undertake training to become a nurse at a hospital of Jamsetjee Jeejeebhoy Group In Bombay (now Mumbai), Maharashtra, in 1891.

3 First woman surgeon general

Mary Poonen Lukose (1886–1976) from Kerala graduated from the University of Madras (now in Chennai), Tamil Nadu, in 1909, and studied medicine in the UK. She became the first woman surgeon general of India in 1938 and was awarded the Padma Shri in 1975.

4 First woman aerospace doctor

Dr Parvathi Gopal from Bengaluru, Karnataka, joined the Institute of Aerospace Medicine in the Department of High Altitude Physiology in 1992. Her field of work included research and treatment to determine whether a fighter pilot is medically and mentally fit to fly.

5 First woman doctor

Kadambini Ganguly (1861–1923) was the first South Asian female physician trained in Western medicine to graduate in 1888 from the Calcutta Medical College (now Medical College and Hospital, Kolkata, West Bengal).

6 First woman neurosurgeon

Dr Thanjavur Santhanakrishna Kanaka (1932–2018) was the first female neurosurgeon in Asia. She was also the first neurosurgeon in India to perform chronic electrode implants in the brain, having performed deep- brain stimulation as early as 1975.

1998, when Dr Amar Agarwal pioneered the technique called Phakonit, in which a cataract was removed through a 0.9 mm incision at Dr Agarwal's Eye Hospital, Chennai, Tamil Nadu. This technique has now been adopted all over the world.

First cochlear implant

Dr Sandra Desa Souza was the first woman surgeon to perform a cochlear implant surgery in the human ear to treat complete deafness. The surgery was performed at Jaslok Hospital, Bombay, Maharashtra, in November 1987.

Cochlear implant

Smallest medical robot

The smallest medical robot measuring 120 nm (one nanometre is one-billionth of a metre) was created by Soutik Betal, a doctoral research student from India, at the University of Texas, San Antonio, Texas, US, on 10 November 2016. Capable of being remotely controlled electromagnetically and of interacting with biological cells, these robots may be used to advance research in cell-based therapy and to provide direct medication to cells for treating cancers and Alzheimer's disease.

TRANSPLANTS

First successful liver transplant

The first successful liver transplant was performed at the Stanley Medical College in Chennai, Tamil Nadu, on 19 January 1996. It was the third transplant, the first two having been performed at Apollo Hospital, Chennai, and AIIMS, New Delhi, respectively. In both cases, the patients died within a few days.

First womb transplant

Doctors at Galaxy Care Hospital, Pune, Maharashtra, successfully conducted India's first womb transplant on 18 May 2017 by transferring a woman's uterus to her 21-year-old daughter, who was unable to conceive. The procedure, which took 9 hrs using the laparoscopic technique, was performed by a team of 12 doctors.

First successful heart transplant

A team of doctors led by Dr P. Venugopal at the All India Institute of Medical Sciences (AIIMS), New Delhi, performed a successful heart transplant surgery in 5 hrs on 3 August 1994.

First paediatric heart transplant

On 14 June 1997, an 11-year-old boy underwent a successful heart transplant at the Institute of Cardiovascular Diseases, Madras Medical Mission, Chennai, Tamil Nadu. The surgery took three-and-a-half hours.

First successful thumb transplant

Dr Tapeshwar Anand and Dr Mohan Das were part of a team of specialists who performed a 12-hour limb- transplant surgery on a seven-hour-old baby Amy, at St Bart's Hospital, London, UK, on 24 March 2001. Her twin sister's thumb was transplanted on her hand (born thumbless) after her sister died at birth.

MEDICAL MARVELS

First double (liver and kidney) transplant

Ganesh Nehru became the first recipient of a liver from his maternal uncle Mohan Ram and a kidney from his mother Hemlata simultaneously. The double transplant lasted 18 hrs on 17 April 2007 and involved 50 doctors and paramedics, besides intricate coordination between three operating theatres at Sir Ganga Ram Hospital, New Delhi. Dr A.S. Soin was the transplant surgeon in charge of the case.

First scalp replantation

A completely avulsed scalp was replanted microsurgically on Gurkripal Singh by Dr Abraham Thomas and Dr Jaychandran of Christian Medical College and Hospital, Ludhiana, Punjab, in March 1985.

Oldest to undergo hip surgery

- A team of doctors at the Postgraduate Institute of Medical Education and Research (PGIMER), Chandigarh, performed a hip replacement surgery on a 110-year-old woman (age based on her Aadhaar card), Manjauki, on 8 January 2020. The team comprised Prof. Vijay G. Goni, Dr Tanvir Samra, Dr Deepak, Dr Karan, Dr Pradeep and Dr Sumeet.
- Ram Lal, a 105-year-old patient, was the oldest to undergo a bipolar replacement of the right hip when he sustained a fracture around the hip joint. The surgery was carried out under Dr Sujoy Kumar Bhattacharjee, director, joint replacement surgery, at Metro Heart Institute with Multispeciality Hospital in Faridabad, Haryana, on 23 March 2018. The operation lasted 2 hrs 52 mins.

Oldest woman to deliver twins

Seventy-four-year-old Mangayamma Yaramati gave birth to a pair of twin girls on 5 September 2019 at the Ahalya Hospital, Guntur, Andhra Pradesh. Dr Sankayalla Uma Shankar delivered the babies by Caesarean section. Conceived through IVF, the babies were the first children of the couple.

WR Heaviest ovarian tumour removed

- As per public domain information, the world's heaviest ovarian tumour, weighing 50 kg, was removed on 18 August 2020 at the Indraprastha Apollo Hospital, New Delhi, from a 52-year-old patient, by a team of surgeons led by Dr Arun Prasad. The surgery lasted for three-and-a half hours.
- *Malignant*: Kavita Khoiwal, assistant professor, Department of Obstetrics and Gynaecology, AIIMS, Rishikesh, Uttarakhand, along with her team of doctors, operated on a 24-year-old female patient on 21 August 2020 and removed the heaviest abdominopelvic mass. The weight of the cancerous ovarian mass was 41.1 kg, from which 36 litres of mucinous fluid was removed prior to removal and the remaining mass of 5.1 kg was removed subsequently. The size of the mass was 60 cm x 50 cm x 40 cm (23.62 in. x 19.68 in. x 15.75 in.) approximately.

Longest object removed from the brain

Dr Rahul Prakash Modgi, neurosurgeon, and Dr Rajendra Gawatre, anaesthesiologist, operated on Pallavi Vijay Shelke, 17, at Shri Saibaba Hospital,

Shirdi, Maharashtra, on 29 December 2012. They removed a 12 cm (4.72 in.) long iron rod, weighing 47 g, from her right fronto-temporo-parietal region.

Largest urinary bladder stone removed

Dr D.C. Patel operated on Maheshbhai Patel, a 49-year-old suffering from blocked urine, at Shree Sainath Surgical and Maternity Hospital, Dharampur, Gujarat, on 6 April 2017. Dr Patel removed a bladder stone measuring 15 cm x 12 cm x 10 cm (5.90 in. x 4.72 in. x 3.94 in.) and weighing 1.365 kg. He was assisted by Dr Hemant Patel and Dr Nital Patel.

Longest fistula removed

A 110 cm (43.30 in.) long fistula was removed from a patient by Dr Ashwin Porwal at Healing Hands Clinic, Pune, Maharashtra, on 10 May 2019. The surgery was conducted from 3:00 p.m. to 7:00 p.m. using the distal laser proximal ligation (DLPL) technique.

Largest small-intestinal tumour removed

A tumour measuring 21 cm x 19 cm x 13 cm (8.26 in. x 7.48 in. x 5.12 in.) was removed from the small intestine of a patient by Dr Karthik Babu Perumalla at Ramesh Sanghamitra Hospital, Ongole, Andhra Pradesh. The surgery was conducted on 1 March 2019 from 11:00 a.m. to 4:00 p.m.

Largest breast tumour removed

The largest breast tumour recorded, which measured 41 cm x 39 cm x 37 cm (16.14 in. x 15.35 in. x 14.57 in.), was removed from a patient by Dr Vikas Jain at the B.J. Hospital, Gondia, Maharashtra. The surgery was conducted on 25 July 2019 from 3:30 p.m. to 6:00 p.m. The tumour weighed 5.6 kg after it was removed.

Largest bone tumour removed

On 9 June 2021, a team of doctors from the orthopaedics department of ACPM Medical Hospital, Dhule, Maharashtra, removed the largest tumour from the left femur of a 28-year-old patient. The team comprised Dr Yashwant Mahale, Dr James Kuris, Dr Ameya Thaware and Dr Akash Metkar. The tumour measured 43.18 cm (17 in.) in length, 30.48 cm (12 in.) in breadth and 25.4 cm (10 in.) in width. It had a circumference of 102 cm (40.16 in.). The surgery took a total of 3.5 hours.

Team of doctors holding largest bone tumour at ACPM Medical Hospital

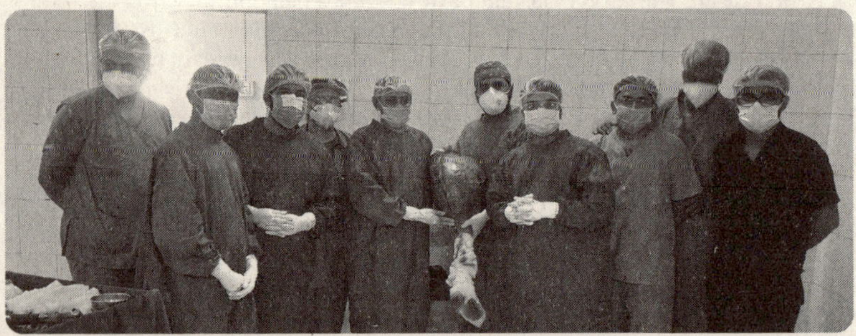

Heaviest kidney removed

Dr Puvvada Sandeep and three other doctors from his team at Ramaiah Medical College, Bengaluru, Karnataka, removed a kidney weighing 7.72 kg on 21 November 2019. Containing 3.12 litres of fluid, the kidney was removed from a 53-year-old patient suffering from bilateral adult polycystic kidney disease (APKD) and chronic kidney disease.

WR Heaviest brain tumour removed

Dr Saraj Kumar Singh, assistant professor, AIIMS, Patna, Bihar, and his assisting team removed a brain tumour weighing 2.280 kg (2,280 g) from a 50-year-old male patient on 22 November 2021 at the hospital. The surgery to excise the tumour began at 12:26 p.m. and ended at 3:42 p.m., lasting 3 hrs 16 mins. The tumour measured 24 cm x 24 cm x 14 cm (9.44 in. x 9.44 in. x 5.51 in.).

Longest foreign body removed

Dr Sanjay Kolte, urologist and kidney transplant surgeon at Sparsh Urology and Kidney Hospital, Dhantoli, Maharashtra, removed a 154 cm (5 ft 0.6 in.) long soft electric wire from the urinary bladder of a patient by percutaneous cystoscopy extraction of foreign body surgery on 28 August 2012.

Largest cystic tumour of the liver removed

Dr N. Bheerappa from the department of surgical gastroenterology at the Nizam's Institute of Medical Sciences, Hyderabad, Telangana, successfully removed the largest known cystic liver tumour (mucinous cystic neoplasm) in 2017. The 24-year-old female patient was operated on for a tumour measuring 40 cm x 28 cm x 15 cm (15.74 in. x 11.02 in. x 5.91 in.).

Largest kidney stone removed

Dr Hemendra Shah at R.G. Stone Urological Research Institute, Mumbai, Maharashtra, removed a 13 cm (5.12 in.) wide kidney stone from a patient on 18 February 2004.

Largest urethral calculus removed

Dr Neeraj Kumar Agrawal removed a 5.6 cm (2.2 in.) long stone from a patient at Neeraj Lifecare and Stone Centre, Bareilly, Uttar Pradesh, on 21 August 2019.

Largest oral (head and neck) tumour removed – in one piece

Dr Saurabh Gupta, assistant professor and consultant, Surgical Oncology, Max Superspeciality Hospital, Shalimar Bagh, New Delhi, as operating surgeon, removed a head-and-neck tumour from a 38-year-old male patient in a left commando surgery. This, along with free alt flap reconstruction, took 11 hrs from 9:00 a.m. to 8:00 p.m. on 30 April 2020. The size of the tumour in this case of oral cancer was 18 cm x 12 cm x 8 cm (7.09 in. x 4.72 in. x 3.15 in.).

Largest thoracic tumour removed

On 13 September 2021, the largest thoracic tumour was successfully removed by Dr Anshuman Darbari of the cardiothoracic department, AIIMS Rishikesh, Uttarakhand. The tumour was removed from a 51-year-old female patient. The tumour measured 26 cm x 24 cm x 12 cm (10.23 in. x 9.44 in. x 4.72 in.).

MEDICAL DEVICES: IMPORT VS EXPORT (USD BILLION)

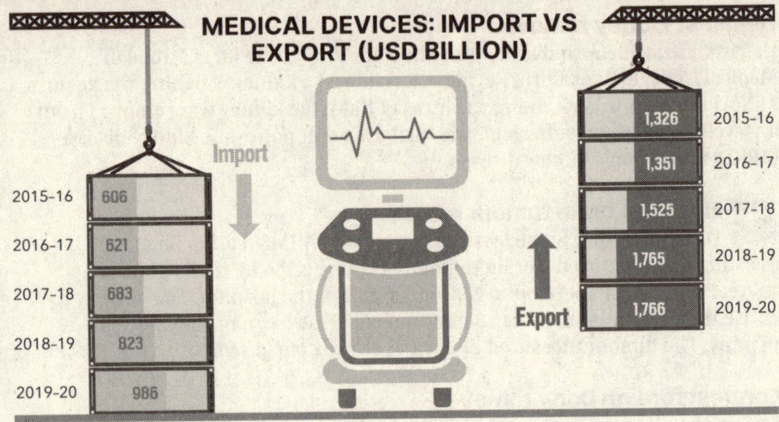

Source: Equitable Access to Medical Devices - India: A Report, March 2023, Public Health Foundation of India (PHFI) and Indian Medical Parliamentarians' Forum (IMPF)

TOP 5 LEADING CAUSES OF DEATH (2019)

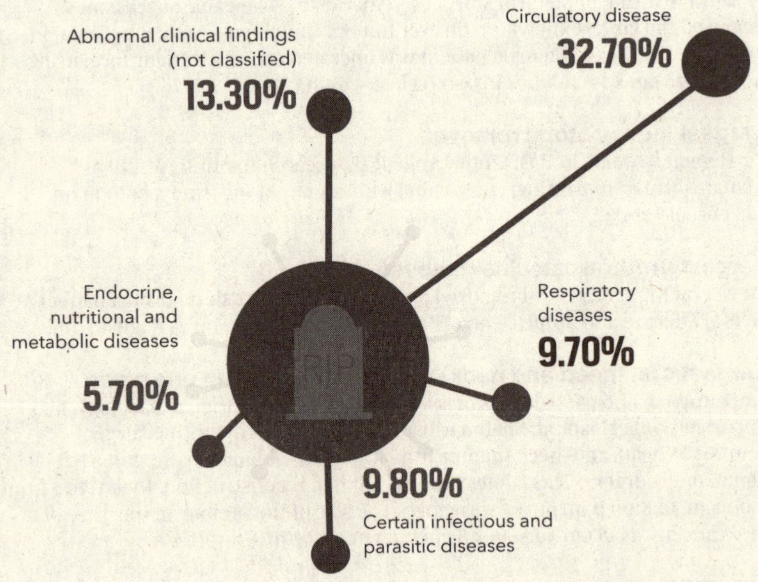

Source: Report on Medical Certification of Cause of Death 2019, Office of the Registrar General, India, Ministry of Home Affairs, Government of India

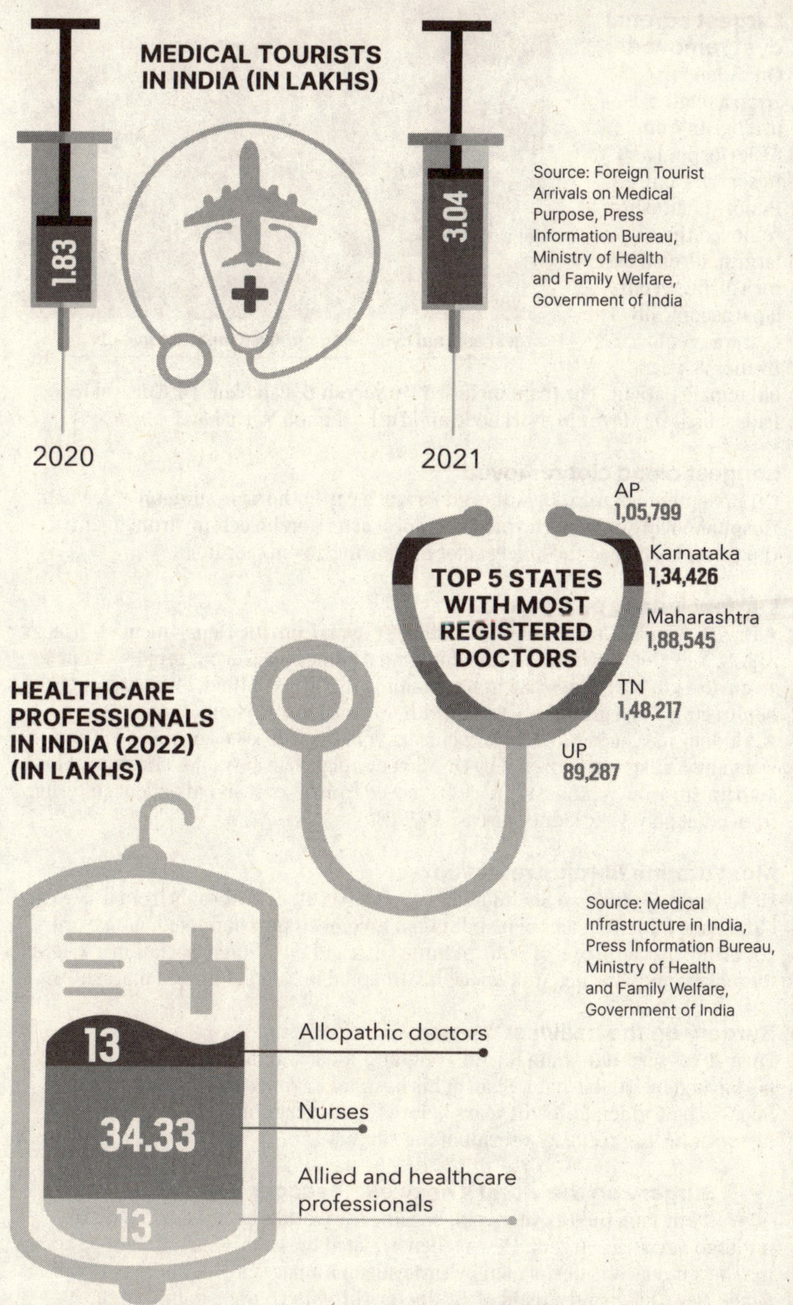
MEDICAL TOURISTS IN INDIA (IN LAKHS)
1.83
3.04
2020
2021
Source: Foreign Tourist Arrivals on Medical Purpose, Press Information Bureau, Ministry of Health and Family Welfare, Government of India
TOP 5 STATES WITH MOST REGISTERED DOCTORS
AP 1,05,799
Karnataka 1,34,426
Maharashtra 1,88,545
TN 1,48,217
UP 89,287
HEALTHCARE PROFESSIONALS IN INDIA (2022) (IN LAKHS)
13
Allopathic doctors
34.33
Nurses
13
Allied and healthcare professionals
Source: Medical Infrastructure in India, Press Information Bureau, Ministry of Health and Family Welfare, Government of India

Largest adrenal cyst removed

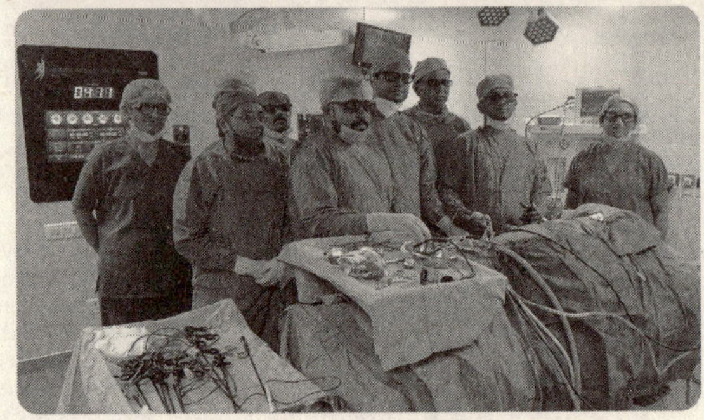
Largest adrenal cyst being removed laparoscopically

On 24 January 2023, a team of urologists from ACE Hospital and Research Centre, Pune, Maharashtra, removed the largest adrenal cyst measuring 23 cm laparoscopically. The cyst was removed from a 58-year-old female patient. The team included Dr Suresh B. Patankar, Dr Gururaj R. Padasalagi, Dr Mayur M. Narkhede and Dr Kashinath V. Thakare.

Longest blood clot removed

On 24 September 2022, Dr Anne Sai Pavan, a cardiothoracic surgeon at Aayush Hospital, Vijayawada, performed a femoral artery embolectomy from 9 p.m. to 11 p.m. and removed the longest clot measuring 20 cm (7.87 in.).

Largest kidney operated on

- Dr A.K. Hemal, Dr S.N. Wadhwa, and their team from the Department of Urology, AIIMS, New Delhi, removed a non-functional kidney measuring 25 cm x 20 cm x 20 cm (9.84 in. x 7.88 in. x 7.88 in.), containing five litres of fluid, by laparoscopic nephrectomy in a unique operation with no incision, on 3 June 1996.
- A kidney measuring 40.5 cm x 22 cm x 12.5 cm (15.94 in. x 8.66 in. x 4.92 in.) and weighing 6.24 kg was removed by Dr Niket Kantilal Shah at Wanless Hospital, Miraj, Maharashtra, on 23 June 2017. It was removed from a 50-year-old patient suffering from adult polycystic kidney disease (APKD).

Most uterine fibroids removed

Dr Ravindra Keshavrao Shelmohkar removed 63 uterine fibroids from a 34-year-old female patient in an open abdominal myomectomy conducted on 14 April 2021 from 9:45 a.m. to 10:45 a.m. at Pune District Education Association's Ayurved Rugnalaya and Sterling Multispeciality Hospital in Nugdi, Pune, Maharashtra.

Surgery on the heaviest woman

Forty-two-year-old Amita Rajani, weighing 300 kg, underwent bariatric surgery performed by Dr Shashank Shah at his hospital in Pune, Maharashtra, in 2015. She was bedridden for eight years before the surgery and had multiple risk factors. She lost 214 kg as a result of the surgery.

WR Surgery on the world's heaviest teenager

Mihir Jain, then 14 years old, became the world's heaviest teenager to undergo bariatric surgery. He weighed 237 kg at the time, with a BMI of 92 kg/sq. m. The surgery was performed by Dr Pradeep Kumar Chowbey at Max Hospital, Saket, New Delhi, and a team of six doctors in 2 hrs 20 mins in July 2018.

THE NATURAL WORLD

PHYSICAL FEATURES

Longest land mountain range

The Himalayan range is the loftiest and most rugged mountain barrier in Asia. Out of the 7,300 mountain peaks in the world, 96 are in the Himalaya–Karakoram range. The range stretches over 2,500 km and varies in width from around 500 km in Jammu and Kashmir to around 200 km in Arunachal Pradesh. Some of the higher ranges are composed of 600-million-year-old Precambrian rocks.

Largest glacier

Siachen Glacier, Ladakh, near the India–Pakistan border, is India's largest glacier. It is 75.6 km long and 2–8 km wide. It is also the second longest glacier outside the polar regions of the earth.

Longest river

The 2,525 km long Ganga River is the longest river in the country. Its source is in the western Himalayas in Uttarakhand, from where the river flows south and east through the Gangetic Plain and Bangladesh, finally merging into the Bay of Bengal.

Largest river system

Of the total river discharge in India, 65 per cent is from the Himalayan group of rivers. The Ganga, Indus, and Brahmaputra Rivers are part of this river system.

WR Largest delta

The triangular land mass formed by the Hooghly River, the Ganga, Padma, and Meghna Rivers combined, and the Bay of Bengal is called the Bengal Delta. It is the largest delta in the world. Two-thirds of this 57,000 sq. km delta is in Bangladesh and the rest lies in West Bengal, India.

Highest peak

Kanchenjunga, with its base partly in India and partly in Nepal, is 8,586 m (28,169 ft) high. Yalung Kang (also on the India–Nepal border) is the second highest at 8,505 m (27,903 ft) and Nanda Devi comes in third at 7,816 m (25,643 ft).

Mt Kanchenjunga

Lonar crater, Maharashtra

Largest crater

The Lonar meteorite crater in the Buldhana District of Maharashtra is India's largest and the world's third largest meteorite crater. It measures 1,800 m (5,906 ft) across and is 170 m (558 ft) deep. It is estimated that it was formed 50,000 years ago by a meteorite that was around 100 m (328 ft) in diameter, weighed a million tonnes and was travelling at a speed of around 90,000 km per hour.

Largest catchment area

The Ganga–Brahmaputra–Meghna system is the biggest river system in the country, with a catchment area of 272 million acres (110 million hectares), which is more than 43 per cent of the catchment area of all the major rivers of the Indian subcontinent.

Largest freshwater lake

Wular Lake, India's largest freshwater lake, has an area of 260 sq. km. It is in Bandipora District, Jammu and Kashmir.

Only cold desert

Ladakh, at an average altitude of 4,878 m (16,004 ft), is the only cold desert in India.

Largest brackish-water lagoon

Chilika Lake in Odisha is the largest brackish-water lagoon and has an area of around 1,100 sq. km.

Largest meteorite shower

On 14 July 1860, a heavy meteorite shower fell at Dharamshala (32°14′N, 76°28′E) in Kangra District, Himachal Pradesh. It consisted of many stones, the largest of which weighed 150 kg.

Largest desert

The Thar Desert is the largest desert in India that stretches over an area of about 200,000 sq. km and spreads over four states: Punjab, Haryana, Gujarat and Rajasthan. It is interspersed with hillocks, gravel plains, salt marshes and lakes.

WR Largest island – freshwater

The island of Majuli, with an area of 352 sq. km in the Brahmaputra River in Assam, is the largest freshwater island in the world.

Largest island – ocean

The island of Middle Andaman (1,523 sq. km) in the Andaman and Nicobar Islands is the largest ocean island in India.

Largest cave

The Amarnath Cave, about 44 km from Pahalgam in Jammu and Kashmir, is the largest cave and a popular pilgrimage. It is a natural cave located at an altitude of 3,800 m (12,467 ft). The cave is 50 m (164 ft) wide and 25 m (82 ft) high. A remarkable stalagmite in the cave is worshipped as a *shivalinga*.

Highest waterfall

Kunchikal Falls in Nidagodu Village near Masthikatte in Shivamogga District, Karnataka, falls down a total height of 455 m (1,493 ft), making it the highest waterfall in India.

Highest temperature

On 19 May 2016, India recorded its highest-ever temperature, 51°C, in Phalodi, a town in Jodhpur District, Rajasthan.

Lowest temperature

The lowest temperature recorded in Dras, Ladakh, was –60°C on 9 January 1995, making it the coldest inhabited place in India.

Minimum rainfall area

Jaisalmer in Rajasthan receives an average rainfall of only about 200 mm (around 7.87 in.) in a year.

Maximum rainfall

Mawsynram, a village in the East Khasi Hills District, Meghalaya, about 65 km from Shillong, gets a mean annual rainfall of 11,873 mm (467 in.) in about 147 days. Earlier the record for the highest average rainfall was held by Cherrapunji (now Sohra) in the same district.

Mawsynram

Lowest surface salinity

Salinity near the surface in the northern Bay of Bengal can be as low as 31 psu because the bay receives fresh water as rain as well as run-off from the Ganga, Brahmaputra, Irrawaddy, and othe rivers.

Highest surface salinity

The surface salinity in the Gulf of Kachchh, off the coast of Gujarat, varies from a maximum of 45.5 psu (practical salinity units) near the head of the gulf to 36.6 psu at the mouth. A practical salinity unit is equivalent to parts per thousand.

WR Longest natural sandstone cave

Krem Puri, found in East Khasi Hills District, Meghalaya, is the world's longest sandstone cave with a length of about 24.58 km. It is also known for its dinosaur fossils from 66–76 million years ago. It is 6 km longer than the previous record holder – the 18.2 km long Cueva Del Saman sandstone cave in Edo Zulia, Venezuela.

Only active volcano

Barren Island, which lies 110 km north-east of Port Blair in the Andaman and Nicobar Islands, is India's only active volcano. On 10 April 1991, it blew up nearly two centuries after it erupted in 1803. It last erupted in 1995.

FOSSILS

Oldest dinosaur fossil discovery

The first dinosaur fossils in India were discovered by a British palaeontologist named W.H. Sleeman in 1828 in Jabalpur, Madhya Pradesh. The specimens were lost in 1877 and found in 2013 in the office of the Geological Survey of India, Kolkata, West Bengal.

MAMMALS

Longest gestation

The elephant has a gestation period of about 20 months.

Shortest gestation

Rodents have a gestation period averaging a month.

Oldest living mammal

One of the oldest living mammals is the Indian one-horned rhinoceros (*Rhinoceros unicornis*). The Indian and Javan rhinoceroses first appeared in the fossil record of Asia 1.6–3.3 million years ago. The species may have diverged much earlier, around 11.7 million years ago.

Smallest mammal

- *Land:* The white-toothed pygmy shrew (*Suncus etruscus*), which has a head-and-body length of 3–5.5 cm (1.18–2.17 in.) and a tail length of 2.5–3.2 cm (0.98–1.26 in.), is the smallest Indian land mammal by weight. It weighs around 1.8 g. This shrew can be found across the Indian subcontinent, except in Jammu and Kashmir and arid areas of Gujarat and Rajasthan.

- *Water:* The smallest water mammal in the country is the finless porpoise (*Neophocaena phocaenoides*), which is only 1.2–2 cm (0.47–0.79 in.) long. It is found in the waters of peninsular India.

Largest land mammal

The adult Asian elephant found in India (*Elephas maximus indicus*) belongs to the species of the largest land mammal *Elephas maximus.* An adult bull elephant averages 2.74 m (9 ft) in height at the shoulder and weighs around 4.5 tonnes. The female elephant or cow measures 2.35 m (7 ft 8.5 in.) at the shoulder and weighs around 3 tonnes. Elephants are found in four clusters in the plains of north, south, east and central India and the north-east.

Largest litter

The Indian mole rat (*Bandicota bengalensis*), found in most plains and forests, is known to have litters of over 12 young ones at a time.

Fastest breeders

The Indian mole rat is the fastest-breeding mammal. The males mature in 58 days after birth and the females in 90–100 days. Females have an average count of 11.32 pregnancies a year with a total break of 32.3 days in between. The female may produce as many as 70 young ones a year.

Slowest breeders

The elephant's main breeding season is the summer and the beginning of monsoon. Only one calf is born at a time and at intervals of three years.

Primate with the longest tail

The tail of the common langur measures around 1 m (3 ft 3.4 in.) on average.

Longest-living

- Humans are the longest-living mammals on land.
- The average lifespan of a blue whale (*Balaenoptera musculus*) is 80–90 years.
- The Indian elephant follows with an average lifespan of around 60 years, but they can live up to 80–90 years.

Blue whale in the Indian Ocean

FASTEST AND SLOWEST MAMMALS

1 FASTEST MAMMAL
Land

The blackbuck (*Antilope cervicapra*), which is native to India, can run at a speed of up to 80 km per hour, making it the fastest mammal on land. It is found in regions ranging from Rajasthan to Punjab in the north, up to Odisha in the east and Tamil Nadu in the south. The cheetah (*Acinonyx jubatus*), recently introduced in India, in Madhya Pradesh, can sprint at speeds of up to 120 km per hour.

Blackbuck in Gujarat

2 Water

Long-beaked common dolphin

The 2–2.5 m (6 ft 6 in.–8 ft 2 in.) long-beaked common dolphin (*Delphinus capensis*), found off the coast of peninsular India, swims at 30 knots or 55.5 km per hour, and is the fastest mammal in water.

1 SLOWEST MAMMAL
Land

The Bengal slow loris (*Nycticebus bengalensis*), which measures 30–40 cm (11.8–15.7 in.), is the slowest land mammal in the country. It is found in Assam.

2 Water

The slowest mammal in water is the 3.2 m (10 ft 6 in.) long dugong or sea cow (*Dugong dugon*), found in the Gulf of Kachchh, off the Malabar Coast, and in the Andaman Islands.

Bengal slow loris on a branch

Dugong or sea cow

The only apes

The western hoolock gibbon (*Hoolock hoolock*) and the eastern hoolock gibbon (*Hoolock leuconedys*) are the only ape species found in India. They are the tallest gibbons; only ape species too. Their average height, standing on hind legs, is about 0.9 m (3 ft).

WR The only camels that swim

The Kharai camels from the Kachchh region in Gujarat are the only ones of their kind in the world that can swim. They live with nomadic camel herders, who are indigenous to the region. The camels have padded hooves that help them navigate wet and salty coastal land and they can swim up to 3 km.

Only herbivorous marine mammals

Dugongs and manatees form the only group of herbivorous marine mammals. They are found in the Gulf of Mannar and Palk Bay, where seagrass meadows provide them with food. Highly endangered, dugongs are also found in the Gulf of Kachchh and near the Andaman Islands. They are 1 m to 3 m (3 ft 3 in. to 9 ft 10 in.) long and weigh around 400 kg.

WR Smallest feline

The world's smallest cat, about half to three-fourths the size of a domestic cat, is the rusty, spotted cat *(Prionailurus rubiginosus)* found in southern and central India. The male has a head-and-body length of 35–48 cm (14–19 in.) and the tail measures 15–30 cm (5.9–11.8 in.). Males weigh around 1.5–1.6 kg, while females weigh about 1.1–1.5 kg.

Feline found at the highest altitude

The snow leopard (*Panthera uncia*) is found at around 3,650–3,960 m (12,000–13,000 ft) in the Himalayan mountains.

Smallest bat

The Indian pygmy bat (*Pipistrellus tenuis*) has a head-and-body length of 3.3–4.5 cm (1.3–1.8 in.). Its tail is 3.5 cm (1.38 in.) and its forearm is 2.5–3 cm (1.0–1.2 in.) long.

Largest/heaviest feline

Male tigers have a head-and-body length of 3.55–4.20 m (11 ft 7 in.–13 ft 9 in.). Females have a head-and-body length of 2.40–2.65 m (7 ft 10 in.–8 ft 8 in.). The height at shoulder is around 90–110 cm (35–43 in.). The average weight of males is 175–260 kg and that of females is 100–160 kg.

Largest bat

The large flying fox (*Pteropus vampyrus*) is the largest bat at 19.8–30 cm (7.8–11.8 in.) in the country and is found in the Himalayas and peninsular India.

Flying fox

Rarest bat

Salim Ali's fruit bat (*Latidens salimalii),* found in southern India and named after the famous ornithologist Salim Ali, is one of the rarest bats in India.

BIRDS

Largest round nests

The nests made by the megapodes (*Megapodius nicobariensis*) reach a height of 1.5 m (4 ft 11 in.) and have a circumference of 10 m (32 ft 10 in.).

Smallest and lightest

The Nilgiri flowerpecker (*Dicaeum concolor*) is only 7 cm (2.7 in.) long and weighs around 4.5 g.

Longest claws

The hind claw of the bronze-winged jacana (*Metopidius indicus*) measures around 6.5–7 cm (2.5–2.7 in.) in length. Its leg (tarsus) is 6.5–6.8 cm (2.5–2.6 in.) long.

Smallest egg

The average size of the egg of the scarlet-backed flowerpecker (*Dicaeum cruentatum*) is 14 mm x 10.3 mm (0.55 in. x 0.4 in.).

Largest egg

The average size of thc sarus crane's egg is 10.4 cm x 6.4 cm (4 in. x 2.5 in.).

Longest beak

The beaks of the rosy pelican (*Pelecanus onocrotalus*) and the Dalmatian pelican (*Pelecanus crispus*) are 43–45 cm (1 ft 4.9 in.–1 ft 5.7 in.) long.

Slowest bird

The Eurasian woodcock (*Scolopax rusticola*) flies at a speed of around 8 km per hour.

Only breeding ground for flamingos

The only known breeding ground in India for the lesser and greater flamingos is the Rann of Kachchh in Gujarat. Thousands of flamingos nest every year in the seasonal marshes of both the Great Rann and the Little Rann of Kachchh.

Flamingo in Gujarat

Shortest legs

The crested tree swift (*Hemiprocne coronata*) has around 7–9 mm (0.27 – 0.35 in.) long legs.

Longest legs

The legs (tarsus) of the sarus crane (*Grus antigone*) measure 31–35 cm (12–13 in.), making them the longest among birds.

Swiftest/fastest dive

The peregrine falcon (*Falco peregrinus*) reaches speeds of over 320 km per hour. It can dive at a speed of up to 360 km per hour – faster than a moving racing car.

Smallest wingspan

The Nilgiri flowerpecker (*Dicaeum concolor*) male has a wingspan of 43–48 mm (1.69–1.89 in.). The female has an even smaller wingspan of 42–45 mm (1.65–1.77 in.).

Largest wingspan

The bearded vulture (*Gypaetus barbatus*) or the lammergeier, found along the lower Himalayas in Jammu and Kashmir, Himachal Pradesh, Uttarakhand, Sikkim, Assam and Arunachal Pradesh, has a wingspan of 2.31–2.83 m (7 ft 7 in.–9 ft 3 in.).

Sarus crane

WR Tallest flying bird

The sarus crane (*Grus antigone*) is the world's tallest bird, standing 1.52 m (5 ft) tall. This greyish crane with a red head is common around the *jheels* of northern and central India. Of the 14–15 species of cranes in the world, six are found in India.

Rarest birds

Possibly the rarest bird is the critically endangered Jerdon's courser (*Rhinoptilus bitorquatus*). The Nicobar megapode (*Megapodius nicobariensis*) or Nicobar scrub fowl, found in the Nicobar Islands, is also one of the rarest Indian birds.

First bird hospital

The Charity Birds' Hospital in Chandni Chowk, Delhi, caters to about 20,000 birds a year and is the only exclusive hospital for birds in the country.

Most intricate nest

The weaver bird species, like the baya (*Ploceus philippinus*), makes the most intricate nests. Shaped like the pipe of a snake charmer, the nests have many chambers.

BUTTERFLIES

Smallest butterfly

The grass jewel butterfly (*Freyeria trochylus*) has a wingspan of only 1.5 cm (0.6 in.).

Largest moth

The Indian atlas moth (*Attacus atlas*) is possibly the largest in the world. The average length of males is 16.7–27.1 cm (6.57 –10.67 in.) and females is 14.2–26.2 cm (5.59–10.31 in.).

Biggest butterfly

The female golden birdwing (*Troides aeacus*) has a wingspan of 19.4 cm (7.6 in.) and was seen in Didihat, Uttarakhand. The male is much smaller with a wingspan of 10.6 cm (4.2 in.).

Butterfly at the highest altitude

The blue Apollo *(Parnassius hardwickii)* is found at altitudes of 4,267–4,876 m (14,000–16,000 ft) in the Green Lake area at the base of Mt Kanchenjunga. This bluish white butterfly, with orange spots, has a wingspan of 4.5 cm (1.8 in.).

AMPHIBIANS

Smallest frogs

In February 2017, Indian scientists found seven new endemic species of *Nyctibatrachus*, or night frogs, which make insect-like calls. Four species of these nocturnal amphibians, including Vijayan's night frog *(Nyctibatrachus pulivijayani)*, were found in the Agasthyamala Biosphere Reserve (spread across several districts in Tamil Nadu and Kerala). They all measure around 12.2–15.4 mm (0.5–0.6 in.).

Largest frog

The Indian bullfrog (*Hoplobatrachus tigerinus*), found all over the country, can grow up to 15 cm (5.9 in.). Some weigh as much as 1 kg.

Indian bullfrog on a leaf

Flying frog

The Malabar gliding frog *(Rhacophorus malabaricus)*, found in Karnataka and the Wayanad District of Kerala, glides from the top of a tree to the base of another using its concave body and webbed feet as a parachute.

Rarest frog

The black, narrow-mouthed Malabar frog or Kerala Hills frog (*Melanobatrachus indicus*), found in thc Anaimalai Hills of the Western Ghats, inhabits moist evergreen forests at 1,220 m (4,000 ft) and is considered one of the rarest frogs in the country.

REPTILES

LIZARDS

Largest lizard
The water monitor (*Varanus salvator*) reaches a length of 2.5 m (8 ft 2 in.) and can weigh up to 14 kg. It is a carnivorous lizard of the Sundarbans, Odisha and the Andaman Islands. Land monitor lizards (*Varanus bengalensis*) also grow up to 61–175 cm (24–69 in.) from snout to tail end.

Longest tongue
The chameleon's tongue is three-fourths the length of its body (30 cm/11.8 in.) and has a viscid club-shaped tip. It can flick out its tongue and catch prey in 1/25th of a second.

Longest tail in relation to body
The long-tailed grass lacertid (*Takydromus sexlineatus khasiensis*) measures only 5 cm (2 in.), but its tail is 35 cm (13.7 in.) long – a ratio of 1:7. It is found in the Khasi Hills of Meghalaya.

Only flying lizards
Norvill's flying lizard (*Draco norvillii*), found in north-east India, and the Indian flying lizard (*Draco dussumieri*) in the Western Ghats and south India are endemic to India. Their average length is 23 cm (9 in.) and they can glide through the air for around 17 m (55 ft 9 in.).

Only legless lizard
The Asian glass lizard or Burmese glass lizard (*Ophisaurus gracilis*) is found at altitudes of 820–1,500 m (2,690–4,920 ft) in Darjeeling, West Bengal, and the Khasi Hills, Meghalaya. It crawls and uses its tongue in a snake-like fashion.

GECKOS

Smallest gecko
A 4 cm (1.6 in.) Persian sand dwarf gecko (*Tropiocolotes persicus*), or the dwarf or pygmy gecko, was recorded in Rajasthan in 2011.

Largest gecko
The *Hemidactylus frenatus* or the common house gecko, found in Bihar, Bengal and north-east India, grows to around 34 cm (13.4 in.) in length. It feeds on insects, rats, birds and small snakes.

Rarest gecko
The golden hill gecko (*Calodactylodes avreus*), found in the Tirumala Hills of Andhra Pradesh, is a very rare species. Its body is golden yellow with brown spots.

The Amaravathy Sagar Crocodile Farm is the largest crocodile nursery in India. It was established in 1976.

'Flying' gecko

The gliding gecko *(Ptychozoon kuhli)*, found in the Nicobar Islands and north-east India, can glide over 13 m (43 ft). It has skin flaps on the side of its head, body and tail, which help it glide when the animal launches into the air.

A flying gecko on a leaf

CROCODILES

Shortest crocodile

The mugger crocodile (*Crocodylus palustris*), found in streams, is only 3 m (9 ft 10 in.) long. It is found almost all over India except at higher altitudes such as in the Himalayan mountains.

Heaviest crocodile

The estuarine or saltwater crocodile (*Crocodylus porosus*) is the heaviest reptile in the country. The adult male crocodile may weigh around 1,000–1,300 kg while the adult female weighs around 76–100 kg.

Longest crocodile

The estuarine or saltwater crocodile grows to a recorded length of 7 m (23 ft). It is found in tidal estuaries, marine swamps and coastal waters in and around the Sundarbans, Odisha and the Andaman and Nicobar Islands.

First known white crocodile

Gori, an albino white crocodile, was artificially hatched at the Bhitarkanika Dangamal Crocodile Research Centre in Odisha on 26 June 1975.

Rarest crocodile

The rarest of the three crocodile species found in India, the gharial (*Gavialus gangeticus*) grows to 6.25 m(20 ft 6 in.) and is the only living member of the family Gavialidae in India. The surviving population is found in the tributaries of the Ganga River like the Girwa (Uttar Pradesh), Son (Madhya Pradesh), Ramganga (Uttarakhand), Gandak (Bihar), Chambal (Uttar Pradesh, Madhya Pradesh, and Rajasthan) and the Mahanadi River (Odisha). It is classified as critically endangered by the International Union for the Conservation of Nature (IUCN).

First/largest crocodile bank

The Madras Crocodile Bank Trust and Centre for Herpetology, 40 km from Madras (now Chennai), Tamil Nadu was founded in 1976 by the naturalist Romulus Whitaker and had over 8,000 crocodiles of 10 different species.

SNAKES

Longest sea snake

The yellow sea snake (*Hydrophis spiralis*) grows 1.8 m (6 ft) long. Specimens up to 3 m (10 ft) long are not uncommon. It is found both in the Bay of Bengal and the Arabian Sea.

WR Longest snake

The reticulated python (*Python reticulatus*) is the longest snake in the world. It is found in the Nicobar Islands. The average length is between 3 and 6 m (10 and 20 ft). While the reticulated python prefers small mammals, it can take larger animals up to the size of a full-grown wild boar.

Only snake that builds a nest

The female king cobra (*Ophiophagus hannah*) is the only snake that builds a nest and is found in the Western Ghats, parts of north India, eastern India, the north-east and the Andaman Islands. It builds a 30 cm (11.8 in.) nest by scraping leaves, weeds and loose vegetation together.

Fastest snake

Rat snakes and bronze-back tree snakes can reach a speed of 10 km per hour.

Loudest hiss

Russell's viper (*Daboia russelii*) hisses the loudest among all Indian snakes – nearly as loud as the hiss of a pressure cooker.

Only 'flying' snake

The ornate flying snake (*Chrysopelea ornata*) is capable of gliding by launching itself from a height. An instance of this species gliding for a distance of 50 m (164 ft) has been recorded. This snake inhabits the hilly forests of the south-west and the north-east, besides the Andaman Islands.

Ornate flying snake

Only snake with heat sensors

The pit viper (subfamily Crotalinae), found in the hilly parts of India, is able to locate warm-blooded prey using two heat sensors between its nostrils and eyes.

Snake at the highest altitude

No other species of snake has been found at an altitude higher than the Himalayan pit viper (*Gloydius himalayanus*). Herpetologist Frank Wall (1868–1950), who lived in Sri Lanka and India, claimed to have seen one at an altitude of 3,658 m (12,000 ft) in Kashmir and one was captured at the foot of the glacier at Dharamshala at an altitude of 4,877 m (16,000 ft).

FISH AND MOLLUSCS

Oldest freshwater fish

Fossil remains of the Dipnoi subclass of fish or lungfish (*Ceratodus agassiz*) were found in the Maleri beds of the Godavari Valley in the late Triassic period (237–201.3 million years ago). The genus *Ceratodus* evolved in the northern hemisphere in the early Triassic period (251–247 million years ago).

Lightest/smallest fish

The dwarf pygmy goby (*Pandaka pygmaea*) is 1 cm (0.39 in.) long and weighs 4–5 mg.

Only fish with suction plates

The remora or suckerfish (family Echeneidae) can swim but is usually found attached to sharks, turtles, dolphins and even ships. The first dorsal fin is modified into a suction apparatus, and the erection of the plate where the fish joins its host creates a vacuum, enabling the fish to stay attached.

Heaviest fish

The whale shark *(Rhincodon typus)* is the largest and heaviest shark in India, weighing up to 60 tonnes.

Only fish without a bony skeleton

Sharks (and their relatives, the guitarfish and swordfish) do not have a bony skeleton. They have cartilage or gristle. They are predominantly marine fish with a few freshwater representatives.

Only male fish producing young

Seahorses (Genus *Hippocampus*) are predominantly marine. The male fish carries a kangaroo-like pouch in its belly. The female passes her eggs into this pouch where the father incubates them. The young are thus born from the father.

A seahorse

TORTOISES AND TURTLES

1 Largest rookery

The 12 km long sandy beach in the Gahirmatha region of Odisha is one of the largest rookeries for marine sea turtles. During February and March, olive ridley turtles (*Lepidochelys olivacea*) come out here in hundreds of thousands to mate and nest. The olive ridley is one of the seven endangered species of turtles in the world due to the disturbance and destruction of their habitat.

2 Largest turtle

The leatherback sea turtle (*Dermochelys coriacea*) has a shell length averaging 2.5 m (8 ft) and weighs 700 kg. It feeds mainly on jellyfish.

3 Largest terrapin

The Batagur terrapin (*Batagur baska*), found in the river estuaries of the Sundarbans, West Bengal, is the largest terrapin and a critically endangered species. The carapace of this terrapin is 59 cm (23 in.) long.

4 Smallest tortoise

The Indian star tortoise (*Geochelone elegans*) grows to a length of around 15 cm (5.9 in.).

5 Smallest carapace

The Cochin cane forest turtle (*Vijayachelys silvatica*) has a carapace that is 13 cm (5.1 in.) long.

6 Rarest freshwater turtle

India's rarest freshwater turtle is possibly the Assam leaf turtle (*Cyclemys dentata*), found in the hill streams of Assam. It grows to a length of around 24 cm (9.4 in.).

Olive Ridleys galore!

Between 23 February and 2 March, Odisha's Ganjam District saw the arrival of a record 6.37 lakh Olive Ridley turtles for mass nesting. This huge number was attributed to the emergence of new beaches that remained unaffected by extreme weather conditions. These turtles, labelled as vulnerable by the IUCN, dig holes in the sand using their flippers, lay eggs, and cover them before returning to the sea. The eggs hatch after 40–60 days and the hatchlings make their way back into the sea. The Gahirmatha Beach in the Kendrapara District of Odisha also sees the arrival of turtles and is known as the world's largest rookery.

Only anadromous fish

Hilsa (*Tenualosa ilisha*) is India's only anadromous fish, which migrates from the sea or estuarine waters up rivers for breeding. This fish is found mostly in the Gangetic estuary.

WR Largest recorded subterranean fish

A fish measuring around 45 cm (17.7 in.) was discovered in a cave in Meghalaya in February 2019. It was discovered by Daniel Harries, a biologist from Heriot-Watt University in Edinburgh, UK.

Shortest-lived fish

Small fish such as the *Pandaka pygmaea* and those from the families Oreichthys and Gambusia (such as mosquito fish) live hardly for a year.

Longest-lived fish

The common carp, a freshwater fish that is found in ponds, lakes and large rivers, is said to live for over 50 years if left alone.

Largest clam

The giant clam (*Tridacna gigas*) grows to a length of 1 m (3 ft 3.4 in.) and weighs over 100 kg. This clam has been exploited throughout its Asia-Pacific range, but is fortunately plentiful in the coral reefs of the Andaman and Nicobar Islands.

PLANTS

Oldest plant fossils

Fossils, which are 1.6 billion years old and appear to contain red algae, were found embedded in mats of cyanobacteria in phosphate-rich sedimentary rocks in Chitrakoot in central India, in May 2017. Until this discovery, the oldest known red algae were 1.2 billion years old.

Longest-lived tree species

The banyan tree (*Ficus benghalensis*), found in most parts of India, is known to have lived for more than 250 years.

Fastest-maturing trees

The eucalyptus and the subabul (*Leucaena leucocephala*) trees mature very fast and are both ready for cutting in 6–7 years.

Tallest trees

The fir (*Abies pindrow*) and deodar (*Cedrus deodara*) grow to an average height of 76.2 m (250 ft).

Biggest tree trunk

The deodar (*Cedrus deodara*) found in Jammu and Kashmir, Himachal Pradesh, and Uttarakhand have trunks with a circumference of around 12 m (39 ft 4 in.) or more.

Largest hollow tree

A baobab or monkey-bread tree (*Adansonia digitata*), which is a species of

African origin, stands amid the ruins of the eastern part of the historic Golconda Fort near Hyderabad, Telangana. Reportedly, its 3.3 sq. m (35.5 sq. ft) hollow trunk can comfortably accommodate 10–12 people.

Tallest flower

- The gigantic Himalayan rhubarb (*Rheum nobile*) grows 0.9–1.2 m (3–4 ft) long. It is found even at 4,268 m (14,000 ft) in the Himalayan ranges.
- The corpse flower (*Amorphophallus titanum*) or 'titan arum', though not a native species, is the tallest flower (2.4 m/7 ft 10 in.) in India, and the largest by diameter (more than 1 m/3 ft 3.3 in.).

The gigantic Himalayan rhubarb

Largest tree canopy

A banyan tree identified in Anantapur District of Andhra Pradesh in 1988, by freelance photographers 'Regret Iyer' and K.S. Ramakrishna from Bangalore (now Bengaluru), Karnataka, was reported to have a canopy covering 2.1 hectares (5.19 acres) and was believed to be over 600 years old.

Plants at the highest altitude

- The *Ermania himalayensis* grows at 6,000 m (19,685 ft) in the Himalayas.
- *Christolea himalayensis*, a herb usually about 10–15 cm (3.9–5.9 in.) tall, is found at 5,000–6,000 m (16,404–19,685 ft).

Longest creeper

The elephant creeper (*Argyreia nervosa*) grows to a length of 1.5 km, making it the longest creeper in the country and one of the longest in the world.

Largest family of plants

The Family Poaceae is the largest plant family in the country, and is represented by as many as 263 genera and 1,291 species. Poaceae or Gramineae is a ubiquitous family of monocotyledonous flowering plants known as grass. The Poaceae family includes cereal grass, bamboo and grasses of natural grasslands as well as the grasses of cultivated lawns and pastures.

Rare flowering

Found in southern and eastern India, the talipot palm (*Corypha umbraculifera*) flowers once in 25–80 years and then dies.

Lightest wood

Balsa (*Ochroma lagopus*) has a specific gravity of 0.12 to 0.15.

Heaviest fruit

The jackfruit tree (*Artocarpus heterophyllus*) is planted (but also grows wild) in the Western Ghats and elsewhere in India. The tree bears fruit of enormous size – weighing up to 40 kg.

Largest leaf

The leaf of the water lily (*Victoria amazonica*) may measure up to 1.5 m (5 ft) in diameter.

Heaviest wood

Anjan (*Hardwickia binata*) wood is the heaviest, with a specific gravity of 0.61–0.73.

Tallest bamboo/grass

The tallest bamboo (*Dendrocalamus giganteus*), known as dragon bamboo, is found in Assam and West Bengal. It grows up to 40 m (130 ft) with a diameter of around 20–25 cm (8–10 in.).

CONSERVING NATURE AND WILDLIFE

Oldest botanical garden

The Acharya Jagadish Chandra Bose Indian Botanic Garden was established in 1787 in Shibpur, Howrah, near Kolkata in West Bengal. It has about 12,000 living plants and 2.5 million dried plant specimens in the herbarium, from all over the world. The garden covers 276.75 acres (112 hectares) in 25 sections.

Oldest zoos

- Raja Rajendra Mallick Bahadur started the Marble Palace Aviary and Zoo in Calcutta (now Kolkata), West Bengal, in 1854 specifically for the education and entertainment of the public.
- The Thiruvananthapuram Zoological Gardens in Kerala is said to have been set up by Maharaja Swathi Thirunal in 1859. Spread over 30 acres (12 hectares), it is the oldest extant zoo.

First marine reserve

The Marine National Park and Sanctuary in Jamnagar District, Gujarat, forms the first marine reserve in India. Including Pirotan Island and other islands, it was given the status of a national park in 1980. It is rich in corals, octopuses, giant snails, sponges, crabs, lobsters and fish.

On the Verge of Extinction

As per the IUCN list, 73 species in India are now under the critically endangered category. This includes 9 mammals, 18 birds, 26 reptiles, and 20 amphibians. The number has risen from 47 in September 2011. Of the 73 species, 8 mammals and 5 reptiles are endemic to India while several amphibian species are restricted to the Western Ghats, the north-east, and the Andaman and Nicobar Islands. To provide the highest level of protection to these animals, the government is now considering including the most critically endangered species in the Schedule-1 of the Wildlife (Protection) Act, 1972.

Arignar Anna Zoological Park, Vandalur

Largest zoological park

Arignar Anna Zoological Park at Vandalur, near Chennai, Tamil Nadu, is the largest zoological park in South Asia. Spread over 602 hectares (1,487.57 acres), it has more than 100 species of birds, 50 species of mammals, and 20 species of reptiles.

First conservation organization

The Indian Board for Wildlife (IBWL), with S. Dharmakumar Sinhji as its vice chairman, was set up in 1952 by the Government of India. It was replaced by the National Board for Wildlife (NBWL) in September 2003.

First virtual herbarium

Since February 2017, a virtual digital herbarium of specimens preserved in the Kerala Forest Research Institute at Peechi in Thrissur District, Kerala, can be accessed at the URL http://kfriherbarium.in.

Oldest NGO to be engaged in conservation and biodiversity research

On 15 September 1883, eight men established the Bombay Natural History Society at the then Victoria and Albert Museum (now Dr Bhau Daji Lad Museum) in Bombay (now Mumbai), Maharashtra. It was established to exchange information on natural history and exhibit interesting specimens. They were E.H. Aitken, Dr G.A. Maconochie, Dr D. MacDonald, J. C. Anderson, Colonel C. Swinhoe, J. Johnston, Dr Atmaram Pandurang and Dr Sakharam Arjun, along with H.M. Phipson.

First wildlife magazine

Indian Wildlife was published by Jim Corbett in the 1930s.

Highest national park

The Kanchenjunga Biosphere Reserve or the Khangchendzonga National Park in Sikkim is the highest national park at 8,585 m (28,166 ft) above mean sea level.

WR Largest camera trap tiger census

India's tiger census of 2018 became the largest camera trap wildlife survey in the world. Camera traps (outdoor photographic devices fitted with motion sensors that start recording when an animal passes by) were placed in 26,838 locations across 141 different sites and surveyed an effective area of 121,337 sq. km as part of the survey. Individual tigers (excluding cubs numbering 2,461) were identified using the stripe pattern recognition software from the photographs clicked by camera traps.

State and UT with the most wildlife sanctuaries

Andaman and Nicobar Islands have 96 wildlife sanctuaries (389.39 sq. km) and Maharashtra has 46 (7,592.3 sq. km).

State and UT with most national parks

Madhya Pradesh leads with 10 national parks, with an area of 365,725 sq. km dedicated to them. Andaman and Nicobar Islands follow with nine national parks across 115,394 sq. km.

Largest collection of bamboo species

Prashant Atmaram Date, a bamboo farmer and entrepreneur from Lakhalgaon Village, Nashik Taluk and District, Maharashtra, has the largest collection of bamboo species in the country. He has a total of 94 species of 22 genera in one place called 'Date Bambusetum', where they are placed in flowerpots. Different species have been collected from bamboo-growing states for conservation away from their place of origin.

First national park

Jim Corbett National Park (earlier Hailey National Park and then Ramganga National Park), established in 1936, stretches over 521 sq. km across the two hill districts of Pauri Garhwal and Nainital, Uttarakhand. It is home to around 110 tree species, 50 species of mammals, 580 bird species, and 25 species of reptiles. It was the first to come under the Project Tiger initiative. The elevation of the park ranges from 400 m to 1,200 m (1,300 ft to 4,000 ft).

The Kosi River in Jim Corbett National Park

GARDENING

Tallest rose plant

Arunsinh Solanki grew a rose plant 11.88 m (39 ft) tall at his home in Godhra in Gujarat, as recorded on 13 May 2019.

Tallest prickly amaranth plant

In August 2017, T. Damodar and his wife Shobha T. Damodar from Belagavi, Karnataka, grew the tallest prickly amaranth plant (*Amaranthus spinosus*), which measured 4.03 m (13 ft 3 in.) in height. Normally this plant grows to a height of 0.3 m to 2.43 m (1–8 ft).

WR Tallest coriander plant

Dalbir Maan (b. 1 June 1982) grew a 2.28 m (7 ft 6 in.) tall coriander plant at his home in Melbourne, Australia, as recorded on 18 November 2020.

Tallest bougainvillea

Prof. Dr Ramesh Babu (b. 12 February 1957) has grown a 10.33 m (33 ft 11 in.) tall *Bougainvillea spectabilis* in his garden in Bengaluru, Karnataka. The over 16-year-old bougainvillea with white blossoms had a spread of 6.09 m (20 ft) and a base girth of 0.2 m (7.8 in.) as on 29 January 2020. Normally, bougainvillea grows to an average height of 6.09 m (20 ft).

Longest Drumstick

Rekha K.N. (b. 6 September 1973) from Kochi, Kerala, grew the longest drumstick (*Moringa oleifera*) on her drumstick tree. As on 17 April 2023, the drumstick measured 116.84 cm (46 in.).

Longest drumstick

Biggest lemon

K. Mohanchandran from Kothanur, Bengaluru, Karnataka, grew a lemon measuring 28 cm x 14 cm (11 in. x 5.5 in.) in his garden. The lemon had a circumference of 49 cm (19.2 in.) and weighed 2.365 kg on 22 February 2020.

Longest mango leaf

A mango tree with a leaf measuring 61 cm (2 ft) was found at the primary school of Budapur in Varanasi, Uttar Pradesh, by Dr Bhola Vishwakarma, one of the schoolteachers, on 30 October 2018.

Largest taro leaf

A taro (*Colocasia esculenta*) leaf measuring 76.0 cm x 64.5 cm (2 ft 5.9 in. x 2 ft 1.39 in.) was cultivated in Boudhgarh, Boudh District, Odisha, by Jayaram Rana on 7 January 2020.

NON FOSSIL FUEL INSTALLED CAPACITY (GW)

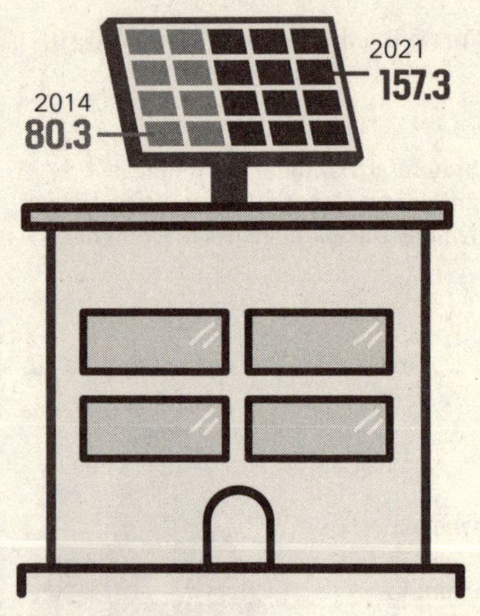

Source: Press Information Bureau Release December 2021, Ministry of New and Renewable Energy, Government of India

GOVERNMENT ANNUAL EXPENDITURE ON ENVIRONMENTAL PROTECTION (IN CRORES)

4,166

1,791

2015–2016

2020–2021

Source: Overview of EnviStats Vol I Environment Statistics, Ministry of Statistics and Programme Implementation, Government of India

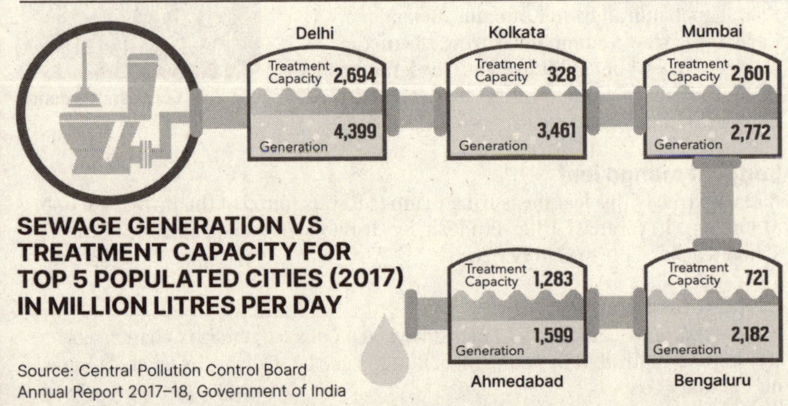

SEWAGE GENERATION VS TREATMENT CAPACITY FOR TOP 5 POPULATED CITIES (2017) IN MILLION LITRES PER DAY

Source: Central Pollution Control Board Annual Report 2017–18, Government of India

INDIA'S INVESTMENT IN RENEWABLE ENERGY (2015-21) IN USD BILLION

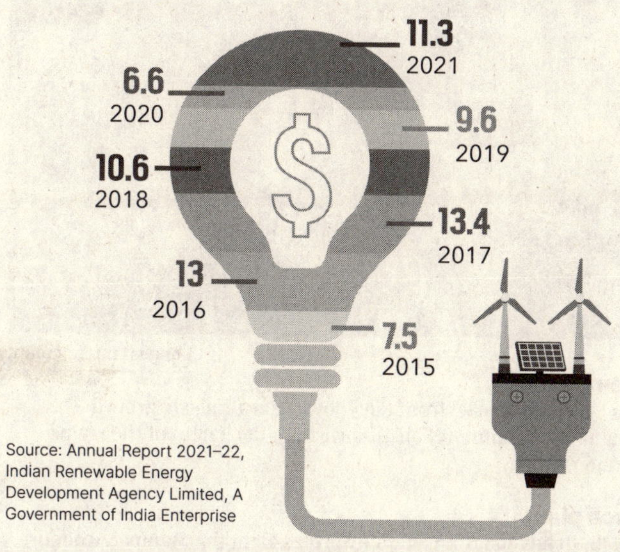

Source: Annual Report 2021–22, Indian Renewable Energy Development Agency Limited, A Government of India Enterprise

OZONE DEPLETING SUBSTANCE – PRODUCTION VS CONSUMPTION (IN MT)

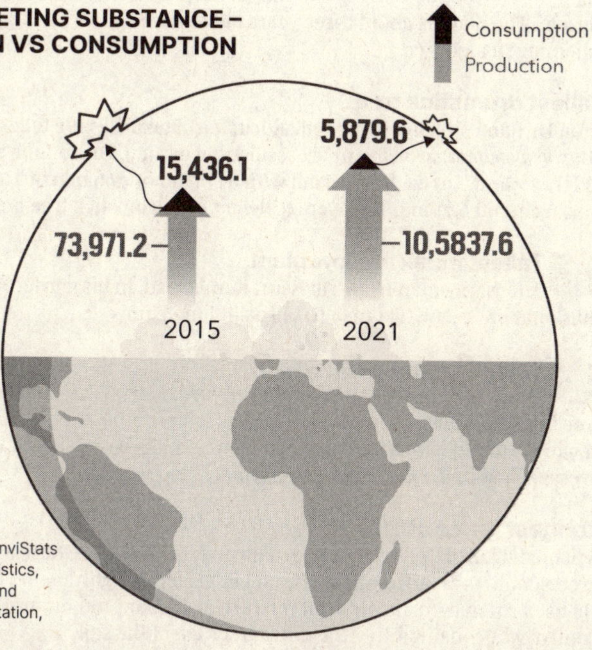

Consumption
Production

Year	Consumption	Production
2015	15,436.1	73,971.2
2021	5,879.6	10,5837.6

Source: Overview of EnviStats Vol I Environment Statistics, Ministry of Statistics and Programme Implementation, Government of India

Longest money plant

Longest money plant

Sapna Popli (b. 13 September 1982) from Lucknow, Uttar Pradesh, grew the longest money plant in her home. As on 21 April 2023, the length of the stem measured 38.4 ft (460.8 in.).

Longest tapioca plant

Satheesha Nayak (b. 16 July 1969), an anatomy professor at the Manipal Academy of Higher Education, Udupi, Karnataka, has grown the longest tapioca (cassava) plant, measuring 16.76 m (55 ft 10 in.), as on 30 January 2022, in his kitchen garden. The plant is about three years old and was provided support on an adjoining mango tree.

Tallest drumstick tree

Prof. Dr Ramesh Babu from Bengaluru, Karnataka, has the tallest drumstick tree (*Moringa oleifera*) growing in his residential garden. On 20 June 2019, the 11-year-old tree was 8.2 m (26 ft 11 in.) tall with a spread of 3.66 m (12 ft) and a base girth of 47.6 cm (1 ft 6.74 in.). The average height of a drumstick tree is 6.1 m (20 ft).

WR Tallest musk mallow plant

A.K. Narayanan from Thrissur, Kerala, had, in his garden, a three-year-old musk mallow plant, 2.74 m (9 ft) tall as in June 2016.

WR Tallest jamun tree

Prof. Dr Ramesh Babu from Bengaluru, Karnataka, has the tallest *jamun* tree (*Syzygium cumini*) in his garden. On 20 June 2019, the 15-year-old tree was 11.9 m (39 ft) tall with a spread of 6 m (20 ft) and a base girth of 1.04 m (41 in.). The average height of a jamun tree is 9.1–10.6 m (30–35 ft).

Longest green chilli

Krishnalal L.S. (b. 19 April 1982) of Thiruvananthapuram, Kerala, grew the longest green chilli, measuring 31 cm (12.1 in.) in his terrace garden in February 2020. He used a home-made nutrient mixture or organic and natural material for pest control while maintaining the nutrient grade of the soil.

ENVIRONMENT AND SUSTAINABILITY

First state/UT to place a ban on plastic bags

Sikkim became the first state to ban plastic bags in 1998. Local communities in Yuksom Village were upset by the harmful impact of plastics on the environment and formed the Khangchendzonga Conservation Committee (KCC), which banned plastic bags and bottles in 1996 and collected around 800 kg of plastic waste from trails and trek routes. Encouraged by their success, the state government announced a state wide ban on plastic bags on 4 June 1998.

First forest healing centre

India's first forest healing centre was inaugurated on 7 March 2021 in Ranikhet, Uttarakhand. Spread across an area of around 13 acres (5.26 hectares), it was developed by the research wing of the Uttarakhand Forest Department as a space where visitors can take walks, hug trees and engage in calming activities such as meditation and sky-gazing. The centre draws inspiration from the Japanese therapy of forest bathing (*shinrinyoku*) and ancient Indian traditions.

First green village

Khonoma Village, located in the Sechu-Zubza Subdivision of Kohima District, Nagaland, has become the country's first 'green village'. The first steps were taken by setting up the Khonoma Nature Conservation and Tragopan Sanctuary in 1998, leading to a ban on hunting in a 20 sq. km area. Ecological studies suggest that the village has 250 plant species, 204 species of trees, 45 varieties of orchids, and 19 varieties of bamboo. The fauna includes 25 varieties of snakes, kinds of lizards, 11 types of amphibians, and 196 bird species, including the Blyth's tragopan, which is categorized as vulnerable on the IUCN Red List.

First Indian winners of the Champions of the Earth Award

Tulsi Tanti, chairman and managing director of the wind turbine manufacturer Suzlon Energy Ltd, was the first Indian recipient of the Champions of the Earth Award in 2009 in the 'entrepreneurial vision' category. Since then, India has won five more awards. The latest recipients of the awards were Prime Minister Narendra Modi for policy leadership and the fully solar-powered Cochin International Airport for 'entrepreneurial vision' in 2018. The award is given by the United Nations Environment Programme.

Most waste collected – beach clean-up – single day

The Maharashtra Navnirman Paryavaran Sena, headquartered in Matunga, Mumbai, Maharashtra, set three records in waste collection on 11 December 2021, based on data available from 16 local governmental bodies:

- *Most waste collected – multiple venues*: 13,194 registered volunteers, among others, collected 59.2 tonnes of waste from 37 locations in seven districts of Maharashtra.
- *Most waste collected – single venue*: Volunteers collected 27 tonnes of waste

The Indian government has spent 78 billion USD as investment in renewable energy from 2014 to 2021.

from a single location – Uttan Beach, Bhavander, Thane District, Maharashtra.

• *Most participants in a waste collection campaign – multiple venues*: The clean-up campaign saw the participation of 13,194 registered volunteers across 37 locations in seven districts of Maharashtra.

First country to have a cooling action plan

The India Cooling Action Plan (ICAP) is the first cooling action plan in the world. It addresses cooling requirements across all sectors to reduce direct and indirect emissions. ICAP aims to balance socio-economic and environmental needs while reducing refrigerant transition and cooling demand, enhancing energy efficiency and evolving better technology options.

First solar-heated tent

Considered to be the first in the world, a 10-seater portable tent that can be heated using solar panels was built by engineer and innovator Sonam Wangchuk along with the Himalayan Institute of Alternatives of Ladakh (HIAL)

Solar Trees to the Rescue

The Council of Scientific and Industrial Research's Central Mechanical Engineering Research Institute (CSIR-CMERI) made and installed the largest solar tree in Ludhiana. The photovoltaic panels cover an area of 309.83 sq. metres and generates 50 kW of electricity. A solar tree resembles a regular tree while the canopy is made of solar panels which convert solar energy into electric energy. This electricity is transported via the branches and trunk into a battery at the base. This is a huge step forward in sustainable energy development and will revolutionize agriculture by providing energy for several farming activities. What is interesting is that these do not require a roof for installation and can be installed in fields as well!

for the Indian Army. Built in four weeks at a cost of ₹5 lakh (0.5 million), the tent weighs less than 30 kg and was specifically developed for Indian soldiers and army personnel serving in areas with very low temperatures.

WR Plog run with most participants

The biggest plog run (combining jogging with picking up litter – from Swedish *plockaupp*) was organized on Gandhi Jayanti on 2 October 2018 from 55 locations of Bengaluru, Karnataka. Plastic waste weighing 6.5 tonnes (6,500 kg), including bottles and litter, was collected by 6,518 participants in four hours from 7:00 a.m. to 11:00 a.m. The participants, representing five organizations – BBMP (Bruhat Bengaluru Mahanagara Palike), Go Native, Namma Nimma Cycle Foundation, Let's Be the Change, United Way Bengaluru – and an individual, Ramakrishna Ganesh, created awareness on urban cleanliness by proper disposal of waste, especially plastic.

Tallest scrap-metal structure – group

A group of 120 students, training to be fitters, welders, electricians, plumbers, and painters at the Government ITI in Berhampur, Ganjam District, Odisha, created the tallest scrap-metal structure, a 21.33 m (70 ft) tall guitar, over a period of three months from 17 July 2019. The 'Best out of waste' mission sought to integrate skill development with waste management in an eco-friendly manner. The guitar was exhibited at the open-air Scrap Sculpture Museum of the ITI, along with 10 other smaller sculptures, which were also created from waste.

Widest scrap-metal structure – group

The Home Designers organization from Jodhpur, Rajasthan, created the widest replica of a blue whale, measuring 104 ft (31.7 m) in width from scrap metal. The team comprised 100 people who began work on the structure on 6 January 2023. It took 10 days to complete the structure.

Most trees planted – 15 mins

Under the supervision of the National Service Scheme (NSS) Programme Officer Shyam Sunder of the Government Dungar College, Bikaner, Rajasthan, a total of 1,05,000 saplings were planted at three locations in Gajsukhdesar Village in 3 min 50 sec by a team of 15,000 participants comprising NSS volunteers, schoolchildren and villagers on 4 August 2008. The total land covered under the plantation was 1,200 bighas (300 hectares).

Most trees planted – 1 hour

As part of the Green India Challenge, an initiative by J. Santhosh Kumar, a member of Parliament (Rajya Sabha) from Telangana, 3,54,900 trees were planted in 1 hr on 4 July 2021 in Durga Nagar, Adilabad, Telangana. The 16,900 people involved in the plantation drive planted 21 trees each.

WR Most saplings distributed – single day

The Department of Environment, Forest and Climate Change and the Department of Tourism, Government of Uttar Pradesh, along with the Prayagraj District Administration, Uttar Pradesh, distributed 76,824 saplings on 9 August 2019. This was part of their larger campaign for tree plantation.

CLEANEST IN INDIA!

1 Cleanest city

The Swachh Bharat Mission 2022 ranked Indore in Madhya Pradesh as the cleanest city of the country for the sixth time in a row, among cities with a population of more than 10 lakh (one million). Surat in Gujarat and Navi Mumbai in Maharashtra were ranked the second and the third cleanest cities, respectively, in the same category. Among the country's smaller cities with a population less than 10 lakh, Tirupati in Andhra Pradesh was ranked first, followed by Mysuru in Karnataka and New Delhi (NDMC).

2 Cleanest state

The Swachh Bharat Mission, the Central government's annual cleanliness survey to promote urban sanitation standards, ranked Chhattisgarh the cleanest state of India in 2021, for the third consecutive year. Maharashtra and Madhya Pradesh were ranked second and third, respectively.

First Green Energy Archaeological Site

The Shore Temple in Mahabalipuram (also known as Mamallapuram), Tamil Nadu, is a seventh century UNESCO World Heritage site that became India's first green energy archaeological site in September 2023. This means that the temple will be illuminated with clean and sustainable solar power completely. The change was possible after the successful implementation of Green Heritage Project, a collaborative initiative between the Renault Nissan Technology & Business Centre India (Renault Nissan Tech) and Hand in Hand India (HiH). As part of the project, three solar plants of 10 kW capacity have been set up in the region to harness solar energy and reduce carbon footprint in the area. The project promotes sustainable ecotourism with minimal ecological footprint.

Other highlights of the Green Heritage Project at the temple include women-operated electric buggies, solar-operated reverse osmosis plant that provides clean drinking water, dedicated parking shed with three charging units for electric vehicles among others.

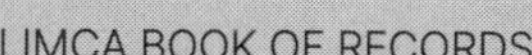

Most trees planted – single day

The Department of Forests and Wildlife, Uttar Pradesh, planted 258,747,661 saplings in a day on 5 July 2020, with the participation of various departments of the state as well as the general public. Starting at 5:55 a.m., the plantation work at selected plantation sites in all 75 districts concluded at 6:00 p.m. This was part of their larger campaign for tree plantation.

Most trees planted – in a quarter

The Maharashtra Forest Department, with the support of individual volunteers, planted 35,13,76,361 seedlings across the state between 1 July and 30 September 2019. The plantation work was done by 9,51,963.5 million people at 23,986.8 million plantation sites. To integrate the work of the forest department, the government hosted a Plantation Monitoring Information System (PMIS) and captured the plantation data of forest and non-forest agencies.

Planting a sapling

Largest single rooftop solar plant – by area

On 17 May 2016, a rooftop solar power plant was inaugurated at the Dera Baba Jaimal Singh (Radha Soami sect) premises at Beas, Amritsar District, Punjab. Spread over 42 acres (17 ha), the plant is the largest single rooftop facility and can generate 11.5 MW of electricity. The solar panels are laid over 82 acres (33.18 hectares) on eight rooftops and the project is planned to cater to 8,000 households.

Largest biogas plant – by capacity

As a step towards clean and green energy, Asia's largest compressed biogas (CBG) plant with a total capacity of 33.23 tonnes CBG per day was commissioned on 12 August 2022 at Bhuttal Kalan village in Sangrur District, Punjab.

First railway station with Green Building Certification

Kevadia railway station in Gujarat, from whose third-level platform one can view the Statue of Unity, is India's first railway station with a Green Building Certification by the Indian Green Building Council (IGBC). The railway station features LED lights and star-rated branded electrical appliances to save electricity; water management through rainwater harvesting; a sewage treatment plant; waterless eco-urinals; and drip irrigation. Additionally, the segregated green waste will be reused to produce fertilizers.

Tallest scrap-metal structure – solo

Sandeep Pisalkar from Vadodara, Gujarat, created a replica of the iconic Eiffel Tower, measuring 21.33 m (70 ft) in height, with 40 tonnes (4,000 kg) of automobile scrap. The three levels of the structure were created separately and then assembled with the help of a crane. The material used included petrol tanks from trucks, C-channels, angles and clutch plates. It was exhibited at the Waste to Wonder Park, New Delhi, in February 2019.

TRANSPORT

AIR

First flight

On 18 February 1911, Henri Pequet flew a Humber-Sommer biplane carrying mail from Allahabad (now Prayagraj), Uttar Pradesh, to Naini Junction. It flew a distance of 10 km. However, Proper and official civil aviation began on 15 October 1932, when aviator and industrialist J.R.D. Tata flew 2092 km on the aircraft D.H. *Puss Moth*. The flight took place under the aegis of Tata Air Services. It delivered mail from the Drigh Road Aerodrome in Karachi (now in Pakistan) to Juhu Aerodrome in Bombay (now Mumbai) Maharashtra, and then continued to Madras (now Chennai).

First pilot licence

J.R.D. Tata, an aviator, entrepreneur and chairman of Tata Group, became the first licensed pilot in India when he received his pilot licence No. 1 in 1929.

First airline

Tata Airlines, set up by J.R.D. Tata soon after he piloted India's maiden civil flight in 1932, was later converted into a public company in 1946 under the name Air-India Ltd, with him as its chairman. In March 1953, it was raised to be a public corporation and became Air India. The state-run carrier was privatized to the Tata Group in 2021.

First airfield

The grass aerodrome at Juhu in Mumbai, opened in 1932. It was the base for Tata Airlines.

First aircraft designer

S.V. Setty, an assistant engineer with the Public Works Department, Mysore (now Mysuru), Karnataka, in 1911–12, designed, piloted, and helped manufacture planes at Avro (a British company). With an eight cylinder engine, the Avro biplane had a 9.76 m (32 ft) span and weighed 362.8 kg without a pilot or passenger. The plane touched a speed of around 72–80 km/hr.

First helicopter school

Hindustan Aeronautics Ltd (HAL), based in Bangalore (now Bengaluru), Karnataka, established a training school on 1 May 2000 for potential aviators

Crash of the Princess

Twenty-nine months after the Malabar Princess's first flight, it crashed on 3 November 1950 into the terrains of Rochers de la Tournette in the French Alps. The 48 passengers who were on board were all killed. These included the captain, co-pilot, navigators, and a radio operator. The debris was found by another aeroplane two days later. The crash inspired many films and books.

to obtain commercial as well as private helicopter pilot licences.

Passenger traffic amounted to over 327 million at airports across India in financial year 2023.

First flying club

The Aero Club was established in Mumbai, by industrial magnate Sir Victor Sassoon in 1928. In September 1929, the club was affiliated to the Royal Aero Club, UK. It was recognized by the Government of India as the coordinating body for flying clubs in India. In 1948, the club was affiliated to the Federation Aeronautique Internationale.

First international flight

The *Malabar Princess* of the Air India International Corporation, with Captain K.R. Guzder in command, flew from Bombay to London, UK, via Cairo (Egypt), and Geneva (Switzerland), on 8 June 1948, carrying 35 passengers.

First aeronautical society

On 17 December 1948, the Aeronautical Society of India was inaugurated at Bengaluru to promote advancement in the field of aeronautics and dissemination of knowledge about aeronautical science and aircraft engineering to the public.

First radio plane

The twin-engine aeroplane called de Havilland DH-89 Dragon Rapide, which was on the Karachi- Bombay-Colombo route, was equipped with wireless transmission facilities on 1 December 1937.

First crash

On 17 July 1950, a DC-3 aircraft was recorded to have crashed near Pathankot, Punjab, tragically killing all 22 passengers.

First cargo service

An air cargo service started on 21 May 1927, between Calcutta (now Kolkata), West Bengal, and Bagdogra in Darjeeling District of West Bengal, by West Bengal Air Transport, operated for only a week.

First air ticket booking office

The first air ticket booking office was opened in 1939 in a building in the Churchgate Reclamation area in Bombay. The space now houses the Asiatic Department Store.

First air freight service

Air Freight Pvt. Ltd was set up in 1945 as handling agents for Tata Airlines and Air India International. It was also the first air cargo clearing agent.

First indigenously assembled plane

The first HS-748 was assembled at the Aircraft Manufacturing Depot, Kanpur, Uttar Pradesh, and delivered to Indian Airlines on 27 June 1967.

Air India flight

First all-jet carrier

In 1962, Air India became the world's first all-jet carrier when it replaced Super Constellation planes with a fleet of Boeing 707.

First indigenous aircraft

The Hindustan Trainer-2, built by Hindustan Aeronautics Ltd (HAL), Bangalore, made its maiden flight in August 1951. Meant for military use, it was also used by flying schools.

First Boeing 737-900 aircraft

Jet Airways acquired the first Boeing 737-900 aircraft in May 2003. The aircraft can seat up to 190 passengers and is the longest among the Boeing 737 family. It has a maximum flight range of 5,084 km. In 2018, Jet Airways took the delivery of the first 150 Boeing 737 MAX acroplanes, becoming the first Indian carrier to fly the new variant.

First indigenous helicopter

The advanced light helicopter (ALH) was built at HAL, Bangalore, in 1992. The ALH was used both in defence and civil operations.

First jet

Air India entered the jet age on 20 April 1960, when its Boeing 707 *Gauri Shankar* flew to London. Soon after, on 14 May 1960, it flew to New York. With this, India became the first Asian country to operate a transatlantic flight. The aircraft was written off after a landing accident at Bombay on 22 June 1982.

First air taxi

India's first air taxi service started at Chandigarh Airport on 14 January 2021 under the UDAN-RCS (Regional Connectivity Scheme) of the Central government. With the capacity to seat a pilot and three passengers, the daily flight was of 45-minute duration and it plied on the Chandigarh–Hisar route at a cost of ₹1,755 per seat.

First air varsity

The Central Training Establishment in Hyderabad (now in Telangana), an independent training centre of Indian Airlines Ltd, was upgraded to a deemed university in 1997. The centre is equipped with infrastructure and training facilities for courses in civil aviation.

First air traffic control system

A state-of-the-art Air Traffic Control (ATC) system, supported by Raytheon flight data and equipped with radar-processing hardware, was installed at the Indira Gandhi International Airport (IGIA), New Delhi, on 14 January 1999. It provided three-dimensional radial, bearing, and height information regarding the location and situation of any aircraft within a range of 250 nautical miles.

First heliport

India's first heliport was inaugurated at Rohini, Delhi, on 28 February 2017. Built by Pawan Hans Ltd, it is spread over an area of 25 acres (10.12 hectares) and has four hangars, nine parking bays, and a terminal building that has a capacity of 150 passengers. The first such facility in South Asia, it helps in offshore transport, emergency medical services, promoting heli-tourism, and reducing the congestion on the IGIA, Delhi.

First airport to install full-body scanner

The first full-body scanner system was installed on a trial basis at Terminal 1D of the Indira Gandhi International Airport, New Delhi, on 10 April 2010. Initially the system was used only on volunteering passengers and the scanning process took less than a minute. The scanning system, called SmartCheck, was built by American Science and Engineering (AS&E). The system works on the X-ray backscatter technology.

Highest commercial airport

Kushok Bakula Rimpochee Airport (or Leh airport) in Leh, Ladakh, is the highest commercial airport at 3,256 m (10,682 ft) above mean sea level. The airport is named after Kushok Bakula Rinpoche, whose Spituk Monastery is very close to the airfield. The Indian Air Force handed over the airport to the Airport Authority of India in 2016.

First airport to install waste recycling machines

The Rajiv Gandhi International Airport (RGIA) in Hyderabad, Telangana, became the first airport in the country to install waste recycling machines. It was launched as a pilot project in October 2017. Operated by GMR Hyderabad International Airport Ltd (GHIAL), the airport has equipment to crush and recycle plastic PET (polyethylene terephthalate) bottles, steel or aluminium cans and plastic bags into reusable raw material. These 'Swachh Bharat Recycling Machines' were designed and created by Mumbai-based company Wild West Media, and can be used to manufacture upcycled goods like bags, wallets, and denim. Passengers may make a donation or claim discount coupons in return for submitting their waste and plastic products. The RGIA is also the first airport to have its own composting plant, which processes the food waste generated at the airport.

Largest passenger airport terminal

On 3 July 2010, Terminal 3 of the Indira Gandhi International Airport, New Delhi, became India's and South Asia's largest aviation hub, with the capacity to

The Indira Gandhi Rashtriya Uran Akademi (IGRUA) was established on 7 November 1985.

handle more than 40 million (four crore) passengers a year. The airport handled over 69.23 million (6.923 crore) passengers in 2018–19.

The number of airports in India have gone up from 74 in 2014 to 147 in 2022.

First Boeing 787 Dreamliner

The Boeing 787 Dreamliner, a fuel-efficient aircraft, can carry up to 290 passengers and fly 15,750 km at a stretch. It touched down for the first time at the Indira Gandhi International Airport, New Delhi, on 13 July 2011.

WR Highest airfield

The Daulat Beg Oldi airstrip in Ladakh, is the highest airfield in the world. It is situated at an altitude of 5065 m (16,617 ft). The Indian Air Force landed a C-130J Super Hercules aircraft at this airfield, reactivating it in 2013.

Oldest fleet

Founded in 1932 as Tata Airlines and renamed in 1946 as Air India Ltd, this airline has a fleet size of 125 aircrafts (excluding subsidiaries), with an average age of 8.2 years, making it the oldest fleet in India. The airline has its headquarters in New Delhi.

Oldest to obtain a commercial pilot's licence

Captain Rajagopal Nagarajan (b. 25 April 1962) from Coimbatore, Tamil Nadu, joined the commercial pilot's course after retiring from the Indian Air Force. He obtained the commercial pilot's licence (CPL) from the Civil Aviation Authority, Philippines, at 48 years on 11 December 2009.

First woman commercial pilot

The first woman commercial pilot was Prem Mathur for Deccan Airways in 1951.

Most air freight traffic

Indira Gandhi International Airport, New Delhi, handled over 737,000 tonnes of freight traffic by the end of financial year 2021.

WR First fully solar-powered airport

The Cochin International Airport in Kochi, Kerala, became the first airport in the world to run completely on solar power on 18 August 2015. The solar

Cochin International Airport, Kochi

Fourth Runway at Delhi Airport

Indira Gandhi International Airport became one of the first airports in India to have four runways. Jyotiraditya Scindia, inaugurated the fourth runway. These are called the elevated taxiways. These runways have increased the air traffic capacity from 1400-1500 to 2000 movements per day. The airport can now serve more than 109 million passengers annually.

plant installed at the airport has 46,000 solar panels and can produce 50,000 to 60,000 units of electricity every day. The airport won the Champion of Earth Prize, awarded by the United Nations, in 2018.

First dual-way elevated Taxiway

On 14 July 2023, the country's first dual-way elevated taxiway was inaugurated at the Indira Gandhi International Airport, New Delhi. The elevated taxiway reduces taxi distance for aircraft by 7km and annual carbon dioxide emissions by 53,000 tonnes. The Eastern Cross Taxiway is 2.1 km long and 44 m wide to allow the safe passage of two big aircraft.

WR Highest number of women pilots

In a report released by Air Line Pilots Association, International (ALPA), in 2018, India led the charts in the number of female pilots among all countries. Around 13 per cent of the pilots in the country are women whereas the global average is only 5 per cent. This means that out of every eight flights in India, one is flown by a woman. Airlines such as IndiGo, SpiceJet and Air India have the highest recruitment numbers for women pilots.

WR First woman Airbus commander

Captain Indraani Singh, who joined Indian Airlines in April 1986, was the first Indian and Asian woman to fly the Airbus A320, in 1989, and became the world's first woman commander of the wide-bodied Airbus A300 in August 1996.

First woman airbus pilot

On 14 May 1987, Durba Banerjee became the first woman to co-pilot a flight – Airbus A300 – on the Calcutta–New Delhi–Calcutta route.

First woman chairperson of the International Civil Aviation Organization (ICAO) Aviation Security Committee

Shefali Juneja was elected chairperson of the ICAO Aviation Security Committee on 17 September 2021. A specialized agency of the UN, ICAO was formed to support and help nations with diplomacy and cooperation in air transport. India held the position 12 years ago. Shefali was also appointed as the representative in the council of ICAO in 2019.

First woman to obtain a pilot's licence

Urmila K. Parekh became the first woman to obtain a pilot's licence in 1930.

First woman chief executive officer of an airline

Harpreet A. De Singh was appointed chief executive officer (CEO) of Alliance Air, a regional subsidiary of Air India, on 30 October 2020. Previously executive director for flight safety in Air India, she became the first woman CEO of an airline. She was also the first woman pilot to be selected by Air India in 1988.

Longest direct-route flight with an all-woman cockpit crew

Air India's flight AI-176 made history on 11 January 2021 when an all-woman cockpit crew flew a distance of 16,000 km from San Francisco, California, to Bengaluru, Karnataka. The flight departed on 9 January 2021 and was flown by four pilots – Captain Zoya Aggarwal, Captain Papagari Thanmai, Captain Shivani Manhas and Captain Akansha Sonaware. The longest commercial flight to be operated by an Indian airline and longest flight entering India, its flying time was 17 hours and its route remarkably included flying over the North Pole.

First woman offshore captain

Captain Mayuri V. Deshmukh (b. 11 November 1982) with Commercial Helicopter Pilot License 991 became the first woman offshore captain in the country when she flew from Juhu to Mumbai High, Mumbai, Maharashtra, as captain from 11:07 a.m. to 1:25 p.m. on 8 March 2022. She was working for Pawan Hans Ltd (PHL) at the time. She has complied with the syllabus laid down by the Directorate General of Civil Aviation (DGCA) and validated by Oil and Natural Gas Company Ltd.

WR First three-point disembarkation system

IndiGo, a leading Indian airline with its headquarters at Gurugram, Haryana, introduced a three-point disembarkation system in a global first on 4 August 2022. To mark its 16th anniversary, the airline introduced a disembarkation process that was carried out from two forward and one rear exit ramp.

Longest length of runways

The Indira Gandhi International Airport, New Delhi, has the longest stretch of airport runways in the country, with a length of 4,430 m (14,534 ft).

Largest passenger airline

IndiGo, with its headquarters at Gurugram, Haryana, is the largest passenger airline in India by passengers carried and fleet size. Since its inception in August 2006, it has grown from one plane to a fleet of 269 aircraft. It is also the largest individual Asian low-cost carrier in terms of jet fleet size. It has a destination count of 100 with 74 domestic destinations and 26 international ones.

RAIL AND METRO

First passenger train

India's first passenger train chugged away from Bori Bunder (later renamed Victoria Terminus, and then Chhatrapati Shivaji Maharaj Terminus) station in Mumbai to Thane, Maharashtra, on 16 April 1853. It was pulled by three locomotives named *Sindh*, *Sultan* and *Sahib*, and carried 400 passengers in 14 railway carriages. This historic journey, which was of about 1 hr 15 mins duration, was flagged off with a 21-gun salute.

First rail construction company

R.M. Stephenson, a British railway engineer, formed the East Indian Railway (EIR) Company in 1844 for the construction of railways. In a contract signed on 17 August 1849, the EIR and the Great Indian Peninsula (GIP) Railway Company, England, were authorized to construct and operate railway lines at Kolkata, West Bengal, Mumbai, Maharashtra.

First indigenous railway carriages

The first railway coaches made in India were built by two coach-building firms in Kolkata, West Bengal: Steward and Company, and Seton and Company. John Hodgson was the chief engineer of the East Indian Railway Company then, and the coaches were employed for the first train journey from Howrah to Hooghly in West Bengal on 15 August 1854.

First double-decker train

India's first double-decker train was the *Flying Ranee*, a superfast train that runs between Mumbai Central and Surat station. It began operating in 1906, was halted in 1939 due to the Second World War, and resumed in 1950 as a daily service train.

First double-decker coaches

The Bombay, Baroda and Central India (BB&CI) Railway Company in Mumbai, introduced the first double-decker coaches in 1862.

Fastest train

The fastest train in India is the Vande Bharat Express or Train 18, which reached a top speed of 180 km/hr during test runs. Its current operating speed is 130 km/hr. The train runs on four routes: New Delhi–Varanasi, New Delhi–Shri Mata Vaishno Devi Katra, Mumbai Central–Gandhinagar, New Delhi-Amb Andaura.

First tramway company

The Calcutta Tramway Company was registered in London, in 1880. The Government of West Bengal nationalized it in 1976.

First locomotive factory

The first locomotive factory in India was set up at Chittaranjan in Paschim Bardhaman District, West Bengal, in 1950. The first diesel locomotive, with an imported engine, was manufactured at the Varanasi Diesel Locomotive Works, Varanasi, Uttar Pradesh, on 4 January 1964.

First tramcars

A horse-drawn tramcar ran on a 3.8 km route between Sealdah and Armenian Ghat Street in Calcutta (now (Kolkata), West Bengal, on 24 February 1873.

First deluxe train

The first deluxe train, the *Deccan Queen*, began between Victoria Terminus, Bombay and Poona (now Pune), Maharashtra, on 1 June 1930. It had 61 first class, 156 second-class and 19 attendants' seats.

First air-conditioned train

Before 1936, some coaches on the Bombay, Baroda and Central India (BB&CI) Railway Company, Mumbai, had double walls lined with lead-zinc sheets filled with ice. The Frontier Mail (now renamed the Golden Temple Mail), which runs between Mumbai and Amritsar, was the first train to get air-conditioned (AC) coaches in 1934.

First electric train

The first electric train operated on the Harbour branch of the Great Indian Peninsula Railway from Victoria Terminus to Kurla in Mumbai, Maharashtra, over 16 km, on 3 February 1925.

First public-private partnership railway station

The Habibganj railway station in Bhopal, Madhya Pradesh, is the first railway station to be built under a public-private partnership and on par with international standards. The redevelopment work began in partnership with the Bansal Group on 9 June 2017. It lies on the main Jhansi-Bhopal-Itarsi route. The plan includes airport-like facilities, such as shopping complexes, forex kiosks and eateries, making it the first of its kind in the country.

NUMBER OF PASSENGERS INJURED OR KILLED IN TRAIN ACCIDENTS

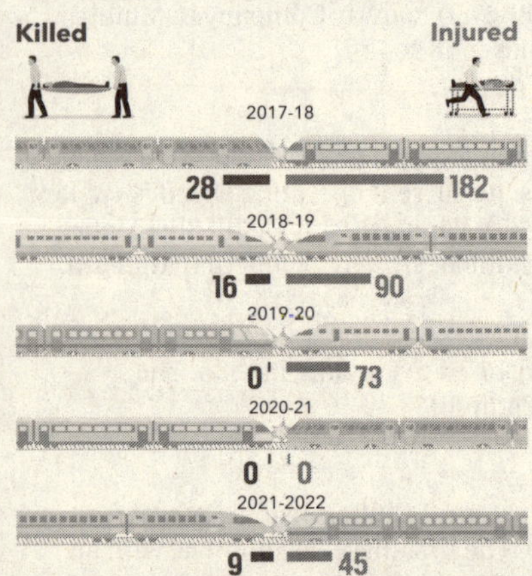

NEW LINES LAID IN THE YEARS 2021-22

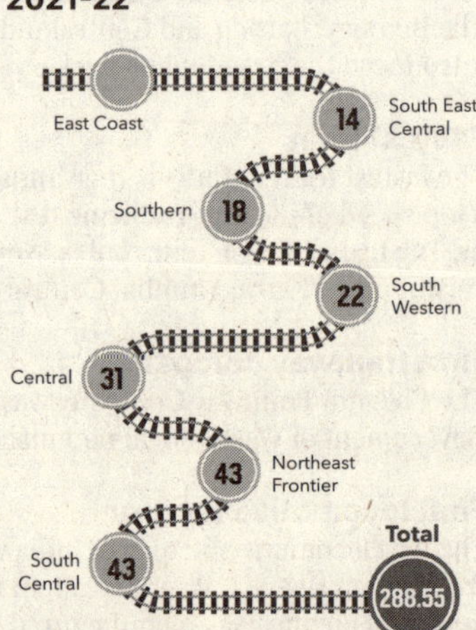

Source: Indian Railways Year Book 2021-22, Ministry of Railways, Government of India

First Vistadome trains

A special seven-coach Vistadome passenger train was introduced on the Visakhapatnam–Araku route in Andhra Pradesh on 16 April 2017 by the Indian Railways. It has features such as see-through glass on all sides, glass roofs, LED lights, a GPS-based information system and an observation lounge that offers panoramic views throughout the journey.

Vistadome train

First green corridor

The Manamadurai–Rameswaram stretch of the Southern Railway was inaugurated as India's first green corridor in July 2016, by installing bio-toilets in 150 coaches of 13 pairs of express and passenger trains on the 114 km long train route. Developed by Indian Railways and the Defence Research and Development Organization (DRDO), the toilets have no discharge of human waste.

Most coaches produced in a year

The Integral Coach Factory, which is located at Perambur in Chennai, Tamil Nadu, manufactured 4,166 railway passenger coaches in 2019–20.

Oldest steam engine

The *Fairy Queen*, officially called the East Indian Railway Nr. 22, has the world's oldest working steam engine. This train started running in 1855 but was stopped in 1908. It was restored in 1997 by Perambur Loco Works in Perambur in

ELECTRIFICATION OF RAILWAY LINES (IN ROUTE KILOMETERS)

Year	Route kilometers
1951	388
1961	748
1971	3,706
1981	5,345
1991	9,968
2001	14,856
2011	19,008
2019	34,319
2020	39,329
2021	44,802
2022	50,394

Source: Indian Railways Year Book 2021-22, Ministry of Railways, Government of India

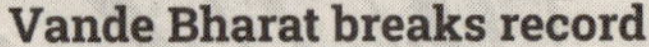

Vande Bharat breaks record

The Vande Bharat express, India's semi-high-speed train, had broken its own record in 2022. The train had reached 100 kmph in just 52 seconds. Before this, it had reached 100 kmph in 54.6 seconds. The express broke the record of Japan's famous bullet train which reaches 100kmph in 55 seconds.

Chennai, Tamil Nadu. In July 1997, this heritage train resumed its route between Delhi and Alwar, Rajasthan, and it still runs occasionally.

Most locomotives produced in a year

The Chittaranjan Locomotive Works in Paschim Bardhaman District, West Bengal, produced 486 locomotives in the financial year 2021–22. It surpassed the Railway Board's production target for the period.

First woman train driver

Surekha Yadav Bhosale was the first woman to drive an Indian Railways train in 1988. She drove the first 'Ladies Special' local train, which started in April 2000 in Mumbai, Maharashtra. She was the first woman to join the Indian Railways as a trainee assistant driver in 1986. She also became Asia's first woman train driver in 2011, driving the *Deccan Queen* from Pune to Chhatrapati Shivaji Maharaj Terminus in Mumbai.

Station with most platforms

Howrah Junction, West Bengal, serves around one million passengers every day. It has 23 platforms, making it the station with the most platforms in India.

First stations

Bori Bunder, Byculla, Sion and Thane stations on the Bori Bunder–Thane line in Maharashtra, were the first railway stations built at the time of the inaugural run of the first passenger train from Bori Bunder to Thane in 1853.

Longest rail tunnel

The Pir Panjal railway tunnel or the Banihal railway tunnel, is 11.215 km long. Located in the Pir Panjal range of the Himalayas in Jammu and Kashmir, it opened in 2013.

Busiest railway station

Kanpur Central station, Uttar Pradesh, is the busiest railway station in the country in terms of the number of trains that pass through it every day. As many as 230 trains pass through the station daily. This railway station also has the world's largest interlocking route system.

WR Station with the longest platform

Shri Siddharoodha Swamiji railway station in Hubballi, Karnataka, has completed the construction of the 1,505 m (4,937 ft 7.97 in.) long Platform No. 1, thus becoming the station with the world's longest railway platform. The platform was inaugrated by Prime Minister Narendra Modi on 12th March 2023.

WR Longest rails manufactured

The Bhilai Steel Plant, the largest plant of the Steel Authority of India Ltd (SAIL), became the only rail maker in the world capable of producing 260 m (853 ft) long rails, on 23 February 2005. It first manufactures 65 m (213 ft) long rails, which are welded together to form the 260 m tracks for high-speed trains.

First corporatized train

The Indian Railways launched the Tejas Express, India's first corporatized train, on 4 October 2019. The infrastructure is owned and run by the Indian Railway Catering and Tourism Corporation (IRCTC), a subsidiary of the Indian Railways, while the services on board are outsourced to private contractors. They include catering, housekeeping, ticketing and refund, among others. The train shuttles between Lucknow and New Delhi, and has only two halts in between – Kanpur and Ghaziabad. Running all week, except Tuesdays, it is contracted under the public– private partnership model.

WR Only railway station listed as a UNESCO World Heritage Site

The first train in the country was flagged off on 16 April 1853 from Bori Bunder (now Chhatrapati Shivaji Maharaj Terminus) in Mumbai, Maharashtra. The historic station is one of the busiest railway stations in India and the only one declared as a UNESCO World Heritage Site. The building, featuring a Victorian Gothic style of architecture, was designed and constructed by draughtsman Axel Herman and architect Frederick William Stevens in 1888.

Chhatrapati Shivaji Maharaj Terminal, Mumbai

Longest double decker viaduct, Nagpur

Longest double decker viaduct

The longest double decker viaduct in India was built by Maharashtra Metro Rail Corporation Limited on Wardha Road, Nagpur. It has a length of 3.14 km. The double decker viaduct carries a highway flyover at the first level and a metro rail at the second level. Along with the already existing highway at ground level this viaduct is a three-tier transportation system.

Longest train route

The Dibrugarh–Kaniyakumari Vivek Express has the longest train route on the Indian Railways network, and the ninth longest in the world. It joins Dibrugarh in Assam to Kaniyakumari in Tamil Nadu, covering 4,286 km, while halting at 56 stations along the route. It starts at 11:05 p.m. and reaches at 9:50 a.m. on the fifth day, with a scheduled journey time of 82 hrs 45 mins.

Longest double decker viaduct

The longest double decker viaduct in India was built by Maharastra Metro Rail Corporation Limited on Wardha Road, Nagpur. It has a length of 3.14 km. The double decker viaduct carries a highway flyover at the first level and a metro rail at the second level. Along with the already existing highway at ground level this viaduct is a three-tier transportation system.

First fully solar-powered railway station

The Guwahati railway station in Assam is India's first fully solar-powered station. Commissioned in 2017, the project has 2,352 solar panels on the roof. This solar project aims

Guwahati Railway Station, Assam

to make the railways environmentally responsible and reduce their carbon footprint. The panels have an average power generation capacity of 2,048 kWh per day.

The number of passengers carried by Indian Railways for the year 2021–22 was 3,519 million.

First metro

A 16.3 km underground mass rapid transit system in the country was inaugurated on 24 October 1984 in Kolkata, between Dum Dum and Tollygunge. The carrying capacity of this metro was 1.73 million passengers a day. The trains for the metro system were manufactured at the Integral Coach Factory, Perambur, Madras (now Chennai), Tamil Nadu, during 1981–82.

Deepest metro station

The Hauz Khas station on the Magenta Line and the Yellow Line of the Delhi Metro is the deepest metro station, located at a depth of 32 m (105 ft).

Largest metro network*

The Delhi Metro, set up by the Delhi Metro Rail Corporation (DMRC), spread across 391 km, is the largest metro rail network in India in terms of both route length and ridership. It has 12 lines and 286 metro stations.

Most metro stations on a double decker viaduct

The double decker viaduct on Wardha Road has three metro stations along the length of 3.14 km. Each station has a length of 77.5 m. The three stations are Ujjwal Nagar, Jaiprakash Nagar, and Chhatrapati Square.

Deepest metro tunnel

Delhi Metro Rail Corporation (DMRC) completed a metro tunnel at a depth of 45 m (147 ft 7 in.) on 30 April 2009. The 1,556 m (5,105 ft) long tunnel below the underground Rajiv Chowk metro station in New Delhi is part of the 22.7 km long Airport Express Line.

First underwater metro

The East-West corridor project, India's first underwater metro service under the Kolkata Metro Rail Corporation was completed by June 2023. The metro line connects Salt Lake to Howrah via Kolkata with a 520 m (1,706 ft) stretch below the Hooghly River. It successfully completed a trial journey from Howrah Maidan to Esplanade and vice versa.

First driverless metro

The Magenta Line in the Delhi Metro became the first 'driverless' metro line in India. The 12.64 km long line started operating on 25 December 2017, and connected Kalkaji Mandir, New Delhi, to Botanical Garden, Noida, while halting at nine stations. The line was extended by 24.34 km to Janakpuri West in May 2018. Initially, it was run by an operator, with high levels of automation based on the Communication Based Train Control technology, and is planned to be driverless in the future.

**Including Noida–Greater Noida Aqua Line and Rapid Metro Gurugram*

INDIA'S HIGHEST CLASS OF ROADS

India has a total length of 4,719 km of expressways. Some of them are still being developed by the Ministry of Road Transport and Highways. Expressways are highways with six to eight lane road networks and are the highest class of roads in India. They incorporate road network features such as grade separation, lane dividers, access ramps, and elevated sections. Some of the popular expressways in India are:

India's widest expressway – Delhi-Meerut Expressway

It has 14 lanes and is 82 km long. It connects Delhi to Meerut via Dasna and Ghaziabad.

India's first 8-lane expressway

Delhi-Noida direct flyway is India's first 8-lane expressway and has a length of 9.2 km.

India's longest expressway – Purvanchal Expressway

It has a length of 340.8 km and passes through nine districts of Uttar Pradesh. It is a six lane expressway that is expandable up to eight lanes.

India's first 6-lane expressway

The Mumbai-Pune expressway is also known as Yashwantrao Chavan expressway. It is 94.5 km and connects Mumbai to Pune city.

First expressway in South India

The Bangalore-Chennai expressway, which is still under construction, is a four-lane expressway and is 258 km long. It will connect Bangalore to Chennai.

ROAD

First highway

Lord William Bentinck, the then Governor General of India (1828–35), began metalling work on the 2,400 km long historic Grand Trunk Road from Calcutta (now Kolkata), West Bengal, to Peshawar (now in Pakistan) and beyond. During his tenure, the initial steps were taken to build a metalled road from Calcutta to Delhi.

First state transport system

In June 1932, the Nizam's State Railways Transport Department (NSRTD), Hyderabad (now in Telangana), set up a road transport service on a 24 km route, with 27 buses operating through three depots. Each bus could seat as many as 25 passengers.

First regular public transport

The first regular long-distance public road transport was introduced between Aligarh and Kanpur in Uttar Pradesh in November 1841.

First traffic police

The Traffic Department of Calcutta Police in Calcutta came into force in 1874 with 17 sepoys in its ranks.

First trolley bus

Twelve trolley buses were imported to replace tramcars on the Gowalia Tank–Mazagon route in Bombay (now Mumbai), Maharashtra, on 11 June 1962. They were withdrawn in March 1971 in favour of buses.

Earliest route

In 1926, the Brihanmumbai (then Bombay) Electricity Supply & Transport Undertaking (BEST) purchased motor buses, choosing two points to try them out. The route covered present-day Afghan Church to Crawford Market through Dadar tram terminus, King's Circle, Opera House, Lal Bagh and Arthur Road in Mumbai, Maharashtra.

First Indigenous Automatic Car

Minus Zero, a Bengaluru-based start-up company, has developed India's first automatic car called zPod. It is the country's first self-driving car which means that it does not have a steering wheel but runs due to strategically placed high-resolution cameras that help it analyse the driving conditions. Minus Zero claims that the vehicle will not need human intervention to operate.

First zero-emission electric car

REVAi, the environment-friendly electric car, is manufactured by the Reva Electric Car Company, Bengaluru, Karnataka, a joint venture formed by Amerigon Inc. of California, USA, and the Maini Group of Industries based in Bengaluru. This eco-friendly car was first flagged off from New Delhi in March 1998 and sold in 26 countries by 2011. It was acquired by Indian conglomerate Mahindra & Mahindra in May 2010, and the company launched the electric hatchback e20 in 2013.

First car

The first motor car was reportedly imported in 1892 by the then maharaja of Patiala in Punjab. It was a De Dion Bouton car.

First motor bus

The motor bus was introduced in Mumbai, Maharashtra, on the Afghan Church–Crawford Market route on 15 July 1926. With a cruising speed of 20 km/hr, it carried 24 passengers, with 2–3 standing ones. Twenty-six buses were bought for ₹12,000 each.

First stainless-steel bus

The first bus with a stainless steel body was built at the Maharashtra State Road Transport Corporation workshop in Aurangabad, Maharashtra. It was inaugurated on the Bombay–Ratnagiri route, Maharashtra, on 12 February 1988.

First Indian car manufacturers

Hindustan Motors Ltd, registered in 1942 to manufacture vehicles, was followed by Premier Automobiles (1944) and Standard Motor Products of India Ltd (1948). The first Indian-built car, Hindustan 10, not fully indigenous but identical to the series M10 HP Morris, rolled out of the factory located in Hooghly District, West Bengal, in 1946.

First indigenous payment eco-system for transport

The National Common Mobility Card (NCMC) based on the 'One Nation, One Card' model was launched in Ahmedabad, Gujarat, on 4 March 2019, by the Ministry of Housing and Urban Affairs, Government of India. It allows users to make payments across multiple transportation platforms such as metros, toll taxes, buses, and parking across India.

First CNG autos

Bajaj Auto Ltd launched the first of its Compressed Natural Gas (CNG) autorickshaws in Delhi on 29 May 2000. With a 3-kg CNG tank and a standby 3-litre petrol tank, it is powered by a 175 cc, four-stroke, overhead camshaft engine, that gives 50 km per kg of CNG and meets the Bharat-II emission norms.

Representative image of a CNG Auto

First satellite navigation system

Sanjay, a navigation system using a Global Positioning System (GPS) receiver and mapping software, was launched on 15 February 1999 in New Delhi. Once installed in the vehicle, the user could access Delhi's road map and get audio information about routes. It also tracks the vehicle from elsewhere. Developed indigenously at the I.B. Saxena Design Lab in New Delhi, it uses 24 satellites.

Indian Automobile Industry reported the highest ever annual passenger vehicle sale in the year 2022. A total of 37.93 lakh units were sold in the country.

First battery-bus fleet

In 1987, for the first time, the Delhi administration introduced 76 battery operated buses on 11 routes in Delhi, through the Delhi Energy Development Agency. Each bus had a laden weight of 3,800 kg, a cruising speed of 40 km/hr and a maximum speed of 60 km/hr.

First electric buses

- The first electric bus service in India is reported to have commenced in Himachal Pradesh for Rohtang Pass, near Manali, at an altitude of 3,962.4 m (13,000 ft). The bus has been developed by Goldstone Infratech and the Automobile Research Association of India. It had the capacity to carry 30 passengers and can run 200 km on fully charged batteries.
- India's first electric double-decker bus was launched at Y.B. Centre in south Mumbai, Maharashtra, on 19 August 2022. The bus – the 'Switch EiV 22' – will be run by the Mumbai civic transport body. Two new electric buses, including the first air-conditioned double-decker bus in the country, will join the fleet of the Brihanmumbai Electric Supply & Transport Undertaking (BEST).

First Advanced Traffic Control system

The Delhi Police installed the first Advanced Traffic Control system at 47 intersections of the capital city in April 2000. The intelligent sensors in this high-tech system are equipped to assess the volume of traffic at each intersection and control the traffic light system accordingly.

First fully electrical SUV

Hyundai launched India's first fully electric SUV, the Kona Electric, on 9 July 2019. The eco-friendly vehicle can cover approximately 452 km on a single charge and was introduced with four drive modes: Eco, Eco+, Comfort, and Sport.

First electric cabs

Nagpur in Maharashtra is India's first city to have an electric mass mobility system. It has a fleet of 200 electric vehicles including taxis, buses, e-rickshaws and autorickshaws, owned by cab aggregator Ola. This multimodal electric vehicle project, the first of its kind in India, was inaugurated on 26 May 2017.

Highest filling station

The Indian Oil Corporation Ltd operates a filling station at Kaza, Spiti

Valley, Himachal Pradesh, at an elevation of about 3,740 m (12,270 ft) above the mean sea level.

The total length of national highways in India was **144,634 km** as of November 2022.

Shortest national highway

National Highway 327 B, located in West Bengal, is the shortest national highway in India. Only 1.2 km long, it starts from its junction with NH-327 near Panitanki in Darjeeling District, connecting Mechi Bridge and terminating at the Indo-Nepal border.

WR Longest Highway Construction in a Single Day

National Highway Authority of India (NHAI) has broken a world record by laying 75 km highway in under five days. The highway was laid as a single-layer of bituminous concrete in a single lane between Amaravati and Akola.

WR Highest national highway

The 490 km long Manali–Leh national highway has an average elevation of over 4,000 m (13,123 ft). Its highest elevation is 5,328 m (17,480 ft) at Tanglang La in Ladakh.

WR Longest highway tunnel

Atal Tunnel, a 9.2 km long tunnel on the Manali–Leh highway, was inaugurated on 3 October 2020. It cuts down the distance between Manali and Leh by 46 km and reduces travel time by four hours. Equipped with CCTVs and fire hydrants, the tunnel is the only one in India to have an emergency exit tunnel inside.

Largest automotive company

Tata Motors Ltd (earlier Tata Engineering and Locomotive Company), founded in 1945 and headquartered in Mumbai, Maharashtra, is the largest automotive company with a portfolio of cars, sports vehicles, buses, trucks and defence vehicles. The company's consolidated net revenue for the fiscal year 2021–22 was ₹2,78,454 crore (₹2,784.54 billion) with 1,086,734 vehicles sold.

Highest Turnover

Hindustan Shipyard Limited is a ship building company that is located in Vishakhapatnam, Andhra Pradesh. It recorded the highest turnover for the financial year 2021–22. The turnover was 667 crore. There was a 40% growth over the previous year.

Most bituminous concrete poured – single day
Travelling over an approximate linear distance of 18,701 km, Hyderabad-based IJM (India) Infrastructure Ltd (IJMII) poured 15,656 metric tonnes (6,068.217 cum) of bituminous concrete in 20 hrs 40 mins on 25 February 2021. The laying of the 26.82 km Solapur–Bijapur single lane of the four-lane NH-13 between Maharashtra and Karnataka was implemented under the National Highway Authority of India.

State/UT with the largest fleet of buses
Tamil Nadu State Transport Corporation (TNSTC) has a fleet of 22,000 buses. It is the largest government-owned bus transport corporation in the country (2019).

WATER

Earliest compass
According to the *Bombay Gazetteer*, Vol. XIII, Part II, Appendix A, a crude forerunner of the modern magnetic compass, Matsya Yantra was used around the fifth century CE. It featured an iron fish that floated in a vessel of oil, and pointed north.

Earliest representation of ships
A rectangular seal portraying a vessel with a sharply upturned prow and stem was unearthed in an excavation at Mohenjo-daro (now in Pakistan). It was dated to 3000 BCE.

Oldest ships
- HMS *Foudroyant (Trincomalee)* used for training, was built in Mumbai in 1817 and is now a museum ship in Hartlepool, UK. The *Trincomalee* carried 46 guns and displaced 1,065 tonnes.
- MV *Safeena* of Ellon Hinengo Ltd, Port Blair, Andaman and Nicobar Islands, built at the government dockyard in Rangoon (now Yangon), Myanmar, in 1942, is the oldest passenger ship.

First steamboat
The steamboat *Diana* was built in India in 1819 by Jessop & Co. Ltd in Calcutta, and launched on 12 July 1823.

First ship to sail from India
The first ship carrying the flag of an Indian Shipping Company, SS *Loyalty* of the Scindia Steam Navigation Company, sailed with a full complement of passengers from Bombay to the British Isles. A hospital ship, *Loyalty* was bought on 17 February 1919 and converted to a passenger vessel. National Maritime Day is observed on 5 April, the day on which the ship undertook this voyage in 1919.

First woman marine pilot
Reshma Nilofer Naha (b. 4 February 1989) is the first and only Indian woman marine pilot in the country. She joined the Kolkata Port Trust in 2011 and became a trained marine pilot in January 2018. As a river pilot, she guides ships in and out of Sagar, and Haldia and Kolkata ports through the Hooghly River.

First shipping company

Freedom fighter V.O. Chidambaram Pillai set up the Swadeshi Shipping Company at Tuticorin (now Thoothukudi), Tamil Nadu, in 1906.

First diesel engine ship

MV *Dwarka*, a modern D-class passenger and cargo ship of the British India Steam Navigation Company, entered service in 1947. Weighing 4,851 gross tonnes, it was 121.6 m (399 ft) long and 16.8 m (55 ft) wide. It had a service speed of 13.5 knots.

First hovercraft ferry

A diesel hovercraft service began between Surat and Ghogha Port in Gujarat on 10 December 1992, linking the two ports, 55 nautical miles (101.85 km) apart, in two hours.

First overseas cargo service

On 3 February 1948, a continental line for an overseas cargo service between India and European countries was inaugurated by the Scindia Steam Navigation Company, with the sailing of the cargo steamship SS *Jalabala* from present-day Mumbai, Maharashtra.

First solar ferry boat

The first solar-powered boat was launched in the country in December 2017. Named *Aditya*, the boat is 21.18 m (69 ft 7 in.) long and 7.0 m (22 ft 11 inc.) wide. Constructed by the NavAlt Solar and Electric Boats Pvt. Ltd, it accommodates 78 rooftop solar panels and sails at a maximum speed of 7.5 knots. The boat seats 75 passengers and operates on the 2.5 km Vaikom–Thavanakadavu route in Kerala.

The Indian government has spent 78 billion USD as investment in renewable energy from 2014 to 2021.

First corporatized port

Ennore Port (now Kamarajar Port Ltd) on the Coromandel Coast, Chennai, Tamil Nadu, was the first Indian port that was a public company, and later became a corporatized port in 1999.

Largest covered dock

Hindustan Shipyard houses the largest covered dock at Visakhapatnam in Andhra Pradesh. The dock measures 240 m x 53 m x 11.25 m (787 ft x 174 ft x 37 ft) with an intermediate twin gate and undocking draft of 8 m (26 ft). It can accommodate ships of up to 80,000 deadweight tonnage.

First indigenous hovercraft

A twin-engine, air-cushioned hovercraft, made in 1987 by the Scientific Instrument Co. Ltd, Allahabad (now Prayagraj), Uttar Pradesh, had a 55 HP thrust engine for propulsion and an 8 HP engine for lift, with a payload capacity of 500 kg and a speed of 45 km/hr.

First private sector port

Pipavav Port in Gujarat, which was inaugurated in November 1996, has three dry cargo berths built as a single-length jetty of 725 m (2,379 ft), and a liquid cargo berth.

India had a fleet strength of **1,520** vessels as on 31st December 2022.

Oldest operating port and largest riverine port

Calcutta Port, Bengal (formerly called Kolkata Port, and now renamed Syama Prasad Mookerjee Port, West Bengal), built by the East India Company and operating since 1870, is the oldest operating port in India. It is also the only major riverine port and the largest riverine port in the country.

First superfast catamaran service

A superfast catamaran service between Mumbai, Maharashtra, and Goa became operational from 14 November 1994. The 40 m long, 400-seater, twin-hull luxury catamaran was imported by Damania Shipping Ltd from Norway. It moved at 40 knots, covering 225 nautical miles (417 km) in 6 hrs 30 mins.

First roll-on–roll-off ferry service

A roll-on–roll-off ferry service began on 22 October 2017 between Ghogha Port and Dahej in Gujarat. The 31 km service reduces the travel time between the two towns from 7–8 hours to just over an hour. It can carry 1,000 passengers and 150 vehicles.

Oldest shipping company

The Scindia Steam Navigation Company was started by Narottam Morarji, Walchand Hirachand, Lallubhai Samaldas, and Kilachand Devchand on 27 March 1919.

WR Longest River Cruise

The MV *Ganga Vilas* is a vessel made in India that was flagged off on its journey from Varanasi on 13 January 2023 by Prime Minister Narendra Modi. The cruise covered a distance of 3,200 km in over 46 days. It reached Dibrugarh on 28 February 2023. It covered 27 river systems in India and Bangladesh.

MV Ganga Vilas

BUSINESS AND ECONOMY

PLANNING

First to work on economic planning

Prashanta Chandra Mahalanobis (1893–1972), an Indian scientist and applied statistician, laid down the framework for the formal foundation of economic planning in India. A member of the first Planning Commission of independent India, Mahalanobis was the first to use statistical tools to forecast, plan, analyse, and evaluate social and economic welfare policies and implementation in India.

First budget

The first Indian budget was presented by James Wilson on 18 February 1860 in colonial India. Wilson, who founded *The Economist* magazine, was a finance member of the Council of India, which advised the Indian viceroy at the time.

First Planning Commission

The first Planning Commission was set up in 1951 under the chairmanship of then prime minister Jawaharlal Nehru, with Gulzari Lal Nanda as the deputy chairman.

First five-year plan

The first five-year plan of free India was launched in 1951, with a total outlay of ₹2,378 crore (23,780 million).

First annual plans

The first annual plans replaced the full five-year plan for an interim period in 1966. These annual plans continued till 1969 and came into force again during 1990–92.

First Union budget

The first Union budget of independent India was presented by then finance minister R.K. Shanmukham Chetty, on 26 November 1947. This was an economic review without any new taxes levied, as the Union budget for 1948–49 was only 95 days away. After this, a budget for a short period was called an 'interim' budget.

First interim budget

An interim budget, to enable government expenditures to continue until the regular budget, was presented first in 1957 by the then finance minister T.T. Krishnamachari.

First book on political economy

Written in Sanskrit by Chanakya in the 4th century BCE, the *Arthashastra* is an ancient Indian treatise on statecraft, economic policy, and military strategy. It was influential till the 12th century, after which it disappeared. A copy of it was rediscovered in 1905 by R. Shamasastry, a Sanskrit scholar, who published it in 1909. Its first English translation was published in 1915. The *Arthashastra* places the knowledge of economics at the heart of a

Chanakya on a coin

king's education. Its discussion of taxation and expenditure gave expression to three traditional Indian principles: the taxing power of the state is limited, taxation should not be felt to be heavy or exclusive or discriminatory, and tax increases should be graduated.

Dr Manmohan Singh was governor of the Reserve Bank of India from 1982 to 1985. He was finance minister from 1991 to 1996 and prime minister of India from 2004 to 2014 (two terms).

Longest budget speech

Dr Manmohan Singh holds the record for the longest budget speech in India. His 1991 budget speech consisted of 18,650 words.

First paperless budget

The Union budget for 2021 was presented on a 'Made-in-India' tablet on 1 February 2021 by Finance Minister Nirmala Sitharaman, doing away with the long-standing tradition of printing the budget papers and also the convention of carrying them in a briefcase. The budget, presented amid the COVID-19 pandemic, was distributed electronically to members of Parliament (MPs).

First Union budget papers in Hindi

While introducing the budget for 1955–56, then-finance minister Sir C.D. Deshmukh circulated the Hindi version of the budget speech for the first time. Hindi versions of the Annual Financial Statement and the Explanatory Memorandum were also circulated from then on.

Longest budget speech in terms of duration is held by Nirmala Sitharaman. Her 2020 budget speech went on for 162 minutes.

Shortest budget speech

The shortest budget speech record is held by Hirubhai Mulljibhai Patel. His budget speech in 1977 had only 800 words.

WORKFORCE AND HUMAN RESOURCES

Earliest public association

The earliest public association in modern India was the Landholders' Society, an association of the landlords of Bengal (now West Bengal), Bihar and Orissa (now Odisha), founded in 1837. It was established to look after the interests of landowners.

Oldest trade union

The Madras Labour Union, the first organized trade union, was formed in 1918–19 by labour veterans Annie Besant, B.P. Wadia, Thiruvarur Viruttachala Kalyanasundaram, Sakkarai Chettiar, G. Ramanujalu, and G. Selvapathy Chetty.

First Legislations for Women

The Bombay Maternity Benefit Act was passed in 1929. It was the first law introduced for the benefit of working women. The writers of the law were Dr Babasaheb Ambedkar, N.M. Joshi, and M.K. Dixit. Later in 1961, independent India had had its own Maternity Benefit Act. The latest amendment to this law took place in 2017. The Equal Remuneration Act was passed in 1976.

Workers on board

Delhi Cloth Mills (DCM) was the first company to recognize labour rights by inducting a workers' representative into its board in 1938.

Oldest banking employees' trade union

The All-India Bank Employees Association (AIBEA), founded on 20 April 1946, is the oldest and largest trade union of bank employees.

Oldest insurance trade union

The All India Insurance Employees Union (AIIEU), established in January 1951, comprised 80 per cent of the nearly 200,000 employees of the Life Insurance Corporation of India (LIC) and the General Insurance Corporation of India (GIC).

First labour strike

The first labour strike in India was that of the palanquin bearers of Calcutta (now Kolkata), West Bengal, in 1827 in pre-Independence India. They refused to wear badges and demanded fare on the basis of the distance they covered instead of time.

First Labour Day

The International Workers' Day celebrations were first organized by communist leader Singaravelar, or Malayapuram Singaravelu Chettiar, (1860–1946) in Madras (now Chennai), Tamil Nadu on 1 May 1923.

First industrial association

The Industrial Association of Western India was formed in 1890 at the annual conference held at Poona (now Pune), Maharashtra.

First organized strike

In 1877, labourers struck work at the Empress Mills in Nagpur, Maharashtra, following a wage cut. In 1884, as many as 5,000 textile workers of Bombay (now Mumbai), Maharashtra, submitted a petition asking for regular payment of wages, a weekly holiday, and a midday recess.

Only Plan to go Through Four Governments

The initial groundwork for the Eighth Five Year Plan (1992–97) was conducted by the Congress (I) government, the approach paper was finalized during National Front rule, the final document was prepared in the Janata Dal (S) regime, and the Congress (I) delivered the revised plan in 1992.

First all-India farmers' organization

The All-India Kisan Sabha was formed in 1936 in British India. It was the first pan-India organization of farmers.

First labour legislation

- The Industrial Employment (Standing Orders) Act of 1946 was followed by protective regulations, such as the Factories Act and the Minimum Wages Act in 1948.
- The first effort to protect unorganized labour was the Coal Mines Provident Fund and Bonus Schemes Bill introduced in 1948, which became an Act in the same year.

Highest FDI in a year

India recorded the highest-ever annual foreign direct investment (FDI) inflow of US $83.57 billion in the financial year (FY) 2021–22.

Largest strike

On 26 November 2020, over 250 million (25 crore) workers struck work for 24 hours in a nationwide general strike organized by a joint platform of 10 trade unions.

Largest employer

- In the government-controlled sector, the largest employer is the Indian Railways with 1,175,925 regular employees as reported on 01 February 2023.
- In the private sector, Tata Consultancy Services continues to be the largest employer with 615,318 employees as on 30 June 2023 in 46 countries.

First LGBTQIA+ job fair

The RISE (Reimagining Inclusion for Social Equity) job fair organized by the Pride Circle on 12 July 2019 in Bengaluru, Karnataka, was the first job fair exclusively for the LGBTQIA+ community. The fair attracted 450 candidates competing for 250 job opportunities in 35 companies. The employers included Goldman Sachs, Uber, Accenture, and Intel.

Longest-serving chairperson

Jehangir Ratanji Dadabhoy Tata, a recipient of the Bharat Ratna in 1992, held the post of chairman of Tata Sons for 53 years (1938–91).

Highest Forex Reserves

India's foreign exchange reserves increased by $8.895 billion to touch an all time high of US $642.453 billion in the week ended 3 September 2021, according to Reserve Bank of India (RBI) data.

COINS AND CURRENCY

Earliest gold coins

The Kushanas (130 BCE–185 CE) issued the earliest gold coins in India. They weighed 121 or 123.1 grains (1 grain = 0.068 g approx.) and appear to be based on the auric standard (122.9 grains) of the Romans with whom the Kushanas had regular trade.

Cowries

First lead coins
The first lead coins were found in the Deccan, dating back to the reign of Sri Satai (c. 150 BCE).

Earliest coinage
Ingots of silver, with only three dots as a mark, probably represent the earliest form of coinage on the Indian subcontinent (in circulation as early as 600 BCE).

Earliest known use of cowries as currency
Cowries were used as legal tender in the Bengal kingdom of Lakhnauti during the reign of Ghiyasuddin Bahadur Shah I (r. 1322–24 CE).

Oldest surviving gold coins
The oldest surviving gold coins are from the reign of Kushana emperor Vima Kadphises (c. 45–78 CE) and they were struck in three denominations – the double stater, the stater or dinara, and the quarter stater. On the obverse of these appears either the king's head or bust, or the king seated cross-legged on a couch, or sitting in a chariot drawn by two horses.

Highest denomination rupee notes
The highest-denomination note ever printed by the Reserve Bank of India was the ten-thousand rupee note issued in 1938. This was demonetized in January 1946. The ten-thousand rupee note was re-introduced in 1954, only to be demonetized again in 1978.

First 200-rupee note
The RBI issued the first-ever currency notes in the denomination of ₹200 on 25 August 2017.

First mint
The East India Company started the first mint in India in 1640 at Fort St George, Madras (now Chennai), Tamil Nadu.
In 1671, the first English mint was installed in Bombay (now Mumbai), Maharashtra through a letter of patent issued by King Charles II of England, but the first coin was minted there only a few years later in 1678.

First coins for the visually impaired
On 7 June 2019, Prime Minister Narendra Modi released a new series of coins, specially conceived

FIRST ISSUE OF RUPEE NOTES

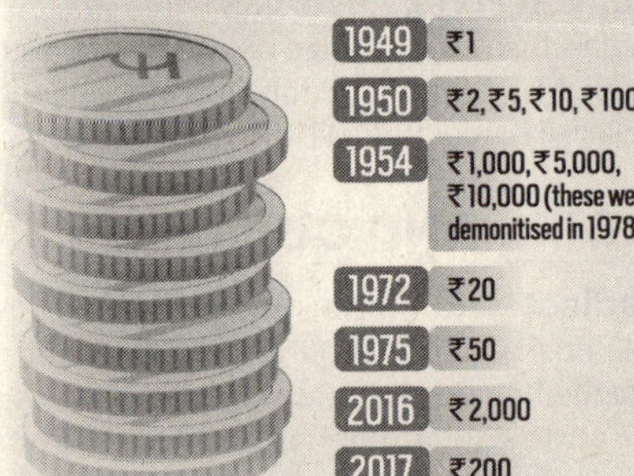

Year	Notes
1949	₹1
1950	₹2, ₹5, ₹10, ₹100
1954	₹1,000, ₹5,000, ₹10,000 (these were demonitised in 1978)
1972	₹20
1975	₹50
2016	₹2,000
2017	₹200

to help visually impaired people to identify them, in New Delhi. Designed by the National Institute of Design in Ahmedabad, Gujarat, the series has coins in denominations of ₹1, ₹2, ₹5, ₹10, and ₹20. These coins are characterized by increasing size and weight from lower to higher denominations. The newly included coin of ₹20 was designed as a 12-sided coin with no serrations. The other denominations are circular.

BANKING

Oldest private bank

The Punjab National Bank Ltd, the first private bank wholly owned and run by Indians, opened in 1895.

First bank

The Bank of Hindostan was established in 1770 by Alexander and Co. of Calcutta (now Kolkata), West Bengal and survived three economic crises before shutting down in the 1830s.

First government banking agency

The Imperial Bank of India, formed in 1921 by merging the Presidency Banks of Bengal, Bombay, and Madras, became the State Bank of India (SBI) on 1 July 1955.

First regional rural banks

The first regional rural banks (RRB) in India were opened in Moradabad and Gorakhpur in Uttar Pradesh, Bhiwani in Haryana, Jaipur in Rajasthan, and Malda in West Bengal on 2 October 1975.

First foreign bank

The Chartered Bank, established in 1853 in Madras, was the earliest foreign bank in India. In 1969, it merged with the Standard Bank in London, UK, and was incorporated as the Standard Chartered Bank.

First bank for housing development

The National Housing Bank (NHB), a subsidiary of the Reserve Bank of India, was established on 9 July 1988.

First Indian bank to open a branch overseas

The Bank of India was the first Indian bank to open a branch outside India, in London, UK, in 1946, and also the first to open a branch in Paris, France, in 1974.

First cooperative bank

The Greater Bombay Cooperative Bank Ltd was registered on 5 November 1952 under the Bombay State Cooperative Act, with 50 members and an initial capital of ₹21,000.

First automated teller machine facility

The Hong Kong and Shanghai Banking Corporation (HSBC) started 24-hour banking facilities by installing automated teller machines (ATMs) at its main office in Bombay on 4 September 1987.

First credit card issued by an Indian bank

The Central Bank of India introduced the Central Card in 1980.

The State Bank of India has more than **65,000** ATMs.

First floating ATM

The State Bank of India launched a floating ATM installed on a *jhankar* (ferry) plying between Ernakulam and Vypin (one among a group of islands forming part of Kovhi) in Kerala on 9 February 2004. The ship was owned by the Kerala Shipping and Inland Navigation Corporation.

First ATMs on wheels

In December 2002, the Industrial Credit and Investment Corporation of India (ICICI) Bank introduced an ATM on wheels using vans equipped with ATM machines and parked at four locations in Mumbai suburbs – Vile Parle (East), Juhu, Andheri (West), and Kandivali – for fixed hours. The mobile ATM was connected to the central database of the bank through GPRS (General Packet Radio Service) technology for a fixed number of hours every day.

Most branches

The State Bank of India (SBI) has most number of branches, over 22,000.

First Indian bank listed on the New York Stock Exchange

On 22 September 1999, ICICI Bank was listed on the New York Stock Exchange (NYSE), with its American Depository Shares priced at US $9.80. After the Bank of Tokyo-Mitsubishi, it was the second Asian bank to be listed on the NYSE.

First export–import bank

The Government of India set up the Export–Import Bank of India (EXIM Bank) in 1982 as a statutory corporation wholly owned by the Union government to provide financial assistance to exporters and importers and to coordinate the operations of export–import institutions.

First institution for agri loans

On 12 July 1982, the National Bank for Agriculture and Rural Development (NABARD) was established, with its headquarters in Bombay, to implement the National Bank for Agricultural and Rural Development Act, 1981. The agricultural credit functions of RBI and refinance functions of the then Agricultural Refinance and Development Cooperation (ARDC) were transferred to NABARD.

First government-owned all-woman bank

Bharatiya Mahila Bank (BMB), India's first government-owned bank only for women, with the vision of economic empowerment of women, opened its first branch at Nariman Point in Mumbai, Maharashtra, on 19 November 2013. It was incorporated on 5 August 2013 and received a banking licence from the RBI on 25 September 2013. It was merged with the State Bank of India in April 2017.

First Indian governor of the Reserve Bank of India

Sir Chintaman Dwarakanath Deshmukh, a member of the Indian Civil Service, was the first Indian governor of the Reserve Bank of India (RBI) – appointed governor in 1943.

First indigenous payment card

The National Payments Corporation of India (NPCI) introduced the RuPay debit card in Mumbai, Maharashtra, on 26 March 2012.

The bank with the largest network

The India Post Payments Bank (IPPB), launched in 2017 with 155,000 access points, became the largest banking network in the country. It is also the bank with the largest rural network, with 110,000 access points.

Largest international bank by number of branches

As reported by the Reserve Bank of India, the Standard Chartered Bank, with the UK as its country of incorporation, leads the list of international banks in India with the highest number of branches, totalling 107.

Biggest bank fraud

On 14 February 2018, Punjab National Bank (PNB), India's second-largest government-owned lender at the time, declared the largest ever bank fraud in India's financial history. It involved fraudulent letters of undertaking worth around ₹11,400 crore (114 billion) issued by PNB at its Brady House branch in Fort, Mumbai, Maharashtra, to overseas branches of other Indian banks.

State/UT with the most ATMs

Maharashtra ranks first in the country as the state with the highest number of ATMs and WLAs (White Label ATMs) deployed, with 28,024 ATMs as reported in September 2022. Tamil Nadu, with 23,524 ATMs, comes second in the list.

Bank with most foreign offices

The State Bank of India had 80 foreign offices in 36 countries to service the bank's foreign customers, in addition to retail operations (by July 2020). The focus of these offices is India-related business.

First Indian bank with a merchant banking subsidiary

The State Bank of India was the first bank to set up a wholly owned merchant banking subsidiary when it set up SBI Capital Markets Ltd in April 1986.

First bank with a satellite network

The State Bank of India installed the first satellite network in September 1988, connecting 134 offices in 64 cities. This network facilitated communication by voice, facsimile, and message switching via digital electronic exchanges.

First woman managing director and chief financial officer of World Bank Group

Anshula Kant, born in Roorkee (now in Uttarakhand), was appointed managing director (MD) and chief financial officer (CFO) of the World Bank on 12 July 2019. Kant is responsible for managing the International Development Association (which offers concessional loans and grants to the world's poorest developing countries), finance, and risk management of the Group. Previously a financial officer of the State Bank of India, Kant became the first woman to become MD and CFO of the international financial institution.

First bank to establish a mutual fund

The State Bank of India launched the SBI Mutual Fund in July 1987. Managed by its subsidiary, SBI Capital Markets Ltd, it was established under the amended Banking Regulations Act, 1949, to attract funds from small investors in rural and semi-urban areas.

First woman to head a foreign bank in India

Naina Lal Kidwai was the first Indian woman to lead a foreign bank (ANZ Grindlays, where she worked from 1982 to 1994) in India. She was also the first Indian woman to graduate from Harvard Business School (1982). Her contribution in the areas of trade and industry earned her the Padma Shri in 2007.

First demonetization

In 1946, currency notes of ₹1,000 and ₹10,000 denominations were removed from circulation in the first instance of demonetization. Both notes were then reintroduced in 1954, with the introduction of ₹5,000 and ₹500 notes.

First woman bank manager

Shanta Kumari became the manager of the Syndicate Bank, Seshadripura, Bangalore (now Bengaluru), Karnataka, in 1962.

INSURANCE

First general insurance company

Triton Insurance Company Ltd, set up by the British in 1850, was the first general insurance company in India.

First life insurance company

The Oriental Insurance Company, the first life insurance company in India, started in Calcutta in 1818, but served only the Europeans in India then.

Largest insurance company

The Life Insurance Corporation of India (LIC) was founded on 1 September 1956. It grew into what is now the biggest public sector insurance company in the country and leads in the insurance sector.

Currently LIC has **2,048** fully computerized branch offices, **113** divisional offices, **8** zonal offices, **1,381** satallite offices, and a corporate office.

First Indian life insurance company

The Bombay Mutual Life Assurance Society was the first Indian life insurance company. It started in 1870.

FINANCIAL INSTRUMENTS

First automatic exchange and screen-based trading

The automated Over the Counter Exchange of India (OTCEI), set up in 1992 in Bombay, Maharashtra, was the ideal avenue for small- and medium-sized companies with an issued capital ranging from ₹30 lakh (3 million) to ₹25 crore (250 million). This exchange failed to live up to its promise and the National Stock Exchange (NSE) came into being in November 1994. It started the first screen-based trading system, in which a network of computers is linked to a central computer located in the stock exchange.

First domestic mutual fund

The Unit Trust of India's (UTI) scheme launched in 1964 was the first domestic mutual fund in the country.

India's first depository

The National Securities Depository Limited (NSDL) was jointly promoted by the IDBI, UTI, and NSE. It started operations in August 1996. C.B. Bhave was the first managing director of the NSDL. In September 2016, when the depository completed 20 years of operations, it had 15 million demat accounts.

First offshore mutual fund

Unit Trust of India (UTI) and Merrill Lynch promoted the ₹75 million India Fund in 1986.

First rating agency

Crisil, formed in 1988, was the first rating agency in India. It was set up jointly by the LIC, lClCl, GIC, and various banks.

First secured promissory notes

Tata Iron and Steel Company Ltd (TISCO), now Tata Steel Ltd, issued secured promissory notes in June 1992.

First global depository receipts issue

Reliance Industries Ltd issued global depository receipts worth US $150 million in March 1992.

First woman president of a stock exchange

Forty-five-year-old Omana Abraham became the first woman president of a stock exchange in India when she was nominated president of the Cochin Stock Exchange in Kochi, Kerala, in 1991.

Highest price for stock exchange membership

A broking card for the Bombay Stock Exchange was auctioned for ₹4.1 crore (41 million) to Jardine Fleming Asia, which later shut down. Before that, Baring Securities India Ltd had paid ₹3 crore (30 million) for one in 1995.

First private sector mutual fund

Shyam Kothari, head of the H.C. Kothari group of companies, floated the

MILESTONES IN LIFE INSURANCE

1 1818

First life insurance company on Indian soil started by Europeans – called Oriental Life Insurance Company

2 1870

First Indian life insurance company started its business – called Bombay Mutual Life Assurance Society

3 1912

First statute to regulate the life insurance business enacted – called the Indian Life Assurance Companies Act

4 1938

First act to regulate the insurance sector enacted – the Indian Insurance Companies Act

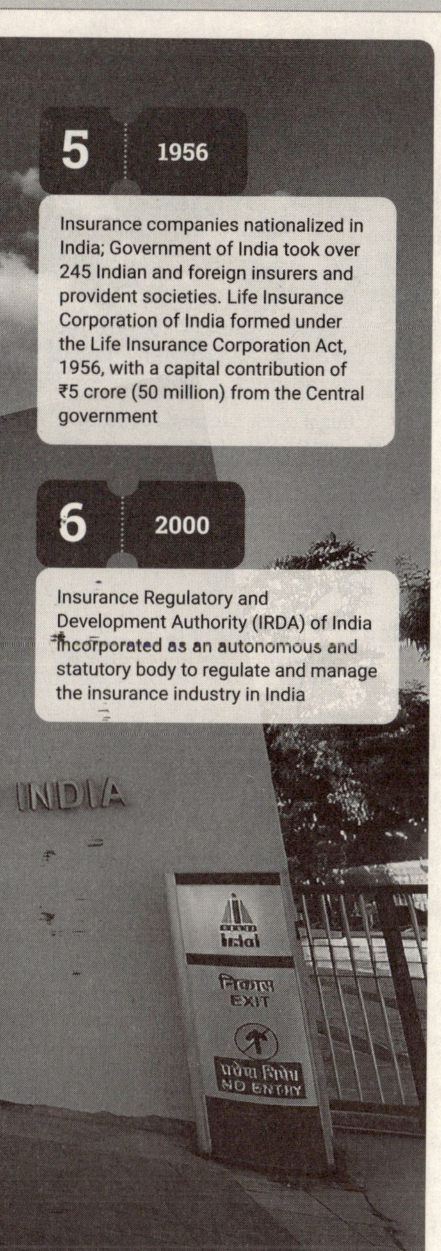

Kothari Pioneer Bluechip Fund in November 1993.

First PSU to go public

Indian Petrochemicals Corporation Ltd (IPCL) went public on 16 November 1992, with a ₹320 crore (3.2 billion) equity issue.

First sectoral fund

The first sectoral mutual fund by the name of CanExpo was offered by Canara Bank during February–March 1994 as the first emerging industry fund.

Largest mutual fund

HDFC Asset Management Company Ltd is the largest mutual fund company in India, with assets worth ₹450,376.22 crore (4,503.76 billion) under its management, as reported in December 2021.

FINANCIAL INSTITUTIONS

Stock exchange with most listed companies

The BSE, with 4,817 listed companies, is the largest exchange going by the number of listed companies on the exchange.

Stock exchange with highest volume of derivative contracts

The NSE has been the world's largest derivatives exchange, reporting an equity derivatives volume of ₹17,350 trillion in 2022 (₹16,952 trillion for the whole of the FY2022–23). The number of contracts traded during the highest point was 1,958 crore (19.58 billion). The number of contracts was 1,860 crore (18.6 billion) for the whole year.

Stock exchange with highest turnover

The National Stock Exchange is the stock exchange with the highest turnover. On 26 September 2023 it recorded a single-day turnover of ₹1.27 lakh crore (US$ 15.25 billion), highest ever in its history.

National Stock Exchange building at the Bandra Kurla Complex in Mumbai

Oldest stock exchange

The Bombay Stock Exchange (BSE) was born under the shade of a giant banyan tree way back on 9 July 1875. Indian brokers doing business in stocks and shares decided to form an association in Bombay to protect the interests of Indian share brokers and stockbrokers. It was also Asia's first stock exchange.

State/UT with the highest contribution to equity trading

Maharashtra leads among states in its contribution to equity trading, with 2.31 crore investors as on September 2022.

Shares of most companies held by an individual

Rajiv Maheshwari (b. 10 April 1961) held shares of 5,348 companies in dematerialized form in National Securities Depository Ltd (NSDL) and Central Depository Services (India) Ltd (CDSL) depository accounts as on 12 June 2023.

First Woman Director of a Stock Exchange

Forty-year-old Deena Mehta became the first woman director of the Bombay Stock Exchange (BSE), elected by securing 382 of 413 votes in March 1997. This was the first time in 122 years that the BSE elected a woman to its board.

POWER AND ENERGY

First builder of the steam engine

Goluk Chandra, who was a blacksmith in Titigur (now Titagarh), near Barrackpore in West Bengal, indigenously built a steam engine to pump groundwater, without any European help, in 1828.

First commercial use of electricity

Electricity was first introduced commercially on 10 November 1897 at Sidrapong Hydroelectric Power Station in Darjeeling, West Bengal.

First nuclear power plant

The Tarapur Atomic Power Station (TAPP) in Palghar, Maharashtra, with an installed capacity of 380 MW, was commissioned in 1969. It started with two boiling-water reactor units with an initial generating capacity of 210 MW each (de-rated to 160 MW), fuelled by enriched uranium. It was built by Bechtel Corporation and General Electric Company, US, under an agreement between the Government of India, the United States, and the International Atomic Energy Agency.

In Forbes' the Global 2000 List for 2023, NTPC has secured 433rd position, a straight jump from its 485th position in 2022.

First electrification

Calcutta (now Kolkata, West Bengal) was the first city in India to go electric when it received current in 1899 with the commissioning of Calcutta Electric Supply Corporation's (CESC's) first generating station at Emambagh Lane the same year.

Largest power supplier

The National Thermal Power Corporation (NTPC) Ltd, set up in 1975, is the country's largest power company. Currently, it has an installed capacity of 73,024 MW (including joint ventures). NTPC's own stations include 26 coal-based, 7 gas-based, 1 hydroelectric, 16 renewable energy-based stations. Under joint ventures, the company has 9 coal-based, 4 gas-based, 8 hydroelectric, and 18 renewable energy projects.

Largest private sector thermal power station

The 4,620 MW Mundra Thermal Power Station at Mundra in the Kachchh District of Gujarat is the largest privately operating thermal power plant in India, with nine generating units. It is a coal-based power plant, owned and operated by Adani Power.

First private sector power company

Tata Power Company Ltd (TPCL) was the first private sector power company to start operations, in 1910 in Bombay.

First state electricity board

On 1 May 1955, the West Bengal State Electricity Board was the first electricity board in the country to become operational.

First heavy water plant

The first heavy water plant was set up at Nangal in the Rupnagar District of Punjab in 1962. Heavy water or deuterium oxide was the basic fuel used by first-generation nuclear power plants.

First indigenous atomic power plant

Madras Atomic Power Station (MAPS) at Kalpakkam near Chennai, Tamil Nadu, was India's first fully indigenously built nuclear power station under the Indira

Gandhi Centre for Atomic Research (IGCAR). Each of its two units generates 220 MW of electricity. The first indigenous 40 MW Fast Breeder Test Reactor (FBTR) was commissioned in August 1985 here.

Victoria House at Esplanade, Kolkata: headquarters of CESC

First steam-powered plant

The Calcutta Electric Supply Company (CESC) set up a steam-powered plant in 1899 at Emambagh Lane near Prinsep Ghat in Calcutta, marking the start of thermal power generation in India.

First hydropower station

Sidrapong Hydroelectric Power Station in the foothills of Arya Tea Estate near Darjeeling, West Bengal, is the oldest hydroelectric power plant in India. It was commissioned on 10 November 1897 with a capacity of 2 x 65 kW. This was increased in phases to meet the rising demands and reached 1,000 kW (1 MW) by 1916.

First solar-powered thermal plant

The country's first 50 MW solar-powered thermal power plant, developed by Chhattisgarh-based Godawari Green Energy Ltd (GGEL) in Nokh Village in Jaisalmer District, Rajasthan, went operational in 2013.

Largest grid-connected rooftop solar plant

The country's largest grid-connected rooftop solar plant, with a capacity of 7.52 MW, started operations in May 2016 at Dera Beas in Amritsar District, Punjab.

Largest thermal power plant

Vindhyachal Super Thermal Power Station in Singrauli District, Madhya Pradesh, with an installed capacity of 4,760 MW, is ranked as the biggest thermal power

Renewable Energy Mini-Ratna Approved for Listing

Indian Renewable Energy Development Agency Limited (IREDA) is currently a wholly owned Government of India, mini-ratna (Category-I) CPSE incorporated in 1987. It is engaged in financing of Renewable Energy (RE) and Energy Efficiency (EE) projects in India. The Cabinet Committee on Economic Affairs (CCEA) has, in March 2023, approved for listing of IREDA on the Stock Exchanges through an Initial Public Offer (IPO) by part sale of the government's stake in it and to raise funds for IREDA through issue of fresh equity shares.

Representative image of an underwater pipeline

plant in the country. It is a coal-based power plant, owned and operated by NTPC Ltd.

Longest underwater hydrocarbon pipeline

India's longest underwater hydrocarbon pipeline completed in April 2023. It stretches 1,656 km, from the river island Majuli in Assam to Jorhat in upper Assam. The pipeline runs under the river Brahmaputra. Its diameter is 24 inches and cost ₹9,265 crore.

First oil well

- Oil was first located at Borbil (later Digboi) in Assam in 1890, but systematic drilling for oil had begun in Upper Assam in 1866 and oil was struck at Makum near Margherita at a depth of 36 m (118 ft) on 26 March 1867.
- The first offshore well was sunk in the Bombay High oilfield in 1974.

First pipeline

The Guwahati–Siliguri petroleum product pipeline (between Assam and West Bengal) was commissioned by the Indian Oil Corporation in 1965.

First refinery

The Assam Railways and Trading Co. built a small refinery at Margherita in present-day Tinsukia District, Assam, in 1893 to refine oil from Makum and Digboi areas.

WR Oldest running refinery

The Digboi Refinery, under the Indian Oil Corporation, started in 1899 in Assam, is the world's oldest running refinery.

First private branded LPG

Reliance Gas was launched in 1998 by Reliance Petroleum Ltd in collaboration with the local LPG bottlers for the packaging of the product.

State with highest installed capacity of renewable power

Tamil Nadu has surpassed Karnataka with the highest installed capacity of grid-connected renewable power. As of 31 January 2022, Tamil Nadu's total installed renewable capacity stood at 15,914 MW as compared to Karnataka's total clean energy capacity of 15,795 MW.

Highest-ever crude throughput and distillate yield

Numaligarh Refinery Limited (NRL) recorded its highest-ever crude throughput of 3.093 million metric tonnes (MMT) against its nameplate capacity of 3.0 MMT in the FY 2022-23. The company has also announced a distillate yield of 87.6 per cent, which is its highest since inception. NRL has kept its capital expenditure at ₹6,615 crore (66.15 billion) in FY 2022-23, which is the highest ever to date, surpassing its earlier record of ₹3,605 crore (36.05 billion) in the FY 2021-22.

First company to market LPG

The first company to market liquefied petroleum gas (LPG) in India was BPCL in 1955. Now BPCL reaches around 25 million households with 2,137 LPG distributors across the country.

MINING

WR Largest coal-producing company

Coal India Limited (CIL), a government-owned coal-mining corporate headquartered in Kolkata, West Bengal, came into being in November 1975 when the Government of India took over private coal mines. It is now the single largest coal producer in the world. Operating through 84 mining areas, it has seven wholly owned coal-producing subsidiaries, as well as a mine planning and consultancy company, across eight states in India. Coal India Ltd (CIL) and its subsidiaries accounted for 596.221 million tonnes during 2020–21, while its production during 2022–23 was 893.19 MT.

Oldest gold mine

India's oldest gold mine was located in Kolar, Karnataka. The production here in the mid-1970s was 3,000 kg a year, but was on a decline ever since, and the mines were closed in 2001.

First lithium resource

Geological Survey of India has found lithium for the first time. They discovered 5.9 million tonnes of inferred resources of lithium in Salal-Haimana area of Reasi District, Jammu and Kashmir, in February 2023.

First coal mining

The first tonne of coal was struck in Raniganj Coalfield in 1775 by Suetonius Grant Heatly, the then collector of the East India Company for Palamu and Hazaribagh, in present-day Jharkhand. Records show that John Summer and Grant Heatly jointly obtained a licence from the then British Governor General Warren Hastings in 1774 to exploit what they then called 'Panchet coal'. They were later joined by another Englishman called Redfern.

Mineral production in India went up by 10.7 per cent in July 2023 as compared to the level in July 2022. In terms of production level of individual minerals, coal topped the chart in July 2023: 693 lakh tonnes.

State/UT with the most mines

There are 1,319 reporting mines (excluding minor, fuel, and atomic minerals) in the country as recorded in 2021-22. Among these, Madhya Pradesh tops the chart with 263 mines, followed by Gujarat (147), Karnataka (132), Odisha (128), Chhattisgarh (114), and Andhra Pradesh (108), Telangana (92), Rajasthan (84), and Maharashtra (67). In terms of the value of mineral production, Odisha leads with ₹32,841 crore (328.41 billion), followed by Rajasthan (₹22,776 crore/ 227.76 billion), and Andhra Pradesh (₹17,906 crore/ 179.06 billion).

Rocks or colourful stone at Panna National Park, which is extensively mined for diamond

Only diamond mines

India's only diamond mines are at Panna in Madhya Pradesh and are administered by the government-owned National Mineral Development Corporation (NMDC).

India's first international Bullion Exchange

The India International Bullion Exchange (IIBX), India's first international bullion exchange, is located at Gujarat's GIFT (Gujarat International Finance Tec-City) in Gandhinagar. It was inaugurated on 29 July 2022. This exchange is the third such exchange in the world. India's first bullion exchange will sell physical gold and silver. The jewellers registered as trading partners with the exchange, with a minimum net worth of ₹25 crore as a prerequisite, will be able to buy and sell gold and silver in the exchange. Jewellers abroad will also be able to do the same, following certain conditions, after registering with the International Financial Services Centre Association (IFSCA).

Oil India Limited (OIL), a state-owned enterprise of the Government of India has registered its highest ever profit since inception, whopping ₹6,810.40 crore for FY 2022-23.

INDUSTRIES AND COMPANIES

First factory

The first factory in India, which was a dye-manufacturing unit, was set up by the East India Company with the permission of the then Mughal emperor Jahangir in Surat in 1609, marking the beginning of colonialism.

First commercial production of iron and steel

- In 1830, a unit was set up at Porto Novo (now Parangipettai) in Cuddalore District, Tamil Nadu, to produce iron, but it failed.

- In 1853, the East India Iron Company set up two blast furnaces in South Arcot and Coimbatore Districts, Tamil Nadu. These closed in 1858.
- In 1875, the Barakar Iron Works, Kulti, Bengal, produced pig iron.
- Steel production began in 1892 at the Metal and Steel Factory at Cossipore (now Kashipur, West Bengal), moving to Ichapore (now Ishapur, West Bengal) in 1905.

First cigarette company

Imperial Tobacco Company (ITC) was established in Calcutta (now Kolkata, West Bengal) in 1910.

First ice-cream company

Joy Ice Creams Pvt. Ltd, which was founded by L.C. Java, was the first company to manufacture and market ice cream. In 1948, Java bought a homogenizer and pasteurizer, and set up a small business that became India's first ice-cream company.

First rubber estate and company

The first rubber company, called Malankara Rubber and Produce Company, was started in 1910 by P. John on a 70-acre (28.3-hectare) estate in Thodupuzha, Idukki District, Kerala.

First cotton textile mill

Though the British had established a cotton textile mill in 1817, the first truly Indian textile mill was set up in July 1854 in Bombay (now Mumbai, Maharashtra), by Cawasji N. Davar. It was called the Bombay Spinning and Weaving Company.

First tea company

- Tea seeds were first imported into India from China in 1774. In 1837, the East India Company set up the first tea estate at Chabua, Dibrugarh District, Assam.
- The Alubari Tea Company, established in 1856 in Darjeeling (now in West Bengal) under the Kurseong and Darjeeling Tea Company, was the first to commercialize tea.

A tea garden in Darjeeling, West Bengal

Oldest engineering company

Jessop & Company Ltd, the oldest engineering company in the country, was established in 1788 by two engineers from Britain – Henry and George Jessop.

Oldest jute mill

Wellington Jute Mill in Rishra, near Serampore (now Srirampur), West Bengal, was established by George Auckland in 1855 as the Rishra Twine and Yarn Mills Ltd, with machinery bought from John Kerr of the Douglas Foundry, the leading manufacturers of flax and manufacturing machines in Dundee, Scotland. The mill had an output of eight tonnes a day. It shut down in 1868 and resumed as Calcutta Jute Mills, which later became Wellington Jute Mills. It is now under AI Champdany Industries Ltd.

First tyre company

The Dunlop Rubber Company (India) Ltd was established on 19 August 1926, with its registered office in Bombay (now Mumbai, Maharashtra) and an authorized share capital of ₹50 lakh (5 million). Dunlop opened its first tyre factory in India at Sahagunj, Hooghly District, West Bengal, in 1936.

The defunct Dunlop tyre factory at Sahagunj

First foreign collaboration

Carr, Tagore and Company was the first Indo-British collaboration under the Charter Act of 1833. There were four partners: W. Carr, Dwarakanath Tagore, D.M. Gordon, and William Prinsep. It closed in 1847.

First champagne manufacturer

In 1987, its very first year, Shyam Chougule's Champagne India, a subsidiary of Indage in Narayangaon, Pune District, Maharashtra, with a 42-acre (17 hectare) vineyard, entered the export market. Champagne Indage Ltd, as it was renamed after being restructured, was the market leader in wines then, with a production of about 100,000 cases a year.

First five-star hotel

The Taj Mahal Hotel in Mumbai, Maharashtra, said to have been built back to front, was founded by Jamshetji Nusserwanji Tata in 1904. The story goes that in those days there were very few hotels that permitted entry to Indians and Tata himself had been denied admission to Pyrke's Apollo Hotel, close to the present-day Taj Mahal Hotel. This motivated Tata to build the hotel.

First plastic factories

A plastic factory was established in 1926 at Jessore, now in Bangladesh. It manufactured combs, soapboxes, ashtrays and other articles from imported celluloid sheets and rods. In 1933, two units for compression moulding were started with machinery that was imported from Germany. The first thermosetting plastic produced in India, starting in 1946, was phenol formaldehyde.

First retail chain for computers

Computer Point launched the country's first retail chain for computers and computer accessories by establishing the first showroom in Bombay (now Mumbai), Maharashtra, on 31 December 1984. It also had stores in other cities, like New Delhi.

A Lambretta scooter at an exhibition in Odisha

First scooter manufacturing company

Lambretta, the first scooter introduced by Automobile Products of India (API), was manufactured in 1956.

First car factory

In 1928, General Motors had commenced the assembly of cars and trucks in Bombay (now Mumbai), Maharashtra, using imported components. The first indigenous car-manufacturing company was the Birlas' Hindustan Motors, which was established at Uttarpara near Calcutta (now Kolkata), West Bengal. The first Indian car, 'Hindustan 10', rolled off the assembly line in 1948.

First batch of microchips

The first microchips rolled out of Semiconductor Ltd, located in Chandigarh, in March 1984.

WR India leads in the export of measles vaccines

Ninety per cent of measles vaccines in the world are supplied by India, which also supplies 65 per cent of DPT and BCG vaccines in the world.

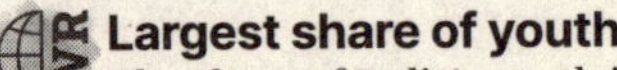

WR Largest share of youth

The share of India's youth in the total population, the highest in the world,

Dilli Bazaar

Delhi government has announced the first government initiative to bring physical markets of the state on to various digital platforms. Dilli Bazaar, the government's planned e-portal will launch with storefronts of 10,000 shops in Delhi. The government plans to bring more than a hundred thousand shops under the portal within six months of its launch. As sellers will have zero set-up cost, they will be able to sell their products at cheaper rates than through other e-commerce platforms.

is 34.8 per cent (as per the 2011 census) or 42.2 crore (422 million). The National Youth Policy defines 'youth' as persons between 15 and 29 years.

First car to be exported

Hindustan Motors Ltd's Ambassador was the first car to be exported in 1975–76 to Guyana in South America.

Inside an old Ambassador car

First power loom

The first power loom for jute cloth was started in 1958 by Henderson and Company, agents of Borneo Jute Company, in present-day Baranagar, Kolkata, in West Bengal. On becoming a limited company, it was named the Baranagore Jute Manufacturing Company and had 512 looms at its peak.

State/UT with the lowest score on the poverty scorecard

Bihar, with a score of 28, was the lowest-scoring state on Sustainable Development Goals (SDGs) India Index's no-poverty scorecard at the end of 2020–21.

Lowest level the rupee touched

The rupee touched an all-time low of 83.2425 against the US dollar on forex outflows on 12 October 2023.

First winner of the Nobel Prize in Economics

Dr Amartya Kumar Sen (b. 3 November 1933) received the Nobel Prize in economic sciences in 1998, becoming the first Indian and Asian to do so. Born in Santiniketan, West Bengal, he is considered to be a pioneer of welfare economics.

First infrastructural index

The Government of India launched a City Liveability Index on 23 June 2017 to measure the quality of life in 116 major cities, based on a set of 79 parameters, such as the availability of roads, education, healthcare, mobility, employment opportunities, emergency response, grievance redressal, pollution, availability of open and green spaces, cultural and entertainment opportunities, and so on.

The contribution of the automobile sector to the National GDP is about 7.1 per cent. It provides direct and indirect employment to over 19 million people. The export of the total number of automobiles increased from 4,134,047 in 2020–21 to 5,617,246 in 2021–22, marking a positive growth of 35.9 per cent.

RETAIL

First virtual mall

The Digital Mall of Asia is a virtual e-commerce platform, an amalgamation of digital space and real estate, making it the first virtual mall in the country. The mall is open in Delhi, Noida, Pune, Ahmedabad, Bengaluru, Chennai, Gurugram, Hyderabad, Jaipur, Lucknow, and Mumbai. Each location has a different digital interface and e-shops can be bought or acquired on rent. The mall works 24 hours a day, 7 days a week.

STATE-WISE GROWTH OF GST REVENUES AS ON JUNE 2023

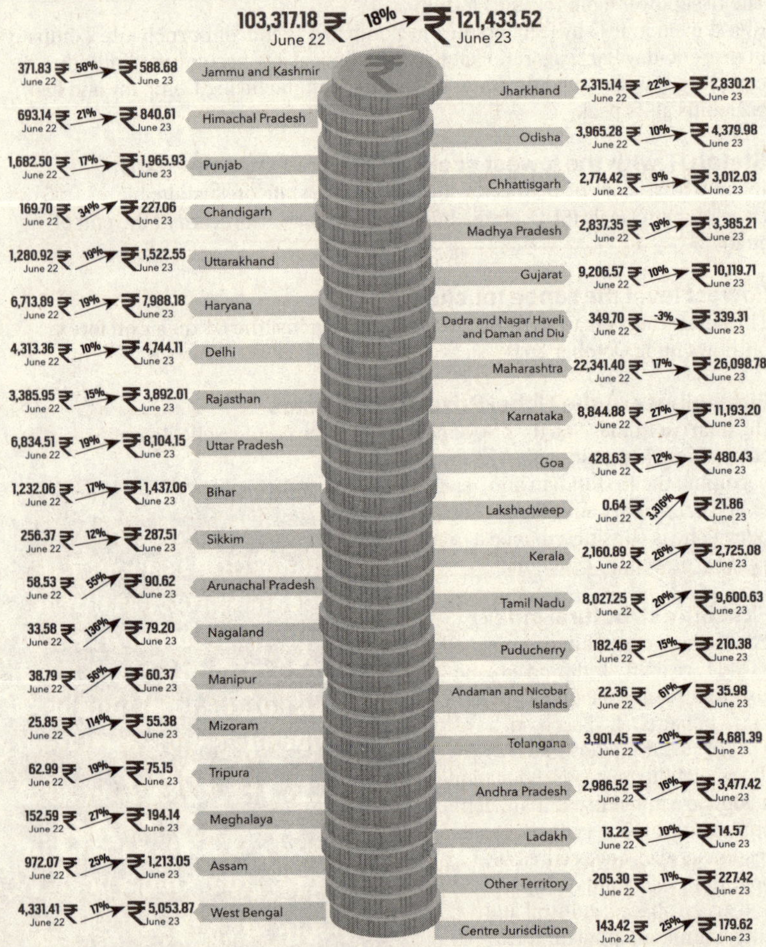

Source: Ministry of Finance, Government of India's press release on Press Information Bureau

Walmart superstore in Lucknow

Biggest business deal

In August 2018, Walmart Inc., a US multinational retail corporation, announced the deal agreements that made it the largest shareholder in the Flipkart Group, an e-commerce company founded by Sachin Bansal and Binny Bansal in 2007 and based in Bengaluru, Karnataka. Walmart bought roughly 77 per cent stake in the e-retailer for around US $16 billion (approx. ₹1,000 billion then). This was India's largest acquisition and also the world's biggest purchase of an e-commerce company.

Highest number of stores opened in a single day

On 29 October 2018, the Chinese electronics company Xiaomi opened 500 retail stores, called Mi Stores, in rural regions of India, thereby setting a record for the most number of stores opened in a single day. These stores are on the lines of the larger 'Mi Home' stores in metropolitan cities.

Largest hoarding

A hoarding of Mumbai-based Ego Media Private Limited was installed on Government Railway Police Grounds, Ghatkopar East, in Mumbai, Maharashtra, on 5 April 2023. It measured 1583.068 sq. m (17,040 sq) by area, making it the largest in India. It is 36.576 m wide and 43.282 m high (120 ft by 142 ft).

GST records

Gross goods and services tax (GST) collection reached an all-time high in April 2023, when it reached ₹1,87,035 lakh crore, of which CGST is ₹38,440 crore, SGST is ₹47,412 crore, IGST is ₹89,158 crore (including ₹34,972 crore collected on import of goods) and cess is ₹12,025 crore (including ₹901 crore collected on import of goods). Highest tax collected on a single day ever was ₹68,228 crore. It happened through 9.8 lakh transactions on 20 April 2023.

TRENDS IN GST COLLECTION (₹ CRORE)

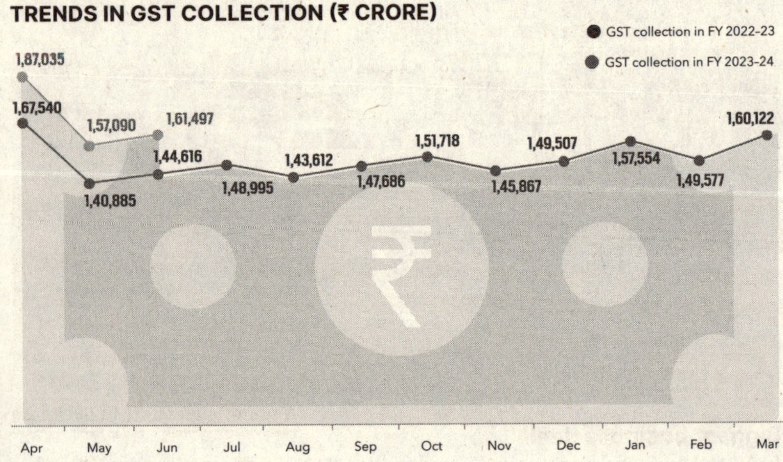

Source: Ministry of Finance, Government of India's press release on Press Information Bureau

ADVERTISING

First patented brand

Horlicks, the first patented brand in the country, was launched in the last decade of the 19th century. In the 1940s, Hindustan Thompson Associates (HTA), an advertising agency, which is now J. Walter Thompson India (JWT), coined the 'Balanced Nourishment' concept for the malt-based beverage to make Horlicks more relevant to India.

First known advertisements

Advertising in India began with the first printed newspaper, called Hicky's Bengal Gazette, and printed from the 1780s onwards in Calcutta (now Kolkata), West Bengal. The advertisements consisted of a series of simple messages 'classified' into different categories for easy reference of readers, or they were lists of the latest merchandise from England.

First multinational advertising agencies

- Alliance Advertising was set up during the First World War (1914–18), and other foreign (American) agencies such as L.A. Stronach and D.J. Keymer followed later.
- The first fully multinational agency in the country was Hindustan Thompson Associates (now JWT) in 1926.

The Indian advertising industry was valued at over ₹85,700 crore (857 billion) in 2022.

First ad association

On 21 September 1945, the Advertising Agencies Association of India (AAAI) was registered as a society in Calcutta. In 1961, its headquarters moved to Bombay.

First full-service Indian advertising agency

In 1934, Venkatrao Sista opened Sista Advertising and Publicity Services in Bombay as the first Indian agency offering creative work and space selling in the media. Sista, who came to the financial capital of India as a stenographer of the Great Indian Peninsular Railway, will always be associated with Khatau Voiles, popularized by his agency's campaign.

First Indianized foreign brand

Lux toilet soap, sold as the 'favourite beauty soap of film stars', signed on Hindi cinema actor Leela Chitnis as its first Indian model in 1941, in order to Indianize the brand.

Most awards at the Cannes Lions

In 2017, India won 40 medals including a Grand Prix award.

Cannes Lions

First ad agency abroad

Interads, a Delhi-based ad agency, was the first Indian advertising agency to open a foreign branch in Moscow, Russia, in 1962.

First ads on TV

The first product to be advertised on TV was Gwalior Suitings in an advertisement that appeared in January 1976.

First commercials on radio

The first commercial came on Vividh Bharati in 1967.

First colour TV ad

An advertisement made for Bombay Dyeing was the first colour TV ad in 1982, the year that colour TV came to India.

Largest LED display screen – on water (aboard a ship/boat/vessel)

On 21 March 2021, Zen Media Ltd LLP, a digital-first Make-in-India start-up, launched Broadcoasters, LED screens on waters in India, used as an advertising platform on a ship. The vessel *My Blue Papillon*, in the waters near the Bandra-Worli Sealink, carried a screen measuring 20 m (65.61 ft) x 5 m (16.40 ft)– with a total area of 100 sq. m (1076.39 sq. ft). The LED screen was powered with a display of 10,000 NITs (Network Interface Taps) and auto-sensors to adjust picture brightness as per daylight.

Firsts at the Cannes Lions

In 1996, the advertising fraternity bagged three awards at the International Advertising Festival in Cannes, France.

Longest sustained advertising campaign

The Amul 'utterly butterly' topical ad series is the longest sustained campaign, with its tongue-in-cheek, pithy comments on current affairs. The first ad featuring the now iconic 'Amul girl' appeared in March 1966. Started by Sylvester da Cunha in 1966 and run by da Cunha Communications, Mumbai, Maharashtra, the Amul Butter campaign has continued for more than 50 years.

ADVENTURE

AERO SPORTS

First jump from a microlight

Wing Commander U.K. Palat skydived from a powered hang-glider piloted by Captain K.A. Vasan from 8,000 ft at 7:40 a.m. on 18 October 1999 in Bangalore (now Bengaluru), Karnataka.

First international paramotor medallist

Appasaheb Bhimraj Dhus (b. 26 December 1970) from Maharashtra, is the first Indian to win international medals in paramotor games. He won a gold medal in the Pure Economy Task category of the World Paramotor Championship Test Event at Lopburi, Thailand, held from 28 April to 7 May 2017. In the same event, Captain Prafulla Raj Singh won a silver medal in the Pure Navigation Task category.

First Indian woman to skydive over seven continents

Shital Mahajan (b. 19 September 1982) from Pune, Maharashtra, completed 705 skydives across seven continents during 2017–18, adding to her skydive at Skydiver Empuriabrava in Spain (Europe) in 2014. She skydived at Skydive Go Fly in Boituva, Brazil (South America); Skydive Utti in Sky Dance Skydiving Center, US (North America); Sydney Skydivers in Sydney (Australia); Patriot Hill, Antarctica; Skydive Pretoria, Johannesburg, South Africa (Africa) and Skydive Pattaya, Thailand (Asia), taking the total to seven continents.

First paraglide from a high cliff

Anand Munje (b. 7 November 1956) from Kitty Hawk GroundSchool, Pune, Maharashtra, launched a flight from the 1,646 m (5,400 ft) high Kalsubai Peak, part of the Western Ghats in Maharashtra, on 25 February 1997. The flight covered 4 km in 11 mins.

First aerial world circumnavigation in a single-engine plane

Ravinder K. Bansal (b. 26 February 1949) from Clarence, New York, US, undertook an aerial circumnavigation in a Cessna 400 and flew solo, covering 36 cities over 20,959 nautical miles. He started from Buffalo, New York, US, on 4 July 2017 and returned on 20 August 2017. The expedition was undertaken to raise funds for the Rotary Ambala Cancer and General Hospital.

First woman skydiver

Rachel Thomas (b. 9 August 1955) from Chittaranjan, West Bengal, was the first Indian woman to skydive from 2,133.6 m (7,000 ft) over the North Pole. She achieved this feat on 20 April

A person jumping out of a plane

2022 to commemorate to commemorate 150 years of the Indian Railways. An employee of the Indian Railways, Thomas was also the first woman to represent the country in a skydiving competition in 1987. She was honoured with the Padma Shri in 2005.

A person in the act of bungee jumping

Highest bungee jump – woman
Sudhalakshmi Thanigai Arasu (b. 2 July 1965) performed a 220 m (721 ft 9 in.) high bungee jump on 13 August 2010 at Diga Verzasca, Switzerland.

First at the Mantar Paragliding XC Open Championship
Prakash Chand Thakur won the first prize at the Mantar Paragliding XC Open Championship, organized from 18 to 24 July 2017 by the Asian Continental Paragliding Association in Mantar, Indonesia.

First balloon bungee jump
Major M.K. Yadav jumped from a hot-air balloon, which was at a height of 3,310.73 m (10,862 ft) on 18 August 1995 over Leh, Ladakh.

First BASE jump
- *Men*: Lieutenant Colonel Satyendra Verma (b. 24 August 1969), then an officer of the Indian Army from the Corps of Signals, carried out a BASE (Building, Antenna, Span, and Earth) jump from the 137.16 m (450 ft) high deck of the Pitampura TV Tower, New Delhi, on 29 October 2010. This feat was part of the centenary celebrations of the Corps of Signals and the silver jubilee of the Army Adventure Wing.
- *Women*: Archana Sardana (b. 1 April 1972) from Visakhapatnam, Andhra Pradesh, is India's first female BASE jumper. She performed 25 BASE jumps off a 122 m (400 ft) high bridge above a canyon in Utah, US, on 13 July 2010.

First to complete a BASE jump during day and night
Mayank Nagpal (b. 21 September 1983) from New Delhi became the first Indian to complete a BASE (Building, Antenna, Span and Earth) jump from all four platforms, during both day and night. For the World BASE number, he jumped from Perrine Bridge, US (5 September 2014), a cliff called Crooked Stick in Idaho, US (11 September 2014), a mobile antenna in Gua Damai Xtreme Park, Malaysia (6 October 2015), and an under-construction building in Delhi, India (31 December 2016). For the Night BASE number he jumped from Perrine Bridge, US (7 September 2014), an antenna in Idaho, US (on 8 September 2014), an under-construction building in Delhi (26 June 2017) and Gua Damai Cliff, Malaysia (28 September 2018).

Aero India – Asia's Largest Aero Show

The 14th edition of Aero India, Asia's largest aero show, was inaugurated by PM Modi on 13 February 2023. The five-day event saw the participation of 73 Chief Executive Officers from India and abroad, defence ministers from 32 countries, and chiefs of air staff from 29 countries. The event focussed on displaying indigenous equipment technologies, during which 115 Indian companies displayed 227 Indian products. More than 80 countries participated in this event. The Sukhoi and Tejas fighter jets gave inspiring performances and the Sarang and Suryakirana teams thrilled the crowds.

Highest BASE jump

Mayank Nagpal (b. 21 September 1983) from New Delhi performed the highest BASE jump from the 3,080 m (10,105 ft) high point of Eiger Mountain in the Bernese Alps, Switzerland, on 24 July 2019.

Lowest BASE jump

Lieutenant Commander Mahesh V. Birajdar from the Indian Navy performed the lowest BASE jump from a 116 m (380 ft 6 in.) high span over a river in the Solang Valley, Himachal Pradesh, on 30 January 2011.

Highest hot-air balloon take-off

Indradhanush, the hot-air balloon of the Ballooning Club of India, piloted by the then club president, Vishwa Bandhu Gupta along with pilot R.K. Wason, took off from the Kushok Bakula Rimpochee Airport (3,310.7 m/ 10,862 ft) in Leh, Ladakh, on 29 September 1988.

Highest and longest wingsuit flight

Lieutenant Colonel Satyendra Verma (b. 24 August 1969), a retired Indian Army officer, on 31 March 2018, jumped from 5,913.12 m (19,400 ft) using a hot-air balloon platform at Phalodi, Rajasthan. He flew in his wingsuit for 4 mins, covering 10 km across the Jodhpur desert.

Highest flight

Megha Jain (b. 21 September 1988) from New Delhi made the highest flight in an MiG-29 fighter jet, touching 18,400 m (60,367 ft 5 in.) at a top speed of 1,850 km/hr over Sokol Airbase in Nizhny Novgorod, Russia, on 16 February 2017.

Most microlight expeditions

Mountain Eagles, the Indian Army microlight formation flying team, based at

A microlight flying

Army Adventure Nodal Centre (Microlight and powered Hang-gliding), Mhow, Madhya Pradesh, conducted three expeditions in 13 months from February 2015. The first, with seven aircraft, covered 1,800 km in 10 flying days between 13 and 26 February 2015. In the second one, commemorating the golden jubilee of the India–Pakistan war in 1965, three microlights covered 3,050 km in 10 flying days from 5 to 14 September 2015. The third one, at the 15th reunion of the Corps of Signals, was from 9 to 17 February 2016, with six aircrafts covering 1,500 km in nine flying days. The core team remained the same in all three expeditions.

Highest skydive landing

Warrant Officer Anshu Kumar Tiwari (b. 3 February 1978) and Wing Commander Gajendra Yadava from the Indian Air Force jumped off an aircraft and landed at Khardungla Pass, 5,481 m (17,982 ft) above mean sea level on 8 October 2020.

Longest motor glider flight

Captain Surendra Prasad Sinha (b. 26 July 1968), director, Flying Operations, Civil Aviation Department, Government of Jharkhand, flew a Sinus 912 VT-GEE two-seater aircraft for 1,098.24 km for eight flying hours, making it the longest motor glider flight in the country. Along with his co-pilot Captain Anil Gill, he took off from Karnal, Haryana, on 13 March 2014 and reached Ranchi, Jharkhand, the next day.

Longest cross-country microlight expedition

The Cross India Air Expedition 2011, organized by the Indian Air Force, covered 7,600 km in 80 hrs 15 mins over 19 days. Wing Commander Akhilesh Chauhan piloted the two-seater microlight, while Squadron Leader Asha Vashisht, Squadron Leader N.D. Gholba, and Sergeant M.P. Singh joined him as co-pilots at different stages of the journey. The flight took off from the air force station at Hindon, Ghaziabad, Uttar Pradesh, on 8 February 2011, proceeded to Udhampur, Jammu and Kashmir, and traversed the length of the country, flying over Delhi, Jodhpur (Rajasthan), Vadodara (Gujarat), Pune (Maharashtra), Bangalore (now Bengaluru, Karnataka), Sulur (Tamil Nadu) and Thiruvananthapuram (Kerala). It returned to Hindon by the same route on 27 February 2011.

Longest paramotor expedition

The Indian Air Force paramotor team, with Wing Commander M.P.S. Solanki as their leader, conducted a circumnavigation-of-India expedition called 'Pradakshina', covering 10,041.7 km in 53 days from 3 February to 26 March 2016. Flagged off from the air force station at Kalaikunda, West Bengal, the team flew along the periphery of the country before returning to Kalaikunda. They followed a clockwise route along the eastern and western coasts and the north-western and eastern regions, covering an average of 218.3 km per day.

NOTHING CAN STOP THEM!

1 Highest zipline by a disabled person

Vijay Kumar Devarkhyani (b. 13 March 1989) from Delhi zipped across Tower 1 and Tower 3 at a height of 473 ft for a distance of 250 ft at 9:58 p.m. on 19 May 2013 at the 40th level of Crown Regency Hotel and Tower, Philippines.

2 First Asian triple amputee to complete a bungee jump

Tinkesh Kaushik (b. 21 June 1993) from Jhajjar, Haryana, became the first Asian triple amputee to perform a bungee jump from the world's highest canyon swing. He performed the jump from a height of 160 m (525 ft) on 25 November 2018 at The Last Resort, Kathmandu, Nepal.

3 First visually impaired person to paraglide

Divyanshu Ganatra, who lost his eyesight due to glaucoma at 19 years, performed a solo paraglider flight over Kamshet near Pune, Maharashtra, on 30 April 2014. The flight up to 213.36 m (700 ft) lasted 1 min 30 seconds.

4 First to paraglide with a prosthetic leg

Lieutenant Colonel Dharam Dutt Goel (b. 14 August 1976) from Pune, Maharashtra, successfully performed solo paragliding on 19 October 2013 at Al-Hilal, Himachal Pradesh, thereby becoming the first Indian with a prosthetic leg to paraglide. He performed the paraglider flight from an altitude of 2,400 m (7,874 ft) for 25 mins.

5 First disabled skydiver in Asia

Major Devender Pal Singh (b. 13 September 1973) from Gurugram, Haryana, is the first disabled skydiver in Asia. A war-injured amputee veteran, Major Singh skydived from an altitude of 2,743.2 m (9,000 ft) on 28 March 2019 at the military cantonment in Nashik, Maharashtra.

A person performing wingsuit jump

Daring dives

Wing Commander Gajanand Yadava of the Indian Air Force (IAF) created four national records in the field of wingsuit skydive jumping in 2019 in Agra, Uttar Pradesh:

1. First wingsuit skydive jump from a high-speed aircraft (An-32),
2. Highest wingsuit jump from an altitude of 7,437.12 m (24,400 ft),
3. First to do a night-time wingsuit jump from 2,438.40 m (8,000 ft),
4. The only jumper to undertake a high-altitude night-time wingsuit jump from 3,657.60 m (12,000 ft), where he opened the chute at 914.40 m (3,000 ft) after doing wingsuit flying for 2,743.2 m (9,000 ft), Part of the IAF's skydiving team Akashganga and a parachute jump instructor, Wing Commander Yadava, has taken more than 2,900 jumps to date and was awarded the Tenzing Norgay National Adventure Award 2019 in the air adventure category.

Most podium finishes in FAI F3M Championship

Harshil Virendra Mane (b. 3 March 1999) from Pune, Maharashtra, has six international podium finishes in the FAI F3M category championship of aeromodelling, the highest number by an Indian. He is also the first aeromodeller representing India in international championships including the World Cups conducted by the Federation Aeronautique Internationale (FAI).

Longest-harness hang-glider flight

Havildar Sanjeev Kumar from the Indian Army Hang-Gliding Team, completed the longest-harness hang-glider flight from Suratgarh to Barmer, Rajasthan, on 12 December 2018. He covered 465.33 km on Fox hang-gliders powered by a Mosquito NRG harness. He covered the distance in 8 hrs 43 mins.

The National Air Sports Policy launched by the Ministry of Civil Aviation covers 11 aero sports.

Most skydiving jumps

Rajkumar Balakrishnan (b. 1 April 1977) from Theni, Tamil Nadu, started performing skydiving jumps in February 2006 and completed his 10,000th jump on 23 March 2018.

Most hours logged in free fall

Rajkumar Balakrishnan (b. 1 April 1977) from Theni, Tamil Nadu, has logged a total of 84 hours in free fall while skydiving, up to 6 July 2018.

Oldest woman skydiver

Usha Arun Mahajan (b. 20 November 1945) from Pune, Maharashtra, successfully performed a tandem skydive from an altitude of 13,500 ft on 1 October 2017 in Pennsylvania, US, at the age of 71 years 10 months 11 days.

Microlight aircraft flight

First: Flying at a cruising speed of 56 km/hr on a 90 kg tricycle-shaped aircraft, Lieutenant Anil Kumar Yadav covered 3,000 km from Jaisalmer, Rajasthan, to Calcutta (now Kolkata), West Bengal, in 31 days starting 21 September 1994.
Fastest: Squadron Leader B.K. Das flew a microlight aircraft from Jaisalmer, Rajasthan, to Dibrugarh, Assam, covering 3,250 km during 1 to 23 February 1999.

ROAD EXPEDITIONS

FOUR-WHEELER

First All-India expedition – group

Arun Kumar Basra and Kamaljit Singh Virdi from Rapid Action India completed an all-India car expedition in their Fiat Padmini, covering 15,179 km in 19 days 19 hrs 5 mins. They were flagged off from Delhi on 5 January 1998 and returned on 25 January 1998.

First Four Corners of India expedition – solo

Dr S.S. Chaudhari (b. 7 March 1962) from Jalgaon, Maharashtra, completed a solo drive connecting the four corners of India, covering 13,834 km in 26 days 22 hrs 15 mins. Driving a Maruti SX4 car, he set out from Kanniyakumari, Tamil Nadu, on 30 October 2014. He reached Tezu, Lohit District, Arunachal Pradesh, on 8 November 2014; Leh, Ladakh, on 16 November 2014; Koteshwar, Kachchh District, Gujarat, on 22 November 2014; and concluded the expedition at Kanniyakumari on 26 November 2014.

First North–South India round expedition – solo

Suresh Joseph (b. 14 May 1958) from Tamil Nadu is the first person to complete the trailblazing North–South India round expedition trip in 2012 and, in the process, breaking the record of the fastest North–South solo expedition. He started his expedition from Kanniyakumari, Tamil Nadu, on 2 July 2012 and reached Leh, Ladakh, on 7 July 2012, covering 3,811 km in 129 hrs 30 mins. Four days later, he was back on the trip, taking off from Leh on 11 July 2012. He reached Kanniyakumari on 15 July 2012. He drove a Maruti Swift car for the journey.

First Trans-Himalayan expedition – solo

Suresh Joseph (b. 14 May 1958) from Tamil Nadu set out in a Ford Endeavour to create a new record for a Trans-Himalayan solo trip, which he accomplished in 18 days 13 hrs 15 mins. Starting his journey from Jammu in Jammu and Kashmir

Fastest GQ expedition – group – women

Sukraty Saxena, Rupam Devedi, Swaranjali Saxena, and Apala Rajvanshi completed the Golden Quadrilateral (GQ) expedition, covering a distance of 6,263 km in 6 days 14 hrs 5 mins. They started their expedition at 1:35 a.m. on 10 May 2023 from India Gate, New Delhi, and concluded it at 4:30 p.m. on 16 May 2023 at Subroto Park Air Force Station, New Delhi.

From left to right: Apala Rajvanshi, Sukraty Saxena, Swaranjali Saxena and Rupam Devedi

First disabled person to reach Umling La – solo

Eric Paul (b. 14 January 1988) from Delhi was the first disabled person to reach Umling La on 6 July 2022 at 2:57 p.m. He started on 1 July 2022 from Delhi and covered a distance of 1,260 km in 126 hrs 27 mins. He is paralysed from below the chest and drove his hand-controlled car to this high altitude.

on 21 August 2015, he reached Tezu in Arunachal Pradesh on 8 September 2015. Joseph covered 5,845 km across nine Indian states, Nepal and Bhutan, and crossed altitudes of up to 2,554.2 m (8,380 ft).

First West–East India round expedition – solo

Daljit Singh Matharoo (b. 29 September 1986) completed a solo West–East–West India expedition, covering 7,715 km in 217 hrs 25 mins. He broke the record for the fastest solo East–West India expedition by covering 3,832 km in 94 hrs 44 mins. He started in his Maruti Zen car from Koteshwar, Kachchh District, Gujarat, on 27 April 2018, and reached Tezu, Arunachal Pradesh, on 1 May 2018. He started back on 1 May 2018 and reached Koteshwar on 6 May 2018.

Fastest East–West India expedition – group

Apurba Kumar Deka (b. 27 March 1975), Animesh Deka (b. 15 January 1982), and Md Zillur Rahman (b. 2 December 1975) from Guwahati, Assam, completed the fastest East–West India expedition from Tezu, Arunachal Pradesh, to Koteshwar, Gujarat, covering 3,771.4 km in 70 hrs 52 mins. The team drove a Renault Duster car, starting their journey on 27 October 2015 and ending the expedition on 30 October 2015.

Fastest East–West India expedition by a disabled person – solo

Eric Paul (b. 14 January 1988), a wheelchair-bound paraplegic from Rohini, New Delhi, completed the East–West India solo expedition in a hand-controlled Maruti Swift, covering 3,697 km in 4 days 18 hrs 55 mins. He started from Tezu, Arunachal Pradesh, on 30 November 2017 at 4:13 a.m., reaching Koteshwar, Gujarat, at 11:43 p.m. on 4 December 2017.

Longest journey within a country – solo

Shashi Kapila (b. 3 November 1942) from New Delhi completed the longest journey in a Honda Mobilio car, covering 8,227 km in 105 hrs 15 mins. He started from Delhi at 6:00 a.m. on 12 November 2016 and reached back at 12:28 p.m. on 22 November 2016. The farthest location he travelled to was Kanniyakumari.

Fastest Four Corners of India expedition – solo

Suresh Joseph (b. 14 May 1958) from Tamil Nadu successfully completed the four corners of India tour (Kanniyakumari, Tamil Nadu; Koteshwar, Gujarat; Leh, Ladakh; and Tezu, Arunachal Pradesh), covering 13,214 km in 403 hrs. Driving a Mahindra XUV500, he started his expedition on 7 May 2015 and ended it on 12 June 2015.

Longest journey within a country – group

Sagar Thakar (b. 30 June 1982) and Kanak Barsadia (b. 14 February 1984) from Surat, Gujarat, completed the longest journey in a Maruti Swift Dzire car, covering 60,830 km in 82 days. They set off from Bardoli, Gujarat, on 20 March 2017 and reached back on 12 June 2017.

Fastest North–South expedition – group

Sameer A.S. (b. 14 December 1986), Noufal K.N. (b. 30 May 1985), and Bibin Krishnan (b. 20 April 1984) from Kerala set a record for the fastest North–South

India group expedition, covering 3,870 km in 49 hrs 34 mins. The trio started from Leh, Ladakh, at 7:05 a.m. on 1 September 2021, reaching Kanniyakumari, Tamil Nadu, at 8:39 a.m. on 3 September 2021.

Fastest North–South expedition – solo

Dhruveer Singh Gandhi (b. 6 March 1985) from Mumbai, Maharashtra, completed the North–South expedition, covering a distance of 3,819.17 km in 56 hrs 20 mins. He started his expedition at 4:45 a.m. on 10 September 2021 from the office of the deputy commissioner GST Division, Srinagar, and concluded it at 1:05 p.m. on 12 September 2021 at the deputy superintendent of police's office at Kanniyakumari.

In 2023, Indian Army organized Jashn-e-Gurez festival in Jammu and Kashmir's Gurez valley. A mix of adventure sports and cultural activities, it saw a footfall of 1,500 people from across the country.

Longest distance travelled across countries – solo

Hitendra Sharma (b. 11 January 1978) from Gwalior, Madhya Pradesh, successfully undertook a solo expedition by road, covering 30,195 km across 11 Asian countries in a Honda Amaze car in 92 days. Starting from Gwalior in Madhya Pradesh, India, on 10 February 2017, he reached Bangladesh, driving through India, Myanmar, Thailand, Laos, Vietnam, Cambodia, Malaysia, Singapore, Bhutan, and Nepal, and returned to India on 21 May 2017.

TWO-WHEELER (MOTORCYCLE)*

UP TO 150 CC

First Trans-Himalayan expedition – solo

Rajeev Kumar Mondal from Burdwan, West Bengal, successfully completed a solo two-wheeler expedition along the Trans-Himalayan route covering 7,120 km in 303 hrs 58 mins of travel time. Kick-starting the expedition on a 150 cc Hero Honda Achiever from Guwahati, Assam, on 5 May 2013, he first went to Arunachal Pradesh and then, passing through Bhutan, West Bengal, Nepal, Uttarakhand and Himachal Pradesh, reached Srinagar in Jammu and Kashmir on 12 July 2013. He crossed 22 passes including Khardung La at 5,602 m (18,380 ft).

151–450 CC

First North–South India round expedition by a disabled person – solo

Vadivel Baluchamy (b. 14 June 1990), a disabled person from Madurai, Tamil Nadu, completed the first North–South solo round expedition by a disabled person, covering 9,136 km in 576 hrs 23 mins. He started on a Royal Enfield Classic 350 bike from Kanniyakumari on 30 August 2018 at 4:25 p.m. and travelled to Leh, Ladakh. He returned to Kanniyakumari on 22 September at 8:18 p.m.

* Records for expeditions on two-wheelers (motorcycles) may be categorized according to engine capacity: up to 150 cc, 151–450cc, and over 450 cc.

Siachen is now open for the public!

Siachen, a glacier in the Karakoram Range, is located at 5,753 m (18,875 ft) above mean sea level. As it was the highest military base camp of the highest battlefield in the world, permission from the army was required earlier for any tourist visits. However, now no prior permission or NOC is required for tourist visits. Tourists only need to pay an environment fee to visit the camp. This is extremely beneficial for the Tourism Department of Ladakh.

Fastest East–West India expedition – solo

Dr S.T. Thomas (b. 8 January 1987) from Tamil Nadu covered 3,729 km from Tezu, Arunachal Pradesh, to Koteshwar, Gujarat, in 68 hrs 18 mins to set a new record in the East–West India two-wheeler expedition category. He started his journey on his Honda CBR 250R bike on 20 March 2016 and concluded the expedition on 23 March 2016.

Fastest Four Corners of India expedition – solo

Vishvesh Dhirendrakumar Mehta (b. 10 June 1980) from Jamnagar, Gujarat, completed the fastest solo expedition connecting the four corners of India, covering 11,217 km in 313 hrs 51 mins. Riding a Royal Enfield Classic 350, he set out from Koteshwar, Gujarat, on 21 May 2019 and returned to Koteshwar after covering Kanniyakumari, Tamil Nadu; Leh, Ladakh; and Tezu, Arunachal Pradesh, on 8 June 2019. His break time was 113 hrs.

Fastest North–South India expedition – solo

Sridhar Ramulu Chidumalla (b. 2 January 1978) from Mumbai, Maharashtra, completed the fastest North–South solo expedition on a Royal Enfield motorcycle, covering 3,849 km in 74 hrs 45 mins. He started from Leh, Ladakh, on 25 June 2018 and reached Kanniyakumari, Tamil Nadu, on 28 June 2018.

Fastest GQ expedition by a disabled person – solo

Vadivel Baluchamy (b. 14 June 1990), completed the fastest Golden Quadrilateral (GQ) expedition by a differently abled person, covering 6,723 km in 14 days 9 hrs 30 mins. He started on a Royal Enfield Classic 350 bike from Chennai, Tamil Nadu, on 25 September 2017 and travelled to Kolkata, Delhi and Mumbai, returning to Chennai on 9 October 2017.

Longest journey within the country – solo

Krishanu Kona (b. 27 September 1991) from Delhi travelled 50,338 km on his motorcycle in 224 days to set the record for the longest motorcycle journey in India. He started on a Bajaj Pulsar NS200 bike on 30 August 2015 from Delhi and returned on 9 April 2016.

Longest distance covered within the country by a disabled person – solo

Mahinder Singh Raghuwanshi (b. 2 October 1987), who has 70 per cent disability and a prosthetic limb, covered 5,331.5 km on an Enfield Bullet 350 bike in 17 days. He started from his hometown Mhow, Madhya Pradesh, on 3 June 2016, and went up to Khardung La (5,359 m/17,582 ft) in Leh, Ladakh, returning to Mhow on 19 June 2016.

OVER 450 CC

Fastest All-India expedition – solo

Prashant Kumar (b. 14 July 1987) from Bengaluru, Karnataka, completed the all-India expedition on 7 November 2019 on his Triumph Tiger XCA 800 bike, covering 16,305 km in 23 days 9 hrs 46 mins. He started from Hyderabad, Telangana, on 15 October 2019 and returned on 7 November 2019, travelling through the then 29 states and five Union Territories.

Fastest GQ expedition – solo

Souvig Sarkar (b. 22 October 1986) from Mumbai, Maharashtra, completed the GQ solo motorcycling expedition, covering 5,962.09 km in 87 hrs 42 mins on a Triumph Street Triple RS motorcycle, between 18 and 22 October 2019.

GENERAL

First to cross Umling La pass – solo

Pallavi Fauzdar (b. 20 December 1979) from Delhi was the first to cross Umling La pass on 4 August 2017 at 3:16 p.m. It is the highest motorable pass in the world, situated at an altitude of 5,882.64 m (19,300 ft) above sea level. On her expedition, she even named the Bonni La pass, situated at an altitude of 5,083 m (16,677 ft), which was unnamed before.

Largest rally (less than 100 km) by women riders – multiple venues

The largest two-wheeler rally by only women riders was organized by the Akhil Bharatiya Terapanth Mahila Mandal on 8 March 2020, International Women's Day. As many as 6,205 women rode distances ranging from 1.5 to 10 km at locations like Udaipur, Ahmedabad, Balotra, Surat and Delhi. The rally was held

BSF BRAVE HEARTS

1 Longest ride while standing anywhere on the bike – solo

Vishwajeet Bhatia (b. 22 January 1983) of the Border Security Force (BSF) successfully covered 95.42 km while standing on the side footrest of the Royal Enfield 350. He completed the ride in 2 hrs 36 mins on 28 December 2022 at 25 Battalion, BSF, R.K. Wadhwa parade ground, Chhawla, New Delhi. He performed this stunt without any belts, harnesses, or supporting equipment.

2 Longest ride while standing on a structure – solo – woman

Satabdi Dhar (b. 23 December 1990) of the Border Security Force performed a continuous ride on a 2.49 m (8.2 ft) ladder fitted on a Royal Enfield 350 for 2.5 hrs on 26 December 2022. She covered a distance of 76 km at 25 Battalion, BSF, R.K. Wadhwa parade ground, Chhawla, New Delhi. She performed this stunt without any belts, harnesses, or supporting equipment.

Satabdi Dhar

3 Longest ride while standing on a structure – group

Inspector Awadhesh Kumar Singh (b. 19 April 1980) and Constable Sudhakar (b. 8 July 1987) of the Border Security Force performed a continuous ride on a 3.35 m (11 ft) ladder fitted on a Royal Enfield 350 for 2.5 hrs. They covered a distance of 75 km at 25 Battalion, BSF, R.K. Wadhwa parade ground, Chhawla, New Delhi. They performed this stunt without any belts, harnesses, or supporting equipment.

4 Longest ride on a structure facing backwards – solo

Inspector Awadhesh Kumar Singh (b. 19 April 1980) of the Border Security Force performed a continuous ride on a 3.42 m (11 .3 ft) pole fitted on a Royal Enfield 350 for 4 hrs 37 mins while facing backwards. He covered a distance of 169 km at 25 Battalion, BSF, R.K. Wadhwa parade ground, Chhawla, New Delhi. He performed this stunt without any belts, harnesses, or supporting equipment.

5 Longest ride while standing anywhere on the bike – solo – woman

Inspector Himanshu Sirohi (b. 4 May 1988) of the Border Security Force successfully covered 178 km while standing on the side bracket of a Royal Enfield 350. She completed the ride in 6 hrs 2 mins on 24 December 2022 at 25 Battalion, BSF, R.K. Wadhwa parade ground, Chhawla, New Delhi. She performed this stunt without any belts, harnesses, or supporting equipment.

6 Longest ride while sitting on a bike facing backwards – solo – woman

Constable Rajwinder Kaur (b. 1 May 1986) of the Border Security Force performed a continuous ride while sitting facing backwards on a Royal Enfield 350. She covered a distance of 32 km in 1 hr on 28 December 2022 at 25 Battalion, BSF, R.K. Wadhwa parade ground, Chhawla, New Delhi. She performed this stunt without any belts, harnesses, or supporting equipment.

7 Largest moving human pyramid – women

On 27 December 2022, the female team of 38 women led by Inspector Himanshu Sirohi of the Border Security Force formed a human pyramid on nine Royal Enfield 350 bikes. They covered more than 1 km in 2 mins 10 secs at Kartavya Path between Vijay Chowk and India Gate, New Delhi. They performed this stunt without any belts, harnesses, or supporting equipment.

as part of their 'I Respect' campaign to emphasize the need for women to respect one another for their choices.

TWO-WHEELER (BICYCLE)

GEARED

Fastest East–West expedition – solo

Naresh Kumar Rajendran (b. 3 June 1992) from Vellore, Tamil Nadu, completed the fastest East–West solo expedition on a geared bicycle by covering 3,613 km in 10 days 8 hrs 57 mins. He started from Tezu, Arunachal Pradesh, at 4:00 a.m. on 5 December 2018 and ended at Koteshwar, Gujarat, at 12:57 p.m. on 15 December 2018.

Fastest GQ expedition – geared bicycle – solo

Bharat Pannu (b. 8 May 1983) from Bengaluru, Karnataka, completed the Golden Quadrilateral (GQ) solo expedition, covering a distance of 5,938.2 km in 14 days 23 hrs 52 mins on his geared bicycle. He started his expedition at 12:08 a.m. on 16 October 2020 from India Gate, New Delhi, and concluded it at 12:20 a.m. on 31 October 2020.

Fastest North–South expedition – solo

Nimesh Mansukhbhai Jivrajani (b. 11 February 1980) from Bhavnagar, Gujarat, completed a solo North–South India expedition on a geared bicycle, covering 3,400 km in 14 days 16 hrs 15 mins. He started from Jammu, Jammu and Kashmir, at 5:40 a.m. on 24 December 2018 and reached Kanniyakumari, Tamil Nadu, at 10:00 p.m. on 7 January 2019.

Longest distance covered within the country – geared – solo

Karan Singh Jagawat (b. 1 March 1948) covered a distance of 20,948 km on his geared cycle in 178 days. He started his journey on 23 April 2017 from Jaipur, Rajasthan, and returned to Jaipur on 18 October 2017. He travelled through Koteshwar, Gujarat; Tezu, Arunachal Pradesh; Khardung La, Ladakh; and Kanniyakumari, Tamil Nadu.

GEARLESS

Fastest North–South expedition – solo

Saurabh Bharat Zagade (b. 28 October 1996) from Pune, Maharashtra, completed a solo North–South India expedition on a gearless bicycle, covering a distance of 3,440 km in 14 days 7 hrs. He started the expedition from Dharmal, Jammu and Kashmir, at 6:25 a.m. on 15 April 2019 and reached Kanniyakumari, Tamil Nadu, at 1:25 p.m. on 29 April 2019.

Fastest North–South expedition – group

Ashwani Kumar Singh (b. 14 August 1995) from Deoria, Uttar Pradesh, and Akash Yadav (b. 1 February 1990) from Azamgarh, Uttar Pradesh, completed the fastest North–South India tour by cycle, covering 4,197 km in 14 days 15 hrs 37 mins. The duo started from Leh, Ladakh, on 13 June 2016 and reached Kanniyakumari, Tamil Nadu, on 27 June 2016.

GENERAL

Representative image

Largest bicycling marathon

Organized by Vodafone India, the second edition of the Vodafone Cycling Marathon held in Bengaluru, Karnataka, on 1 March 2015, attracted 6,123 cyclists. The event was held under four different categories: Champion Race (60 km), Passion Race (40 km), Green Ride (20 km) and Fashion Ride (5 km). It was conducted under the aegis of the Cycle Federation of India, supported by Bengaluru City Traffic Police. Around 5,000 cyclists took part in the first edition of this marathon.

Oldest Super Randonneuse

Ela Ghose (b. 8 April 1961) successfully completed four brevets organized by Noida Randonneurs and Delhi Randonneurs (a part of Audax India Randonneurs) under the aegis of Audax Club Parisien of France, and earned the title of Super Randonneuse in the 2018–19 season. A randonneuring event is called a randonnée or brevet, and a rider who has completed a 200 km event is called a randonneur. The Super Randonneur/Randonneuse title is awarded on the completion of a series of four brevets within a single (cycling) year, say, November 2018–October 2019. The four brevets cover 200 km (completed within 13.5 hrs), 300 km (completed within 20 hrs), 400 km (completed within 27 hrs) and 600 km (completed within 40 hrs).

Longest tandem bicycling – women

Sheetal Bambulkar (b. 27 October 1978) from Mumbai, Maharashtra, and Dr Meera Velankar (b. 11 December 1975) from Bengaluru, Karnataka, completed a tandem cycling brevet ride of 206 km in 12 hrs 27 mins in Vadodara, Gujarat, on 20 December 2015.

First tandem bicycling

Ashok N. Bhanushali (b. 21 May 1974) from Mumbai, Maharashtra, and Dr Meera Velankar (b. 11 December 1975) from Bengaluru, Karnataka, completed India's first 300 km brevet ride on a tandem bicycle. The feat was part of an event organized by Surat Randonneurs on 10 July 2016. The duo started the ride from M.T.B. College, Surat, Gujarat, and covered a distance of 309 km in 17 hrs 36 mins.

Most consecutive cycling expeditions – 100 km

Gurpreet Singh (b. 28 June 1972) from Jalandhar, Punjab, cycled at least 100 kms consecutively for 300 days from 19 May 2020 to 14 March 2021 with geared Merida Sculptura 400 and Trek FX2 bicycles in Jalandhar, Punjab.

All-India tour on a mono-wheeler

Subrata Chakraborty (b. 5 November 1976) from Kolkata, West Bengal, completed an all-India solo expedition on a monocycle, covering 10,500 km in 256 days. He started his journey from Raj Bhavan, Kolkata, on 8 September 2000 and returned to Kolkata on 21 May 2001. He passed through 17 states of the country, viz., West Bengal, Odisha, Andhra Pradesh, Tamil Nadu, Kerala, Karnataka, Goa, Maharashtra, Gujarat, Rajasthan, Haryana, Delhi, Uttar Pradesh, Madhya Pradesh, Bihar, Assam, and Arunachal Pradesh.

Fastest Asian to cycle across the world

Vedangi Kulkarni (b. 1998) from Pune, Maharashtra, became the fastest Asian to cycle across the world. She started her expedition from Perth, Australia, in July 2018 and reached Kolkata, West Bengal, on 23 December 2018. She crossed 29,000 km in 159 days, pedalling up to 300 km every day.She covered 14 countries including New Zealand, Canada, Iceland, Portugal, Spain, France, Belgium, Germany, Denmark, Sweden, Finland, and Russia, and endured temperatures ranging between –20°C and 37°C.

WATER SPORTS

First sail down the Ganga River

Captain P.P. Sabharwal and Captain S.N. Dubey performed the first sail down the Ganga River in a racing craft from Chandi Ghat at Haridwar, Uttarakhand, to Kolkata, West Bengal, from 26 to 28 July 1960. The total distance they covered was 1,931.23 km.

First circumnavigation of the globe – group

On 28 September 1985, ten sappers, led by Colonel T.P.S. Chowdhury, set off on INS *Trishna*, for a 55,000 km sail in an 11.3 m (37 ft) long, 10.5 tonne fibreglass yacht. They sailed from Mumbai, Maharashtra, to Maldives and Mauritius, and then to St Helena Island. Crossing the Equator for the second time, they sailed into the Port of Belem in Brazil, then through the Panama Canal towards the Galapagos Islands, the Polynesian Islands and Bali, reaching Mumbai on 10 January 1987.

First circumnavigation of the globe by a disabled sailor

Major Ashok Kumar Singh, a permanent member of the INS *Trishna* crew and winner of the National Adventure Award in 1994, went around the globe in 1985. It was the longest journey undertaken by a disabled person.

First sailing expedition on the Brahmaputra River and longest on any Indian river

Sixty NCC cadets of Assam undertook a 220 km long sailing expedition on the capricious Brahmaputra River in three whaler boats of the NCC naval units, with safety and support vessels provided by the Indian Army Eastern Command. The maiden expedition named 'Lachit-1' was flagged off at Biswanath Chariali, Assam, and flagged in at Pandu Port, Guwahati, on 16 October 2019.

First circumnavigation – man – solo

Commander Dilip Donde of the Indian Navy completed a solo circumnavigation of the globe in 276 days. He covered 21,600 nautical miles sailing on INSV *Mhadei*, a 17 m (56 ft) long sailing boat fitted with high-tech navigation and communication equipment. He embarked on the voyage on 19 August 2009. On return, his boat touched base at Sunk Rock Lighthouse at Mumbai harbour on 22 May 2010. The expedition was part of the Indian Navy's 'Sagar Parikrama' project.

First circumnavigation – woman – solo

On 15 October 1988, Ujwala Rai became not only the first Indian woman, but also the first Asian one, to sail around the world after a 17-month voyage in *Jaykus III*, a 9.75 m (32 ft) Vancouver-class sailboat.

First catamaran sailing expedition

A team of sailors from the Artillery Water Sports Association, Hyderabad, Telangana, completed the Sarvatra Sailing Expedition, a 1,364 km long marine voyage along the eastern coast of India. The longest such expedition in the country, it was launched from Marina Beach, Chennai, Tamil Nadu, on 18 December 2011 and culminated at Gopalpur, Odisha, on 3 January 2012. They also set records of sailing 153 km non-stop in a day on 21 December 2011 and of 15 hours of non-stop sailing on 31 December 2011.

First expedition on the Beas River

A team of 13 people from Atal Bihari Vajpayee Institute of Mountaineering and Allied Sports (ABVIMAS), Manali, Himachal Pradesh, was the first to raft across the length of the Beas River from 23 to 26 October 2019. Led by Colonel Neeraj Rana, the director of ABVIMAS, the 230 km long rafting expedition was undertaken with two rafts and three kayaks from Manali to Dehra Gopipur Bridge at Pong Dam.

First sailing expedition around the Indian peninsula

Alok Kumar Yadav (b. 20 June 1984) from EME Sailing Association completed the first sailing expedition around the Indian peninsula. He started from Haldia, West Bengal, along the east coast on 21 October 2018 and reached Porbandar, Gujarat, on the west coast on 1 December 2018. He covered a distance of 4,597 nautical miles in 41 days.

First rafting event in the country

The Indo-US Upper Ganga Rafting Expedition in 1984 was the first rafting expedition in India led by American Ken Warren and Avinash Kohli. The expedition rafted sections of the Rivers

Rafting on the Ganga

FIRST IN ASIA!

1 First to complete the Ocean's Seven Challenge

Rohan Dattatrey More (b. 30 October 1985) from Pune, Maharashtra, became the first Asian swimmer at the age of 32, to complete the Ocean's Seven challenge on 9 February 2018 when he swam across the Cook Strait between North and South Islands of New Zealand in 8 hrs 37 mins. He became the ninth swimmer in the world to complete the difficult open-water swimming challenge that includes the English Channel, the North Channel, the Molokai Channel, the Catalina Channel, the Tsugaru Channel, the Strait of Gibraltar and the Cook Strait.

2 Youngest in the world to complete the Ocean's Seven Challenge

WR Prabhat Koli (b. 27 July 1999) from Navi Mumbai, Maharashtra, became the youngest person in the world, at the age of 23, to complete the Ocean's Seven Challenge on 1 March 2023. He completed the challenge in 8 hrs 41 mins, crossing the Cook Strait between New Zealand's North and South Islands amid bad weather. He is also the recipient of Tenzing Norgay National Adventure Award.

The Cook Strait, New Zealand

3 First Asian woman to swim across the seven seas

Bula Chowdhury (b. 2 January 1970) from West Bengal was the first Asian woman to swim across the seven seas: the Arctic Ocean, the North Atlantic Ocean, the South Atlantic Ocean, the Indian Ocean, the North Pacific Ocean, the South Pacific Ocean, and the Antarctic Ocean. She crossed the English Channel twice in 1989 and 1999, and in 2005 she became the first woman to swim across sea channels off five continents. She received the Arjuna Award in 1990 and the Padma Shri in 2008.

4 First and youngest Asian woman to swim in Antarctic waters

Bhakti Sharma (b. 30 November 1989) from Udaipur, Rajasthan, is the first Asian woman and the youngest in the world to set a record in open swimming in Antarctic waters. She swam 2.3 km in 41 hrs 14 mins, in temperatures of around 1°C, breaking the record of L. Cox (US) and L. Pugh (Britain). She was awarded the Tenzing Norgay National Adventure Award in 2010.

5 Fastest Asian swimmer to cross Gibraltar Strait

Shubham Dhananjay Vanmali (b. 20 December 1995) from Mumbai, Maharashtra, became the fastest Asian swimmer to cross the Strait of Gibraltar, completing 16.7 km from Isla de Tarifa in Spain to Point Cires in Morocco in 3 hrs 16 mins on 14 August 2014. Earlier, Vanmali had also swum the English Channel (England to France), crossing the channel in 12 hrs 42 mins on 4 August 2014, and the 35 km long stretch from Dharamtar in Raigad district, Maharashtra to the Gateway of India in Mumbai, in 8 hrs 1 min 17 secs on 21 January 2014.

Bhagirathi and Alaknanda Rivers till Devprayag, and the Ganga River from Devprayag to Rishikesh in Uttarakhand.

First saturation dive

Commodore Vimal Kumar of the Indian Navy conducted the first saturation dive in May 1985 in a decompression chamber, using a mix of helium and oxygen, on INHS *Ashvini* in Mumbai, Maharashtra. Pratap Singh and T. Vinod Rao were pressurized to a depth of 67 m (219 ft 10 in.) on 16 May 1985 and stayed in saturation for six days.

First deep-bounce dive

Commodore Vimal Kumar of the Indian Navy was the first person to dive to a depth of 160 m in a diving bell in the Black Sea in 1970. He explored the bottom of the sea for about 10 mins. After surfacing, he underwent a decompression schedule for 10 hrs.

First canoeing expedition

Sheo Shankar Gope and Ravindra Kumar Bhuyan were team leaders of a canoeing expedition that started from Kolkata, West Bengal, on 6 July 1991. They paddled upstream on the Ganga and sailed a distance of 2,000 km, touching Bhagalpur, Mokama, Patna, Allahabad (now Prayagraj) and Etawah, reaching Delhi on 25 September 1991.

First backstroke swimming across the Strait of Gibraltar without neoprene

Tejesh Vishnu Parsekar (b. 30 May 1990) from Mumbai, Maharashtra, became the first Indian and second in the world (since 1928) to successfully complete backstroke swimming across the Strait of Gibraltar from Isla de Tarifa, Spain, to Perejil Island near Morocco on 16 August 2010. He was the first in the world to complete it without neoprene (protective suit). He covered 19. 4 km in 5 hrs 21 mins.

First to swim from mainland to Anacapa Island

Prabhat Raju Koli (b. 27 July 1999) from Mumbai, Maharashtra, successfully swam from Hollywood Beach, Oxnard, to Anacapa Island in 6 hrs 22 mins 17 secs on 10 July 2019. The route was 20 km long in open sea.

WR First woman to cross the English Channel – solo

Arati Saha (b. 24 September 1940) from West Bengal became the first Indian woman to cross the English Channel on 29 September 1959. She swam from Cape Gris Nez, France, to Sandgate, England, in 16 hrs 20 mins.

First to swim the English Channel thrice – solo

- *Men*: Taranath Narayan Shenoy (b. 1958) from Maharashtra became the first person to cross the English Channel thrice by 1985. Deaf and nearly blind, he had previously swum across the channel in 1983 and 1984.
- *Women*: Rashmi Sharma (b. 1988) from Kolkata, West Bengal, became the first woman to cross the English Channel thrice by 2009. She had previously swum across the channel in 2006 and 2007.

An aerial view of Strait of Gibraltar

King of Gibraltar

B. R. Ghadge of Mumbai Police, Maharashtra, crossed the shark infested and freezing Strait of Gibraltar (Spain–Morocco) four times. He was conferred the title 'King of Gibraltar' by the Gibraltar Strait Association in August 2002 as he completed the fourth feat in 6 hrs 10 mins on 2 August 2002. He was the first Indian to cross the 26 km long Toroneos Gulf, Greece, in 10 hrs 43 mins on 20 July 2002.

First to complete the Round-Trip Angel Island marathon

Shubham Dhananjay Vanmali (b. 20 December 1995) from Mumbai, Maharashtra, was the first Indian to complete the Round-Trip Angel Island marathon swimming. He completed the 16.1 km marathon swim in 10 hrs in San Francisco, California, US, on 24 May 2018. He is also the youngest male swimmer and 12th in the world to complete this challenging bay-water swim marathon.

First woman to swim the Strait of Gibraltar

Aarti Pradhan from Maharashtra became the first Indian woman to swim the Strait of Gibraltar in 1988. She covered the distance of 22.2 km in 7 hrs 17 mins from Isla de Tarifa, Spain, to Morocco. She received the Arjuna Award in 1988.

Most stand-up paddle-boarding

Kumaran M. (b. 2 March 1981) from Chennai, Tamil Nadu, had completed stand-up paddle-boarding on 19 different waterbodies, including 17 in India and one each in Sri Lanka and Malaysia, as on 30 June 2016.

First to complete the Triple Crown

Taranath Narayan Shenoy (b. 1958) from Maharashtra became the world's second swimmer and the first Indian to complete the Triple Crown of Open Water Swimming when he crossed the 32.2 km long Catalina Channel (or San Pedro Channel), separating Santa Catalina Island from the Southern California mainland, US), on 25 August 1987. Deaf and nearly blind, he had previously swum the 20 Bridges Swim (a 45.9 km circumnavigation of Manhattan Island, New York City, US) on 9 August 1987 and the English Channel on 18 August 1983.

Most rivers rafted in a month

National Institute of Mountaineering and Allied Sports (NIMAS), Dirang, Arunachal Pradesh, conducted an expedition with seven members, namely, Colonel Sarfaraz Singh, Naib Subedar Jadhav Laxman Vishnu, Havaldar Loushambam Labango Singh, Havaldar Darshan Singh, and Lance Naik Patil Suraj Ravindra and Lance Naik Himmat Singh, and Mr Tosap Rime, and rafted seven rivers in one month. They rafted on Kameng, Dibang, Noa Dihing, Lohit, Subansiri, Siyom, and Siang in Arunachal Pradesh from 23 November 2020 to 23 December 2020, covering a total distance of 720.21 km.

First surfing and stand-up paddle competition

The Surfing Federation of India, with the Kerala Tourism Department, organized Spice Coast Open, India's first official national surfing and stand-up paddle (SUP) competition at Kovalam Beach, Kerala, from 3 to 5 May 2013. The three-day event had more than 100 participants in surfing contests under five categories and SUP races under two.

Longest stand-up paddle-boarding – group

Sri Krishnan (b. 31 July 1991) and Siddharth C. (b. 6 July 1992) from Chennai, Tamil Nadu, accomplished the longest stand-up paddle-boarding in the open sea, covering 31 km in the Bay of Bengal on 15 April 2016. They started at Kovalam Beach, Kerala, and paddled to reach Marina Beach, Tamil Nadu, covering the distance in 6 hrs 27 mins.

Longest kayaking – solo

Kaustubh Kisan Khade (b. 17 January 1987) from Mumbai, Maharashtra, completed the west coast expedition from Dwarka, Gujarat, to Kanniyakumari, Tamil Nadu, from 17 November 2016 to 7 February 2017. He paddled 1,845 km in 83 days.

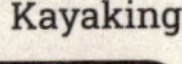
Kayaking

Aerial view of the English Channel

Fastest to swim across the English Channel

Anita Sood from Maharashtra remains the fastest Indian to swim the Great English Channel. She swam in the year 1987 and took 8 hrs 15 mins (England to France).

Longest social campaign through an adventure sport

The National Mission for Clean Ganga, operated under the Department of Water Resources, River Development and Ganga Rejuvenation, Ministry of Jal Shakti, Government of India, organized the Ganga Aamantran Abhiyaan – a river-rafting and kayaking expedition on the Ganga River, conducted between 10 October and 12 November 2019 with a team of nine members. The expedition started from Devprayag and culminated at Ganga Sagar after covering 2,500 km. They spread the message of water conservation and river rejuvenation.

Longest kayaking – group

Tarun K. Roy and Brij Mohan Bisht from New Delhi completed the Himalaya-to-Ocean Ganga Expedition from Rishikesh, Uttarakhand, to Ganga Sagar Island in the Bay of Bengal from 5 January to 19 March 2003. They paddled 2,443 km in 74 days.

Longest open-sea swimming by a paraplegic

M.S.A. Shaikh (b. 17 July 1986) from Mumbai, Maharashtra, a paraplegic with 100 per cent disability due to a spinal cord injury, participated in open-sea swimming from Sinquerim to Baga and back to Candolim Beach, Goa, on 8 April 2017 at the UMOJA #BeachFest 2017. He completed the 8 km swim in 4 hrs 4 mins.

WR Long-distance swimming by a paraplegic woman

Deepa Malik (b. 30 September 1970) is an Indian athlete from New Delhi. She swam against the current in the Yamuna River at Allahabad (now Prayagraj), Uttar Pradesh, covering a distance of 1 km in 35 mins 36 secs on 15 June 2008. She received the Khel Ratna in 2019.

Longest white-water rafting expedition

Aqua Scullers, the nine-member rafting team of the Indian Air Force, completed the longest white-water rafting expedition on the Ganga River, covering over 3,000 km from Gangotri in Uttarakhand to Ganga Sagar in West Bengal in 16 days from 19 October to 4 November 2013. The first such expedition undertaken by the Indian Air Force, it included the Himalayan portion of the river from Gangotri (3,049 m/10,003 ft) to Haridwar (295 m/968 ft), a very challenging white-water stretch with Grade IV–V rapids.

Non-stop rafting expedition

Eight members of the Bihar Adventure Foundation, led by Sanjay Kumar Dutta, set off on a non-stop rafting expedition on the Ganga River. They began from Haridwar, Uttarakhand, on 29 October 1991 and covered 2,400 km in 621 hrs, ending at Calcutta (now Kolkata), West Bengal, on 24 November 1991.

Marathon windsurfing

Rahul Rastogi from Hyderabad, Telangana, was the first Asian to windsurf 400 km from Kavaratti, Lakshadweep, to Kozhikode, Kerala. He started on 22 April 1988 and completed the marathon three days later. His average windsurfing timing was 14 hrs a day.

Swimming at the highest altitude

Petty officer R.L. Sharma and leading seaman Dhani Ram swam a distance of 4,746 m (15,571 ft) across the breadth of Kedartal, a glacial lake at an altitude of 4,750 m (15,584 ft) in Uttarakhand, on 25 September 1995.

Oldest to cross English Channel

Srikaanth Viswanathan (b. 15 July 1972) from Bengaluru, Karnataka, crossed the English Channel on 21 July 2018, at the age of 46, becoming the oldest Indian to do so. He started swimming at 5:00 a.m. and completed the crossing at 7:07 p.m., crossing the channel in 14 hrs 7 mins.

Oldest to complete the Triple Crown

Srikaanth Viswanathan (b. 15 July 1972) from Bengaluru, Karnataka, at the age of 47, completed the 20 Bridges Swim in New York City, US, in 8 hrs 7 mins on 31 August 2019, becoming the oldest Indian to complete the Triple Crown of Open Water Swimming. He had previously swum across the English Channel (14 hrs 7 mins) on 21 July 2018 and the Catalina Channel (13 hrs 4 mins) on 16 August 2019.

Yachting at the highest altitude

Captain Gautama Dutta from Mumbai, Maharashtra, carted his laser boat to an altitude of 5,460 m (17,913 ft) at Devtal Lake, Uttarakhand, and yachted there on 18 September 1993.

Fastest to complete Cape2Rio race

Indian Navy's Captain Atool Sinha (b. 1 August 1968) from Pune, Maharashtra, skippered INSV *Mhadei* in the Transatlantic Intercontinental Cape2Rio Race 2017 and completed the race in a record time of 20 days 19 hrs 27 minutes. The crew began the race on 1 January 2017 at 12:00 noon and finished the race on 22 January 2017 at 7:27 a.m., covering a distance of 3,800 nautical miles (7,038 km). The boat had six crew members including the skipper.

Deepest underwater cycling – ocean – solo

Nishant K. Patel (b. 15 February 1982) from Mumbai, Maharashtra, successfully attempted underwater cycling at a depth of 32.7 m (107 ft 3 in.) on 25 October 2016. He covered a distance of 100 m in 6 mins 47 secs in the Bay of Bengal off Puducherry coast. He used a Firefox Vortex 20 cycle and tied weights of 5 kg in the front and 2 kg at the back of the cycle to avoid floating. He had a 12-litre (200 bar) air tank attached for breathing support.

MARATHONS

First to complete Grand-to-Grand Ultramarathon

Arpita Maitra (b. 31 October 1978) from Kolkata, West Bengal, became the first Indian to successfully complete the Grand-to-Grand Ultra (G2G) marathon, a gruelling week-long foot race from the Grand Canyon to the Grand Staircase in the US, in which she covered the 273 km route in 76 hrs 21 mins 43 secs in six stages from 22 to 28 September 2013.

First 4 Deserts Grand Slam winner

Atul Patki (b. 8 November 1965), a US citizen of Indian origin, completed the 4 Deserts Ultramarathons Series on 8 November 2014. He became the first Indian to complete all four 250 km events in one calendar year.

WR First to complete all Six World Marathons

Siddhartha Ghosh (b. 21 February 1975) from Kolkata, West Bengal, was the first person to complete all Six World Marathons in one calendar year during 2013. He is also the first recipient of the Six Star World Marathon certificate and has received the same five times consecutively from 2012 to 2016. The World Marathon Majors consist of six races annually across cities and are accredited by the International Association of Athletics Federations.

Most half-marathons organized in a single day – multiple venues

The Indian Air Force organized half-marathons simultaneously across 100 air force stations as part of the centenary celebrations of the Marshal of the Indian Air Force Arjan Singh on 14 April 2019. The marathon began at 5:30 a.m. and concluded at 9:30 a.m., and saw the participation of 12,600 air force officers. The marathon distance was 21 km and it was conducted in three age categories: below 35 years; between 35 and 45 years; and 45 years and above. Marshal of the Indian Air Force Arjan Singh was the first and only officer of the Indian Air Force to hold a five-star rank.

Participants in a half marathon

First to complete the 7 Emirates Run

M.A. Shaikh (b. 29 September 1974) from Mumbai, Maharashtra, became the first

Indian to successfully complete the 7 Emirates Run, an ultramarathon across all seven emirates of the United Arab Emirates (UAE). He covered a distance of 575 km in 12 days from 21 November to 2 December 2014.

First to complete the GQ run

Michelle Kakade (b. 9 October 1968), a long-distance runner from Pune, Maharashtra, became the first person to cover the Golden Quadrilateral (GQ) on foot. The GQ is a highway network connecting Mumbai, Delhi, Kolkata, and Chennai. She covered 5,968.4 km in 193 days, 1 hr 9 mins from 21 October 2015 to 1 May 2016.

First to complete the World Marathon Challenge – full marathon

Aditya Raj (b. 22 June 1983) from Gurugram, Haryana, became the first Indian to complete the World Marathon Challenge in 2020, in which runners travel across the globe, completing seven marathons (each 42.2 km) in seven days on seven continents. Starting on 6 February 2020 in Novo, Antarctica, Raj travelled to Cape Town in Africa, Perth in Australia, Dubai in Asia, Madrid in Europe, and Brazil in South America, finishing his seventh marathon in Miami, North America, on 12 February 2020. His total running time was 36 hrs 47 mins 36 secs.

First Ultraman triathlete

Arunaabh Shah (b. 11 August 1990) from Delhi completed the Ultraman Triathlon (a 10 km swim, 421.1 km of cycling and an 84.3 km run) in Australia on 16 May 2016. He is the first Indian to do so in Ultraman's 33-year-long history.

First Ironman triathlon

The first Indian Ironman triathlon was held in Goa with over 1,000 participants on 20 October 2019. Considered the most prestigious endurance triathlon event worldwide, the race included 1.9 km of swimming, 90 km of cycling and 21.1 km of running, which were all done sequentially in a single day. Bishworjit Singh Saikhom from Pune, Maharashtra, completed the triathlon in 4 hrs 42 mins 44 seconds, securing the first place.

First disabled Ironman

Praveen Kumar (b. 17 July 1985) from New Delhi became India's first disabled Ironman on 17 November 2018 in the Ironman event organized in Langkawi, Malaysia. He completed a 3.86 km long swim in 1 hr 36 mins 7 secs, 180 km of cycling in 7 hrs 49 mins 50 secs and a 42 km long run in 5 hrs 40 mins 55 secs. Kumar is a battle-casualty soldier who was injured during the terrorist attack in Mumbai, Maharashtra, in November 2008.

First to finish the Ultraman World Championship

Gaurav Makkar (b. 26 November 1979) from Gurugram, Haryana, became the first Indian to finish the Ultraman World Championship. The championship is a three-day, 515 km multi-sport race held annually in Hawaii, US. He completed a 10 km swim (in 4 hrs 24 mins), a 421 km bicycle ride (in 16 hrs 20 mins) and an 84 km run (in 8 hrs 56 mins) during 23–25 November 2018. He also completed the Ultraman Florida 2018 during 16–18 February 2018, thereby completing two Ultraman races, the most by an individual in a year.

Longest cross-country run

Long-distance runner Raj Vadgama (b. 18 June 1967) from Mumbai, Maharashtra, successfully undertook 'Bharathon 10,000', a unique run across 70 cities in 17 states of India to spread the message of unity. He covered a distance of 9,902 km from 15 August 2014 to 26 January 2015, making it the first and longest such self-supported cross-country run. He ran 60 km a day for 165 days.

Longest relay race

As part of its golden jubilee celebrations, while also paying tribute to former president A.P.J. Abdul Kalam, the Border Security Force (BSF) Sector Headquarters in West Bengal organized the BSF Golden Jubilee Baton Relay Race 2015. The event saw 1,785 BSF jawans in commando uniform cover a distance of 174.2 km in relay format in 8 hrs 55 mins 36 secs on 24 August 2015.

Longest distance covered while running – single day

Ullas Narayana from Bengaluru, Karnataka, ran 250.3 km in 24 hours on 1 December 2018, becoming the first to cover this distance in a day. He completed the non-stop run at the 2018 International Association of Ultra Running (IAU) 24-Hour Asia and Oceania Championships in Taipei, Taiwan.

Most half-marathons in a year

Vijay Boddupalli (b. 1 September 1988) from Chennai, Tamil Nadu, completed 17 half-marathons, the most by an individual in a year, from 1 June 2017 to 31 May 2018. The 17th half-marathon was completed at the H2O Run on 22 April 2018. The half-marathons were conducted across seven states in India.

Most half-marathons by an individual

Adil S. Nargolwala (b. 31 August 1969) from Gurugram, Haryana, completed his 164th half-marathon, the most by an individual, at the Ironman Virtual Club 5 (70.3 (miles/113 km) race on 1 May 2020. These half-marathons were conducted at venues both in India and abroad, and included road as well as trail events. He had also completed at least one marathon in each of the seven continents by 15 January 2019.

Most full marathons in a year

Sivabalan Pandian (b. 21 September 1958) from Mumbai, Maharashtra, completed 114 full marathons, the most by an individual in a year, from 6 January to 31 December 2019. These full marathons were conducted at venues both within India and abroad. The count also includes 14 ultramarathons.

Most ultramarathons in a year

Sivabalan Pandian (b. 21 September 1958) from Mumbai, Maharashtra, has run and completed 18 ultramarathons in a year from 16 June 2018 to 23 December 2018.

WR Oldest marathoner

Fauja Singh (b. 1 April 1911) of Indian origin, residing in the UK, is the world's oldest marathon runner. He completed the London Marathon, covering a distance of 42.16 km in 6 hrs 2 mins on 22 April 2012. His marathon record, for age 90-plus, was 5 hrs 40 mins at the Toronto Waterfront Marathon held in Canada in 2013.

Most consecutive half-marathon distance runs

Abhishek Singh Pandher (b. 27 September 1977) from Ahmedabad, Gujarat, completed 685 half-marathon distance (21.09 km) runs in 685 days from 15 July 2020 to 30 May 2022. The runs were conducted in Gujarat and Madhya Pradesh.

Most triathlons completed in a year

Adil S. Nargolwala (b. 31 August 1969) from Gurugram, Haryana, completed the most triathlon races in a year in 2019. He completed the Triathlon Sprint at the Delhi International Triathlon 2019, the Triathlon Olympics at the New Delhi Triathlon Championship, the Ironman (70.3 miles/113 km) in Kazakhstan, the Ironman in Sweden, and the Ultraman India Race conducted in Delhi-NCR.

Most visually impaired athletes completing marathons

Six visually impaired athletes –Nandeesh J., Sunita N.D., Renuka Rajput, Kavya Ramesh, and Ajay and Mala Kolkar – ran a full marathon in 7 hrs 21 mins on 21 October 2018 at Sree Kanteerava Outdoor Stadium, Bengaluru, Karnataka. Helped by guide runners, the students, who were from the Samarthanam Trust for the Disabled, Bengaluru, were led by their coach, Bhumika Patel.

Only Asian to complete Ironman triathlons in six continents

Kaustubh Radkar has completed the Ironman triathlon in six continents between March 2014 and November 2016, and is the only Asian to do so. He has completed 25 Ironman triathlons since he ran his first triathlon in 2008.

Fastest at Badwater Ultramarathon

Brij Mohan Sharma (b. 1 January 1974) of the Indian Navy, from Mumbai, Maharashtra, is the fastest Indian at the Badwater Ultramarathon, one of the world's toughest foot races, held in California, US, from 18 to 20 July 2016. He completed the 217 km run in 40 hrs 47 mins.

MOUNTAIN ADVENTURES

First club

The Himalayan Club was founded in February 1928 in the room of Field Marshal Sir William Birdwood, then commander-in-chief of the British Indian Army.

First mountaineering expedition

In 1951, Gurdial Guru Singh from Dehradun, Uttarakhand, led an expedition to the 7,120 m (23,360 ft) high Trishul 1 Peak in the Garhwal Himalayas, Uttarakhand.

First to summit the Volcanic Seven and youngest to climb both the Seven Summits and Volcanic Seven summits

At 34 years, Satyarup Siddhanta (b. 29 April 1983) from Bengaluru, Karnataka, completed the Volcanic Seven Summits (Messner list) on 15 December 2017 becoming the first Indian to do so. The Volcanic Seven Summits include Mt Kilimanjaro (5,895 m/19,341 ft – Africa), Mt Ojos del Salado (6,893 m/22,615 ft – South America), Mt Elbrus (5,642 m/18,510 ft – Europe), Mt Damavand (5,628 m/18,465 ft – Asia), Mt Giluwe (4,367 m/14,327 ft Australasia), Mt Pico de Orizaba (5,610 m/18,406 ft – North America), and Mt Sidley (4,181–4,285 m/ 13,717– 14,058 ft

– Antarctica). He also completed the Seven Summits challenge on 15 January 2019, becoming the youngest Indian to climb both the Volcanic Seven Summits and Seven Summits.

First to walk the Siachen Glacier

Siachen Glacier, lying along India's border with China, is about 700 sq. km in area and situated at an altitude touching 5,753 m (18,875 ft) above mean sea level. Under Indian Army protection since 1984, it is the highest battlefield in the world. In 1984, Captain (now Colonel) Ashok Pratap Tanwar became the first person to cover the entire glacier on foot. Appointed as the official photographer of a military formation, he walked the length and breadth of the 76 km long and 3–5 km broad glacier.

First to complete the Seven Summit challenge

Mastan Babu Malli (3 September 1974–24 March 2015) was an Indian mountaineer best known for his 2006 world-record–setting feat of climbing each continent's highest peak in the shortest period at the time – a total of 172 days – with the first climb on 19 January 2006 and the seventh on 10 July 2006. This feat made him the fastest Seven Summiteer in the world by 2006, and the first Indian and South Asian to climb the Seven Summits.

Most Himalayan summits

Sange Sherpa from Darjeeling, West Bengal, has six summits to his credit, which include Mt Everest thrice, Aqtash in 1993, Jaloni in 1994, and Nanda Devi in 2000. He is the only person in the world to climb Mt Everest from three faces: from South Col in 1992, North Col in 1996, and Kangshung face in 1999. He received the National Adventure Award in 1998.

First mountaineering institute

The Himalayan Mountaineering Institute at Darjeeling, West Bengal, the first in India, was formed in 1954 by the then Prime Minister Jawaharlal Nehru, along with Major Nandu Jayal of the Corps of Engineers of the Indian Army, who was its first director.

Himalayan Mountaineering Institute, Darjeeling

Oldest to climb the Seven Summits

Ankur Bahl (b. 25 January 1961) from Haryana, became the oldest, at 57 years, to complete the Messner list of the Seven Summit challenge in 2018, which involves the summiting of the highest mountains in each continent. These include Mt Kilimanjaro (5,895 m/19,341 ft – Africa), Mt Elbrus (5,642 m/ 18,510 ft – Europe), Mt Denali/McKinley (6,190 m/ 20,310 ft – North America), Mt Aconcagua (6,961 m/22,838 ft – South America), Mt Everest (8,848.86 m/ 29,031 ft 8 in. – Asia), Mt Kosciuszko (2,228 m/7,310 ft – Australia), and Mt Vinson (4,892 m/16,050 ft– Antarctica).

First woman to scale Mt Everest

Bachendri Pal (b. 24 May 1954) became the first Indian woman to reach the summit of Mt Everest in 1984.

First Indian to summit the three highest peaks of South America

Vikas Shukla (b. 6 December 1989) from Bhusawal, Maharashtra, is the first Indian to summit the three highest peaks of South America. He scaled Mt Aconcagua (6,961 m/ 22,838 ft) on 16 February 2019; Mt Pissis (6,793 m/22,287 ft) on 24 February 2019; and Mt Ojos del Salado (6,893 m/ 22,615 ft) on 1 March 2019.

First to summit Mt Everest without supplemental oxygen

Phu Dorjee was the first to summit Mt Everest (then measured at 8,848m/29,028 ft) without supplemental oxygen on 9 May 1984 through the south east ridge route. He was part of the third Everest expedition led by Captain M.S. Kohli in 1965. Dorjee died in 1987 on the Kangchenjunga Expedition of the Assam Rifles.

First to summit four unscaled peaks above 6,000 m

A team of eight mountaineers from the Nehru Institute of Mountaineering, in collaboration with Uttarakhand Tourism Development Board, summited four unscaled and unnamed peaks in the Gangotri region of the Garhwal Himalayas in eight days between 9 October and 16 October 2018. The team, led by Colonel Amit Bisht, SM, scaled peaks 6,566 m (21,542 ft), 6,557 m (21,512 ft), 6,126 m (20,098 ft), and 6,086 m (19,967 ft) high.

Oldest to scale Mt Everest

- *Men*: S.C. Negi (b. 8 March 1950), additional deputy inspector general of the Border Security Force, became the oldest to scale Mt Everest on 24 May 2006 at the age of 56 years.
- *Women*: Sangeeta Sindhi (b. 9 February 1965) from Gurugram, Haryana, became the oldest Indian woman to summit Mt Everest on 19 May 2018 at the age of 53 years.

Fastest scaling of Mt Everest

Kazi Sherpa climbed Mt Everest in 20 hrs 24 mins in 1998, breaking the earlier record of 22 hrs 29 mins.

TREKKING

First women's team to complete Snowman Trek

A team of 11 women led by iconic Indian mountaineer Bachendri Pal successfully completed the Snowman Trek in Bhutan, considered one of the toughest in the world. Starting at Paro Valley on 4 June 2011, the trek was completed at Sephu Village on 27 June 2011. It involved crossing 11 high mountain passes and other difficult terrain. This expedition was sponsored by the Tata Steel Adventure Foundation in Jamshedpur, Jharkhand.

Fastest to scale most 8,000 m peaks

Baljeet Kaur became the first Indian to summit four out of the 14 peaks at altitudes of 8,000 metres or more in less than a month. The 27-year-old from Solan, Himachal Pradesh, started her journey by summitting Mt Annapurna I

Rescued from Mt Annapurna in Nepal!

Baljeet Kaur, a 28-year-old from Himachal, summited Mt Annapurna for the second time without supplemental oxygen in April 2023. The climb to Mt Annapurna, the 10th highest mountain in the world at 8,091 m, is one of the most treacherous climbs in the world. On her way down, Baljeet Kaur went radio-silent near Camp IV on 17 April and was found alive a day after she went missing. She was airlifted and taken to Annapurna base camp thereafter. Around the same time, another Indian mountaineer Anurag Maloo went missing after he fell into a crevasse from 6,000 m, and was rescued three days later.

(8,091 m) on 28 April 2022 and Mt Kanchenjunga (8,586 m) on 12 May 2022, and became the first Indian woman to summit these peaks in less than two weeks. She continued her journey two weeks later and summitted Mt Everest (8,849 m) on 21 May 2022 and Mt Lhotse (8,517 m) on 22 May 2022, the first and fourth highest mountains in the world, respectively.

Oldest trekker

Gopal Vasudev Lele (b. 8 March 1932) from Pune, Maharashtra, then 81 years of age, made a week-long trek to Rupin Pass (4,680 m/15,354 ft) in Himachal Pradesh from 21 to 28 September 2013. He completed a 70-degree climb. Lele had completed 20 treks since 1972.

Longest desert trek – group

The 22nd battalion of the Mahar Regiment, part of the Golden Katar Division of the Indian Army, successfully completed the 'Golden Katar Desert Trek 2017–18'. A ten-member team of soldiers trekked 700 km through the Thar Desert, Rajasthan, in 21 days from 22 December 2017 to 12 January 2018. The arduous journey on foot through the Great Indian Desert began from Bakhasar, Barmer District, and concluded in Gajjewala, Bikaner District, Rajasthan.

Fastest Everest Base Camp trek by a disabled person

Mahinder Singh Raghuwanshi (b. 2 October 1987) completed the longest trekking in Nepal, with a prosthetic leg, to the Everest Base Camp from an altitude of 2,859.9 m to 5,642.7 m (9,383 ft to 18,513 ft). He started his trek on 28 April 2018 and ended it on 11 May 2018, covering 150 km in 14 days. He started his trek from Lukla, Nepal, and covered Kala Patthar (5,550 m/ 18,209 ft), Cho La (5,368 m/ 17,612 ft), Gokyo (4,790 m/15,715 ft), Renjo La (5,360 m/17,585 ft) and Everest Base Camp (5,364 m/17,598 ft). He was accompanied by a friend and a guide.

THE POLES

First at the Arctic
Sharat Kumar Roy (1897–1962) was the first to reach the Arctic as a member of the Rawson–Macmillan Arctic Expedition in 1927.

First to reach North Pole by surface
Dr M.R. Shetty from Bangalore (now Bengaluru), Karnataka, reached the North Pole by surface on 5 August 2001 with a 100-strong team, by *Yamal*, a nuclear-powered ice-breaking ship, starting from Longyearbyen, Svalbard's administrative centre in Norway, on 1 August 2001.

First at Antarctica
Meher Moos (b. 1944) from Maharashtra was the first woman to set foot on the icy continent of Antarctica way back in 1976, long before any of the scientific expeditions went there.

First route recce to the South Pole
Major Anand Swaroop and Captain R.R. Bhat of the Corps of Engineers of the Indian Army were the first to recce the route from the Maitri base, Antarctica, to the Polar/Antarctic Plateau in 2000.

First at the Geographic South Pole
On 17 January 1989, Colonel J.K. Bajaj became the first Indian to reach the Geographic South Pole at 22:15 hrs (GMT). He was the only Indian in this 11-member international expedition that skied over 1,200 km in 50 days to the Geographic South Pole. The five-nation expedition was organized by Mountain Travel, US, and the International Adventure Network, Canada.

First organization to reach 'three' poles
Indian Navy teams have been to three poles: Mt Everest, the vertical pole, in 2004; the Geographic South Pole in 2006; and the Geographic North Pole in 2008. Commander Satyabrata Dam and two POMAs (petty officer medical assistants) Vikas Kumar and Rakesh Kumar were the first to reach all three poles.

First to ski to the North Pole
Ajeet Bajaj is the first Indian to ski to the North Pole and complete the polar trilogy, which entails skiing to the North Pole and South Pole, and crossing the Greenland Ice Sheet. He started his ski expedition to the North Pole from the Russian Arctic Polar Research Station called Barneo and reached the North Pole on 26 April 2006, along with three other skiers.

Longest stay in Antarctica
Shaik Mastan (b. 12 February 1968) from Gudavalli Village, Guntur District, Andhra Pradesh, had the longest uninterrupted stay of 490 days in Antarctica at the Indian Antarctic research station, Bharati, from 16 November 2011 to 19 March 2013. He was a member of the 35th Indian expedition to Antarctica.

SPORTS

GENERAL

First Indian president of the International Cricket Council

Jagmohan Dalmiya became the first Indian president of the International Cricket Council (ICC) in 1997. He served till 2000.

First Indian chairman of the ICC

N. Srinivasan was the first ICC chairman from India (2014–15).

First Indian independent chairman of the ICC

Shashank Manohar was the first independent chairman of the International Cricket Council in 2016 and he was re-elected for another two years.

First Indian president of the World Squash Federation

Indian squash administrator Narayana Ramachandran was president of the World Squash Federation (WSF) for two terms from 2008 to 2016.

First Indian president of the International Kabaddi Federation

Sports administrator Janardan Singh Gehlot was the founder president of the International Kabaddi Federation from 1985 to 2013. He became the life president from May 2013.

First Indian on the Federation Internationale de Football Association (FIFA) executive panel

Praful patel was the first Indian to be elected to the FIFA Executive Council in April 2019. He was also the president of All India Football Federation and was the senior vice president of the Asian Football Confederation.

First Indian woman to be a member of International Olympic Committee's (IOC) Athletes' Commission

Badminton player Saina Nehwal was appointed a member of the IOC's Athletes' Commission in October 2016.

First sportsman to be nominated to the Rajya Sabha

Wrestler Dara Singh was the first sportsman to be nominated to the Rajya Sabha, the Upper House of the Indian Parliament, in 2003.

First Indian to become a FIFA World Cup match commissioner

Former All India Football Federation president Priya Ranjan Dasmunsi was the match commissioner in a FIFA World Cup 2006 game. It was a group stage match between Australia and Croatia.

Priya Ranjan Dasmunsi

First sportsperson to be awarded the Padma Shri

Triple Olympian gold medallist Balbir Singh Sr (1924–2020) became the first sports person to be awarded the Padma Shri in 1957. The versatile centre forward hockey player played a key role in India's victories in the Olympics in 1948 in London, in 1952 in Helsinki, and in 1956 in Melbourne.

M.C. Mary Kom

First sportsperson to receive the Padma Vibhushan

In 2008 the Padma Vibhushan was first awarded to sports persons and the first to receive the award was the chess wizard Viswanathan Anand. The two other recipients of the award are mountaineer Edmund Hillary and cricket icon Sachin Tendulkar, who also received it in 2008.

First woman sportsperson to receive the Padma Vibhushan

Boxer M.C. Mary Kom was honoured with the Padma Vibhushan in 2020.

First sportsperson and coach to receive an honorary doctorate degree

Pullela Gopichand, former badminton sports star and chief Indian coach, was bestowed an honorary doctorate degree by The Indian Institute of Technology, Kanpur, Uttar Pradesh, on 28 June 2019 in recognition of his contribution to badminton. Gopichand was the second Indian to win the All England Open Badminton Championships in 2001. In 2008, he switched to coaching and launched his academy in Hyderabad, Telangana.

First sportsperson to receive an honorary doctorate degree

Man: Raja Randhir Singh, former shooter, was conferred with an honorary doctorate degree in literature by the Lakshmibai Institute of Physical Education, Gwalior, Madhya Pradesh on 8 September 2000. He had represented India in six Olympic Games: Tokyo (1964), Mexico City (1968), Munich (1972), Montreal (1976), Moscow (1980) and Los Angeles (1984).
Woman: P.T. Usha was conferred with an honorary doctorate degree by Kannur University, Kerala, on 1 November 2000 for her contribution to athletics. She represented India in four Olympic Games, five Asian Games, and five Asian Championships. She also won the most medals ever by an Indian athlete at the Jakarta Asian Championships in 1985, with five gold medals and a bronze medal.

First Indian Fencer to Win a Medal at the Asian Fencing Championships

C.A. Bhavani Devi became the first Indian fencer to win a medal at the Asian Fencing Championships by winning the bronze medal in 2023. She defeated Misaki Emura with a remarkable score of 15-10 in the quarter-finals but in the semi-finals she had to settle for a bronze because she lost 14-15 to Uzbekistan's Zaynab Dayibekova.

First sweep in the Asian Para Games

At the 2018 Asian Para Games, Indian para-athletes occupied all three positions in high jump when Sharad Kumar (1.90 m), Varun Bhati (1.82 m), and Thangavelu Mariyappa (1.67 m) got the gold, silver, and bronze medals respectively, in the T-42/63 category (lower limb deficiency, leg length difference, impaired muscle power, and impaired range of movement).

First woman to head a state cricket association

Rupa Gurunath became the first woman president of the Tamil Nadu Cricket Association (TNCA), a BCCI State Association, on 27 September 2019.

First Indian woman to participate in the World Transplant Games

Reena Raju from Bengaluru, Karnataka, was the flag bearer in the opening ceremony at the World Transplant Games 2017 in Malaga, Spain. She represented India in the 100 m sprint and badminton mixed doubles. She was the first Indian to undergo a repeat heart transplant on 22 October 2017 at Frontier Lifeline Hospital, Chennai, for cardiac allograft vasculopathy.

First sports magazine

Bengal Sporting was first published in 1837. It was edited by British journalist Joachim Hayward Stocqueler.

First recipient of the Olympic Order (Gold)

The Olympic Order (Gold), the highest award of the Olympic movement, is given for distinguished contribution to the movement. Former Indian prime minister Indira Gandhi was its first recipient in 1983. The Olympic Order is also awarded in silver and bronze categories.

First international rugby 15s win

The Indian women's rugby team scripted history by clinching their first ever international 15s victory against a higher-ranked Singapore for a bronze medal in the Asian women's Division 1 Rugby 15s Championship 2019.

First to win a world title in motorsport

Aishwarya Pissay from Bengaluru, Karnataka, became the first Indian to win a world title in motorsport. She won the Federation Internationale de Motocyclisme (FIM) Bajas World Cup (women's category) with 65 points on 13 August 2019 in Varpalota, Hungary. She won the first round in Dubai, UAE, was placed third in Portugal, fifth in Spain, and fourth in Hungary.

Best performance in the Olympic Games

India capped off its best-ever performance in the 2020 Tokyo Olympics with a haul of seven medals, including a gold, two silver, and four bronze medals.

First fencer to qualify for the Olympics

C.A. Bhavani Devi became the first Indian fencer to qualify for the 2020 Tokyo Olympics on 14 March 2021 at the Women's Sabre World Cup in Budapest, Hungary. Chennai-based Devi secured her slot through the Asia/Oceania Zone of the Adjusted Official Ranking (AOR).

Best performance in the Asian Para Games

Indian para-athletes won 72 medals in the 2018 Asian Para Games in Jakarta, Indonesia, bagging 15 golds, 24 silvers, and 33 bronzes.

Best performance in the South Asian Games

India bagged 174 gold, 93 silver, and 45 bronze medals in the 13th South Asian Games 2019 in Kathmandu, Nepal.

India has won **35** medals in the Olympics since **1900**.

Best performance in the Asian Games

India participated in the 2018 Asian Games in Jakarta and Palembang, Indonesia (from 18 August to 2 September) and had the best-ever haul with 69 medals, including 15 gold, 24 silver, and 30 bronze medals from 465 events. After 67 years, since the inaugural edition of the Games in Delhi in 1951, India matched its best haul of 15 golds.

Best performance in the Commonwealth Games

India's best performance was in the 2010 CWG held in New Delhi, when India won 101 medals in all.

Youngest Commonwealth Games captain

Seventeen-year-old Prachi Tehlan was the youngest captain representing India in netball at the 2010 Commonwealth Games, New Delhi.

Youngest sportperson to receive the Padma Bhushan

Badminton player P.V. Sindhu, at 24 years, became the youngest sportsperson to receive the Padma Bhushan in 2020. Sindhu is the third badminton player to be awarded the honour after Pullela Gopichand received it in 2014 and Saina Nehwal in 2016.

Most national awards

Woman: M.C. Mary Kom, six-time world champion, was the recipient of the

Arjuna Award in 2003, the Rajiv Gandhi Khel Ratna Award in 2008–09, the Padma Shri in 2006, the Padma Bhushan in 2013, and the Padma Vibhushan in 2020. *Man:* Pullela Gopichand, the second Indian to win All England Open Badminton Championships in 2001, was the recipient of the Arjuna Award in 1999, the Rajiv Gandhi Khel Ratna Award in 2000–01, the Dronacharya Award in 2009, the Padma Shri in 2005, and the Padma Bhushan in 2014.

ARCHERY

GENERAL

Deepika Kumari

First to win back-to-back titles

Deepika Kumari became the first Indian archer to win titles back-to-back when she won the cadet individual recurve title in 2009 at Ogden in Utah, US, and the junior individual recurve gold in 2011 at Legnica, Poland.

First Indian compound archery women's team to be ranked world no. 1

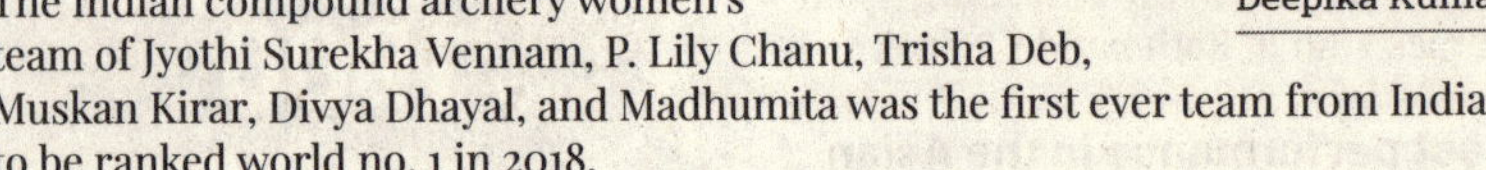

The Indian compound archery women's team of Jyothi Surekha Vennam, P. Lily Chanu, Trisha Deb, Muskan Kirar, Divya Dhayal, and Madhumita was the first ever team from India to be ranked world no. 1 in 2018.

First compound para medal

Indian compound mixed pair of Shyam Sundar Swami and Jyoti Bullyan made history with a silver at the World Archery Para Championships 2022 in Dubai, UAE.

ASIAN CHAMPIONSHIP

First medal in the Asian Championships – men

Limba Ram became the first Indian archer to win an Asian Archery Championships medal in 1988.

Most medals in the Asian Championship

Indian recurve archers won one gold, four silver, and two bronze medals at the 2021 Asian Archery Championships in Dhaka (Bangladesh). In the Asian Championships in 2019 too, in Bangkok, Thailand, during 22–28 November 2019, India had won seven medals: one gold, two silver and four bronze medals.

ASIAN PARA-GAMES

First gold medal in the Asian Para Games

Harvinder Singh won India's maiden archery gold in the Asian Para Games 2018 in the men's individual recurve. He outplayed China's Zhao Lixue 6–0 in the W2/ST category.

COMMONWEALTH GAMES

Most medals in the Commonwealth Games

The Indian team won three gold, a silver, and four bronze medals in archery at the 2010 Commonwealth Games in Delhi.

INTERNATIONAL

First individual international medal

Shyam Lal won a bronze in the 50 m event at the fifth Asia Cup championship in Calcutta (now Kolkata), West Bengal, in January 1988. He represented India in the 1988 Seoul Olympics in South Korea.

First Junior World Championships title – men

Palton Hansda won the World Junior Archery Championships (compound – men's) in 2006 at Merida in Mexico.

First Archery World Cup team gold – women

Rimil Buriuly, Bombayla Devi Laishram, and Deepika Kumari toppled Olympic champions South Korea 219–215 to win the first back-to-back World Cup titles at the Archery World Cup (stage 4) at Wroclaw, Poland, on 25 August 2013, after winning the first medal at the World Cup (stage 3) in Medellin, Colombia, in July.

First international gold

In October 1989, India took the gold in the team event at the Asian Archery Championships in Beijing, China, with 1,850 points, while reigning Olympic champion South Korea stood second with 1,842 points. The Indian team comprised Limba Ram, Shyam Lal, and Skalzang Dorje.

First Olympics representation – men

The Indian national archery team, with Shyam Lal, Limba Ram, and Sanjeeva Singh, participated in the individual and team archery events at the Olympics in 1988 at Seoul, South Korea.

First international gold – women

Dola Banerjee outclassed Tatyana Dorkhova of Ukraine 102-96 in the women's recurve final at the 18th Golden Arrow Grand Prix Championship 2005 at Antalya, Turkey.

First World Cup compound title – men – individual

Abhishek Verma won an archery World Cup (stage 3) event at Wroclaw, Poland, on 15 August 2015.

Abhishek Verma

Hat-trick of bronzes – men

Atanu Das bagged three bronze medals in the 2019 Asian Archery Championships in Bangkok, Thailand. He clinched the men's recurve individual bronze, the recurve mixed team bronze (with Deepika Kumari), and the third bronze with Tarundeep Rai and Jayanta Talukdar in the team recurve event.

First World Cup compound title – men – team

The men's compound archery team of Abhishek Verma, Chinna Raju Srither, and Amarjeet Singh bagged the World Cup (stage 1) on 20 May 2017 in Shanghai, China, scoring 226–221 against Colombia.

First Olympics representation – women

Dola Banerjee, Reena Kumari, and Sumangala Sharma were the first women to represent India in archery at the 2004 Olympic Games in Athens, Greece.

First World Championships medal

The Indian men's archery team won a silver medal, behind Korea, at the 43rd World Outdoor Target Archery Championship 2005 in Madrid, Spain. The recurve team comprised Tarundeep Rai, Gautam Singh Sardar, Jayanta Talukdar, and Robin Hansda.

First silver at the Youth Olympics

Fifteen-year-old Akash Malik from Haryana became India's first archery silver medallist at the Youth Olympic Games 2018 in Buenos Aires, Argentina, on 17 October 2018.

Most medals in a World Cup – team

India won one gold, two silver, and two bronze medals in the Archery World Cup (stage 4) at Wroclaw, Poland, in August 2014. The team of Deepika Kumari, Bombayla Devi Laishram, and Laxmirani Majhi won the gold in the women's recurve team event. The men's recurve team, with Tarundeep Rai, Jayanta Talukdar, and Atanu Das, won a silver medal. Abhishek Verma and Purvasha Shende clinched the silver in the compound mixed pair event. Deepika Kumari bagged two bronze medals in the women's recurve individual event and in the mixed team event with partner Jayanta Talukdar.

First international gold – individual

Jayanta Talukdar won an individual gold medal at the Federation Internationale de Tir a l'Arc (FITA) Meteksan World Cup, in 2006 in Merida, Mexico.

Most medals in the World Championships

India won a silver and two bronzes in the World Archery Championships during 10–15 June 2019 at 's-Hertogenbosch, Netherlands. The men's team of Tarundeep Rai, Atanu Das and Pravin Yadav won silver.

Jayanta Talukdar

The women's compound team of Jyothi Surekha Vennam, Muskan Kaur, and Raj Kaur won the bronzes.

First gold medal in a World Cup

Dola Banerjee from West Bengal is the only Indian archer to win gold in a World Cup final, in the women's individual recurve event at the World Cup in Dubai, UAE, in November 2007.

Most gold medals at the World Cup by an individual

India won three gold medals in the Archery World Cup (stage 3) 2021 in Paris, France: the individual gold – Deepika Kumari; the mixed team event – Deepika Kumari with her husband Atanu Das; and the women's team event trio of Deepika Kumari, Komalika Bari, and Ankita Bhakat.

Dola Banerjee

Only Indian couple to represent India at the Olympic Games

Atanu Das and Deepika Kumari are the only Indian archer couple to represent India at the Olympic Games 2020. They married in June 2019 amid the pandemic.

Youngest world champion

Aditi Swami became the youngest-ever senior world champion at the age of 17 as she won the gold medal at the World Archery Championships 2023 in Berlin, Germany.

Two medals in World Cup Stage 3

Jyothi Surekha Vennam claimed two medals in the World Cup (Stage 3) in Paris in June 2022. When she was four years old, she crossed the Krishna River in 3 hrs 20 mins 6 secs to cover 5 km three times across, entering the *Limca Book of Records*. Starting with two bronze medals in the World Youth Archery Championships in 2013, she went on to win 10 medals in the Asian Archery Championships, nine medals in

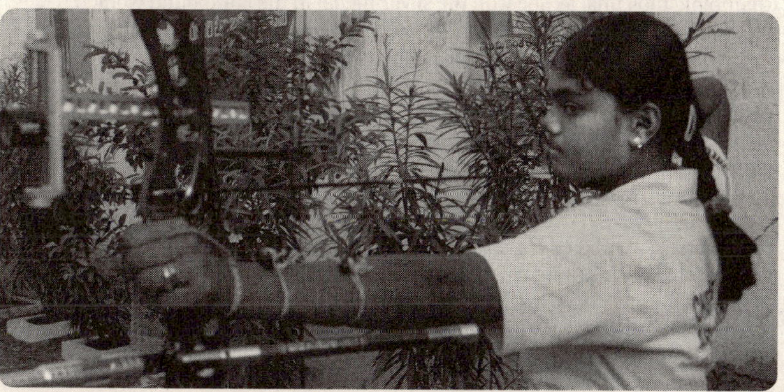

Jyothi Surekha Vennam

the World Cup and six medals in the World Archery Championships. She has nearly 100 medals in national and international competitions.

Three gold medals in the World Cup

Deepika Kumari won three gold medals in the World Cup (stage 3) in Paris in 2021. India took the top honour in the women's team, mixed team, and women's individual events.

Three individual gold medal in World Cup

Compound archer Abhishek Verma won three individual gold medals at the World Cup with his latest coming at the World Cup Stage III 2023 in Medellin. He earlier won gold medals in Paris 2021 and Wroclaw, Poland, in 2015.

Aditi Gopichand breaks U-18 world record

Aditi Gopichand broke the U-18 world record with 711 points out of possible 720 (72 arrows) during the qualification round of the World Cup Stage 3 in Medellin. The 16-year-old broke the previous age group record of 705 held by Riko Arreola of the US.

First Indian to win Youth World Champion in recurve – men

Parth Salunke became the first Indian male archer to win recurve under-21 men's individual championship during the World Archery Youth Championships 2023 in Limerick, Ireland. The 19-year-old archer defeated Korea's Song In Jun in the gold medal match.

PARALYMPICS

First archery medal in Paralympics

Harvinder Singh clinched India's first-ever archery at the 2020 Paralympics. He won the bronze medal in the men's singles recurve archery at the 2020 Summer Paralympics in Tokyo, Japan.

World's first armless archer to reach World Championships final

Sheetal Devi became the first female armless archer to make a World Championships final as she won the silver medal in the compound women individual category in Pilsen, Czech Republic. She lost the gold medal match to Turkey's Oznur Cure after defeating compatriot Sarita in the semis.

World record in Women's Team

Sarita and Sheetal Devi set a new world record in the Compound Women Team Open category with a score 1386/1440 in the qualification round. The duo also won the bronze medal, defeating Iran.

First World Archery Para Championships gold

Sarita and Rakesh Kumar set world record in the Compound Mixed Team Open category with a scored of 1398 out of possible 1440 in the qualification round. The duo went on to win the gold medal as well by beating Brazil in the final, winning India's first para archers to win gold medal in World Archery Para Championships.

ATHLETICS

Oldest gold medallist

Bhagwani Devi, at 94 years, won a gold medal in the 100m sprint at the World Masters Athletics Championship on 11 July 2022 in Tampere, Finland.

ASIAN ATHLETICS CHAMPIONSHIPS

Best performance in the Asian Athletics Championships

India clinched five gold, one silver and three bronze medals in the 2017 Asian Athletics Championships in Bhubaneswar, Odisha, to top the medal tally for the first time in the championships.

Joint-highest medal tally at Asian Athletics Championships

India won 27 medals (six gold, 12 silver, and nine bronze medals) at the Asian Athletics Championships, equalling the joint-highest tally of medals at the event as the nation did in 2017 in Bhubaneswar, Odisha

Triple excellence in shot put

Former shot putter Bahadur Singh Chouhan is the only Indian to receive the Arjuna Award, the Dronacharya Award as well as the Padma Shri. Between 1973 and 1985 he won three gold, two silver, and three bronze medals at the Asian Games and Asian Championships.

First to win gold at Asian Athletics Championships – women

Jyothi Yarraji won the first gold for India in the women's 100 m hurdles at the Asian Athletics Championships held in Bangkok in July 2023. She clocked in 13.09 seconds.

ASIAN GAMES

First double gold at the Asian Games

Lavy Pinto won the first double gold at Asian Games in the 100 m and 200 m races in Delhi, 1951. Six other athletes have won at least two golds each in a single Asian Games event.

Biggest point-haul in pentathlon - women

Swapna Barman set the pentathlon record with a point haul of 4119 points (out of 5000) while clinching the Asian Indoor Championships silver medal. She surpassed the old record held by Purnima Hembram of 4062 points (in 2017).

Swapna Barman

First Asian Games medals – women

In the 1951 Asian Games in Delhi, Roshan Mistry won the silver in the 100 m race,

Milkha Singh

while Mary D'Souza (200 m) won a bronze. The women's 4 x 100 m relay team of Nilima Ghose, Stephie D'Souza, Mary D'Souza, and Roshan Mistry also won a silver.

Most individual golds in the Asian Games

Two sportspersons have won four gold medals each at the Asian Games:

- Milkha Singh won four golds in two Asian Games in 1958 and 1962.
- P.T. Usha won four golds in the 1986 Asian Games at Seoul, South Korea, in the 200 m, 400 m, 400 m hurdles, and the 4 x 400 m relay.

First Asian Games gold – men – individual

Ranjit Singh won a gold in the 800 m marathon on 8 March 1951 at Delhi, clocking 1 hr 59 mins 3 secs. Indian men won 10 golds in this edition of the Asian Games.

First Asian Games gold – women – individual

Kamaljeet Sandhu won the 400 m race in 57.3 secs at the sixth Asian Games held in Bangkok, Thailand, in 1970.

Only Asian Games gold medal in marathon

Chhota Singh won a gold in the men's marathon in 1951 in Delhi with a timing of 2 hrs 42 mins 58 secs.

First to win three golds successively in the Asian Games

Manjeet Kaur was the first Indian to win three consecutive gold medals in the women's 4 x 400 m relay race in the Asian Games (2002, 2006, and 2010).

Longest career – men

Bahadur Singh Chouhan who represented India in the inaugural Asian Track and Field (ATF) meet in 1971, also participated in the ninth one at Delhi in 1989. He won gold medals in shot put in the Asian Games in 1978 and 1982, and a silver medal in 1974.

First gold medal – women – team

Christine Brown, Stephie D'Souza, Violet Peters and Mary D'Souza won the gold in the 4 x100 m relay, clocking 49.5 secs at the second Asian Games held in Manila, Philippines, in 1954.

Longest career – women

- P.T. Usha represented India from 1980 to 1998 in four Olympic Games, five Asian Games, and five ATF meets.
- Shiny Wilson represented India 72 times in international meets from 1981 to 1995. She won the 800 m in her last major meet – the ATF meet in 1995 in Jakarta, Indonesia.

ASIAN YOUTH ATHLETICS CHAMPIONSHIPS

Best performance in the Asian Youth Athletics Championships

India clinched six gold, eleven silver, and three bronze medals in the 2022 Asian Youth Athletics Championships, held in Kuwait between 13 and 16 October 2022, topping the medal tally.

COMMONWEALTH GAMES

First gold medal in throws at the Commonwealth Games – men – individual

This feat was achieved by the 6 ft 9 in. tall Vikas Gowda in discus throw. Gowda won this event in 2014 in Glasgow, Scotland, with a throw of 63.64 m.

First to win a gold medal in triple jump in the Commonwealth Games

Eldhose Paul became the first Indian to win a gold medal in the men's triple jump at the Commonwealth Games 2022, recording a massive 17.03 m.

First Commonwealth Games gold medal – women

The first Commonwealth Games gold medal for women came when Krishna Poonia won the discus throw (61.51 m), while the quartet of Sini Jose, Mandeep Kaur, Manjeet Kaur, and Ashwini Chidananda Akkunji won the women's 4 x 400 m relay (3 mins 27.77 secs) at the 2010 New Delhi Games.

First medal in race walk – women

Priyanka Goswami is the first Indian woman to win the silver medal in the women's 10,000 m race walk at the 2022 Commonwealth Games. It is India's second medal in the race walk at the Commonwealth Games after Harminder Singh's bronze in the 20 km event in the 2010 Commonwealth Games.

First javelin throw medal in the Commonwealth Games – women

Annu Rani, a javelin thrower, is the first Indian woman to win a medal, a bronze, in the 2022 Commonwealth Games in Birmingham, UK.

First medal in the Commonwealth Games – women

Anju Bobby George won the bronze medal in long jump with a best of 6.49 m at the 2002 Commonwealth Games in Manchester, UK, followed by Neelam J. Singh, who won a silver in the women's discus throw.

Anju Bobby George

First title in the Commonwealth Fencing Championship

Chennai-born fencer C.A. Bhavani Devi made history in November 2018 by becoming the first Indian to win the gold medal at the Commonwealth Championship. The 42nd ranked Indian fencer and the first ever Indian fencer to have qualified for an Olympics (Tokyo 2020) Bhavani Devi defeated second-seeded Australian Veronika Vasleva 15-10 in the senior women's sabre individual category final in London, UK, in the Commonwealth Championship in August 2022.

Tejaswin Shankar

First high jump medal in the Commonwealth Games

Tejaswin Shankar, the 2015 Commonwealth Youth Games gold medallist in high jump, became the first Indian to win a medal – a bronze – in high jump with a jump of 2.22 m at the 2022 Commonwealth Games.

Best Commonwealth performance

India won 12 medals – two golds, three silvers, and seven bronzes – during the 19th Commonwealth Games in New Delhi in 2010.

COMMONWEALTH AND ASIAN GAMES

Gold medal in Commonwealth and Asian Games

Milkha Singh won gold in the 440 yards (the quarter-mile dash) race at the 1958 British Empire and Commonwealth Games in Cardiff, Wales, with a timing of 46.6 secs. He also won the 400 m races back-to-back in the Asian Games in Tokyo, Japan (1958), in 47.0 secs, and Jakarta, Indonesia (1962), in 46.9 secs. He was the first Indian to win individual gold medals in both the Asian Games and the Commonwealth Games. He was also the first Indian athlete to win a gold medal in the Commonwealth Games.

INTERNATIONAL

First Indian elected to the International Association of Athletics Federations (IAAF) Council

Adille J. Sumariwalla was elected to the IAAF (now World Athletics) Council at the IAAF Congress in 2015.

First individual gold medal in track events at the IAAF World U-20 Championships

Hima Das won the gold in the400 m race in the IAAF (now World Athletics) World U-20 Championships in Tampere, Finland, on 12 July 2018 with a timing of 51.46 secs. She holds the current Indian national record in 400 m with a timing of 50.79 secs set at the 2018 Asian Games in Jakarta, Indonesia.

First international medal in a marathon – women

Asha Agarwal won the Hong Kong Marathon on 27 January 1985. She later won the Asian Track and Field gold at Jakarta, Indonesia, in 1985, and the Trinidad Marathon in 1986.

WOMEN ATHLETES OF INDIA

1 P.T. Usha

Payyoli Tevaraparampil Usha, born in Kozhikode District of Kerala, grabbed five medals in the 1986 Asian Games, four of which were gold medals. From 1983 to 1989, P.T. Usha earned up to 13 gold medals at the ATF Meets (Asian Championships). She was the first Indian woman to reach the final of an Olympic event. She was part of India's 4x100 m relay at the 1998 Asian Championships and set the current record of 44.43 seconds. She had been conferred with the Padma Shri and Arjuna Award.

2 Anju Bobby George

She is India's only medalist at the IAAF World Championships and a gold medalist in the IAAF World Athletics Finals. She won a gold medal in the Asian Games in Busan in 2022 with a jump of 6.53m.

3 Shiny Wilson

She represented India in four Olympic Games, three Asian games, six Asian Championships, and seven SAF Games apart from other international meets. She was the first Indian track athlete to make it to the semi-final stage at the Olympic Games. She achieved this in 1984 where she finished fourth in a time of 2 minutes 4.69 seconds. She was also the first woman to carry the Flag in the Athlete's Parade at an Olympic Games. She returned to the track within months of childbirth and set a 800m national record.

4 Dutee Chand

She is the current national champion in the women's 100 m event and the first Indian to win a gold medal in 100 m race in an international event. She was the first Indian sprinter to win a gold at the Universiade in 2019. She clocked in 11.32 seconds in the 100 m race. Dutee is India's first athlete to openly come out as a member of the LGBTQ+ community.

5 Kamaljeet Sandhu

She won a gold medal at 1970 Bangkok Asian Games in 400 m race where she finished the distance in 57.3 seconds. In 1971 she received the Padma Shri and in the same year she was one of the finalists in the World University Games that was held at Turin, Italy, in 400m race. At the 1972 Munich Olympics she participated in the women's 400 metres.

First clean sweep in a major international meet

Krishna Poonia, Harwant Kaur, and Seema Antil bagged the gold, silver, and bronze medals respectively in the women's discus throw in the 2010 Commonwealth Games in New Delhi.

At the 2021 World U-20 Championships India had **28** competitors participating in **19** events.

First athlete to win a medal at the IAAF Continental Cup

Arpinder Singh, the 2018 Asian Games gold medallist in triple jump, was the first Indian to win a medal in the IAAF Continental Cup. He won a bronze medal in triple jump with a distance of 16.59 m.

First Indian to win gold at the IAAF World U-20 Championships

Neeraj Chopra, by clinching the gold on 23 July 2016 at the IAAF (now World Athletics) World U-20 championships in Bydgoszcz, Poland, with a winning javelin throw of 86.48 m, became the first Indian to win a gold medal at any event in the championships and the first Indian to set a junior world record in athletics. In 2018, he became the second Indian after the legendary runner Milkha Singh to win both Commonwealth and Asian Games gold medals in the same year, breaking the national record on both occasions. At 20 years, he was the youngest ever flag bearer of the Indian contingent at the 2018 Jakarta Asian Games.

First to receive IAAF Veteran Pin

Indian track and field legend P.T. Usha was presented the Veteran Pin by the World Athletics governing body – IAAF (now World Athletics), on 24 September 2019.

First World U-20 Athletics Championships twin medals

Quarter-miler Rupal Chaudhary is the first Indian to win twin medals in a single edition of the 2022 World U-20 Athletics Championships. She won silver in 4x400 m relay and a bronze medal in the women's 400 m.

First to finish among podium places at Diamond League

Murali Sreeshankar became the first long jumper to finish among the podium places of a Diamond League as he finished third in the Paris Diamond League 2023 with an attempt of 8.09 m. He is overall the third Indian to finish in top three of Diamond Leagues after discus thrower Vikash Gowda (2015) and Neeraj Chopra (2022).

MARATHONS

Most appearances in marathons

Sunita Godara has completed 85 half- and 69 full marathons in 24 different countries. Starting with the Rath Marathon in 1984, she finished first in 25 marathons, second in 12, and third in 14 of them. She has won 25 gold medals in half-marathons.

OLYMPICS

First Olympic marathoner

Phadeppa Dareppa Chaugule represented India in the 1920 Antwerp Olympic Games. He finished 19th in 2 hrs 50 mins 45.2 secs.

First women at the Olympics

Mary D'Souza and Nilima Ghose participated in the 1952 Helsinki Olympics. They were both eliminated in the heats of the 100 m and 200 m races, and 80 m and 100 m hurdles, respectively.

Best performances in the Olympics

Milkha Singh and P.T. Usha finished fourth in the 400 m and the 400 m hurdles in the 1960 Rome and the 1984 Los Angeles Olympic Games respectively.

WORLD ATHLETICS

First gold at World Athletics final

In the World Athletics Championships held in Monte Carlo in September 2005, Anju Bobby George from India came second in long jump. The gold medallist, Tatyana Kotova from Russia, was later disqualified following a failed retest for doping, and Anju Bobby George was upgraded to gold medallist, India's first, in January 2014.

First woman captain

Shiny Wilson captained the Indian athletes' contingent at the 1992 Olympic Games in Barcelona, Spain.

Shiny Wilson

First Indian to win gold at World Athletics Championships

Neeraj Chopra wrote history when he became the first Indian to win a gold medal at the World Athletics Championships. He had a big throw of 88.17 m in the men's javelin final.

WORLD CHAMPIONSHIPS

First World Championships medal

Anju Bobby George won a bronze in long jump at the 2003 World Championships in Paris, France, in August, with a leap of 6.70 m. She surpassed this at the 2004 Olympics in Athens, Greece, finishing sixth with 6.83 m.

WORLD UNIVERSIADE

First gold at the World Universiade

Dutee Chand, the current national champion in the women's 100 m race, became the first Indian to win the gold at the World Universiade, Naples, Italy, in the 100 m race with a timing of 11.32 secs on 10 July 2019. She is also the first Indian to win a gold in the 100 m race at a global championship. She also won a silver in the 100 m race at the 2018 Asian Games in Jakarta.

Muhammed Anas Yahiya, Amoj Jacob, Muhammed Ajmal Variyathodi, and Rajesh Ramesh.

India at World Athletics Championships 2023

India broke the world Asian record for the men's 4x400 m relay at the World Athletics Championships in Budapest, Hungary. It qualified for the finals. After the first run Muhammed Anas Yahiya came in the sixth place. But the run by Amoj Jacob put India in the second place. Muhammed Ajmal Variyathodi and Rajesh Ramesh broke the Asian record clocking in at 2 minutes 59.05 seconds. The earlier Asian record of 2 minutes 59.51 seconds was held by Japan.

PARA ATHLETICS

First participation in the Paralympics

In 1968, India made its Paralympics debut at the Tel Aviv Games. India did not participate in the first two Games, in 1960 and 1964. India completed again in 1972 and then consistently from the 1984 New York Games in the USA to Tokyo 2020 in Japan.

First triple medal in the Paralympics

India's Joginder Singh Bedi had won three medals – a silver each in javelin and shot put, and a bronze in the discus throw – at the 1984 Paralympics in Stoke Mandeville and New York, USA.

First gold in javelin

Sumit Antil won the gold medal in the men's javelin throw F64 category at the 2020 Summer Paralympics in Tokyo, Japan. He holds the current world record, having thrown 68.55 m in the Paralympics final.

First bronze medal at the World Para Athletics Championships

Varun Kumar Bhati won the bronze medal in the men's T-42 category high jump and Karan Jyoti Dalal settled for bronze in the discus throw F-55 at the World Para Athletics Championships in London in 2017.

First Paralympics gold – women

Deepa Malik became the first Indian woman to win a medal at the Paralympics by bagging a silver medal in shot put in the 2016 Paralympic Games. She also won gold in the F-53/54 javelin event at the para athletic Grand Prix held in Dubai in 2018.

Deepa Malik

Best performance in the World Para Athletics Championships

India won two gold, two silver, and five bronze medals (a total of nine) at the World Para Athletics Championships 2019 held in Dubai, UAE.

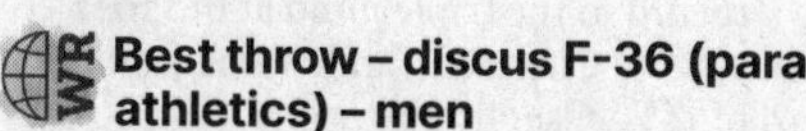

Best throw – discus F-36 (para athletics) – men

Yogesh Kathuniya smashed the world record in men's discus F-36, when he threw 45.18 m to win the gold medal in the World Para Athletics Grand Prix in Berlin, Germany, on 1 July 2018.

First para athlete to get the Rajiv Gandhi Khel Ratna Award – women

Deepa Malik was the first woman para-athlete to receive the Rajiv Gandhi Khel Ratna Award in 2019.

Best javelin throw

Sumit Antil's world record javelin throw of 68.55 m in the F64 category came at the 2020 Tokyo Olympics. He threw the spear to a record distance of 68.62 m in the Open National Para Athletics Championships.

First ever IAS officer to win a silver medal

Suhas Yathiraj, a 2007 Indian Administrative Service (IAS) officer of Uttar Pradesh cadre bagged the silver medal in the men's SL4 category at the Tokyo 2020 Paralympics.

NATIONAL GAMES

Fastest 100 m hurdles – women

In the women's-only 100 m hurdles, Jyothi Yarraji became the first Indian woman to finish the race with a sub-13 timing, as she clocked 12.82 seconds at the 61st National Open Athletics Championships in Bengaluru on October 2022.

Highest pole vault

Woman: At the 36th National Games, Rosy Meena Paulraj cleared a height of 4.20 m to break the eight-year-old record of 4.15 m held by V. S. Surekha in the women's pole vault in the National Games 2022. A week later, she rewrote her own record by vaulting 4.21 m on 15 October 2022 at the National Open Athletics Championships 2022 in Bengaluru.

Man: At the 36th National Games, held between 29 September and 12 October 2022, Siva Subramani (5.31 m) eclipsed his own record of 5.30 m in the men's pole vault, set four years back.

Fastest race walk

Ram Baboo clocked 2 hours 36 minutes 34 seconds to break the previous national record in the men's 35 km race walk 2 hours 40 minutes 16 seconds by nearly four minutes in the 36th National Games in 2022.

Oldest gold medallist

Rambai, at 105 years, won gold in the 100 m race at the National Open Masters Athletics Championships on 21 June 2022 in Vadodara, Gujarat.

Longest triple jump – women

On 13 June 2022, Aishwarya Babu made a record in the triple jump at the 2022 National Inter-State Athletics Championships in Chennai, Tamil Nadu, leaping 14.14 m and breaking the national record of 14.11 m set by Mayookha Johny.

Youngest athletics champion

Henry Rebello won the triple jump at Bangalore (now Bengaluru), Karnataka, in 1946 when he was only 17 years old. He set a record of 50 ft 2 in. at the 1948 National Games, which was surpassed only after a gap of 23 years by Mohinder Singh in 1971.

BADMINTON

INTERNATIONAL

OLYMPIC GAMES

First medallist

Saina Nehwal became the first Indian medallist, winning a bronze medal in London, UK, in 2012.

First silver medallist

P.V. Sindhu finished runner-up in Rio de Janeiro, Brazil, in 2016.

First two-time medallist

P.V. Sindhu remains the only two-time medallist with the silver medal in Rio de Janeiro, Brazil (2016), and the bronze medal in Tokyo, Japan (2020).

WORLD CHAMPIONSHIPS

First doubles medallists – men

Satwiksairaj Rankireddy and Chirag Shetty finished with a bronze in the men's doubles in Tokyo, Japan, in 2022.

First individual medallist – men – singles

Prakash Padukone claimed the men's singles bronze medal in Copenhagen, Denmark, in 1983.

Jwala Gutta and Ashwini Ponnappa

First individual medallist – women – singles
P.V. Sindhu received the women's singles bronze medal in Guangzhou, China, in 2013.

First doubles medallists – women
Jwala Gutta and Ashwini Ponnappa became the first Indian bronze medallists in women's doubles in London, UK, in 2011.

First silver medallist – men – singles
K. Srikanth finished runner-up in the men's singles in the 2021 edition at Huelva, Spain.

Saina Nehwal

First two-time silver medallist – women - singles
P.V. Sindhu finished runner- up in women's singles in Glasglow, Scotland (2017) and Nanjing, China (2019).

First silver medallist – women – singles
Saina Nehwal finished runner-up in the women's singles in Jakarta in 2015.

First world champion
P.V. Sindhu claimed the honour by winning the women's singles in 2019.

K. Srikanth

Highest number of medals
P.V. Sindhu has five medals – a gold, two silver and two bronze medals – from the premier championship.

Two medals from one edition – men
K. Srikanth, with the silver medal, and Lakshya Sen, with the bronze, made it to the podium in Huelva, Spain, in 2021.

Two medals from one edition – women
P.V. Sindhu, with the silver medal, and Saina Nehwal, with the bronze, were on the podium of the women's singles at Glasgow, Scotland in 2017.

ASIAN GAMES

First medal – men – team
The men's team comprising Prakash Padukone,

Dinesh Khanna, Davinder Ahuja, Partho Ganguli, and Raman Ghosh won a bronze medal in Tehran, Iran in 1974.

The 2023 India Open badminton tournament was the first India Open to have a Super 750 status.

First medal – women – team

The women's team comprising Ami Ghia, Madhumita Goswami, Amita Kulkarni, Hufrish Nariman, Kanwal Thakur Singh, and Vandana Chiplunkar claimed a bronze medal in New Delhi, India in 1982.

First to win a medal – men – singles

Syed Modi claimed a bronze in New Delhi, India in 1982.

First to win a medal – mixed – doubles

Leroy D'Sa and Kanwal Thakur Singh received a bronze medal in New Delhi, India, in 1982.

Multiple medal-winner in a single edition

Leroy D'Sa received three bronze medals – for the men's team, the doubles, and the mixed doubles – in New Delhi, India in 1982.

First to win a medal – women – singles

Saina Nehwal received a women's singles bronze in Jakarta-Palembang, Indonesia, in 2018.

First to win a medal – men – doubles

Leroy D'Sa and Pradeep Gandhe claimed a bronze medal in New Delhi, India, in 1982.

Two medallists in a single event

P.V. Sindhu (silver) and Saina Nehwal (bronze) made it to the podium in the women's singles in Jakarta-Palembang, Indonesia, in 2018.

P.V. Sindhu - Badminton Star

Sindhu was in the Forbes' list of highest paid female athletes in 2018, 2019, 2021, and 2022. She is a recipient of the highest of sports honours such as Arjuna Award and Rajiv Gandhi Khel Ratna, and also civilian awards such as Padma Shri and Padma Bhushan. She entered the international circuit at a young age of 14 in the year 2009. In February 2023 she was part of the Indian team that won a bronze medal at the Badminton Asia Mixed Team Championships.

COMMON-WEALTH GAMES

First medallist – women – singles

Aparna Popat received a bronze medal in women's singles in Manchester, England, in 2002.

First medallist – men – singles

Dinesh Khanna claimed a bronze medal in 1966 in the British Empire and Commonwealth Games. (In 1978, these Games were rechristened as the Commonwealth Games.)

Prakash Padukone

First gold medallist – men – singles

Prakash Padukone won the men's singles title in Edmonton, Canada, in 1978.

First medallists – men – team

The team comprising P. Gopichand, Abhinn Shyam Gupta, George Thomas, Jaseel P. Ismail, Marcos Bristow, Nikhil Kanetkar, and Vincent Lobo claimed a silver medal in Kuala Lumpur, Malaysia, in 1998.

First medallist – women – doubles

Ami Ghia and Kanwal Thakur Singh claimed a bronze in Edmonton, Canada, in 1978.

First medallists – women – team

The team comprising Manjusha Kanwar, P.V. V. Lakshmi, Madhumita Bisht, Aparna Popat, Archana Deodhar, K. Neelima Chowdhary, and C. Deepthi won a bronze medal in Kuala Lumpur, Malaysia, in 1998.

First gold medallist – mixed – team

The team comprising K. Srikanth, Saina Nehwal, P.V. Sindhu, H. S. Prannoy, Ashwini Ponnappa, Sikki Reddy, Ruthvika Shivani, Chirag Shetty, Satwiksairaj Rankireddy, and Pranaav Chopra won the title in Gold Coast, Australia, in 2018.

First silver medallist – mixed – team

The team comprising Saina Nehwal, P. Kashyap, Jwala Gutta, Ashwini Ponnappa, Chetan Anand, Aditi Mutatkar, Sanave Thomas, Rupesh Kumar, Aparna Balan, and V. Diju finished runner-up in Delhi, India, in 2010.

First bronze medallist – mixed – team

The team comprising Anup Sridhar, Aparna Popat, Chetan Anand, Jwala Gutta, Shruti Kurien, Saina Nehwal, Trupti Murgunde, V. Diju, Sanave Thomas, and Rupesh Kumar claimed the bronze in Melbourne, Australia, in 2006.

First gold medallists – men – doubles

Chirag Shetty and Satwiksairaj Rankireddy won the title in Birmingham, UK in 2022.

First gold medallist – women - singles
Saina Nehwal won in New Delhi, India, in 2010.

First gold medallists – women – doubles
Jwala Gutta and Ashwini Ponnappa won gold in Delhi, India, in 2010.

Most gold medals from one edition
India won three gold medals – from men's singles (Lakshya Sen), women's singles (P.V. Sindhu), and men's doubles (Chirag Shetty and Satwiksairaj Rankireddy) – in Birmingham, UK, in 2022.

Most medals from one edition
India won six medals – women's singles gold (Saina Nehwal), mixed team gold and men's singles silver (K. Srikanth), women's singles silver (P.V. Sindhu), men's doubles silver (Chirag Shetty and Satwiksairaj Rankireddy), and women's doubles bronze (Ashwini Ponnappa and N. Sikki Reddy) – in Gold Coast, Australia, in 2018.

ASIAN CHAMPIONSHIPS

Dinesh Khanna

First bronze medal – men – singles
Suresh Goel claimed a men's singles bronze in Lucknow, India, in 1965.

First medal – women – singles
Meena Shah claimed a women's singles bronze in Lucknow, India, in 1965.

First gold medal from Asian championships
Dinesh Khanna won the men's singles gold medal in Lucknow, India, in 1965.

First medal – men – doubles
Dipu Ghosh and Raman Ghosh received a bronze at Jakarta, Indonesia, in 1971.

First silver medal – men – doubles
Prakash Padukone and Syed Modi received the silver medal in Peking, China, in 1978.

First medal – mixed – doubles
Owen Roncon–Sarojini Apte and A.I. Sheikh–Achala Karnik received bronze medals in Lucknow, India, in 1965.

First medal – women – doubles
Jwala Gutta and Ashwini Ponnappa received a bronze medal in Gimcheon, South Korea, in 2014.

WORLD JUNIOR CHAMPIONSHIPS

First silver medallist – boys – singles
Siril Verma received a silver medal in the boys' singles in Lima, Peru, in 2015.

First medallist – boys – singles

R.M.V. Gurusaidutt claimed a bronze medal in the boys' singles in Pune, India, in 2008.

First medallist – girls – singles

Saina Nehwal received a silver medal in the girls' singles in Incheon, South Korea, in 2006.

BWF SUPER SERIES MASTERS FINALS/BWF WORLD TOUR FINALS

First medallist – women – singles

Saina Nehwal received a bronze in Kota Kinabalu, Sabah, Malaysia, in 2008.

First gold medallist – women – singles

P.V. Sindhu won the title in Guangzhou, China, in 2018 when the event was rechristened as BWF World Tour Finals.

First medallist – men – singles

K. Srikanth received a bronze medal in Dubai, UAE, in 2014.

First silver medallists – mixed – doubles

V. Diju and Jwala Gutta finished runner-up in the mixed doubles in Johor Bahru, Malaysia, in 2009.

Highest world ranking – women – singles

Saina Nehwal became the world no. 1 in the women's singles in April 2015.

First silver medallist – women – singles

Saina Nehwal received a silver in Liuzhou, China, in 2011.

Highest world rankings – mixed – doubles

Jwala Gutta and V. Diju were ranked world no. 6 in August 2010.

Highest world ranking – men – singles

K. Srikanth became the world no. 1 in the men's singles in April 2018.

Highest world ranking – women – doubles

Jwala Gutta and Ashwini Ponnappa were ranked world no. 10 in August 2015.

First duo to win Super 1000 title

Satwiksairaj Rankireddy and Chirag Shetty became the first Indian pair to win Super 1000 title as they won the men's doubles final at Indonesian Open 2023. They are also the first Indian pair to win a BWF World Tour Title at all levels.

Satwiksairaj Rankireddy (*right*) and Chirag Shetty (*left*)

Highest world ranking – men – doubles

Chirag Shetty and Satwiksairaj Rankireddy were ranked world no. 7 in November 2019.

OTHER INTERNATIONAL COMPETITIONS

First medal in the Thomas Cup – men – team championship

India defeated 14-time champion Indonesia at the Thomas Cup 3-0 to win the prestigious title in 2022 for the first time ever, with World Championships medallist Lakshya Sen, K. Srikanth, and the current world no. 8 doubles duo of Chirag Shetty and Satwiksairaj Rankireddy.

First winner of the World Cup – men – singles

Prakash Padukone won in Kuala Lumpur, Malaysia, in 1981.

First winner at the All England Championship

Prakash Padukone won in London, UK, in 1980.

First finalist at the All England – men – singles

Prakash Nath reached the men's singles final in 1947 in London, UK.

First medal in the Uber Cup – women's – team

India claimed its first bronze medal in New Delhi, India, in 2014.

Two semi-finalists at the All England

Prakash Nath and Davinder Mohan reached the men's singles semi-finals in 1947. Interestingly, the two players chose not to play each other. They tossed a coin, Prakash Nath called it right and advanced to the final.

Most titles – women

Saina Nehwal won 10 titles in the BWF Superseries from 15 appearances in the final.

Most titles – men

K. Srikanth won six titles in the BWF Superseries in seven appearances in the final.

PARALYMPICS

First gold medallist – men – singles

Pramod Bhagat became the first gold medallist after winning the men's singles in the SL3 category in the 2020 Tokyo Paralympics.

First silver medallist – men – singles

Suhas Yathiraj became the first silver medallist in men's singles in the SL4 category in Tokyo, Japan, in 2020.

First bronze medallist – men – singles

Manoj Sarkar became the first bronze medallist in the men's singles SL3 category in Tokyo, Japan, in 2020.

DOMESTIC: NATIONALS

The Indian national badminton team is currently ranked 5th in the world.

First National champions

Vijay Madgavkar (men's singles in 1934); T. P. Boland (women's singles in 1935); D. Minas–V. Minas (men's doubles in 1934); T. P. Boland–Cameron (women's doubles in 1935); and N. Knight-I. Brydges (mixed doubles in 1936).

Most titles – men – singles

Prakash Padukone holds a unique record of winning all his nine singles titles in a row from 1971 to 1979.

Most titles – men – doubles

Rupesh Kumar was part of the men's doubles title-winning pair for nine successive years from 2002 to 2010. Rupesh partnered Markose Bristow in 2002 and 2003, and thereafter joined hands with Sanave Thomas.

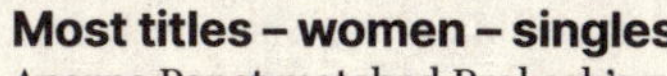

Aparna Popat

Most titles – women – singles

Aparna Popat matched Prakash's record by winning her nine singles titles on the trot from 1997 to 2005.

Most titles – women – doubles

Jwala Gutta formed part of the title-winning combination 10 times between 2000 and 2013. She won with Shruti Kurien in 2000 and again from 2002 to 2008. She paired with Ashwini Ponnappa in 2009 and 2013.

Most versatile and successful player in the Nationals

Madhumita Goswami-Bisht, in an international career spanning almost a quarter of a century from 1978, won eight National women singles, nine women's doubles and twelve mixed doubles titles.

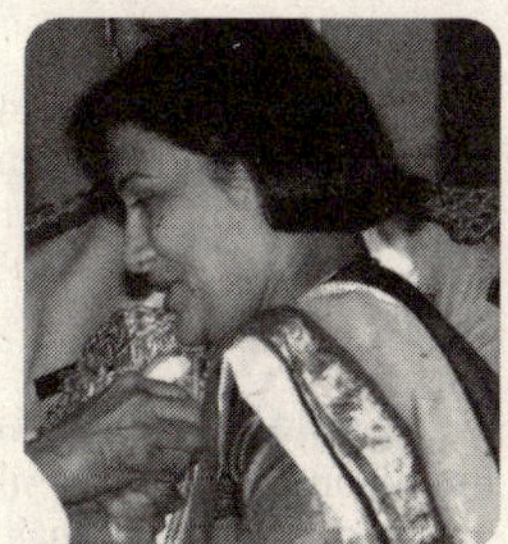

Madhumita Goswami-Bisht

Most titles – mixed – doubles

Madhumita Goswami-Bisht won the mixed doubles title 12 times with five different partners. She won in 1981, 1986–88 (with Sanat Mishra); in 1989–90 (with Harjeet Singh); in 1994–97 (with Vinod Kumar); in 2000 (with Vincent Lobo); and 2001 (with Markose Bristow).

First badminton gold – Paralympics

Pramod Bhagat of Odisha won India's first ever Paralympics Gold in badminton. (Badminton made its debut at the 2020 Tokyo Olympics). He clinched Gold in men's singles badminton (SLB) event.

BASKETBALL

Prashanti Singh

First appearance in the Asian Games

India took part in the first Asian Games at New Delhi in 1951, under the captaincy of Ranbir Chand. In its best performance at the Games to date, the team came fourth.

Most appearances in the Asian Games – women

Prashanti Singh is the only woman basketball player to represent the Indian team in two Asian Games, in 2010 and 2014. She also represented the national team in the 2006 CWG. She has won 22 medals in national championships and federation events.

First Indian-born player in the NBA

Satnam Singh Bhamara set a milestone in the history of Indian basketball when he was drafted into the National Basketball Association (NBA), the premier professional basketball league in the USA, in June 2015. Selected by the Dallas Mavericks, he played his Summer League debut match against the New Orleans Pelicans, scoring four points for his team, on 11 July 2015.

First and only sisters representing the country

Prashanti, Pratima, Priyanka, and Divya Singh, four sisters from Varanasi, Uttar Pradesh, have all played basketball for India.

Longest sequence of Nationals titles

- Services won the men's national title 26 years in a row from 1957 to 1982.
- Railways won the women's title 17 years in a row from 1986 to 2002.

Best win

Indian basketball's biggest win was at the 2014 FIBA Asia Cup, held in Wuhan, Hubei, China, winning against home favourites and against the most successful Asian team, China, by seven points.

BOXING

Most golds in an international meet

India won 10 gold and 2 silver medals at the 1995 South Asian Games (SAG; formerly SAF) in Chennai, Tamil Nadu, India. This achievement is second only to South Korea's haul of all 12 gold medals in the 1986 Seoul Asian Games.

India is at the 3rd spot in the International Boxing Association's (IBA) latest world ranking.

Most successive professional wins

Vijender Singh demolished former Commonwealth champion Charles

Adamu to claim his 12th straight win in November 2019. The winning streak ended when he was defeated by Russian opponent, Artysh Lopsan, in Goa, India, in March 2021.

Best youth boxer – men

Sachin Siwach was named Asian Boxing Confederation's Best Youth Boxer of 2017.

Oldest existing boxing association

The Maharashtra Amateur Boxing Association was formed in 1924.

AIBA

First boxer in the AIBA athletes' commission

In November 2019, veteran Indian boxer Laishram Sarita Devi was elected unopposed to the AIBA's first ever athletes commission to represent the Asian bloc. She is an eight-time Asian Championship medallist, with five being gold medals.

AIBA LEGEND

First Indian woman boxer to receive AIBA Legends Award

M.C. Mary Kom received the AIBA Legends Award at AIBA's 70th anniversary gala in Montreux, Switzerland, in 2016.

First male boxer to win the APB Best Boxing trophy

Asian Games gold medallist Vikas Krishan was awarded the APB Best Boxing trophy at AIBA's 70th anniversary in Montreux, Switzerland in 2016.

World no. 1

- In 2009, AIBA announced Vijender Singh as the top-ranked boxer in the annual middleweight category.
- In January 2019, M.C. Mary Kom (48 kg category) was the top-ranked boxer in the AIBA World Ranking (women).

ASIAN CHAMPIONSHIPS

Most medals in the Asian Championships – women

M.C. Mary Kom (46 kg), L. Sarita Devi (54 kg), Jenny R. Lalremliani (63 kg) and Jyotsna (80 kg and 86 kg) won two golds each at the 2003 and the 2005 Asian Women's Boxing Championship, in Hisar, Haryana, India, and Kaohsiung, Taiwan, respectively.

Best performance at the Asian Championships

Indian boxers won two gold, four silver and seven bronze medals in Bangkok, Thailand, in April 2019 to finish at the third position with 13 medals. Pooja Rani (81 kg) and Amit Panghal (52 kg) won gold medals; Deepak Singh (49 kg), Kavinder Singh Bisht (56 kg), Ashish Kumar (75 kg) and Simranjit Kaur (64 kg) won silvers; Nikhat Zareen (51 kg), Manisha Moun (54 kg), Sonia Chahal (57 kg), L. Sarita Devi (60 kg), Shiva Thapa (60 kg), Ashish (69 kg) and Satish Kumar (91 kg) won bronze medals.

ASIAN GAMES

First Asian Games medal – men

Hari Singh won the silver in the middleweight category at the 1958 Manila Games in the Philippines. Sunder Rao and Ranganathan won the bronze in the lightweight and the welterweight categories respectively.

First Asian Games gold – men

Padam Bahadur Mal won the gold medal in the lightweight category in 1962 in the Asian Games held in Jakarta, Indonesia.

Most Asian Games golds

Hawa Singh (heavyweight) won two golds at the 1966 and 1970 Asian Games, both held in Bangkok, Thailand.

Best performance in Asian Games – women

India won a gold and two bronze medals at the 2014 Incheon Asian Games in South Korea. M.C. Mary Kom won the gold in the women's flyweight (51 kg) event. L. Sarita Devi (lightweight, 60 kg) and Pooja Rani (middleweight, 75 kg) won bronze medals.

Best performance in the Asian Games

India won two gold, three silver and four bronze medals in the 2010 Asian

M.C. Mary Kom: Boxer Extraordinaire

Magnificent Mary, as she was called, was the only female boxer to have qualified for the 2012 Olympics where she participated in the flyweight category and won a bronze medal. She is a six-time world champion in women's boxing, having secured gold medals in the AIBA World Boxing Championships. Mary Kom's achievements also include being an Olympic bronze medalist, winning the medal at the 2012 London Olympics. Her dedication to the sport is evident in her numerous accolades, including Padma Bhushan and Padma Shri awards, which are India's fourth highest and third highest civilian honors, respectively. Mary Kom's journey in boxing began at a young age, and she has become an inspiring figure for aspiring athletes, particularly women, for breaking barriers and excelling in a traditionally male-dominated sport.

Games, its best haul at an Asian Games. The gold medallists were Vikas Krishan (60 kg) and Vijender Singh (75 kg). Silver medals were won by V. Santosh Kumar (64 kg), Dinesh Kumar (81 kg), and Manpreet Singh (91 kg). The bronze went to Suranjoy Singh (52 kg), Paramjeet Samota (+91 kg), M.C. Mary Kom (51 kg), and Kavita Goyal (75 kg).

COMMONWEALTH CHAMPIONSHIPS

Most Commonwealth Championship gold medals

India won six gold medals and the overall title at the Commonwealth Championship in New Delhi in March 2010. Amandeep Singh (49 kg), Suranjoy Singh (52 kg), Jai Bhagwan (60 kg), Vijender Singh (75 kg), Dinesh Kumar (81 kg), and Paramjeet Samota (+91 kg) won a gold medal each.

COMMON WEALTH GAMES

First Commonwealth Games gold

Mohammed Ali Qamar won the gold medal in the lightweight category, defeating Darren Langley 27–25 at the Commonwealth Games in Manchester, UK, in 2002.

Best performance at the Commonwealth Games

At the 2018 CWG in Gold Coast, Australia, India won three gold, three silver, and three bronze medals. M.C. Mary Kom in women's lightweight (48 kg), Gaurav Solanki in flyweight (52 kg), and Vikas Krishan in middleweight (75 kg) won gold medals. Amit Panghal in light flyweight (49 kg), Manish Kaushik in lightweight (60 kg), and Satish Kumar in superweight (+91 kg) won silver medals. Mohammed Hussamuddin in bantamweight (56 kg), Manoj Kumar in welterweight (69 kg), and Naman Talwar in heavyweight (91 kg) won bronze medals.

INTERNATIONAL

Most international titles

- Heavyweight boxer Kaur Singh won gold at four major international events: the 1980 Asian Boxing Championship (Bombay, now Mumbai, Maharashtra) and 1982 (Seoul, South Korea), the 1982 Delhi Asian Games and the 1982 King's Cup in Bangkok, Thailand.
- Super heavyweight boxer Rajkumar Sangwan also won four golds: at the 1991 Asian Invitational Championship in Bangkok, Thailand; the 1993 China Invitational Championship in Beijing, China; the 1993 South Asian Federation (SAF) Games at Dhaka, Bangladesh; and the 1994 Asian Boxing Championship at Tehran, Iran.

NATIONALS

First National Championship

The very first National Boxing Championship in the country, organized by the Indian Amateur Boxing Federation, was held in Bombay, Maharashtra, from 18 to 22 March 1950.

OLYMPICS

First Olympic appearance
India entered a boxing team in seven divisions for the first time at the 1948 London Olympics but could not reach the quarter-finals.

First Olympic medal – men
Vijender Singh won a bronze medal (middleweight) in the 2008 Beijing Olympics.

First Olympic medal – women
Six-time women's world champion M.C. Mary Kom won a bronze medal (51 kg) in the 2012 London Olympics. Lovlina Borgohain (69 kg) became the second Indian woman to win a bronze medal at Tokyo 2020 after losing to Turkey's Busenaz Surmeneli 0-5 in the semi-finals.

WORLD BOXING CHAMPIONSHIPS

First medal in the World Boxing Championships – men
- Amit Panghal was the first Indian male boxer to win a silver medal in the World Boxing Championships 2019. Seven Indians have won World Championships medals until now: Amit Panghal (2019, silver), Vijender Singh (2009, bronze), Vikas Krishan (2011, bronze), Shiv Thapa (2015, bronze), Gaurav (2017, bronze), Manish Kaushik (2019, bronze), and Akash Kumar (2021, bronze).
- Parveen Kumar won a bronze medal in the lightweight category in the World Junior Championships in Budapest, Hungary, in November 2000.

First World Boxing Championships medal – women
- M.C. Mary Kom from Manipur bagged a silver medal in the 48 kg category in the US in December 2001.
- Manju Rani became the second Indian to enter the World Boxing Championships final and won the silver at Ulan-Ude, Russia, in 2019.

WR Most medals in the World Boxing Championships
In October 2019, M.C. Mary Kom became the first boxer in the world (male or female) to win eight World Championship medals (six gold, a silver, and a bronze).

Best performance in the World Boxing Championships – women
India won four gold, one silver, and three bronze medals in the fourth World Women's Boxing Championship 2006 in New Delhi. M.C. Mary Kom (46 kg), L. Sarita Devi (52 kg), Jenny R. Lalremliani (63 kg), and Lekha K.C. (75 kg) won gold medals. N. Usha (57 kg) won a silver. The bronze winners were Chhotu Loura (50 kg), Aruna Mishra (60 kg), and Renu (82 kg).

WORLD CHAMPIONSHIPS

Most World Championship titles – women
M.C. Mary Kom is the first female pugilist to win the World Championship crown six times (2002, 2005, 2006, 2008, 2010, and 2018). She also won the most world

titles (five) in a row between 2002 and 2010. Others to have won gold medals in the World Championships are Sarita Devi (2006) , Jenny R. Lalremliani, (2006), Lakha K.C. (2006), and Nikhat Zareen (2022).

First medal in the World Championship – senior – men

Vijender Singh won a bronze medal in the 2009 Milan World Cup in Italy.

WORLD CUP

First medal at the World Cup – men

Zoramthanga defeated teammate Dharmender Yadav 17–4 on points to win the light flyweight bronze on 17 November 1990 in Bombay, Maharashtra.

Most medals in the World Cup – men

The Indian team won a silver and a bronze medal, and the sixth position overall, in the AIBA Boxing World Cup in October 2019 in Yekaterinburg, Russia.

YOUTH BOXING CHAMPIONSHIPS

Most medals at the Youth Boxing Championships

The Indian team won five gold, two silver, and five bronze medals at the Youth Boxing Championship in November 2019 in Ulaanbaatar, Mongolia.

Best performance in the World Youth Women's Boxing Championships

Seven Indian women boxers clinched gold medals in their respective weight categories in the AIBA Youth World Boxing Championships in Kielce, Poland, in August 2021. They were Gitika (48 kg), Naorem Babyrojisana Chanu (51 kg), Poonam (57 kg), Vinka (60 kg), Arundhati Choudhary (69 kg), T. Sanamacha Chanu (75 kg), and Alfiya Pathan (+81 kg).

CHESS

GENERAL

Most times world champion

Viswanathan Anand has won the World Chess Championship five times (2000, 2007, 2008, 2010 and 2012).

Oldest to regain the world rapid title

Viswanathan Anand, at 48, became the oldest world champion in the rapid format (25-minute time format) in Riyadh in December 2017. He regained the title won in 2003. Two days later, he also became the oldest medallist in the blitz format (five-minute time format) by claiming the bronze medal.

Asian champions – men

Five men – K. Sasikiran (2003), Surya Shekhar Ganguly (2009), P. Harikrishna (2011), Parimarjan Negi (2012), and S.P. Sethuraman (2016) – have been crowned Asian champions.

Most successful Commonwealth champion

Abhijeet Gupta is the only player to win the title five times, including three times in a row from 2015 to 2017.

Asian champions – women

Seven Indian women have won the title on nine occasions – Rohini Khadilkar (1981 and 1983), Anupama Gokhale (1985 and 1987), Bhagyashree Thipsay (1991), K. Humpy (2003), Tania Sachdev (2007), D. Harika (2011), Bhakti Kulkarni (2016), and Padmini Rout (2018).

Asian junior champions – men

V. Ravi Kumar (1978); Viswanathan Anand (1984 and 85); Abhijit Kunte (1997); Tejas Bakre (1998); K. Sasikiran (1999); P. Harikrishna (2000); Deepan Chakravarthy (2002); P. Magesh Chandran (2003); S. Arun Prasad (2004); P. Karthikeyan (2007); Aswin Jayaram (2008 and 2009); M. Shyam Sundar (2010 and 2011); N. Srinath (2012, 2013 and 2014); and Aravindh Chithambaram (2016).

Asian junior champions – women

Anupama Abhyankar (1985); Saheli Dhar (1993); K. Humpy (2000); M. Kasturi (2001); Tania Sachdev (2002); Y. Pratibha (2003); Mary Ann Gomes (2006, 2007, 2008); Padmini Rout (2009); Bhakti Kulkarni (2011); and Ivana Furtado (2012 and 2017).

Domination in Advanced Chess

Viswanathan Anand won a hat-trick of titles in 1999, 2000 and 2001 in Leon, Spain. In 2000 and 2001 he beat Alexei Shirov of Spain in the final to win the tournament. In Advanced Chess, players have the benefit of using database searches on their computers before making a move.

Four successive Asian Junior titles

Indians twice won the title for four years in a row. The Indian boys won from 1997 to 2000 and again from 2007 to 2010.

Commonwealth Champions

Twelve Indians have won the Commonwealth title. They are: Pravin Thipsay (1985), D.V. Prasad (1986), P. Mithrakanth (1996), Atanu Lahiri (1999), K. Sasikiran (2000), P. Harikrishna (2001), Dibyendu Barua (2003), R.B. Ramesh (2007), R.R. Laxman (2010), M.R. Lalith Babu (2012), Abhijeet Gupta (2013, 2015, 2016, 2017 and 2019) and P. Karthikeyan (2018).

Pravin Thipsay

Board Prize with a perfect score

Viswanathan Anand scored seven points from seven rounds to win the top Board Prize in the Asian Team Championship in 1989.

Viswanathan Anand

Golden sweep – Asian Youth Championships

India won 18 medals, including all eight gold medals at stake, in the Asian Youth Championship in 2006. Sweety Patel (girls' U-8), Sahajasri (Girls U-10), Padmini Rout (girls' U-12), Bhakti Kulkarni (girls' U-14), Prince Bajaj (boys' U-8), G.V. Sai Krishna (boys' U-10), Vidit Gujarati (boys' U-12) and S. Nitin (boys' U-14) were the gold medal winners.

Grand Slam victories

In chess, the tournaments in Wijk Aan Zee, Netherlands, Linares, Chile and Dortmund, Germany, were considered the equivalent of the Grand Slam in golf. Anand won at Wijk Aan Zee five times, and at Linares and Dortmund, both three times.

First GM norm

Pravin Thipsay was the first to achieve GM norm in the 1985 Commonwealth championship in London, UK.

First GM norm in National Championships

P. Konguvel was the first Indian to date to gain a nine-game norm from the National 'A' Championship at New Delhi in June 2001.

First Grandmaster (GM)

Viswanathan Anand became India's first GM on 28 December 1987 at the Sakthi Finance Grandmaster tournament in Coimbatore, Tamil Nadu.

First International Master (IM) – men

Manuel Aaron of Tamil Nadu became an International Master in 1961.

First International Master (IM) – women

S. Vijayalakshmi got the International Master's title in Sept 2000.

First Olympiad gold

Dibyendu Barua won the gold on the second board of the Olympiad in Novi Sad (erstwhile Yugoslavia) in 1990.

First Olympiad gold on top board

D. Gukesh won the gold on top board in Mahabalipuram, Tamil Nadu in 2022.

First Olympiad medal

Rafiq Khan won a silver medal in the 1980 Olympiad.

Rameshbabu Praggnanandhaa

A chess grandmaster, a chess prodigy, and an international master at the age of 10, Rameshbabu Praggnanandhaa became the youngest player in 2022 to defeat the world champion Magnus Carlsen. Praggnanandhaa became world's number 20 chess player. He was the runner-up at the Chess World Cup after being defeated by Magnus Carlsen in 2023.

First time when India won medals in both sections of Olympiad

India won bronze medals in open and women sections of the Olympiad in Mahabalipuram, Tamil Nadu, in 2022.

First international recognition

Mir Sultan Khan, born in 1905 in Mittha Village, Punjab, received international recognition at a time when there was no system of Elo ratings. In 1928, he won the all-India title scoring 8.5 out of 9 points at the British Championship. He won again in 1932 and 1933. He also defeated world champion Jose Casablanca of Cuba at the Hastings tournament. Considered among the 10 best players in the world then, he returned to India in 1933 but played little chess. He died in Sargodha, Pakistan, on 25 May 1966.

First medal in the Chess Olympiad

India won its maiden medal from the Tromso Chess Olympiad in 2014 in Norway. In the open section, India was represented by Parimarjan Negi, K, Sasikiran, S.P. Sethuraman, B. Adhiban, and M.R. Lalith Babu claimed the bronze medal, ahead of traditional powerhouses like Russia, Armenia and Ukraine.

First medal in Asian Games

K. Humpy won the gold in the Doha Asian Games, Qatar, in 2006.

First team medal in Asian Games

The trio of K. Sasikiran, P. Harikrishna, and K. Humpy won the mixed team gold in Doha, Qatar, in 2006.

First WIM

Jayshree Khadilkar became a WIM (Woman International Master) in 1978.

First to win the Asian Junior girls' title thrice

Mary Ann Gomes won the title in 2006 (New Delhi), 2007 (Mumbai) and 2008 (Chennai).

First WGM norm

Bhagyashree Thipsay was the first to achieve a Woman Grand Master

There have been 81 chess grandmasters in India as of February 2023.

(WGM) norm in 1986 in the Lloyds Bank Master's tournament when she was twenty-one.

First woman to lead a team in the open section

K. Humpy led India 'B' in the open section of the Asian Team Championship at Jodhpur, Rajasthan, in 2003.

Two World Cups

Viswanathan Anand is the first person in the world to successfully defend the men's World Cup title. He did so at Hyderabad, Telangana, in October 2002.

First World Junior title

Viswanathan Anand was 17 years 225 days when he won the title on 2 August 1987 at Baguio in the Philippines. P. Harikrishna (2004) and Abhijeet Gupta (2008) are the other junior title winners.

WR First country to win both World Junior titles in a single edition

India became the first country to win both the World Junior titles in a single edition in 2008 when Abhijeet Gupta and D. Harika won the open and girls' sections respectively in the World Junior Chess Championship in Gaziantep, Turkey. Parimarjan Negi claimed the silver to give India a rare 1-2 finish in the open section.

First World Sub-junior medal

Viswanathan Anand claimed a bronze after sharing the second place in 1984.

MOSTS

Highest cheque

Viswanathan Anand won €1.20 million for retaining the World Chess title in Sofia, Bulgaria, in May 2010. This is the biggest cheque received by an Indian sportsperson.

P. Harikrishna

Most International age group titles (in a single year)

Tejas Bakre won three gold medals in eight months in 1998: the Asian Junior at Rasht (Iran) in May, the World Youth Games championship in Moscow, Russia, in July and the Asian Sub-Junior in Mumbai, India, in December.

Most National titles (in a season)

P. Harikrishna won five National titles in 1997–98 season – the 1997 National Sub-juniors held in January 1998 at Aurangabad, Maharashtra, the U-12 in Ahmedabad, Gujarat, the U-18 in Bikaner, Rajasthan, the U-14 rapid chess title in Guntur, Andhra Pradesh, and the 1998 National Sub-junior at Aurangabad, Maharashtra.

Most medals

Indians won 21 medals – seven gold, seven silver, and seven bronze – in the Asian Youth Championship held in New Delhi in 2005. This was the biggest haul by India in a continental competition.

Most National titles

- *Men*: Manuel Aaron won nine National titles, five of them in a row from 1969 to 1974.
- *Women*: S. Vijayalakshmi has claimed the National title six times, including five times in a row from 2002.

Most titles in a year

Viswanathan Anand won a string of eight titles in the year 2000. Starting with the World Blitz Cup, he won the Wydra International at Haifa, Israel, the Advanced Chess title in Leon, Spain, the Giants Classic in Frankfurt, Germany, the Dortmund International (joint winner), Germany, the World Cup in Shenyang, China, and the Corsica Masters in France, finishing with the World Championship title in December 2000.

City to host most Commonwealth Championships

New Delhi hosted the Commonwealth Championship six times between 2007 and 2019.

Most participants in an International Open

As many as 2,810 entries were received across three sections of the 17th Delhi International Open held in January 2019.

Most prize money offered in an International Open

The 2019 Delhi International Open offered 1.01 crore rupees as prize money across three sections.

FASTEST

Fastest to achieve norms

P. Harikrishna achieved three norms – his IM norm in the Asian Championship in Udaipur, Rajasthan, the Goodricke tournament in Kolkata, West Bengal, and the Commonwealth Championship in Sangli, Maharashtra, – in less than two months in 2000.

YOUNGEST

Youngest to achieve an IM norm

R. Praggnanandhaa became the youngest Indian to make an IM norm. At 10 years and six months, he gained the distinction in Cannes (France) in February 2016.

Youngest Indian in the World Cup and the Chess Olympiad

D. Harika played in the World Cup at 11 years 9 months in Hyderabad, then in Andhra Pradesh in 2002. She also became the youngest to play for India in the Chess Olympiad after her undefeated performance in Mallorca, Spain, in 2004.

Youngest International Master

R. Praggnanandhaa, at the age of 10 years 9 months, became the youngest International Master in chess history in May 2017 by making his third and final IM norm at Bhubaneswar, Odisha. His earlier two norms had come in Cannes, France, and Moscow, Russia.

D. Gukesh

Youngest Grandmaster

D. Gukesh became the country's youngest and the world's second youngest Grandmaster in January 2019 at the age of 12 years, 7 months and 17 days.

Youngest Grandmaster – female

K. Humpy is the youngest female to become a GM at 15 years 58 days.

Youngest National champion

Sixteen-year-old G. Akash became the youngest National champion in 2012.

Youngest National Junior – champion

Abhijeet Gupta of Bhilwara became the youngest National Junior champion at Nagpur in 2002. He won the U-19 event at the age of 13 years 10 days.

Youngest international title winners

Sanskruti Wankhede and Vallabh Kavi were the winners of the Asian Schools' chess (U-5) girls' and boys' titles, respectively, in New Delhi in 2011.

Youngest to beat a GM

Hetul Shah (9) defeated Nurlan Ibrayev from Kazakhstan in the first round of the Parsvnath International Open chess tournament in New Delhi on 11 January 2009, to become the youngest Indian to beat a Grandmaster. He broke the record of Parimarjan Negi who had achieved the feat at the age of eleven.

Youngest to win the Commonwealth title

P. Harikrishna, then fifteen, won the gold in London, UK, in 2001 after a three-way tie with two British players.

Youngest to win the World Junior title

P. Harikrishna won the World junior title in Kochi, Kerala, in November 2004 when he was 18 years 204 days old.

There are 42 Woman International Masters (WIM) as of May 2023.

Youngest WIM

K. Humpy became the youngest Woman International Master (WIM) in Asia at twelve years, three months, four days.

Youngest winner of Asian Junior (U-20) title

M. Kasturi, then 14 years old, won the Asian Junior title in Teharan, Iran, in 2001.

Youngest to qualify for the National Championship

- Dibyendu Barua, then 12, remains the youngest to qualify for the National championship in 1978.
- D. Harika holds the unique record of being the youngest girl to qualify for the men's National championship in 2004 as well as for the women's National championship in 2001.

Youngest world champion in any sport

Ivana Furtado claimed the World Girls' U-8 crown at the age of seven years and 226 at Batumi, Georgia on 29 October 2006.

BEST

Best achievement

- *Men*: Viswanathan Anand's rating of 2817 in March 2011 is the highest recorded by an Indian.
- *Women*: Among women, Koneru Humpy's rating of 2623 in July 2009 is the highest.

Best performance in Asian Team Championship

Indian men won the gold and women won the silver medal at Esfahan, Iran, in 2006.

Highest title

K. Humpy won the World Junior Girls (U-20) Championship in August 2001 at 14 years.

Best performance (Category 21)

Viswanathan Anand beat a field of seven super Grandmasters at Madrid, Spain, between February 21 and 10 March, 1998. The Category 21 tournament attracted seven of the top nine GMs of the world. Anand beat Alexey Shirov, Peter Svidler, Vassily Ivanchuk, Vaselin Topalov 1.5-0.5; lost to Gary Kasparov 0.5-1.5 and drew 1-1 with Vladimir Kramnik.

ONLY

First/only winner of Asian Junior and Sub-junior titles

Tejas Bakre won the Asian Junior and Asian Sub-junior titles at the same time, in 1998.

Only Indian to win against computers

Viswanathan Anand simultaneously played six computers and won 4-2, in the Aegon Man versus Computer Chess Event in 1997.

Only Asian to win at Wijk Aan Zee

Viswanathan Anand is the only Asian to win the Hoogovens Chess Tournament (Corus tournament since 2000) at Wijk Aan Zee, Netherlands, in 1989, though jointly with three others. He won the title again in 1998, jointly with Vladimir Kramnik, and outright in 2003, 2004 and 2006.

Only Indian to win rapid/ blindfold event
Viswanathan Anand won the first-of-its-kind Melody Amber Blindfold and Rapid chess event in 1994, 1997, 2003, and jointly in 2006.

K. Humpy

Only Indian to reach the final of World Championship
K. Humpy reached the final of World Championship 2011 where China's Hou Yifan won 5.5-2.5 with two games to spare in their 10-game title match.

Only Chess Oscar award winner
Viswanathan Anand is the only Indian to receive the Chess Oscar (founded in 1967) by the Russian chess magazine *64 - Chess Review*. He has claimed the Chess Oscar six times (in 1997, 1998, 2003, 2004, 2007, and 2008).

Only semi-finalist of World Championship and World Cup
K. Humpy reached the semi-finals of the World Championship in Elista, Russia, in 2004 and the World Cup held at Hyderabad, then in Andhra Pradesh, in 2002.

Only Indian with three World Championship bronze medals
D. Harika claimed three successive bronze medals from the Women's World Championship in 2012, 2015 and 2017.

Only girl to win the National U-12 – open section
K. Humpy won the U-12 title in Ahmedabad, Gujarat, in 1999.

CRICKET

WOMEN'S CRICKET

GENERAL

Most career runs in women's international cricket
Mithali Raj has scored 10,868 runs in her international career, with 669 runs in Tests, 7,805 in ODIs and 2,364 in T20Is.

Shafali Verma

Youngest to debut across all formats
Shafali Verma became the youngest Indian cricketer to make her debut across all three formats of the game when she played her first One-Day International (ODI) on 27 June 2021, against England in the UK, when she was 17 years and 150 days old. She made her Test debut on 16 June 2021 in Bristol, UK, against England. Her T20I debut came at the

age of 15 against South Africa in September 2019 in Surat, Gujarat. She is also the youngest woman ever to play an ODI, and the first Indian and fourth woman to score a half-century in both innings on a Test debut.

Mithali Raj

WR Longest career
Mithali Raj's cricketing career spans more than 23 years.

Most career wickets across formats
Jhulan Goswami, with 355 wickets in 284 matches, has the most wickets across formats.

First and only double century
Mithali Raj scored 214 runs in 407 balls, against England at Taunton, UK, on 16 August 2002. She also has the best batting average of 51.00 in 10 matches.

TESTS

Most career dismissals by a wicketkeeper
Anju Jain has the most career dismissals by a wicketkeeper with 23 dismissals from 1995 to 2003, including 15 caught and 8 stumped.

Biggest victory margin
India won by an innings and 34 runs while playing against South Africa in Mysuru, Karnataka, on 16 November 2014.

Narrowest victory margin
India won by 5 wickets against West Indies in Patna, Bihar, on 17 November 1976, and then against England at Taunton, UK, on 1 September 2006.

Lowest total
The lowest total ever was 65 runs for 10 wickets in 46 overs against the West Indies at Jammu, Jammu and Kashmir, on 29 November 1976.

Highest total
The highest total by the women's cricket team is 467 in 177.1 overs versus England at Taunton, UK, on 17 August 2002.

Most runs
Sandhya Agarwal has 1,110 runs in 13 matches. She also holds the record for the most centuries, with four in 13 Tests and 23 innings.

WR Best bowling – innings
Neetu David's eight wickets for 53 runs against England at Jamshedpur, Jharkhand, on 27 November 1995, makes her the only bowler in women's Test cricket to have claimed eight wickets in an innings.

Women's IPL

The Women's Indian Premier League (IPL) is a significant milestone in the evolution of women's cricket in India. Launched in 2019, the Women's IPL, also known as the Women's T20 Challenge, features exhibition matches that run parallel to the men's IPL matches. The tournament aims to provide a platform for women cricketers to showcase their skills and gain exposure on a global stage. While the Women's IPL is not a full-fledged league like its male counterpart, it has garnered attention due to the participation of international and Indian women cricketers. Players like Harmanpreet Kaur, Smriti Mandhana, and Mithali Raj have been instrumental in promoting the tournament.

Women's Delhi team

WR Most balls delivered

Former Indian player and left-arm spinner Diana Edulji is the only woman to deliver more than 5,000 balls (5,248) in Test matches.

Most wickets in a Test

Right-arm pacer Jhulan Goswami took 10 wickets in the match against England at Taunton, UK, on 1 September 2006.

Most career wickets in Tests

The record for most wickets in a Test career belongs to Diana Edulji, with 63 wickets taken from 1976 to 1991.

Best bowling average

Jhulan Goswami, with an average of 17.36 with 44 wickets in 12 matches, has an unmatched bowling average in women's Test cricket in India.

Most career catches by a fielder

Sudha Shah has taken 21 catches in as many matches, an Indian record for a fielding position.

ONE-DAY INTERNATIONALS

Highest partnership

Deepti Sharma and Poonam Raut made a 320-run stand for the first wicket at the India versus Ireland match at Potchefstroom, South Africa, on 15 May 2017.

Best bowling average – minimum 50 wickets

Neetu David holds the record with an average of 16.34 (141 wickets in 97 matches).

Highest individual score

Deepti Sharma was 188 not out at the India versus Ireland match at Potchefstroom, South Africa, on 15 May 2017.

Clean sweep victories in a bilateral series

The Indian team won all five matches in a bilateral series twice – against England in January 2002, and then against West Indies during February–March 2004.

Century on debut

Mithali Raj scored a century on her debut with 114 runs (not out) versus Ireland at Milton Keynes, UK, on 26 June 1999.

Most runs scored

Mithali Raj has scored 7,805 runs in 232 matches. She is the only woman cricketer to score more than 7,000 runs.

Harmanpreet Kaur

Most career runs

Harmanpreet Kaur has scored 2,694 in 137 matches with a batting average of 27.48.

Most career dismissals by a wicketkeeper

Anju Jain has 81 dismissals to her credit, including 30 caught and 51 stumped.

Most career stumpings by a wicketkeeper

Anju Jain holds a world record with 51 stumpings across her career.

Most career catches by a fielder

Jhulan Goswami has notched up 69 catches in 204 matches.

T20 INTERNATIONALS

Largest victory margin

- The largest victory margin in terms of runs is 142 runs versus Malaysia on 3 June 2018 at the Kinrara Academy Oval, Kuala Lumpur, Malaysia.
- In terms of wickets, the largest victory margin has been by 10 wickets against the Australian team on 29 January 2016 at Melbourne, Australia.

Highest partnership

Shafali Verma and Smriti Mandhana put on a 143-run stand for the first wicket versus West Indies at the Darren Sammy National Cricket Stadium, Saint Lucia, on 9 November 2019.

Narrowest margin of victory

- By runs, the narrowest margin was 3 runs on two occasions. The first was against the West Indies at North Sound, Antigua, on 19 February 2012, and the second was against New Zealand in Melbourne, Australia, on 27 February 2020.
- By wickets, India's narrowest margin has been against New Zealand, of 3 wickets at Aldershot, England, on 27 June 2011.

Highest team total

India's highest team total was 198 for 4 wickets in the third match versus England at Brabourne Stadium in Mumbai, Maharashtra, in the Tri-Nation Women's T20I Series in March 2018.

Lowest team total

India scored only 62 runs in 18.2 overs versus Australia at Billericay, Essex, UK, on 23 June 2011.

Best bowling

Jhulan Goswami took 5 wickets for 11 runs in a T20I match against Australia at Visakhapatnam, Andhra Pradesh, on 23 March 2012.

Most career wickets

Poonam Yadav has notched up 98 wickets in 72 matches.

Best bowling average (minimum qualification of 30 matches)

Poonam Raut has a record bowling average of 9.66.

Most career dismissals by a wicketkeeper

Tania Bhatia has 67 dismissals (23 caught and 44 stumped) in 50 matches.

Most career catches by a fielder

Harmanpreet Kaur holds the record of 53 catches in 137 matches, the highest number of career catches.

Since the first Women's Twenty20 International against England in August 2006, India has played 151 matches.

MEN'S CRICKET

GENERAL

Player with the most IPL titles

Rohit Sharma has earned the most IPL titles, totalling six: one with the Deccan Chargers, Hyderabad (2009) and five with the Mumbai Indians (2013, 2015, 2017, 2019 and 2020).

TESTS

First victory

India, captained by Vijay Hazare, defeated England by an innings and 8 runs on 10 February 1952 at Madras (now Chennai), Tamil Nadu. The victory came in the fifth match of a five-match series and India managed to draw the series 1–1.

Sunil Gavaskar

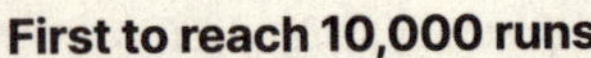

First to reach 10,000 runs

Indian cricket legend Sunil Gavaskar first went past the 10,000 mark in 125 matches, reaching 10,122 Test runs in his last series against Pakistan in 1987.

Highest team innings score

The highest innings score was 759 runs for 7 wickets against England at Chennai, Tamil Nadu, in 2016.

Highest score on debut (series)

Legendary batsman Sunil Gavaskar scored 774 runs in his very first Test series against West Indies in 1971, a record that remains unbroken.

WR Most consecutive wins at home (series)

India recorded their 15th consecutive Test series wins at home when they beat Sri Lanka in a two-match series in March 2022, beating Australia to the top spot in the longest winning streak by any team.

WR Most career wickets

Anil Kumble holds the record with 619 wickets in his Test career spanning from 1990 to 2008.

Most career runs

Sachin Tendulkar's total of 15,921 runs is an unbroken world record for the most career runs in men's Test cricket.

Most wickets in a debut series

In the India–England Test series from 5 February to 8 March 2021, Axar Patel took 27 wickets in the four-match series. He holds the record jointly with Dilip Doshi, who took the same number of wickets during a six-match home series against Australia in 1979.

WR Most individual centuries

Sachin Tendulkar scored 51 centuries – 3 versus West Indies in 19 Tests, 11 versus Australia in 35 Tests, 2 versus Pakistan in 18 Tests, 7 versus England in 28 Tests, 4 in 22 Tests versus New Zealand, 9 in 25 Tests versus Sri Lanka, 7 in 25 Tests versus South Africa, 5 in seven Tests versus Bangladesh, and 3 in nine Tests versus Zimbabwe.

Most runs in an over

Jasprit Bumrah scored 35 runs (not out) in an over off England bowler Stuart Broad at Edgbaston, Birmingham, in May 2022. He hit two fours off the first two deliveries, followed by a wide ball, then a six, followed by a no ball, and the next three balls were hit for fours. The penultimate ball went for a six and he scored a single off the last ball.

WR Most sixes in a series

Rohit Sharma scored 17 sixes in the Test series against South Africa on 20 October 2019 in Ranchi, Jharkhand.

Highest individual score in a day

Virender Sehwag, in his knock of 293 against Sri Lanka in Mumbai, Maharashtra, during 2009–10, made 284 runs on the second day of the Test match – the highest individual score in a single day to date.

Highest run chase

India's run chase of 406 runs for 4 wickets against West Indies in Port-of-Spain, Trinidad, in 1976, is its highest successful chase to date.

Fastest Indian opener to score 1,000 runs

Right-handed batsman Rohit Sharma achieved this landmark in his 17th innings as the Indian opener against England on 5 March 2021.

Sachin Tendulkar

Sachin Tendulkar, born on April 24, 1973, in Mumbai, India, is an iconic figure in the world of cricket. He is often referred to as the "Little Master" or "Master Blaster." He is the highest run-scorer in international cricket, with 100 international centuries to his name, a feat unparalleled in the sport. Making his debut for the Indian cricket team at the age of 16, Tendulkar's incredible consistency and versatility allowed him to excel in all formats of the game. He played a pivotal role in India's 2011 ICC Cricket World Cup victory, a moment that captured the hearts of millions. Tendulkar received the Bharat Ratna, India's highest civilian award, in recognition of his contributions to the nation through cricket. His impact on the sport goes beyond statistics, as he remains an inspiration and role model for aspiring cricketers worldwide.

Rahul Dravid

Lowest team innings score
India recorded an all-time low of 36 runs against Australia in Adelaide in December 2020. It is the fifth lowest in the world.

WR Highest run aggregate
Sachin Tendulkar's score of 15,921 runs from 1989 to 2013 in 200 Tests is a world record. This score, from 329 innings, amounts to an average of 53.78.

WR Highest century partnerships
Rahul Dravid has been part of the most three-figure partnerships, on 88 occasions; 3 times for the first wicket, 34 times for the second, 26 times for the third, 8 times for the fourth, 12 times for the fifth, 3 times for the sixth and 2 times for the eighth wicket. He partnered with Sachin Tendulkar in 100-plus stands in a world record 20 times and with V.V.S. Laxman 12 times. Dravid's highest stand was with Virender Sehwag in a 410-run stand against Pakistan at Lahore in 2006. Dravid and Tendulkar have added 6,920 partnership runs, the most by any pair in history.

WR Most 1,000+ runs in a calendar year
Sachin Tendulkar has scored more than 1,000 runs in a calendar year on six occasions. He made 1,000 runs in 12 Tests in 1997; 1,088 runs in 10 Tests in 1999; 1,003 runs in 10 Tests in 2001; 1,392 runs in 16 Tests in 2002; 1,063 runs in 13 Tests in 2008; and 1,562 runs in 11 Tests in 2010.

Wicket off first ball on debut
Nilesh Kulkarni is the first and only Indian, and the 15th in the world, to capture a wicket off the very first ball on debut, when he bowled out Marvan Atapattu of Sri Lanka in Colombo, Sri Lanka, in 1997.

Highest individual innings
Rohit Sharma scored 118 versus Sri Lanka in Indore, Madhya Pradesh, in 2017.

Wicket off first ball in a match
Syed Abid Ali took the wicket of Roy Fredricks off the very first ball in Port-of-Spain, Trinidad, against the West Indies in 1971. Kapil Dev emulated him twice by dismissing Mohsin Khan at Jalandhar, Punjab, against Pakistan during 1983–84, and Jimmy Cook at Durban versus South Africa in 1992–93.

Best bowling figures on Test debut
Narendra Hirwani took 16 wickets for 136 runs against West Indies at Madras (now Chennai), Tamil Nadu, during 1987–88.

WR Best bowling in a match
Narendra Hirwani took 16 wickets for 136 runs versus West Indies at Madras (now Chennai), Tamil Nadu, during 1987–88.

Best bowling in an innings

Anil Kumble took 10 wickets for 74 runs against Pakistan at Delhi in one innings during 1998–99. He became the second bowler after England's Jim Laker to do so, and is now joined by Ajaz Patel of New Zealand.

Anil Kumble

Most catches in an innings

The world record of five catches is held by four individuals (along with eight foreign players): Yajurvindra Singh (versus England at Bengaluru, Karnataka, in 1977); Mohammad Azharuddin (versus Pakistan at Karachi, Pakistan, in 1989); K. Srikkanth (versus Australia at Perth, Australia, in 1992); and Ajinkya Rahane (versus Sri Lanka at Galle, Sri Lanka, in 2015).

Most career dismissals by a wicketkeeper

M.S. Dhoni has dismissed 294 batsmen (caught 256 and stumped 38) in 90 Tests. The record for dismissals is six, shared by four players: Syed Kirmani, who caught five and stumped one against New Zealand at Christchurch, New Zealand, in 1975–76; M.S. Dhoni, who caught six against New Zealand at Wellington, New Zealand, in 2008–09; Wriddhiman Saha, with five caught and one stumped against West Indies at North Sound, Antigua, in 2016; and Rishabh Pant, with six caught in Adelaide in December 2018 versus Australia.

Dismissing all 11 batsmen in a match

S. Venkataraghavan dismissed all 11 batsmen in the Delhi Test against New Zealand in 1964–65. His final tally was 12 for 152. He became the second bowler after England's Jim Laker and one among only six bowlers in the world to do this.

Most dismissals by a wicketkeeper in a match

Rishabh Pant shares the world record with England's Jack Russell (versus South Africa, 1995) and South Africa's A.B. de Villiers (versus Pakistan, 2013), with 11 dismissals in Adelaide, versus Australia, in December 2018.

Most catches in a match

With eight catches in the match against Sri Lanka at Galle, Sri Lanka, in 2015 (three in the first innings and five in the second), Ajinkya Rahane holds the world record for most catches in a match.

Most dismissals by a wicketkeeper in a series

N.S. Tamhane holds the record with 19 dismissals in five Tests against Pakistan in the 1954–55 series.

Wicketkeeper with the fastest 100 dismissals

Risabh Pant reached the milestone of 100 dismissals in only 26 matches, with

92 catches and 8 stumpings. He achieved it in the first Test against South Africa at SuperSport Park, Centurion, in December 2021.

Highest score and fastest 100 on debut

Shikhar Dhawan scored 187 runs in 174 balls (33 fours, 2 sixes) in his Test debut against Australia at Mohali, Punjab, in 2013. Dhawan reached his 100 in just 85 balls – the fastest by a debutant (where full figures are available).

ONE-DAY INTERNATIONALS

First bowler to take more than three wickets on debut

Prasidh Krishna is the only bowler to take four wickets in an ODI debut. He finished 4/54 in his debut ODI on 23 March 2021, against England, at the Maharashtra Cricket Association Stadium in Pune.

Highest team total

The Indian men's cricket team scored 418 runs for 5 wickets in 50 overs against West Indies at Indore, Madhya Pradesh, on 9 December 2011.

First to score 100 centuries in international cricket

Sachin Tendulkar was the first to score 100 international centuries (51 Test and 49 ODI hundreds). He scored his 100th century at the 4th ODI of the Asia Cup versus Bangladesh on 16 March 2012.

Most wickets in an innings

Mohammed Shami took seven wickets in a match against NZ in 2023 World Cup.

Highest score on debut

K.L. Rahul scored an unbeaten 100 against Zimbabwe at Harare, Zimbabwe, on 11 June 2016 – the only Indian to make an ODI century on debut.

Sachin Tendulkar

Most career Man of the Match awards

Sachin Tendulkar has won 62 Man of the Match awards in his career. He won the first Man of the Match award in the 1992 World Cup against Pakistan.

Lowest team total

India scored only 54 runs in 26.3 overs against Sri Lanka at Sharjah, UAE, on 29 October 2000.

Most ODI century partnerships

Sourav Ganguly and Sachin Tendulkar have 26 century-plus stands as a pair.

Fastest 50 runs on debut

Krunal Pandya became the fastest-scoring debutant to post a half-century in an ODI match in just 26 balls, finishing at 58 not out in 31 balls on 23 March 2021 at the Maharashtra Cricket Association Stadium in Pune, Maharashtra, against England. He became the 15th Indian to score over 50 runs on an ODI debut.

12 international teams have official test status with ICC.

WR Most runs in all World Cups

Sachin Tendulkar scored 2,278 runs in 45 World Cup matches from 1992 to 2011. He also holds the world record for the most centuries in World Cups, with 6 in 45 World Cup matches; this was equalled by Rohit Sharma in 17 matches.

Most career catches

Mohammad Azharuddin took 156 catches in ODIs.

Most player of the series awards

In the India–England Test series during February–March 2021, R. Ashwin became the first Indian with more than 30 (he took 32) wickets and a century in a four-match Test series, and only the fifth player in the world to do so. He also became the first Indian to take 30 or more wickets in a Test series twice. Ashwin's nine Player of the Series awards in Test cricket are the most won by an Indian, just behind Sri Lankan player Muttiah Muralitharan (11) in this format.

WR Most centuries in ODIs

Virat Kohli scored the most centuries in 292 one-day internationals with 50 centuries so far. He has surpassed Sachin's previous record of 49.

Most career wickets

Anil Kumble holds the record with 337 wickets.

WR Most total career runs

Sachin Tendulkar has made a total of 18,426 runs in his ODI career spanning 463 matches.

Highest individual innings

Rohit Sharma's 264 runs versus Sri Lanka on 13 November 2014 at Kolkata, West Bengal.

WR Most sixes in World Cup

Rohit Sharma became the batter to score the most sixes in ODI World Cups with 54 sixes.

Best strike rate

Hardik Pandya has achieved a record strike rate of 115.59 across 66 matches.

Best bowling

Stuart Binny took 6 wickets for 4 runs against Bangladesh at Mirpur, Bangladesh, on 17 June 2014.

WR Most runs in a single World Cup edition

Virat Kohli became the batter to score the most runs in a single World Cup edition with 765 runs in 2023, breaking Sachin's earlier record of 673 runs from 2003.

WR Most centuries in a single World Cup

Rohit Sharma notched up five centuries in the 2019 World Cup, breaking Kumara Sangakkara's previous record.

First wins in the World Cup and ICC World Twenty20

India won its first World Cup under the captaincy of Kapil Dev in 1983 and its second World Cup under the leadership of M.S. Dhoni in 2011, thus becoming the third nation after West Indies and Australia to win the World Cup more than once. Dhoni also led India to its first ICC World Twenty20 win in its inaugural 2007 edition.

Fastest century

K.L. Rahul scored the fastest century in World Cup 2023 with 62 balls.

WR Most career catches

Rahul Dravid holds the record for most career catches, with 210 catches in 164 matches (including one catch for the ICC World XI): 47 versus Australia, 30 versus England, 26 versus West Indies, 21 versus South Africa, 21 versus Zimbabwe; 19 versus Pakistan; 17 versus New Zealand; 16 versus Sri Lanka; and 13 versus Bangladesh.

India has won **131** T20I matches.

T20 INTERNATIONALS

Highest team total

The highest team total is 260 for 5, for India versus Sri Lanka in Indore, Madhya Pradesh, on 22 December 2017.

Lowest team total

India scored 74 runs in 17.3 overs against Australia at Melbourne on 1 February 2008.

Highest run chase

The Indian team made 211 runs for 4 wickets on 12 December 2009, chasing Sri Lanka's 206 runs for 7 wickets, at Mohali, Punjab.

Most career wickets

Bhuvneshwar Kumar has the most T20I career wickets with 90 in 86 matches.

Best bowling average (minimum 10 wickets)

L. Balaji's bowling average of 12.10 is the best on record for T20I matches.

Best individual bowling

Deepak Chahar took 6 wickets for 7 runs while playing against Bangladesh at Nagpur, Maharashtra, on 10 November 2019.

Most runs in T20
Virat Kohli has 4,008 runs in 115 matches.

WR Most career dismissals as a wicketkeeper
M.S. Dhoni holds the record of most career dismissals, with 91 dismissals in 98 matches, including 57 caught and 34 stumped.

WR Best batting average (minimum 50 matches)
Virat Kohli has the best batting average of 52.73 in 115 matches.

Fastest to 50
Yuvraj Singh's 50 runs in 12 balls against England in Durban, South Africa, on 19 September 2007, is the fastest half-century in T20Is.

WR Only captain to win all three ICC trophies
M.S. Dhoni is the only captain to lead his team to victory in all the three major ICC tournaments: the World T20 in 2007, the Cricket World Cup in 2011 and the Champions Trophy in 2013.

CUE SPORTS

DOMESTIC

First National Championship – billiards
The first National Championship was held in 1931 in Calcutta (now Kolkata), West Bengal, with only eight entries. M.M. Beg won the title.

First National Championship – snooker
The first National Snooker Championship was held in 1939 in Calcutta, West Bengal. P.K. Deb won the title.

Most national titles – billiards and snooker
Pankaj Advani has won the national titles for both billiards and snooker a record 32 times.

Pankaj Advani

Highest break – snooker

Geet Sethi had the maximum possible break of 147 against Latif Nazarali at the 54th National Championship in Guntur, Andhra Pradesh, in 1988.

First billiards and snooker hat-trick

Geet Sethi achieved a hat-trick of three consecutive National Championship titles in billiards and snooker from 1985 to 1987. He also won the national titles for both sports in 1988.

INTERNATIONAL

First world snooker champion

Om B. Agarwal won the IBSF International Billiards and Snooker Federation World Snooker Championship at Dublin, Ireland, in 1984.

First world billiards team title

India 'B' won a gold while India 'A' bagged a silver in the inaugural World Billiards Team Championship in Glasgow, Scotland, in August 2014. The winning team, with Pankaj Advani, Rupesh Shah, Devender Joshi and Ashok Shandilya, beat India 'A' 5–4.

First world champion on debut

Geet Sethi became world champion on debut when he beat legendary billiards player Bob Marshall, fifty years his senior, to win the 25th World Amateur Billiards Championship in 1985 in Delhi. He was also the first unseeded player to become world champion.

World 6-red title

Laxman Rawat won the 6-red title versus Muhammad Asif of Pakistan in Mandalay, Myanmar, on 20 September 2019.

First win at the World Ladies Billiards and Snooker Championship

Chitra Magimairaj and Varsha Sanjeev won the senior gold medal and the U-21 gold medal, respectively, at the World Ladies Billiards and Snooker (WLBS) Championship in Leeds, UK, in April 2016.

First snooker team World Cup title

Pankaj Advani and Manan Chandra won the inaugural (IBSF) Snooker Team World Cup in 2018 in Doha, Qatar.

First World Ladies Billiards and Snooker Association title

R. Umadevi won her maiden, and India's first, World Ladies Billiards and Snooker Association title, beating the then world no. 13, Eva Palmius, 2–0 in the final at Cambridge, England, in April 2012.

R. Umadevi

First World Games snooker title

Aditya Mehta won the Quadrennial World Games snooker gold at Cali, Colombia, in July 2013.

Aditya Mehta

First Asian Games title

Billiards was introduced at the 1998 Bangkok Asian Games. India won two golds, a silver, and a bronze. Ashok Shandilya won the gold, beating the world champion Geet Sethi 5–4. In the doubles, Ashok Shandilya and Geet Sethi won a gold, beating Devendra Joshi and Balachandra Bhaskar, who won the bronze.

Most billiards gold medals in the Asian Games

Pankaj Advani won two gold medals in the 2006 Doha Asian Games and in the 2010 Asian Games at Guangzhou, China.

First Asian snooker title

Yasin Merchant beat Udon Khaimuk of Thailand by eight frames in New Delhi on 15 July 1989 to win the Asian Confederation of Billiard Sports (ACBS) Championship.

Most world titles – billiards and snooker

Pankaj Advani has the world champion titles for both billiards as well as snooker a record 24 times. Pankaj Advani claimed at least one International Billiard and Snooker Federation world title every calendar year.

Best performance in the Asian Games – snooker

At the 2010 Asian Games held in Guangzhou, China, the Indian team won a silver, while Aditya Mehta (individual) and Alok Kumar (8-ball pool) won bronze medals.

Best performance at the Asian Billiards Sports Championship

India won a gold, a silver and three bronze medals in the inaugural Asian Billiards Sports Championship at Al Fujairah, UAE, held from 24 September to 2 October 2016. Siddharth Parikh (billiards 100-up) won the gold medal and Vidya Pillai won the silver (6-red, women). The bronze medallists were Sourav Kothari (billiards 100-up); Kamal Chawla (6-red, men); Amee Kamani and Arantxa Sanchis (6-red, women); Manan Chandra, Sundeep Gulati, and Ishpreet Singh Chadha (team snooker).

WR **Highest break in the World Billiards Championship**

Geet Sethi had a break of 1,276 over two sessions in 80 mins against Bob Close of England in the quarter-final of the World Professional Championship in Mumbai, Maharashtra, on 1 October 1992.

WR Highest break under three-pot rule – billiards

Michael Ferreira scored 630 against S.B. Agrawal at the World Championship in Delhi in 1981, a world record for the highest break under the three-pot rule.

Most billiards grand doubles

Pankaj Advani has won four world doubles in billiards (time and points format) in 2005, 2008, 2014, and 2018.

Most Asian titles

Pankaj Advani 24-time snooker and billiards world champion retained the Asian snooker title by defeating former champion Amir Sarkhosh of Iran. Advani had won the title in 2019 before the 2020 edition got scrapped due to COVID-19. Advani's tally of Asian titles across both snooker and billiards stands at 13, including two Asian Games gold medals in 2006 and 2010.

Most competitive 147 breaks in snooker

Aditya Mehta became the first Indian to make 147 maximum breaks in 2014 at the Paul Hunter Classic snooker tournament.

Youngest world champion – snooker

Pankaj Advani was 18 years old when he won the amateur World Snooker Championship title in October 2003.

Youngest to win the World Professional title

Pankaj Advani was 24 years old when he won the World Professional Billiards title at the Northern Snooker Centre, Leeds, England, on 6 September 2009. He outclassed 41-year-old Mike Russell, who has won the World Professional Billiards title a record nine times.

Two titles in 6-red snooker

Pankaj Advani was the world's first player to hold both world and continental titles in 6 red snooker at the same time. He is also the only player to win world titles in both 15-red and 6-red snooker.

Oldest woman champion – billiards

Kamala Devi Chandrababu from Tamil Nadu beat Judy Walia from Karnataka 109–63, 65–112, 53–76, 98–72, 95–74 in the 1995 National Championship at Bangalore (now Bengaluru), Karnataka. At 63 years, it was her fourth championship and the second national title after 1991.

FOOTBALL

GENERAL

Oldest football tournament

The Durand Football Tournament is the third oldest tournament in the world and the oldest in Asia and India. Started by British diplomat and civil servant Sir Henry Mortimer Durand in 1888 for the British troops in India, it was held in

Simla (now Shimla, Himachal Pradesh). In 1940, the tournament was moved to New Delhi. The latest edition, the 131st in the history of the tournament, was held from 16 August to 18 September 2022, with Bengaluru FC winning the tournament.

First Indian team to win the Durand Cup

Mohammedan Sporting won the Durand Cup in 1940 when it was first moved to Delhi and the final played at Irwin Amphitheatre (now Dhyan Chand National Stadium). Mohammedan Sporting beat Royal Warwickshire Regiment 2–1 in the final.

Mohun Bagan was founded in **1889** and is one of the oldest clubs in Asia.

Most wins at the Durand Cup

Mohun Bagan has won the Durand Cup 16 times and finished runner-up 11 times. East Bengal has won 16 times and been runner-up 10 times.

Most clean sheets

The men's national team created a new record of eight consecutive clean sheets between 22 March 2023 and to 24 June 2023. It surpassed the previous record of six clean sheets kept during 1952–53.

Most individual goals at the Durand Cup

Mohammed Habib scored 12 goals for East Bengal in seven matches (both the semi-finals and the final were replayed) in the 1972 Durand tournament.

First football academy

The Tata Football Academy (TFA) was started at Jamshedpur, Jharkhand, in 1986 with Mohammed Habib and Ranjan Chowdhury as coaches, and Subimal 'Chuni' Goswami as technical director. It has produced over 100 junior and senior international players for India. It was followed by the Williamson Magor Football Academy in Assam and the Chandigarh Football Academy that started in the 1990s.

First Olympic referee

Komaleeswaran Sankar became an Olympic referee when he was selected for the football tournament of the 2000 Sydney Olympics, one among the four match officials chosen from Asia. Sankar, who became a referee in 1988 and a national referee in 1994, retired in 2007 at the age of forty-five, as mandated by FIFA rules.

First World Cup referee

Komaleeswaran Sankar was the first World Cup referee from India when he was chosen to officiate at the 2002 World Cup in South Korea and Japan. His first match was a Group G league match between Mexico and Croatia on 3 June 2002. He officiated in three matches.

First Indian club to enter the Asian Football Confederation Cup final

- Bengaluru FC was the first Indian club to enter the final of Asia's prestigious club competition, the Asian Football Confederation (AFC) Cup, in October 2016.

They lost the final match against Iraq Air Force 0–1 in Doha, Qatar, on 5 November 2016.

- Dempo SC (Goa) was the first club to enter the semi-finals of the Cup in September 2008.

First international tournament win by a club

- Mohammedan Sporting won the Aga Khan Gold Cup in Dhaka (then Pakistan, now Bangladesh) on 11 October 1960, defeating Makassar XI, Indonesia, 4–1 in the final.
- East Bengal, coached by Subhas Bhowmick, won the LG ASEAN Club Cup Championship on 26 July 2003 in Jakarta, Indonesia, beating BEC Tero Sasana of Thailand in the final 3–1.

First professional coach

Amal Dutta, India's first professional coach, started his career in 1963, coaching East Bengal. He also coached the other two big Kolkata clubs: Mohun Bagan and Mohammedan Sporting (Dhaka).

First foreign coach

English professional footballer Harry Wright was appointed coach of the Indian football team in 1963. He held the position till 1964, leading India to one of its best performances – a runner-up position at the 1964 Asian Football Confederation (AFC) Cup.

First Indian club to win a major trophy

The first win in a major domestic tournament was by Mohun Bagan of Calcutta, who beat East Yorkshire Regiment of Ghaziabad 2–1 in the Indian Football Association (IFA) Shield tournament final at the Calcutta Football Club Ground on 29 July 1911.

First in English professional club

- Mohammed Salim from Calcutta, West Bengal, was the first from the Indian subcontinent to play for a European club, Celtic FC, in 1936.
- Bhaichung Bhutia was the first Indian footballer to join an English club when he signed a contract to represent second division outfit, Bury FC, from 1999 to 2002.
- Aditi Chauhan was the first Indian woman to play in the English league football on 16 August 2015, as a goalkeeper for West Ham United. She attended Loughborough University, completing an MSc in sports management and represented their football team from 2014–15. Chauhan joined Gokulam Kerala FC for the 2019–20 Indian women's league.

Syed Nayeemuddin

First Indian to be national coach of a foreign country

Syed Nayeemuddin was appointed national coach of Bangladesh in July 2007. He was also the first Indian to coach a club side abroad – the Brothers

Union of Bangladesh in 2004. In India, he won 33 trophies with Mohammedan Sporting, East Bengal and Mohun Bagan. As national coach, he led India to victory in the 1987 South Asian Federation (SAF) Games in Calcutta (now Kolkata), West Bengal, the 1997 Kathmandu South Asian Football Federation (SAFF) Championship in Nepal, and the 2005 Karachi SAFF Championship in Pakistan.

First hat-trick in Mohun Bagan versus East Bengal match

On 13 July 1997, Bhaichung Bhutia scored a hat-trick for East Bengal versus Mohun Bagan in the KBL Federation Cup semi-final, in which East Bengal won 4-1.

Bhaichung Bhutia

First tiebreaker

- The first tiebreaker in a final came when Mohammedan Sporting won the tie 3–1 against Mohun Bagan at the 1983 Peerless Trophy final at Calcutta, West Bengal.
- The first tiebreaker match occurred in a third round match of the Durand Tournament played on 17 February 1972 at Delhi. Mohun Bagan beat Indian Navy 5–3.

First hat-trick in Indian football

Norman Pritchard scored a hat-trick for St Xavier's College, Calcutta, West Bengal, against Sovabazar Club in the 1889 Trades Cup.

First woman player to sign a contract with a foreign club

Ngangom Bala Devi made history when she signed a contract with Scottish Giant Rangers FC, a professional football club in Glasgow, UK. She donned a no. 10 jersey for the club and created yet another record on 6 December 2020 when she scored the final goal against Motherwell Women in the Scottish Women's Premier League, becoming the first Indian woman to score in a professional European Club.

Most matches officiated

S.S. Hakim officiated in 33 international matches and was a referee in the final of every major domestic tournament including three Nehru Cups. He represented India in the 1960 Rome Olympics and was the team's assistant coach for the 1982 Delhi Asiad. He is the only individual to have played football, coached the national team, and functioned as an international referee.

Most appearances as coach in the Nehru Cup

Syed Nayeemuddin coached the Indian team in the Nehru Cup on four occasions – in 1987 at Kozhikode, Kerala; in 1988 at Siliguri, West Bengal; in 1989 at Margao, Goa; and in 1997 at Kochi, Kerala.

Most successful Indian coaches in domestic tournaments

P.K. Banerjee led domestic teams to 53 trophies, Amal Dutta to 35, and Syed Nayeemuddin to 33 of them.

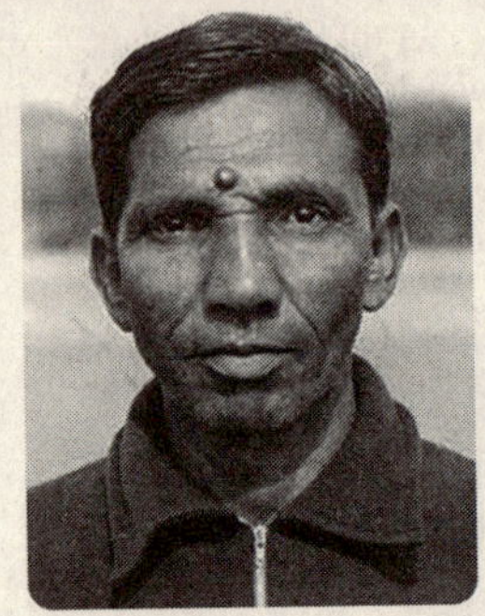

S.A. Rahim

Most appearances as coach in the Olympics

S.A. Rahim (1909–63) from Hyderabad (then in Andhra Pradesh) was the coach of the Indian football team in three consecutive Olympic Games in 1952 (Helsinki), 1956 (Melbourne) and 1960 (Rome).

Most successful coach at the Asian Games

- S.A. Rahim led as coach on five successful occasions – twice at the Asian Games (1951 and 1962), and thrice at the Quadrangular Tournament (1953, 1954, and 1955).
- The foreign coach with the best record is Bob Houghton of the UK with three trophies: the Nehru Cup (2007 and 2009) and the AFC Challenge Cup in 2008.

Most individual goals in an international club match

Bhaichung Bhutia scored six goals, a double hat-trick, for East Bengal against Army FC of the Philippines in the LG ASEAN Cup in Jakarta, Indonesia, on 16 July 2003.

Longest sequence of wins

Mohun Bagan won 42 consecutive matches in the 1994 season till they lost to Dempo SC (Goa) in the Scissors Cup final in November 1994.

Longest unbeaten-streak at home

Indian football team is currently on a 17-match unbeaten streak at home under head coach Igor Stimac. The streak began with a draw against Bangladesh back in 2019.

Only Indian coach to gain success with a foreign club

In his eight-year stint in Bangladesh, Syed Nayeemuddin helped his club, Brothers Union of Bangladesh, win three trophies.

Best record against foreign clubs

East Bengal has the best record against foreign clubs: played 239 matches (both exhibition and tournaments), won 97, drawn 40 and lost 102. They scored 343 goals and conceded 348.

Fastest goal

Midfielder Dipankar Roy scored a goal in 9.33 seconds after kick-off for Bengal versus Karnataka in the 2000 Santosh Trophy held in Thrissur, Kerala.

SANTOSH TROPHY RECORDS

Most wins in Santosh Trophy

The National inter state championships for the Santosh Trophy started in 1941. The football trophy was instituted in the name of maharaja of Santosh, the former president of IFA, the parent body of Bengal football. Bengal won the title 32 times and finished runners-up on 14 occasions. Punjab have won eight times,

Kerala seven times, Services six times and Goa five times. Bengal holds the record of winning the trophy six times in a row from 1993 to 1998 and five times in a row from 1975 to 1979.

Most individual goals in a single edition

Playing for Punjab, Inder Singh scored 23 goals in the 1974 edition in Jalandhar.

Most individual goals in the final match

Playing for Bengal, Mohammed Habib scored five goals in the 6-1 win over Services in Nowgong, Madhya Pradesh, in 1969.

Inder Singh

Highest number of goals by an individual in a single match

Burma (now Myanmar) striker Fred Pagsley, while playing for Bengal, scored seven goals against Rajputana in Mumbai in 1945. Punjab's Inder Singh scored seven goals against Gujarat in Jalandhar in 1974.

Biggest margin of victory

Bengal beat Tripura 18-0 in Jalandhar in 1974; Punjab beat Gujarat 17-0 in Jalandhar in 1974; Kerala beat Andaman and Nicobar Islands 17-0 in Siliguri in 2014.

All-time top scorers

Inder Singh (Punjab) has 45 goals. Mohmmed Habib and Shyam Thapa (both Bengal) have 34 and 31 goals to their credit, respectively..

Success for different teams

Peter Thangaraj won the Santosh Trophy for three different teams – Services (1960), Bengal (1962) and Railways (1966).

INDIAN SUPER LEAGUE (ISL)

Maximum titles

ATK (now ATK Mohun Bagan) has won three titles in 2014, 2016, and 2019-20 season.

Most individual goals by an Indian footballer

- Sunil Chhetri has played in all editions of the Indian Super League since 2014, scoring 51 goals. He played for Mumbai City FC and Bengaluru FC.
- Jeje Lalpekhlua, while playing for Chennaiyin FC and SC East Bengal, has 24 goals.

Biggest margin of victory

FC Goa defeated Mumbai City FC 7-0 in Margao, Goa, in 2015.

Most goals scored in a match

A total of 11 goals were scored when Odisha FC defeated SC East Bengal 6-5 in the 2020-21 season.

Most individual goals by a foreign footballer

Bartholomew Ogbeche

- Punjab's Nigerian footballer Bartholomew Ogbeche has played four seasons in ISL for NorthEast United, Kerala Blasters, Mumbai City FC and Hyderabad FC, scoring a total of 53 goals.
- Punjab's Spanish striker Ferran Corominas, who played for FC Goa starting July 2017, has record 48 goals to his credit for one club.

Most goals scored by a team

FC Goa has scored 267 goals, followed by Chennaiyin FC's 199 goals.

Most wins by a team

FC Goa have won 62 matches, followed by Mumbai City FC, who have won 61 matches.

Hat-trick records

A total of 31 hat-tricks have been scored. Brazilian Andre Mortiz, while playing for Mumbai City FC against FC Pune City, scored the competition's first hat-trick in October 2014. Canadian Iain Hume (ATK and Kerala Blasters) and Nigerian Bartholomew Ogbeche have scored three hat-tricks each in the ISL. Sunil Chhetri (Mumbai City FC and Bengaluru FC) has two hat-tricks to his credit.

DOMESTIC EVENTS

First to win three National Football League titles

Mohun Bagan has won three National Football League (NFL) titles: in 1997–98, 1999–2000 and 2001–02. East Bengal emulated this when they won their third NFL crown in 2003–04. Their earlier wins were in 2000–01 and 2002–03.

Most individual goals in a match in NFL

- Bhaichung Bhutia scored the most goals in an NFL match when he scored five goals playing for JCT against Mahindra in the first NFL in 1997. JCT won the match 6–1.
- In the fourth NFL, Francis Silveira of Churchill Brothers scored four goals in a match against Dempo SC (Goa) for a 5–0 win.

Most individual goals in a match in the I-League

The most goals by a player in an I-League match are seven by Ranti Martins for Dempo SC (Goa) in their 14–0 win versus Air India in Margao, Goa, on 30 May 2011.

First International match

With seven barefoot players, India entered the 1948 Olympics under captain Talimeren Ao from Bengal but lost to France 1–2. Sarangapani Raman scored the lone goal. Since then, India has played eight matches in four Olympic Games – 1948, 1952, 1956 and 1960 – won one, drawn one, lost six; scored 10 and conceded 27 goals. After 1960, India has been eliminated in the pre-Olympic stage.

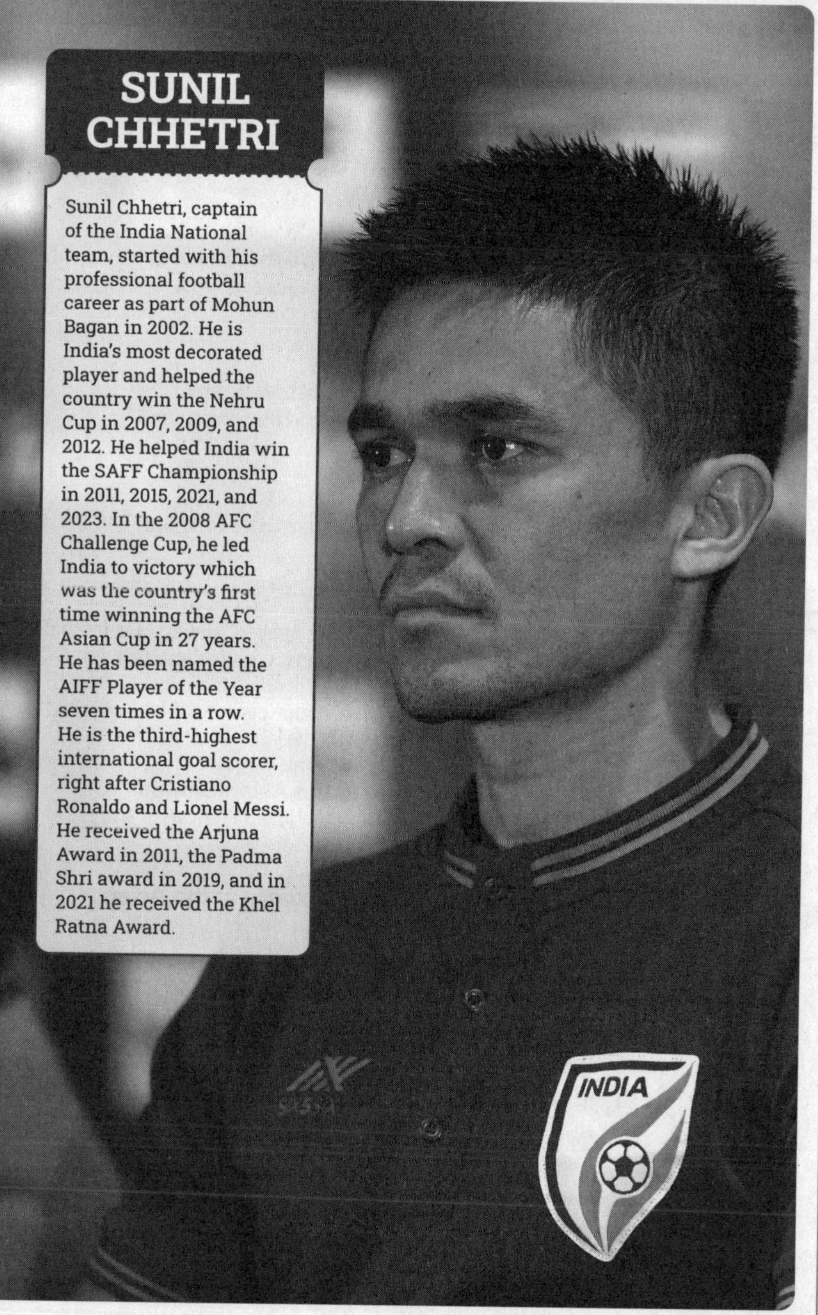

SUNIL CHHETRI

Sunil Chhetri, captain of the India National team, started with his professional football career as part of Mohun Bagan in 2002. He is India's most decorated player and helped the country win the Nehru Cup in 2007, 2009, and 2012. He helped India win the SAFF Championship in 2011, 2015, 2021, and 2023. In the 2008 AFC Challenge Cup, he led India to victory which was the country's first time winning the AFC Asian Cup in 27 years. He has been named the AIFF Player of the Year seven times in a row. He is the third-highest international goal scorer, right after Cristiano Ronaldo and Lionel Messi. He received the Arjuna Award in 2011, the Padma Shri award in 2019, and in 2021 he received the Khel Ratna Award.

Most goals by a club in the NFL/ Indian League (I-League)

East Bengal has scored 690 goals in 460 matches. Other teams to score are Churchill Brothers with 664 goals in 406 matches and Mohun Bagan with 619 goals in 446 matches.

India first sent a football team to the Olympics in the year **1948**.

Most individual hat-tricks in the NFL and I-League

Nigerian striker Odafa Onyeka Okolie has scored 14 hat-tricks: nine for Churchill Brothers four for Mohun Bagan and one for Sporting Clube de Goa.

INTERNATIONAL

Most appearances by a player for Indian Football Team

Sunil Chhetri is India's most capped player. He made 143 international appearances for the Indian National Team.

Only win in Olympics

On 1 December 1956, India beat hosts Australia 4-2 to register their only win in Olympics.

Best performance at the Olympics

India became the first Asian nation to reach the semi finals of an Olympic football event, beating Australia 4-2 at the 1956 Melbourne Games. India took the lead against Yugoslavia but lost 1-4. In the play-off for the bronze, India lost 0 3 to Bulgaria, ending at fourth position. Samar 'Badru' Banerjee was India's captain and S.A. Rahim was the coach.

Subimal 'Chuni' Goswami

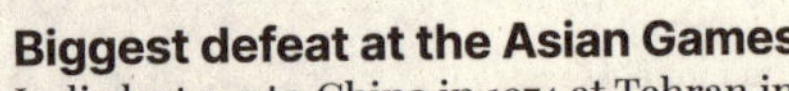

Biggest defeat at the Asian Games

India lost 1-7 to China in 1974 at Tehran in Iran. Magan Singh scored the lone goal.

Biggest margin of victory at the Asian Games

India beat Hong Kong 5-2 at the 1958 Asiad in Tokyo, Japan, in its biggest margin of victory at the Asian Games. Mohammad Rahmatullah scored two goals while Subimal 'Chuni' Goswami, D. Damodaran and T. Balaram scored a goal each. India scored three goals in extra time, the first time India played extra time in an international match.

Biggest margin of victory

In the 1963 pre-Olympics, India won 7-0 against Ceylon (now Sri Lanka) at Bangalore (now Bengaluru), Karnataka, and later 7-0 against Bangladesh in the Aga Khan Tournament at Dhaka, Bangladesh, in 1977.

Most goals in the Asian Games:
P.K. Banerjee scored the highest number of individual goals for India in the Asian Games. He scored six goals – one in 1958, four in 1962, and one in 1966.

P.K. Banerjee

Best performance at pre–World Cup
With three wins, two draws and one defeat (0–1 versus UAE in an away match in Al Ain), India's performance in the 2001 World Cup qualifiers has been the best yet. It is also the only series of matches where the Indian team scored more goals (11) than they conceded (5).

Biggest margin of victory at pre–World Cup
India beat Brunei 5–0 at Bangalore, Karnataka in a Group 8 qualifier on 20 May 2001. Jules Alberto, I.M. Vijayan, Bhaichung Bhutia, Jo Paul Ancheri and Abdul Hakeem scored for India.

Worst defeat at pre–World Cup
India lost 0–7 to South Korea at Seoul, South Korea, in the 1993 World Cup qualifiers.

Worst defeats
In international tournaments, India's worst defeats have been 1-10 to Yugoslavia at the 1952 Helsinki Olympics and 1–9 to Burma (now Myanmar) in the 1971 Merdeka Tournament in Kuala Lumpur, Malaysia.

Most successful team in Intercontinental Cup (AIFF)
India became the most successful team in the AIFF's Intercontinental Cup with their second title. India defeated Lebanon 2-0 in the final of the 2023's edition in Bhubaneswar. North Korea are the only other winners as the competition has been played thrice since 2018.

Most wins by a team
Mumbai City have won 76 matches, followed by FC Goa, who have won 70 matches.

India's longest unbeaten run in a year
In 2017, India remained unbeaten in nine matches, three away games and six at home:
- 1–0 versus Myanmar; 1–0 versus the Kyrgyz Republic; 2–0 versus Macau; 4–1 versus Macau; and 2–2 versus Myanmar (all Asian Cup qualifiers).
- 3–2 versus Cambodia; 2–0 versus Nepal; 2-1 versus Mauritius; and 1-1 versus St Kitts and Nevis (all friendly matches).

INDIVIDUAL RECORDS

Highest caps earned: Sunil Chhetri has played the maximum number of matches for India (131). The other in the top five are: Bhaichung Butia (107), I.M. Vijayan (88), Shabbir Ali (81), and Mahesh Gawli (79).

Highest number of goals scored: Sunil Chhetri has scored the highest number of goals for India (92). The other in the top five are: Bhaichung Bhutia (42), I.M. Vijayan (39), Shabbir Ali (30), and P.K. Banerjee (26).

Fastest international goal: I.M. Vijayan scored against Bhutan within 12 seconds after kick-off in a Group A league match played on 28 September 1999 at the SAF Games at Kathmandu, Nepal.

Hat-trick in Olympics: Neville D'Souza is the only Indian to score a hat-trick in Olympics. He scored three goals in a row in India's 4-2 win over Australia on 1 December 1956.

First Hat-trick on debut: K. Appalaraju scored a hat-trick in his first international appearance against Ceylon (now Sri Lanka) on 22 December 1963 in the pre-Olympics.

Maximum hat-tricks: Sunil Chhetri is the only Indian to score three hat-tricks in international matches. Chhetri's three hat-tricks came against Tajikistan (13 August 2008, AFC Challenge Cup, New Delhi), against Vietnam (10 October 2010, Friendly, Pune), and against Chinese Taipei (1 June 2018, Hero International Cup, Mumbai).

Back to back hat-tricks: K. Appalaraju and I.M. Vijayan scored back-to-back hat-tricks in international matches. Appalaraju scored against Ceylon (now Sri Lanka) on 22 December 1963 in the pre-Olympics in Colombo and against the same team on 29 December 1963 in the pre-Olympics in Bangalore. I.M. Vijayan scored against Pakistan in Kathmandu on 26 September 1999 in the SAF Games and against Bhutan on 28 September 1999 in the same SAF Games in Kathmandu.
Most successful captain: Bhaichung Bhutia has five tournament wins to his credit as captain: the LG Cup in Vietnam (2002), the SAFF Cup in Karachi, Pakistan (2005), the Nehru Cup in Delhi (2007 and 2009), and the AFC Challenge Cup in Hyderabad and Delhi in 2008. He is also the second highest international scorer, with 42 goals in 107 matches.

Youngest match winner at the Nehru Cup:
Bhaichung Bhutia was 19 years old when he scored a goal to beat Uzbekistan 1-0 in 1995 at Calcutta (now Kolkata), West Bengal.

GOLF

GENERAL

Oldest to get hole-in-one

Lieutenant General Ajit Singh at the grand old age of 90 achieved his first hole-in-one on 18 October 2005 at the Delhi Golf Club on the 9th hole (par 3; 160 yards).

Oldest club

The Royal Kolkata Golf Club founded in 1829 is the oldest club outside Britain. The Kolkata Ladies Golf Club was established in 1891.

Highest golf course

The Yak Golf Club is located at an altitude of 13,025 ft at Kupup, Sikkim.

Indian Open record

Jyoti Randhawa won the Indian Open in October 2007 at the Delhi Golf Club course for the third time and equalled the record of Australia's Peter Thomson.

First international success in the U-10 category

Tanya Wadhwa of Delhi finished third in an U-10 International Golf tournament in San Diego, USA in July 2001.

Sponsorship bonanza

Golf offered the most prize money in any individual event on the domestic circuit. The prize fund offered in 2010 was ₹8.80 crore spread over 29 tournaments.

Indian Open winners

Nine Indians have won this prestigious title spread over 13 times. They are: P.G. Sethi, Kolkata, 1965; Ali Sher, Delhi, 1991 and 1993; Feroze Ali, Kolkata, 1998; Arjun Atwal, Kolkata, 1999; Jyoti Randhawa, Gurugram, 2000; Vijay Kumar, Delhi, 2002; Jyothi Randhawa, Delhi, 2006 and 2007; C. Muniyappa, Gurugram, 2009; Anirban Lahiri, Delhi, 2015; S.S.P. Chawrasia, Delhi, 2016 and Gurugram, 2017.

Indian men winning international tournaments

So far, 25 Indians have won 88 international titles on various tours. Jeev Milkha Singh heads the list with 13 victories, followed by Gaganjeet Bhullar (11), Arjun Atwal (10) and Jyoti Randhawa (9).

Most Indian tournaments on the Asian Tour

In 2002, for the first time, three tournaments – the Royal Challenge Indian Open, the Hero Honda Masters, and the Honda-SIEL tournament figured on the Asian Professional Golf Association Tour.

Most consecutive medals – disabled athlete – international tournaments

Ranveer Singh Saini (b. 24 November 2000) from Gurugram, Haryana, won three successive medals at the Special Olympics World Summer Games in golf tournaments in Los Angeles, USA (2015), Abu Dhabi, UAE (2019), and Berlin World Games (2023).

Indians at the Majors

So far, eight Indians – Anirban Lahiri (17 times); Jeev Milkha Singh (14 times); Jyoti Randhawa, Arjun Atwal, Shiv Kapur, Shubhankar Sharma (five times each); Gaganjeet Bhullar and Gaurav Ghei (once each) – have made 52 appearances at the Majors.

'Rookie' on a rampage

The Rookie Golfer of the Year award was introduced in 1997–98 on the domestic tour. To date, S. Chikkarangappa remains the most successful 'rookie' on the Tour. He won ₹32,65,313 and finished second to Rashid Khan on the 2013 Order of Merit.

Indians topping the Asian Tour Order of Merit

Jeev Milkha Singh won the Asian Tour Order of Merit in 2006 and 2008. Jyoti Randhawa (2002), Arjun Atwal (2003), Anirban Lahiri (2015) and Shubhankar Sharma (2018) are the other Indians to top the Order of Merit.

FIRST

First sweep of gold medals in the Asian Games

Golf was introduced in the Asian Games in 1982. Besides the team gold, India won the individual gold and silver medals through champion Lakshman Singh and runner-up Rajiv Mohta. Two other members of the gold-winning team were Amit Luthra and Rishi Narain.

First international recognition

India was invited to the 1969 World Cup qualifying event at Singapore. Ruda Valji and Shadi Lal represented India.

First to win all three National titles

Arjuna Award-winner Amit Luthra is the first Indian to have won all three National titles: the Junior National (1979), men's National (1993, 1994) and Senior Nationals (2015, 2016).

First Olympians

Anirban Lahiri, S.S.P. Chawrasia and Aditi Ashok represented the country in the 2016 Rio Olympics in Brazil.

First to gain qualification for the PGA Tour

Arjun Atwal became the first Indian to gain qualification for the full US Tour after making it through the Qualifying school for the year 2004.

First to qualify for the British Open

Gaurav Ghei was the first Indian to qualify for the premier event in 1997.

Arjun Atwal

First victory in Nomura Cup

India's first major victory in an international team event came in the 1973 Nomura Cup at Jakarta where the squad of Raj Kumar Pitamber, P.G. Sethi, Vikramjit Singh, and Lakshman Singh was crowned Asia-Pacific Golf champions.

First to gain a full 'card' on PGA Tour

Arjun Atwal became the first Indian to gain a full card (exemption from playing qualifying rounds) after his stupendous showing in the 2005 season.

First to play in the US Open

Jeev Milkha Singh was the first to play the US Open in 2002.

First European–Asian Tour win

Arjun Atwal is the first Asian to win two co-sanctioned titles on the Tour. He won the Caltex Singapore Open in February 2002 and the Carlsberg Malaysian Open in February 2003. Both these events enjoy joint sanction of the European and Asian PGA Tours.

First to play the Masters at Augusta

Jeev Milkha Singh was the first to play the Masters at Augusta, Georgia, US, in 2007.

First to play the PGA Championship

Arjun Atwal was the first to play the PGA Championship in 2005.

First participation in World Cup

Arjun Atwal and Jyoti Randhawa formed the first Indian team to take part in the World Cup in 2005.

First to play in three WGC events in a year

Jyoti Randhawa became the first Indian to play in three events in the World Golf Championship (WGC) series in 2005.

First to play in a Major

Jeev Milkha Singh became the first Indian to qualify for a Major when he made it to the 2002 US Open in July.

First to qualify for European PGA Tour

Jeev Milkha Singh was the first to qualify for the European Tour for the 1998 season.

First to make the 'cut' in a Major

Jeev Milkha Singh became the first Indian to make the 'cut' of a Major championship playing all four rounds of the 2002 US Open.

Jeev Milkha Singh

Jeev Milkha Singh is the first Indian golfer to have played in the Masters Tournament and the Ryder Cup. Jeev's career boasts multiple victories on the European Tour and the Asian Tour, showcasing his skill and consistency across diverse golfing landscapes. His triumphs include wins at prestigious events like the Scottish Open and the Volvo Masters. Beyond his achievements on the course, Jeev's sportsmanship and dedication have earned him respect among fellow players and fans alike. He has paved the way for Indian golfers to shine on the global stage and continues to inspire the next generation of talent in the country.

Aditi Ashok

First to win on the Japanese PGA Tour
Jyoti Randhawa won the Suntory Open in 2003.

First to win the Ladies Indian Open
Aditi Ashok became the first to win the Ladies Indian Open in November 2016.

First win on PGA Tour
Arjun Atwal won the 2010 Wyndham Championship.

First win on the European Tour
Arjun Atwal won the 2002 Singapore Masters.

First win on the European Tour in Europe
Jeev Milkha Singh won the Volvo Masters in Spain in October 2006.

First team to qualify for World championship
The Indian team of Gaurav Ghei and Digvijay Singh qualified for the 2003 World Golf Championship held at Kiawah Island, US, after finishing joint-second in the Nations Cup.

First to secure her card (playing rights) winner on the Ladies European Tour
By winning the Lalla Aicha Tour School, Aditi Ashok secured the Ladies European Tour card for 2016 season. She also became the youngest to win the title.

First woman to qualify for the Olympic Games
Aditi Ashok is the first woman to qualify in golf for the Olympic Games in Rio in 2016. She attained her best finish – fourth – in the 2020 Tokyo Olympics.

Best finish on the LET Order of Merit
Aditi Ashok finished second on the 2016 LET Order of Merit and also won the 'Rookie of the Year' award.

First to represent the country in four multi discipline Games
Aditi Ashok has participated in the 2013 Asian Youth Games, the 2014 Youth Olympic Games, the 2014 Asian Games, and the 2016 and 2020 Olympic Games.

First to qualify for the Ladies PGA Tour
Aditi Ashok gained the playing rights for the 2017 LPGA Tour via the LPGA Final Qualifying School.

First to win LET title outside India
Aditi Ashok won the 2016 Qatar Ladies Open.

First to win on the Ladies European Tour (LET)

Aditi Ashok is the first to win a title on the Ladies European Tour by claiming the 2016 Ladies Indian Open.

Rashid Khan

MOSTS

Highest prize money (women)

Aditi Ashok collected US $60,000 in becoming the first to win the Ladies Indian Open title in November 2016.

Highest prize money earner in a domestic season

Rashid Khan won two events from fourteen tournament appearances in the 2019 season and collected ₹66,27,650 as prize money.

Most birdies

Jyoti Randhawa broke the course record at Shanghai with a seven-under par 65 that included eight birdies at the Volvo China Open Golf tournament in 2000. He finished in a tied fourth place.

Tournament with highest prize money

The ₹1.50 crore McLeod Russel Tour Championship in 2014 became the first domestic tournament to offer such high prize money in any individual domestic sport.

Most lucrative season

During the 2017–18 PGAI Tour, 97 golfers earned over ₹1 lakh, including 79 over ₹2 lakh, 67 over ₹3 lakh, 51 over ₹5 lakh, 29 over ₹10 lakh, 19 over ₹15 lakh, 13 over ₹20 lakh, and six players over ₹25 lakh during the season.

Most international titles

Jeev Milkha Singh has won 14 tour titles spread over three tours – four on the European Tour, six on the Asian Tour and four on the Japanese Tour.

First appearance in the Commonwealth Games

Manjit Singh, B.S. Nandi and N.B. Bhosle represented India at the 1978 Edmonton Commonwealth Games in Canada.

Most titles on the Asian Tour

Jyoti Randhawa has won eight titles: the 1998 Hero Honda Masters, the 1999 Hero Honda Masters, the 2000 Indian Open, the 2000 Singapore Open, the 2004 Volvo Masters of Asia, the 2006 Indian Open, the 2007 Indian Open and the 2009 Thailand Open.

Quickest to reach the million mark in prize money
Ashok Kumar won ₹10,010,334 in the 2004-05 season of the Indian Tour after just nine events.

Most career prize money from the domestic Professional Golf Tour of India (PGTI)
Shamim Khan has earned ₹43,803,143 from 265 tournament appearances.

Most titles in an Indian Tour season
Mukesh Kumar won six titles during the 2004-05 season.

Five titles in a season twice on the Indian Tour
Ashok Kumar won five titles in 2004 and repeated the feat in 2007.

BEST

Best Indian performance on the PGA Tour
In the 2022 season, Anirban Lahiri has earned $3,084,598 – the highest by an Indian on the PGA Tour – from 24 events. His best came in the Players Championship where he finished runner-up, earning a $2.18 million pay cheque.

Anirban Lahiri

Best finish in a Major
Anirban Lahiri finished tied-fifth in the 2016 PGA Championship

Best finish in the European Tour Order of Merit
Jeev Milkha Singh finished 12th on the 2008 European Tour Order of Merit.

Best world ranking
Jeev Milkha Singh was placed 28th in the World ranking list in 2009.

Best performance based on prize money received
Arjun Atwal became the first Indian to win a title on the PGA Tour by claiming the honours in the Wyndham Championship in August 2010. The first qualifier to win the title in 24 years on the PGA Tour, Atwal collected $918,000 – the highest ever by an Indian golfer.

LOWEST

Lowest winning score on the European Tour
Arjun Atwal's scored title-winning 24-under 260 in the Carlsberg Malaysian Open in February 2003.

Lowest winning score on the Asian Tour
Jeev Milkha Singh scored 26-under par in the Philip Morris Championship in

Seoul, when he won the four-round tournament on the Asian Tour. This is the lowest score by an Indian in winning an international title.

Least putts on the European Tour

Jeev Milkha Singh needed just 94 putts for four rounds of the 2001 Desert Classic. Jeev fell one short of the world record of 93, which stands in the name of Kenny Knox from the US since 1990.

Lowest winning score on the Indian Tour

Mukesh Kumar fired 30-under 250 to win the DDA Open tournament at the Qutub Golf Course in New Delhi in April 2005.

Lowest round on the Indian Tour

Mukesh Kumar carded 11- under 59 in the third round of the DDA Open tournament at the Qutub Golf Course, New Delhi, in April 2005.

ONLY

Only Indian to win two European Tour titles in a year

Anirban Lahiri won the Malaysian Open and the Indian Open – both co-sanctioned events on the European Tour – in 2015.

Only Indian to win four European Tour events in India

S.S.P. Chawrasia's all four European Tour titles have come in India: the 2008 Emaar MGF Indian Masters, New Delhi, the 2011 Avantha Masters, Gurugram, the 2016 Indian Open, New Delhi, and the 2017 Indian Open, Gurugram.

S.S.P. Chawrasia

Only team title in the US

Former Test cricketer Kapil Dev led India to the TAG Heuer Invitational Golf title in Boston in September 2004. The team comprising Kapil Dev, Rakesh Rao, Nikhil Dewan, and Rohit Duggal shot seven 65-under to win ahead of China, Indonesia, South Africa, and two teams from North America, among others.

Only Indian to win four titles on Japanese Tour

Jeev Milkha Singh has won four titles on the Japanese Tour: the 2006 Casio World Open, the 2006 Golf Nippon Series JT Cup, the 2008 Nagashima Shigeo Invitational Sega Sammy Cup, and the 2008 Golf Nippon Series JT Cup.

Quickest to win two European Tour titles

Shubhankar Sharma won two European Tour titles in the space of 55 days. He won the Joburg Open in December 2017 and Maybank Championship in February 2018.

YOUNGEST

Shubhankar Sharma

Youngest to win two back-to-back international titles

Shubham Juglan won the IMG Academy golf championship in San Deigo and the International Golf Academy titles in Vegas – both for children aged 9–10 – in successive weeks in 2015.

Youngest to win European Tour title

Shubhankar Sharma, at 21 years and 4 months, won the Joburg Open to become the youngest Indian winner on the European Tour.

Youngest winner on the domestic PGTI Tour

Playing only his second pro event, amateur Karandeep Kochar became the youngest winner on the PGTI Tour by beating the field in the 2016 Players Championship in Kolkata. Kochar, at 17 years and five months, broke Shubhankar Sharma's record of 17 years and eight months set in 2014.

Youngest to win Asian Tour Order of Merit

Shubhankar Sharma became the youngest to win the Asian Tour Order of Merit in December 2018.

Youngest to get hole-in-one

Viraat Badhwar (b. August 28, 1995) was all of 6 years 11 months and 19 days when he scored a hole-in-one at the sixth hole (par-3 at 155 yards) using a 3-wood at the Peacock Course, Delhi Golf Club on 17 August 2002.

Longest hole-in-one

Amit Luthra scored a hole-in-one at the second hole of Delhi Golf Club (par-4 at 258 yards) using a 5-iron on 16 March 1998.

GYMNASTICS

DOMESTIC

First National Championship

The first National Gymnastics Championship was held in 1952 in Madras (now Chennai), Tamil Nadu where Khushi Ram emerged as the all-round individual champion and Punjab won the team championship.

Most successive titles – team

Services won the team National Championship six times in a row between 1954–55 and 1961–62. They won it again six times in a row between 1963–64 and 1971–72. (The tournament was not held for some years in between.)

Most individual titles in the Nationals

- Kalpana Debnath from Madhya Pradesh won the all-round individual title four years in a row from 1976–77 to 1979–80.
- Rajesh Kumar from Chandigarh won the all-round individual title four times in a row between 1990–91 and 1994–95.

INTERNATIONAL

First World Cup medal

Aruna Reddy, then 22 years old, from Hyderabad, Telangana, became the first Indian gymnast to win a medal at the Gymnastics World Cup when she won a bronze in vault in Melbourne, Australia, with a score of 13.649 points on 24 February 2018.

First medal in the Commonwealth Games – men

Ashish Kumar won the first-ever medals (and a rare two at that) in gymnastics: a bronze in the individual floor exercise (score: 14.475) and a silver in the vault (with 15.312 points) at the 2010 Commonwealth Games, New Delhi.

First appearance in the World Championship

Daljit Inder Singh, Manjit Singh and Vithal Karande participated in the 1970 World Championship held at Ljubljana (in present-day Slovenia).

First Olympic appearance

Khushi Ram and Vir Singh were the first gymnasts to represent India at the Olympics in 1952 at Helsinki.

First medal in the Asian Games – men

With a score of 14.925, Ashish Kumar won a bronze in the floor exercise at the 2010 Guangzhou Asian Games in China, which was India's first and only medal in gymnastics at the Asian Games.

First medal in the Asian Championship

Ashish Kumar won a bronze medal in the floor exercise at the third Senior Asian Gymnastics Championship at Pandit Deen Dayal Upadhyay Indoor Stadium, Surat, Gujarat, on 2 August 2006.

Most Olympic representations

Anantram Dogra is the only gymnast who has represented India in two Olympic Games – in Melbourne in 1956 and in Tokyo in 1964. He was also selected for the 1960 Rome Olympic Games, but the Indian Army team was called back due to an emergency.

HOCKEY

GENERAL

First Indian to head the International Hockey Federation (FIH)

Dr Narinder Dhruv Batra was the first non-European president of the FIH. He was elected twice to the prestigious post, first in 2016 and re-elected in 2022.

Dilip Tirkey

Most Arjuna Awards for any sport in a year

Normally, two or three hockey players (both men and women collectively) used to get the Government of India's top sporting award. However, with the success of Indian men's team at the Tokyo Olympics, all the 16 members (except the duo of goalkeeper P.R. Sreejesh and captain Manpreet Singh, who have already received the award earlier) were awarded the honour. P.R. Sreejesh and Manpreet Singh were given the Khel Ratna award.

First Olympian to head Indian hockey

Dilip Tirkey from Odisha, who had participated in three Olympic Games (in 1996 in Atlanta, US, in 2000 in Sydney, Australia, and in 2004 in Athens, Greece), was unanimously elected president of Hockey India on 23 September 2022.

Most FIH Hockey Star Awards

Indian players and coaches swept all the annual FIH Hockey Star Awards in 2021. The winners include Player of the Year: Harmanpreet Singh (men) and Gurjit Kaur (women); Best Goalkeeper: P.R. Sreejesh (men) and Savita Punia (women); Best Rising Star: Vivek Sagar Prasad (men) and Sharmila Devi (women); Best Coach: Graham Reid (national men's team coach) and Sjoerd Marijne (national women's team coach).

DOMESTIC

Oldest tournament – men

The Beighton Cup was started in Calcutta (now Kolkata), West Bengal, in 1895 and is considered to be the oldest tournament. Presented by T.D. Beighton, the legal remembrancer of the then Government of Bengal, the Cup was held initially in the form of local matches, evolving into a regular tournament. Its latest edition was held in December 2016, with Indian Oil defeating Bharat Petroleum 5–3.

Oldest tournament – women

First National Championship that was in 1947 in the then Bombay is the oldest domestic tournament for women.

First National Championship – men

The first National Championship, then known as the Inter-Provincial Championship, was staged in 1928 at Kolkata (then Calcutta). India became a member of the International Hockey Federation in 1927 and thus became eligible to participate in the 1928 Olympics. The Calcutta edition was held to select the team for participation in the 1928 Olympic Games in Amsterdam.

Most wins in the National Championship – men

Indian Railways team has won 25 times.

First Domestic League – women

The Khelo India Women Hockey League for U-21 (2021) was the first domestic league for women.

Most wins in the National Championship – women

Indian Railways team has won 30 times.

First National Championship – women

Various attempts were made to start a National Championship. However, these efforts did not bear any results, after an edition was initially held. Subsequently, when the Bombay Inter-Provincial Hockey Association started in 1947, it got the much elusive consensus of all the states and thus a legacy was born.

INTERNATIONAL

First international appearance - men

In 1926, the Indian Army team went to New Zealand to play 21 matches. They won 18, drew two, and lost one match. They scored 192 and conceded 24 goals.

First major success by a foreign coach

Australian Terry Walsh was India's coach at the time of the gold medal win at the 2014 Incheon Asian Games in South Korea. In the final, India drew with Pakistan 1–1 but won 4–2 in the penalty shoot-out.

First women professional players

Penalty corner expert Jasjeet Kaur Handa and Subhadra Pradhan played for HC Den Bosch club in the Dutch League in 2007.

First medal and most successful team in the Olympics

The Indian hockey team won its first Olympic medal in 1928, under the captaincy of Jaipal Singh Munda. From 1928 to 1956, the team was unbeaten, winning six gold medals. Since then, India has been adding medals to its Olympic tally, and currently, with a total of eight gold, one silver and two bronze medals, it is the single most successful team at the Olympic Games.

First foreign coach

- *Men*: Gerard Rach from Germany, India's first foreign coach, was with the team at the 2004 Athens Olympics, and till January 2005.
- *Women*: Herman Kruis from the Netherlands was the first foreign coach for the women's hockey team, and was in charge of the Asia Cup in Hong Kong in September 2007.

First Commonwealth Games success – women

At the 2002 Commonwealth Games in Manchester, UK, the Indian women's hockey team won the gold medal, defeating England 3–2. The team was led by Suraj Lata Devi.

Inaugural FIH Hockey 5s Championship win

The International Hockey Federation (FIH) introduced a new tournament in 2022. India, led by Gurinder Singh, won, by defeating Poland (4-3) in the final on 7 June 2022 in Geneva, Switzerland.

Dhyan Chand

WR Most Olympic goals – individual

Dhyan Chand scored 33 goals in three Olympics – 10 in 1928, 12 in 1932 and 11 in 1936.

WR Most medals in the Olympics

The world record for the most medals in hockey at the Olympics is held by Leslie Claudius and Udham Singh, who were in four medal-winning teams – with three golds and one silver. Claudius was in the team that won the gold in 1948, 1952, and 1956, and silver in 1960, while Singh played for the gold-winning team in 1952, 1956, and 1964, and the silver-winning team in 1960.

First Asia Cup win – women

Coached by M.K. Kaushik, the Indian women's hockey team won the Asia Cup for the first time, beating Japan 1–0 in the final at the National Stadium (now Dhyan Chand National Stadium), New Delhi, in February 2004.

First Asian Men's Hockey Champions Trophy win - Men

India won the inaugural edition of the tournament held in Ordos City, China, during August–September 2011, by defeating Pakistan 4–2 in the final via penalty strokes.

First Asian Women's Hockey Champions Trophy win - Women

India, led by Deepika Thakur, won the Asian Women's Champions trophy held in Singapore in 2016, beating China in the final on shoot-out.

WR Most goals in the Olympics – team

India scored 43 goals in six matches at Moscow in 1980, a record for the most goals in an Olympics. In the 1936 Berlin and 1956 Melbourne Olympics, India notched up 38 goals in five matches. It did not concede a single goal in 1928 and 1956.

Most Junior Asia Cups – men

India under-21 hockey team lifted the Men's Hockey Junior Asia Cup 2023 after defeating Pakistan 2-1 in the final played in Salalah, Oman. This was India's record fourth Asian title at the age group ahead of Pakistan's three. India previously won in 2004, 2008 and 2015.

Most international caps – women

Vandana Katariya became the first Indian woman player to play 250 matches in national colours in January 2022. At 31, the forward has played 287 matches for India. Savita Punia and Deep Grace Ekka are the other two current players with 250 or more matches.

Women's Hockey

Women's hockey in India has a storied history marked by moments of triumph and determination. The Indian women's national hockey team earned its first Olympic medal in 1980, securing the gold at the Moscow Games. Led by iconic players like Rani Rampal, the team has since made significant strides on the international stage. Their consistent performances have resulted in podium finishes in various tournaments, including the Asian Games and the Asian Champions Trophy.

First Junior Asia Cup win

India won the fifth Junior Asia Cup in Karachi, Pakistan, in March 2004, beating the hosts 5–2. Tushar Khandekar scored a memorable hat-trick in the final.

Most capped player

Dilip Tirkey is the most capped player in India (412).

Playing for teams with most Olympic golds

The record for playing for teams winning the most Olympic golds – three each – is held by seven Indians: Richard Allen and Dhyan Chand (1928–36); Balbir Singh, R.S. Gentle, Leslie Claudius, and R. Francis (1948–56); and Udham Singh (1952, 1956, 1964).

Most appearance in the Women's World Cup

Deepika Thakur is the only Indian woman hockey player to appear in three World Cups (2006, 2010, 2018). India did not qualify for the 2014 edition.

Most appearances in the World Cup

Ashok Kumar of Indian Airlines played in four World Cups from 1971 to 1978, a record for the most appearances at the World Cup.

Most goals in a World Cup

In the fifth World Cup in Bombay (now Mumbai), Maharashtra, during 1981–82, India scored 29 goals in seven matches, winning five and losing two.

Best performance in the Commonwealth Games

Hockey was first introduced in the Commonwealth Games in 1998. India's best performances at the Commonwealth Games include three silver medals (in 2010 in New Delhi, in 2014 in Glasgow, and in 2022 in Birmingham).

Best performance on a foreign tour

Dhyan Chand, who led the team to New Zealand in 1935, played 48 matches and won them all. India scored 584 goals and conceded 40 goals. Dhyan Chand alone scored 201 goals, his brother Roop Singh scored 187 and F.C. Wells scored 112 goals.

Best performances in the Champions Trophy

India reached the final in the 2016 Champions Trophy in London, UK, and the 2018 Champions Trophy in Breda, Netherlands. In both, India lost 1–3 to Australia in penalty shoot-out. The traditional tournament has not being held after 2018.

Richard J. Allen
(*standing extreme left*)

Best goalkeeping in the Olympics
Richard J. Allen did not concede a single goal in the five matches in the 1928 Olympics. He let in only two goals in 1932 and one in five games in 1936, conceding only three goals in three successive Olympics – a rare feat.

Best performance in the World Cup – men
India, led by Ajitpal Singh, beat Pakistan 2–1 in the final of the third World Cup at Kuala Lumpur, Malaysia, in 1975, displaying its best performance at the World Cup.

Biggest victory margin in the Olympics
India created a world record for the biggest victory margin at the Olympics when they beat the US 24–1 on 11 August 1932 at Los Angeles, US.

Best performance in the World Cup – women
India, led by Ajinder Kaur, finished fourth in 1974.

Biggest victory margin in the Asian Games – men
India's biggest victory margin at the Asian Games was 26–0 versus Hong Kong in the League phase of the 2018 Jakarta Asian Games in Indonesia.

Biggest victory margin in the Asian Games – women
India's biggest victory margin at the Asian Games came in the League phase of the 2018 Bangkok Asian Games when it beat Kazakhstan 21–0 on 21 August 2018.

Biggest win in the Asia Cup finals
India beat South Korea 7–2 in the final of the 2007 Asia Cup in Chennai, Tamil Nadu, on 19 September 2007.

Biggest win over Pakistan
India's 7–1 win over Pakistan on 17 June 2017 in the World Hockey League semifinal in London, UK, is their biggest victory margin over their arch-rivals.

Best recovery in the Men's Hockey Champions Trophy

- The Indian team rallied from 0–3 at Amstelveen, Netherlands, to beat Pakistan 5–4 in 1982.
- India trailed West Germany 1–5 in 1985 at Perth, but in the last seven minutes levelled at 5–5. Centre half Joaquim Carvalho scored an equalizing penalty stroke.

Highest goal scorer at the World Cup

Defender Rajender Singh, who played a solitary World Cup, scored all 12 goals in the 1981–82 tournament in Bombay, Maharashtra, making him the highest goal scorer at the World Cup.

Highest goal scorer in the Asia Cup

Centre forward Sheikh Mohammed Nayeem scored 11 goals in the second Asia Cup in Dhaka, Bangladesh, in 1985.

Highest goal scorer and double hat-trick in the Youth Asia Cup

Defender Jugraj Singh scored 14 goals, including a double hat-trick, in the Youth Asia Cup in Malaysia in June 2001.

Fastest goal

Ajit Singh scored within 15 seconds of the start of the League match against Argentina in the 1976 Montreal Olympics – the fastest goal on artificial turf.

Only captain in successive Olympics

Pargat Singh was the captain first at Barcelona in 1992 and then in 1996 at the Atlanta Olympics in the US, but India did not win a medal at either Games.

Only goalkeeper in three finals

Goalkeeper Shankar Laxman played in three Olympic finals – in 1956 in Melbourne, in 1960 in Rome, and in 1964 in Tokyo.

Only double hat-trick in the Olympics

Mohammed Shahid scored seven goals, including a double hat-trick, against Thailand (11–0) on 24 September 1986 in the Seoul Olympics in South Korea.

Only hat-trick in succession

At the 1952 Helsinki Olympics, centre forward Balbir Singh scored three goals in the semi-final against Great Britain and netted five, including a hat-trick, against the Netherlands in the final.

Balbir Singh (*centre*)

Only hat-trick in the Olympics – women
Vandana Katariya scored a hat-trick against South Africa on 31 July 2021 in the 2020 Tokyo Olympics in Japan.

Youngest to win a gold in the Olympics
Cinnadorai Desamuthu was the youngest player to be in a gold-winning team, aged 19 years and 272 days, when India won in the 1952 Helsinki Olympics.

Oldest players in the Olympics
- Udham Singh (b. 1928) was 36 when he played in the 1964 Tokyo Olympics. Prithipal Singh (b. 1932) was also 36 when he was joint captain of the Indian team at the 1968 Mexico Olympics.

KABADDI

First Nationals
- The first kabaddi Nationals for men were held in 1951 in Maharashtra. The host state won the title.
- The first Nationals in kabaddi for women were held in 1955 in Calcutta (now Kolkata), West Bengal. Maharashtra won here too.
- The first championships for junior boys and girls were held in 1974 and 1976 respectively at Asansol, West Bengal.

First appearance of kabaddi in the Asian Games
Kabaddi was played for the first time in the 11th Asian Games in 1990 in Beijing, China. Pakistan, Japan, China, Nepal, Bangladesh and India participated, with India winning the gold medal.

First demonstration in the Olympics
Kabaddi and other indigenous games were the demonstration games in the 1936 Olympic Games held in Berlin, Germany.

First participation in the Asian Junior Championship
The championship was held for the first time at Faridabad, Haryana, in January 2000, with teams from Bangladesh, Nepal, Sri Lanka, and Thailand. India won the gold.

First demonstration at the Asian Games
Kabaddi was an exhibition sport at the 1982 Asian Games held in New Delhi.

First Asian Championship
The first Asian Championship for men was held at Calcutta (now Kolkata), West Bengal, in 1980, in which teams from Bangladesh, Nepal and India played. India won the gold medal.

First Pro Kabaddi League
The first Pro Kabaddi League was held in 2014, with eight teams participating. Sixty games were played, with the Jaipur Pink Panthers winning the inaugural title, defeating U-Mamba 35–24.

Women's Kabaddi

The Indian women's kabaddi team has emerged as a dominant force in the world of kabaddi. Since the inception of the Women's Kabaddi World Cup in 2012, India has consistently showcased their prowess, securing gold medals in all editions until 2019. Led by exceptional players like Payel Chowdhury and Priyanka Negi, the team's performances have captivated fans with their remarkable agility, strategy, and teamwork. Women's kabaddi has gained popularity across the country due to their achievements, motivating more women to participate in sports and fostering a sense of empowerment.

First team to win three consecutive Pro Kabaddi titles

Patna Pirates won three consecutive Pro Kabaddi League titles in 2016–17.

Most Asian Games titles – women

Kabaddi first made an appearance as a competitive sport for women in the 2010 Guangzhou Asian Games in China, 20 years after it was introduced for men. The Indian team won gold in 2010 and 2014, but got a silver in the 2018 Asian Games in Jakarta, Indonesia, losing to Iran in the final.

Most World Cup wins – men

The Indian team has won all three Kabaddi World Cups, organized by the International Kabaddi Federation, in 2004, 2007, and 2016, beating Iran in the finals of all three.

Most Asian Games titles – men

The Indian team has since won the Asian Games gold seven times – in 1990, 1994, 1998, 2002, 2006, 2010 and 2014.

Most World and Asian Championship medals – women

Sarala Shetty of Bank Sports Board is the only Indian to win the Asian Kabaddi Championship eight times. Captain of the Indian team on eight occasions, she has also won three World Championship medals.

Most expensive non-cricket player

Raider Monu Goyat from Haryana became India's most expensive non-cricket sportsperson when Haryana Steelers bought him at ₹1.51 crore (15.1 million) for season 6 of the Pro Kabaddi League 2018.

Most expensive player in Pro Kabaddi League (PKL)

Pawan Sehrawat became the most expensive player in PKL as Tamil Thalaivas bought him for Rs 2.26 crore at the 2022 auction. Iran's Fazel Atrachali became the most expensive foreign player at Rs 1.38 crore in 2022.

Most Asian titles — men and women

India won their record eighth Asian Kabaddi Championship title after defeating Iran in the final 42-32 in Busan, South Korea, in July. India, under captain Pawan Sehrawat, remained unbeaten in all six games played in the campaign. This was the eighth title in nine editions for India with Iran, a one-time champion.

LUGE

WR Youngest luge Olympian

India's single representative at luge in the Winter Olympics, Shiva Keshavan from Manali, Himachal Pradesh, was the youngest luge Olympian in history, when he participated in the 1998 Nagano Olympics in Japan at the age of 16 years. Keshavan holds the record of participating in six winter Olympics: 1998 Nagano, Japan; 2002 Salt Lake City, US; 2006 Turin, Italy; 2010 Vancouver, Canada; 2014 Sochi, Russia; and 2018 Pyeongchang, South Korea. He won the Asian Luge Championships in 2011, 2012, 2016, and 2017. He set a new Asian speed record of 134.3 kmph in 2011.

MARTIAL ARTS

WUSHU

Youngest Wushu Medallist

Pranathi. G (b. 17 November 2014) won her first National Championship at the age of 7. She won two bronze medals at the Sub-Junior National Wushu Championships.

First world wushu champion – men

Praveen Kumar of the Indian Army became the first Indian to win the gold medal on 23 October 2019 in the weight 48 kg category of the 15th World Wushu Championship.

JUDO

Youngest champion

Sandeep Bayala was 15 years old when he won the Nationals at Srinagar in 1982.

First National Championship

The first National Championship was held in Hyderabad in 1965. Till 1981, it was held every two years.

First international medal

India, represented by Sandeep Bayala (below 65 kg), Cawas Billimoria (below 95 kg), Shyam Singh Gurjar (+95 kg), and Bannu Singh (open), won four bronze medals in the 1986 Asian Games in Seoul.

First medal in the Asian Games – women

Poonam Chopra won a silver medal in the 56 kg weight category at the 1994 Hiroshima Games in Japan.

The **1986** Asian Games was the first international event in which an Indian team participated.

First medal in the Asian Championship – women

Poonam Chopra won a bronze medal in 56

kg weight category at the Asian Championship in 1993 in Macau, China.

Pooja Kadian

First judoka to win a world title

Sixteen-year-old Linthoi Chanambam clinched a historic gold medal at the World Cadet Championship on 22 August 2022. She won the title across age groups.

First world wushu champion – women

In 2017, Pooja Kadian became the first Indian to be crowned World Champion in the women's 75 kg weight category.

Most wins in the Nationals

Sandeep Bayala of Delhi Police has won 11 titles successively during 1982–93.

Oldest competitor

Banu Singh was 39 years old when he represented India at the Seoul Games in 1986. He won a bronze in the open category.

Best performance in the Commonwealth Games

India won two silver and two bronze medals in 2018 at Gold Coast in Australia.

POWER-LIFTING

Most Commonwealth Championship golds – individual

Sampa Guha won four gold medals in the first Commonwealth Championship in Newcastle, UK, in September 2005.

Most medals in one edition of the Asian Championship

V.S.N.L. Renuka won four golds in the 48 kg category in squat, bench, deadlift and overall lift of 310 kg at the Asian Powerlifting Championship in Zarafshan, Uzbekistan, in 2000.

Best performance in the World Championship

India won all three medals in the World Championship in Akita, Japan, in November 2000. N. Anbu (52 kg) won gold in the deadlift and an overall silver, while Jentry Francis (56 kg) won the bronze medal.

Most medals in Asian Championship

In the biggest haul at the Asian Championship to date, Indian powerlifters won 49 medals (22 gold, 19 silver and 8 bronze medals), besides the Women's Team Championship and overall medals (men and women), at the 18th Asian Senior, Junior, Sub-junior and Masters (men and women) Championship 2006 at Taebaek City, Korea.

Best performance in the Asian Junior Championship

At the Asian Junior Championship, Indian boys won the team trophy with four gold, four silver and two bronze medals at New Delhi in May 2001. In the same championship, Indian girls also won the team trophy with three gold, two silver, and two bronze medals.

Farman Basha

Best performance in the Asian Sub-junior Championship

The Indian boys' team won the team trophy with five gold and two silver medals at the inaugural Asian Sub-junior Championship held at New Delhi in May 2001. In the same championship, the Indian girls' team bagged four gold and two silver medals.

First medal in powerlifting in the Asian Para Games

Farman Basha won India's first medal – a bronze – in the 48 kg category at the inaugural Asian Para Games held in Guangzhou, China, in December 2010.

First medal in the Commonwealth games in para powerlifting

Sakina Khatun won the bronze medal in the lightweight category at the 2014 Commonwealth Para Games held in Glasgow, UK.

Best performance in the Commonwealth Championship – men

India bagged a total of five gold, three silver and four bronze medals, and were declared runner-up in the team event in the second Commonwealth Championship at Christchurch, New Zealand, held from 6 to 9 December 2007.

Back-to-back Olympia Pro-Powerlifting wins

Mukesh Singh Gehlot from Delhi is the only Indian to win an individual medal in successive IPL Olympia Pro-Powerlifting. He won the gold on his debut in IPL Olympia Pro-Powerlifting 2017 in the 100 kg open category and a bronze in Las Vegas, USA, in 2018.

First gold in para powerlifting

Sudhir Lath claimed the gold medal in the men's heavyweight para powerlifting event at the 2022 Commonwealth Games in Birmingham. The 27-year-old, who has an impairment due to polio, lifted 212 kg.

SHOOTING

First Asian Games medals

- *Men:* India's Asian Games medal haul started with Dr Karni Singh winning silver in the trap event in 1974 at Tehran, Iran.
- *Women:* Soma Dutta won a silver in the individual rifle 3-position event and a bronze medal in air rifle at the 1986 Seoul Games, South Korea.

First ever individual Olympic gold medal

Abhinav Bindra won India's first individual Olympic gold medal by claiming the honour in the men's air rifle event on 11 August 2008 in Beijing, China.

First Olympic finalist

Anjali Vedpathak-Bhagwat of the Central Industrial Security Force (CISF), Mumbai, Maharashtra, reached the air rifle final in the 2000 Sydney Olympics. She finished eighth with 493.1 points.

Abhinav Bindra

First World Championship gold

- Ace shooter Abhinav Bindra won India's first gold medal in a World Championship in air rifle at Zagreb, Croatia, on 24 July 2006.
- Manavjit Singh Sandhu won the first shotgun gold medal in a World Championship by beating 124 shooters to the title in the trap event at Zagreb, Croatia, two days after Bindra's effort.

First Asian Games gold

- Randhir Singh won gold in the trap event in the 1978 Games in Bangkok, Thailand, and a bronze in 1982.
- Jaspal Rana won the men's individual 25 m centre-fire pistol event in the 1994 Hiroshima Asian Games with 588 points, a new Asian record then. It was the only individual gold medal for India that year and the first Asian Games gold in that event.

First Commonwealth Games gold

- *Men:* Ashok Pandit won the gold in the free pistol event in Auckland, New Zealand, in 1990.
- *Women:* Roopa Unnikrishnan clinched the gold in the rifle prone event in the 1998 Commonwealth Games in Kuala Lumpur, Malaysia. In the 1994 Games in Victoria, Australia, Unnikrishnan won two medals – a silver in the small-bore rifle 3-position and a bronze in the pairs with Kuheli Ganguly.

First World Cup pistol medal

Sonia Rai from Himachal Pradesh won the bronze in the women's air pistol in the World Cup at Resende, Brazil, on 28 April 2006. She shot a 482.2, after 384/400 in the qualification phase.

WR Gold in the World Cup

Saurabh Chaudhary won the gold medal in the 10 m air pistol event in the World Cup at Munich, Germany, in May 2019. He shot a 246.3 to break his own world record of 245.5 set in the World Championship. He won gold medals in the 2018 Youth Olympics in Buenos Aires, Argentina, and in the 2018 Asian Games in Jakarta, Indonesia.

Out of the 35 Olympic medals that India has, 4 are for shooting.

First World Cup silver and gold medals

Anjali Vedpathak-Bhagwat won the gold in

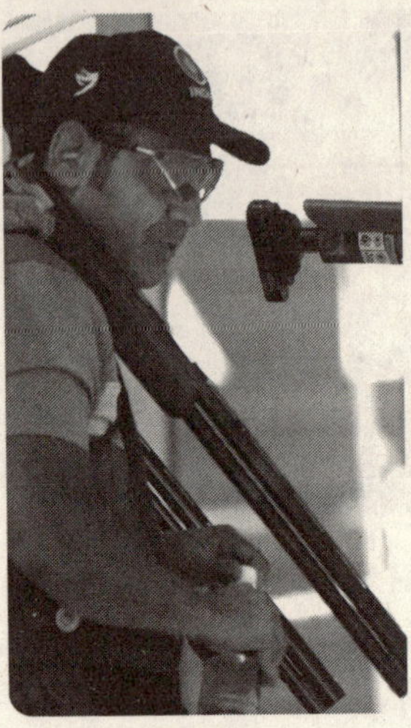
Mairaj Ahmad Khan

the air rifle event in the World Cup at Milan, Italy, in 2003. She had earlier won the silver in Munich, Germany, in 2002.

First medal haul in the Asian Championship

India won two gold, one silver and two bronze medals in Jakarta, Indonesia, in 1983, in its first haul in the Asian Championship. Ashok Pandit and Mohinder Lal won the gold in the centre-fire pistol team event with a world record.

First skeet gold in the World Cup

Olympian Mairaj Ahmad Khan became the first Indian to win a skeet gold in a World Cup in Changwon, Korea, in July 2022. The 46-year-old Mairaj beat Kin Minsu of Korea 37-36 for the gold. Khan shot 119 in qualification and had to win a shoot-off with four others for the last two slots in the second stage. Mairaj had lost the shoot-off for the gold in the World Cup in Rio de Janeiro in 2016, and won the silver.

First mixed air pistol gold medal in the World Cup – team

Heena Sidhu and Jitu Rai won the gold in the mixed air pistol team event in the World Cup in Delhi in 2017, when it was officially made a medal event.

World champion with a world record

Rudrankksh Patil became the world champion in men's air rifle in the World Championship in Cairo, Egypt, in October 2022. He had shot a world record 633.9 in the first stage of qualification. Eighteen-year-old Rudrankksh beat Danilo Dennis Solazzo of Italy 17-13 for the gold. He beat two Chinese shooters, including the reigning world and Olympic champion Yang Haoran. He became the second Indian to become world champion in air rifle after Abhinav Bindra in 2006. Rudrankksh also led the Indian team to the gold later, along with Arjun Babuta and Kiran Jadhav, as the trio beat China 16-10.

Rahi Sarnobat (*right*)

First woman to win a gold in the Asian Games

Rahi Sarnobat became the first Indian woman to win a gold in the Asian Games (25 m pistol event) in 2018 at Jakarta, Indonesia.

First Nationals

The first shooting national tournament was held in Delhi from 9 to 16 November in 1952.

First gold in the Asian Championship

Dr Karni Singh won an individual gold in the trap event in 1971 in Seoul, South Korea. This was India's first gold in the Asian Championship.

WR World record in skeet in the Asian Championship

Angad Vir Singh Bajwa shot a perfect 60 out of 60 to win the gold medal in the men's skeet final in the Asian Championship held in Kuwait, UAE, in November 2018.

First team gold in the Asian Clay Championship

Mansher Singh, Moraad Ali Khan, and Manavjit Singh won India's first team gold at the Asian Clay Shooting Championship at Chengdu, China, in July 1995 with a tally of 357/375, equalling Kuwait's Asian record at the 1994 Hiroshima Asian Games in Japan.

First ever Olympic medal in shooting

Rajyavardhan Singh Rathore won the silver medal in double-trap shooting, behind Ahmed Al Maktoum of the UAE, in the 2004 Athens Olympics in Greece. Rathore made his maiden Olympic appearance in the 2004 Olympic Games in Athens, Greece, merely about six years after he had taken up the sport. A year before, he had won the gold medal in the 2003 World Cup in Sydney, Australia.

First to win two golds in a World Cup

Manu Bhaker, then 16 years old, from Jhajjar, Haryana, won the 10 m air pistol gold medal and partnered with Om Prakash Mitharval for the 10 m air pistol mixed team gold in the 2018 World Cup in Mexico.

WR World record at the Asian Championship

Suma Shirur shot a perfect 400 out of 400 to win the gold medal in the women's air rifle in the Asian Championship at Kuala Lumpur, Malaysia, in February 2004. She shares the record with eight others.

Most individual medals in the Asian Shooting Championship

Ronak Pandit won seven gold medals and a silver medal in the junior pistol events of the Asian Championship in Kuala Lumpur, Malaysia, in 2004.

Most career golds at the South Asian Games

Jaspal Rana won 23 golds and a silver in three editions of the SAF Games (now South Asian Games). He won eight golds each at Madras (now Chennai), Tamil Nadu, in1995 and at Kathmandu, Nepal, in 1999; and seven golds and a silver at Islamabad, Pakistan, in 2004.

Jaspal Rana

Best haul in the Asian Clay Shooting Championship

The best performance in the Asian Clay Shooting Championship was five gold medals in Bangkok, Thailand, in September 2005.

Double world record

Ronjan Sodhi

- Ronjan Sodhi gained the unique distinction of equalling both the qualifying and final world records in double trap while winning the gold in the World Cup in Belgrade, Serbia, in 2008. He shot 147 in the qualifying phase and ended with 194.
- Gagan Narang won the World Cup final gold medal in men's air rifle with two world records in Bangkok, Thailand, in November 2008.

Best haul in the World Championship

- The Indian team won 34 medals including 12 gold medals in the World Championship for rifle and pistol in Cairo, Egypt, in 2022. It is the best ever performance by India in a World Championship and India finished second in the medals table behind China.
- In 2018, India had won 27 medals in the World Championship in Changwon, Korea, finishing third behind China and Korea.

Best haul in the World Cup

The Indian team topped the medals table with a record total of 30 medals in the World Cup in Delhi in March 2021, with ten gold, eight silver and four bronze medals. The US came a distant second with four gold, three silver, and one bronze medals. Yashaswini Singh Deswal (women's air pistol), Aishwary Pratap Singh Tomar (men's rifle 3-position), and Chinki Yadav (women's sports pistol) won the individual gold medals.

Best performance at the World Cup on debut

Shahzar Rizvi created a world record at the ISSF World Cup when he scored 242.3 points in the final of the 10 m air pistol event on 3 March 2018 at Guadalajara, Mexico. In his debut performance at the World Cup, Rizvi won the gold medal beating the reigning Olympic champion Christian Reitz of Germany.

Best Asian Games haul

Indian shooters won three gold, five silver and six bronze medals in the Asian Games at Doha, Qatar, in 2006, for their best haul of 14 medals in an edition of the Asian Games. India had won only 17 medals in all the previous editions put together.

Back-to-back gold medals in the Junior World Cups

Elavenil Valarivan (b. 2 August 1999) won gold medals in air rifle in the 2018 Junior World Cup in Sydney, Australia, and Suhl, Germany. She also won the mixed air rifle team gold with Divyansh Singh Panwar in the Junior World Cup in Suhl, with a junior world record of 498.6 in the final.

Best haul in the Junior World Championship

The Indian juniors topped the medal standings in the Junior World

Championship in Lima, Peru, in October 2021, with a total of 31 medals, including 12 gold and 13 silver medals. Manu Bhaker (women's air pistol), Naamya Kapoor (women's sports pistol), Aishwary Pratap Singh Tomar (men's rifle 3-position), Vijayveer Sidhu (men's standard pistol), Rhythm Sangwan (women's standard pistol), and Arjun Singh Cheema (men's free pistol) won the individual gold medals.

Youngest to win a World Cup gold – women

At Guadalajara, Mexico, in March 2018, Manu Bhaker (b. 18 February 2002) was the youngest to win a gold medal in the women's air pistol, and the air pistol mixed gold with Om Prakash Mitharval. She also clinched the gold medals in the Junior World Cups in Sydney, Australia, and Suhl, Germany, in 2018. She also won the air pistol gold, ahead of compatriot and former world record holder Heena Sidhu, in the 2018 Commonwealth Games in Gold Coast, Australia.

Best haul in the Commonwealth Games

Indian shooters bagged 27 medals in the 2006 Commonwealth Games in Melbourne, Australia, with 16 gold, seven silver and four bronze medals. Gagan Narang bagged four gold medals (a feat he repeated in the 2010 Commonwealth Games, New Delhi), while Vijay Kumar and Omkar Singh bagged three gold medals each.

Best haul in the Olympics

India's win of two medals in the 2012 London Olympics was the best in terms of numbers. Gagan Narang won the bronze medal in the air rifle and Vijay Kumar won the silver in the rapid fire pistol.

Youngest to win a Junior World Championship gold – men

In 2017, Anish Bhanwala (b. 26 September 2002) became the youngest Indian shooter to win a Junior World Championship gold medal in standard pistol.

Most medals in a World Cup

India topped the medals table in the 2019 World Cup in Rio de Janeiro, Brazil, with five gold, two silver and two bronze medals.

Most medals in a Junior World Cup

India topped the medals table in the 2018 Suhl World Cup in Germany with 26 medals: fifteen gold, two silver and nine bronze medals. This bettered the country's share of 22 out of 66 medals in the 2017 Sydney World Cup in Australia, when it won nine gold, five silver and eight bronze medals, to be placed second behind China with 25 medals.

Most medals in four consecutive World Cups

India has topped the medals table in four consecutive World Cups in rifle and pistol events. India topped the table in the 2018 Munich World Cup (with five gold medals and one silver medal), the 2019 New Delhi World Cup (with three golds), the 2019 Beijing World Cup (with three golds and a silver), and the 2019 Rio de Janeiro World Cup (with five golds, two silver, and two bronze medals).

SQUASH

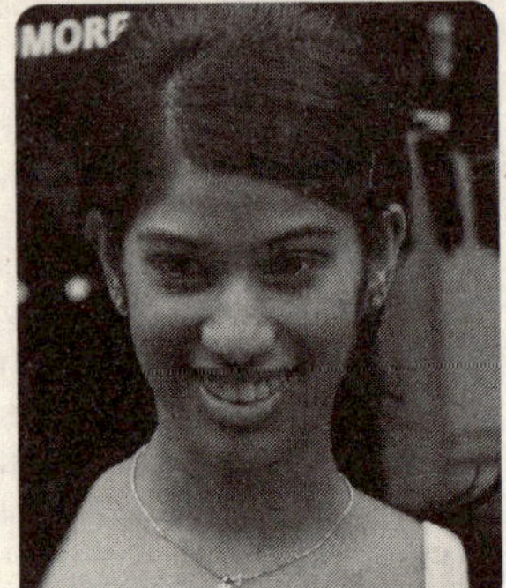

Joshna Chinappa

First professionals

In the early 1990s, the first professionals were Arjun Singh (men) and Misha Grewal. The latter became a professional in 1993, and played the women's professional circuit in Asia, Europe, and the US. Her best rankings were second in Asia and 27th in the world.

First international success – women

Joshna Chinappa became the first Indian woman to claim a Women's International Squash Players Association (WISPA) title, defeating Malaysia's Low Wee Wern 11–8, 11–5, 11–3 in the NSC Super Satellite (no. 3) Squash Tournament final at National Squash Centre, Kuala Lumpur, Malaysia, in November 2008.

First champion

Rajkumar Narpat Singh won the first squash Nationals in 1953 and made a hat-trick, holding the title for two more years.

First junior and senior Nationals title

Anil Nayyar won both the junior and senior titles in the Nationals in 1964, when he was 18 years old.

First individual medals in the Asian Championships

- Bhuvaneshwari Kumari won the bronze in the 1990 and 1992 Asian Championships.
- Misha Grewal won a silver in the Asian Championship in 1996 at Amman, Jordan.

First silver in the Asian Junior Championship

The Indian girls' squad bagged a silver medal in the Asian Junior Championship in Chennai, Tamil Nadu, in February 2003. They lost 0–3 to Malaysia in the final.

First junior world no. 1

Saurav Ghosal was the first Indian to be ranked junior world no. 1 when he won the British Junior Open in 2004.

First to win world ranking titles

In August 2003, Ritwik Bhattacharya became the first Indian to win back-to-back international Professional Squash Association (PSA) world ranking tournaments in New Zealand when he won the North Island Championship and the Royal Oak Open titles. In 2005, he annexed two more titles – the Esportiu Rocafort Squash Open in Barcelona,

Bhuvaneshwari Kumari's first national triumph was in **1977** at **16** years.

Spain, and the Rochester ProAm Squash Championship in New York, US. He has won four international squash titles.

Bhuvaneshwari Kumari

Most titles in a row in the Nationals – women

Bhuvaneshwari Kumari was the women's national champion 16 times in a row from 1977 to 1992, a record that remains unbeaten.

First to win the Asian junior title – girls

Joshna Chinappa was the first to win the Asian junior title (U-19) in 2003. Later, Dipika Pallikal also won the title in July 2010.

First doubles champions in the Nationals

In the first National Doubles Squash Championship held in Chennai, Tamil Nadu, in 2004. Joshna Chinappa and Dipika Pallikal, representing Tamil Nadu, won the women's title and Saurav Ghosal and Harinder Pal Singh Sandhu, also representing Tamil Nadu, won the men's title.

Best performance in the Asian Juniors

Anaka Alankamony from Chennai, Tamil Nadu, became the youngest winner of the Asian Junior title (U-19) at 16 years when she beat Tsz-Wing Tong of Hong Kong 6–11, 11–8, 10–12, 11–7, 11–7 at Amman, Jordan, in June 2011. India enjoyed triple success in this event: Ramit Tandon (U-19 boys' and Saumya Karki (U-17 girls') won silver medals in India's largest haul at the event.

First Indians to win World Doubles titles

Dipika Palikkal became the first Indian to win two gold medals at the World Doubles Squash Championship winning the gold in women's and mixed finals. Dipika partnered Joshna Chinappa in the women's final and teamed up with Saurav Ghosal in the mixed doubles in the 2022 edition in Glasgow. The trio are the first Indians to win World Doubles title since the inception of the tournament in 1981.

First Indians to win Asian Mixed Doubles Championship

Dipika Pallikal Karthik and Harinderpal Singh Sandhu won the inaugural Asian Mixed Doubles Squash Championship 2023 in Huangzhou, China. The duo defeated the Malaysian pair of Rachel Arnold and Ivan Yuen 11-10, 11-8 in the final.

Best performance in the World Championships

Saurav Ghosal was the first Indian to reach the quarter-finals of the World Championship in Manchester, UK, in October 2013. Though he lost to world no. 1 Ramy Ashour in the match, this is India's best performance to date at the World Championships.

Dipika Pallikal

First Commonwealth Games gold

India bagged its first gold medal when Dipika Pallikal and Joshna Chinappa defeated Laura Massaro and Jenny Duncalf of England 11–6, 11–8 to win the women's doubles event in the Commonwealth Games in Glasgow, UK, in 2014.

Best in the Asian Games

For the first time, India won the men's team event gold medal in the 2014 Incheon Asian Games in South Korea, beating Malaysia 2–0. Saurav Ghosal, Harinder Pal Singh Sandhu and Mahesh Mangaonkar represented India in this event. The women's team of Dipika Pallikal, Joshna Chinappa and Anaka Alankamony won the silver medal, losing to Malaysia 0–2 in the 2014 Asian Games team event final.

Most National titles won

Joshna Chinappa won 18 national titles, the most yet by an Indian.

Most titles in a row in the Nationals – men

Major K.S. Jain and Brigadier R.K. Manchanda hold the men's record for the highest number of titles won in the Nationals, with six wins in a row. Jain won the title from 1958 to 1963, while Manchanda was the champion from 1978 to 1983.

Best performance in the World Team Championships

The Indian men's team, led by Saurav Ghosal, made a second successive appearance among the top eight in the World Team Championship in June 2013. The women's team also reached the quarter-finals in 2012. This is India's best performance in the World Team Championships.

Youngest to represent India

Saurav Ghosal and Joshna Chinappa were the youngest to represent India in an international event. Ghosal was 16 years old and Chinappa was 15 when they played for India in the 2002 Asian Games in Busan, South Korea.

Youngest champion – men

Adrian Ezra and Ritwik Bhattacharya were both 17 when they won the senior national singles title in 1989 and 1997, respectively, making them the youngest national squash champions to date.

Youngest national champion – women

Joshna Chinappa became the youngest national women's champion at 14 years in 2001.

Oldest champion

Brigadier R.K. Manchanda was 37 years old when he won the Nationals title in 1983, thus becoming the oldest national champion in squash. He also became the oldest finalist in 1987 when he was 41 years old. He reached the final in the Nationals a record 11 times, as did Anil Nayyar. Manchanda won six of the 11 finals in which he competed.

Highest rankings

- Saurav Ghosal is the first Indian to break into the top 10 in the Professional Squash Association (PSA) world rankings. He was ranked 10th with 6,455 points in April 2019.
- Joshna Chinappa is the highest-ranked Indian woman in the 27th position with 2,345 points (*at the time of going to press*).
- In 2012, Dipika Pallikal and, in 2016, Chinappa were placed 10th in the world rankings.

SWIMMING

First swimmer in the Olympics

D.D. Mulji of Bengal was the first Indian swimmer in the Olympics, taking part in the 1928 Amsterdam Olympics. Indian women participated in the Olympics for the first time at the 1952 Helsinki Olympics, with Dolly Nazir and Arati Saha representing India.

First swimmers in the Asian Games

Nine Indian swimmers participated in the inaugural Asian Games in 1951: Sachin Nag, Bimal Chandra, Issar Mansoor, Santosh Bhattacharjee, Kanti Shaw, Protip Mitra, Shambu Shaw, J.J. Naigamwalla, and Bhubaneswar Pandey. The first Indian women to participate in Asian Games were Kumari Rima Dutta in the fifth Asian Games held at Bangkok in 1966.

First woman to participate in the Asian Games

Kumari Rima Dutta participated in the fifth Asian Games in Bangkok, Thailand, in 1966.

First water polo team in the Asian Games

- In 1951, the Indian water polo team first participated in Asian Games and won a gold medal. The team members were Ganesh Dass (captain), G. Rattansey, D. Daver, Isaac Mansoor, Jhair Ahir, Rober Dean, and Kanti Shaw.
- The Indian water polo team participated in Asian Games in 1970 in Bangkok and won the silver medal. The team included Pijus Mitra (Captain), Samir Kapadia, Tarun Goswami, Abdul Mutlib, Ashok Biswas, Bharat Merchant, Chand Ram, Umed Singh, Avinash Sarang, Pattabhi Raman, and Deep Narayan Singh.

First diver in the Asian Games

Three Indian divers participated in the first Asian Games in 1951. They were: K.P. Thakkar, Ashu Dutta, and T.T. Dand. Thakkar of Maharashtra won gold medals in the high-board and springboard events, while Dand won a bronze in high-board diving.

First to participate in the Commonwealth Games

- Divers Dum Bahadur and Vasant Gadge were the first to represent India in the aquatics events at the 1978 Commonwealth Games in Edmonton, Canada.
- In 1982, for the first time, Indian swimmers participated in the Commonwealth Games at Brisbane, Australia. The team members were Wilson Cherian, Khazan Singh Tokas, T. Thoiba Singh, Sanjeev Chakraborty, Persis Madaan, Geeta Anand and Giselle Bharucha.

First Asian Games gold

India won its first Asian Games gold when Sachin Nag clocked 1 min 4.7 secs to win the 100 m freestyle in the 1951 Asian Games in Delhi. In the same Asian Games he won two bronze medals as well. He represented India in two Olympics: in 1948 in London and in 1952 in Helsinki.

First to reach a Commonwealth Games final

During the 2010 Commonwealth Games in New Delhi, two Indian men – Virdhawal Khade and Sandeep Sejwal – reached the finals in their best events. Khade was placed seventh in the 50 m butterfly, while Sejwal came eighth in the 50 m breaststroke.

First relay team in a the Commonwealth Games final

The quartet of Virdhawal Khade, Anshul Kothari, Arjun Jayaprakash, and Aaron D'Souza qualified for the 4 x 100 m freestyle relay final at the 2010 Commonwealth Games in New Delhi. They clocked 3 mins 27.14 secs to better their qualifying timing, but only finished sixth.

First 100 m freestyle – under 1 min.

- The first Indian swimmer to swim under 1 min. in the 100 m freestyle category was Basakha Singh, clocking 59.75 secs in 1971.
- The best performance is by Virdhawal Khade, who clocked 49.47 secs in October 2008. Among women, Shikha Tandon of Karnataka holds the record, with 58.91 secs in 2003.

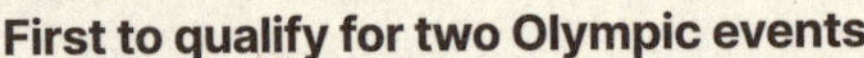

First to qualify for two Olympic events

Shikha Tandon of Bengaluru, Karnataka, qualified for the 50 m and 100 m freestyle events in the 2004 Athens Olympics, but did not win.

Shikha Tandon

First National Championship

The first National Championship was held in Bombay (now Mumbai), Maharashtra, in 1945.

First to win a medal in the Asian Indoor Games

Shikha Tandon won a bronze in the 100 m backstroke event at the Asian Indoor Games in Bangkok, Thailand, in November 2005.

First 200 m freestyle – under 2 mins

Virdhawal Khade of Maharashtra, who clocked 1 min 49.86 secs, holds the record.

Srihari Nataraj

First swimmer to make Olympic 'A' cut – 100 m backstroke – men

Srihari Nataraj became the second Indian swimmer to qualify for the 2020 Tokyo Olympics after FINA approved his 'A' standard qualification time in men's 100 m backstroke time trial at the Sette Colli Trophy in Rome. He clocked 53.77 secs in time trial.

First swimmer to make Olympic 'A' cut 200 m butterfly – men

On 26 June 2021, Sajan Prakash became the first-ever Indian swimmer to breach the 'A' Olympic qualification time by clocking 1 hour 56 minutes 38 seconds in the men's 200 m butterfly event at the Sette Colli Trophy in Rome, Italy. He made the Tokyo Games 'A' standard, set at 1 hour 56 minutes 48 seconds, by 0.10 seconds at the FINA-accredited Olympic qualifier. Earlier, he was the only Indian male swimmer who represented India in the 2016 Rio Olympics and was the only one to qualify with B timings for Rio.

First para swimmer to win bronze at the Commonwealth Games

Prasanta Karmakar was the first Indian para swimmer to claim a bronze medal in the 50 m freestyle in the S-9 category at the 2010 Commonwealth Games in New Delhi.

First visually impaired swimmer to win a gold

Kanchanmala Pande won gold in the 200 m medley event in the S-11 category on 8 December 2017 at the World Para swimming Championship in Berlin.

First Indian para swimmer to qualify for the Paralympic Games

Sharath Gayakwad was the first Indian para swimmer to qualify for the 2012 London Paralympic Games. He secured the ninth position. He also has a bronze at the 2010 Asian Para Games.

First Indian para swimmer to win gold in the Para Asian games

Suyash Narayan Jadhav won the gold medal in men's 50 m butterfly S7 (6 –7) category at the Para Asian Games held at Jakarta, Indonesia, in 2018. He clocked 32.71 secs.

Participation in two consecutive Paralympics

Suyash Narayan Jadhav represented the country at Rio in 2016 and the 2020 Tokyo Paralympics (in 2021).

Suyash Narayan Jadhav

Participation in two consecutive Olympic Games

Sachin Nag represented India in the 1948 London Olympics and the 1952 Helsinki Olympics. Sajan Prakash represented India at Rio in 2016 and the 2020 Tokyo Olympics (in 2021).

TABLE TENNIS

GENERAL

Most National singles titles in a row

A. Sharath Kamal among men and Indu Puri among women have won most National singles titles in a row. Kamal won the title five times between 2006 and 2010. Indu was champion six times between 1980 and 1985.

Junior/ Senior titles in a year

Four girls have won both titles in one calendar year – Rinku Gupta Acharya (Madhya Pradesh) in 1988; Mantu Ghosh (Bengal) in 1991; Kasturi Chakraborty (Bengal) in 1998, and Poulomi Ghatak (Bengal) in 1998-99.

No games conceded

Farokh Khodaiji was the first to achieve this feat, winning the men's singles title in 1967 in Guwahati, followed by Kaity Chargeman in the women's singles in Calcutta in 1970 and Chetan Baboor in the men's singles in 1999.

FIRST

First gold medallist in the Asian Championship

Gool Nasikwala won the singles, doubles, and mixed doubles gold medals in the 1952 Asian Championship in Singapore.

A total of 43 medals have been won by Indian paddlers in major tournaments.

First Indian to reach World championship quarter-finals

Krishna Nagaraj reached the men's singles quarter-finals in the 1956 World Championship in Tokyo, Japan.

First doubles pair in World championship quarter-finals

Mouma Das and Manika Batra became the first to reach the women's doubles quarter-finals in the 2017 World Table Tennis Championship.

First woman to play in two Olympics

Mouma Das became the first woman player to qualify for two Olympic Games (2004, Athens, and 2016, Rio).

First Commonwealth Games winner – women – singles

Manika Batra won the women's singles gold at Gold Coast in 2018.

First Commonwealth Championship team title – men

India won the Commonwealth men's team title in Kuala Lumpur in 2004.

A. Sharath Kamal

A. Sharath Kamal, born on 12 July 1982, is a prominent Indian table tennis player who has made significant contributions to the sport. With a career spanning several decades, Sharath Kamal is recognized as one of India's top table tennis players. He has represented the country in multiple Olympic Games and Commonwealth Games, showcasing his skill and consistency on the international stage. Sharath Kamal has secured several national championships and international titles, cementing his status as a seasoned professional. Notably, he became the first Indian paddler to break into the top 30 of the International Table Tennis Federation (ITTF) world rankings.

First Commonwealth Games gold –men – team
The Indian men's team won the first Commonwealth Games table tennis gold medal in Melbourne in 2006.

Youngest to qualify for the Olympic Games
Manika Batra became the youngest to play Olympic Games in Rio (2016) at the age of 21 years and 2 months.

First Commonwealth Games winner – men – singles
A. Sharath Kamal won the men's singles gold at Melbourne in 2006. He regained the medal in Birmingham in 2022.

First Commonwealth Games gold medal – mixed doubles
A. Sharath Kamal and Sreeja Akula won the mixed doubles gold in Birmingham in 2022.

First to be a medallist in five successive Commonwealth Games
A. Sharath Kamal is the only player to win Commonwealth Games medals in five successive editions – 2006, Melbourne; 2010, New Delhi; 2014, Glasgow; 2018, Gold Coast; and 2022, Birmingham.

First Commonwealth Games gold – women – team
India's women team won the first Commonwealth Games team gold medal in Gold Coast in 2018.

First to regain Commonwealth Games gold – men – team
A. Sharath Kamal was the only member of the Indian team that won the men's team gold in 2006 and again in 2022.

First Commonwealth Games gold – men – doubles
A. Sharath Kamal and Subhajit Saha won the men's doubles gold in New Delhi in October 2010.

First time when six Indian men and three women broke into the top 100 in world rankings

G. Sathiyan (ranked 49th), Sharath Kamal (51st), Soumyajit Ghosh (58th), Harmeet Desai (60th), Sanil Shetty (68th), and A. Amalraj (87th) were in the top 100 of world rankings in January 2018. At the same time, Manika Batra (62nd), Mouma Das (74th) and Madhurika Patkar (81st) also made the grade.

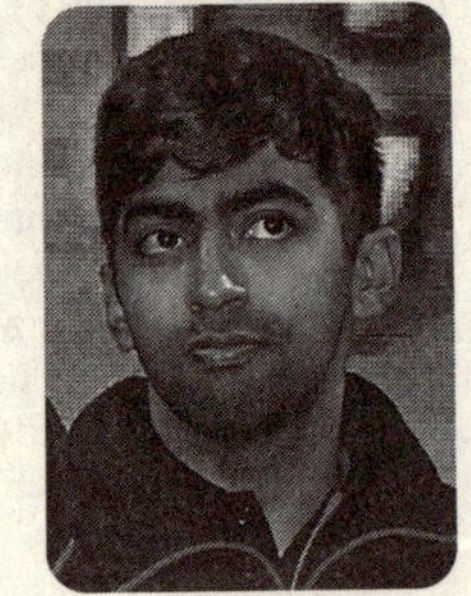
Harmeet Desai

First title triumph in the ITTF Junior tour

Harmeet Desai defeated Soumyajit Ghosh in the 2011 Austrian Open junior boys' final to become the first Indian to win a title on the ITTF (International Table Tennis Federation) Junior Tour.

First Commonwealth Games medal– women – doubles

Poulomi Ghatak and Mouma Das claimed the bronze in the women's doubles in New Delhi in October 2010.

First ITTF Pro-Tour title

A. Sharath Kamal won the Egypt Open to become the first Indian to win an ITTF Pro-Tour event in July 2010.

First Indian to be ranked world no. 1 in U-18

Manav Thakkar became the first Indian to be ranked world no. 1 in the boys' U-18 category in February 2018.

First medal in Asian juniors

India won the bronze medal in the 2006 Asian Junior Championship at Kitakyushu, Japan, by reaching the semi-finals of the girls' event.

First National champion

- *Men*: M. Ayub won the men's singles title in Calcutta (now Kolkata) in 1938.
- *Women*: P. Lima won the women's singles in Bombay (now Mumbai) in 1939.

First team medal in the World Junior Championship

The Indian boys' team, comprising Soumyajit Ghosh, Harmeet Desai, and G. Sathiyan, won India's first- ever bronze medal in the 2011 Junior Championship held in Bahrain.

First international league

The first edition of the Ultimate Table Tennis (UTT) was held in July 2017 in Chennai, New Delhi, and Mumbai. Six teams took part the event and Falcons Club won the title by beating Shaze Challengers 14-9 in the final.

First to win Asian Cup medal – women

Manika Batra became the first Indian woman to win a medal at the Asian Cup in 2022 as she defeated Japan's World No. 6 Hina Hayata in the bronze medal match. She also became the first Indian woman paddler to reach the semis of the continent.

First Indian in the ITTF's Umpires and Referees Committee

Neelakanta Ganeshan was the first Indian inducted as a member of International Table Tennis Federation's Umpires and Referees Committee (URC) in June 2017.

First pair to win Asian Junior Championship in mixed doubles

Payas Jain and Yashaswini Ghorpade became India's first mixed doubles pair to win Asian Junior Table Tennis Championship in 2022 as the duo defeated China's Han Xinyuan and Qin Yuxuan in the final.

First professional

Chetan Baboor played as a professional with Enig Club in Kalmar, Sweden, from 1998.

First pair to win WTT Contender title

Manika Batra and G. Sathiyan became the first Indian pair to win WTT Contender title after beating Hungary's Nandor Ecseki and Dora Madarasz 3-1 (11-9, 9-11, 12-10, 11-6) in the final in Budapest in 2021.

LONGEST

Longest mixed doubles reign

Farokh Khodaiji and Kaity Khodaiji of Mumbai won the Susan Barna Cup five years in a row during 1967-71. They had earlier won the title in 1965.

MOST

Most medals from Commonwealth-level competitions

Mouma Das has claimed 19 medals in both team and individual events of the Commonwealth Games and Commonwealth Championships between 2001 and 2018.

Most medals from the Commonwealth Games

Indians won eight medals, including three golds, in the 2018 edition of the Games in Gold Coast, Australia. India claimed gold medals in men's team, women's team, and women's singles (Manika Batra); silver medals in men's doubles (A. Sharath Kamal and G. Sathiyan) and women's doubles (Manika Batra and Mouma Das); and bronze medals in men's singles (A. Sharath Kamal), men's doubles (Harmeet Desai and Sanil Shetty), and mixed doubles (Manika Batra and G. Sathiyan).

Most Commonwealth Games medals won by an individual player in a single edition

- *Men*: A. Sharath Kamal won four medals in the 2022 Commonwealth Games in Birmingham, UK.
- *Women*: Manika Batra won four medals in the 2018 Commonwealth Games in Gold Coast, Australia

Most World Championship appearances

Mouma Das has played in 16 editions of World Championship since 1997.

Most state representations at the Nationals

N. Ravichandran represented five different units, including four states in the National Championships: Tamil Nadu, Punjab, Goa, and Puducherry apart from the Central Revenue Sports Board at National- level tournaments.

Most appearances in the National Championship

S. Ramaswamy, who first played the Nationals in Allahabad in 1976, appeared in 30 successive National Championships until February 2006.

Most team titles – men/ women

Bombay won the team title for the Barna Bellack Cup 16 times. Maharashtra won the team title for the Corbillion Cup 14 times. The championship was first introduced in 1946 at Madras (now Chennai) where Bombay (now Mumbai) won the title and remained unbeaten till 1952.

Most gold medals in the South Asian Federation (SAF) Games

A. Sharath Kamal won four gold medals – men's team event, men's singles, doubles, and mixed doubles – in Colombo in August 2006.

Most National titles – singles

- *Men*: Sharath Kamal has won 10 National singles titles in the men's singles section. Sharath broke Kamlesh Mehta's record of eight singles titles in 2019.
- *Women*: I ndu Puri won the women's singles title eight times — 1972, 1975 and from 1979-84.

TABLE TENNIS IN INDIA

Table Tennis was invented in England and was called ping-pong until 1901. The game was brought to India and until the establishment of Table Tennis Federation of India (TTFI), British people dominated the game. TTFI was established in Calcutta in 1937 and is an active member of the International Table Tennis Federation (ITTF). India has hosted the World Championships, an important table tennis tournament, for three times. Some of the key players and their achievements are:

1 Manika Batra

The Delhi-born player won her first international medal when she was just 16, in the Under-21 category at the Chile Open in 2011. She won three medals in the Commonwealth TT Championships in 2015 and made her Olympic debut in Rio 2016. She won a Khel Ratna award, and became the first female Indian table tennis player to make the singles round of 32.

Manika Batra

2 Sathiyan Gnanasekaran

He clinched the ITTF Pro-Tour crown at the Belgium Open in 2016 and teamed up with Sharath Kamal in 2017 to win a bronze at an ITTF Major in Sweden. He won a team title in the men's event at the 2018 Commonwealth Games and won a bronze at the Asian Games in the same year. He won the Arjuna Award. Sathiyan made his Olympic debut in 2020 at Tokyo, Japan.

3 Sharath Kamal

A four-time Olympian, has won the national table tennis championship a record 10 times. He is also the first Indian to win an ITTF Pro- Tour title and to win a singles gold medal at the Commonwealth Games. He made his Olympic debut at Athens, Greece, in 2004.

4 Soumyajit Ghosh

He was the youngest player who qualified for the 2012 Olympics in London, UK, and won the doubles bronze medal at the World Junior Championships in 2010. He beat champion Sharath Kamal in the finals of the 74th National Table Tennis Championship and became the youngest National champion. He won the ITTF Pro title in 2017 and became the third Indian to do so.

5 Mouma Das

She won her first International gold medal in the second Children of Asia International Sports Games in Yakutsk, Russia, and has played more than 400 international matches against 75 different countries. She has won multiple medals at the Commonwealth games and a gold in the Women's Team Competition in 2018. She was awarded the Arjuna Award in 2013 and in 2018 she partnered with Manika Batra to win a silver at the Commonwealth Games.

Most participants in a tournament

An unprecedented 4,104 entries were received across 17 categories in the first Indian Table Tennis Marathon 2019 held between 1 and 5 May 2019 at the Table Tennis Federation TT Hall, Sant Sujan Singh Ji International School, Swaroop Nagar, New Delhi. A record 4,102 matches were played.

YOUNGEST

Youngest to win the National title

Mantu Ghosh was 16 when she won the title at Jaipur in 1990-91.

HIGHEST

Highest world ranking

- *Men*: G. Sathiyan attained his career-high world ranking of 24 as of 1 May 2019.
- *Women*: Manika Batra reached her career-best world ranking of 38 as of 3 May 2022.

BEST

Best team performance in the World Championship

India finished 10th – its best finish till date – in the men's team events of the 1959 World Championship in Dortmund (Germany). In 2018, India produced its second best performance and took the 13th place.

Best Indian performance (individual): beating three top-20 players in one event

A. Sharath Kamal defeated three players from the world's top 20 list in the Asian Cup held in Jaipur in March 2015. They included world no. 8 Chuang Chih-Yuan (Chinese Taipei), world no. 15 Gao Ning (Singapore), and world no. 16 Joo Sae Hyuk (Korea).

Best performances in the Commonwealth Games – doubles

A. Sharath Kamal holds the distinction of winning the men's doubles medal in four successive Commonwealth Games. He partnered Subhajit Saha to win the gold in the 2010 Commonwealth Games in New Delhi. In 2014, he joined hands with Anthony Amalraj to claim the silver in the men's doubles in Glasgow, UK. In 2018, he and G. Sathiyan settled for a silver medal in Gold Coast, Australia, and again in 2022 in Birmingham, UK.

Second division titles in World championship

Indian men and women won the second division titles in the 2016 World Championship in Kuala Lumpur, Malaysia, on 5 March 2016. In the final, Indian men beat Brazil 3-2 and the women defeated Luxemburg 3-1.

Best doubles performance in the Commonwealth Championship

Chetan Baboor and S. Raman won two successive Commonwealth Championship titles in 1997 and 2000.

TENNIS

BILLIE JEAN KING (FEDERATION) CUP

First world play-offs qualifying team

Earlier known as the Federation Cup, the Billie Jean King Cup is a team event for women's tennis players who represent their country in singles and doubles matches. The Indian Fed Cup team created history by progressing to the play-offs for the first time ever in March 2020, defeating Indonesia in the Asia–Oceania Group I event in Dubai, UAE, and finishing second behind China. They lost the world group play-off tie against Latvia. The team comprised Ankita Raina, Rutuja Bhosale, Zeel Desai, Karman Kaur Thandi and Sania Mirza.

Karman Kaur Thandi

Best women's singles result

Karman Kaur Thandi's singles title in the US $60,000 International Tennis Federation women's tournament in Saguenay, Canada, with a 3-6, 6-4, 6-3 victory over Katherine Sebov (Canada) in the final in October 2022 was a big breakthrough for Indian women's tennis. It was the biggest singles title for an Indian woman since Sania Mirza won the $75,000 tournament in Dubai, UAE, in 2010. The biggest title ever by an Indian woman was Mirza winning the US $140,000 Women's Tennis Association event in Hyderabad in 2005. The 24-year-old Karman became no. 1 in India with a rank of 217.

Somdev Devvarman

ASIAN GAMES

First gold – men – doubles

Leander Paes and Gaurav Natekar won the gold medal in the Hiroshima Asian Games, held in 1994 in Japan – making this the country's first doubles gold medal at the Asian Games. They won by defeating the South Korean duo of Chang Euijong and Kim Chi-wan.

First singles gold

Somdev Devvarman won the gold medal at the 2010 Guangzhou Asiad in China, defeating Denis Istomin of Uzbekistan 6–1, 6–2.

First gold medallist – doubles – mixed

India got its first mixed doubles gold at the Asian Games when the team, with Leander Paes and Sania Mirza, won the gold in the Doha Asian Games in Qatar in 2006. They defeated the Japanese pair of Satoshi Iwabuchi and Akiko Morigami 7–5, 5–7, 6–2.

DAVIS CUP

Most successful player – doubles

Leander Paes became the most successful doubles player in the history of the Davis Cup with a record 45th victory in March 2020, when he and his partner Rohan Bopanna won India's Davis Cup match against Croatia in the do-or-die round of the World Group Qualifiers.

First appearance

India played in the Davis Cup for the first time in 1921 against France in Paris and won 4–1. The Indian team comprised S.M. Jacob, Mohammed Sleem, A.A. Fyzee, and L.S. Dean.

Best Davis Cup record in Asia

Though India has not yet won the Davis Cup, they have managed to reach the finals three times (in 1966, 1974 and 1987). Japan is the only other Asian nation to have figured in the Davis Cup finals (once in 1921).

The total number of medals won by tennis players in major tournaments in India is 41.

Most appearances

Leander Paes holds the record of playing the most Davis Cup matches – 128 in 58 ties (as of March 2020). His win/loss records are 48/22 in singles and 45/13 in doubles.

Junior Davis Cup regional champs

The Indian under-16 team of Rushil Khosla, Bushan Haobam, and Debasis Sahoo under the captaincy of Sajid Lodi won the Asia-Oceania Junior Davis Cup title in Delhi, to make the World Group along with Japan and Australia in 2022. In the World group played in Turkey, India, represented by Rushil Khosla, Kriish Tyagi and Vansh Nandal, finished 14th among 16 countries.

GRAND SLAM TOURNAMENTS

WIMBLEDON

First to play at Wimbledon

Sardar Nihal Singh was the first Indian to play at Wimbledon in 1908. He lost in the first round to Briton Herbert Wilson Fox, who beat him 11–9, 6–2, 6–4.

First men's title – doubles

The dominant Indian tennis pair of Leander Paes and Mahesh Bhupathi, then popularly known as Lee-Hesh, won India's first men's doubles title at Wimbledon in 1999, defeating Paul Haarhuis (the Netherlands) and Jared Palmer (US) 6–7, 6–3, 6–4, 7–6.

First junior boys' title

Ramanathan Krishnan won the first junior boy's Wimbledon title in 1954, defeating Ashley Cooper of Australia 6–2, 7–5. Twenty-five years later,

Ramanathan's son Ramesh Krishnan won the same title in 1979, creating a unique father-and-son record. Both were recipients of the Padma Shri in 1962 and 1998 respectively. Ramanathan Krishnan was also awarded the Padma Bhushan in 1967.

First title – doubles – mixed

Leander Paes was the first Indian to win a mixed doubles title when he won it with Lisa Raymond (US) in 1999. They defeated the pair of Anna Kournikova (Russia) and Jonas Björkman (Sweden) 6–4, 3–6, 6–3. Paes was awarded the Padma Shri in 2001.

First seeded at Wimbledon

Dilip Bose was the first seeded Indian player, at no. 15, in Wimbledon singles in 1950. He was a product of the Calcutta South Club (now in Kolkata, West Bengal), one of Asia's oldest tennis clubs.

First junior girls' title – doubles

Sania Mirza and her Russian partner Alisa Kleybanova won the junior girls' doubles title in 2003.

First Indian woman at Wimbledon

Jenny Sandison was the first woman to represent India in tennis at Wimbledon, way back in 1929. However, she lost in the first round to French player Simone Barbier 2-6, 3-6.

FRENCH OPEN

First and only junior champion

Ramesh Krishnan won the juniors title in 1979, the first and only Indian to achieve this feat, and was ranked the world's no. 1 junior player. He became India's Davis Cup captain in 2007.

First all-Indian title – mixed doubles

Mahesh Bhupathi and Sania Mirza won India's first ever all-Indian mixed doubles title in 2012, defeating Klaudia Jans-Ignacik (Poland) and Santiago González (Mexico) 7–6 (7–3), 6–1.

First title – doubles – mixed

Mahesh Bhupathi and his Japanese partner Rika Hiraki won the French Open title in 1997, defeating the American team of Lisa Raymond and Patrick Galbraith 6–4, 6–1. With this Bhupathi became the first Indian to win a Senior Grand Slam title.

Mahesh Bhupathi

First all-Indian men's title – doubles

Leander Paes and Mahesh Bhupathi won India's first men's doubles title in 1999. The pair defeated Goran Ivanisevic (Croatia) and Jeff Tarango (US) 6–2, 7–5.

US OPEN

First title – doubles – women

Sania Mirza was the first Indian to win a women's doubles title in 2015 at the US Open in New York, with Swiss player Martina Hingis. The pair defeated Casey Dellacqua (Australia) and Yaroslava Shvedova (Kazakhstan) 6–3, 6–3.

First title – doubles

Mahesh Bhupathi and his partner Max Mirnyi of Belarus won the US Open doubles title in 2002, defeating the Czech pair of Jiri Novak and Radek Stepanek 6–3, 3–6, 6–4.

Yuki Bhambri

First title – doubles – mixed

Mahesh Bhupathi, with his Japanese partner Ai Sugiyama, won the mixed doubles US Open title in 1999, the first Indian to win a mixed doubles title here. The pair defeated Kimberly Po and Donald Johnson of the US 6–4, 6–4.

First junior boys' champion

Yuki Bhambri defeated Alexandros-Ferdinandos Georgoudas of Greece 6–3, 6–1 to win the Junior Boys' Championship in 2009.

First and only junior boys' title

Leander Paes is the first and only Indian to win the junior boy's crown at the US Open in 1991. He beat Karim Alami (Morocco).

AUSTRALIAN OPEN

First men's title – doubles

Leander Paes became the first Indian to win a men's doubles title at the Australian Open, along with Radek Stepanek (Czech Republic) in 2012. They defeated Bob Bryan and Mike Bryan of the US 7–6 (7–1), 6–2.

First title – doubles – mixed

Leander Paes, with Martina Navratilova of the US, won the mixed doubles title in 2003, becoming the first Indian to do so. They defeated Eleni Daniilidou (Greece) and Todd Woodbridge (Australia) 6–4, 7–5.

First all-Indian title – doubles – mixed

Mahesh Bhupathi and Sania Mirza won India's first all-Indian mixed doubles Australian Open title in 2009, defeating the pair of Nathalie Dechy (France) and Andy Ram (Israel) 6–3, 6–1.

ATP TOUR

First Indian to win 2 ATP Challengers singles titles in Europe

Sumit Nagal is the first Indian to win two ATP Challengers titles in Europe after he won the Tampere Open title in Finland in July 2023. He surpasses Somdev Devvarman, Rohan Bopanna and Harsh Mankad, who have won a title each. It was also his fourth ATP title overall and second of the season.

Rohan Bopanna

World's oldest player to win ATP Masters title — doubles

Rohan Bopanna at 43 became the oldest tennis player to win the ATP Masters 1000 title after he and Mathew Ebden won the Indian Wells in March 2023. Bopanna surpassed the record of Canada's Daniel Nestor, who won the Cincinnati Masters doubles title in 2015 at the age of 42.

First Indian to win ATP Challenger on European clay

Sumit Nagal became the first Indian to win ATP Challenger on European clay after winning the ATP Rome Challenger in April 2023. He defeated Jasper De Jong in the final 6-3, 6-2.

NATIONALS

First Nationals – grass court

The first tennis Nationals were held in 1946 at the Calcutta South Club lawns in Calcutta, West Bengal. Sumant Misra beat Manmohan Lal in the final, becoming the first national champion. Khanum Singh (née Haji) was the first women's national champion.

Most Nationals titles

Ramanathan Krishnan won eight grass-court titles in 1953, 1956, 1958 to 1960 and 1962 to 1964.

WEIGHTLIFTING

First medals in the World Championships

Kunjarani Devi from Manipur bagged three silvers at Manchester, UK, in 1989 in India's debut performance at the World Championships. The Indian squad won seven medals in all at the event. Shyamala Shetty and Chhaya Adak won silver medals for individual lifts, while Lalita Polley claimed two bronze medals.

First Olympic-qualifying gold

Saikhom Mirabai Chanu won the gold medal in the women's 49 kg category at the EGAT Cup International Weightlifting Championship, an Olympic-qualifying event in Chiang Mai, Thailand, on 7 February 2019. She lifted 82 kg in snatch and 110 kg in clean and jerk to total 192 kg, and took gold on her return to international competition after a nine-month lay-off due to an injury. She had won the gold medal on her last appearance in 2018 at the Gold Coast Commonwealth Games in Australia.

First Junior weightlifting gold

Harshada Sharad Garud became the first Indian boy or girl to win a World Junior Weightlifting Championship by lifting a total of 153 kg (clean and jerk 83 kg + snatch 70 kg).

First back-to-back gold medals

Khumukcham Sanjita Chanu made history for the second time when she bagged the gold medal in the women's 53 kg weightlifting event at the 2018 Commonwealth Games at Gold Coast, Australia. Her first gold was at the 2014 Commonwealth Games in the 48 kg category.

First silver medal at the Olympic Games

Saikhom Mirabai Chanu scripted a remarkable performance by winning a silver in the 2020 Olympic Games held in Tokyo, Japan, on day one. With an 87 kg lift in snatch and a 115 kg lift in the clean and jerk section, Chanu finished with a total of 202 kg.

First Asian Games medals – women

Women's weightlifting was introduced in the 1990 Beijing Asian Games in China, where India won two silvers: Bharati Singh (82 kg category) and Jyotsna Dutta (+82 kg); and two bronzes: Kunjarani Devi (44 kg) and Chhaya Adak (52 kg).

First Asian Games medal

Kamineni Eswara Rao won the silver in the 90 kg category in the 1951 Asian Games held in New Delhi. He was also adjudged the 'Strongest Man of India' at the 1954 Senior Nationals.

Women's Weightlifting

Women's weightlifting in India has experienced a remarkable journey of growth and success. With the emergence of talents like Karnam Malleswari, who won India's first Olympic medal in weightlifting with a bronze at the 2000 Sydney Olympics, the sport gained national attention. Subsequently, athletes like Mirabai Chanu have continued to shine on the global stage, clinching medals at international events including the World Weightlifting Championships and the Commonwealth Games. The Indian women weightlifters have defied stereotypes and challenges, showcasing their strength and determination. Their achievements have not only bolstered the sport's popularity in the country but also motivated aspiring athletes, particularly women, to pursue weightlifting as a competitive endeavour.

Saikhom Mirabai Chanu

Most medals in the Commonwealth Games – women

Yumnam Renu Bala Chanu has won two golds in the Commonwealth Games. Her first came in the women's 58 kg category in Melbourne in 2006. She repeated this in the 2010 Delhi Commonwealth Games in the same category.

Yumnam Renu Bala Chanu

First gold in the Commonwealth Games – men

E. Karunakaran won gold in the flyweight class in the 1978 Edmonton Games in Canada.

First gold medal at the Youth Olympic Games

Jeremy Lalrinnunga became the first Indian to win a gold medal at the Youth Olympic Games 2018 held in Buenos Aires, Argentina.

WR Clean and jerk at the Asian Weightlifting Championships

Saikhom Mirabai Chanu set a new world record in the women's 49 kg clean and jerk with a lift of 119 kg on 17 April 2022 at the Asian Weightlifting Championships in Tashkent, Uzbekistan.

Most medals in the Commonwealth Games

India won five gold, two silver, and two bronze medals at the 2018 Gold Coast Commonwealth Games, Australia, the most at the Commonwealth Games in weightlifting. Saikhom Mirabai Chanu made a record-breaking performance in the clean and jerk event in the 48 kg category. Khumukcham Sanjita Chanu (53 kg) set a Commonwealth Games record in snatch, and Punam Yadav won a gold in the 69 kg category. In the men's section, Sathish Sivalingam (77 kg) and Ragala Venkat Rahul (85 kg) won gold medals too. P. Gururaja (56 kg) and Pradeep Singh (105 kg) won silvers, and Vikas Thakur (94 kg) and Deepak Lather (69 kg) won bronzes.

Best performance at an Asian meet

India's weightlifters bagged five gold medals and a bronze at Busan, South Korea, in July 1995. Karnam Malleswari won three gold medals, and Kunjarani Devi claimed two gold medals and the overall title. Arun Murugesan won a bronze in snatch in the 54 kg category for men.

Most medals in world and Asian meets

Kunjarani Devi, who holds the record for the highest number of world and Asian meet medals, won 55 medals overall – 21 in six World Championships and the remaining in the Asian Games, and the Asian and Commonwealth Championships.

Most National titles

Balbir Singh Bhatia won 15 National and all-India titles.

Most gold medals in World Championships

Karnam Malleswari won the gold in the World Championships twice – in 1994 (Istanbul, Turkey) and 1995 (Guangzhou, China).

Oldest national champion

Alok Nath Ghosh won the National Championship title in 1974 at 40 years. He had won the first national title in 1958 in Cuttack, Odisha. His first title was for Services and the last one was for the Railways.

Youngest Commonwealth Games medal winner

Eighteen-year-old Deepak Lather (69 kg) from Haryana became the youngest Indian weightlifter to win a medal at the 2018 Commonwealth Games in Glasgow, UK, by clinching a bronze medal.

Youngest National champion

P.K. Mahanand from Hyderabad won the All-India Championship at Calcutta (now Kolkata), West Bengal, in 1955 at the age of eighteen.

WRESTLING

First at the Olympics

U. Zaw Weik (75 kg), the first to represent India at the Olympics, was placed 15th in the 1936 Olympics in Berlin, Germany.

First Olympics medal – men

Khashaba Dadasaheb Jadhav from Satara, Maharashtra, won a bronze in the bantam- weight category (57 kg) in the 1952 Helsinki Olympics.

First winner of both Olympic and World Championship medals

Sushil Kumar is the first Indian to win medals at both the Olympics and the World Championships. He won a bronze at the 2008 Beijing Olympics in the 66 kg freestyle category and a silver medal in the same category at the 2012 London Olympics. He also won a gold in the same category at the Moscow World Championship in Russia in 2010.

First Olympic medal – women

Sakshi Malik created history as the first Indian woman to win an Olympic medal, a bronze, for wrestling, in the women's freestyle 58 kg category in the Rio Olympics in Brazil on 17 August 2016.

First woman at the Olympics

Geeta Phogat from Bhiwani, Haryana, was the first Indian woman wrestler to compete at the Olympics during the 2012 London Games. However, she did not advance to the quarter- finals.

Geeta Phogat

First medal at the World Championship – men

India's first medal in the World Championship was a bronze in the freestyle category (67 kg) won by Udey Chand from Hisar, Haryana, in the 1961 World Championships at Yokohama, Japan. He participated in three Olympics: at Rome, Italy, in 1960; at Tokyo, Japan, in 1964; and at Mexico City, Mexico, in 1968.

Antim Panghal

First to win gold in U-20 World Championships – women

Antim Panghal became the first to win gold in the U-20 World Championships on 10 September 2022 in Sofia, Bulgaria.

First woman triple winner – World Championships, Asian Games and Commonwealth Games

Vinesh Phogat became the first Indian woman to win medals at the World Championships, Asian Games and Commonwealth Games. While she won bronze at the 2019 World Championships in the 53 kg freestyle and a bronze at the 2014 Incheon Asian Games in the 48 kg category, she was also the first Indian woman to win a gold medal in the 2018 Asian Games in Jakarta and Palembang, Indonesia, in the 50 kg category. She won three consecutive Commonwealth crowns at Glasglow, UK, in 2014, Gold Coast, Australia, in 2018 and Birmingham, UK, in 2022.

First medal at the World Championships – women

Alka Tomar of the Noida College of Physical Education won a bronze in the women's 59 kg class at the Senior World Wrestling Championship in Guangzhou, China, during September–October 2006. She was the first Indian woman wrestler to win a World Championship medal after a gap of 39 years.

First World Championship gold medallist

Sushil Kumar from Delhi was the first Indian to win a World Championship gold medal in the 66 kg freestyle category in Moscow, Russia, in 2010.

First medal in the Commonwealth Games

- Rashid Anwar won a bronze medal at the 1934 Commonwealth Games held in London, UK, in the 74 kg category. This was the country's first medal won in the Commonwealth Games.

- Lila Ram won the first gold medal in the 1958 Games at Cardiff, Wales, in the heavyweight (100 kg) category.

India has won a total of **423** medals for wrestling in all major tournaments so far.

First and only Indian woman wrestler to win the Laureus World Sports Award

Vinesh Phogat is the first and only Indian wrestler to be awarded the Laureus World Sports Award 2019 in the comeback-of-the-year category. Phogat not only returned from her injury but also won the gold medal in both the 2018 Commonwealth Games at Gold Coast, Australia, and the 2018 Asian Games in Jakarta and Palembang, Indonesia.

First medal in the Asian Games

Vinesh Phogat, competing in the 50 kg freestyle category, bagged India its first gold medal in wrestling in the Asian Games in 2018 in Jakarta, Indonesia. She is the first Indian woman to win a gold medal in wrestling and to win back-to-back Asian Games medals, having won a bronze in 48 kg in Incheon, South Korea, in 2014.

First Asian Games gold – men

Gold medals were won by Maruti Mane in 90 kg freestyle, Malwa Singh in 52 kg Greco-Roman and Ganpat Andalkar in 100 kg Greco-Roman, section at the 1962 Asian Games in Jakarta, Indonesia.

First Asian Championships gold medal – women

Navjot Kaur from Punjab became the first Indian woman to win the gold at the Senior Asian Wrestling Championships on 2 March 2018 at Bishkek, Kyrgyzstan. She beat Japan's Miya Imai 9–1 to win in the women's 65 kg category.

First Coach of the Year award

Late Yashvir Singh was the first Indian coach to be recognized as the Coach of the Year in 2010 by the Federation Internationale des Luttes Associées (FILA), the then apex body that governed wrestling.

First Junior World Champion

- The first gold medallists at the Junior World Championship were Ramesh Kumar (69 kg) and Palwinder Singh Cheema (130 kg) in 2001.
- Deepak Punia became India's junior world champion after 18 years, winning the gold medal at Tallinn, Estonia, on 14 August 2019. He defeated Russia's Alik Shebzukov in the 86 kg men's freestyle category.

First Junior Wrestler of the Year award

Deepak Punia (86 kg freestyle) became the first Indian wrestler to receive the Junior Wrestler of the Year title in 2019 from the United World Wrestling.

First Indian couple to win silver medals

Sakshi Malik (65 kg) and Satyawart Kadian (97 kg) became the first Indian wrestler couple to win silver medals in the 2020 Asian Championships in New Delhi.

Back-to-back World Championship medals

Sajan Bhanwal became the first Indian to win back-to-back medals in the World Championship in the 77 kg category in the Greco-Roman style. He won a silver on 20 August 2019 in Trnava, Slovakia, and a bronze at the Tampere World Championship, Finland, in 2017.

First medals in Greco-Roman Championships – Under-17

- Vinod Kumar (1980) and Pappu Yadav (1990) bagged the U-17 world title.
- Suraj Vashisht (55 kg) won it again after 32 years in July 2022 in Rome.

First gold medal in the Asian Games

The first Indian to win a gold medal in the Asian Games was Kartar Singh in the 1986 Seoul Asiad in South Korea in the 100 kg category.

Best performance in the Asian Championship

India won a record haul of 20 medals (five gold, six silver and nine bronze) across formats and genders in the 2020 Asian Championship. The gold medallists were: Sunil Kumar (87 kg Greco-Roman [GR]); Pinki (55 kg women's freestyle [WFS]); Sarita Mor (59 kg WFS); Divya Kakran (68 kg WFS); and Ravi K. Dahiya (57 kg men's freestyle [MFS]). The silver medals were won by Nirmala Devi (50 kg WFS); Sakshi Malik (65 kg WFS); Bajrang Punia (65 kg MFS); Gourav Baliyan (79 kg MFS); Satyawart Kadian (97 kg MFS); and Jitender (74 kg MFS). The bronze went to Arjun Halakurki (57 kg GR); Ashu (67 kg GR); Aditya Kundu (72 kg GR); Hardeep (97 kg GR); Vinesh Phogat (53 kg WFS);Anshu Malik (67 kg WFS); Gursharan Preet Kaur (72 kg WFS); Rahul Aware (61 kg MFS); and Deepak Punia (86 kg MFS).

Anshu Malik

First Indian woman to win a silver medal at the World Championship

Anshu Malik (57 kg) became the first Indian female wrestler to win a silver medal at the 2021 World Championship in Oslo, Norway.

First gold in Greco-Roman wrestling

- Pappu Yadav was the first grappler to win a gold medal in the 48 kg Greco-Roman category at the 1993 Asian Wrestling Championships held in Ulaanbaatar, Mongolia.
- On 19 February 2020, Sunil Kumar (87 kg) won a gold in Greco-Roman wrestling in the Asian Championships, which came 27 years after the first gold in 1993.

Best performance at the Commonwealth Games – men

At the Commonwealth Games in 2010 in Delhi, the Indian men's team won seven gold, three silver and three bronze medals in freestyle and the Greco-Roman style. The gold medals were won by Yogeshwar Dutt (60 kg), Sushil Kumar (66 kg), and Narsingh Panch Yadav (74 kg), all in freestyle wrestling; and Rajender Kumar (55 kg), Ravinder Singh (60 kg), Sanjay Kumar (74 kg), and Anil Kumar (96 kg), all in Greco-Roman wrestling. The silver medals were won by Anuj Kumar (84 kg) and Joginder Kumar (120 kg) in freestyle, and Manoj Kumar (84 kg) in the Greco-Roman style. The bronze medals were bagged by Anil Kumar (55 kg in freestyle); and Sunil Kumar (66 kg) and Dharmender Dalal (120 kg), both in the Greco-Roman style.

Ranked as world no. 1

In March 2021, the UWW announced Bajrang Punia (65 kg) and Vinesh Phogat (53 kg) as top-ranked wrestlers.

Vinesh Phogat (*left*) and Bajrang Punia (*right*)

Best performance in the Greco-Roman event of the Asian Championships

India's best performance in the Greco-Roman category was at the 2020 Asian Championships in New Delhi where Indian grapplers won one gold and four bronze medals. Sunil Kumar (87 kg) won the gold medal while Arjun Halakurki (55 kg), Ashu (67 kg), Aditya Kundu (72 kg), and Hardeep (97 kg) won the bronzes.

Most consecutive Commonwealth Games titles – women

Vinesh Phogat became the first to win three consecutive Commonwealth Games crowns at Glasgow, UK, in 2014; Gold Coast, Australia, in 2018; and Birmingham, UK, in 2022.

Best performance at the World Championship

India has a record haul of five medals at the 2019 World Championship held at Nur-Sultan, Kazakhstan. Deepak Punia won a silver in the 86 kg category. Bronze medals were won by Bajrang Punia (65 kg), Rahul Aware (61 kg), Ravi Dahiya (61 kg) and Vinesh Phogat (women, 53 kg).

Best performance in the Commonwealth Games – women

Women's wrestling was introduced in the 2010 Delhi Commonwealth Games, where India bagged three gold medals, two silver medals and one bronze medal in freestyle. Geeta Phogat (55 kg), Alka Tomar (59 kg) and Anita Sheoran (67 kg) won gold medals. The silver medals were won by Nirmala Devi (48 kg) and Babita Phogat (51 kg). Suman Kundu (63 kg) won the bronze medal.

Most medals in the Asian Games – men

Kartar Singh won the gold at Bangkok, Thailand, in 1978, a silver in 1982 at Delhi, and another gold at the 1986 Seoul Asian Games in South Korea. He competed in the 90 kg category in 1978 and 1982, and in 100 kg in 1986 (all in freestyle).

Most gold medals in the Asian Championship

Sushil Kumar won the title in 2003, 2008, and 2010. Thereafter Ravi Kumar Dahiya won triple gold in Asian Championship titles in 2020, 2021, and 2022.

Most medals in the Commonwealth Championships

The Indian contingent, with 42 wrestlers, bagged 40 medals – 15 gold, 20 silver and 5 bronze – in the 2011 Commonwealth Championships in Melbourne, Australia.

Most medals in the Asian Championship

Between 2013 and 2022, Bajrang Punia won a record eight medals in the 60 kg to 65 kg categories. He won bronze in 60 kg (2013, New Delhi), silver in 61 kg (2014, Astana, Kazakhstan), gold in 65 kg (2017, New Delhi), bronze in 65 kg (2018, Bishkek, Kyrgyzstan), gold in 65 kg (2019, Xian, China), and silver in 65 kg (2020, New Delhi; 2021, Almaty, Kazakhstan; 2022, Ulaanbaatar, Mongolia).

Most gold medals in the Commonwealth Games – men

Sushil Kumar of the Indian Railways and an alumnus of the Noida College of Physical Education, Noida, Uttar Pradesh, won India's first ever men's triple gold in the Commonwealth Games (2010, Delhi; 2014, Glasgow, UK; and 2018, Gold Coast, Australia).

Most individual medals in the World Championship

Bajrang Punia won the World Championship medal three times between 2013 and 2019. He won the bronze medal in the 60 kg category in 2013, a silver in the 65 kg category in 2018, and a bronze in 2019.

Most medals at the Asian Girls Championship (U-15)

Indian girl wrestlers won seven medals in the Asian Girls Championships (U-15) in November 2018 in Fujimi, Japan. The gold medallists were: Pooja Rani (33 kg), Komal (36 Kg), and Sweety (43 kg). Silver medals were won by Pinki (39 kg), Antim Panghal (46 kg), and Bhagyashree Fand (58 kg). Pratibha Janghu (54 kg) won the bronze.

Youngest champion in the Asian Games

Malwa Singh won the gold medal in the Greco-Roman style in the light flyweight category at the 1962 Asian Games in Jakarta, Indonesia, at the age of 14 years, thus creating history by becoming the youngest wrestling champion from India.

Youngest gold medallist at the Commonwealth Games

Ved Prakash was 14 years old when he won the gold medal in the light flyweight class at the 1970 Commonwealth Games in Edinburgh, UK.

Most individual medals in the Commonwealth Championships – men

Sushil Kumar won the title five times between 2003 and 2017. He won the gold medal in 2003 (London, UK), 2005 (Cape Town, South Africa), 2007 (London, UK), 2009 (Jalandhar, India), and 2017 (Johannesburg, South Africa).

Sushil Kumar

ASIAN GAMES 2022

India's Medal History at the Asian Games

Edition	Gold	Silver	Bronze	Total medals	Rank
New Delhi 1951	15	16	20	51	2
Manila 1954	5	4	8	17	5
Tokyo 1958	5	4	4	13	7
Jakarta 1962	10	13	10	33	3
Bangkok 1966	7	3	11	21	5
Bangkok 1970	6	9	10	25	5
Tehran 1974	4	12	12	28	7
Bangkok 1978	11	11	6	28	6
New Delhi 1982	13	19	25	57	5
Seoul 1986	5	9	23	37	5
Beijing 1990	1	8	14	23	11
Hiroshima 1994	4	3	16	23	8
Bangkok 1998	7	11	17	35	9
Busan 2002	11	12	13	36	7
Doha 2006	10	17	26	53	8
Guangzhou 2010	14	17	34	65	6
Incheon 2014	11	10	36	57	8
Jakarta 2018	16	23	31	70	8
Hangzhou 2022	28	38	41	107	4
Total	183	239	357	779	5

India's Asian Games 2022 medals tally

Sport	Gold	Silver	Bronze	Total
Shooting	7	9	6	22
Athletics	6	14	9	29
Archery	5	2	2	9
Squash	2	1	2	5
Cricket	2	0	0	2
Kabaddi	2	0	0	2
Badminton	1	1	1	3
Tennis	1	1	0	2
Equestrian	1	0	1	2
Hockey	1	0	1	2
Rowing	0	2	3	5
Chess	0	2	0	2
Wrestling	0	1	5	6
Boxing	0	1	4	5
Sailing	0	1	2	3
Bridge	0	1	0	1
Golf	0	1	0	1
Wushu	0	1	0	1
Roller skating	0	0	2	2
Canoe	0	0	1	1
Sepaktakraw	0	0	1	1
Table tennis	0	0	1	1
TOTAL	28	38	41	107

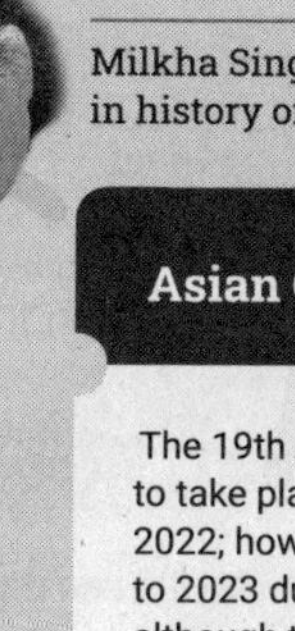

Milkha Singh won most individual gold medals in history of the Asian Games.

Asian Games 2022 Huangzhou

The 19th Asian Games were all scheduled to take place from 10 to 25 September 2022; however, they had to be postponed to 2023 due to Covid-19 pandemic. Hence, although the games were held in 2023, they are still known as the 2022 Asian Games.

Esha Singh

Best-ever gold medal show

India's gold medal haul of 28 medals at Asian Games 2022 is their best-ever gold medal haul and surpasses their previous best of 16 medals in 2018.

Most medals won by an athlete

Shooter Esha Singh was the most successful athlete in terms of medals won at the Asian Games 2023 with a gold and three silver medals. The 18-year-old pistol shooter won women's 25 m pistol team event and also won silver medals in 25 m air pistol (individual), 10 m air pistol (individual), and 10 m air pistol (team).

First 100-medal haul

India crossed the 100-medal mark for the first time in 2022 Asian Games. Women's Kabaddi gold was the 100th medal as the national Kabbadi team defeated Chinese Taipei in the final.

Youngest medallist at Asian Games 2022

Roller-skater Sanjana Bathula (b. 21 June 2008) and Squash player Anahat Singh (b. 13 March 2008) is the youngest Indian medallist at the Asian Games 2022. Anahat won a two bronze in women's team and mixed doubles.

Oldest medallist at Asian Games 2022

Jaggy Shivdasani (b. 1958) won the silver medal with the bridge men's team event and became the oldest Indian to win a medal at Asian Games 2022.

Most gold medals at Asian Games 2022

Compound archers Ojas Deotale and Jyothi Surekha, who won the mixed team gold medal together, were the most successful Indian athletes at Asian Games 2022 with three gold medals each. The other events they won gold medals in were men's individual, men's team, women's team, and mixed team.

Avinash Sable

First Athletics Medal at Asian Games 2022

Shot putter Kiran Baliyan won India's first athletics medal at the Asian Games 2022. Her bronze medal in the field event was also India's first shot put medal since the inaugural 1951 Asian Games, where Barbara Webster won a bronze medal as well.

Most medals won by a discipline

Indian track and field athletes won 29 medals, the most by any discipline at the Asian Games 2022.

First Indian sprint hurdler to win a medal

Jyothi Yarraji became the first Indian 100 m hurdler to win a medal at the Asian Games. The national record holder took the silver medal with a timing of 12 minutes and 91 seconds.

Dipika Pallikal

First men's doubles gold

Satwiksairaj Rankireddy and Chirag Shetty became the first Indian pair to win a gold medal in men's doubles at the Asian Games.

First women's doubles medal

Ayhika Mukherjee and Sutirtha Mukherjee became the first Indian women's doubles pair to win a medal at the Asian Games 2022. The duo won the bronze medal with a historic win over Chinese pair of Chen Meng and Wang Yidi, World No. 2 and 4 respectively.

First pair to win mixed doubles gold medal

Dipika Pallikal and Harinderpal Singh Sandhu became the first pair to win mixed doubles gold medal at the Asian Games 2022 after the format was introduced for the first time in the history of the Games.

First team to complete hat-trick of gold medals

Indian women's kabaddi team became the first team to win the gold medals thrice in their discipline at the Asian Games after defeating Chinese Taipei in the final. The national team previously won gold medals in 2010 and 2014 after women's kabaddi was introduced in 2010 edition.

Neeraj Chopra

Best medal haul in archery

Indian archers returned with a haul of nine medals, which was their best-ever show at the Asiad. India's previous best medal haul was three medals at 2014 Incheon.

First 1-2 finish in Men's Javelin throw

Neeraj Chopra and Kishore Kumar Jena finished at the top of the podium in men's javelin throw, making for India's first-ever 1-2 finish in the event. Neeraj also defended his 2018 title, when he became the first Indian javelin thrower to win gold medal at Asian Games.

Asian Games 2022–India's medal winners

No.	Athletes	Sport	Event	Medal
1	Team India	Shooting	Women's 10 m air rifle team	Silver
2	Team India	Rowing	Men's lightweight double sculls	Silver
3	Team India	Rowing	Men's pair	Bronze
4	Team India	Rowing	Men's eight	Silver
5	Ramita Jindal	Shooting	Women's 10 m air rifle	Bronze
6	Team India	Shooting	Men's 10 m air rifle team	Gold
7	Team India	Rowing	Men's four	Bronze
8	Team India	Rowing	Men's quadruple	Bronze
9	Aishwary Pratap Singh Tomar	Shooting	Men's 10 m air rifle	Bronze
10	Team India	Shooting	Men's 25 m rapid file pistol team	Bronze
11	Team India	Cricket	Women's T20 cricket	Gold
12	Neha Thakur	Sailing	Girl's Dinghy - ILCA4	Silver
13	Eabad Ali	Sailing	Men's Windsurfer - RS:X	Bronze
14	Team India	Equestrian	Team dressage	Gold
15	Team India	Shooting	Women's 50 m rifle 3 positions team	Silver
16	Team India	Shooting	Women's 25 m pistol team	Gold
17	Sift Kaur Samra	Shooting	Women's 50m rifle 3 positions	Gold
18	Ashi Chouksey	Shooting	Women's 50 m rifle 3 positions	Bronze
19	Team India	Shooting	Men's skeet team	Bronze
20	Vishnu Saravanan	Sailing	Men's dinghy ICLA7	Bronze
21	Esha Singh	Shooting	Women's 25 m pistol	Silver
22	Anantjeet Singh Naruka	Shooting	Men's skeet	Silver
23	Naorem Roshibina Devi	Wushu	Women's 60 kg sanda	Silver
24	Team India	Shooting	Men's 10 m air pistol team	Gold
25	Anush Agarwalla	Equestrian	Individual dressage	Bronze
26	Team India	Shooting	Women's 10 m air pistol team	Silver
27	Team India	Shooting	Men's 50 m rifle 3 positions team	Gold
28	Team India	Tennis	Men's doubles	Silver
29	Esha Singh	Shooting	Women's 10 m air pistol	Silver
30	Palak Gulia	Shooting	Women's 10 m air pistol	Gold
31	Team India	Squash	Women's team	Bronze
32	Aishwary Pratap Singh Tomar	Shooting	Men's 50 m rifle 3 positions	Silver

No.	Athletes	Sport	Event	Medal
33	Kiran Baliyan	Athletics	Women's shot put	Bronze
34	Team India	Shooting	Mixed team 10 m air pistol	Silver
35	Team India	Tennis	Mixed doubles	Gold
36	Team India	Squash	Men's team	Gold
37	Karthik Kumar	Athletics	Men's 10,000 m	Silver
38	Gulveer Singh	Athletics	Men's 10,000 m	Bronze
39	Aditi Ashok	Golf	Women's golf	Silver
40	Team India	Shooting	Women's trap team	Silver
41	Team India	Shooting	Men's trap team	Gold
42	Kynan Chenai	Shooting	Men's trap	Bronze
43	Nikhat Zareen	Boxing	Women's 50kg	Bronze
44	Avinash Sable	Athletics	Men's 3000m steeplechase	Gold
45	Tajinderpal Singh Toor	Athletics	Men's shot put	Gold
46	Harmilan Bains	Athletics	Women's 1500m	Silver
47	Ajay Kumar Saroj	Athletics	Men's 1500m	Silver
48	Jinson Johnson	Athletics	Men's 1500m	Bronze
49	Nandini Agasara	Athletics	Women's heptathlon	Bronze
50	Murali Sreeshankar	Athletics	Men's long jump	Silver
51	Seema Punia	Athletics	Women's discus throw	Bronze
52	Jyothi Yarraji	Athletics	Women's 100m hurdles	Silver
53	Team India	Badminton	Men's team	Silver
54	Team India	Roller skating	Women's speed skating 3000m relay	Bronze
55	Team India	Roller skating	Men's speed skating 3000m relay	Bronze
56	Team India	Table tennis	Women's doubles	Bronze
57	Parul Chaudhary	Athletics	Women's 3000m steeplechase	Silver
58	Priti Lamba	Athletics	Women's 3000m steeplechase	Bronze
59	Ancy Sojan	Athletics	Women's long jump	Silver
60	Team India	Athletics	Mixed 4x400m relay	Silver
61	Team India	Canoe Sprint	Men's canoe double 1000m	Bronze
62	Preeti Pawar	Boxing	Women's 54kg	Bronze
63	Vithya Ramraj	Athletics	Women's 400m hurdles	Bronze
64	Parul Chaudhary	Athletics	Women's 5000m	Gold
65	Mohammed Afsal	Athletics	Men's 800m	Silver
66	Praveen Chithravel	Athletics	Men's triple jump	Bronze
67	Tejaswin Shankar	Athletics	Men's decathlon	Silver
68	Annu Rani	Athletics	Women's javelin throw	Gold
69	Narender Berwal	Boxing	Men's +92kg	Bronze
70	Team India	Athletics	Mixed team race walk	Bronze

No.	Athletes	Sport	Event	Medal
71	Team India	Archery	Mixed team compound	Gold
72	Team India	Squash	Mixed team	Bronze
73	Parveen Hooda	Boxing	Women's 57kg	Bronze
74	Lovlina Borgohain	Boxing	Women's 75kg	Silver
75	Sunil Kumar	Wrestling	Greco-Roman 87kg	Bronze
76	Harmilan Bains	Athletics	Women's 800m	Silver
77	Avinash Sable	Athletics	Men's 5000m	Silver
78	Team India	Athletics	Women's 4x400m relay	Silver
79	Neeraj Chopra	Athletics	Men's javelin throw	Gold
80	Kishore Jena	Athletics	Men's javelin throw	Silver
81	Team India	Athletics	Men's 4x400m relay	Gold
82	Team India	Archery	Women's compound team	Gold
83	Team India	Squash	Mixed doubles	Gold
84	Team India	Archery	Men's compound team	Gold
85	Saurav Ghosal	Squash	Men's singles	Silver
86	Antim Panghal	Wrestling	Women's 53kg	Bronze
87	Team India	Archery	Women's recurve team	Bronze
88	HS Prannoy	Badminton	Men's singles	Bronze
89	Team India	Sepaktakraw	Women's regu	Bronze
90	Team India	Archery	Men's recurve team	Silver
91	Sonam Malik	Wrestling	Women's 62kg	Bronze
92	Kiran Bishnoi	Wrestling	Women's 76kg	Bronze
93	Aman Sehrawat	Wrestling	Men's freestyle 57kg	Bronze
94	Team India	Bridge	Men's team	Silver
95	Team India	Hockey	Men's team	Gold
96	Aditi Swami	Archery	Women's compound individual	Bronze
97	Jyothi Surekha Vennam	Archery	Women's compound individual	Gold
98	Ojas Pravin Deotale	Archery	Men's compound individual	Gold
99	Abhishek Verma	Archery	Men's compound individual	Silver
100	Team India	Kabaddi	Women's kabaddi	Gold
101	Team India	Badminton	Men's doubles	Gold
102	Team India	Cricket	Men's team	Gold
103	Team India	Kabaddi	Men's kabaddi	Gold
104	Team India	Hockey	Women's team	Bronze
105	Deepak Punia	Wrestling	Men's freestyle 86kg	Silver
106	Team India	Chess	Men's team	Silver
107	Team India	Chess	Women's team	Silver

A

Aadhaar, state/UT with highest coverage, state/UT with least coverage 241

Académie des Beaux – Arts Photography Awards – William Klein, first winner 167

academy, first for visual arts 170, first radio jockey training, first defence 112

actor, first woman stunt, highest-earning, oldest debut, most pairings 158

Acts, a timeline that shaped modern India 224

Aditya L1 320

administration, early 222

admiral, first four-star 274

advertising, **agency**, first full-service Indian, first multinational 425, first abroad 426; **association**, first 425; **advertisement**, first known 424, first on colour TV, first on radio, first on TV, longest sustained campaign 426

Aero India, aero show 430

aeronautical society, first 377

affiliation, first tri-services 265

agency, first rating 409

agriculture, first theme park 82, first society 83, first university, first research institute 84

agri-plane, first 100

AIIMS, a hub of medical firsts 328

air, crash of the Princess 376, first taxi 378

AIRAWAT, among top 500 314

aircraft, first designer 376, first indigenous, first Boeing 737-900 378; **airfield**, first 376, highest 380; **airline**, first 376, largest passenger 382, first Boeing 787 Dream liner 380, first, first supersonic, first indigenous (trainer), first indigenous light combat 288, first indigenous fighter, first indigenous AEW&C class of 289, oldest fleet 380

air force, first forward surgical centre 291, first S-400 defence system 290, first technical officer 285

air freight, first service 377, most traffic 380

airmail, first letter by 209, first 212

airlift, first of Indian troops, biggest rapid 291

airport, first to install a body scanner, first to install waste recycling machines, highest commercial, largest passenger terminal 379, first fully solar-powered 380; **club**, first flying 377

algebra, invention of 296

algorithm, first to invent new and speedy 314

alliance, first Indo-European 222

alumni association, first college 109

ammunition, first indigenous 278

amphitheatre, oldest medieval 59

amusement park, first 73, first indoor 73, first marine 74, first water 75

anaesthetist, first woman 335

Anand, **Viswanathan**, 465, 495, 496, 497, 499, 500, 502, 503

Anganwadi centres 238

Antarctic, first expedition 309, first women 310

anther culture, first 310

anthology, earliest known 178

apes, only 350

app, first Aadhaar-based payment 219, first related to health launched by defence service 291

aquarium, largest underground 80
arch, only natural 63
archaeological site, first green 373
archery, first international gold 469, youngest world champion 471, Aditi Gopichand breaks U-18 record 472; **Asian Championship**, most medals, first medal (men) 468, hat-trick of bronze medals 469; **Asian Para Games**, first gold 468; **Commonwealth Games**, most medals won 469, first compound para medal, first compound team (women) ranked no.1, first to win back-to-back, 468; **Internationals**, First gold, first gold (women), first medal (individual), 469; **Olympics**, first representation (men) 469, first representation (women) 470 only couple to represent India 471; **Paralympics**, first ever medal, first armless archer to reach final, world record in women's team, first world para championships gold 472; **World Championships**, first junior title (men) 469, first medal, most medals 470; **World Cup**, first compound title (men) (individual), first team gold (women) 469, first compound title (men) (team), most medals 470, most gold medals won (individual), two medals in stage 3, first gold medal 471, three gold medals, three individual gold 472; **Youth Olympics**, first silver 470; **Youth World Champion**, first Indian to win in recurve - men 472
architect, first 52
Arihant-class submarines 276
arithmetic, first textbook on 297
armament checker, first administrative unit 265, first special operations division, first and oldest extant 266
armoured personnel, first indigenous 267
army, **Ashok Chakra**, first 264; **Padma Bhushan**, first republic day commander and first to receive 264; **UN Military Gender Advocate award**, first Indian Peacekeeper to win the UN Military Gender Advocate award 264; **George Cross**, first 264; **Param Vir Chakra**, first (Army) 264
art, first summit, first modern school, first fine arts exhibition 169, first bank 170, highest price for an Indian piece at an auction 171; **competition**, largest (multiple venues) 171; **sand**, tallest castle 175; **district**, first public 172; **festival**, largest 133
artillery, first company, first unit 264, first administrative unit 265, lightest towed artillery 267
ash gourd, longest 92
Ashva Dvar 258
Asian Games, India's best performance 467
Asian Games 2022, India's medal history at, India's medal tally, Asian Games 2022 Huangzhou 581; best ever gold medal show, first 100 medal haul, youngest medallist at, most medals won by a discipline, most won by an athlete, oldest medallist at, most gold medals at, first athletics medals at 582,

first men's doubles gold, first women's doubles, first Indian sprint hurdler to win a medal, first pair to win mixed doubles gold, first team to complete hat-trick in gold medals, best medal haul in archery, first one-two finish in men's javelin throw 583, India's medal winners 584
Asian Para Games, India's first clean sweep 466, best performance 467
association, earliest public 401, first industrial 402
asteroid, discovery of 301
Asthana Nartaki, only 133
astrolabe, earliest extant, first manual on 298
astronomy, two firsts in 298, first university to teach 300; **observatory**, first 299, first chain 298, highest 299, highest 300; **society of India**, first woman president 301
athletics, **Asian Athletics Championships**, best performance, joint-highest medal tally, first to win gold - women, triple excellence in shot put, 473; **Asian Games**, first double gold, first medal (women) 473, first gold (men) (individual), first gold (women) (individual), first gold (women) (team), first to win three successive gold medals, most individual golds, only gold in marathon 474; **Asian Indoor Championships**, biggest point-haul in pentathlon – women, 473; **Asian Youth Athletics Championships**, best performances, 475; **career**, longest (men), longest (women), 474; **Commonwealth Games**, first title in fencing, first gold (women), first individual gold medal in discus throw (men), first medal (women), first medal in javelin throw (women), first medal in racewalk (women), first to win gold medal in triple jump 475, best performance, first medal in high jump, Gold medal in Commonwealth and Asian Games 476; **International**, first Indian to be elected into the IAAF council, first individual gold in track events in World U-20 championship, first medal in a marathon (women) 476, Diamond League, first clean sweep in a meet, first Indian to win gold in World U-20 championship, first win in IAAF continental cup, first to receive veteran pin by the IAAF, first world U-20 Athletics Championships twin medals 478; **marathoner**, most appearances 478, oldest gold medallist 473; **Nationals**, fastest 100 m hurdle, highest pole vault 481, fastest race walk, oldest gold medallist, longest triple jump - women, youngest athletics champion 482; **Olympics**, best performances, first marathoner, first woman captain, first women in 479; **para athlete**, best javelin throw (men), first gold (women), first IAS officer to win a silver medal, first to get Rajiv Gandhi Khel Ratna Award (woman) 481; **Paralympics**, best discus throw (men), first gold - women 481, First gold in javelin, first

participation in, first triple medal, 480; **World Athletics**, first gold 479; **World Championships**, first medal 479; **World Para athletic championship**, best performance 481, first bronze medal 480, **World Universiade**, first gold 479

ATM, first floating, first on wheels 406, state/UT with the most 407

atomistic, earliest theory 301

auditorium, largest 75

auto, first CNG 393

automated teller machine, first facility 405

automotive, largest company 395

awards, most national won (*see under each sport*) 467

A-web, update 228

B

baby, heaviest at birth, lightest 325

badminton, **Asian Championship**, first bronze medal (singles) (men), first gold, first medal (doubles) (men), first medal (doubles) (mixed), first medal (doubles) (women, first medal (singles) (women), first silver medal (doubles) (men) 486; **Asian Games**, first individual medal (men), first individual medal (woman), first medal (men) (doubles), first medal (mixed doubles), first team medal (women), two medallists (single event), mutiple medal winner in a single edition 484; **BWF Super Series Masters Finals/BWF World Tour Finals**, first gold medallist (singles) (women), first medallist (singles) (men), first medallist (singles) (women), first silver medallist (doubles) (mixed), first silver medallist (singles) (women) 487, highest world ranking (doubles) (men) 488, highest world ranking (doubles) (mixed), highest world ranking (doubles) (women), Highest world ranking (singles) (men), highest world ranking (singles) (women) 487; **Commonwealth Games**, first bronze medallist (team) (mixed) 485, first gold medallist (doubles) (men) 485, first gold medallist (singles) (men) 485, first gold medallist (singles) (women), First gold medallists (women) (doubles), first gold medallist (team) (mixed), first medallist (doubles) (women), first medallist (individual) (men), first medallist (individual) (women), first medallist (team) (men), first medallist (team) (women), first silver medallist (team) (mixed), 485, most gold medals from one edition, Most medals from one edition 486; **International competitions**, first duo to win Super 1000 title 487, First finalist at the All England – men – singles, first medal in Thomas Cup championship (team) (men), first medal in Uber Cup (team) (women), first winner at All England Championship, first winner of world cup (men) (singles) 488, most titles (men), most titles (women), two semi-finalists at All England 488; **National Competitions**, first champions, most titles (doubles) (men), most titles (doubles) (mixed), most titles (doubles) (women), most titles (singles) (men), most titles (singles) (women), most versatile and successful player 489; **Olympics**, first medallist, first silver medallist, first two-time medallist 482; **Paralympics**, first badminton gold 489, first bronze medallist (singles) (men), first gold medallist (singles) (men), First silver medallist – men – singles 488; **World Championships**, first doubles medallist (men) 482, first doubles medallist (women) 483, first medal (individual) (men) 482, first medal (individual) (women), first silver medallist (individual) (men) first silver medallist (individual) (women), first two-time silver medallist (individual) (women), first world champion, two medals from one edition (men), highest number of medals, two medals from one edition (women) 483; **World Junior Championship**, first medallist (singles) (boys), first medallist (singles) (girls), first silver medallist (singles) (boys) 486

Baha'i, first house of worship 60

balancing, longest time balancing a hockey stick on the little finger 5, longest time hockey stick on the middle finger 4

ball, **cricket**, longest duration of non-stop hitting a dangling 3

ballet, first film 132

balloon, **hot-air**, highest takeoff 430

ballot, first use of single paper and single box 226

bamboo, first tissue culture 312, tallest grass 362, largest collection of species 364

band, first on MTV 144

bank, biggest fraud 407, first, first cooperative 405, first credit card issued by an Indian 406 first export-import 406, first foreign, first for housing development 405, first government-owned all-woman 406, first Indian to open a branch overseas 405, first Indian with a merchant banking subsidiary 407, first listed on the New York Stock Exchange 406, first regional rural 405, first to establish a mutual fund 408, first with a satellite network 407, first woman manager, first woman to head foreign in India 408, most branches 406, largest international by number of branches 407, oldest private 405, with most foreign offices, with the largest network, 407

banking, first government agency 405

Bappu-Wilson effect, discovery 300

barrage, largest 73

barrister-at-law, first 244

BASE jump, first 429, first to complete during day and night 429, highest, lowest 430

basketball, longest shot 4; **Asian Games**, first appearance, most appearances (women), best win, first and only sisters representing the country 490; **Nationals**, longest sequence of titles 490; **NBA**, first Indian-born player in 490

bas-relief, largest 54

basundi, most varieties 10

bat, smallest, largest 350, rarest 351

bathing, biggest tank 61
battle, **ground**, highest 270
Belur Math, smallest model 32
benches, most donated – 1 year 50
Bengal Chemicals, rejuvenated 306
Bengal Gazette banned 195
besan chillas, most varieties 14
Bhagavadgita, most translated work 182
Bharatanatyam, first campaign for revival 131, largest ensemble 133
bill, longest 9
biocentre, first 311
biocide, first neem-based 99
biocontrol agents, first 100
biogas plant, largest by capacity 374
biotechnology, first department 326
bird, largest round nest 351, most intricate nest 352, smallest and lightest, longest claws, longest beak, slowest 351, swiftest/fastest dive, longest legs, shortest legs 352; **egg**, smallest, largest 351; tallest flying, largest wingspan, smallest wingspan, rarest, first hospital 352
biryani, most varieties 14
blood, first bank 329, longest clot removed 342
boat, first missile, first indigenous patrol 276
book, earliest known Telugu work, earliest extant English work, first printed in local languages, first printed to use Bengali type, first printed in Bengali 179, largest market, most travel bookshops, largest bookshop 185, largest sales (Children's hardback), largest sales (fiction on release – hardback), largest lifetime sales-hardback, largest sales (Adult non-fiction hardback) 184, oldest surviving, earliest known grammar text 178, first known printed, earliest known Gujarati work, earliest known Malayalam work, earliest original Odia work, earliest known Kannada works 178, earliest known Tamil work, earliest known Marathi works 179, smallest, thickest 181, longest audiobook, first book fair 182, first comic convention, first village, oldest bookshop, biggest retail chain - high street 183; **title**, top 10 front-list 2022 186; **novel**, longest 180
booking office, first air ticket 377
bosons, discovery 304
boxes, first 211
boxing, **AIBA**, first in athletes commission 491; **AIBA legend**, first Indian man to receive APB best boxing trophy, first Indian woman to receive award, world number one 491; **Asian Championships**, most medals (women), best performance 491; **Asian Games**, best performance, best performance (women), first gold (men), first medal, most Golds 492; **association**, oldest existing, best youth boxer (men) 491; **Commonwealth Championship**, most golds 493; **Commonwealth Games**, best performance, first gold 493; **International**, most titles 493; most golds in an international meet, most successive professional wins 490, **Nationals**, first championship 493; **Olympics**, first appearance, first medal (men), first medal (woman) 494; **World Boxing**

Championship, first medal (men), first medal (women), best performance (women), most medals 494; **World Championship**, first medal senior (men) 495, most titles (women) 494; **World Cup**, first medal, most medals (men) 495; **Youth Boxing Championship**, best performance in the World Youth Women's Boxing Championships, most medals 495
brain, longest object removed from 337
branches, most 265
brand, first Indianized foreign 425, first patented 424
breakwater, longest 70
breast milk, first bank 329
bridge, biggest cantilever, busiest, cable-stayed rail 68, first cable-stayed road, first iron 67, highest bailey 68, highest rail 69, highest suspension 68, longest bailey 68, longest balanced 67, longest built during war 273, longest over water 69, longest road-and-rail 70, longest sea, only bascule 68, tallest 70, widest double-decker steel 69
British House of Commons, first representative in the 174
British inscription, oldest 54
broadcasting, first company 203, first private FM broadcaster, first controller of broadcasting, first service 202, first 203
broiler, first chicken variety 97
broom, largest 40
browser, most popular 220
budget, first, first interim 400, first paperless, first papers in Hindi 401, first Union 400, longest speech 401, shortest speech 401
buffalo, first female cloned by hand-guided technique, first cloned 94, first milk powder 96
building, first all-steel, first reinforced concrete, tallest 77
bull, first frozen semen bank, first artificial insemination 93, heaviest and highest-priced 96, most calves cloned from 95
Bullion Exchange, India's first international 417
bungee, first Asian triple amputee to complete a jump 432, highest jump (woman), first balloon jump 429
burpees, most by a woman in 1 hr 26
bus, first trolley 392, first motor, first stainless-steel 393, state/UT with largest fleet 396, first battery fleet, first electric 394
bust, largest 50
butterfly, smallest, biggest, at the highest altitude 353

C

cab, first electric 394
cable link, first submarine 215
cakes, most varieties made and displayed 14
calculus, largest urethral removed 339
calf, first cloned from frozen semen 94
camels, the only that can swim 350
camera, largest collection of 166, largest museum 165
campaign, longest social through an adventure sport 453
canal, earliest system, longest 70
canapés, most varieties of 12
cancer, first centre for rehabilitation 326

Cannes Film Festival 159
Cannes Lions, first at the 426, most awards at the 425
canoeing, first expedition 450
Cape2Rio, fastest to complete race 454
car, first, first zero-emission electric, first Indian manufacturers, 393, **SUV**, first fully electrical 394
card, first indigenous payment 407
cardiologist, first 331
cargo, **service**, first 377, first overseas 397
Carnatic music, earliest treatise 135, first codifier of concert format 135, first English periodical on dance 129, first all-woman Hindustani-Carnatic music band 143, first whistling LP 144, marathon vocal performance 145
carrier, first all-jet 249; **aircraft**, largest, first dry dock 277
carriers, birds and animals 214
cartoon, first gallery 171
Carvaan, first portable digital audio player 143
carving, smallest pencil-lead 175
castor, first hybrid 92
catalogue, first modern of stars 299
catamaran, first superfast service 398
cataract, pioneering removal 334
catchment area, largest 345
cavalry, first unit, first regiment 265, first use of air 270
cave, largest 346, longest natural sandstone 347
cellular service, first 218
censor, first boards 156
Census, first 247
Central Production Centre, first 205
certificate, first gender-neutral 115
chaat, most varieties 9
chain, longest and largest human 9, longest paper 8
chairperson, longest-serving 403
Champions of the Earth Award, first Indian winners 369
chancellor, youngest 117; **vice**, first Indian 115
Chandrayaan-2, **Chandrayaan-3** 318
channel, first TV station to get to get a second, first private, first business, first 24-hour news, first infotainment 205, first high definition, first 24-hour 206
charcuterie, longest platter 8
Chattopadhyay, **Bankim Chandra** 105
Chemical Landmark Plaque, awarded to outside Europe 306
chemicals company, first, first heavy 305
chemistry, first department 305, terpene 306
chess, board prize with a perfect score 497, domination in advanced chess 496, first grandmaster 497; **Asian**, champions (men) 495, champions (women), four successive junior titles, junior champions (boys), junior champions (girls) 496, golden sweep at youth championships 497, fastest to achieve norms 500, first junior title 499, first sub-junior champion 499, most participants in International Open, most prize money in International Open 500, youngest winner of Asian junior u-20 501, first/only winner Asian junior and sub-junior 502; **Asian Games**, first medal,

first team medal, first to win Junior girls' title thrice 498; best achievement, best performance, best performance Asian Team 502, chess Oscar award 503; **Commonwealth**, city to host most championships 500, most successful champion 496, youngest to win title 501; first international recognition 498, first woman to lead a team in open section 499; **GM norm**, first, first in national championship 497; **Grandmaster**, youngest, youngest (female), youngest to beat 501; **Grand Slam**, victories 497; highest cheque 499, highest title 502; **International Master**, first (men), first (women) 497, most international age group titles 499, youngest 501, youngest to achieve norm, most medals 500, most times world champion 495; **National**, most titles, most titles in a year 500, most titles (season) 499, youngest champion , youngest junior 501, only girl to win U-12 503, youngest to qualify for championship 502; oldest to regain world rapid title 495; **Olympiad**, first gold, first gold on top board 497, first in both sections, first medal in chess 498, youngest in World Cup and Olympiad 500; only to win against computers 502, rapid/ blindfold event 503; **WGM**, first norm 498; **Wijk Aan Zee**, only Asian 502; **WIM**, first 498, youngest 501; **World Cup**, first country to win both world junior titles (single edition), two world cups 499; youngest international title winners, youngest to win the World Junior title 501, youngest world champion in any 502, only semi-finalist of world championship and world cup 503, only Indian with three bronze medals, only Indian to reach final 503

Chetak, first flight commander 284

Chhau, first woman to perform 131, only dance form varied in three states 133

Chhetri, **Sunil**, Indian footballer 524, 525, 526, 527, 528

chief, first of foreign air force 284, longest tenure 284, first air 187

Chief Election Commissioner, first, longest tenure as, shortest tenure as 226

Chief Justice, first, first woman (*See also Woman*) 245

chief minister, first elected abroad 238, first 'film star', most in a year, oldest, shortest term, with longest tenure and most consecutive terms, youngest 239

chilli, hottest 92, longest green 368

chimney, tallest 76

chip, first indigenous 312

chocolate, **largest**, wall, painting 42, fall 43

cholera exotoxin, discovery 311

Christian Medical College and Hospital, firsts 332

Christmas tree, tallest man-made 7

church, largest 65, oldest 61, tallest 65

cinema, first hall 155, largest multiplex 76

circuit board, smallest with printed water level controller 34

circumnavigation, first aerial world in a single-engine plane 428, first by a man - solo 446, first by a woman - solo 447, first of the globe by a group, first of the globe by a differently abled sailor 446
citizen, first to have a 'no caste, no religion' certificate 246
city, cleanest 372
civic body, oldest 246
clean-up, **beach**, most waste collected in a single day 369
clinic, **first**, online, hormone replacement therapy, liver 327
clock, largest wall 39
club, first flying 377
coaches, **double-decker**, first 383, most produced in a year 385
Coast Guard, first director general, first and only Integral ICG contingent operating abroad 292, Tatrakshak Medal, first (Coast Guard) to receive President's 293
coconut, first hybrids 92, longest and biggest, largest producer 91
code, first British Indian 244, first penal 243
coinage, earliest 404
coins, earliest gold 403, first for the visually impaired, first lead, oldest surviving gold 404
cold storage, state/UT with most capacity 89
collage, largest (group) 171
collections, Amitabh Bachchan memorabilia 15, aircraft models 18, matchboxes featuring horses 16, maps 15, Autographs – national awardees 17, *Chitra Kathayen* comics 17, Hair clips 17, Stickers 16, Newspaper clippings featuring Mahatma Gandhi 17, Owl-shaped jewellery 17, Models of owls 18, Obituaries – from a single family 20, Cinema press booklets – on a single personality 20, Autographs of Ajit Laxman Wadekar 18, ₹5 commemorative coins, Largest collection of stamps – mountain-theme 41, credit cards 15, lighters 21, lapel pins 21, antique matchbox labels – uncut sheets 24, Badges - political theme 24, Railway platform tickets 21, napkins 19, one-quarter British anna coins 46, collection of stamps-Ramayana theme, collection of stamps-bird-theme from most countries 41, ₹100 commemorative coins, coins – Covid-19 theme, largest collection of coins – experimental 46, smallest-value stamps 45, commemorative currency notes- from most countries, 5-rupee notes with the same serial number 47, press clippings featuring Sridevi 15, ties 16, Hindi-language newspapers 15, foreign-language newspapers 15, playing cards 16, Nokia handsets 20, Airmail envelopes 16, Seer 18, Soap covers – single brand 20, Toothpaste wrappers 20, Newspaper clippings featuring Lata Mangeshkar 20, Pradhan Mantri Yojana matchboxes 21; **magazines**, largest collection of magazines, hindi, regional languages 22, first issues 23, airline, personality covers – featuring a single personality 23

college, first for physical education, first for the hearing-challenged, first for sanitation workers 112, first home science 111, first modern 104, first intermediate 105, first of veterinary science, first to offer bachelor's degree in veterinary medicine 113, for women 109, first of nursing 108, oldest dentist in South-east Asia 107, first science 108
columns, most published in a year 201
command, only training 275
commander, first Indian station 284, first squadron 284
commander-in-chief, first 262, **defence**, first chief of integrated and staff, first chief of staff 262
commission, first public service 240
Commonwealth Champions 496
Commonwealth Games, best performance, youngest captain 467
communist, first elected government in power 239
company, first cigarette, first ice-cream, first rubber estate 418, first scooter manufacturing, 419, first tea 418, first tyre 419, largest coal-producing 416, oldest engineering 419, first shipping 397
compass, earliest 396
computer, first to obtain PhD in science 313, first analogue, first digital 312, first indigenous palmtop, first powerful commercial 313, fastest super 313, first indigenous super, powerful indigenous 314
computing, first human brain-like 313
concrete, most bituminous poured (single day) 396
Congress, **Indian National**, first woman president, longest-serving president 225
conservation, first organization, oldest NGO engaged in conservation and biodiversity research 363
control system, first air traffic 378
conveyor, longest 76
cooking, **vessel**, largest 76
copper kiln, earliest 315
cottages, first floating 78
cotton, earliest cultivation 83, first hybrid 88
counter-insurgency, first school 271
country, first to have a cooling action plan 370
course, first pharmacy education 107, oldest in pharmacy 114, first correspondence 112
cow, first cloned 95, first cross-bred 96, oldest 97
crane, first hand-operated, 74
crash, first air 377
crater, largest 345
creeper, longest 361
cricket, **International Cricket Council**, first Indian chairman, first Indian president 464; **association**, first woman to head a state 466, Indian independent chairman 464; **men's One Day Internationals**, best bowling, best strike rate 513, fastest 50 runs on debut, first bowler to take more than three wickets on debut, first to score 100 centuries 512, first wins in the World Cup and World Twenty20 514, highest individual innings

510, highest score on debut, highest team total, lowest team total 512, most career catches, most career wickets 513, most centuries in a single World Cup 514, most centuries partnerships 512, most Man of the Match awards (career) 514, most player of the series awards, most runs in all World Cups 513, most career wickets 513, highest individual innings 510, most sixes in an innings, most total career runs 513, winning Man of the Match four consecutive times 514, most career catches 513; **men's T20 International**, best batting average (minimum 50 matches) 515, best individual bowling performance 514, fastest to 50 515, best bowling average (minimum 10 wickets), highest run chase, highest team total, lowest team total, most career wickets 514, most runs in T20, only captain to win all three ICC trophies 515; **men's Tests**, best bowling figures on debut, best bowling in a match 510, best bowling innings, dismisses all 11 batsmen in a match 511, Fastest Indian opener to score 1,000 runs 509, first to reach 10,000 runs, first victory 508, highest century partnerships, highest individual innings 510, highest individual score in a day 509, Highest run aggregate 510, highest run chase 509, highest score on debut and fastest century on debut 512, highest score on debut (series), highest team innings score 508, lowest team innings score 510, most 1,000+ runs in a calendar year 509, most career dismissals by a wicketkeeper 511, most career runs, most career wickets, most consecutive wins at home series 508, most catches (innings) 511, most catches (match) 511, most dismissals by a wicketkeeper (match), most dismissals by a wicketkeeper series 511, most individual centuries 508, most runs in an over 509, most sixes in a series 509, most wickets in a debut series 508, wicketkeeper with fastest 100 dismissals 511, wicket off first ball (debut)/ (match) 510; **IPL**, player with most titles (men) 508; **women's**, longest career 504, most career runs in international cricket (women's) 503, most career wickets across formats 504, youngest to debut 503; **women's One Day Internationals**, best bowling average (minimum 50 wickets), highest individual score, highest partnership, century on debut, clean sweep victories in a bilateral series, most career catches by a fielder, most career dismissals by a wicketkeeper, most runs scored, most stumpings by a wicketkeeper 506; **women's T20 International**, best bowling 507, best bowling average 507, highest partnership, highest team total, largest victory margin, lowest team total 507, most career catches by a fielder, most career dismissals by a wicketkeeper 507, most

career runs 506, most career wickets 507, narrowest 507; **women's Tests**, best bowling average, best bowling (innings), biggest victory margin, first and only double century, highest total, lowest total, most balls delivered, most career catches by a fielder, most career wickets 505, most runs 504, most wickets 505, narrowest victory margin, most career dismissals by a wicketkeeper 504
crocodile, longest 355, first known white, rarest, first/largest bank 233, shortest, heaviest 232
crop, only genetically modified cash approved for commercial cultivation 88
cross-country, longest run 457
cruiser and flagship, first 275
crunches, most bicycle - 1 min. (woman) 30, most abdominal - 1 min., most 31
cryptocurrency, biggest crime 243
cue sports, **Asian billiards**, best performance 517; **Asian Games**, first title, best performance in snooker, most billiards gold medals 517; **billiards and snooker**, most Asian titles 518, most world titles 517; first snooker team World cup title 516, highest break under three-pot rule (billiards) 518, World 6-red title 516; **Nationals**, first billiards championship, first snooker championship, most national titles billiards and snooker 515, highest break (snooker) 516, two titles in 6-red snooker, most competitive 147 breaks (snooker), oldest woman champion (billiards) 518; **WLBS championship**, first title, first win 516; **World Billiards**, first team title 516; highest break in the championship 517; **world champion**, first on debut 516, youngest snooker 518; **World Games**, first world championship 516; first snooker title 517 **World Professional**, youngest to win 518
curd-churning machine, smallest 34
currency, earliest known use of cowries as 404
cycles, fastest assembling 7
cycling, deepest underwater - ocean – solo 455
cyst, largest adrenal removed 342

D

daguerreotype, first use 164
daily (newspaper), first with an international edition, first financial 196, multi-edition with the largest readership, largest - Hindi/English, largest read regional-language daily 199
dairy, largest development programme 97
dam, **dam and canal**, earliest 70; highest earth-fill, largest river, oldest cement masonry, oldest extant 72
dance, **competition**, first celebrity, first to win an international 132; **dance-drama**, first dance theatre form recognised by UNESCO 132, first known form 128, oldest surviving dance-drama form 128, performed by women alone 133; **dancer**, earliest scriptural mention 128, only with an artificial foot, only Persianized classical 133; earliest evidence

of formalized 128, first revivalist school 129, first schools 129, first classical to be revived 130, first Indian-European fusion 132, oldest recipient of President's award 133, only extant pre-Vedic 132, first modern work on 132, first national seminar 130
deal, biggest business 423
decimal system, earliest use 296
delta, largest 344
demolition, India's biggest 78
demonetization, first 408
dental, first college 326
department, first government-run for disorders of sex development 331
depository, first, first global receipts issued 409
desert, largest 345, only cold 345
desk calendar, biggest 39
destination, first live entertainment, theatre, and leisure 74
Devi, Bhavani C.A., 466, 467, 475
Dharmachakra, biggest 37
dictionary, first official sign language 180, largest-selling bilingual 184
differential calculus, discovery of 297
Dilli Bazaar 420
dim sums, most varieties 11
disc, first compact 142
disembarkation system, first three-point 382
dissection, first 331
dive, first deep bounce, first saturation 450
dives, daring 434
diyas, fastest lighting – group 7
DJ, disabled 142
dock, first naval yard 279, first floating dry, largest indigenous floating, first naval, first unified theatre 279, largest covered 397
doctor, first doctor-to-doctor online session, first western medicine 330, first woman, first woman aerospace 335
dome, largest corbelled cornice 54, pillar-less 80
doodle art, largest (group) 175
Doordarshan, first director general of 206
drainage system, earliest extensive 52
drama, earliest dramatic references 146, first club 148; **plays**, earliest, oldest extant, early political 146, earliest street 147, first Marathi musical 149, performed in most languages (single day) 148, longest, most performances as a personality - stage and screen, most performances as a character - (mythological) stage, most stage plays performed in a day - solo 150, first modern (translations), first foreign translation of a Sanskrit, first protest 147, first and only on Broadway and West End 148; **playwright**, earliest 146, **school**, longest serving director of NSD 150
drill, smallest 31
Drone, first show 273, first pilotless 279
drum, first mention 138
drumstick, longest 365, tallest tree 368
DTH service, first 206

E

eco-hotel, first 79
economic, first to work on planning 400

editor, first letter to 199, longest letter to 201, longest spell as 200
education first minister, first national council 102, first steps 104
egg, biggest of hen 98
election, first EVM'S/postal ballot papers with candidate photographs 227, first presidential 231; **ambassador**, first transgender 227; **candidate**, youngest winning 229; **electorate**, largest, state/ UT with the largest, state/ UT with the smallest 229; **general elections**, first 226, fewest independent candidates elected, fewest women elected, highest voter turnout 228, Lowest voter turnout 227, most female candidates, most independent candidates, most independent candidates elected, most women elected 228; most expensive 229; **vote**, first app launched for vigil 227, first electronic machines 226, first NOTA option, first 'others' category, first teenage 227, most IDs Distributed in 1 hr, state/UT with the largest turnout, state/ UT with the smallest turnout, verifiable paper audit trail in all constituencies for the first time 229
electric bike model, smallest 31
electricity, first commercial use 412, first state board 413
electrification, first 413
elevator, first 74
email, first free service 219
employer, largest 403
endoscopy, first lab 328
Enrolment, stats at a glance 106
enzyme, first insulin blocking isolated 311
escalator, tallest 77
expedition, longest with a mixed crew 281
expedition, **four-wheeler**, fastest GQ – group – women 436, first all-India – group, first four corners of India - solo, first North-South India round – solo, first trans-Himalayan – solo 435, first West-East India round – solo, fastest East-West India – group, fastest East-West India by a disabled person – solo, fastest Four Corners of India – solo, longest journey within a country - solo, longest journey within a country – group, fastest North-South group 438, longest distance travelled across countries – solo, fastest North-South expedition – solo 439; **two-wheeler**, **151–450 cc**, fastest East-West – solo 440, first North-South round by a differently abled person – solo 439, fastest Four Corners of India – solo 440, fastest North-South – solo 440, fastest GQ by a disabled person – solo, longest journey within the country – solo, longest distance covered within the country by a disabled person – solo 441; first disabled person to reach Umling La – solo 437, human pyramid, largest moving – women 443; **over 450 cc**, first to cross Umling La – solo, fastest All-India – solo, Fastest GQ expedition – solo, 441; **rally**, largest by woman riders – under

100 km – multiple venues 441; **ride, longest**, while standing anywhere on the bike – solo, while standing on a structure – solo – woman, while standing on a structure – group 442, on a structure facing backwards – solo 443, while standing anywhere on the bike – solo – woman, while sitting on a bike facing backwards – solo – woman 443; **up to 150 cc**, first trans-Himalayan – solo 439; **two-wheeler (bicycle)**, **geared**, fastest North-South – solo, fastest East-West – solo, fastest GQ – solo, longest distance covered within the country – solo 444; **gearless**, fastest North-South – solo, fastest North-South – group 444; oldest super randonneuse, longest tandem – women, first tandem, most consecutive – 100 km, all-India tour on a mono-wheeler 445, fastest Asian across the world 446, largest marathon 445

explorer, largest mineral 308

export, first car to be 421, India leads in measles vaccines 420

F

Facebook, largest user base 219

factory, first 417, first car 420, first plastic 419

FAI F3M Championship, most podium finishes 434

family planning, first governmental programme 325

famine commission, first 83

farm, first and largest cattle 97, highest stud 96, only camel 93, largest single 86, largest average holdings in a state/UT 86, smallest average holdings in a state/UT 88; **loan**, biggest waiver, first nationwide waiver 82; most sold equipment with largest market share 100

fax, first net service 218

FDI, highest in a year 403

feline, smallest, largest/heaviest, found at highest altitude 350

fencing, **Olympics**, first fencer to qualify for 467

ferry, first roll-on-roll-off service 398, first solar boat, first hovercraft 397

fertilizer, first factory, state/UT with highest use per hectare 99

fibre, first multicore, first optical 302

fibre-optic link, first 215

fibroids, most uterine removed 342

filling station, highest 394

film, largest archives 120, first Indian in English, edited in most languages/dialects, first cinemascope, first in 70 mm, first advertisement for a, first concern 153, first serial, first one-actor, one-set, first adult 155, first animated, first use of surround sound, first 3D, longest-running 155, first shot in India, first shot by an Indian, first exhibited, first indigenous feature 152, first in multilingual versions 153, longest footage, most episodic films in a single feature, shortest, most number of songs in a Hindi 160, most aspects handled, tallest cut-out, largest poster, most produced, most expensive produced, largest city/studio 162, most

feature directed, highest screens, horror produced 163; **music**, most songs recorded in a day 160, maximum roles in a single 157, most as a lead, roles in most number 158; **awards**, first academy, first foreign, first academy for best documentary (short subject) 157; **Hollywood**, first to act in a film 157; **box-office**, first hit 157; **studio**, first 156
fingerprint, first bureau 242
fish, first marine aquarium for ornamental, first transgenic rohu 98, oldest freshwater, lightest/smallest, only with suction plates, heaviest, only without a bony skeleton, only male producing young 357, only anadromous, largest recorded subterranean, shortest-lived, longest-lived, largest clam 360
fisherwoman, first and only licensed 97
fishing station, first deep-sea 97
fission, first observation of spontaneous 305
fistula, longest removed 338
flamingo, only breeding ground 351
fleet replenishment tanker, first indigenous 278
flight, first 376, first international 377, first to the true North Pole, only vintage 291, highest and longest wingsuit, highest 430, longest motor glider 431, longest direct-route with an all-woman cockpit crew 382
flower, tallest 361
flower carpet, largest 44
flute, marathon performance 145
flying, **spy**, first 266
food, most packets, distributed among the poor 50, most, donated – single day – multiple venues 47
football, most rolls from eye to eye 5; **academy**, first 519; **Asian Games**, biggest defeat, biggest margin of victory 526; **club**, best record against foreign 522, first Indian to enter Asian Football Confederation Cup Final 519, first Indian to win a major trophy, first in English professional club 520, first hat-trick 521, first international tournament win 520, first woman to sign a contract with a foreign 521, most goals in NFL/I-league, 526; **coach**, first national of a foreign country, first foreign, first professional 520, most appearances in Nehru Cup 521, most appearance in Olympics, most successful at the Asian Games 522, most successful in domestic tournaments 521, only Indian to gain success with a foreign club 522; **Durand Cup**, first team to win, most individual goals, most wins 519; **FIFA**, first Indian in FIFA executive panel 464, first international match 524, first World Cup match commissioner, 464, India's longest unbeaten run in a year, 527, most individual in international club match 522, worst defeats 527; **AIFF Intercontinental Cup**, most successful team 527; **Indian League**, most individual goals in a match 524; **Indian Super League**, biggest margin of

victory 523, hat-trick records 524, maximum titles 523, most goals by a team 524, most goals in a match 523, most wins by a team 524; **individual records**, back-to-back hat-tricks, fastest international goal, hat-trick in Olympics, hat-trick on debut 528, highest caps earned (top five) 527, maximum goals scored (top five) 528, Maximum hat-tricks 528, most goals in Asian Games 527, most successful captain, youngest match winner at Nehru Cup 528, highest number of goals 523; fastest goal, longest sequence of wins, longest unbeaten streak at home 522, most clean sheets 519; **National Football League**, first to win three, most individual goals in a match 524, most individual hat-tricks in NFL and I-League 526; **Olympics**, biggest margin of victory, only win in, overall performance, 526; **pre-World Cup**, best performance, biggest margin of victory, worst defeat 527; **referee**, first in Olympics, first in World Cup 519, most matches officiated 521; **Santosh Trophy**, all-time top scorers, biggest margin of victory, highest number of goals by an individual in a single match, most individual goals in a single edition, most individual goals in finals 523, most wins 522, success for different teams 523; **tiebreaks**, first 521; **tournament**, oldest 518; **win**, longest sequence 522

foreign body, longest removed 339

foreign collaboration, first 419

forest, first healing centre 369

fort, earliest known fortified city 52, longest fortification wall, one of the oldest 58, only in a tiger reserve, on three hills, with largest metal ordnance 55

fossil, first dinosaur 307, first megafossil from Himalayas 307, oldest biological 310, oldest dinosaur discovery 347

freefall, most hours logged 435

frog, largest, smallest, flying, rarest 353

fruit, first train 82

G

Gaja Dvar 258

garden, oldest botanical 362

Garuda Dvar 258

gateway, highest 58

gazebo, largest 79

gecko, smallest, largest, rarest 354, 'flying' 355

gene, first national bank, first synthesis of workable 311

geologists, first, first official 307

geology, first course 308

geomagnetic, **observatory**, first 307; **reversals**, periodicity 308

geometry, earliest treatise, first mention 296

geoscientific data centre, first data 309

gharana, oldest 138

GIFT, first twins 324

glacier, largest 344

glasshouse, largest 75

Global Satellite Launch Vehicle (GSLV), first flight 320

gnat, first 289

goat, first cloned pashmina 94, heaviest 96

Golden Reel Award, first Asian 144
gold violin, smallest 35
golf, **Asian Games**, first sweep of gold medals 530; **Asian Tour**, lowest winning score on 534, most titles 533, youngest to Order of Merit 536; best world ranking 534; **British Open**, first to qualify for 530; **European Tour**, best finish in Order of Merit 534, first win in Europe, first win on 532, least putts on 535, lowest winning score on 534, only Indian to win four events in India, only Indian to win two titles in a year, quickest to win two titles 535, youngest to win title 536; **first**, to represent the country at four multi-discipline Games 532, international recognition, Olympians, to win all three Nationals titles 530; first international success in U-10 category 529, highest golf course, Indian at the majors, Indian men winning international tournaments 529; **Indian Open**, winners 529; Indians topping the Asian Tour Order of Merit 530; **Indian Tour**, five titles in a season twice on 534, lowest round on, lowest winning score on 535, most titles in a season 534; **Japanese Tour**, only Indian to win four titles on 535; **Ladies European Tour**, best finish on the Order of Merit, first to secure her card (playing rights) winner on, First to win LET title outside India 523, first to win on 533; **Ladies Indian Open**, first to win 532; **Ladies PGA**, first to qualify 532; longest hole-in-one 536; **Majors**, best finish in 534, first to make the 'cut' in a, first to play in a 531; **Masters at Augusta**, first to play 531; most birdies 533, most Indian tournaments on Asian tour 529, most international titles, most lucrative season 533, oldest club, oldest to get hole-in-one 528; **Olympics**, first woman to qualify for the 532; only team title in the US 534; **PGA** best Indian performance on the tour 534, first to gain qualification for on the tour 530, first to play the championship 531, first to win on a Japanese tour 532, first to win on tour 530, 532; **PGTI**, most career prize money won 534, youngest winner on the domestic tour 536; **prize money**, best performance based on received 534, highest earner in a domestic season, highest (women) 533, quickest to reach the million mark in 534, tournament with highest, 533; Rookie on a rampage, sponsorship bonanza, 529; **US Open**, first to play in 530; **WGC**, first to play in three events in a year 531; **World Championship**, first team to qualify for 532; **World Cup**, first participation in 531; **youngest**, hole-in-one, to win two back-to-back international titles; Commonwealth Games, first appearance in 536
government, tiers of Indian 235
governor, youngest 241
graffiti, first officially recognized woman artist 170

Grammy, best world music album, only Indian to win both Oscar and, first award-winning Indian percussionist 143
gramophone, first company 139, first voices 139, first record 140, first singer recorded 139, only museum 140
Gregory series, first to give 297
GST, records 424, state-wise growth of revenues 422, trends in collection 424
guitar, smallest functioning 31
gun, first foundry 266
gurdwara, highest 65
gymnastics, **Asian Championship**, first medal 537; **Asian Games**, first medal 537; **Commonwealth Games**, first medal in (men) 537; first national championship 536, most individual titles in the nationals 537; **Olympics**, first appearance 537; most representations 537; **World Championship**, first appearance in 537, most successive team titles 536 **World Cup**, first medal 537
gymnosperms, discovery 311

H

hair, longest 8
HAL HJT-16 Kiran 290
hall, largest vaulted 54, largest chaitya 65
halwa, most varieties prepared 8
Hamsa Dvar, 259
hang-glider, longest-harness flight 434
harmonica, most people playing together 145
harp, first player 141
Hasselblad, first Indian to receive award 166
healthcare, largest scheme 324
helicopter, first Apache 290, first indigenous 378, first indigenous advanced light 289, first lifted battalion, first operations 270, first pilot 286, first school 376, first training school 280
heliport, first 379
helium isotope, discovery in cosmic rays 305
helmet, first bulletproof 267
hepatitis E virus, first clone 311
herbarium, first virtual 363
High Court, first judge 245, oldest 246, with most judges 243
Highest turnover 395
highway, first 392, shortest national, longest tunnel, highest national, longest construction in a single day 395
hoarding, largest, 423
hockey, **Asia Cup**, first win (women) 540, highest goal scorer 543, biggest victory margin (men)/(women), biggest win in finals 542; **Asian Men's Hockey**, first win 540; **Asian Women's Hockey**, first win 540; **awards**, first women professional players 539, most Arjuna for any sport in a year, most FIH hockey star 538; best performance in a foreign tour 541, biggest win over Pakistan 542; **Champions Trophy**, best performance, best recovery in men's 541; **coach**, first foreign, first major success by foreign 539; **Commonwealth Games**, best performance 541, first success (women) 539 ; **FIH Hocky 5s Championship**,

inaugural win 539; first domestic league (women) 539, first national championship (men) 538, first national championship (women) 539, first Olympian to head Indian hockey 538; **International Hockey Federation**, first Indian to head 537; **Junior Asia Cup**, first win; most capped player 541, most international caps (women) 540, most wins in national championship (women) 539, most wins of national championship (men), oldest tournament (men), oldest tournament (women) 538; **Olympics**, best goalkeeping in, best victory margin 542, most goals (individual) 540, fastest goal 543, first medal and most successful team 539, most goals – team, most medals 540, oldest player 544, only captain in successive, only double hat-trick in, only goalkeeper in three finals 543, only hat-trick (women) 544, playing for teams with most golds 541, youngest to win gold 544; **World Cup**, best performance (men), best performance (women) 542, highest goal scorer 543, most appearances, most appearances in women's, most goals 541; **Youth Asia Cup**, highest goal scorer and double hat-trick 543

homoeopathic, company, first, college 326, international congress 332

Honorary doctorate, first Indian sportsman and coach to receive, first Indian sportsman to receive 465

hospital, first 325, with stealth neuro-navigation system 327, corporate 329, with a rooftop helipad 328, oldest eye 325

hotel, first five-star 419

houseboat, first 74

hovercraft, first and longest deep-sea passage 293, first berthing platform 294

human organ, regeneration 312

hydraulic engineering, first known example of ancient 53

hydroelectric project, first 70

hypothalamus, discovery of feeding centre in 330

I

IAF, first AESA radar for 289

ice-skating, oldest rink 76

idol, tallest Ganesha 66

igloo, café, first stay 78

IIT, first 109

Imperial Civil Service, first Indian in the 240

implant, first cochlear 336

index, first infrastructural 421

India at World Athletics Championships 2023 480

Indian Air Force 282

Indian executive system 233

Indian Medical Service, first to pass the examination 115

Indian Postal Order, first electronic 209

Indian Sign Language Research and Training Centre (*See also dictionary*) 181

Indian Statistical Institute, first woman director 117

India's Musical Genius 141

Indigenous Automatic Car 392

infantry, oldest unit, oldest

brigade 265
infinite series, first study of 297
ink, **indelible**, first use 227
institute, first for farm machinery training and testing 98, first for population sciences, first metro technology 109, first of oceanography 110, first national for the visually impaired, first yoga 112, first national of Watersports 114, first statistical, first gemmological, first of mass communication 110, first of fashion technology, first for studying footwear design, first national of management 111, first to teach modern architecture 108, first veterinary research 113, oldest extant for the blind 103
insulin, first to extract from plant 311
insurance, **company**, first general, first Indian life, first life, largest 408, milestones in life 410
Intelligence Bureau, first Indian director of the 242
International Booker Prize, first Indian citizen to win Booker Prize 191, first novel in Indian language to win 188
International Court of Justice, first Indian president 246
International Geological Congress, first president of 308
International Society of Soil Sciences, first Indian president 86
International Subscriber Dialling (ISD), first 216
Internet, first provider of services 218, first 3G operator 218, first and only 4G, top subscription areas - wired and wireless, highest data consumption 219, fastest 4G service provider 220
Internet Service Provider (ISP), first private 219
Integrated Automatic Aviation Meteorological System, first 278
iron, earliest furnace , earliest use 315, first ore deposits 309, smallest 34
iron and steel, first commercial production of 417
irrigation, earliest 83, first use of lift 99, largest groundwater system 85
island, **largest**, freshwater 345, ocean 346
IUCN, on the verge of extinction 362
IVF, first baby 325, oldest mother 324

J

jackfruit, heaviest 91
jazz, first Indo fusion album 143
jet, first 378, first bomber, first 288, first indigenous tandem seat trainer 289
jigsaw puzzle, **biggest**, solved – group 37, solved – solo 38
Jnanpith, first recipients 188
job, first LGBTQIA+ fair 403
journalist, first Indian origin to win Pulitzer Prize 200, longest career as 201
jowar, tallest 89
judge, first transgender 247
Judicial, evolution of the system in India 244
juggling, most patterns on a balance board 3
juice blender, smallest 34
jumping jacks, **most**, 1 min. 30, 1

hr, woman – 1 min. 31

K

kabaddi, **Asian Championship**, first, first participation in junior 544; **Asian Games**, first appearance, first demonstration 544, most Asian titles (men and women), most titles (men), most titles (women) 545, first nationals 544; **International Kabaddi Federation**, first Indian president 464, most expensive non-cricket player 545; **Olympics**, first demonstration 544; **Pro Kabaddi League**, first 544, first team to win three consecutive titles, most expensive player 545; **World and Asian Championship**, most medals (women) 545; **World Cup**, most wins (men) 545
kaju katli, largest 39
Kamal, **A. Sharath**, 353, 354, 355, 357
Kaprekar Constant, discovery 297
Kathak, first known teacher 131
Kathakali, thickest make-up 130
kayaking, **longest**, solo 452, group 453
kebab, longest 8
kicks, most full-contact on a kick-pad – alternate legs in 1 hr 24 31
kidney, heaviest removed 339, largest operated on 342
Kirti Chakra, first prisoner of war to receive 263
kites, most on a single line 12
Knitting, solo-marathon 6
Kodak, first express outlet 165
Kohli, **Virat**, 515
Kom, **M.C. Mary**, Boxer Extraordinaire 492
Krishnan effect, discovery 304
Kuchipudi, first couple to win Padma Shri, first solo 130

L

laboratory, first forensic science 242
Labour Day, first 402
lagoon, largest brackish-water 345
lake, largest freshwater 345, oldest man-made 53
lamb, first from frozen embryo 93
language, oldest living 178
laser, first carbon dioxide 307
lassi, most varieties 14
lawyer, first transgender 247
leaf, largest 362, longest mango, largest taro 365
LED display screen, largest on water (aboard a ship/boat/vessel) 426
Legion d'Honneur, first to win 157
legislation, first for women 402, first labour 403
Legislative Assembly, first state 258, shortest session of state legislative assembly 260
Legislative councils, most elections won 240
lemon, biggest 365
letter, first window delivery 207, first office for dead 210
library, first mobile, first sports 118, only underground, largest university 119, only bookshop-cum-library on a lake, largest, first boat, first university 118, first national medical 119, first 117, oldest, first online Braille 118, first operational digital network 117, biggest public system 118

lieutenant general, first woman 262
lighthouse, first unmanned, oldest, oldest functional, tallest, tallest from mean sea level 73
Linnean medal, first biologist to win 312
literacy, first 100 per cent literate district 102
literary, first agency 183; **award winners**, first Grinzane Cavour, first Commonwealth writers' Prize, first Newbery Medal 192, first DSC Prize for South Asian literature 189, first winner of the Pulitzer Prize, Rabindranath Tagore literary prize, first Saraswati Samman, JCB Prize, first Kamaladevi Chattopadhyay NIF Book prize, highest monetary prize 192, first Neustadt Prize 188, first Ondaatje Prize 189; **festival**, first virtual 183, first children's, largest 182, first Yuva Puraskar 189
lithium, first resource 416
livestock, largest population 96
lizard, largest, longest tail in relation to the body, only flying, only legless, longest tongue 354
loan, first institution for agri 406
locomotive, first factory 383, most produced in a year 386
locust, oldest control programme 84
logo, biggest Swachh Bharat made by arranging motorcycles 37
LPG, first company to market 416, first private branded 415
luge, youngest Olympian 546
Lunar probe, first 318
lunges, most in 1 hr 27
lyricist, most prolific 160

M

Made-in-India, launches 268-269
magazine, first for visually challenged 197, first in Hindi 196, first women's in English, first women's in an Indian language 197, first sports 466, first wildlife 363, most read English, most read Hindi, most read in a regional language, longest-running Indian women's 200, oldest children's 199
magic square, earliest 296
Mahalanobis distance, invention of 298
mail, first automatic processing centre 211, first by steamboat 207, first in hot-air balloon 209
Makara Dvar 258
Malik, Sakshi 574, 576, 577
mall, first virtual 422
mammal, fastest land, slowest land, fastest water, slowest water 349, longest gestation, shortest gestation 347, only herbivorous marine 350, oldest living 347, longest-lived 348, smallest 347, largest land, largest litter, fastest breeders, slowest breeders 348
man, tallest 6
mandala artwork, largest solo, largest group 174
mangoes, largest producer of 92
manufacturer, first champagne 419
manuscript, first Mughal illuminated 169
marathon, **4 Deserts Grand Slam**, first winner 455; **7 Emirates Run**, first to complete 455; **full**, most in a year 457; **GQ**, first to complete the run 456; **half-marathons**, most in a year, most by an individual 457,

most consecutive distance runs 458, most organized in a single day – multiple venues 455; **marathoner**, oldest 457, most visually impaired athletes completing 458; **Six World Marathons**, first to complete all 455; **triathlon**, first disabled 456, most completed in a year 458, first Ironman 456, only Asian to complete in six continents 458; **Ultraman**, first to finish the world championship, first triathlete 456; **ultramarathons**, fastest at Badwater 458, first to complete grand-to-grand 455, most in a year 457; **world challenge**, first to complete – full marathon 456
marine, first research institute 309
marker and ink, marathon portrait solo 176
market (bazaar), first permanent crafts 77, first underground 77
marshal, first 284, first field 262
martial arts, best performance in CWG, oldest competitor 547; **Judo**, first international medal 546, first judoka to win world title 547, first medal in Asian Championship (women), first medal in Asian Games 546; **National**, first championship 546, most wins in nationals 547, youngest champion 546; **Wushu**, first world champion (men), youngest wushu medallist, world champion (women) 546
Master Craftsman Award, most national awards won in a family 171
mathematics, earliest mention of series, 296
mausoleum, longest taken to build 59
mayor, youngest 241
maze, largest 54
medical, college 326, school to offer oncology degrees, 325, conference 333, first, organized service 326, laser facility 327, rural college 328, most innovations by a professional 331, smallest robot 336, symposium 332
medicine, earliest treatise, first Persian text 324
memento, biggest 37
memory, fastest to recall 2,500 digits of π, fastest to identify flags of all countries of the world, fastest to identify all the bones of the human body, fastest solving of the mirror cube while blindfolded, most 2-digit numbers multiplied correctly – 1 min. 2, most squares correctly calculated –3-digit numbers – 1 min 3, most cubes correctly calculated – 3-digit numbers – 1 min. 3, most dinosaur names identified in a minute 5, most binary numbers memorized – 5 mins 3, most number of national anthems sung by an individual 2
Mental Calculation World Championship, first winner 2
mesons, discovery 304
metallurgist, first to work with plutonium 315
metal-scrap structure, tallest-group 371, tallest-solo 374, widest-group 371
meteorite, largest shower 345
methane, first plant 310
metro, first, deepest station,

deepest tunnel, first driverless, first underwater, largest network 389
microchips, first batch of 420
microlight, aircraft flight 435, first jump from a 428, longest cross-country expedition 431, most expeditions 430
microwave oven, smallest 34
military, first intelligence school 271, first dog school 272
milk, top producing country 96
mill, first cotton textile 418, oldest jute 419
minaret, first revolving 60, only shaking 63, tallest brick 56
mine, oldest gold 416, only diamond 417, state/UT with most 416
mining, first coal 416, first underwater system 308
minister, **Cabinet**, longest-serving, shortest tenure 235; **Union**, first to die in harness 236, first to resign 235
mint, first 404
missile, first anti-ship 277, first indigenously developed naval anti-ship 279, first corvette 277, first indigenous anti-radiation 290, longest-range nuclear 267
mission, first dedicated commercial satellite, first interplanetary 321, first remote sensing 317
mobile, first call using a phone 217, first tower at the highest altitude 218; **app**, first store 219, most number of downloads 219, most downloaded 220
mocktails, most varieties prepared 15
Molecular Distillation Unit, first 302
momo, largest 46
monastery, highest 65, largest 62
monument, most names engraved 74, oldest Buddhist 60
mosque, earliest 59, first single-aisle 59, largest 65, only one in marble 65
moth, largest 353
motorsport, first Indian to win a world title in 466
mountain, longest land range 344
mountaineering, first club, first expedition, first to summit the Volcanic Seven and youngest to climb both the Seven Summits and Volcanic Seven summits 458, first institute 459, first to summit four unscaled peaks above 6,000 m, fastest to scale most 8,000 m peaks, first to summit three highest peaks of South America 460; **Himalaya**, most summits 459; **Mt Everest**, first woman, fastest scaling, oldest to scale 460, first to summit without supplemental oxygen 460; **Seven Summit**, first to complete 459, oldest to complete 459
MSO, first Indian to win 298
multimedia notebook, first smallest 314
municipalities, first 240
mural, oldest extant 168
museum, first election, first insect 122, first interactive of music 123, first wax, first dinosaur 122, first sports – organization 121, first sports –personal collection 122, first of textiles 120, first railway, first partition 121, first national of Indian cinema, first transport 120, first kite, first underground, first of toilets 121, first of utensils 124,

first culinary arts, first science 123, largest chain of science 124, first archaeological site 123, first Prime Minister's, largest terracotta 124, only leprosy 125, first public in a university, largest and oldest 120, conflictorium 125
music, first raga 134, earliest reference to performances 131, earliest form of, earliest notes 134, earliest mention of ragas 135, first medieval treatise on 134, first to standardize 135, earliest royal composers 134, most prolific composer 135, first fusion melody, oldest sabha for dance and music 138, first school, first recorded 142, first set of records 143, most events in a day 145, only director couple 144; **album**, first fusion 143; **award**, first Asian to win Golden Reel 144; **festival**, first virtual 144; **instruments**, first electronic 140; marathon duet 145, oldest, oldest south Indian stringed, oldest known percussion, earliest 138, first three-in-one classical 139; **performers**, first at Royal Albert Hall 139, first duo to introduce jugalbandi 140, longest innings as conductor 144, most recorded artiste 142; **singing**, earliest ballad 135; **songs**, first recorded 139, only multilingual classical, earliest form of classical 134, earliest Prakrit 135
Music of India 136
mustard, first hybrid 90
mutual fund, first domestic, first offshore, first private sector 409, largest 411
MV Ganga Vilas 398

N

National Anthem, first rendition 223
National flag, first design of the 222
National Photography Awards 2023 168
national song, first rendition 223
Natya Shastra, earliest known treatise on performing arts 128, first modern translation 129
Nautch girls 129
navy, first academy 279, first school 280, first air squadron, first exclusive base, first unmanned aerial squadron 275, first combat management system, first virtual reality centre 281, first commander-in-chief, first chief of naval staff 274
NEET, first to score 100 per cent 116
news, first bulletin 203
newspaper, first 195, first vernacular 196, first non English, only handwritten 195, first Hindi 196, first for visually impaired 195, first run entirely by women 196, first to be printed in colour 199, most pages in 201, most pages in a supplement 201, oldest extant in English 201, oldest extant in regional language 200, state/UT with most registered 199; **article**, most published in a year – single publication 201, most in a year – multiple publication 201; **news agency** first 194, first to supply news in Urdu 195
newsreader, first 206

Nobel Prize, first in physics 304, first winner in economics 421
note, first 200-rupee, first issue of rupee 404, first secured promissory 409, highest denomination rupee 404
nova, first to observe 300
nuclear, first advanced heavy water 304, first implosion 302, first reactor 304, first shelter 273, only safety institute 304
nukkad natak, marathon performance 147
numbers, earliest use of irrational 296
nurse, first woman 335
nursing, first college 326

O

oceanography, first course, first vessel 309
Odissi, earliest sculptures, earliest text to mention 128
officer, first commissioned 262
official residence, largest 76
oil, first well 415
olive ridleys 359
Olympic Games, first Indian woman to become a member of IOC's Athletes' Commission 464, best performance in 467
Olympic Order, first Indian recipient (See also individual sports) 466
onion, first hybrid 91
online, most participants in a training/workshop, longest lesson, longest seminar 50
opera, first full-fledged 148, first in English by an Indian 149
operating system, most popular 220
operation, first active 291
operators' association, first 216
ordnance, first board 271
organic producers, largest number in the world 88
organisms, earliest multicellular discovered 310
organization, first all-India farmers' 403, largest media 202
origami, largest artwork solo (widest) 176
Ottanthullal, marathon performance 134
ozone, first to measure 303

P

pacemaker, first bi-ventricular 334
paddy, tallest plant 89
Padma Bhushan, youngest to receive 467
Padma Shri, first sportsman to be awarded 465
Padma Vibhushan, first sportsperson to receive, first woman sportsperson to get 465
Paes, Leander, 567, 568, 569
painting, earliest discovered 168, earliest rock 169, first gallery 169, first auction of contemporary Indian abroad 169; **marathon**, sand painting 176, acrylic colours – solo 176; **largest**, single wall– solo, portrait – acrylic paints – solo 174, oil paint – solo 175, natural colours – solo 175; **painter**, first realist 170
palace, facade on a wall 55, only with a bird sanctuary 58, largest chandelier 59; **oldest**, site excavated 53
panchayat, first 241
papaya, tallest plant 91
paper-making machine, first 194

paragliding, first from a high cliff 428, first at the Mantar XC Open Championship 429, first visually impaired person to, first to with a prosthetic leg 433
parallel dips, most in 1min. 27
paramotor, first international medallist 428, longest expedition 431
Param Vir Chakra, first (Air Force) 287, first (Army) 264
parcel, first service 211
park, largest zoological, highest national 363, first national, state/UT with most national 364
Parliament, animals on doors 258, committees, the story of the Indian 250 first couple 260, first hung 259, first session 258, first visually impaired member 258, longest term as speaker, most bills passed in a year 260, timeline of how the new House took shape 254; **Lok Sabha**, first deputy speaker 258, first dissolution 259, first speaker 258, highest average age, shortest term as speaker, lowest average age, shortest term 260; **Rajya Sabha**, first woman secretary general 259, longest tenure as chairman 260
pastries, most varieties 9
peak, highest 344
pearl, first culture 99
pencil art, largest drawing (solo) 171, largest portrait (solo) 174, marathon session 176
periodical, first vernacular, State/UT with the most newspaper and periodical publications 199
Periodic table, fastest to arrange all elements in order, fastest identification of all elements of the 2
pesticide, first 99, first synthetic 100, state/UT with highest use of chemical pesticides and biopesticides 99
PhD, first Indian to receive from a foreign university 115, first to obtain in library science 115, first to obtain a doctorate 116, most awarded by a university in a year 116
philately, first miniature sheet 213, first society 213, largest bureau 213, first exhibition 214, first national museum 214; **Federation Internationale de Philatelie (FIP)**, first Indian president 213
phirni, most varieties 10
phosphocreatine, discovery 306
photographer, first commercial 174, first woman photojournalist 164; **studio**, earliest commercial 164, first personal, oldest extant portrait 165
photography, earliest book 164, first photo-film manufacturing company, first course in, first society 165, largest unit for production/distribution, marathon (models) 166, marathon (city/structures) 166, first fellow of the British Photographic Society 167; **exhibition**, first photo 164, first permanent in space 168; **album**, earliest recorded commercial 164; **awards**, first to recieve the Hasselblad 166, first Asian to win the International Photography Award, first winner of the Wildlife Photographer of the Year title 167
pigeon pea, first hybrid 88

piglets, most in a single litter 96
pillar, oldest rust-free iron 52; **stambha**, earliest 53
pilot, first licence 376, first naval 274, oldest to obtain commercial licence 380, first Indian 281
pipeline, first 415, longest underground 76, longest underwater hydrocarbon 415
plan, first five-year, first annual 400, only to go through four governments 402
plane, first radio, first indigenously assembled 377
planetarium, oldest 299
plank, longest 27
planning, first commission 400
plant, at the highest altitude, largest family of, heaviest fruit, lightest wood, rare flowering 361, heaviest wood 362, first heavy water 413, first solar-powered thermal, largest grid-connected rooftop solar 414, longest tapioca, tallest musk mallow 368, oldest fossils 360, tallest rose, tallest prickly amaranth, tallest coriander, tallest bougainvillea, longest money 368
plastic, first state/UT to place a ban on bags 369
plog run, most participants 371
ploughed field, earliest 82
poet, first in English in India 180
Polar Satellite Launch Vehicle (PSLV), first flight 320
Poles, first at the Arctic, first at Antarctica, longest stay in Antarctica, first organization to reach 'three' 462; **North**, first to reach by surface, first to ski to 462; **South**, first at the geographic, first route recce to 462
Pole Star, first observation of 299
police, first all-woman station, first act, first dog squad, first transgender sub-inspector 242
political economy, first book on 400
political organization, first 225
political party, first constitution, oldest 225, first electoral win by an Indian 235, national party with most votes 260
pollen cryobank, first 84
polling station, highest 231
poppy, first non-narcotic 90
port, largest private, oldest operating and largest riverine 398, first corporatized 397, first private sector 398
postal communication, earliest 207
postal inspector, first woman 209
postal stamp, largest 44
postcard, biggest 37, first 209
postgraduate, first degree 114, most master's degree obtained 117, qualifications from most number of universities 116
postmaster, longest-serving 211
Postmaster General, first Indian 209
post office, first all-woman, first mobile 210, first drive-in, first online 211, first savings account 210, first delivery peons 209
potato chip, largest moulded 40
poultry, largest company 98
poverty, state/UT with lowest score on the scorecard 421
power, first hydro station 414, first indigenous atomic plant, first nuclear plant, first private company, largest private sector thermal station, largest supplier 413, largest thermal plant 414,

state with highest installed capacity of renewable 415
powerlifting, **Asian Championship**, best performance in Asian junior championship 547, best performance in sub-junior championship 548, most medals, most medals in one edition 547; **Asian Para Games**, first medal 548; **Commonwealth Championship**, best performance (men), first gold in Para Powerlifting, first medal in Para Powerlifting 548, most golds (individual) 547; **Olympia Pro**, back-to-back win 548; **World Championship**, best performance 547
power loom, first 421
Praggnanandhaa, Rameshbabu, 498
president, first woman 231, longest tenure 232, most from a state 233, of India, oldest, shortest tenure, youngest 232
press, first printing 194, first newsprint 196, first multilingual 194, first regulation 195
primate, with the longest tail 348
prime minister, first 233, first deputy 234, first to die in harness 233, first to resign, oldest, only woman, shortest tenure, youngest 234
printing, first lithographic 194
prison, first open 242, largest complex 243
Pritzker Prize, first architect 77
Privy Council, first Indians 240
programme, first master's in Hindu studies 114
pseudonym, first 180
PSU, first to go public 411
publication, state/UT with most Indian-language, most circulated Government, State/UT with most in a single language 200
public prosecutor, first 244
publisher, first independent 183, largest literary 182
publishing house, first feminist 183, largest trade 182
Pulitzer Prize, in 2022 197, first to win for a health/medicine-related publication 331; **winner**, first for feature photography 167
push-ups, most, half-knuckle in 1 min., diamond in 1 min., clap in 1 min., superman in 1 min., abdominal in 1 hr 26, side-jump in 1 min. 27, two-finger-both arms in 1 min. 26, most in 1 hr, two-thumb in 1 min., fingertip-one-arm in 1 min., by a woman in 1 min., contortion in 1 min. 25, tandem in 1 min. 30

Q

qawwali, marathon performance 145
quantum Zeno paradox, discovery 305
quasicrystals, new class 315
queue complex, biggest 61
quiche, most varieties of 10
quilling, largest artwork (solo) 174
quiz, first live on TV, first show on radio 125, first national TV quizmaster 126, longest-running open 125, most participants – offline quiz – multiple venues – single day, longest-running school, longest-running televised,

longest-running state-level, most participants in a single day – online, most participants in an offline – multiple venues – single day 126

R

radiation, first synchrotron facility 303
radio, first frequency modulation (FM) service, highest station, first national of play, first national of music, first sponsored 203, first of talks, first phone-in 204, most commercial anchored 203, first private FM station, first private station 202
radio phone link, first 216
radio source, first double 301
rafting, first event in the country 447, longest white-water expedition, nonstop expedition 454, most rivers in a month 452
rail, first construction company, first indigenous carriages 383, first green corridor 385, longest tunnel 386, longest rail manufactured 387, **station**, first 386, first fully solar-powered 388, first public-private partnership 384, with most platforms 386, busiest, with longest Platform, only listed as a UNESCO World Heritage Site 387, first with a green building certification 374
rainfall, maximum, minimum area 346
Rajya Sabha, first sportsman to be nominated 464
Ramayana, *Adipurush* and the tradition of remakes 154
Ramoji film city 162 (*See also film*)
Ramon Magsaysay Award, first scientist to receive 86
ramps, most constructed – single day 50
rapper, first female 144
rasgulla, most varieties of flavoured 14
Ravana, tallest effigy 7
Ravanhatha, longest 145
Reconnaissance Vehicle, first set of next-gen armoured engineer 270
refinery, first, oldest running 415
regiment, most decorated 264, special operations division 266, first para in action 270
registration centre, first computerized 210
rehabilitation, first low-vision centre 337
reign, shortest 223
relay, first between radio stations 204, first direct 202
relay race, longest 457
Remount and Veterinary Corps 272
Renewable Energy Mini-Ratna, approved for listing 414
replantation, first scalp 337
replica, biggest of ₹1 coin 37, largest of ₹500 note 40
republic, earliest on the subcontinent 222
Republic Day, first parade 223
research, early vet 92, first dairy institute 93, first institute for freshwater aquaculture 97, oldest fisheries institutes 98, institute located at highest altitude 85, largest scientific and industrial organization 306, only centre for tropical tuber crops, only weed centre 85
reserve, first marine 362

Reserve Bank of India (RBI), first Indian governor 406
reserves, highest Forex 403
reservoir, largest water 72
restaurant, first floating, first revolving 75
retail, first chain of computers 420
revenue, telecom in FY2023 217
reverse dips, most in 1 min. 27
revolver, first indigenous 267
rice, first Basmati hybrid 86
rifle, first regiment 265, first indigenous sniper 270, first factory 266
river, longest, largest system 344
road, earliest route 392
roaming, first national/ international service 217
robot, first sentry 270
rocket builder, India's first private 321
roof, largest retractable 76
rookery, largest 358
ropeway, highest and longest 80, longest river 80
Royal society of London, first Indian Fellow 86
Roy, Arundhati, another laurel 191
RRR 163
Rubik's cube, fastest to form the English alphabet while blindfolded 3, most solved in 5 mins, most solved in 1 hour 3, most solved in 15 mins 2
rugby, first international 15s victory 466
rugby stadium model, smallest 31
rule, first colonial 222, longest colonial 223
running, longest distance covered – single day 457
runway, fourth at Delhi airport 381, longest length 382
rupee, lowest level touched 421

S

Sahitya Akademi, first fellowship 188; **award**, first Bhasha Samman Awards 185, first recipients of 185, first Translation Prize 190
sailing, first down Ganga river, first on Brahmaputra River and longest on any Indian river 446, first on Beas River, first catamaran expedition, first around the Indian peninsula 447
samosa, most varieties 14
sandwich, longest 8
Sangeet Natak Akademi, first winners 131, first winners for creative dance 130; **text**, only pan-Indian 132
sanitary pad, largest arrangement in the shape of a 39
Sansad TV 255
Santa Claus, tallest 6
sapling, most distributed in a single day 371
saree, most styles draped 14
sarpanch, youngest 241
satellite, first centre 317, first fully indigenous 316, first indigenous launcher 320, first indigenous series, 317, first linkage, first private channel 205, first oceanographic 317, first private launched 321, first weather-cum-communications 317, heaviest launched 322, highest-resolution imaging 317, 100-plus launched in a single mission, lightest in orbit 322
satellite navigation system, first 394
satyagraha, first 223
saxophone, first woman professional players 140

school, earliest for girls, first for the hearing-impaired, first Indian abroad 103, first medical 105, first medical to offer degrees in Oncology 107, first military, first model-training 111, first of mines 110, first solar-powered, largest chain of government 104, largest open, largest science fair – multiple venues – single day, largest science fair – single venue – single day, oldest extant 103, oldest of art 114, only of tropical medicine 108
scientist, first chartered in aviation 117
scissors, smallest 35
screening, most people (multiple venues) 331, most people (single venue) 332
scripture, in the largest format 181
sculpture, largest bird 67, marathon session 176
search engine, most popular 219
sectoral fund, first 411
seed, first company 90
seismological zones, first mention 307
self-government, local in India 230
selfie, most people in 166
semiconductor, first laser 302
seminal plasmin, discovery 311
Sengol, the inauguration 256
serial, first 205, first Indian animation 206, first sci-fi 207
service, first express, first registered 211, first insured 210; **post**, under British rule 207
service provider, largest wireline 217, largest wireless, with number of rural subscribers – wireless 218
Shakespeare, **William**, only folio 180
Shardula Dvar 259
shares, of most companies held by an individual 412
sheriff, first Indian 242
ship, earliest representation, oldest, first to sail from India 396, first diesel engine 397, first dedicated cadet training 277, first fast attacker, first 'green' 278, first ocean minesweepers 277, first submarine depot, First submarine rescue ship 276
shoe, largest donation 47
shooting, **Asian Championship**, first gold 551, first medals haul 550, world record in skeet, most individual medals, world record at 551; **Asian Clay Championship**, best haul, first team gold 551, **Asian Games**, best haul 552, first gold 549, first medals 548, first woman to win a gold 550; **Commonwealth Games**, first gold 549, best haul 553; **Nationals**, first 550; **Olympics**, best haul 553, first ever individual gold medal 548, first finalist 549, first ever medal 551; **South Asian Games**, most career golds 551; **World Championship**, best haul, best haul in junior 552, first gold 549, world champion with a world record 550, youngest to win junior gold medal - men 553; **World Cup**, back-to-back golds in Junior, best haul, best performance (debut), double world record 552, first gold and silver medals 549, first mixed air pistol team gold medal 550, first pistol medal 549, first skeet gold 550, first to win two

golds 551, gold in 549, most medals, most medals in four consecutive, most medals in Junior, youngest to win gold (women) 553
shrimp, top producing state/UT 98
Siachen glacier, first to walk 459
silk, only producer of all five commercial varieties 89
silver article, largest 54
simulator, first indigenous training 267
Sindhu, P.V., Badminton Star 467, 482, 483, 484, 485, 486, 487
sines and cosines, use in place of chords 296
Singh, **Jeev Milkha**, 529, 530, 531, 532, 533, 534, 535
sit-ups, **most**, abdominal in 1 min., 1 min. 27
skydiving, first woman 428, first disabled in Asia 433, first woman to dive over seven continents 428, highest landing 431, most jumps 434, oldest woman 435
skyscraper, first 77
slide, oldest 78
SMS, first provider 216
snake, longest sea, longest, only that builds a nest, only 'flying', fastest, loudest hiss 356, only with heat sensors, at the highest altitude 357
Snowman, tallest 7
soap opera, most watched daily 207
social network, largest penetration 220
society, first mathematical 298
soil, earliest treatment experiments 98
soil sciences, first Indian society 83
solar, discovery of radio burst 300, first heated tent 370, first heater 301, largest single rooftop plant by area 374, trees to the rescue 370
SOS, first known use of signal 216
South Asian Games, best performance 467
space, first Indian organization 316, first man in 317, first private sector launches 316, first university for study of outer 320, first venture 316, first woman 321
spacecraft, world's smallest launched 322
sperm, first bank 329
spices, first research institute 84, largest producer of 92
spinning wheel, smallest 36
squadron, first, first bomber, first transport, first to have a jet bomber, first heavy-lift transport, first attack helicopter 287
squash, **Asian Championships**, first individual medals 554, first to win world doubles title, first to win mixed doubles 555; **Asian Games**, best in 556; **Asian Junior Championship**, best performance 555, first silver 554, first to win title (girls) 555; first international success (women) 554, Commonwealth Games, most gold, most national titles won 556; **Junior**, first world No. 1 554; **Nationals**, first champion 554, first doubles champion 555, junior and senior titles 554, most titles, most titles in a row (men) 556, most titles in a row (women)/(men) 555, oldest champion 557, youngest champion (women) 556; **professionals**, first

554; **rankings**, highest 557; **World Championships**, best performance in 555; **world ranking titles**, first to win 554; **World Team Championships**, best performance, youngest champion (men), youngest to represent India 556

squats, most, alternative in 1 min. 30, jump in 1 min., most in 1 min., most by a woman in 1 min., pistol – alternating legs in 1 min. 27

stamp, first autograph-inscribed 213, first featuring wildlife 214, first international exhibition 215, first of independent India 213, first differently-shaped 212, first to be jointly issued with another country 211, first commemorative, first one-rupee charity, first designer (pre-independence) 213, from most countries in honour of a person 211, first, first state to issue (pre-1947), first Indian featuring a woman, first customization of 212

stand-up paddle-boarding, first surfing and competition, longest group 452, most 451

stars variability, discovery of 301

state transport system, first (road) 392

state/UT, first with 100 per cent literacy, highest literacy rate, highest/lowest female literacy rate, highest percentage of graduates, lowest literacy rate, lowest percentage of graduates 102, first modern Indian 237, states v. union territory 248, with the highest sex ratio, with the lowest sex ratio 248; **state**, cleanest 372, first fully organic, first to regulate crops 82, first to enact law on contract farming 83, first linguistic (post-1947), first linguistic (pre-1947) 236, first under president's rule 239, least densely populated 248, least populated, most densely populated, most populated 247, sharing border with most states, with longest international border, with the largest area, with the longest coastline 237, with the smallest area, youngest 238; **UT**, least densely populated, least populated 164, most densely populated, most populated 247, youngest 238

statue, largest Nandi, largest Shivalinga 67, tallest, tallest monolithic, tallest Shani Dev, tallest shivalinga 66

steam, engine, first builder of 412, first powered plant 414, oldest 396

steamboat, first 396

steel, first manufacture 315

steel charkha, biggest 38

stepwell, deepest 53, most elaborate 77

stock exchange, first woman director of 412 first woman president of, highest price for membership 409, oldest, with highest turnover 412, with highest volume of derivative contracts, with most listed companies 411

stone, largest, urinary bladder removed 338, kidney removed 339

store, highest number opened in a single day 423

strike, first labour, first organized 402, largest 403
structures, earliest 52, first spaceframe concrete 75, largest tent 79, oldest extant marble 55, tallest Durga, tallest hollow stone 66, tallest reinforced Earth 79
stupa, largest 54
submarine, first base 276, first nuclear 274, first deep-sea rescue system 280, first indigenous 277
Subscriber Trunk Dialling (STD), first 215
sugar cane, tallest 89
sundial, biggest 301
superconductors, first prediction of hot 303
Super Fab lab, first 314
surface salinity, highest, lowest 347
surgeon, **first**, neurosurgeon, psychosurgeon 330 woman neurosurgeon, woman general 335
surgery, **first**, bloodless breast, laser on trachea, global telecast of, craniopagus 333, video-assisted heart, heart-shrink, Maze III, coronary artery bypass 334, department of minimal access 328, on heaviest woman, on world's heaviest teenager 342, oldest to undergo hip 337, first open-heart, first separation of conjoined twins, earliest cataract 332, father of plastic surgery 333
survey sample, largest 324
swimming, **Angel Island marathon**, first to complete the round-trip 451; **Antarctic waters**, first and youngest Asian woman to 449; **Asian Games**, first diver 557, first gold 560, first swimmer, first water polo teams 557; **Asian Indoor Games**, first medal 558, at the highest altitude 454; **Commonwealth Games**, first to participate 558, first para swimmer to win bronze 559, first relay team in finals, first to participate, first to reach finals 558; **English Channel**, fastest across 453, first to swim thrice solo, first woman to cross 450, oldest to cross 454, woman to cross the English channel – solo, to swim the English Channel thrice – solo 450, at the highest altitude 454, first and youngest Asian woman across Antarctic waters 449, first to swim from mainland to Anacapa Island 450; **Gibraltar Strait**, fastest Asian to cross 449, first backstroke without neoprene, first woman to swim the 450, king of 451; **Nationals**, 200 m freestyle first under two minutes, first 100 m freestyle under one minute 558; **Ocean's Seven challenge**, first in the world to complete, youngest in the world to complete 448; **Olympics**, first swimmer 557, first to qualify for two events 558, first swimmer to make 'A' cut – men's 100 m backstroke event, first swimmer to make 'A' cut – men's 200 m butterfly event 559, participation in two consecutive games 560; **Para Asian Games** first para swimmer to win gold 559; **Paralympic Games**, first visually impaired swimmer to

win a gold 559, first national championship 558, first Indian para-swimmer to qualify, participation in two consecutive games 559; **paraplegic**, long distance swimming by a woman, longest open-sea swimming 453; **seven seas**, first Asian woman to swim across 449; **Triple Crown**, first to complete 451, oldest to complete 454
synagogue, oldest active 61, largest 64

T

table, largest 75
table tennis, **Asian Cup**, first gold medallist in Asian Championship 560, best individual performance 566, first to win medal – women 562; **Asian Juniors**, first medal 562, first pair to win mixed doubles 563; **Commonwealth Championship**, best doubles performance 566; **Commonwealth Games**, first winner men singles 561, first winner women singles 560, first gold men team 561, first gold medal mixed doubles, first team title men 560, first gold women team, first to regain gold men team, first gold men doubles 561, first medal women doubles 562, medallist in five successive games first 561, most medals, most medals from, first professional, most medal won by an individual player in a single edition 563; **International Table Tennis Federation**, first Indian to be a member of Umpires and Referees Committee 563, first title-triumph in junior tour 562, longest mixed doubles reign 563, most senior/junior titles in a year 560, most team titles (men/women) 564; **National**, first champion 562, most appearances, most state representation 564, most singles titles in a row 560, no games conceded 560, youngest to win title 566, most titles singles 564; **Olympics**, first woman to play two 560, youngest to qualify 561; **ranking**, first to be World no. 1 in U-18 562; **South Asian Federation Games**, most gold medals in 564; **tournament**, most participants 566; **World Championship,** first to reach quarter-finals 560, best team performance 566, first doubles pair in the quarter-finals 560, second division titles 566; **ITTF Pro Tour**, first title 354; **World Junior Championship**, first team medal 354; **WTT Contender title**, first pair to win 563; **Table Tennis in India** 564
talkie, first, first female actor 152
tank, earliest, first indigenous 266, highest battle in the world 271
tarts, most varieties of mini 9
tea, first estate 89, highest garden 89, most varieties prepared 11, oldest research station 85
telecast, first, first national 204
telecom, **5G service**, first carrier to demonstrate capability 216
tele-density, state/UT with highest 218

telefilm, first 205
telegram, first Indian radio telegraphy company, first director general, first Indo-European line, last 215
telephone, first automatic exchange, first push-button 216, first internet telephony service, first exchange 217
telescope, first liquid mirror only for astronomical observations 303, first robotic 301, largest optical 300
television, first teleshopping 205, tallest tower 206, first private producer of national news 206; **broadcasting**, first simultaneous, first colour, first colour transmission 204
tempera method, earliest use 168
temperature, highest, lowest 346
temple, biggest bell 62, biggest lamp 61, earliest extant Hindu, earliest extant structure 59, heaviest and highest single stone shikhara 65, largest cave complex 63, largest collection of, largest sun 64, most sculptures in 63, oldest extant with a shikhara 61, oldest leaning, oldest yogini 60, only Nataraja 62, only quadrangular yogini 60, only rat, only with an apsidal sanctum 62, tallest tower 65
Tendulkar, **Sachin**, 122, 184, 465, 508, 509, 510, 512, 513
tennis, **Asian Games**, first doubles gold medallist, first singles gold, first gold medallist doubles mixed 567; **ATP Tour**, first Indian to win 2 ATP Challengers singles titles, first Indian to win ATP Challenger on European Clay, oldest player to win ATP Masters title – doubles 571; **Australian Open**, first all-Indian mixed doubles title, first junior boy's champion, first men's doubles title, first mixed doubles title 570, best singles result 567; **Billie Jean King (Federation) Cup**, first team to qualify world play-offs 567; **Davis Cup**, best record in Asia 568, first appearance, Junior regional champs, most appearances, most successful doubles player 568; **French Open**, first All-Indian men's doubles 570, first and only junior champion, first mixed doubles title 569; **Nationals**, first (grass court), most titles 571; **US Open**, first and only junior boys' title, first doubles title, first mixed doubles title, first women's doubles title 570; **Wimbledon**, first junior boy's title 568, first junior girl's doubles title 569, first men's doubles title 568, first mixed doubles title, first seeded 569, first to play 568, first Indian women, first titles doubles mixed 559
terrapin, largest 359
tetracycline, discovery 306
thali, biggest by dishes 39
theatre, Asia's biggest festival 150, earliest open-air 53, first commercial, most theatrical performances 149, oldest cave 146, origins of social 149, oldest children's, first public hall 148
The Elephant Whisperers 156 (*See also film*)
theory, first on infinite dimensional

representations 298
thermal, new method for conductivity 304
thiosulphuric acid, discovery of isomerism 306
tickets, most booked in advance 161
tie, most knots tied in 1 minute 3
tiger, largest camera trap census 363
tokamak, first 305
tomb, earliest known monumental, first garden 57
tortoise, smallest 359
toys, most, donated – single day 50
tractor, earliest use 89, first semi-autonomous, state/UT with most exports, largest seller 100
trading, first automatic exchange and screen-based 409, state/UT with the highest contribution to equity 412
traditional lamp, biggest 38
traffic, first advanced control system 394, first police 392
train, fastest, first passenger, first double-decker 383, first air-conditioned, first deluxe, first electric 384, first Vistadome 385, longest route 388, first corporatized 387
training centre, first 207, postal network 209
tram, first company 383, first cars 384
translator, most prolific - published literary works 188
transplant, **first**, hear, liver, womb, paediatric heart, thumb 336, double (liver and kidney) 337
transport, first indigenous payment eco-system for 393, first regular public system 392
tree, longest-lived species, fastest maturing, tallest, biggest trunk, largest hollow 360, largest canopy 361, tallest jamun 368; **most**, planted in 15 mins, planted in one hour 371, planted in one day, planted in a quarter 374
trekking, oldest trekker, longest desert – group 461; **Snowman trek**, first women's team to complete 460; **Everest Base Camp**, fastest by a disabled person 461
Trinity of Carnatic Music 135
tumour, heaviest brain removed 339, largest bone removed, largest small-intestinal removed, largest breast removed 338, heaviest, ovarian removed 337, largest, cystic of the liver removed, largest oral (head and neck) removed in one piece, largest thoracic removed 339
tunnel, longest transportation railway 80
turtle, largest, rarest freshwater, smallest carapace 359
type, earliest 194
typewriters, first, first indigenous 194

U

umbrella, biggest 39
underwater, clean-up 294
union, oldest banking employees' trade, oldest insurance trade 402, oldest trade 401
Union Government, first non-congress 234
United Nations, first Indian to design a stamp for 214, first use of Hindi 236
university, first energy studies, first virtual medical 108, first

women's, first technical, first technical for women, first railway 109, first five residential 108, first for the disabled 112, first only for tribal students 114, first of fisheries and ocean studies, first university for the study of outer space 110, first law 111, first Sanskrit, first modern, first act, longest functioning ancient, first five 105, first rural 107, first veterinary 113, largest open 117
University of Delhi 116
Uranus, discovery of rings 300
uterine transplant, first woman to give birth after 324

V

vaccine, first indigenously developed 328, largest company 329
vada, most varieties of 10
vanadium, discovery 308
Vande Bharat, breaks record 386
vanilla, first cultivation 90
varsity, first air 378
vessels, first, latest training, first indigenous offshore patrol 293
vest, first indigenously made bulletproof 267
veterinary, first surgeon 93, state with most institutions 97, first army school 182
Viaduct, longest double-decker 388, most metro stations 389
vice president, first, oldest to assume office, shortest tenure 231
Victoria Cross 263
Victoria Cross, first, youngest to receive 263
video viewership, highest concurrent 220
village, earliest settlement 52, first green 369
virology, first institute of advanced 328
Vishisht Seva Medal, first couple to be awarded 286
volcano, only active 347

W

wall clock, largest 38
war, first of independence 222, first national memorial, first high-altitude warfare school 272; **camel**, first Bactrian to join the army 273, **dogs**, first Indian breed in active duty 273; **International Scout Masters Competition (ISMC)**, first win 273
warship, first indigenous modern 277, first modern builder, first modern ship building yard 279, first multi 278
warship/aircraft, longest serving 279
waterfall, highest 346
wave, highest 310
weightlifting, Asian Championship, record in clean and jerk (women) 573; **Asian Games**, first medal, first medal (women) 572; **Asian Meet**, best performance 573; **Commonwealth Games**, back-to-back gold medals 572, first gold (men) 573, most medals, most medals (women) 573, youngest winner 574; **Nationals**, oldest champion, youngest champion 574; **Olympics**, first silver 572, qualifying gold 571; **World and**

Asian meets, most medals 573; **World Championship**, first medal 571, most gold medals 574, **World Junior Championship**, first gold 572
WhatsApp, largest user base 219
wildlife sanctuary, state/UT with most 364
Wimbledon Centre Court, smallest 35
windsurfing, marathon 454
wireless, first demonstration 302
woman, first advocate 244, first ambassador 240, first cabinet minister 236, first career diplomat 241, first chairperson of the International Civil Aviation Organization (ICAO) Aviation Security Committee 381, first chief Justice 245, first chief minister 239, first director general of CSIR 307, first film-maker 153, first foreign concert tour by instrumentalist 148, first full-time finance minister 235, first IAS officer 240, first Indian on the United Nations law board 246, first instrumentalist 141, first ghatam player 142, first nadaswaram player, first shehnai player 141, first to perform at UN 142, first in the army 262, first in military police 263, first IPS officer 243, first judge of the Supreme Court, first judicial officer 245, first marine pilot 396, first mayor 241, first president of the Indian National Congress (*See also Congress*) 225, first rulers 222, first sarpanch 240, first technical university for (*See also university*) 109, first train driver 386, first vice chancellor, first graduates, first bachelor of medicine, law graduate, first to obtain a PhD in a scientific discipline, first doctor 115, highest number of pilots 381, first commercial pilot 380, first Airbus commander, first airbus pilot 381, first to obtain a pilot's licence, first chief executive officer of an airline, first offshore pilot 382, oldest to deliver twins 337, youngest sarpanch 241, first legislator 259, first all-woman crew to circumnavigate the world 281, first air marshal, first flight commander 284, first commissioned pilot by Order of Merit, first combat pilots, first medical officer (Air Force) 285, first in defence services staff, first pilot to lead the Republic Day fly-past 286, first hovercraft pilot, first pilot, first combatants 292, first maritime reconnaissance pilot, first pilot of naval aircraft 274, first officer as 'Observers' 275
Women athletes of India 477
Women in Indian Air Force 285
Women's Hockey 541
Women's IPL 505
Women's Kabaddi 545
Women's Weightlifting 572
woollen caps, **most donated**, group–single day–single venue 49, caps donated 48
workers, on board 402
World Bank Group, first woman managing director and chief financial officer 407
World Food Prize, first winner 86
World Transplant Games, first Indian woman to participate 466
wraps, most varieties 10

wrestling, **Asian Championship**, best performance 577, best performance at Asian Championship 579, first gold (women), first Indian couple to win silver 576, most medals 579, most medals (U-15) (girls) 580; **Asian Games**, first gold, first gold (men), first medal 576, youngest champion 580; **Asian Games, Commonwealth Games and World Championships**, first winner of all (women) 575; **award**, first coach of the year, first junior wrestler of the year 576; **Commonwealth Championship**, most individual medals (men) 580, most medals 579; **Commonwealth Games**, best performance (men) 578, best performance (women) 579, first medal 575, most consecutive title (women), most gold medals (men) 579, youngest gold medallist 580; **Greco-Roman**, first gold 578; **Greco-Roman Championship**, first medals (U-17) 577; **Junior World Champion**, first 576; **Laureus World Sports Award**, first and only woman to win 576; **Olympic and World Championship**, first winner of both 574; **Olympics**, first at the, first medal (men), first woman at the 574; **World Championship**, back-to-back medals 577, first to win gold in U-20 575, best performance 579, first gold medallist 575, first medal (men), first medal (women) 575, most individual medals 580

Y

yachting, at the highest altitude 454
yak, first test-tube calf 96
yield, highest-ever crude throughput and distillate 415
yoga, **longest**, *ekapada shirshasana*, *bakasana*, *janu shirshasana* 28, *setu bandhasana*, *ashtavakrasana*, *vishvamitrasana*, *Hanumanasana*, *parshva poorna dhanurasana* 24, *padma mayurasana*, *mayurasana* – with one hand, *purvattanasana*, *mandukasana*, *nirlamba ushtrasana* 25, *paschimottanasana*, *padangushthasana* 29
youth, largest share of 420
YouTube, most subscribed channel, most viewed Indian video 220
Yudh Seva Medal, first 293, first and only Sarvottam (Air Force) 286, first woman to be awarded (Air Force) 286

Z

zentangle, largest art 171
zero, first to understand 296
zinc, earliest artefact 315
zipline, highest by a differently abled person 432
zoo, oldest 362
zoologist, first 310

PRELIMS I–XII

Title page: by courtesy of the record holder; **vi–xii**: **Contents**: images have been credited under the respective chapters below.

HUMAN STORY 1–50

Images are by the courtesy of record holders; **4**: **background**: Karolina Grabowska/Pexels.com; **5**: **top (background)**: Shutterstock.com; **22–23**: **background**: Delpixel/ Shutterstock.com; **28–29**: **background**: Shutterstock.com.

STRUCTURES 51–80

Opener Pic, **51**: Shutterstock.com; **52**: Iron pillar: Shutterstock.com; **55**: Forest fort of Ranthambhore: Shutterstock.com; **56–57**: background: Qutb Minar complex: Shutterstock.com; **Insets, top**: Garhi tomb: Shutterstock.com; **bottom**: Tomb of Sikandar Lodi: Shutterstock.com; **58**: **top**: Kumbhalgar fort: Shutterstock.com; **bottom**: Kalinjar Fort: Shutterstock.com; **61**: Paradesi synagogue: Shutterstock.com; **62**: Tawang monastery: Shutterstock.com; **63**: **top**: Bashir mosque: Shutterstock.com; **bottom**: Natural arch Tirumala: Shutterstock.com; **69**: Double-decker steel bridge: by courtesy of the record holder; **72**: Grand Anicut: Shutterstock.com; **72**: India gate: Shutterstock.com; **78–79**: **background**: Tallest Reinforced Earth Structure: by courtesy of the record holder; **80**: Longest ropeway: rima das mukherjee/ Shutterstock.com.

AGRICULTURE 81–100

Opener pic, **81**: REAFON GATES/ Pexels.com; **82**: Sahil Ghosh/ Shutterstock.com; **84**: **top**: Biomaterial in liquid nitrogen: Shutterstock.com; **inset**: Locust: Shutterstock.com; **85**: Micro-irrigation: Shutterstock.com; **88**: Farmer in a mustard field: Shutterstock.com; **89**: Tea gardens in Nilgiris: Shutterstock.com; **90**: Vineyard: Shutterstock.com; **91**: **top**: Jackfruit: Shutterstock.com; **bottom**: coconut: Shutterstock.com; **92**: Indian spices: Shutterstock.com; **93**: Camels in NRCC: Shutterstock.com; **94–95**: **background**: Shutterstock.com; **96**: Horse: Shutterstock.com; **98**: Rohu fish: Shutterstock.com; **99**: CMFRI: by courtesy of Central Marine Fisheries Research Institute (CMFRI), Kochi, Kerala; **100**: **top**: Farmer spraying pesticide: Shutterstock.com; **bottom**: Mahindra tractors: Rangeecha/Shuttestock.com

EDUCATION 101–126

Opener pic, **101**: Shutterstock.com; **102**: Maulana Abul Kalam Azad stamp: GODL–India/India Post; **104**: Serampore college: PD–UK/ US; Bankim Chandra Chattopadhyay: PD–India/US; **108**: **top**: J.J. School of Art stamp: SUDARSHAN BHATLA/ Shutterstock.com; **bottom**: BHU: Rahul Banarasi/Shutterstock.com **111**: RIMC: Hindustan Times; **113**: **background**: Shutterstock.com;

116: University of Delhi: PD/Seek1 at English Wikipedia; **118**: Delhi Public Library: Hindustan Times; **123**: Dinosaur museum: Hindustan Times; **124**: PM museum: by courtesy of PIB.

PERFORMING ARTS 127–150

Opener Pic, 127: SN040288/ Shutterstock.com; **128**: Dancing Girl of Mohenjodaro: CC0 1.0 Universal/ Gary Todd; **129**: Nautch Girls: Wikimedia Commons/Fair Use/ Hooper and Western (http://www.columbia.edu/itc/mealac/pritchett/00routesdata/1800_1899/women/nautchphotos/nautchphotos.html); **130**: Thickest Make-up: DHEEKSHIT K DAS/Shutterstock.com; **131**: Sculpture of Panini: CCA-SA 4.0 International/Author Unknown; **135**: Muthuswamy Dikshitar: rook76/Shutterstock.com **136–137**: **background**: Pikoso.kz/Shutterstock.com; **Insets, clockwise from top**: Mridangam: muthugpd/Shutterstock.com; Tabla: Alexxx Shmel/Shutterstock.com; Bansuri: ANGO.IN/Shutterstock.com; Sarod: silentwings_M_Ghosh/ Shutterstock.com; Sitar: Tattoboo/ Shutterstock.com; Ghatam: Wikimedia Commons/Fair Use/ Sven.petersen; Veena: PRL/ Shutterstock. com; Shehnai: reddees/Shutterstock.com; **139**: Lata Mangeshkar: CCA-SA 4.0 International/LataRamdas.jpg; **140**: M.S. Subbulakshmi: CCA-SA 3.0 Unported/ Saregama Carnatic; **141**: A.R. Rahman: Featureflash Photo Agency/Shutterstock.com; **147**: Jogimara Cave: CCA-SA 4.0 International/Biospeleologist; **149**: Social Theatre: MOROZ NATALIYA/Shutterstock.com; **150**: Akash Bhadsavle: by courtesy of the record holder.

VISUAL ARTS 151–176

Opener pic, 151: Shutterstock.com; **152**: *Alam Ara* advertisement: PD–India; **153**: A. Sreekar Prasad: by courtesy of the record holder; **156**: *The Elephant Whisperers* event: Hindustan Times; **157**: Dastagir: PD–US; **158**: Akshay Kumar: GODL–India/Vice President's Secretariat; **159**: **top**: *Neecha Nagar* poster: Kailash 29792/ Fair use; **bottom**: *Do Bigha Zamin* poster: Kailash 29792/Fair use; **160**: *Mera Naam Joker* poster: Indians/Fair use; **162**: Ramoji film city: Joe Ravi/Shutterstock.com; **163**: *RRR* poster: Krimuk 2.0/Fair use; Mariinskey Palace: CCA-SA 4.0 International/Roman Naumav/ https://creativecommons.org/licenses/by-sa/4.0/deed.en; try of Information and Broadcasting; **bottom**: *Naatu Naatu* audio cover: Ranjith207/Fair use; **164**: Homai Vyaravalla: GODL–India/Ministry of Information and Broadcasting; **165**: Museo Camera Museum: by courtesy of Radhika Chauhan; **166**: Selfie: by courtesy of the record holder; **167**: Sir Prodyot Coomar Tagore: PD; **169**: Bhimbetka: Shutterstock.com; **170**: **top**: *Shakuntala* painting: PD; **bottom**: Raja Ravi Varma: PD/Bhawani Ram; **172–173**: **background**: by courtesy of Aravani Art Project (Artist),

Pranav Gohil (photographer) and St+Art India Foundation; **Insets, from left to right**: by courtesy of Vanita Ganesh; CCO 1.0 Universal Public Domain Dedication/DesiBoy101; **174**: Quilling: by courtesy of the record holders; **175**: Doodle art: by courtesy of record holder; **176**: Sandpainting: by courtesy of the record holder.

LITERATURE 177–192

Opener pic, 177: Shutterstock.com; **179**: *Tholkappiyam*: PD/த*உழவன்; **181**: Sign language: Shutterstock.com; **182**: Bookaroo festival: by courtesy of Parul Gulati; **184**: **background**: Shutterstock.com; **186–187**: **from left to right**: *War of Lanka* cover: by courtesy of HarperCollins India; *Get Epic Shit Done* cover: by courtesy of Juggernaut Books; *The Magic of the Lost Story* cover: by courtesy of Penguin Random House India; *Fantastic Beasts*: *The Secrets of Dumbledore* cover: by courtesy of Hachette India; *The Gutsy Girls of Science* cover: by courtesy of HarperCollins India; *World History in 3 Points* cover: by courtesy of Hachette India; **188**: Bibek Debroy: by courtesy of PIB; **191**: **background**: lev radin/Shutterstock.com.

MEDIA AND COMMUNICATION 193–220

Opener Pic, 193: Illus_man/Shutterstock.com; **194**: Press Trust of India: MukeshR/Shutterstock.com; **195**: Hicky's Bengal Gazette: Wikimedia Commons/Fair Use/James Augustus Hicky; **196**: *The Times of India*: Art Now/Shutterstock.com; **197**: Danish Siddiqui: PradeepGaurs/Shutterstock.com; **202**: Akashvani Logo: CCA-SA 4.0 International/All India Radio; **204**: Mandi House: Wikimedia Commons/Fair Use/Ekabhishek; **206**: NDTV: rafapress/Shutterstock.com; **207**: Madras General Post Office: Wikimedia Commons/Fair Use/India Illustrated; **212**: First airmail: SUDARSHAN BHATLA/Shutterstock.com; **213**: Stamp of Rabindranath Tagore: spatuletail/Shutterstock.com; **214**: **top**: Birds and animals as carriers of mail: SUDARSHAN BHATLA/Shutterstock.com; **217**: JIO Digital: WESTOCK PRODUCTIONS/Shutterstock.com.

GOVERNMENT 221–248

Opener, Pic, 221: Wikimedia Commons/Fair Use/आशीष भटनागर; **222**: Tomb of Razia Sultan: Pradeep Gaur/Shutterstock.com; **224**: **top**: National Flag: Shutterstock.com; **middle**: Copper coins: Shutterstock.com; **225**: Sonia Gandhi: Government Open Data License–India(GODL)/Ministry of Parliamentary Affairs; **227**: Election Ink: Soumen82hazara/Shutterstock.com; **228**: Chief Election Commissioner: John 1107/Shutterstock.com; **230**: Local Self Government: Saikatpaul/ Shutterstock.

com; **231**: V.V.Giri: Sudarshan Bhatla/Shutterstock.com, **232**: Droupadi Murmu: Government Open Data License-India(GODL)/ President's Secretariat; **234**: Indira Gandhi: Shutterstock.com; **236**: Mehrangarh Fort: Shutterstock.com; **238**: Panchayat Anganwadi Centre: Neeraj Chaturvedi/ Shutterstock.com; **243**: **top**: Allahabad High Court: Harshit Srivastava S3/Shutterstock.com; **244–245**: **background**: Supreme Court: mrinalpal/Shutterstock.com; **246**: Greater Chennai Corporation: Sira Anamwong/Shutterstock.com; **248**: Puducherry: PRASANTH_K_RAJ/Shutterstock.com.

PARLIAMENT 249–260

Opener pic, 165: by courtesy of PIB; **251**: Old Parliament Building: Hindustan Times; **253**: New Parliament: by courtesy of PIB; **254–255**: **background and insets**: by courtesy of PIB; **172**: Inside New Parliament: by courtesy of PIB; **257**: **top, bottom**: by courtesy of Amit Bhattacharya.

DEFENCE 261–294

Opener Pic, 261: Hamara/ Shutterstock.com; **262**: Sam Manekshaw: Hindustan Times; **263**: top: Victoria Cross: Steve Ellis/Shutterstock.com; **264**: Param Vir Chakra: rook76/Shutterstock.com; **266**: First Indigenous Tank: CCA-SA 4.0 International/Swapnil. Karambelkar; **267**: Longest-range missile: Government Open Data License-India(GODL)/President's Secretariat/DRDO; **268**: HAL 'Prachand': Government Open Data License-India(GODL)/IAF; **bottom**: ALH Dhruv: BoeingMan777/ Shutterstock.com; **269**: **top left**: Udaygiri: Government Open Data License-India(GODL)/Ministry of Defence, **top right**: Nistar and Nipun: Government Open Data License–India(GODL)/ Hindustan Shipyard Limited; **bottom**: Offshore Patrol Vessel: by courtesy of PIB; **272**: Remount and Veterinary Corps: CCA-SA 4.0 International/Indian Army; **274**: INS Chakra: Wikimedia Commons/Fair Use/Unknown sailor or employee of U.S. Navy; **276**: Arihant Class Submarine: CCA-SA 4.0 International/Abjura; **277**: INS *Viraat*: Government Open Data License–India(GODL)/Indian Navy; **282–283**: **background**: BoeingMan777/Shutterstock.com, **top left**: Aerial Defense: CC BY-SA 2.0 Generic/g4sp, **bottom left**: Aerial Warfare: CCA-SA 4.0 International/Echo1Charlie; **top right**: Rustom UAV: Aerospace Trek/Shutterstock.com; **middle right**: HADR: Kmatton/ Shutterstock.com; **285**: Women in Indian Air Force: Government Open Data License–India(GODL)/ Ministry of Defence of India; **286**: Yudh Seva Medal: Government Open Data License–India(GODL)/ Indian Navy; **288**: HAL Tejas: Courtesy of Sohang Kapur; **290**: HAL-HJT16: CCA-SA 3.0 Unported /Aeroprints.com; **292**: ICGS *Sachet*: Government Open Data License–India(GODL)/Indian Coast Guard.

IMAGE COPYRIGHT INFORMATION

SCIENCE AND TECHNOLOGY 295–322

Opener Pic, 295: Sergey Nivens/ Shutterstock.com **299**: Pole Star: Shutterstock.com; **302**: Crescograph: CCA-SA 3.0 Unported/Wikimedia.org; **303**: Liquid Miror Telescope: by courtesy of Deparment of Science and Technology, Government of India (dst.gov.in); **306**: Bengal Chemicals: by courtesy of Brotish Kar; **307**: Dinosaur Fossil illustration: Shutterstock.com, **309**: GSI: by courtesy of Brotish Kar; **312**: Linnean Medal: Wikimedia Commons/Fair Use; **314**: Supercomputer: Shutterstock.com; **316**: First Indigenous Satellite: by courtesy of Indian Space Research Organization (ISRO); **318–319**: images of Chandrayaan-3: by courtesy of ISRO; **321**: Kalpana Chawla: Nasa.gov **322**: Sriharikota: Kaarthikeyan.SM/Shutterstock.com.

MEDICAL SCIENCES 323–342

Opener pic, 323: Jonathan Borba/ Pexels.com; **325**: IVF under microscope: Shutterstock.com; **326**: Calcutta Medical College: by courtesy of Brotish Kar; **327**: Doctors operating: Mazhar Ahmad/ Shutterstock.com; **328**: Endoscopy equipment: Shutterstock.com; **329**: Apollo app: sdx15/Shutterstock.com; **329**: **background**: Shutterstock.com; **330**: WHO: Elenarts/Shutterstock.com; **331**: PGIMER: PradeepGaurs/ Shutterstock.com; **333**: Sushruta: Anuja Mukhopadhyay/ Shutterstock.com; **334**: Dr. Naresh Trehan: World Economic Forum/ CCA-SA 2.0 Generic (https://commons.wikimedia.org/wiki/File:Naresh_Trehan_at_the_World_Economic_Forum_on_India_2012.jpg); **335**: **background**: Shutterstock.com; **336**: Cochlear implant: Shutterstock.com; **338**: Largest bone tumour: by courtesy of the record holder; **342**: Largest adrenal cyst: by courtesy of the record holder.

THE NATURAL WORLD 343–374

Opener pic, 343: Anirudh Vidyabhushan/Pexels.com; **344**: Mt Kanchenjunga: Shutterstock.com; **345**: Lonar crater: Shutterstock.com; **346**: Mawsynram: Shutterstock.com; **348**: Blue whale: Shutterstock.com; **349**: **top background**: Dolphin: Shutterstock.com; **Inset**: Blackbuck: Shutterstock.com; **bottom background**: Loris: Shutterstock.com; **inset**: Dugong: Shutterstock.com; **350**: Flying fox: Shutterstock.com; **351**: Flamingo; **352**: Sarus crane: Shutterstock.com; **353**: Bullfrog: Shutterstock.com; **355**: Flying gecko: Shutterstock.com; **356**: Flying snake: Shutterstock.com; **357**: Seahorse: Shutterstock.com; **358–359**: background: Shutterstock.com; **361**: Himalayan rhubarb: Shutterstock.com; **363**: Arignar Anna Zoological Park: Albin Raj/ Shutterstock.com; **364**: Kosi River:

Shutterstock.com; **365**: and **368**: by courtesy of the record holders; **370**: Solar tree: Shutterstock.com; **372**: **background**: Saud Visuals/Shutterstock.com; **Inset**: Waterfall: Shutterstock.com; **373**: **background**: CCA-SA 4.0 International/Swarna1311 (https://commons.wikimedia.org/wiki/File:Shore_Temple_-Mamallapuram_-Tamil_Nadu_-N-TN-C55.jpg); **374**: Tree planting: Shutterstock.com.

TRANSPORT 375–398

Opener Pic, 375: Iam_Anuphone/Shutterstock.com; **376**: Malabar Princess: CCA-SA 4.0 International/Swissair; **378**: Air India: viper-zero/Shutterstock.com; **380**: Cochin International Airport: PREJU SURESH/Shutterstock.com; **381**: Delhi Airport: saiko3p/Shutterstock.com; **385**: Vistadome Train: Lalam photography/Shutterstock.com; **386**: Vande Bharat Express: Jimmy Kamballur/Shutterstock.com; **387**: Chhatrapati Shivaji Terminal: saiko3p/Shutterstock.com; **388**: **top**: Longest double decker viaduct: by courtesy of the record holder; **bottom**: Guwahati Railway Station: vector photo gallery/Shutterstock.com; **390–391**: **background**: Dinesh Hukmani/Shutterstock.com; **392**: First indigenous automatic car: Suti Stock Photo/Shutterstock.com; **393**: CNG Auto: Neng etta/Shutterstock.com; **395**: Hindustan Shipyard Limited: CCA-SA 4.0 International/Ramki01061966; **398**: MV *Ganga Vilas*: by courtesy of Antara Cruises.

BUSINESS AND ECONOMY 399–426

Opener Pic, 399: Shutterstock.com; **400**: **top**: Chanakya coin: AnilD/Shutterstock.com; **401**: Dr Manmohan Singh: PradeepGaurs/Shutterstock.com; **404**: Cowrie: Shutterstock.com; **410–411**: IRDA: by courtesy of Pritha Ghosh; **412**: National Stock Exchange building: R.M. Nunes/Shutterstock.com; **414**: Victoria House at Esplanade: by courtesy of Brotish Kar; **415**: Underwater pipeline by courtesy: Shutterstock.com; **417**: Panna National Park: Shutterstock.com; **418**: Tea Garden: Ron Ramtang/Shutterstock.com; **419**: Dunlop: factory: by courtesy of Prabir Ghosh; **420**: Lambretta: Soumitra Giri/Shutterstock.com; **421**: Hindustan motors steering: Aravind Sivaraj/Shutterstock.com; **423**: Walmart superstore in Lucknow: Priya dwivedi/Shutterstock.com; **425**: Cannes Lion: Nattapat.J/Shutterstock.com; **426**: Amul: alien27ravi/Shutterstock.com.

ADVENTURE 427–462

Opener pic, 427: Pixabay/Pexels.com; **428**: Jumping out of plane: Shutterstock.com; **429**: Bungee jumping: Shutterstock.com; **430**: Air jets: Aerospace Trek/Shutterstock.com; **431**: Microlight flying: Werner Gillmer/Shutterstock.

com; **432–433**: background: Shutterstock.com; **434**: Wingsuit jumping: Shutterstock.com; **436**: GQ expedition: by courtesy of the record holder; **437**: **top and bottom**: Umling La expedition: by courtesy of the record holder; **440**: Siachen: Shutterstock.com; **442–443**: by courtesy of the record holders; **445**: Cycling: Shutterstock.com; **447**: Rafting: Shutterstock.com; **448–449**: **background**: Shutterstock.com; **451**: Strait of Gibralter: Shutterstock.com; **452**: Kayaking: manoj_kulkarni/Shutterstock.com; **453**: English channel: Shutterstock.com; **455**: Marathon: sugitas/shutterstock.com; **459**: Himalayan Mountaineering Institute: saiko3p/Shutterstock.com; **461**: Mt. Annapurna: Shutterstock.com.

SPORTS 463–586

Opener Pic, **463**: Oleksii Sidorov/Shutterstock.com; **464**: Priya Ranjan Dasmuni: Government Open Data License–India(GODL)/Ministry of Information and Broadcasting, **464**: MC Mary Kom: cameranest/Shutterstock.com; **466**: C.A. Bhavani Devi: by courtesy of The Hindu; **468**: Deepika Kumari: CCA-SA 3.0 Unported/Rajivranprasad; **469**: Abhishek Verma: Government Open Data License–India(GODL)/President's Secretariat, **470**: Jayanta Talukdar: Government Open Data License–India(GODL)/President's Secretariat; **471**: **top**: Dola Banerjee: Government Open Data License–India(GODL)/President's Secretariat, **bottom**: Jyothi Surekha Vennam: by courtesy of The Hindu; **473**: Swapna Barman: CCA-SA 4.0 International/Athletics Federation of India, **474**: Milkha Singh: CCA-SA 3.0 Unported/Sanyam Bagha, **475**: Anju Bobby George: CCA-SA 4.0 International/Jyothishvijay; **476**: Tejaswin Shankar: by courtesy of Hindustan Times; **477**: background: Denis Kuvaev/Shutterstock.com; **479**: Shiny Wilson: Government Open Data License–India(GODL)/Ministry of Information and Broadcasting; **480**: India at World Athletics: by courtesy of Hindustan Times, **481**: Deepa Malik: Government Open Data License–India(GODL)/Prime Minister's Office, Government of India, **483**: **top**: Jwala Gutta and Ashwini Ponnappa: Government Open Data License–India(GODL)/Ministry of Youth Affairs and Sports; **middle**: Saina Nehwal: CCA-SA 3.0 Unported/Bollywood Hungama; **bottom**: K. Srikanth: Wikimedia Commons/Fair Use/Pierre-Yves Beaudouin, **484**: P.V. Sindhu: Government Open Data License–India(GODL)/Prime Minister's Office, **485**: Prakash Padukone: CCA-SA 3.0 Unported/Mussarat Kang; **486**: Dinesh Khanna: CCA-SA 4.0 International/Vkg wifi; **487**: Satwiksairaj Rankireddy and Chirag Shetty: by courtesy of Hindustan Times, **489**: **top**: Aparna Popat: Government Open Data License–India(GODL)/President's Secretariat; **bottom**: Madhumita Goswami-Bisht: Government Open Data License–India(GODL)/

President's Secretariat; **490**: Prashanti Singh: CCA-SA 3.0 Unported/Risingprincess; **492**: Government Open Data License–India(GODL)/Government of India; **496**: Pravin Thipsay: CCA-SA 4.0 International/ Swaralithipsay; **497**: Viswanathan Anand: CC BY-SA 2.0 Generic/ GFHund; **498**: Rameshbabu Praggnandhaa: CC BY-SA 2.0 Generic/Frans Peeters; **499**: P. Harikrishna: CCA-SA 4.0 International/Krysztof Szeląg; **501**: D. Gukesh: CC BY-SA 2.0 Generic/Frans Peeters; **503**: **top**: K. Humpy: Government Open Data License–India(GODL)/President's Secretariat; **bottom**: Shafali Verma: CCA-SA 4.0 International/ Bahnfrend, **504**: Mithali Raj: CCA-SA 3.0 Unported/Sadhguru (https://www.youtube.com/ watch?v=KJF5C00BSRY); **505**: Women's IPL team: by courtesy of The Hindu, **506**: Harmanpreet Kaur: CCA-SA 4.0 International/Bahnfrend; **508**: Sunil Gavaskar: CCASA 3.0 Unported/Bollywood Hungama; **509**: Sachin Tendulkar: Olga Popova/Shutterstock.com; **510**: Rahul Dravid: CCA-SA 3.0 Unported/Bollywood Hungama, **511**: Anil Kumble: CCA-SA 3.0 Unported/lensbug.chandru; **512**: Sachin Tendulkar: PIXATHON/ Shutterstock.com; **515**: Pankaj Advani: by courtesy of Hindustan Times; **516**: R. Umadevi: Government Open Data License–India(GODL)/Ministry of Women and Child Development; **520**: Syed Nayeemuddin: CCA-SA 3.0 Unported/Biswarup Ganguly; **521**: Baichung Bhutia: CCA-SA 3.0 Unported/Baichung Bhutia, **522**: S.A. Rahim: Wikimedia Commons/Fair Use/The Hindu; **523**: Inder Singh: CCA-SA 4.0 International/Vickrem3; **524**: Bartholomew Ogbeche: CCA-SA 4.0 International/Rufyrosh, **525**: Sunil Chettri: daykung/ Shutterstock.com; **526**: Chuni Goswami: Wikimedia Commons/ Fair Use/Vidmarp; **527**: P.K. Banerjee: Wikimedia Commons/ Fair Use/Unknown Author; **530**: Arjun Atwal: CC BY-SA 2.0 Generic/Keith Allison; **531**: Jeev Milkha Singh: mooninblack/ Shutterstock.com; **532**: Aditi Ashok: pendakisolo/Shutterstock. com; **533**: Rashid Khan: by courtesy ofHindustan Times; **534**: Anirban Lahiri: CCA-SA 4.0 International/Punishar; **535**: S.S.P. Chawrasia: CCA-SA 3.0 Unported/ Pvt Pauline; **536**: Shubhankar Sharma: masuti/Shutterstock. com; **538**: Dilip Tirkey: Government Open Data License–India(GODL/ Ministry of Youth Affairs and Sports; **540**: Dhyan Chand: Wikimedia Commons/Fair Use/ Faizhaider; **542**: Richard J. Allen: Wikimedia Commons/Fair Use/ Unknown author; **543**: Balbir Singh: Wikimedia Commons/ Fair Use/Balbir Singh; **547**: Pooja Kadian: Government Open Data License–India(GODL)/President's Secretariat; **548**: Farman Basha: CCA-SA 3.0 Unported/Laura Hale; **549**: Abhinav Bhindra: Open Government Licence version 1.0/ British High Commission, India,

IMAGE COPYRIGHT INFORMATION

550: **top**: Mairaj Ahmad Khan: CCA SA 2.0 Generic/U.S. Army; **bottom**: Rani Sarnobhat: Government Open Data License–India(GODL)/ Ministry of Youth Affairs and Sports; **551**: Jaspal Rana: Government Open Data License–India(GODL/Ministry of Petroleum and Natural Gas; **552**: Ronjan Sodhi: Government Open Data License–India(GODL)/President's Secretariat, **554**: Joshna Chinappa: CC BY-SA 2.0 Generic/Simitha T.Singam; **555**: Bhuvaneshwari Kumari: CCA-SA 4.0 International/Tpsn98290; **556**: Dipika Pallikal: CHEN WS/ Shutterstock.com, **bottom**: Bhuvaneshwari Kumari: CCA-SA 4.0 International/Tpsn98290; **352**: Shikha Tandon: Government Open Data License–India(GODL)/ President's Secretariat; **559**: **top**: Srihari Nataraj: CCA-SA 4.0 International/Martin Ruksch, **bottom**: Suyash Narayan Jadhav: by courtesy of Meenakshi Pahuja, **561**: A. Sharath Kamal: Government Open Data License–India(GODL/Ministry of Youth Affairs and Sports; **562**: Harmeet Desai: CC BY-SA 2.0 Generic/ XIAOYU TANG; **356**: **background**: Stefan Holm/Shutterstock.com, **567**: top: Karman Kaur Thandi: CC BY-SA 2.0 Generic/si.robl; **bottom**: Somdev Devvarman: CCA-SA 3.0 Unported/Photo by DAVID ILIFF; **569**: Mahesh Bhupathi: CCA-SA 3.0 Unported/ Robbie Mendelson; **570**: Yuki Bhambri: CC BY-SA 2.0 Generic /si.robi, **571**: Rohan Bopanna: Wikimedia CC BY-SA 2.0 Generic/si.robi; **572**: Government Open Data License–India(GODL/ Ministry of Youth Affairs and Sports; **573**: Yumnam Renu: Government Open Data License–India(GODL)/ President's Secretariat; **574**: Geeta Phogat: CCA-SA 3.0 Unported/ BollywoodKilla (https://www.youtube.com/ watch?v=zgfGIZI4ctE); **575**: Antim Panghal: by courtesy of Hindustan Times; **577**: Anshu Malik: CCA-SA 4.0 International/Jørgen Løken; **578**: Bajrang Punia and Vinesh Phogat: by courtesy of Hindustan Times; **580**: Sushil Kumar: CCA-SA 3.0 Unported/Ten Sports; Asian Games Special: **581**: Milkha Singh: cameranest/Shutterstock.com; **582**: **top**: Esha Singh: CCA-SA 4.0 International/Esha Singh/ BBC World Service India Pvt. Ltd., **bottom**: Avinash Sable: CC BY-SA 2.0 Generic/U.S. Army; **583**: **top**: Dipika Pallikal: CC BY-SA 2.0 Generic /julesgriff, **bottom**: Neeraj Chopra: CCA-SA 4.0 International/ Anass Sedrati

PREAMBLE

Limca Book of Records ('*LBR*'), as a record-keeping publication, has been compiling records since 1987 and has seen over 30 editions. It is India's first and longest continuously published book of records.

It is, however, a private book, run and managed by a private organization with no public funding whatsoever. The retail price is also subsidized by the owner Coca-Cola India Private Limited ('CCIPL'). The *LBR* also accepts absolutely no funding or payment or any other charges from record applicants or record holders for entries or for processing or for publication acceptance.

Consequently, it is important to understand that all decisions are taken by applying a set of standards that are specific and stringent, but equally are subjective, and based on what the editors and staff of *LBR* and Consultants ('*LBR* Team') think are most suitable for the book. And that decision is solely *LBR*'s and *LBR* is not answerable to or the decision is not affected by any other individual, entity, or by what another entity, may do or accept.

I. INTRODUCTION

1. *LBR* is a catalogue of achievements made by Indians. It catalogues unique milestones and landmarks including, but not limited to, firsts, bests, mosts, inventions, discoveries, and honours and awards received by Indians at home or abroad in all fields – both human and natural – that can be qualified in superlatives and that conform to the prevailing editorial policy in force during any year.

While this is primarily a catalogue of superlatives and achievements, it is also a book of records, and a work of reference, and therefore in the spirit of empirical record keeping, it will record other milestones that may be negative or not celebratory or laudatory but are notable, such as 'longest trial in a court of law' or records pertaining to disasters or crime. Any such record is a statement of fact on record, and is not meant to downplay any entity, nor encourage anyone to attempt to beat such records.

LBR encompasses an extensive range of information and is thus divided into several chapters and record categories. Prospective entries under these chapters and categories may include, but are not limited to, any of the following headings: a record, a quantifiable skill, a superlative or historical landmark/phenomenon/man-made or natural event/process/structure considered as remarkable as a record by the *LBR* Team.

2. Anyone with a reasonable claim for a record may write to *LBR* for possible inclusion (subject to acceptance under *LBR* criteria).

3. Entry into *LBR* and attempt of any record are subject to compliance with the general Terms and Conditions (the 'Terms') as well as the specific rules and guidelines applicable to each type of record attempt or claim (the 'Attempt'). Where pre-existing terms are not there to cover a particular record or Claim, a relevant policy shall be decided by the *LBR* Team and that shall be binding. Earlier policies and parameters go under continuous review and modifications, and the *LBR* Team is not bound to any previously existing parameters.

4. Individuals or groups interested in attempting to set or break a record must understand and accept *LBR's* general policy, study the Terms and the specific rules and guidelines applicable to the Attempt, and sign the Disclaimer and Indemnity Form (available before the commencement of any Attempt) in order to be considered for inclusion in *LBR*. Records already set and sent for inclusion ex post facto are also bound by all these Rules and Guidelines; acceptance of all Terms and Conditions is a necessary qualifier to any record being accepted.

5. All Terms, rules, and guidelines apply to a person/persons making a record Attempt ('Applicant'/'Applicants') who send an Application to *LBR* as well as any and every person/persons ('Participant'/'Participants') part of such an Attempt (for example, in an Attempt by a group or organization).

6. *LBR* is owned by CCIPL, which reserves the right to modify these Terms and any other rules and guidelines established in relation to an Attempt or general policy. CCIPL does not implement or involve itself in editorial policy and does not process submissions. *LBR* is collated and published by publishers Hachette Book Publishing India Pvt. Ltd/Hachette India, who will process the entries, make all decisions on acceptance and inclusion, and publish the book autonomously as is required for an independent book of records. Publication dates and content design are decided and implemented in conjunction with CCIPL.

All such modifications of the Terms and Conditions, and policy, will be updated (a) on the website: https://www.coca-colaindia.com/limca-book-of-records; and (b) on the webpage: https://www.hachetteindia.com/home/rulesandguidelines (for the latest rules and guidelines, and updates), and anyone attempting to enter their record in *LBR* must review the Terms and the corresponding rules for each Attempt regularly to remain informed of any changes or modifications therein.

7. *LBR* and its representatives do NOT charge any fee or accept any money for the application, review, processing, or acceptance of records [please see clauses III.18 and III.19 of 'General Guidelines' pertaining to certificates and discount on sale of copies to Applicants].

II. ELIGIBILITY CRITERIA

1. To be eligible for consideration by the *LBR* Team for a successful Attempt, 'Applicant' must fulfil the following conditions:

a. The Applicant should be a resident Indian or non-resident Indian (NRI)/ overseas citizen of India (OCI), and must submit ID and residence proofs and other documents as required by law to establish this.

b. The Applicant must have read and consented to the Terms, the specific rules and guidelines applicable to the Attempt, and must have signed and submitted the Disclaimer and Indemnity Form before undertaking the Attempt.

c. *LBR* does not accept applications of children below 13 years except in certain memory-related categories, select skill, and art-based categories, and those under certain national and international Sports categories as decided by the *LBR* Team, and as per certification by relevant national and international sports organizations and authorities. The Applicant must fall in one of the two age groups, as specified below, and must adhere to the eligibility criteria for that age group.

2. The Attempt must be corroborated by a valid proof of age:

a. Age Group I – Between 13 and 18 years

b. Age Group II – Above 18 years

3. Age Group I:

a. An Applicant undertaking an Attempt under this age group must be older than thirteen (13) years and younger than or up to eighteen (18) years at the time of the Attempt.

b. Consent from a parent or legal guardian must be submitted, after such parent or legal guardian has read the Terms as provided and consented to the same. The parent or legal guardian is also required to have read and consented to the Disclaimer and Indemnity Form, and provide a Certificate of Medical Fitness, signed and stamped by a certified doctor, in certain Attempts as decided and indicated by the *LBR* Team, and follow any other rules specified in relation to the category of the Attempt, before undertaking the Attempt.

c. Certain categories of records may not be permitted for Applicants from this age group, as may be notified by CCIPL and/or *LBR* from time to time. Any record in this age group must be cleared with *LBR* before it occurs to see if it will be considered suitable as a record entry and *LBR*'s decision shall be final regarding its own criteria for inclusion and safety.

d. Attempts that are detrimental to the health of such persons, or that are potentially dangerous, or that are in violation of any law in force, will not be accepted for entry in *LBR*.

e. Any Attempt by minors beyond 15 minutes will be considered as endurance and would lead to the rejection of the claim. Any record attempt below that time duration (or even if the activity is strenuous within that time frame) that the *LBR* Team deems as stressful or strenuous for a minor, or as dangerous, harmful, or injurious in any other way, may also be rejected at the discretion of the *LBR* Team.

f. Guardians/parents must sign a Disclaimer and Indemnity Form assuring against any exertion, stress, or harm caused to the minor record Applicant and indemnifying *LBR* and CCIPL against any such occurrence.

g. Memory records are available to this age group and are subject to the decision of the *LBR* Team and representatives of *LBR*.

h. Certain records, such as the lightest/heaviest baby born or a medical feat performed on a child below 13 years may be accepted at the discretion of the *LBR* Team under the Medical Sciences chapter, wherein the child/baby itself is not an active actor in the record.

4. Age Group II:

a. The Applicant must be above eighteen (18) years of age.

b. The Applicant must have carefully read and consented to the Terms, and the specific rules and guidelines set down for the Attempt. Before engaging in the Attempt the Applicant must have submitted the Disclaimer and Indemnity Form as well as a Certificate of Medical Fitness (with the medical practitioner's registration number mentioned on it) to attempt any physical feat or one involving mental exertion, or one deemed so by the *LBR* Team.

III. GENERAL GUIDELINES

A. GENERAL

1. Standard norms and rules should be adhered to while setting national and world records. In some cases there may be additional event-specific norms that need to be observed.

2. The onus of proving a record claim rests on the Applicant. The claim, signed by the Applicant, should be backed by adequate and satisfactory documents without which it will not be accepted. Materials submitted as supporting evidence, such as press clippings, audio/video tapes, flash/pen drives, CDs, DVDs, hard drives, and photographs, become the property of the publisher Hachette Book Publishing India Pvt. Ltd/Hachette India and the Copyright Owner, and only copies should be submitted with the originals kept safe by the claimant for Life after the claim has been accepted (see also Section V [Evidence]). Forms such as the Application Form duly signed by the Applicant and validating/witnessing authorities as indicated by the representatives of *LBR* and/or the rules and guidelines need to be submitted in the original (hard copy) and a copy retained by the Applicant/Applicants for Life after the claim has been accepted. *LBR* does not take any responsibility for lost material/s if the record is questioned or objected to by any person. In case of a query or objection raised, the responsibility of providing the evidence again for reverification (see also Reverification of Evidence clause V.15) and all expenditures therein lies with the Applicant.

3. It is not necessary or binding for someone from *LBR* to be present at the record-making event, but proper authentication of the same must be ensured. Authentication should be by someone who is competent and in a responsible position, such as a gazetted officer, district magistrate, or principal of a government school/college, unless specified otherwise.

4. The Applicant/s must update themselves with the latest record before making any Attempt to break it. Potential record-breakers should inform *LBR* at least 30 days in advance about the record Attempt details and procedure in order to avoid disqualification on technicalities.

5. Confirmations from Consultants are not to be treated as final. The final confirmations are only issued by the *LBR* Editorial Team. Applicants are advised to check the existing record with the *LBR* Team just before their Attempts as well, so that they may be intimated of any updates.

6. While breaking an existing record, the Applicant/s must follow the rules, technical specifications and set precedents. For example, if the needle-threading record specifies a no. 13 needle, no other needle may be used.

7. Records should be absolute and not technical offshoots. For example, if one is setting a typing record, it is assumed that it is normal typing. One-finger or two-finger typing will not be registered as separate records. Records have to be quantifiable and comparable, and overly specific variables may not be considered.

8. While *LBR* does accept new categories, these will have to be of high interest value and have definable and comparable parameters, and these are entirely subject to the *LBR* Team's decision. For example, even if no record exists, a 'two-hour marathon for guitar playing' will not be accepted.

9. Not every record set by women is eligible for entry as the sub category 'First woman to ...'.

10. Collections should have a basic 'standard'. Limited numbers of obscure articles may not be accepted unless of exceptional interest value, and that shall be decided upon by the *LBR* Team.

11. For distance records, only basic types of vehicles are recognized: four-wheelers and plus, two-wheelers, geared bicycles, gearless bicycles, tandem bicycles, and electric vehicles.

To ensure measurability, distance against time will be the criterion. Cross-country or intra-country motoring/cycling or other vehicular records must get prior clearance from the *LBR* Team for inclusion. In non-speed records, vehicles may be categorized according to engine capacity: up to 60 cc; 61–100 cc; 101–350 cc; 351–500 cc; and above 500 cc.

12. Before attempting any driving record, Applicants have to submit a copy of the following document/documents, as applicable, attested by a gazetted officer or notary public: their valid driving licence/earlier experience certificate in case of motor sport or bicycling record; pilot's licence/aero-sports course certificate/earlier experience certificate in case of aero-sports record; mountaineering/

mountain sports course certificate/earlier experience certificate in case of a mountain sports record; and water sports course certificate/earlier experience certificate in case of a water sports record to the *LBR* office for prior approval.

13. All claimants must send in supporting photographs for their Claim to the *LBR* Team. In physical evidence with documents or photographs, these should not be stapled to the entry. Detachable clips should be used. In cases where applicable and as indicated by the *LBR* Team, time- and date-stamped video recordings of the Attempt must be provided.

14. Attempts that may result in physical harm, such as 'hitting head against a wall', or mental/emotional duress for the Applicant, such as 'isolating oneself for 100 days', will not be considered, and are entirely left to the decision of the *LBR* Team.

15. Any record in the book may be reconsidered or dropped without prior intimation.

16. Certificates issued are valid only for the date or period specified and will be considered ended if surpassed by a new record, and/or change in criteria, measuring methods, or if disputed and found to be erroneous on reverification (see clause V.15).

17. For reasons of space or any other reasons, a confirmed entry may be dropped at the time of going to press. The *LBR* Team may inform the Applicant of the change in status but is not bound to do so.

18. Record holders within India are entitled to ONE complimentary copy of their certificate and its postage, if eligible, and further copies need to be ordered by writing to the *LBR* Team and on payment (including GST) as indicated. Record holders outside India are entitled to ONE complimentary copy of their certificate but will need to pay courier and/or postal charges (including applicable taxes/surcharges). Requests for reissue of older certificates issued in previous years are considered on a case-by-case basis and such certificates are reissued on payment within reasonable time as per printing schedules, provided the record is accessible in *LBR*'s archived editions.

19. Record holders are not entitled to any remuneration or free copies of *Limca Book of Records*. They may, however, avail a 30 per cent discount on the cover price of the book by writing to the *LBR* Team and following the payment process.

20. If new record holders do not receive their certificate within two months after the release of the book, they should contact the *LBR* office.

21. The *LBR* Team reserves the sole right to decide on the suitability of all records for inclusion in the book. The Team's decision on all such matters is final. Any attempt to browbeat or threaten the *LBR* Team or representatives shall result in instant disqualification.

22. ATTEMPTS BY MINORS

a. Records by minors below 13 years are not accepted, except under certain memory-related categories, select skill-and art-based categories, and certain recognized national and international tournament categories as decided by the respective Consultants for specific sports.

b. Records that are against the law (e.g., driving at an age not qualified for licence) or those that require excessive physical exertion (like a marathon) detrimental to a minor's health will not be accepted.

23. OBJECTIONS/DISCREPANCIES

a. Any typographical error or inaccuracy in the statement of a record or certificate should be pointed out by the record holder immediately.

b. Objections raised by any person regarding any published entry shall be entertained only within a period of three (3) years from the date of publication or acceptance/certification of a record/entry. However, discrepancies identified by the *LBR* Team suo motu shall be addressed regardless of passage of time. Applicants must note that, in accordance with the prevailing laws, there is no limitation in respect of criminal liability should it arise.

B. CHAPTERS AND CATEGORIES

LBR reserves the right to include or exclude any chapter or category, or section or record category as otherwise listed below and is under no obligation to publish all or any of the listed chapters or categories in *LBR* or any of its publications.

The list provided here is only for illustrative and explanatory reasons, and for the clarity of persons seeking to engage in an Attempt. Further, the following list consists only of chapters and categories that have been published in current and previous editions and is non-exhaustive. *LBR* may, at its sole discretion, include additional chapters or categories, delete a chapter or category, or even merge two or more chapters or categories as the *LBR* Team deems appropriate. Any such addition, deletion or merging of chapters or categories creates no obligation on the part of *LBR* Team and/or CCIPL to inform any person making an Attempt of such addition, deletion, or merger. Records after acceptance may also be changed or deleted if suitable circumstances warrant it, and this also shall be the sole decision of the *LBR* Team.

1. THE HUMAN STORY

This chapter contains records, talents, and information, and includes, but is not limited to, unique achievements, uncommon talents, collections, community development initiatives, and other human feats. Applicants under this category are required to not break any laws, and must sign and submit the Disclaimer and Indemnity Form, Self-Declaration of Medical Fitness and Certificate of Medical Fitness, as applicable, at least one month prior to the Attempt. *LBR* prohibits and will not accept any Attempt that is likely to cause harm or be of nuisance to the general public, or is likely to cause unnecessary waste of essential goods or resources such as food items, or is likely to harm the environment; and of course possible physical, mental, or emotional harm to oneself.

a. Records involving alcohol consumption as an event or performance measure will not be considered.

b. Yoga or endurance, or speed or strength records are only for Age Group II unless specifically permitted otherwise in writing.

c. Applicants from Age Group I can perform for a maximum of 15 minutes in mass participation records involving strength, speed, or performance. Any Attempt longer than that will be considered endurance on the part of minors and rejected. In such records attempting 'mosts' in terms of numbers, minors will not be counted, such as in a two-hour-long dance performance. The allowance may depend upon the nature of the Attempt. For example, minor Applicants/Participants might participate in an Attempt involving reading for more than 15 minutes but will not be allowed at any mass physical feat claim for more than that time period, such as most Participants performing the plank together. Such applications, if accepted by the *LBR* Team, will need a Medical Fitness Certificate confirming that no harm will be caused to the Applicant/Participant by such an Attempt.

d. For the section on Online feats, we will accept both single and multiple sessions for a single event. The number of platforms will not be a parameter.

e. *LBR* does not have categories related to religious traditions and ceremonies, unless they form general records.

f. Records indicating or involving harm to physical or mental health, such as 'maximum blood donated in a day', or 'starving for the most number of days', or 'isolating oneself for the longest period' will not be considered.

g. For collection claims, minor changes like changes in colour and/or slight tweaks will be considered as duplicated, and will not be counted separately.
h. For claims related to 'smallest/largest/biggest' forms of an object, the form has to closely resemble the original object as a replica and creative representations will not be accepted from both functionality and outer look and feel perspectives.

2. STRUCTURES

This chapter contains records related to general, modern, residential, religious, mechanical and historical structures, bridges, dams and flyovers, and various other specialized structures.

a. There are no set parameters of the claim regarding fastest construction as each construction would have multiple aspects of difference and the *LBR* Team does not wish to encourage the fastest construction of public services or private buildings.

3. AGRICULTURE

This chapter contains records and information, and it may include, but shall not be limited to, topics such as agricultural crops, farm machinery, milk and milk products, poultry, animal sciences, fisheries, agricultural research, and awards. Specific rules are to be complied with for Attempts under this chapter.

4. EDUCATION

This chapter contains records and information related to literacy, schools, higher education, archives, libraries, museums, and quizzes. *LBR* has discontinued the 'youngest' category as a record claim. Record claims with qualifications beyond postgraduation are considered. Record claims pertaining to online courses, or qualifications based on the University Grants Commission (UGC)–National Eligibility Test (NET), or publication of research papers will not be considered.

5. PERFORMING ARTS

This chapter contains records related to talent and information in the fields of dance, music, and theatre (including but not limited to puppetry and other local theatre types depending on parameters), and dance drama and dance-martial arts crossovers. The records are further divided into marathon events or group events. All Attempts under this chapter are required to follow the specific rules for both types of events as provided by the *LBR* Team. Record claims pertaining to fastest performances will not be considered.

6. VISUAL ARTS

This chapter contains records and information related to cinema, photography, painting, and some categories of drawing and cartooning. The records related to national and regional commercial and art cinema is based on information collected from the National Film Archive of India (NFAI), public domain, magazines, and national newspapers. The records about box-office collection are obtained from the website www.boxofficeindia.com, the standard source in India for collecting such details, or similar sources.

a. Individual record claims for cinema may be submitted for consideration under this chapter, subject to compliance with the basic criteria laid down:
   i. The film should have been cleared by the Central Board for Film Certification (CBFC) and given a censor certificate.
   ii. Certification requirements for Over the Top (OTT) content/films/drama series will be decided on a case-by-case basis and as per the laws of the land.
   iii. The film should be screened at film festivals or at public theatres/auditoriums.
b. Information related to painting and photography is collected from newspapers, magazines, the Internet, and any other verified source. Individual record claims may be submitted for consideration under this chapter, subject to compliance

with the basic criteria laid down:

i. No miniature paintings in any medium are considered in this chapter currently. They may be eligible for entry in the Human Story chapter depending on parameters.
ii. All rangoli, *alpana* and *kolam* records have been categorized under one category of 'Traditional floor art'.
iii. Considering that art is a subjective concept, the *LBR* Team reserves the final decision regarding the artwork so produced. Random repetition of patterns, block colour patches, strokes of paint, or smearing paint randomly on the canvas would lead to the rejection of the claim. Similarly, geometric shapes, haphazard lines, and arbitrary usage of colour would also lead to rejection. The artwork so produced should have a coherent sense of pattern, colour, and tone. It should depict a certain level of skill and creation of aesthetics. For photography claims, repetitive, fragmented, and haphazard images would not be considered. The images should have a coherent sense of posture, alignment, and lighting.
iv. The largest art competition would be a single-day category following the rules of continuous events and being a maximum of 12 hours.
v. Portrait categories: A portrait should have only a single person in the painting/mosaic. A portrait is considered to be a drawing/painting of the head and shoulder of a person for the purposes of record claims.
vi. Origami claims have been sorted into the following categories:
    1. Largest origami mosaic – solo/group
    2. Single-item origami (single sheet, single item): A) Tallest/Longest; B) Widest
    3. Multiple-item origami (multiple sheets, multiple items): A) Tallest – solo/group; B) Widest – solo/group
    4. Marathon origami (single day, single venue) – solo
    5. Most towel origami made – solo/group – in 1 hour
vii. Claims regarding pencil carvings (graphite) have been sorted into the following categories:
    1. Largest collection of carved pencils
    2. Most pencil carvings done – single day
    3. Most pencil carvings done – 1 hour
    4. Smallest pencil carving

7. LITERATURE

This chapter contains records and information from the field of literature. Applicants willing to undertake an Attempt under this chapter must ensure compliance with the basic criteria laid down:

a. Only published works will be considered unless the work created is an art installation or superlative, or an artefact.
b. No long ghazals/poems, rewriting of religious texts, or anthologies will be considered.
c. A work infringing copyright or violative of any other prevailing laws will not be considered.
d. General category claims: Book(s) self-published or published by a publishing house should be available for purchase online or at bookshops. Sales records must be certified by publishers who have audited accounts, or by Nielsen BookScan.

8. MEDIA AND COMMUNICATIONS

This chapter contains records and information related to the broad fields of (a) media and (b) communications, and may be divided into six sections: (i) print, (ii) radio, (iii) television, (iv) post and philately, (v) telecom, and (vi) Internet, social media and apps (applications). Applicants wishing to undertake an Attempt under this chapter must ensure compliance with the specific guidelines provided by the *LBR* Team.

9. GOVERNMENT

This chapter contains information and records. This category may include, but shall not be limited to, such subjects as nationhood, parties, elections, the Parliament, states, administration, government officials, civics, judiciary, and law and order.

10. DEFENCE

This chapter contains records and information pertaining to all the branches of the armed or paramilitary forces and related military records. This chapter does not accept entries unless routed through the appropriate defence authority/organization with the understanding that no official secrets, or confidential information, are being revealed in the process. An independent entry by current or former defence personnel should be accompanied with a self-declaration that no official secrets or confidential information is being revealed. The chapter is otherwise compiled by the *LBR* Team from news sources originating with government ministries and information sources such as the official websites of the Indian Navy, Army, Air Force and Coast Guard as well as the Press Information Bureau, Government of India.

11. SCIENCE AND TECHNOLOGY

This chapter contains absolute records like oldest planetarium and first nuclear reactor along with discoveries and records in, but not limited to, mathematics, physics, chemistry, biology, engineering, environmental sciences, computers, information technology, and space technology. All Attempts under this chapter are required to follow the specific rules for both types of events as provided by the *LBR* Team. For a new invention to be considered as a record, it must be patented with a recognized national/international body. This chapter also includes records and relevant information compiled by the *LBR* Team.

12. MEDICAL SCIENCES

This chapter contains records and information from the field of medical sciences such as medical breakthroughs, medical camps, 'firsts', and in selective medical procedures, medical devices and equipment.

Claims are acceptable only from registered medical practitioners and related to government-approved medical practices and institutions, such as those affiliated to the Indian Medical Association, the Ministry of Health and Family Welfare, and any others as deemed eligible by the *LBR* Team.

The *LBR* Team will reject any Attempts that may potentially or otherwise harm or endanger persons/patients, e.g., speed-related records, such as 'most kidneys transplanted in a day' or 'most LASIK surgeries performed in a day', whether at a medical centre or in camps, charitable or otherwise.

LBR may accept camp-related statistics that turn out to be records, but may not process or encourage any camps set up to create records, especially speed-related medical science Attempts because such Attempts may jeopardize patient safety and health.

For all surgery-related claims, only successful surgery applications will be accepted, where the patient has not died on the operation table.

13. THE NATURAL WORLD

This chapter contains information and records, and the entries are compiled from multiple and deemed verified reports in magazines, newspapers, and Internet resources available to *LBR* on topics including, but not limited to, geographical features, flora, fauna, environment, and conservation. Information related to flora and fauna is verified with nature conservation authorities, well-known wildlife institutions, government websites, and relevant international websites.

All claims related to rainwater harvesting and pollution control are counterchecked with government sources and/or authoritative expert bodies. Gardening records relating to non-agricultural production and claims, such as largest pumpkin, will require scale-comparative photographs as well as other indicated documentation.

14. TRANSPORT

This chapter contains records and information, and the sections under this chapter include road, rail and metro, water, and air transport. Applicants who claim records under any of these sections shall provide evidence of the same, including authentication documents as required by the *LBR* Team.

15. BUSINESS AND ECONOMY

This chapter contains records and information, and the sections under this chapter may include, but shall not be limited to, the economy, financial institutions, financial instruments, banking, industries and companies, workforce, housing and real estate, and advertising.

Applicants who claim records under any of these sections shall provide proof of the same, including authentication letters from independent observers including at least one expert in the field. Industry company data must be from authentic authorized bodies such as the Registrar of Companies and the Securities and Exchange Board of India (SEBI), or in the case of own company figures, audited figures must be submitted.

a. Claims for 'highest/lowest' sale of product(s) are not accepted.

16. ADVENTURE

This chapter may be divided into various sections, including but not limited to, aero-sports, mountaineering, road expeditions, water sports, marathons (those not classified internationally as athletics track and field events) and other adventure activities. A person undertaking an Attempt under this category may seek the *LBR* Team's guidance/assistance for specific guidelines. Potential Applicants are advised to note that such guidelines or safety advice provided by the *LBR* Team shall merely be explanatory and, non-exhaustive, and will not create any responsibilities or liabilities whatsoever on behalf of the *LBR* Team and/or CCIPL.

a. For all claims related to Ironman triathlon, *LBR* refers to the International Triathlon Union and the Indian Triathlon Federation.
b. For swimming records, only solo as well as up to three-person relay crossings (each covering at least 10 km) will be considered. For marathon swimming – with permitted breaks – breaks of only 1.5 minutes will be allowed for each completed hour. Exceptions may be made for para swimmers or extremely remarkable records, subject to the discretion and decision of the *LBR* Team.
c. A minimum altitude of 6,000 m is required to review any mountaineering claim. Claims regarding Mt Kilimanjaro (5,895 m) will not be considered in accordance with this limit. All mountaineering claims must be verified by the Indian Mountaineering Foundation or a similar credible international body.
d. There are separate categories for women in solo attempts and group attempts where Applicants and, if present, Participants are women.
e. Our categories for expedition records for two-wheelers will now be subdivided as:
   i. Up to 150 cc
   ii. 151 to 450 cc
   iii. Over 450 cc
f. Adventure/Marathon and Endurance Claims:
   i. A detailed logbook must be maintained with entries in chronological order. All entries in this logbook must be witnessed and authenticated by reputed individuals/competent authorities (a gazetted officer, district magistrate, or principal of a government school/college, unless specified otherwise). A sample sheet will be given by the *LBR* Team on request. Emphasis will be on events that highlight special skills.

ii. In cases where applicable and as indicated by the *LBR* Team, time- and date-stamped videos of the Attempt must be provided.
iii. All adventure/endurance events come under five categories. Special instructions on rest breaks for each of them follow:
   1. Marathon: A five-minute break for rest after every completed hour is allowed as per prevailing international norms. These breaks may be accumulated (e.g., a 15-minute break may be taken after 3 hours of non-stop action) but not added to the tally. The logbook must clearly indicate the rest breaks.
   2. Virtually non-stop: Minimal breaks permitted for medical/toilet purposes but no rest breaks. Breaks are to be indicated in the logbook.
   3. Continuous: Performed on a rotating or relay basis.
   4. Normal: Breaks permitted as and when necessary.
   5. Absolute non-stop: No breaks at all.
iv. Attempts jeopardizing individual or public safety and public property are not encouraged.
v. All adventure feats/stunts/sports, etc., require prior written approval from authorities concerned.

17. SPORTS
The Sports chapter of the *LBR* primarily contains records, sportsrelated statistics and information. It is prepared by independent Consultants, who are well-established journalists and/or authorities in particular sports. The Consultants in conjunction with the *LBR* Team are the final authority on all records under this chapter. In cases where an uncommon sport is involved, the decisions will be made in consultation with an expert in the field.

IV. PROCEDURE FOR ATTEMPT

1. *LBR* recognizes two types of Attempts:
a. an Attempt to break a previously existing record; and
b. an Attempt to set a new record.

2. The following procedure must be followed by any person willing to undertake an Attempt to be considered for entry in *LBR*:

An application by the person attempting the record should be either emailed to **lbr.entries@hachetteindia.com** or couriered/mailed by registered post (see clause IV.3: Application Procedure):

a. Such application should contain details regarding the unique achievement, or proposal to set a record, for the consideration of the *LBR* Team, along with the complete address and contact number of the person attempting the same, at least one (1) month before the Attempt in order to avoid disqualification on technicalities. For specific requirements in the procedure for an Attempt please refer to Section III. of these Rules and Guidelines/Terms.
b. The person undertaking the Attempt must approach the *LBR* Team regarding the proper procedure and information or documents required for consideration of a successful Attempt.
c. On completion of an Attempt, the Applicant must provide the *LBR* Team detailed and accurate documentation, as required by the *LBR* Team, and these will then be scrutinized by the *LBR* Team.
d. All entries to an edition are confirmed only after the deadline, i.e., the last date for submission of entries. Any Application made after such a date may be considered for a subsequent edition of *LBR*.
e. On confirmation of an entry, a certificate shall be mailed to the Applicant who carried out the successful Attempt. Such certificates shall be sent after the

particular edition for which the Attempt has been considered is printed or released.

f. For all Attempts to be undertaken, the person undertaking such an Attempt must sign and submit the Disclaimer and Indemnity Form and Certificate of Medical Fitness (in hard copy), as and when required, to the *LBR* Team, prior to the Attempt. The acceptance of any application for entry in *LBR* shall be conditional on the signing of and adherence to the Disclaimer and Indemnity Form, the Terms, and any other specific rules and guidelines established by *LBR* in relation to a particular category of Attempt.

   The following rules will apply to Disclaimer Forms:
   i. Disclaimer forms should have only one party mentioned, i.e., the record claimant. The second party is not applicable.
   ii. Applicants may choose to get the form notarized instead of adding witnesses. Or witnesses can be used, but verification from the notary holds more value.
   iii. Disclaimer forms have to be on a stamp paper of minimum value of ₹10.

3. APPLICATION PROCEDURE

a. All applications must be sent to the following address:
   Limca Book of Records (Editorial)
   Hachette Book Publishing India Pvt. Ltd
   4th/5th Floors, Corporate Centre
   Plot No. 94, Sector 44
   Gurugram 122003, Haryana, India
   Ph: +91 22 35305621
   Fax: +91 124 4148900
   Email: lbr.entries@hachetteindia.com

   Hachette Book Publishing India Pvt. Ltd is a company incorporated under the Indian Companies Act, 1956, with CIN U22222DL2007PTC164081.

b. *LBR*'s primary mode of communication is email (and only via its formal email IDs), which is both retrievable and transparent as well as a formal record. No Attempt should be made based on phone or other verbal conversations, or communication on social media/messaging platforms.

c. There is no need for personal visits to the *LBR* office to hand over record-related applications, documentation, or evidence, and in case the Applicant does visit personally, the application and requisite documents may be handed over at the Reception. Since all claim formats devised are such that they need written submission, everything should be clear from written communication.

d. Submissions must be in English since *LBR* is currently published in the English language (submissions in other languages shall be accepted, but they should be accompanied with an English translation).

e. The primary application shall consist of the following:
   i. Name of the Applicant
   ii. Date of birth of the Applicant
   iii. Complete postal address of the Applicant
   iv. Contact details (Phone number and email ID) of the Applicant
   v. Description of the record the Applicant wishes to apply for; and event plan.
   vi. Confirmation of acceptance of LBR procedures, Terms and Rules and Guidelines via a formal statement on email or signed hard copy.

f. These applications shall be perused by the *LBR* Team, and further correspondence shall take place between the Applicant and the *LBR* Team member concerned, from the assigned chapter/section.

g. On acceptance of the initial application, the general guidelines and record-specific guidelines shall be emailed or couriered to the Applicant by the *LBR*

Team along with the procedure and documentation required.

h. On receipt of the correspondence from a member of the *LBR* Team, the Applicant shall send the following documents (in both soft and hard copies) to the addresses mentioned in clause IV.3(a) above:
   i. A covering letter stating the Attempt details
   ii. A signed copy of the Disclaimer and Indemnity Form sent to the Applicant
   iii. A self-attested copy of the Applicant's government-approved identity proof (such as passport, voter ID card, PAN card, Aadhaar, etc.)
   iv. A self-attested copy of the Applicant's government-approved age proof (such as passport, birth certificate, ration card, etc.) together with the 'Required Documents' as indicated by the *LBR* Team.

i. On authentication and verification of the Required Documents, the Applicant shall obtain a confirmation from the *LBR* Team to proceed with the Attempt.

j. After completing the Attempt in accordance with the provisions of Sections III and IV, and collecting evidence of the Attempt in accordance with the provisions of Section V, the Applicant shall send the following to claim a record (the 'Claim'):
   i. Details of the supposed record, duly authenticated by gazetted officers, or relevant public authorities, or relevant authorities in charge, or other competent authorities. Such authentication must be on the basis of personal verification of every detail of the Claim.
   ii. Material evidence of the event, consisting of all the evidence collected by the Applicant during the Attempt. All CDs/DVDs, flash/pen drives and other data storage media/devices sent to the *LBR* Team, as part of the application process, should have the Applicant's name and the record category written legibly on it.

k. A Claim that is successfully submitted shall be considered for entry in the *LBR*.

l. The application procedure should be completed within the last date of submission. Entries submitted after the deadline may be considered for the subsequent edition unless extension was granted in writing or on email for extenuating circumstances, or at the discretion of the *LBR* Team.

m. In addition to the aforementioned rules, specific requirements provided under the relevant categories must be fulfilled.

V. EVIDENCE

1. The onus of proving a record is on the Applicant. The Claim, signed by the Applicant, should be backed by adequate and satisfactory documentation without which it will not be accepted by the *LBR* Team.

2. The Applicant must, as part of the verification process, submit all supporting documents including at least two authentication letters (originals) on stamp paper, photographs (or CD/DVD/flash drive containing still photos), personal details of the Applicant, including residential address and contact details, along with a covering letter, without which the Claim will not be considered for entry.

3. Outside of moral and creative ownership rights, which will vest in the creator/artist/author, etc., the assigned copyright/publishing rights and any other intellectual property rights in and to any such material evidence shall, to the extent permitted by law, be waived unconditionally by the Applicant and transferred to *LBR* and CCIPL by the submission.

4. The evidence must only be sent after the Required Documents, as indicated by the Rules and Guidelines, have been verified and the primary application has been duly confirmed and evidence asked for by the *LBR* Team.

5. Only the Claim may be supplemented by evidence of the record with the following to be submitted on the currently prevailing and commonly available and accessible data storage media from where it is easily retrievable, such as a flash/pen drive or hard drive, with the onus of providing a back-up copy/original being on the Applicant:

a. Press clippings of local, national or international newspapers, or press cuttings, or news reports in an electronic form, furnishing direct evidence of the record; or
b. Audio recordings from radio, or any such fact of record which could be heard, furnishing direct evidence of the record; or
c. Direct evidence/audio-visual recording of the record; or
d. Any other fact of record that may be in audio, visual, or audio-visual format, furnishing direct evidence of the record; or
e. Photographs of any such fact of record documented by photographs furnishing direct evidence of the record. (It is advisable to submit high-resolution photographs only that are pictures 1,500 pixels wide for horizontal images and 1,500 pixels high for vertical images, of 1 Mb or more.)

6. If any of the evidence mentioned above is in a local language, it must be sent along with a copy of an English translation of the said document attested by a gazetted officer/notary public.

7. The evidence must be clear, distinct and unambiguous.

8. *LBR* reserves the right to refuse the Claim if evidence sufficient to prove the record act beyond reasonable doubt is not furnished, or for any other reason whatsoever at *LBR*'s discretion.

9. For categories where specific evidence is required, a reference is invited to the respective category, mentioned in this document on Rules and Guidelines, for the requirements.

10. The material evidence provided by the Applicant shall NOT be returned. The Applicant is advised to keep all original evidence along with copies.

11. Wherever possible, a person from the *LBR* Team may also visit for verification. In such cases also, the evidence shall be sent along with the Claim.

12. In case of records where giant structures are put in place or super-sized objects are involved, the measurements shall be taken in the presence of appropriate observers and authenticators, such as gazetted officers, principal of a government school/college, an engineering expert, or others as approved by the *LBR* Team.

13. Originals must not be sent, unless specifically requested by *LBR* for scrutiny. *LBR* will not keep copies longer than twelve (12) months after acceptance of the Claim, but record holders should keep their evidence to be produced for disputes for life (see below V. 15: Reverification of Evidence). Evidence and documents of rejected records will be destroyed immediately after informing the Applicant of the decision.

14. All records and evidence are accepted in good faith and normal deep scrutiny. Any submission of fake evidence shall be met with a charge of cheating and other offences as mentioned in the Indian Penal Code and other applicable laws.

15. REVERIFICATION OF EVIDENCE:

a. In case a discrepancy in the record comes to light, as pointed out by any person or independently detected by the *LBR* Team, the onus of providing the evidence again for reverification of the record entry lies entirely with the record holder. If, in the opinion of the *LBR* Team, the discrepancy, irrespective of the reason for its coming to light, is genuine, it shall be communicated to the record holder and evidence sought for reverification; In the meantime, the record will be frozen/suspended and the certificate considered withdrawn until the evidence is reverified by a panel consisting of an *LBR* Team member and a legal consultant. Announcement of such a suspended/frozen record will appear only on the *LBR* website publicly and nowhere else. Subsequent to reverification, the record may either be restored, amended, or struck off completely.

b. *LBR* will not keep any data or records longer than one year (12 months) from acceptance in writing. In the event of any objection or discrepancy needing reverification (see sub-clause [a] above), the record holder must keep all supporting evidence safe and readily accessible.

c. In all matters pertaining to reverification of records/evidence, the *LBR's* decision shall be final and binding.

VI. ACCEPTANCE CRITERIA

1. Each Attempt must be categorized within one of the chapters or categories listed under Section II and III[B]. However, *LBR* reserves the right, to be exercised at its sole and absolute discretion, to accept applications for Attempts.

2. Records must be absolute and not technical offshoots, and they must be quantifiable, comparable, and measurable.

3. No Claim shall be considered valid unless it is sent, along with the required evidence, in the manner prescribed in Sections IV and V.

4. *LBR* reserves the right to publish or delete any chapter, section, category or record in the present or any future edition of *LBR*, without any notice to the Applicants. *LBR* is under no obligation to inform record holders when a record may be dropped. Such decisions shall be the sole prerogative of the *LBR* Team in the larger continuing interests of the book.

5. Records shall be considered for publishing only on the grounds of their interest value and general public acceptance.

6. *LBR* will not consider potentially dangerous Attempts by Applicants, particularly those belonging to Age Group I, being up to thirteen (13) years of age.

7. Further, no entries in violation of any law, rule, regulation, guideline, or any other statutory instrument shall be accepted.

8. Entries for the new edition of *LBR* will be confirmed only after the annual deadline, which is usually 31 May.

9. In all matters pertaining to the *Limca Book of Records*, the *LBR* Team's and/or CCIPL's decision shall be final and binding.

10. Record claims are accepted in good faith and may be considered records and published in the book as such unless disproved with appropriate evidence.

11. It should be borne in mind, that *LBR* by its rejecting a Claim is not stating that the Claim may not be a record, or that the achievement, if any, is belittled. It is merely stating that for its purposes and within the framework of the book, as run by its editorial policy, it does not consider the Claim suitable to feature.

12. Harassment of staff, including overt or covert threats, including threats of legal process for rejecting a Claim, or for any other reason whatsoever, or defaming *LBR* or the *LBR* Team on public platforms will not be acceptable and will be met with all the measures under law. Any such behaviour will also result in automatic disqualification of the Claim.

VII. STATUTORY COMPLIANCE

1. It is mandatory for Applicants to abide by all local, state, and national laws, rules, and regulations applicable in relation to the Attempt. *LBR* expressly prohibits any Attempt that involves violation of any local, state, or national laws, rules, or regulations. Applicants are under an obligation to ensure that all activities related to the Attempt are neither unlawful, nor against public decency and morality.

Applicants must note that *LBR* strongly discourages Attempts that are likely to offend the sentiments of any community. *LBR* also discourages Attempts that may cause harm to the public or animals, or cause any damage to the environment, and Applicants are requested to refrain from making such Attempts. Applicants shall bear sole responsibility for any consequences arising out of any non-compliance with any applicable laws, rules, or regulations insofar as they relate to the Attempt. *LBR* shall not be liable for any harm caused to the public or the environment in the course of the Attempt, and *LBR* shall not be responsible for any non-compliance with any applicable local, state, national, or international laws, rules, and regulations insofar as they relate to the Attempt.

2. With the submission of any Claim a record holder agrees to abide by the Terms and Conditions, and Rules and Guidelines, in full and is thereby covenanting that the submission is true with no falsifying of evidence or no mala fide intent of any sort whatsoever.

VIII. SAFETY PRECAUTIONS

1. The Applicant is requested to take all reasonable safety precautions prior to the Attempt including, but not limited to, the testing of all equipment used for the Attempt, the utilization of prescribed safety equipment in relation to the Attempt, the presence of requisite medical personnel and treatment facilities, and any applicable safety permits required under local, state, or national laws, rules, and regulations.

2. The Applicant understands that the Attempt may be dangerous to them, other Participants, and spectators, and that they must identify such risks, with the help of professional advice, such as the risk of accident, illness, paralysis, injury, loss, or death that may be caused by negligence, forces of nature, or other agencies, known and unknown. The Applicant knowingly and freely assumes all such risks, both known and unknown, and assumes full personal responsibility for the Attempt and its consequences.

3. The Applicant shall bear sole responsibility for taking all such safety precautions and acknowledge that CCIPL, the *LBR* Team, and/or their respective directors, publishers, editors, officers, appointed representatives, Consultants, or agents shall not, in any manner whatsoever, be responsible for making any safety arrangements for the Attempt.

IX. PUBLICITY

1. The Applicants undertake and irrevocably and unconditionally permit CCIPL and *LBR* to cover any Attempt through various media including newspapers, radio, television (news and other channels), Internet, mobile apps, social media, etc., and shall not raise any objection, protest, or demur whatsoever to such coverage or in this regard. Whilst *LBR* shall make all reasonable efforts, there is no obligation on the part of *LBR* to air or otherwise engage in publicizing any Attempt. The Applicants must, at the request of CCIPL/*LBR*, participate in all promotional activity (such as publicity and photography) in relation to a successful Attempt, free of charge, and consent to CCIPL and *LBR* using their name and image in all promotional materials, free of charge, should CCIPL/*LBR* Team wish to do so as mentioned under Section X below.

2. In the case of publicity-related interview and other occasions/opportunities and/or events where the participation or presence of the Applicant may be required, the *LBR*/CCIPL Team will contact the Applicant/s in writing/on email for their consent and willingness for such an interview and/or event.

X. LICENCE TO USE NAME, IMAGE, LIKENESS, RECORD

Applicants hereby grant in perpetuity to CCIPL and *LBR*, their authorized agents, successors, and assigns, the worldwide licence to use the name, image, likeness, pictures, video recordings, audio recordings, etc., of the Applicants in relation to any Attempts undertaken by the Applicants (the 'Licensed Property'). Applicants agree and grant to CCIPL and Hachette Book Publishing India Pvt. Ltd/Hachette India a waiver of their privacy and personality rights, and grant the right to use any element of the Licensed Property for any purpose in connection with *LBR* including, but not limited to, the publication and distribution of *LBR*, the promotion of *LBR*, CCIPL, and any of its divisions or products, and the filing of copyright, trademark, and other similar registrations in relation to *LBR* that involve the Licensed Property. All material submitted in connection with a potential entry in *LBR* (whether in written, audio, electronic or visual form, or a combination of these) or any photographs, video and/or film footage, and/or audio recording taken of Applicants are assigned to *LBR* and CCIPL upon submission and become the property of *LBR* and CCIPL exclusively. *LBR* and CCIPL may use the material in any medium in any reasonable manner they deem fit. Copyright in any such material remains the sole property of *LBR* and CCIPL.

XI. INTELLECTUAL PROPERTY RIGHTS

The name 'Limca' and the 'Limca' logo are registered trademarks of The Coca-Cola Company, USA, and should not be used for any publicity in relation to an Attempt, or after a Claim has been accepted, without the express permission of CCIPL. All rights, titles, and interests including, but not limited to, the Intellectual Property Rights, in *LBR* and in any and all entries received, shall vest solely and exclusively in CCIPL at all times. CCIPL or any person or entity permitted by CCIPL in this regard shall be entitled to use any information in connection with the entry in any media for future promotional, marketing, publicity, and any other purpose, without any permission and/or payment to the Applicant.

XII. RESPONSIBILITY FOR ALL ASSOCIATED COSTS AND INSURANCE

The Applicant understands and acknowledges that all expenses incurred in relation to the Attempt shall be borne solely by the Applicant. CCIPL and/or *LBR* Team shall in no manner be responsible for reimbursing any expenses incurred in the course of the Attempt, or even in the event that the Applicant is successful at the Attempt. CCIPL/*LBR* shall not be responsible for providing any kind of insurance in relation to any Attempt, and shall not be responsible for any emergency medical expenses or any subsequent medical expenses in the event of any incident/accident, illness, or incapacity arising out of the Attempt.

XIII. WAIVER OF CLAIMS AND INDEMNITY

1. Applicants acknowledge and consent on behalf of themselves, their heirs, successors, assigns, personal representatives, and next of kin, to WAIVE ALL CLAIMS AND RELEASE AND HOLD HARMLESS the *LBR* Team, Hachette Book Publishing India Pvt. Ltd/Hachette India and all its employees, directors, parent or affiliate organizations, Consultants, representatives, partners, CCIPL, its directors, publishers, editors, officers, employees and representatives, and its partners, affiliates, subsidiaries, advertising agencies, agents, and their respective directors, officers, employees, and representatives (the 'Released Parties'), with respect to any and all injury, disability, paralysis, death, or loss or damage to person, property, or reputations, arising out of the Attempt, to the fullest extent permitted by law. The Applicants agree to indemnify and hold the Released Parties harmless from all losses, liabilities, damages, costs, or expenses (including but not limited to reasonable legal fees and other litigation costs and expenses) incurred by any of the Released Parties as a result of any claims or suits that any Applicant/s (or anyone claiming by, under, or through such Applicant/s) may bring against any of the Released Parties to recover any losses, liabilities, costs, damages, or expenses that may arise during or result from the Attempt.

2. Further,

a. *LBR* retains an indemnity for human error or typographical error, and the right to revise a record because of that; and the right to withdraw or modify a certificate because of such error lies with the *LBR* Team.

b. The right to suspend records/certification on receipt of disputes or objections lies with the *LBR* Editorial Team. In such cases the record verification will be revisited, and the Claimant of the record must provide reverification (see clause V.15) and, if necessary, further detailing to answer such objections. If the Claimant is not able to furnish a copy of the evidence as per the original claim, the record and certification may be cancelled.

c. The principle of acceptance is basic verification and acceptance in good faith, so records should be clear and detailed. *LBR* reserves the right to do forensic examination or reopen a record case later if found to be suspect.

d. Faking of records and evidence is a criminal offence and shall be dealt with strictly under the prevailing laws. The application/Claim/record shall be cancelled and the Applicant/record holder shall be immediately blacklisted and no further applications/claims from them shall be entertained; and the rights to legal prosecution shall be reserved.

e. For records involving mass participation/huge numbers, for example, 'most people at a concert' or 'most vehicles in a rally', the simple principle of sequentially numbered badges should be there with a logbook of a unique identifier (licence/registration number, individual ID card, or any similar clearly visible device).

f. *LBR* is a private body and its editorial criteria solely belong to it alone and its decisions shall be the ones solely binding on any record.

XIV. SEVERABILITY

Each of the provisions contained in these Terms/Rules and Guidelines is considered to be reasonable by CCIPL, *LBR*, and the Applicants, and each clause, subclause, paragraph and sub-paragraph shall be construed as independent of any other provision. If any provision of these Terms/Rules and Guidelines proves to be invalid, void, or illegal, it shall not in any way affect, impair, or invalidate any other provision, and the remaining provisions shall remain in full force and effect.

XV. DISPUTE

The courts of competent jurisdiction at Delhi shall have exclusive jurisdiction to determine any and all disputes arising out of, or in connection with, any Attempt undertaken or entry made for the purpose of *LBR*. Further, all issues and questions concerning the construction, validity, interpretation, and enforceability of these Terms/Rules and Guidelines, or the rights and obligations of the Applicants and/or CCIPL and/or partners of *LBR*, shall be governed and construed in accordance with the laws of the Republic of India.
Note: For specific guidelines all Applicants are requested to contact the *LBR* Team by email at **lbr.entries@hachetteindia.com.**

APPENDIX 1

The clauses below are subject to ongoing review and modifications, and applicants may check this section from time to time to update themselves on categories that may have been discontinued, modified, or changed.

1. SPECIAL NOTE FOR PROSPECTIVE ATTEMPTS

a. For young children: No marathon records or dangerous records will be considered for children. They can attempt records in mental mathematics, collections, and Rubik's cube. The pre-approved categories are as follows:
   Main categories:
   i. Mental mathematics (without using pen and paper)
   ii. Calculation (using pen and paper)
   Spoken or visual or flashing numbers (for calculation purposes) will be considered as mental maths. Both the major categories have the following subcategories for attempting records:
   1. Five-minute event: The Applicant will be given five (5) minutes to attempt the event. The time will be the major benchmark for making and breaking records.
   2. Marathon event: The Applicants set the quantum of calculations for attempting the record. The time will not be considered for attempting a new record. However, for breaking the record in this category both time and the quantum will be considered as parameters.
   3. Sprint event: The Applicant will be given one (1) minute to attempt a record. Time cut-off will be the major benchmark for breaking records. The Attempt must be made in the approved categories only. The age criteria are U-18 and above 18 only. The documents submitted/record attempted will not be considered on their face value and will be only considered for review after the *LBR* Team approves it. Calculations with or without decimals will be considered as same.
   4. The following events will not be considered for records:
      - Multiplication and division by a single digit
      - Writing/speaking of multiplication tables
      - Squaring of 1-, 2- and 3-digit numbers
      - Multiplication of 2-digit numbers
      - Any record Attempt with even a single error
      - Multiple claims under the same category

b. There are categories in the book, marked with a single asterisks, indicating that they are one-time categories. These categories will not be carried forward into our subsequent editions and are not contestable.

c. Additional pointers to remember before sending the documentation or claims:
   i. Applicants should not send any documents unless requested by the *LBR* Team, post-approval.
   ii. Applicants should not send any documentation if their event has not been approved for consideration by the *LBR* Team.
   iii. Documents received by *LBR* for events that are not pre-approved (in writing or on email) will not be reviewed by the *LBR* Team.

2. A NOTE FOR PAST, PRESENT, AND POTENTIAL RECORD HOLDERS

a. The name Limca and the Limca logo are registered trademarks of The Coca-Cola Company, USA, and should not be used for publicity when a record is being attempted or after the Claim has been accepted, without written permission of the publisher.

b. When records are being attempted, it is not obligatory for the *LBR* Team to provide invigilators. However, where possible they may do so.

c. All Attempts at breaking old records and setting new ones are undertaken entirely at the risk of the Applicant. Neither the *LBR* Team nor CCIPL can be held responsible by the Applicant/person undertaking an Attempt or any third party for any liability that may arise out of such an Attempt.

d. Applicants may use the name '*Limca Book of Records*' while attempting the record as long as:
   i. they do not use the logo of the *Limca Book of Records* or Limca brand or any Licensed Property of CCIPL;
   ii. they do not receive or give money in the execution of such an Attempt using *LBR* as a party or implied party or endorser; and
   iii. they do not offer Participants/partners any kind of inducement using *LBR* as a party. **This is strictly prohibited and will result in the Applicant's name being blacklisted and rejected for any future application/attempts.**

e. The *LBR* Team reserves the complete and incontestable right to decide which chapters, sections, photographs, categories, and records to publish or delete in future editions. *LBR* will not consider potentially dangerous record Attempts by minors or any Attempt that violates a law.

f. *LBR* strives to be completely authentic. However, it sometimes happens that an earlier record may come to light or be applied for after the book is released. In such cases corrections/updates will be carried out in the next edition or as deemed fit by the *LBR* Team.

g. Records that are 'firsts' are not entitled to perpetuity and can be dropped from the book without any prior intimation.

h. For reasons of space or any other reasons whatsoever, a confirmed Claim may also be dropped. *LBR* Team members may inform the Applicant of the change in status but are not bound to do so. Such decisions are the sole prerogative of the *LBR* Team in the larger continuing interests of the book.

i. The record holders are not entitled to any prize money, gift(s) or free copies of *Limca Book of Records*.

j. **In case the record is subjected to reverification, the onus to prove the same is on the Applicant. So the Applicant must retain copies of documentary, images, audio, and video evidence with them should such a situation arise. *The Limca Book of Records* holds the right to revoke any record that fails reverification and to cancel the issued certificate.**

k. In all matters pertaining to *Limca Book of Records*, the *LBR* Team's decision is final.

3. DISCONTINUED CATEGORIES

a. A few categories have been discontinued and will not be featured in any subsequent editions. The website is updated regularly regarding such categories.

b. Youngest category: The youngest category has been dropped. The only exceptional cases are sports, art, creative skills, and any other reputed competitions where there is a quantifiable group. The age categories are specified only to ensure that no records are created against the law (for example, driving at an age not legally permissible) and to ensure that minors do not try to attempt records that require excessive physical exertion (like marathon events or climbing high mountains) and/or those that may be detrimental to their physical, mental, or emotional well-being.
c. Most surgeries/medical procedures within a time duration: The category for most surgeries/medical procedures has been discontinued as the quality of the procedure may be compromised during such claims.
d. Tractor service camps: The category for most tractors serviced has been discontinued as such claims are difficult to monitor and make it an industry-specific claim.
e. Largest blood/organ donation drives.
f. Wrist cracking/wrist rotation.
g. Most couplets written.
h. Holding most burning candles in the mouth.
i. Fastest yoga asanas.
j. Collection of error coins.
k. Longest interview.
l. Limbo skating.
m. One-hand claps.
n. Most postcards sent In a day – solo/group – single/multiple venues.
o. Largest packers and movers of household goods.
p. Most people screened/diagnosed – single/multiple venues.
q. Most postcards sent in a day – individual/group – single/multiple venues.
r. Largest anthology.
s. Collections for '786' notes.
t. Fastest construction of structures.
u. Longest preservation of food items/articles.
v. Claims related to number of research papers written or published.
w. Collections based on alphabetical order (A–Z).

4. WHY WAS YOUR RECORD REJECTED?

Unfortunately, many applications are rejected. The following are the general reasons that lead to the rejection of applications:

a. Not accepted the Terms and Conditions and/or Rules and Guidelines; and/or submission of incomplete form.
b. Insufficient documentation: The details provided do not suffice for verification purposes.
c. Not met criteria: For record purposes, *LBR* has certain criteria and set categories. For instance, in physical feats it has categories for 1 minute or 1 hour claims. Any claim that does not follow the format (e.g., most push-ups in 40 seconds) shall not be accepted.
d. Specific titles: Usually, *LBR* measures record titles by one single parameter so that anybody can attempt and break/surpass that record. If the record claim is too specific or has multiple variables, the *LBR* Team would not consider such claims. For example, 'most push-ups in one minute' would be considered whereas 'most push-ups done in 1 minute by a teacher' shall not be accepted.
e. Inappropriate/Offensive: *LBR* does not accept or encourage inappropriate or offensive claims.
f. Claims involving alcohol/smoking/substance usage: *LBR* does not encourage or accept claims involving alcohol, smoking, or substance use.

g. Animal welfare: Any claim that is not in accordance with animal rights laws or involves any mistreatment of animals is neither encouraged nor accepted in *LBR*.
h. Personality-related claims: Claims related to famous personalities, such as 'most people dressed as' or 'most times performing as' will only be considered for internationally recognized, iconic, and universally acknowledged personalities. The *LBR* Team reserves the right of discretion in any such claim.
i. Record claims involving wastage of food/medical supplies, e.g., artworks made with fresh food materials would not be considered.
j. Environmentally harmful claims: *LBR* does not support any claim that may have any sort of adverse effect on the environment.
k. Fastest musicians: *LBR* does not consider claims such as fastest guitarist, fastest piano player, etc., as it is not possible to judge the quality of music produced in such claims.
l. Firsts: The firsts in a field are generally not accepted unless they mark change in trend, beginning of a new era, or change the traditional way for the matter. The *LBR* Team reserves the right to accept or reject any such claim.
m. Poetry: *LBR* does not accept claims pertaining to poetry due to its subjective nature.
n. Originality/Uniqueness-based claims: Uniqueness/originality cannot be a parameter of competence for a record. The *LBR* Team reserves the right of discretion in any such claim.
o. Sports achievements: For records directly involving performance in sports, *LBR* only accepts those which occur at a top-level professional, international, or pre-eminent amateur levels, or as per the decision of the relevant Consultant in specific cases.

Limca Book of Records
NEXT EDITION: 2025

The last date for new entries and applications (complete with relevant documentation) for the *Limca Book of Records* 2025 edition:

31 May 2024

Please address all correspondence to:

Limca Book of Records (Editorial)
Hachette Book Publishing India Pvt. Ltd
4th/5th Floors, Corporate Centre
Plot No. 94, Sector 44
Gurugram 122003, Haryana, India

Phone: +91 22 35305621

Fax: +91 124 4148900

Email: lbr.entries@hachetteindia.com

Websites: https://www.coca-colaindia.com/limca-book-of-records.

https://www.hachetteindia.com/home/rulesandguidelines.

Note: In order to have an accessible, credible, and reproducible record of interactions, email (and where it is unavailable, registered postal mail or courier service) is the preferred form of communication and correspondence.